THE PROMISE OF THE METROPOLIS

Bangalore's recent emergence as a metropolis and its internationally acknowledged status as India's 'Silicon Valley' have made it known the world over. While providing a well-researched perspective on the city, this book analyses how it has been shaped by the ideologies and principles of planning, instrumentalities of law, and by the mobilization of 'City Beautiful' aesthetics. It also discusses the unanticipated uses of space that fashion a city quite different from the one envisaged by planners and technocrats, revealing ways in which citizenship and democracy are being re-conceptualized.

The book explores certain historical themes, particularly the legacies of the past that have gained legibility in the contemporary city, focusing in particular on its divided history. The fifty years since Independence are discussed in terms of the success with which they overcome divisions marked by the nation, the region, and the global capital.

THE PROMISE OF THE METROPOLIS

Bangalore's Twentieth Century

Janaki Nair

OXFORD
UNIVERSITY PRESS

OXFORD
UNIVERSITY PRESS

YMCA Library Building, Jai Singh Road, New Delhi 110 001

Oxford University Press is a department of the University of Oxford. It furthers the University's objective of excellence in research, scholarship, and education by publishing worldwide in

Oxford New York

Auckland Cape Town Dar es Salaam Hong Kong Karachi
Kuala Lumpur Madrid Melbourne Mexico City Nairobi
New Delhi Shanghai Taipei Toronto

With offices in
Argentina Austria Brazil Chile Czech Republic France Greece
Guatemala Hungary Italy Japan Poland Portugal Singapore
South Korea Switzerland Thailand Turkey Ukraine Vietnam

Oxford is a registered trademark of Oxford University Press
in the UK and in certain other countries

Published in India
by Oxford University Press, New Delhi

First published 2005
Oxford India Paperbacks 2007

Publishing grant from the Prince Claus Fund is acknowledged

ISBN-13: 978-0-19-569044-6
ISBN-10: 0-19-569044-3

Typeset in Sabon 10/14
by Eleven Arts, Keshav Puram, Delhi 110 035
Printed in India at Pauls Press, New Delhi 110 020
Published by Oxford University Press
YMCA Library Building, Jai Singh Road, New Delhi 110 001

For Devayani

To treat the past (better: what has been) in accordance with a method that is no longer historical but political. To make political categories into theoretical categories, insofar as one dared to apply them only in the sense of praxis, because only to the present—that is the task.

Walter Benjamin, *The Arcades Project*

Abbreviations

AIR	All India Reporter
AITUC	All India Trade Union Congress
BATF	Bangalore Agenda Task Force
BCC/BMP	Bangalore City Corporation/Bengaluru Mahanagara Palike
BDA	Bangalore Development Authority
BEL	Bharat Electronics Limited
BEEU	Bharat Electronics Employees' Union
BHEL	Bharat Heavy Electricals Limited
BMRDA	Bangalore Metropolitan Region Development Authority
BMTF	Bangalore Metropolitan Task Force
BUAC	Bangalore Urban Art Commission
CDP	Comprehensive Development Plan
CITB	City Improvement Trust Board
CITU	Centre of Indian Trade Unions
CIVIC	Citizen's Voluntary Initiative for the City
COPU	Committee of Public Undertakings
CPI	Communist Party of India
CPM	Communist Party of India (Marxist)
C&M Station	Civil and Military Station
DSS	Dalit Sangarsh Samiti
DMK	Dravida Munnetra Kazhagam
DVG	D.V. Gundappa

ELRTS	Elevated Light Rail Transport System
EPW	Economic and Political Weekly
GIPA	Gokhale Institute of Public Affairs
GPO	General Post Office
HAL	Hindusthan Aeronautics Limited
HBCs	House Building Co-operatives
HMT	Hindusthan Machine Tools
HUD	Housing and Urban Development
IDPAD	Indo Dutch Programme for Alternatives in Development
ISEC	Institute for Social and Economic Change
ISRO	Indian Space Research Organisation
ITI	Indian Telephone Industries
KHB	Karnataka Housing Board
KLJ	Karnataka Law Journal
KSA	Karnataka State Archives
KUIDFC	Karnataka Urban Infrastructure Development Finance Corporation
KVR	Karnataka Vimochana Ranga
MLJ	Mysore Law Journal
NAL	National Aeronautical Laboratories
NGO	Non-Government Organisation
NGO Forum	Non-Gazetteed Officers' Forum
NRIHA (K)	Non-Resident Indians' Housing Association (Karnataka)
ODP	Outline Development Plan
PAC	Public Affairs Centre
PDF	People's Democratic Forum
ULCRA	Urban Land (Ceiling and Regulation) Act, 1976

Contents

List of Photographs		xi
List of Maps		xiii
List of Tables		xiv
Acknowledgements		xv
Introduction	Where Does the City Begin?	1
One	Bengaluru/Bangalore: The Presence of the Past	23
Two	Remembered and Imagined Cities	77
Three	Conceiving the City: Master Planning and Informal Power	121
Four	The Map is not the Territory: Law and the Production of Space	166
Five	Past Perfect: Architecture and Public Life	200
Six	Language and the Right to the City	234

Seven	Battles for Bangalore: Re-territorializing the City	271
Eight	The 'Body Politic': Gender and the Practise of Power	299
Conclusion	Is 'Singapore' Bangalore's Destiny?	333
Notes		348
Select Bibliography		419
Index		438

Photographs

1	Bangalore Karaga, 1980s	3
2	Kadalekai Parishe, 2000	6
3	Town Hall Junction, 1960s	16
4	Vineyard on Idgah property, 2000	17
5	Central Business District, 2000	19
6	Layers of architecture, 2000	24
7	Mysore Bank Square, 2000	25
8	View of Cubbonpet, 2000	26
9	North View of Bangalore, 1791	29
10	Akkithimmanhalli Tank, 1980	31
11	Annamma procession, 1960	33
12	Gavi Gangadhareswara Temple, 2000	34
13	St Mary's Festival, 1992	37
14	Dyeing Unit, Cubbonpet, 2000	41
15	South Parade, early twentieth century	44
16	Avenue Road, c. 1880	47
17	Colonial Bungalow, 1980	48
18	Commercial Street, early twentieth century	54
19	Murphy Town, 2000	55
20	Shoolay, early twentieth century	57
21	Hounds for the Bangalore Hunt, 1930s	59
22	Courtyard, Palace Guttahalli, 2000	61
23	Mahatma Gandhi Road, 1980	80
24	Hindusthan Machine Tools, 1972	82

25	Health Scribe Offices, 2000	86
26	Diamond District, 2000	93
27	Congress Exhibition, early 1960s	96
28	Attack on KFC outlet, 1996	98
29	Poura Samiti protest, 1970	106
30	*Busa* agitation, 1973	107
31	Performance at Congress exhibition, 1960s	109
32	Adi Parashakthi Shrine, ITI, 1999	138
33	Cattle Fair at Sampangi Tank, early 1960s	142
34	KHB Flats, Byrasandra Tank Bed area, 1999	145
35	Shiva Statue, Kemp Fort, 1998	154
36	Siddhi Vinayaka Temple, Residency Road, 1999	155
37	Highway Anjaneya, Babasanpalya, 1999	156
38	BDA legal offices, 1999	179
39	Ashoknagar Slum Demolition, 1997	193
40	Inauguration of Mysore Assembly, 1953	203
41	Kengal Hanumanthaiya, c. 1956	209
42	Rally on Ambedkar Veedhi, 1981	214
43	Cubbon Park Gates, 1999	216
44	S. Bangarappa rally at Vidhana Soudha, 1992	218
45	Karnataka High Court, 2000	226
46	Visvesvaraya Towers, 2000	230
47	Rajkumar cutout, Kapali Theatre, 2000	236
48	Kannada signs on MG Road, 1970	242
49	*Ramayana Darshanam* procession, 1969	246
50	Kannada Bhuvaneswari in motorcade, 1970s	248
51	HMT Watch Factory, 1971	254
52	Roadside shop, Tilaknagar, 1999	260
53	Cenotaph, 1964	277
54	Rajyothsava celebrations, 1999	281
55	Guards at Shivaji statue, 1994	284
56	Thiruvalluvar statue, 1991/1999	285
57	Praja Vimochana Chaluvali Protest, 1995	289
58	Cubbon Park protests, 1998	295
59	Garment workers, 1991	310
60	Miss World protests, 1996	329
61	Women in Black demonstration, 2003	331
62	K.R. Market flyover, 2000	337
63	International Tech Park, 2004	339
64	Cyber Café, 2000	346
65	Plate Glass shop fronts, 2003	347

Maps

1 Bangalore c. 1791 39
2 Bangalore c. 1850 43
3 Bangalore c. 1897 49
4 Plan of Basavangudi, 1894 52
5 Bangalore, 1924 58
6 Bangalore, 1935 71
7 Bangalore, 1960 78
8 Bangalore, 1980 84
9 Growth of Industries, 1940–90s 88
10 Cubbon Park and environs, 2000 211
11 Location of IT industries, 2000 342
12 Proposed IT corridor 343

Tables

2.1	Growth of population in Bangalore, 1941–2001	101
2.2	Registered vehicles in Bangalore, 2000	102
3.1	Land Use Analysis in Various Planning Documents For Bangalore City, 1952–90	129
4.1	Housing Units and Estimates of Housing Shortages	170
4.2	Growth of Population in Bangalore City and Metropolitan Area, 1901–2001, and Projected Population Growth	171
4.3	Extent of Area Acquired and Utilized in 41 BDA Layouts between 1.1.76 and 31.3.90	178
4.4	Land Utility Study of Five Layouts, 1991	180
6.1	Languages spoken in Public Sector Units	256
8.1	Sex ratio in Bangalore, 1941–2001	320
8.2	Stated Reasons for Unnatural Death of Newly Married Women, 1997–2000	323
8.3	Mode of Unnatural Death of Newly Married Women, 1997–2000	324

Acknowledgements

I began working on Bangalore, a city that I have known from childhood, at a time when I thought that not enough was known about the historical processes that have shaped or ruined the contemporary city. Over the past few decades, the city has changed in many unrecognizable ways, providing the right kind of distance between the native and the object of research, and indeed, to adapt the words of Walter Benjamin, 'the writer has not spent her childhood there in vain'. Yet, very soon after I began the research, I found that Bangalore was attracting the attention of a large number of scholars from all over the world, whose enquiries will no doubt provide a fuller, richer account of its recent rise to metropolitan status. My work will thus join a new but expanding body of literature on what is arguably one of India's most important metros.

I could not have hoped for more generous funding than I have received from two institutions, both based in The Netherlands, over the past five years. The SEPHIS (South–South Exchange Programme for Research on the History of Development) post-doctoral grant enabled a two-year period of research on the most generous terms, funding research assistance and a visit to Singapore in addition to paying my salary. The grant also included funds to begin a small collection of photographs on contemporary Bangalore, from which a selection was displayed at an exhibition entitled 'Beladide Noda Bengaluru Nagara!' in June/July 2000. Throughout this period, Ulbe Bosma and Ingrid Goedhart of SEPHIS have been extraordinarily accommodating, flexible, and above all very encouraging of every effort, even at the expense of taking on more work. I was doubly fortunate to receive funds from the Prince Claus Fund for Culture and Development for a further two years of writing based on the research. This allowed me to remain in Bangalore and complete the manuscript. Geerte Wachter was extremely accommodating, permitting changes in budgets by adding a subsidy for this book. To both these institutions, I am extremely grateful.

My greatest institutional debt is to the Centre for the Study of Culture and Society which risked its fledgling existence by affiliating me as a visiting fellow between 1998–2000, and graciously tolerating my occasional though often disruptive presence. Some of the most critical contributions to this research have come from colleagues at this Centre: Vivek Dhareshwar urged me to read many important works and introduced me to the profoundly influential work of Richard Sennett; Tejaswini Niranjana provided valuable comments on draft chapters; Ashish Rajadhyaksha, Madhava Prasad, and S.V. Srinivas were always encouraging and supportive, in addition to providing technical support, advice with accounts, and a critical if patient hearing. Above all, talks and discussions at the Centre were richly rewarding, and helped to sharpen my own questions and refine lines of enquiry.

The Institute for Social and Economic Change provided me with affiliation when this work was being written, and its director, M. Govind Rao, responded to all my requests with alacrity. I am grateful to all my colleagues and staff at this institute for their assistance and support between 2000–2; Venkatesh accessed what I might poorly describe as his 'hard drive' to locate books that had gone astray while that excellent library was reclassified. I found another unlikely home during this period at the National Centre for Biological Sciences, as visiting social scientist. Being a historian among biologists was a unique and very rewarding experience, and what I may not have learned of biology was more than compensated for by lessons in exemplary enthusiasm from all faculty and staff who welcomed me into their fold. K. Vijayraghavan, Obaid Siddiqi, and Satyajit Mayor in particular were important interlocutors.

To all at the Madras Institute of Development Studies, where this project was first conceived, many thanks. I visited the Centre for Advanced Studies in the National University of Singapore (NUS) and benefited enormously from interactions with all there, especially Brenda Yeoh, Chua Beng Huat, Kong Chong Ho, and Zaheer Babar. Abdul Fakhri, Gyanesh Kudasiya, Medha Kudasiya, Peter Reeves, and Dipinder Randhawa made NUS and Singapore a lively and enjoyable experience.

The warmth and enthusiasm with which I was welcomed into the community at the Centre for Studies in the Social Sciences provided a fresh impetus that helped in the revision of this manuscript. I am grateful to all colleagues, friends in the library and office, and all others who helped me in Kolkata. Abhijit Bhattacharya's assistance with photographs is gratefully acknowledged. Anjushree stepped in to complete a last minute map request.

I found more than a research assistant in P. Sudarshan who worked tirelessly even when he did not quite see the point of the data he was gathering; I have discussed ideas with him, shared drafts, and have generally enjoyed and perhaps even exploited his friendship and support over the years.

For their friendship and encouragement, I would like to thank Ayisha Abraham, Janaki Abraham, Clare Arni, Niladri Bhattacharya, Sabyasachi Bhattacharya, Bharatesh S. Mallur, Moinak Biswas, Uma Chakravarthi, Partha Chatterjee, Indira Chowdhury, Satish Deshpande, Tapati Guha Thakurtha, Sheela Gowda, Ram Guha, Gaiti Hasan, Mary John, Ammu Joseph, Sarah Joseph, Sujatha Kesavan, Sudhir Krishna, Suvritta Khatri, Radhika Lal, Tasqeen Machiwala, Prabhu Mohapatra, Pragati Mohapatra, K.T. Margaret, Jitu Mayor, Parvathy Menon, Shobhana Narasimhan, V.K. Natraj, Pushpamala N., Ann Ninan, Shalini Panjabi, Asad Hajeebhoy, Kiran Sebastian, Mrinalini Sebastian, Samita Sen, Shikha Sen, Sanjay Sharma, Bharat Shekar, Asiya Siddiqi, Christoph Storz, Dilip Subramanian, Lakshmi Subramanian, Susie Tharu, Carol Upadhyay, A.R. Vasavi, S.G. Vasudev, and Sarojini Vittachi. Ayisha helped design photo albums, Satish and Mary ploughed through an untidy manuscript in its early stages and made suggestions that have significantly improved this work, and Vasavi read drafts in addition to sharing child care, fetching books, suggesting references, and transporting me around.

Sanjeev Aundhe, Vinay Baindur, Solomon Benjamin, James Heitzman, Smriti Srinivas, and Balaji Parthasarathy were part of an informal group working on the city that readily shared critical documents, maps, writings, insights, words of caution, and ways of thinking about the bewildering changes in Bangalore. I was fortunate to be a part of this network, which brought some life and meaning to the cyber world we often inhabited. Dilip Subramanian shared a very important set of documents from his own research; N.P. Shankaranarayana accompanied me on jaunts around the city; Suresh Moona gave me photographs; V.K. Natraj provided important references; Edgar D'Mello, Jaspreet Kaur, and Raj Shetty provided new insights on architecture and city space, while Annapurna Garimella shared her work on emerging religiosities. Elizabeth Staley responded to many long distance requests, and Sanjeev Jain shared his articles. Clare Arni, S. Nagamani, and G. Raghav assisted me at various points during this period: to all of them I am very grateful. Two people who helped me with maps, Muthatha Ramanathan and Avinash Veeraraghavan, deserve my thanks for handling all my fantasies and worries with equal ease. To Padma Raju, I owe heartfelt thanks for many hours of labour on the computer. S. Rajagopal and all at Spinfo produced new digital perspectives on the city.

Several people in government and in other offices made the task of data collection somewhat less stressful: I would like to thank in particular B.K. Chandrasekhar, A. Ravindra, Leo Saldanha, Yakub Shariff, P.S.S. Thomas, and Lakshmi Venkatachalam. I thank staff at libraries and archives across the city: the BCC, the BDA, the BMRDA, the Town Planning Department, *Deccan Herald*, *Indian Express*, *Samyuktha Karnataka*, *Lankesh Patrike,* the High Court Library, the Legislature Library, the MEG library, the Survey of India, the Karnataka State Archives, the Gokhale Institute of Public Affairs, the Mythic Society, the Tamil Sangam, the Institute for Social and Economic Change, the United Theological College, Vimochana, CIVIC, and TIDE.

Thanks are also due to those at Oxford University Press, particularly Anil Chandy, for his patience in seeing this manuscript through.

Various parts of this work were shared at seminars and workshops in Bangalore, Chennai, Delhi, Hiroshima, Kolkata, La Paz, Paris, Shimoga, and Singapore, and I am grateful to comments from the audiences at all these locations. Earlier versions of some chapters have appeared: Chapter 5 as 'Past Perfect: Architecture and Public Life in Bangalore', in *Journal of Asian Studies*, 61.4 (Nov. 2002), pp. 1205–36; Chapter 6 as 'Language and the Right to the City', *Economic and Political Weekly*, 35.47 (Nov. 18, 2000), pp. 4141–6; Chapter 7 as 'Battles for Bangalore', www.iisg.nl/~sephis.

My extended family was completely baffled by my preoccupations, and failed to see any value in this work, and yet remained steadfastly loyal: thanks to one and all. Rebecca, Netra, and Manjula relieved me of many domestic chores at various points of this work, and though they disapproved, put up with untidy ways of working.

To Madhava Prasad for his support, love, and encouragement over the years and his critical engagement with every idea in the book, more than thanks is due. Devayani was the wonderful gift that burst into our lives, upsetting all schedules and work routines, deciding new rules for work and play, and showing healthy disrespect for my pre-occupations with the computer in the most pleasurable way imaginable. This would have been a very different and much poorer effort without her inputs. Seeing the city once more through the fresh eyes of one who is poised to inherit its hopes, pleasures, and burdens was a unique and sometimes blinding experience. To her, by way of small recompense for my distractions, I dedicate this work.

Janaki Nair

INTRODUCTION

Where Does the City Begin?

The fundamental problem of India is not Delhi or Calcutta or Bombay but the villages of India .... We want to urbanize the village, not take away the people from the villages to the towns. However well we may deal with the towns, the problems of the villages of India will remain for a long time, and any social standards that we seek to introduce will be judged ultimately not by what happens in Delhi but in the villages of India.

Jawaharlal Nehru in Ravi Kalia, *Chandigarh: The Making of an Indian City.*

The city, or more properly 'the urban', has had a fugitive existence in the political, cultural, and sociological imaginations of modern India. Only recently, and somewhat fitfully, have these imaginations been transformed to admit a consideration of the city as a legitimate object of attention, investigation, and research, and as a site that recasts the meanings of citizenship, democracy, and indeed modernity in contemporary India. The village dominated the vision of politicians, planners, scholars, and cultural producers alike, even when their own origins may have been firmly urban. If the city, and the colonial city in particular, exercised a hold on the Indian imagination at all, we are told in Ashis Nandy's recent considerations of the 'ambiguous journey to the city', disillusion was quick to set in, making the village, real or imagined, an ideal destination. In his account, the Indian city appears as a site that 'vend[s] a dream of total freedom for the individual and the reasoning self' by combining the promise of 'citizenship, civility and civic virtues with a particularly ruthless form of self indulgent, unrestrained, asocial individualism'.[1] The village is thus made to hold a different kind of promise, as it structures the imagination of those seeking an alternative to the tainted, immoral cosmopolitanism of the Indian city.[2] It is the inability to imagine a village except as an antonym of the city, as an idealized, or often, an infantilized/geriatrized Other, that is Nandy's central concern: his cases largely speak of the return journey to a village following disillusionment with the city. Of the city itself, represented in ways that equal the flattened image of the village, his certainties remain, and are spared any critical scrutiny.

Where then does the city begin? It would be no exaggeration to say that the village and its ruins continue to haunt many recent reflections on, and representations of, the city: to this, even a consideration like Nandy's is no exception. Bargur Ramachandrappa wrote in 1992 that despite its turbulent traffic, miles of tarred road, splendid cinemas, and beautiful gardens, Bangalore was no thoroughgoing metropolis. Instead, his essay, entitled 'A Village called Bangalore City', declared that the heart and mind of the city called Bangalore remained rural, untouched by an urbanity which he identified variously with a scientific temper, prosperity, and a sense of history: thus 'cities have puranas *and* histories (*charitre*); but villagers tend to see the puranas *as* history'.[3] To stress this dichotomy between the form and the substance of metropolitan Bangalore, he deployed a number of metaphors: 'jeans pants on the outside and *madi panche* on the inside';[4] 'a brain touched by science' but a heart that remained superstitious; the consciousness of the bullock cart 'soaring in an aeroplane'. These metaphors were aided by his examples of how the rural still stained the urban in a city like Bangalore: migrants whose slum lives resembled village life, the celebration of Karaga (the annual *jatre* of the Dharmaraya temple in the old city, Fig.1), and the Kadalekai Parishe (the annual peanut fair, Fig. 2), the worship of machine tools during Ayudha Puja, and the like.

Ramachandrappa's writing expresses surprise, if not disappointment, at the stubbornness with which the rural dogs urban India, and Bangalore in particular. Even more interesting however is the lens through which Ramachandrappa views the urban, so that the oldest civic ritual of the city, the Karaga, is taken as a sign of the rural.[5] It is almost as if the tools for understanding the city in its own right simply do not exist, and have to be fashioned anew. For many others too, the city remains merely the Other of a real or imagined rural India, either in terms of the ways in which it corrupts

FIG. 1 *The Bangalore* (Pete) *Karaga, is the oldest civic ritual of the city. It performatively traces a sacred geography that links localities of the old city area with an earlier urban horticultural economy of tanks and gardens.*
(Department of Information and Publicity, Karnataka, early 1980s.)

or dehumanizes the city dweller,[6] or as a space where individualism would flourish and generate new civic virtues were it not for the fact that Bangalore is still organically yoked to its rural origins.[7]

The belief that the truth of the Indian nation is in its villages has long structured the political imagination. The sentiment immortalized in Gandhi's words 'For me, India begins and ends in the villages',[8] was echoed, albeit with very different consequences, in the writings of Jawaharlal Nehru, and recast in the writings of B.R. Ambedkar notwithstanding the fact that these three ideologues of the national movement belonged to the city.[9] Nehru in particular saw increased urban migration and urbanization as alarming trends that had to be stemmed and reversed. Although there were early warnings about the costs of ignoring India's burgeoning urban population, particularly in the decade of 1941–51,[10] they were marginal in an economic and political field overwhelmed by the image of India as a land of villages. The turn to the village from the city was also a characteristic of some social movements, most famously the Naxal movement of the late 1960s and 1970s that fanned out of the city to the village.[11]

The emphasis on village India in the early years of Indian independence could not but have left its mark on contemporary scholarship. If urban India has, until recently, occupied only an inconspicuous corner of the field of social sciences, it is because some social scientists, lamented M.S.A. Rao, mistakenly felt there is no justification for urban studies 'since 80 per cent of the people live in villages'.[12] Surinder Jodhka has shown that the belief in the village as the site of India's civilizational continuity, as representing in microcosm the 'real India', structured the agenda of sociological research, especially in its formative phase in the 1950s.[13] For M.N. Srinivas, under whose guidance and tutelage the discipline of sociology expanded, village studies could form the basis for generalizations about Indian social processes and problems.[14] The village enjoyed not only a historical and cultural continuity with the past, but was the repository of all that stood threatened by the forces of modernity sweeping the country.

While the village studies of the 1960s and 1970s served as a useful corrective to prevailing Orientalist notions of the unchanging Indian village, the focus of most studies was on the binding ties and enduring structures of rural society: caste, gender, or occupational hierarchies. Srinivas, however, emphasized the urgency of carrying out field based village studies as soon as possible after Indian independence, as 'We have, at the most, another ten years in which to record facts about a type of society which is changing fundamentally and with great rapidity.'[15] These studies, Jodhka observes, frequently looked for sources that *reproduced* the Indian social order rather than those events that challenged or transformed it.[16] Even when some sociologists made attempts to understand the nature of Indian urbanization, the focus was on the impact of the proximity of the city on village life.[17] Rapidly urbanizing villages, especially as they succumbed or adapted to changes in the political economy of towns, thus formed part of a growing field of study. Some emphasized the deep structures that were shared by village and city,[18] while others carefully charted the ways in which the village survived in the city.[19] Alan Beals' studies on villages around Bangalore, such as Namhalli and Hatarahalli, which were affected by opportunities and political initiatives radiating from the city spoke of fields of power that were thoroughly recast in the space of a few decades.[20] Over ten years later, Mark Holmstrom studied a village that had long lain in the administrative jurisdiction of Bangalore in order to illustrate the compromises achieved between two systems of political authority, one a traditional panchayat or council and the other the modern voluntary association.[21] The structure of village studies even influenced the studies of slums in urban areas: Gertrude Woodruffe's 1959 study of an Adi-Dravida *cheri* in Bangalore followed the model of village studies in tracking the persistence of the caste panchayat as a centre of power in vastly transformed economic circumstances.[22] In many ways, the description of *cheri* life approximated the structures of experience of these migrants from the rural areas of Tamil Nadu.

Nor was a preoccupation with the village the monopoly of sociologists, though they certainly dominated the field: political scientists too focused more on the patterns of rural life in their studies. When the 'urban' did make a slow and hesitant appearance as a category of analysis from the 1960s onwards, it was most hospitably accommodated within such disciplines as demography and geography, as well as urban planning. Far from being a reflection of the absence of urbanization in Indian history,[23] the pronounced tilt in favour of village studies had its roots in colonial representations of the village as the authentic expression of Indian civilizational values.

Finding the City

Patrick Geddes' celebrated 1915 report on planning in six Indian towns and his appointment as professor in the University of Bombay did little to kindle an interest in the modern Indian city. In an early overview of studies of Indian

FIG. 2 *The village in the city: the annual Kadalekai Parishe (peanut fair) occupies the rocky environs of the temple complex at Basavangudi.*
(Clare Arni, 2000)

urbanism, Satish Saberwal rightly remarked that 'this terrain has until recently remained singularly devoid of decisive intellectual landmarks ...'[24] In the early 1950s, following a UNESCO study on migration into Indian cities, the topic of urbanization did gain a separate space within the Indian Sociological Association and the Indian Economic Association.[25] A major impetus for urban studies came from the profiles sponsored by the Planning Commission of 20 major Indian cities. Indeed, 'well articulated demographic profiles of Indian cities at the national, regional and local levels' were among the first contributions to urban studies.[26] The more descriptive mode was followed by geographers, of which R.L. Singh's studies on Banaras and Bangalore were among the most detailed.[27] For the most part, even when city studies followed the structure of ecological studies of the city in the West, they were descriptive rather than analytical.[28]

Predictably, it is the Presidency cities of Bombay and Calcutta that have been best served by scholars from the various disciplines. Nirmal Kumar Bose's pioneering social survey of Calcutta in the early 1960s attempted to correlate land use, occupation, and social institutions, and their spatial distribution, to assess the contemporary city in its own right. It is striking that his morphology of the city led him to conclude, perhaps in defiance of doomsayers then predicting the death of the city, that even such a well defined and long existing metropolis as Calcutta was 'in a state of immature or imperfect urbanization'.[29] The urgency of asserting a continuing vibrancy for a city that was condemned as a 'dying city' is revealed in the investigations of social anthropologists who followed Bose: if the enormous creative energies of Calcutta in the fields of the arts and in science dominated the collection of essays edited by Surajit Sinha,[30] other volumes drew attention to the political and social innovations and movements that were fostered in the old metropolis.[31] By the 1980s, debates on what had gone wrong in Indian planning and development singled out Calcutta as a disturbing example, more directly acknowledging and addressing the dimensions of a city in crisis.[32] Even the excellent compilation of articles to commemorate the city's tercentenary found it necessary to declare Calcutta a 'Living City' rather than a metropolis in decline, one that had long given up its claim to being the *urbs prima* of India.[33] The two volumes are, however, ample testimony to the sheer breadth of scholarly interest in the city's rich cultural, social, and political history, resulting in a document which spans both the colonial and post-colonial period.

Far more ambitious frames have been used in recent studies of a metropolis like Bombay. Bombay's claim to a twentieth century modernity was assessed in two anthologies after the shocked recognition (following the post-Babri Masjid riots in 1993) that its cosmopolitanism was neither uniformly shared by all social groups nor irreversible.[34] Once more, there was celebration of the sheer diversity of cultural traditions that the city had fostered, its architectural heritage, its vibrant economic and social opportunities. There was however also a sober consideration by some contributors, such as Gerard Heuze and Jayant Lele, of the more troubling legacies of the post-Independence period, namely the rise to power of the Shiv Sena and the ways in which it had rewritten urban politics, forging styles that departed from those of nationalist and left wing struggles.[35] The rich and hospitable soil of Bombay within which violent and divisive politics took root and flourished has received fuller treatment in a recent monograph by Thomas Blom Hansen.[36] Hansen's account takes the metropolis not merely as the backdrop against which right wing politics emerged but as constitutive of the process itself. The 'assertive, often violent, mode of being urban' is a sign, not of the Shiv Sena's loyalty to a primordial identity, but of a full-blooded plebeian engagement with modern city life and its technologies of power, in striking contrast to earlier, paternalist modes of political mobilization.[37] By taking urban violence as his starting point, Hansen provides a fresh perspective on the ways in which urban identities mobilize ethnicity and masculinity in the process of refashioning forms of assertion and notions of citizenship itself. Hansen's study is clearly a pioneering attempt at understanding the range of possibilities for self definition offered by the new urban–industrial setting, and shakes free of earlier sociological preoccupations with 'continuity and change'.

The city as a site of new and intensified forms of violence, and communal violence in particular, has prompted other investigations into city history. In particular, the spatial remnants of the pre-colonial city that have become centres of recurrent conflict between ethnic communities has led some to question the relationship between a decaying spatial form, the experience of economic decline and forms of self assertion that have led to a completely new and violent political life. In a study of the walled city of Hyderabad, Ratna Naidu has provided a detailed spatial analysis of the area's proneness to violence to conclude that the phenomenon of 'multiple deprivation', namely pervasive blight and decay of the physical infrastructure and economic order of the old city, play a major role.[38] Few other urban studies have attempted as ambitious a correlation between spatiality and politics as this. Although Naidu admits that 'we could find no evidence for a direct relation between urban decay and communal tension', the economic and spatial deterioration provided the setting within which institutionalized communal politics took shape. Besides, 'a high density and narrow connecting lanes and bylanes enable people to both assemble and disappear at short notice'.[39] The study emphasizes the importance of permanent and temporary occupations of city space, as they indicate a change in the field of forces: the routes through which the Muharram and Ganesha processions pass, for instance, and the dramatic changes in the form and scale of the latter have had serious consequences for deteriorating relations between communities in the densely populated area.[40] The detailed survey thus allows the author to confidently assert that plans and programmes intended to rejuvenate the area are inappropriate, and call for more imaginative approaches to planning.[41]

The problems, among planners for instance, of taking only the physical–material dimensions of city life into consideration, have formed the basis of other studies. Perhaps few Indian cities illustrate the limits of planning in its physical–material sense as well as the city of Chandigarh. This city, which in Nehru's inimitable prose was 'the first large expression of our creative genius flowering on our newly earned freedom' was indeed 'free from the existing encumbrances of old towns and old traditions'.[42] However, Madhu Sarin has critically analysed the multiple ways in which the modernism of Le Corbusier failed to take the social, economic, and cultural priorities of the new city's population into account. She points out that the planning of Chandigarh marked a subtle shift from the more general design and planning of refugee townships because 'instead of centring planning proposals around enabling the majority of urban households to be engaged in productive occupations, the focus shifted to a pre-occupation with visual appearance and aesthetic style and a virtually total control of land use and building use specified on the basis of assumed criteria'.[43] The technocratic imagination thus did not allow for planning the space of the city in terms of work opportunities, and emphasized instead its purely residential or official uses. Indeed, the unplanned areas of Chandigarh are a sign of the ways in which an unresponsive planning mechanism is negotiated by those from lower castes and classes.[44]

Many other Indian cities have not fared as well as the Presidency cities and the new cities in the realm of scholarship. Given its rich architectural legacy, it need not surprise us that the Mughal imperial and British colonial pasts of Delhi have been well documented in chronicles, travelogues, memoirs, and not least, in distinguished histories, such as that by Narayani Gupta.[45] Yet there are few studies which consider the enormous transformations in the contemporary city, particularly by planning practices, emerging aesthetic regimes, and communal violence: Gupta herself admits that the history of Delhi from the 1930s to the 1980s 'cries out to be written', a challenge that does not appear to have been taken up as yet.

Histories of the modern Indian city have focused on the moment when town planning made its simultaneous debut in the metropolitan centre and in the colonies. The imperatives of transforming a 'disloyal', 'unsafe', and indeed unclean city following the Rebellion of 1857 underlay the urgency with which areas of colonial Lucknow were 'Napierized' just as Paris was 'Hausmannized'. Veena Oldenburg thus discusses civic planning as a way of restoring order and as an 'invidious form of social control',[46] and her study charts the profound and deleterious consequences of plans for a new Lucknow. The genesis of town planning as a means of restoring public health and well-being following a major epidemic is somewhat better known[47] than the instances of city planning that are aimed at disarming a population in revolt. Still, as other equally well documented histories of planning bear out, the population was not deprived entirely of the resources to resist, and perhaps even determine, the nature and direction of planning. Mariam Dossal, who has studied a very similar time period as Oldenburg's for Bombay Municipality, provides instances of various plans—for the design of public spaces or water supply and sanitation—remaining unimplemented due to fears of political repercussion.[48] The city of Delhi, which shared Lucknow's history as a major site of the 1857 rebellion, was ruthlessly transformed as the British tried to regain their hold of the region. The demolitions in Delhi that followed the rebellion bore great resemblance to the Lucknow demolitions, and indeed a symptom of the fear of a recurrence of rebellion was the large amount (75 per cent) of its municipal budget that was spent on policing, rather than in improving the infrastructure. Yet attempts to put in place an enduring municipal mechanism were far less tidy or unidirectional even within a municipality packed with loyalists: the conflict between Jains and Hindus, and eventual resolution of the problems posed by their respective processions in the city is a case in point.[49]

Important perspectives on urban life have emerged in the most unexpected quarters. Studies of the working class, which have enjoyed a certain visibility in the Indian social sciences, have, unwittingly perhaps, done much to lay out the experience of the urban from workers' perspectives. [50] Yet fierce and unequal contests over the industrial landscape of Bombay provide new perspectives from the point of those whose lives have been reordered by forces and movements over which they have had little control.[51] Nita Kumar's work on Banaras similarly constructs the life–world of artisanal workers, including perspectives on work and leisure in a city more strongly associated with the sacred geography of Hinduism.[52]

Overall, there has been no enthusiastic embrace of urban studies since M.S.A. Rao first made this observation in 1974: 'Our understanding of Indian social institutions has been largely based on knowledge of village communities ... Hence it is necessary to promote urban studies which would supplement the *rural view* and thus provide a balanced picture of Indian social institutions.'[53] The exuberant announcement of the 'urban turn' has yet to be realized in the new millennium[54] and the postmodernist celebration of fragments of new metropolitan life has emerged against a background of as yet insufficiently researched historical processes. [55]

Beyond India: The City in History

Unencumbered by the obligation to study the realm of the authentic (and therefore rural) community, urban historians and sociologists beyond India have engaged with distinctly urban cultural and political processes that are not anchored in municipal or planning concerns. The city could thus be the theatre for the enactment of new regimes of political power, as in Michael Johns' book on the city of Mexico in the time of Porfirio Diaz.[56] The city could be the space within which remarkable intellectual cultures, such as liberalism, could flourish and also decline.[57] In contrast, studies of city-states such as Singapore reveal the success with which new ideologies of social control, based on the compelling dream of economic advancement, have been materialized in city and housing design[58] and with far more predictable consequences.[59] As James Holston points out in his study of Brasilia, a 'messianic modernism' gripped the imaginations of those who believed that redesigned urban environments held the promise of new social relations, and indeed the new urban heroism of the *superquadra* (the holistic neighbourhoods into which Brasilia was divided) attempted not only to refashion public and private life but to critique capitalist cities as well.[60]

The processes of planning and of the built-for-profit metropolises of the twentieth century have found strong critics, from Lewis Mumford[61] to Richard Sennett, for many of whom the life-giving vitality of the medieval European city was irretrievably lost when capitalism and planning processes redrew Western cities. Curiously, the theme of the neighbourhood in decline has resonated in the work of American sociologists and historians alike: perhaps the most powerful indictment of the short-sightedness of planning was contained in Jane Jacobs' *The Death and Life of Great American Cities*.[62] In all these works, there is a severe indictment of technological success and the inhuman scale of modern cities. Indeed, it was the large-scale delinquency of the poor in large American cities, the breakdown of family life and neighbourhood communities, and the impossibility of racial harmony that provided the impetus for studies associated with the Chicago school.[63]

A far less sentimental tone marks the work of Mike Davis, who writes of racial conflict and urban violence in fin-de-siecle Los Angeles by setting the inadequacies of technocratic solutions to urban problems within the framework of historically unequal social opportunities.[64] Rather than focusing on a process of historical *decline*, Davis's work builds on what a number of scholars elsewhere have spent time theorizing: that well-recognized injustices of the city are inherent to capitalism, and the very tendency to crisis within the urban milieu (and housing markets in particular) is its most important symptom. Insights into the production of space under capitalism, and its attendant inequalities, were enabled by the theories of Marxist sociologists such as Manuel Castells and Henri Lefebvre, and geographers such as David Harvey and Doreen Massey.[65] Lefebvre in particular has developed the theoretical tools for an analysis of the production of space, thus deconstructing categories which emphasize space as a creation of nature. Through a focus on the ways in which conceived and perceived spaces are articulated, the framework allows for an understanding of space that is at once physical-material and mental–ideological, thereby bringing clarity to a range of urban spatial practices. Despite internal disagreements and a rather formal adherence to the Marxist method, such works paved the way not only for an understanding of the role of the state/market in modern urban societies, but of social movements based in cities, of the autonomous meaning and importance of symbolic spaces, and of how cities could exacerbate, as much as they contained the possibility of ameliorating, existing hierarchies of, say, gender or race.

In its latest phase, as the site of the new industrial revolution powered by the rise of information technology, the modern metropolis is no longer defined by a landscape of grim satanic mills. It has been thoroughly recast in its physical–material senses by the shift to high technology manufacturing, comprising microelectronic based and computer-aided manufacturing. The replication of these manufacturing conditions across the globe, the rise of 'technopoles' which are intended to catalyse entire regions and the desire for 'placeless production' have gripped the imagination of scholars worldwide. The literature is vast and still growing: one may cite Manual Castell's recent attempt to synthesize and evaluate these scholarly productions as a useful starting point.[66] By characterizing the new spatial logic of the informational city as the 'space of flows', as opposed to an earlier logic that affirmed the 'space of places',[67] Castells is able to come to grips with an international revolution that has produced the spreadeagled 'corridors' of IT industries as much as it does the well-defined 'technopole' with varying degrees of success.[68] These developments, as Saskia Sassen's monumental study of three metropolises has shown, have done nothing to shake the power of the older financial and commercial hubs in a world of bewildering change: instead, 'the combination of spatial dispersal and global integration has created a new strategic role for major cities' such as London, Tokyo, and New York, adding to their historic importance as centres of international trade and banking several new roles in the organization and production of goods and, in particular, services.[69]

Not all of the developments that have been described for the 'global cities' or even 'technopoles' are mirrored in Indian cities, particularly since they are integrated into the global economy only partially and in enclaves. If anything, as Castells himself was careful to point out in his two latter volumes which discussed the political and cultural consequences of the new informational age, many of the generalizations about the new economy and its effects on cities can only be understood in terms of specific regional histories which negotiate the remnants of other socio–economic or cultural forms and the emergent economic or political forms.

The tools that are more appropriate to making sense of these experiences of city life in newly independent or newly industrializing nations are being forged through increasing attention to the meaning of citizenship itself, and cities as the site of this transformation.[70] Singapore, as I have already noted, has traced a very different trajectory from other post-colonial societies in its embrace of modernity:[71] one scholar, Chua Beng Huat, has described Singapore's political experiments as striking a different path from Western liberal conceptions of liberty and right, by staking out the totally new terrain of 'non-liberal communitarian democracy'.[72] Here, Beng Huat traces the communitarian element in Singapore politics to the legacies of a supposedly Asian tradition, though one that had shaken free of Confucianism.[73] Other scholars have been understandably more wary of invoking any specific 'tradition' in order to retain distinctions between the range of political regimes which share a striking similarity in their treatment of the rights of the urban poor.[74] Nevertheless, it is particularly instructive to stress the uniqueness of the Singapore example at a time when it has begun to dominate the imagination of city planners and politicians who desire an achievable model for cities in Asia and elsewhere.[75]

The yearning to recast the relationship between private and public, and thereby the meaning of citizenship itself, through state fiat in certain post-colonial societies, is now well documented by scholars such as Holston and Beng Huat. The experience of cities where such transformations have occurred through other historical processes can be equally instructive. There is perhaps no single author whose concern has so consistently been with the historic deterioration of public life in Western cities as Richard Sennett. Through several insightful studies of these cities, Sennett carefully traces the pernicious effects of a tyrannical privatization on the meaning and importance of public life. In what was to become an important trilogy of books on urban culture, Sennett pursues similar themes to emphasize the ways in which the quality of life in the planned Western city has changed—he would say deteriorated—in ways that impoverish both private and public life, and indeed, identity in the urban setting.[76] Moving away from traditional social scientific concerns about the deterioration of urban life, or the decline of cities, Sennett seeks ways of understanding the quality of urban life through the effects that it has on the Western personality and, more recently, character.[77]

If Sennett has used a variety of sources, not the least of them literary, to make his critical observations of urban life in the West, the very method of constructing an archive on the city, and the modalities of historical research based on such sources, have been brilliantly demonstrated by Walter Benjamin in his (literary) excavations of the Paris arcades of the nineteenth century.[78] By its very enigmatic incompleteness, Benjamin's monumental work urges the historian of the city to consider no material too minor or inconsequential in building up a critical analysis of city life. Benjamin's approach to the sources for writing a history of the city and his powerful critique of capitalism itself through unsentimental analysis of the fragments of everyday life in the city, constitutes a landmark in urban studies that would be perilous for any contemporary work on the city to ignore. The insights of Sennett and Benjamin, even as they are based on methods that are unconventional, breathe new life into any enquiry into the city, and remain relevant far beyond the time and place that was their chosen focus. The methods and insights of some of these cultural historians will animate the discussion of contemporary Bangalore that follows.

Recognizing the Metropolis: The Place of Bangalore

In his address to the Bangalore Literary Union in 1953, Sir M. Visvesvaraya, Mysore's leading engineer–statesman, who had long stressed the imperatives of economic planning, shared his visions for the future of Bangalore. Among many suggestions, which included the call to Bangalore's citizens to lead a 'disciplined life', was the one he made for a 'Ring Strauss' (sic) around the city, and a plea for a promenade along the lines of Bombay's Marine Drive:

> Another important development should be the construction of a road with a broad paved foot path by its side to connect Lalbagh with the Cubbon Park to facilitate the City Population taking an evening drive or walk in open air so that it may become a centre of recreation.[79]

'What makes Americans long lived, progressive and prosperous,' he continued, 'is the planned, disciplined lives they lead. Our activities on the other hand are unplanned, and our behaviour unplanned and inactive.' With remarkable prescience he referred to the citizens as 'stockholders of the city corporation', suggesting that only an 'enlightened and forceful public opinion' would help the executive in its daily administrative tasks.

Visvesvaraya's suggestions for a new recreational zone that would give the city a distinctive edge may not have been realized, but the mode of recreation has flourished in the most unexpected of sites in the city. Since it was completed in 1999, the section of the Inner Ring Road that connects two residential localities in Bangalore, Indiranagar and Koramangala, and broadly paved on either side, has attracted dozens of people seeking a break from their tedium. They gather every morning and evening for walks, as if on a promenade or to look at flights landing and taking off at HAL airport. If this space has sprung to life in ways that were entirely unanticipated by the planners of the Ring Road, and only confirmed Visvesvaraya's worst fears that Indians were incapable of planned behaviour, it also serves as a metaphor for the many practices that make new meaning of urban life in ways that exceed the technocratic imagination. This is one of the concerns of this book.

Another of Visvesvaraya's hopes appears to have been realized, and perhaps this time in ways that might have met with his approval. The appeal to citizens to see themselves as 'stockholders of the city corporation' appears to have struck root, inaugurating a period of middle class engagement with municipal concerns, and public corporate involvement with the municipality that is unprecedented. The constitution by the newly elected S.M. Krishna Government in 1999 of a body that would oversee the development of Bangalore, namely the Bangalore Agenda Task Force (BATF), is a sign not only of the acknowledgement of the need for building institutions to meet demands that the present system of elected corporators does not adequately fulfill: it is also a belief that the successes of corporate governance be applied to the city as a whole. In effect, it has meant that those for whom the city has been a space of accumulation on an unprecedented scale may determine the development and infrastructure of the city. Thus Janaagraha, an initiative of BATF, defines itself as 'a collaborative movement' which is intended to help citizens make 'informed and effective decisions that truly represent citizen's priorities', a direct call to 'take ownership and get to participate in governance'.[80]

Such initiatives come at a time when the formal aspects of citizenship are called into question with increased vigour by certain other categories of urban residents: slum dwellers, unemployed young men, women's groups. For such groups, the struggle over entitlements to space in the city, whether material or symbolic, is a way of redefining rights as claims, rather than possessions held against the world,[81] contrasting with the ownership of rights advocated by Janaagraha. Yet such claims are increasingly being made in languages that are violent; they reterritorialize city space and redefine public life in ways that are a source of mounting anxiety to the middle class, dismayed by modes of plebeian democracy. The modes by which the city becomes a site of refashioned citizenship is another of the concerns of this book.

Finally, the book is also concerned with a set of relationships that a senior technocrat and administrator like Visvesvaraya would have acknowledged as central to his concern for the production of disciplined citizens: the relationship between built forms, the design and regulation of the use of spaces, and the materiality of the body in the city (Fig. 3). Among the many suggestions he made towards defining a new mode of citizenship were the control of population growth and the institution of a rigorous 48 hour work week, as well as measures by which the voluntary cooperation of citizens might alleviate the temporary and long-term privation suffered during the war years. These suggestions concerned bodily discipline and the material aspects of everyday life,[82] especially as they stressed the imperatives of adhering to planning. A focus on the relationship between the body, politics and the city, and on the woman's relationship to urban life in particular inverts his optic to conclude this account of Bangalore's contemporary history.

FIG. 3 *The Town Hall overlooked a spacious junction and was in close proximity to the offices of the City Corporation, defining, along with Narsimaharaja Square, a continuous civic strip for the city, especially in the early 1950s, when it was the meeting place of the Mysore Legislature.*
(Department of Information and Publicity, Karnataka, early 1960s)

Bangalore too has suffered from the general neglect of urban studies in the social science disciplines. Until the 1970s, it was not even considered as anything more than a modest-sized state capital though it was the site of major public sector industries. Noel Gist made an early attempt at defining the ecological zones of the city, exploring the fit between space and function in different zones as they related to work, commercial activities, residential clustering, and public institutions.[83] The ecological approach received fuller treatment in Venkatrayappa's study of Bangalore city which continued the task of describing zones and their uses in greater detail (Fig. 4).[84] The first rigorous attempt at understanding the city from the perspective of a geographer was R.L. Singh's monograph on Bangalore.[85] In addition to mapping the urban morphology of the city, Singh's work was particularly successful in mapping the city within its regional geographic, and more important economic, systems, tracing the impact that the city had on its *umland*: in his analysis, the city's influence stretched to 15785 sq. km, almost a quarter of the then Mysore state.[86] He traced the evolution of the townscape of Bangalore as it historically bore 'an intimate relationship with the physical setting of site', and indeed as its morphology was geographically determined. Thus, as a 'ridge and valley town' which corresponded to the cantonment and city respectively, the

FIG. 4 *Remnants of the 'garden city': vineyard on Idgah property, Old Madras Road.* (Clare Arni, 2000)

settlement was shaped by the sources of water supply and considerations of proper drainage of the soil.[87]

The most ambitious study of Bangalore's social and economic structure was undertaken in the mid 1970s by two other geographers, V.L.S. Prakasa Rao and V.K. Tewari. [88] Based on a sample survey, which was to serve as a benchmark for several decades to come, its focus was on correlating a variety of social and economic indicators with the use of space. Moving away from the firmly physical geographical approach of Singh, or the entirely descriptive approach of Venkatrayappa, the study produced a far more nuanced account of human aspects of the urban landscape, taking such relationships as class, ethnicity and caste, as well as family size and economic status, into account. It was a snapshot of a city that was not yet a metropolis; indeed, the scale of the city's growth was not even anticipated at the time.

In the four volume *Essays on Bangalore* which was completed in the early 1980s, we may detect the beginnings of an anxiety about the future of a city that was experiencing exponential growth, made alarmingly evident in the census of 1981. The transition to metropolitan status from big city, in a demographic sense, was dealt with in an interesting way. Though some essays attempted to provide historical insights on its industrial structure,[89] problems relating to the city's infrastructure, public health, changing climatic profile, and the supply of essential public goods such as water and electricity, dominated the series. One may detect in these studies the early manifestation of an ideology of 'social municipalism' that characterized private middle class activism from the 1980s. The research agenda thus was determined by the urgency of coping with dramatic population growth: not surprisingly, the management of the city has been the focus of many studies that followed.[90] The management of the everyday city was paralleled by an interest in the management of disaster: James Manor's study of the 1983 liquor tragedy in the city, for instance, pointed to the grave lack of coherent responses from state and private agencies.[91]

Bangalore's recent rise to the status of a metropolis, and its internationally acknowledged status as the premier Indian centre of information technology, IT enabled service industries, and more recently, biotechnology industries, has begun to attract the attention of a wide range of scholars interested in the logic of such growth and its future potential. In some cases, this has been evaluated in terms of its relation both to the city's public sector past and to the demands of an international market.[92] The conclusions in many cases are sobering:[93] even more sobering are studies of the ways in which the planning or administrative apparatuses have been transformed through the

FIG. 5 *A Central Business District has emerged, defined by the high rise commercial buildings (visible in the distance) that ousted the low rise shopping area (visible in foreground) on Mahatma Gandhi Road. The 24 storey Public Utility Building, completed in 1973, continues to dominate the skyline.*
(Clare Arni, 2000)

use of the very technologies that have brought it such fame.[94] James Heitzman's newly published book *Network City*, which examines the city as the space of flows of information, challenges Bangalore's claim to the status of an 'information society' given the unevenness of this economic and political transition.[95] Indeed, the IT industries have taken root and even thrived on the uneven and combined development of capitalism in its latest phase. Yet, although it is far from being either a 'technopole' or a 'global city', there are unmistakable signs of the success of the new economy in defining the city in its own image through the new institutional forms that are being forged. In this sense, Bangalore may well be the site of a new and confident definition of urban space by capitalism (Fig. 5).

The work of scholars who look at the city from the perspective of the urban poor has followed predictable lines in most cases: studies of the slums of Bangalore,[96] for instance, or the informal economy[97] reveal aspects that may not be unique to the city. A far more complex account of the survival strategies of the urban poor in Bangalore, and the ways in which emerging structures of governance affect their prospects is in the recent work of Solomon Benjamin and Bhuvaneswari R.[98] Fewer studies have analysed political trends within the city as a whole. Only more recently has attention been paid to the emergence of social movements within the city, ranging from the trade union movement[99] to the more recent rise of linguistic nationalisms.[100]

This work hopes to lay out a different perspective on the city: one that relates to the three moments or levels of analysis outlined by Henri Lefebvre in his monumental work, *The Production of Space*. The space of the city is eventually produced by far more than the plans and drawings of the technocrat, and extends beyond the physical–material to include the mental–imaginative aspects of the production of and claim on city space. One may thus consider the distinctions made by Lefebvre, between the conceived city, the perceived city and spatial practice, as three possible levels of analysis. Yet the book also goes far beyond Lefebvre's concerns, in charting the styles and forms of contemporary urban democracy, and the city as the site of a continuous redefinition of Indian citizenship.

The book begins by painting the modern history of Bangalore with broad brush strokes, proceeds to analyse the careers of ideologies such as planning and national-modern architecture, moves on to the ways in which symbolic claims reterritorialized the city, and concludes with a consideration of the experience of women as political subjects in the city. In the first chapter, I explore certain historical themes particularly as they relate to the legacies of the past that have gained legibility in the contemporary city, focusing in particular on the divided history of the city (Chapter One). The fifty years since Independence are discussed in Chapter Two in terms of the success with which they overcome such divisions, as the city is marked by the nation, the region, and global capital. It also considers the concomitant development of the idea of citizenship in each of these phases.

The next three chapters are concerned with the conceived city, particularly as it relates to the ideologies of planning (Chapter Three), the law (Chapter Four), and the aesthetics of public architecture (Chapter Five). The two chapters that follow explore the ways in which city space is reterritorialized, through contests over systems of symbols and non-verbal signs in the city. Beginning with the ways in which language defines the right to the city, (Chapter Six), the work moves on to discuss contests over symbols and symbolic spaces (Chapter Seven).

Chapter Eight outlines spatial practices in the city through the example of women. Considerations of gender and the space of the city are few and far between, partly as women's studies in India has, like many of its older cohorts, been somewhat preoccupied with the position of the rural women and with spatial practices in rural areas.[101] This chapter hopes to bring the insights of women's studies to bear on the space of the city. Women are both marginal to the city (at the level of visibility and power) and yet an insistent presence that the zoning laws and the 'temporal neutrality' of the planning apparatuses rarely admit. Above all, the case of women as citizens-in-the-making enables the exploration of a series of relationships between the body and the city space, perhaps more fully than any other social group.

The conclusion points to the ways in which the case of Bangalore may be taken as instructive of the fate of many Indian metropolises. Many of the features of Bangalore's contemporary history are recognizably true of other Indian metros. Its extraordinary demographic growth, its difficulties with implementing planning law, and its engagement with ideologies of language or caste, to name a few features, are the post-colonial experiences of many cities in the Indian subcontinent. However, the city has equally developed distinct modes of civic engagement and spatial practices that reveal the operation of specific histories, so that the possible futures of the metropolis may resemble neither its remembered nor imagined forms. Bangalore, moreover, as I hope this account will make clear, has struck a metropolitan path that is remarkably different from that of older Indian cities such as Calcutta or Bombay. In this sense, it may indeed be the city of the future.

This work on the city of Bangalore is the outcome of a project that was ambitiously titled 'Worlding the City: The Futures of Bangalore'. It has now assumed far more modest proportions as a book that explores the making and meaning of urban space in the five decades since Independence. As a historian who has thus far worked on the nineteenth and early twentieth centuries, I have breached the time line, 1947, behind which most colleagues in the profession have safely stayed. I have thus wilfully strayed into a bewildering world of copious if always incomplete documents and writings, newspapers and books, visual materials and objects, all of which compose the reality of contemporary urban experience. I have plundered these materials and sensory perceptions, and transgressed many disciplinary borders, deploying the methods of the geographer, the ethnographer, the sociologist, and the cultural critic, while extending each of their interpretative frameworks to produce what will surely dissatisfy the more conscientious social science reader. These are transgressions compelled by the subject itself: urban life in contemporary India. Although the work is not structured strictly in chronological terms but is organised thematically, it reaches back when necessary to the city's pre-Independence past, or leans forward into the future. These levels of analysis will, I believe, disrupt any notion of the city as a space of incremental development or even progress.

At an exhibition of photographs of contemporary Bangalore entitled *Beladide Noda Bengaluru Nagara*! that I organized in 2000, a surprisingly large number of people remarked that the photographs, and black and white photographs in particular, brought back warm memories of a better time, a time before the city had achieved its metropolitan status. This, notwithstanding the fact that the exhibit anticipated, and particularly strove to overcome, the framing of the city as an idyllic space that has been lost to 'development', in all its enabling ugliness. This city has been particularly ill-served by 'once upon a time' kind of narratives, and the intention had been to produce a present history of Bangalore. Could the reader be urged to think critically and creatively about our *present*, in as unsentimental a way as possible? To develop the tools by which we may treat the past, including the immediate past, as something that is neither to be mourned or celebrated: this intention, which was only partially achieved in the exhibition, will I hope, be better served by this book.

ONE

Bengaluru/Bangalore: The Presence of the Past

Here there are many streets laid out with much regularity and of great width. Few towns in Hindostan can boast of better houses or of richer inhabitants, if credit can be given to appearances, and although the people had removed the principal part of their wealth on the advance of the British army, still bales of cloth with immense quantities of cotton and grain were strewed in every direction. Indeed the booty dug up by the individuals, out of concealment and deserted homes, strongly indicated ease, comfort and happiness in former times.

Roderick Mackenzie *A Sketch of the War with Tippoo Sultan*, 1793.

The relation between City and Cantonment was strange. It was neither one of friendship nor enmity. The English were not very interested in matters relating to the city. They managed to obtain the ayahs, grooms, butlers and clerks they needed in the cantonment itself. Enough revenues were generated there to maintain their territories. We must admit that they kept their areas clean and beautiful. Broad streets, lined with trees, the large compounds of the military and civil officers, colourful gardens around each home, English women pushing children in prams: we must admit that in addition to the strange appearance of a foreign environment, Cantonment was also beautiful. The spaciousness, wealth of colour, peace, restfulness and beauty: none of this belonged to us, it was produced by the unconscious alienated labour of our people for the foreigners. If we could forget this, we might enjoy it, but not even a moment's interaction with the English allowed you to forget that fact. Even the most ordinary Englishman had the superior air of the British Empire.

A.N. Murthy Rao, 'Bengaluru', *Samagra Lalitha Prabandhagalu*, 1999.

A cityscape of considerable diversity meets the eye looking north-east over Mysore Bank Square in Bangalore. In the foreground, the red brick University Law College reproduces the classical style of the colonial period, replete with pediments, tiled roofs, and balustrades. The multi-storeyed buildings that crowd close behind bear the mark of thrift and dull imaginations, as well as the necessities of efficient use of space. They are like an atonement for the lavish domes of Vidhana Soudha behind, which reach back to a monarchical regional history, echoed once more in the dome that tops the General Post Office. Piercing the sky in the distance are the tall, spare Visvesvaraya towers, locked in visual combat with the historical styles over which they preside. The imperial–colonial, national–historical, and national–modern imaginations thus co-exist in the spacious and thickly tree-covered central administrative district of Bangalore, giving only a hint of the architectural styles that lie beyond (Fig. 6).

The high modernist Mysore Bank Building, the first such structure in the city, dwarfs an older granite structure and looks down on heavy traffic coursing through the square below. In the past, and less frequently today, Mysore Bank

FIG. 6 *Layers of architecture visible from the Mysore Bank Building, looking north east. The law college building is seen in the foreground, behind which are the modern Multistoried Buildings. The domes of the Vidhana Soudha and the Visvesvaraya Towers are visible in the distance.*
(Clare Arni, 2000)

FIG. 7 *The Mysore Bank Square has been the focal point of religious, political and civic gatherings throughout the twentieth century. A Rajyothsava procession of the early 1970s.* (T.L. Ramaswamy, 1971)

Square was the site of religious gatherings, the launching point of nationalist protests, or on the route of celebratory processions. A memorial in granite to those who died in the 'Nariman disturbances' of 1937[1] registers a forlorn presence amidst the terrible profusion of vehicles and sounds, and is the only testimony of the many confrontations between the state and the people that have occurred at this square (Fig. 7).

Mysore Bank Square is a unique space in Bangalore for another reason, representing as it does a pause at the edge of the oldest part of Bangalore, near the Yelahanka Gate of the old city. Looking south-west, away from the central administrative district, the eye sweeps over a more homogenous but nondescript view of the old city area, where narrow three- and four-storey structures are pressed together to abut even narrower, treeless streets. The rooftops are generously sprinkled with TV antennae and naked steel rods, a promise of construction to come. Architectural styles here, if such a name is deserved at all, are strictly subordinated to the pragmatism of commerce, and of combining residence with workplace. The aerial view betrays no sign of the frenetic activity in the by-lanes of the oldest manufacturing district of the city. Here, for at least four-and-half centuries up to the present day, the din of the marketplace has mingled with the noise of manufacture (Fig. 8).

FIG. 8 *Traditional tiled roof or brick structures in the old city area have been almost entirely replaced by flat topped cement concrete buildings. The roofs of Cubbonpet as visible from the Mysore Bank building looking south west.*
(Clare Arni, 2000)

The history of Bengaluru/Bangalore is thus a tale of two cities, a western part or *pete* that dates back to at least five centuries (referred to here as Bengaluru) and the eastern part (or 'Cantonment' referred to as Bangalore) that is no more than two centuries old.[2] In 1949, these two cities, Bangalore City and the Civil and Military Station (earlier the Cantonment) were brought together under a single municipal administration. Yet the integration of these two distinct linguistic, political, and economic cultures, and their spatial identities remains an unfulfilled task to the present day. In many ways, Bangalore continues as a 'divided city', and brings to life some old divisions between its eastern and western parts.[3]

A history of the city must, following Henri Lefebvre's insightful assertion, view space as a far from neutral or natural medium. The modes by which city space is *produced* are central to such a history; moreover, space itself should be understood as referring to more than just the physical, to include mental and social space as well. Lefebvre suggests that at least three elements are crucial to an understanding of the historical production of social space: spatial practice (or lived space), representations of space (systems of verbal and worked out signs), and representational spaces (systems of non-verbal symbols and signs). Such a history of the city goes well beyond the terms in which Bengaluru's history has usually been discussed, as a parade of dates and names, of battles and rulers. Most narratives speak of the men who established, built up, captured, or enlarged Bengaluru, as it was annexed to the dominions of those who resided as far as England or Delhi, and sometimes as close as Bijapur or Mysore.[4] These accounts, and the countless narratives of nostalgia,[5] speak of but do not systematically develop these divisive legacies as they animate the life of the present day metropolis. In order to grasp the time we inhabit, we must produce neither a narrative of progress or decline, and must thus forsake the twin notions of continuity and homogeneity in history. Therefore, historical accounts that follow in this chapter and the next, will reveal something about the historical time to which the people, events, or processes belonged, but much more about the particular time, namely the present, in which they gain visibility.

A Place called Bengaluru

For a settlement that has been in existence for over four and half centuries, the city of Bengaluru boasts of few physical markers or monumental sites as visible signs of its antiquity. The topography of the region to which Bengaluru belongs is unremarkable and there are few signs of an archaic temple town, a commercial centre, or a tract energized by a river or other water source. The earliest settlement was probably a hamlet of no particular commercial or demographic importance to warrant the name of an urban setting, functioning instead as a node that drew the surpluses of the agricultural countryside, and was dominated by rural notables. Indeed, James Heitzman's comparisons of the area with the urbanizing regions of medieval Tamil Nadu during the Chola period strongly affirm Bengaluru's somewhat isolated and rural character until at least the sixteenth century.[6] Located at the ridge top of the main water parting of the Arkavathi and the S. Pinakini rivers, the region relied on tanks which were constructed right across this territory as the principal source of water for agricultural and domestic needs. This network of tanks supported mixed farming and market gardening activities. The low scrub forest which was interspersed afforded excellent opportunities for hunting and gathering, well into the twentieth century.

The region was controlled successively by the Gangas (fifth to tenth centuries), the Cholas (ninth to thirteenth centuries) and the Hoysalas (twelfth to thirteenth centuries), but the city first took shape as a fortified settlement in the sixteenth century. Though colourful tales may exist about how he 'founded' the city, Kempegowda was one of many Telugu warrior chieftains (*palegars*) of the late Vijayanagara state who made incursions into Tamil and Karnataka regions, and established their rule over vast agricultural tracts. Some historians believe that the name 'Bengaluru' is derived from an old settlement near present day Yelahanka, long before the time of Kempegowda, the 'Yelahanka Nadu Prabhu' or chieftain whose name is usually associated with the founding of the town in 1537. It is likely that Kempegowda's rule coincided with the development of a new urban form: a fortified settlement linked to a network of temples and tanks, later attracting many merchants and artisans who took up residence there.[7]

Kempegowda's ancestors, who came from the Kanchi region, had settled in the area around Yelahanka. Driven by the strategic need for a capital from which he could command the resources of the agricultural region around, Kempegowda chose a village called Sivanasamudram ten miles to the south of Yelahanka for his mud fort, and indeed the Bengaluru district was for long known as the Sivanasamudram territory.[8] The mud walls enclosed the principal streets of the town, and Bengaluru, according to one chronicler, was the maidan fortress which, along with the higher strongholds of Savandurga and Magadi, served as a defence for the entire area.[9] The site was located on an elevated ridge that sloped west to east. To the west were rocky hills, while the eastern areas were undulating. The cities of Bangalore would thus become what R.L. Singh has called a 'ridge and valley town, the old city occupying the valley portion and the new one including the Cantonment, the High Ground'.[10] These distinctive physical features would soon be mapped on to the economic, social, and cultural spheres, resulting in what has been referred to as the 'east–west zonation' of the contemporary city.[11]

The town that sprang up within these walls could have taken longer to be settled, functioning initially only as an administrative capital, later drawing in a mercantile class who traded in goods from the hinterland. Twelve *hobli*s yielding a revenue of '30,000 pagodas' were annexed to this town in the early sixteenth century: they included Talaghatapura, Kumbalgud, Hesarghatta, Banawara, Yelahanka, Halasoor (Ulsoor), Varthur, Kengeri, Jigani, Canally (Kanalli), Bavoor (Begur), and Casba Hale Bengaluru, all villages which have been subordinated to the urban agglomeration today.[12]

The decisive thickening of this node, or crossroad, into a recognizable urban centre occurred only in the sixteenth century. 'Emporium Mysuriensis regni celeberrinum' (the most famous market place in the kingdom of Mysore) said the Jesuit letter sent from Mysore province in 1724–5.[13] Certainly the

FIG. 9 *North View of Bangalore, as seen by the triumphant British army, showing the 'bastions that were breached' in the Battle of Bangalore, 1791.*
(Select Views in Mysore, The Country of Tippoo Sultan, from Drawings taken on the spot by Robert Home)

fall of Vijayanagara and the threat of Adil Shahi Bijapur compelled trade and commercial routes to move further south, strengthening places such as Bengaluru, as well as other urban centres of the south such as Senji, Madurai, Thanjavur, and Vellore. The fortified cities were also strategic imperatives against the marauding forces of the triumphant Bijapur Sultan (Fig. 9).[14]

Yet the difference in form between urban centres and rural nodes was still uncertain. Most of the historical accounts collected around the time of the British takeover of Mysore in 1799 focus on three distinct aspects of medieval life in the region: the grants to Brahmin *agrahara*s, establishment of large temple complexes, and the construction of tanks.[15] From these vivid historical markers, we may ask some questions about the economic and social history of the city and its urban form during the medieval period.

Endowing the City

The city of Bengaluru survived for nearly two and half centuries without noticeable physical expansion. Perhaps this has to do with the organization of economic activity in the settlement itself, which for a long period was a node for the collection of surplus from the countryside. Records that refer to the establishment of Brahmin *agrahara*s through the sixteenth and seventeenth centuries make clear that in the early phases of their rule, the warrior élite could extend and maintain their extortion and control of agricultural revenues only through liaison with the Brahmins, the legitimizing authority.[16] The grants serve as a sign of how political alliances were made and kingly status and control asserted. Kempegowda I (1513–59; 1564–9) established the Kari Amman, Doopasamudra, and Jadahally *agrahara*s. Some grants were made to Brahmin scholars: Immadi Kempegowda (1569–1623) established the Kempapura *agrahara* in Bengaluru for 48 scholars of diverse Brahmin orders, in a grant of 1605.[17] Shahji Bhonsle's (1638–44) first act on annexing Bengaluru from Immadi Kempegowda was to endow the Brahmins of Singapura to the north-west of Bengaluru in 1644. Similarly, his successor Venkaji's (1659–85) grant to the Chinnasamudra *agrahara* in 1665 and of Agram village to 'Anyem Bhut Brahmin' in 1670 were ample signs of the precarious command of the politico–military élite over a vast agricultural region. The establishment of the four towers around Bengaluru in Immadi Kempegowda's reign may have been brave symbols of a new power asserting its authority over the agricultural region.

For a site that was not close to a water source and was situated on an elevated ridge, a reliable supply of water for agricultural or domestic purposes was imperative from the earliest days of the settlement. The limited availability of water may have imposed its own limits on the growth of the city population. No wonder then that the provision of water through a system of tanks became a crucial element of city building throughout the twentieth century. Some claim that Bengaluru was referred to as 'Kalyananagara', a city of *kalyani*s or tanks.[18] Kempegowda himself is credited with the construction of the famed Dharmambudi and Kempambudi tanks, as well as Sampangi tank. The founder's namesake and successor Immadi Kempegowda constructed the Gidda Gowda and Karanji tanks, the latter supplying the fortified city;[19] both these tanks appear to have been filled up in the 1920s to make way for a labour colony and a *jutka* stand respectively.[20]

The dependence on tanks did not diminish even when the economic structure of the city had vastly changed. The British did not draw legitimacy for their rule from the patronage of Brahmins and temples, but the supply of water to the old and new cities was as important as in earlier times. The Ulsoor, Miller's tank, and Hesarghatta lake served as reservoirs for the city in the nineteenth century. Tanks required periodic human effort on a massive scale to keep them functional. The Ulsoor tank around 1900 was regarded so dangerous to public health, that it required drainage and de-weeding on a massive scale.[21] By the late nineteenth century, when tanks were becoming clearly inadequate to meet the city needs, Sankey's Reservoir was designed to collect and store rain water, with connections through contour channels to the Miller's tanks and Dharmambudhi tanks. Indeed, said Lewis Rice, so keenly felt was the need for augmented water supplies to the city, that contests were frequently held to design such systems, and 'there is scarcely a site or a tank for miles around Bangalore that has not formed part of one or another project'. Only in 1933 did Tippagondanahalli reservoir first yoke the waters of the Arkavathi river to Bangalore's supply.[22]

The tank economy thus sustained market gardeners through most of the twentieth century, with some water bodies retaining a hold within central areas of the city. Today, some tanks are no more than muddy puddles, and fields and gardens that fringe the tanks survive only on the outer reaches of the city, south-east off Sarjapur Road, or to the north-east as in the Nagawara tank system. Tanks that remain within city limits have been put to new uses, serving as oases of 'nature' within the urban landscape (Fig. 10).

The singularity of the tank as an urban landmark in Bangalore was long

FIG. 10 *Many of Bangalore's tanks, particularly in the heart of the city, have dried up and been built upon as the demand for the housing and commercial space grew. Akkithimmanhalli Tank (or Mud Tank) in Langford Town.*
(Elizabeth Staley, 1980)

recognized, and it was deployed as a refreshing visual element in the city. D.V. Gundappa, in his memoirs of former Bangalore municipal presidents, recalls the visit of Prince Albert in 1889.

> As the Royal Party got down at the City Railway Station and proceeded by horse drawn coaches towards the city, a grand sight greeted it at the Totadappa Choultry corner. The tank in front, the Dharmambudhi tank, was a broad sheet of cool clear water with a float (Theppa) gently gliding upon it. The float carried a party of Bharata Natyam dancers in colourful attire. As the processions turned to the east and took the tank bund, there was another delight—in the small part to the south of the tank *bund*, now called the Municipal Park [the Chik Lal Bagh]. With Theppa, dancing and music to the left and Nagaswaram pipe music to the right, the Royal Party should have felt as in a fairy land.[23]

At the turn of the century, Dharmambudhi tank continued to be a wonderful welcome to the many tired travellers who disembarked from trains at the station nearby: it was 'a vast spread of water' topped by water birds and an accompanying cool breeze.[24] This made for a pleasurable first encounter for those who were new to the city.

Small temples that thrived on the tank bunds brought together two different kinds of attachment to the city, an economic attachment with its functional use of space, and a sense of place produced by what Richard Sennett has called 'narrative time'. With the disappearance of the tanks to which they were dedicated, the shrines took on new, autonomous identities within a religious landscape that was rapidly transformed as new faiths found a foothold in the city.

The Reinscribed Religious Landscape

In his remarkable study of the relation between body and city in Western history, Sennett draws a distinction between space and place in urban form. 'It turns on more than emotional attachments to where one lives, for it involves as well an experience of time ... Economics prompted a conjunction of functional use of space and opportunistic use of time ... Religion prompted emotional attachment to place coupled with a sense of narrative time, a narrative fixed and certain.'[25] Certainly, medieval city building norms in India declared that no city is complete without a major shrine, a tutelary deity who watches over the people and their activities.[26] In the case of Bengaluru, there were many contenders for such a position, but it is Annamma Devi who is popularly acknowledged as the tutelary goddess of the city (Fig. 11).[27]

Boundary goddesses notwithstanding, Kempegowda showed the

FIG. 11 *Annamma, whose temple borders the erstwhile Dharmambudhi Tank, is popularly acknowledged as the tutelary deity of the city. Annamma procession on Subedar Chatram Road.*
(T.L. Ramaswamy, 1960)

exemplary enthusiasm of a new convert in his patronage of a number of large Shaivite temple complexes. Urban Shaivism was markedly different from the rural religion of the Kempegowda clan that patronized Beere Devaru and Kempamma. The complex at Basavanagudi, and Gavi Gangadhareswara temple to the south of the fort area (Fig. 12), and 'Chamaga Roy Swamy Devasthanam' (which could refer to Chennigaraya Swamy temple near Ganigarpet) belong to his time. Immadi Kempegowda is credited with establishment and endowment of the famous Someswara temple in Ulsoor. These temple complexes, as well as the Kadu Malleswara temple (established 1668–9) whose expansion is attributed to Venkaji's reign, lay beyond the city gates on commanding sites, their many and complex activities and servants supported through the grant of revenues from villages around.[28]

Temples in the old city area lent a different meaning to the urban landscape than that of the distant and spacious temple complex. This was no walled temple town, with its tower or *gopuram* and square, a peaceful void around which the rest of the city took shape. Cheek by jowl with houses, shops, factories, gymnasiums, and other civic institutions, these smaller temples

FIG. 12 *Several shrines have been added to the Gavi Gangadhareswara Temple founded by Kempegowda I in the 16th century, to make it one of the most important Shaivite complexes of the city.*
(Clare Arni, 2000)

are a lasting reminder of the waves of immigrant groups that made a home in the city. The trade guilds endowed grander structures, while smaller shrines also thrived. They ranged from the smaller Bisilu Maramma shrines of Doddpet, or the nineteenth century Sitaramanjaneya temple of Chikpet, to the more substantial and well established complexes such as Kasi Visveswara Temple at Balepet or Dharmaraya temple on Old Taluk Cutcherry Road.[29]

In 1807, a few years after the British takeover, as many as 44 temples were identified in the four *petes* or quarters of Bengaluru, each patronized by a different manufacturing caste or trade group.[30] There were several additions to this 'city of temples' throughout the nineteenth century. The temples, with either individual or community patrons, formed then, as they do today, a focal point for the religious and social life of a community. If temples to Shiva and Basava were built by the Balija merchants who were socially and economically dominant in the old city area, large numbers of temples were also built by the artisanal castes. The numerically dominant weaving castes (Devangas) and market gardeners (Tigalas) alike built and supported temples. Not to be left out of this social inscription of the city were less powerful communities such as tank diggers (Woddaru), the Vishwakarmas, and glass bangle selling itinerant tribes (Gajjalawar) who staked a claim to the city through the Vali and Sugreeva, Kalikamba, and the Nagappagudi temples respectively. Itinerant 'dasaravaru' or religious mendicants were associated with a number of smaller temples of Hanumantha and Gopalkrishna, asserting a narrative of renunciation within the social order of Bengaluru.[31] K.V. Iyer, a resident of the old city area at the turn of the nineteenth century, recalled the 'tufted and ash covered Bairagis' who smoked their ganja pipes in Poornia's *choultry*, unmindful of the disciples and families gathered around, epitomising the language of renunciation.[32]

We know less about groups that may have moved away from the city in times of political instability. Nomenclatural changes give us some clues to a transformed demography: Muthyalpet (pearl market) was briefly known as Ballapurpet, after the weavers of Doddaballapur who came to the area, indicating a shift from trading activities to manufacture. The merchants were notorious for their flexible urban ties, showing a remarkable willingness to migrate in times of war or excessive state control of trade, as occurred during the time of Tipu. Still, Ranganathaswamy temple in the erstwhile Muthyalpet was endowed in 1628 by a federation of trade guilds for the performance of various temple services, a sign that the city was not merely an economic space, a site of vast opportunities for monetary transactions and profits, but produced other kinds of attachments.

Throughout the 17th century, the influence of itinerant Sufis redrew the sacred space of the city with dargahs and shrines. The earliest mosque of the Taramandalpet area, Sangeen Jama Masjid, is ascribed to the brief Mughal interregnum in 1687–90, although it has been entirely rebuilt since then. Many dargahs of Sufi saints venerated by Hyder and Tipu, such as the well known Hazrat Sayyad Shah Mohiuddin Quadri (Kambal Posh) and Hazrat Tawakkal Mastan Shah (which is honoured by a visit from the Karaga) add liveliness and variety to the religious landscape. [33] Such a cosmopolitan religious landscape must have called for civic resources to regulate, manage, and foster access to public spaces for festivals and processions. This could not have been without its share of conflicts and contests. Order was however established and justice administered, in both intra-caste and civil disputes, by caste heads and leaders who only occasionally appealed to the law of the ruling élite.[34]

Christianity preceded a British presence in the area. The first missionaries of the Society of Jesus reached Mysore in 1648, and a church to Virgin Mary was built in 1724–5 in the heart of Bengaluru, with its probable location in the Lourdes convent in contemporary Cubbonpet.[35] Even the St Mary's Basilica of current day Shivajinagar to the east of Bengaluru had its origins as a shrine in 1674, well before the area was settled with the establishment of the General Bazaar and Blackpally in the nineteenth century. It was improved by Abbé Dubois in 1799, and thoroughly rebuilt between 1875–82.

Jesuit records speak of the difficulties of securing converts in the city, and of the constant call to 'perform miracles' in order for the new faith to triumph. Christianity on an expanded scale followed the conquest of Mysore by the British in 1799, when St Luke's Church was built for the use of British soldiers in the fort. Once it was relocated to a site in the old city area in 1932, it catered to the Tamil workers of the city area, and was patronized alike by the new city bourgeoisie as well as the old aristocracy.[36] By the 1930s, over 20 per cent of the population of Bangalore C&M Station was Christian, the largest such urban concentration of Christians in India.[37] The skyline of the cantonment included churches of every denomination to meet the needs of European sects and Indian converts alike. Some, such as the East Parade Church on Dickenson Road, began as a chapel in 1831 before moving to its present location in 1865 where it initially catered to British troops, then Tamil converts, and most recently to members of the Malayalam CSI.[38] The religious landscape was thus constantly reinscribed as new faiths and migrant groups found a foothold in the city. Older religious traditions were recast as the city took shape and transformed the topography of the area.

There is perhaps no single annual event, celebrated up to the present day, that unites aspects of Bangalore's tank economy with the religious landscape of the old city area and its complex economic life as the Karaga. For several days during the month of March–April, in preparation for the Karaga performance, the old city area is re-consecrated by the Tigala community, numbering several thousand in Bangalore alone. The nine-day festival ritually redraws a landscape that combines the economy of water bodies and (vegetable and horticultural) garden cultivation, both vanishing aspects of Bangalore city life. A chosen male priest is prepared over a forty-day period through a strict dietary and exercise regimen, to receive the manifestation of the goddess Draupadi, the wife of the Pandavas, at Dharmaraya temple. On the final night of the festival, he journeys through the streets of the old city area, as he himself embodies the goddess, and is the bearer of the pot that symbolizes primal female power tamed and contained in a male vessel. The Karaga thus refers both to the icon and the bearer of the icon who identifies with it. The route taken by the Karaga bearer, surrounded by sword-wielding Veerakumaras, traces a sacred geography that includes the main thoroughfares of the city, paying homage at selected temples and a dargah.[39] (Refer Fig. 1)

This festival, which straddles the border between village and city practices, and indeed between different notions of agricultural and cultural time, is witnessed by over two lakh people, many of whom visit the city from areas around the city.[40] Widely recognized as the most important civic ritual of the city, the *pete* Karaga finds littler echoes throughout the city, in dense settlements like Ulsoor, or in villages that have been engulfed by the metropolis such as Doopanhalli. Its performance today links memories of a different vanishing city to the vastly changed topos of the contemporary metropolis, and is a spectacular annual reaffirmation of ties to the city.

A similar affirmation of ties to the city occurs during the Festival of St Mary in the Cantonment. A promiscuous mingling of commerce and religion happens in the large square that fronts the St Mary's Basilica, on the edge of which the Russell Market built in the 1920s asserts a strong presence. At the end of the nine day feast of St Mary in Shivajinagar, the idol journeys through the crowded Cantonment lanes, echoing the religious journey of the Karaga, and attracting as large a number of witnesses (Fig. 13).[41] Yet a formal similarity between the Karaga and the St Mary's festival must not be taken as implying an overall congruence of the economies of city and Cantonment. The two cities represented two very distinct sets of economic relations, with

FIG. 13 *Crowds throng the market square in front of the St Mary's Basilica at Shivajinagar for the St Mary's Festival.*
(The Printers Mysore, Private Limited, 1991)

the fortunes of the old city dramatically altering in response to changes in political regimes.

Economies Old and New

The old city area bears the imprint of earlier economies both in its design and in the economic activities it supports. Bengaluru, which was a flourishing centre of textile production and a major emporium for goods from several parts of the subcontinent for over two and a half centuries,[42] suffered severe decline in the nineteenth century, revived its fortunes in the twentieth, and remains an important site of 'art' silk production. The walled town with its four principal gates, was intersected by two main streets to form numerous *petes* which were identified with the various trades and professions of the inhabitants. A high street ran from the Yelahanka Gate of the town in the north to the Fort gate in the south, separating the town into Deshadapet on the west and Nagarthpet on the east. Another street which ran east–west from Ulsoor Gate to Sondekoppa Gate intersected the Doddpet at a central chauk, or square.[43] (See Map 1) Traders and merchants as well as artisans were attracted to Bangalore due to the efforts of successive rulers in the seventeenth century.[44] By 1687, when the Mughal emperor sent forces to subdue and capture the area, the city was more than just a strategic gain: the Mughals were supported by the Wodeyars of Mysore who gained control of the city and its environs three years later (1690) for a sum of Rs 3 lakhs.[45]

Who indeed did not want control of what had by this time become an important commercial town? The *Shiva Bharat*, a Sanskrit chronicle written by Paramanand in 1670 to celebrate Shivaji's exploits, spoke of its wealth soon after its capture by the Bijapur army several years earlier:

> This town of Bingrul with its massive fort gates and strong fort walls is an impressive place. Deep ditches, full of water drawn from the big tanks, which are existing in its close proximity surround the fort walls. Within the town are fine buildings the most prominent among which is the palace .... There are many commercial streets in this town with an array of shops displaying costly goods. At some of the squares of the town, fountains have been built from which water springs, giving a pleasing appearance ...[46]

Over a hundred years later, a flood of British accounts bore testimony to the centrality of Bengaluru as the commercial and manufacturing capital of Mysore state under Hyder Ali and Tipu Sultan. 'A great deal of cloth is manufactured in different parts of the country particularly about Bangalore but little of it

MAP 1 *Bangalore, c. 1791*

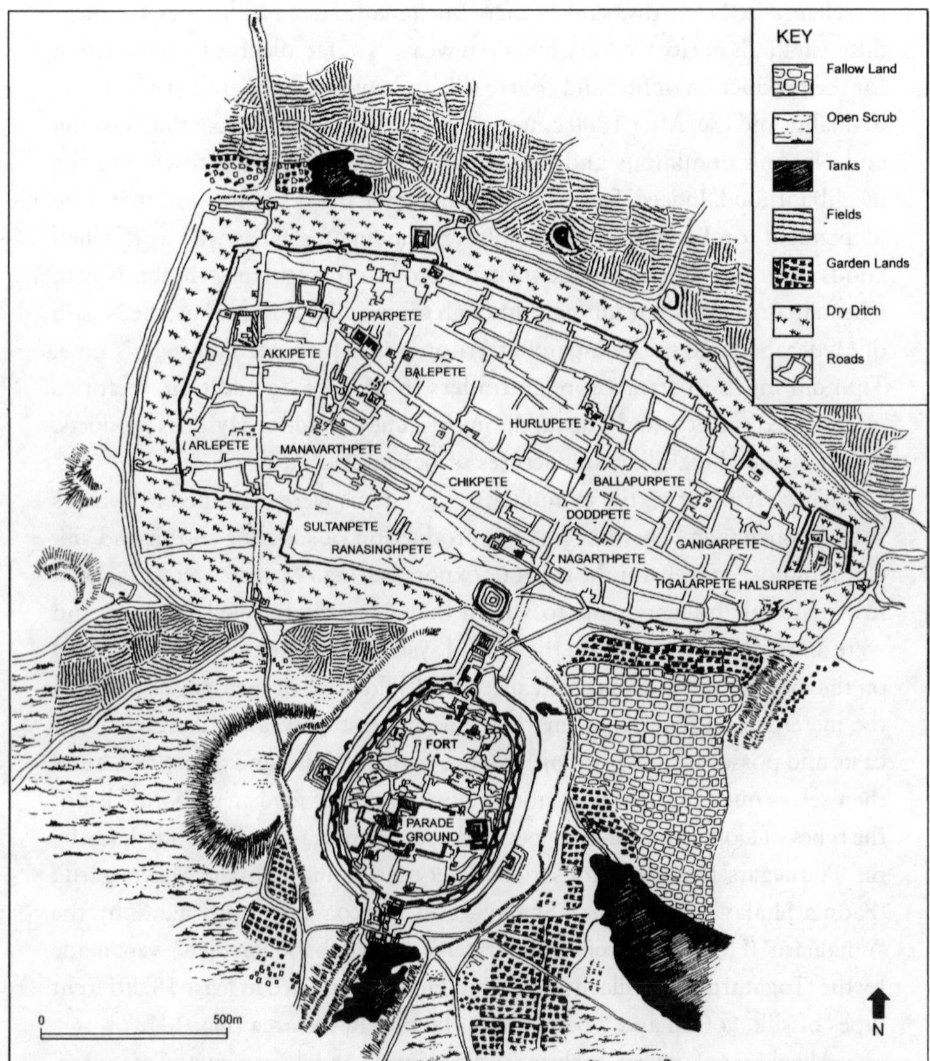

Source: Based on a map of Bangalore showing the Kempegowda Fort, from Intelligence Records of Colonel Read, 1791

is exported,' said Benjamin Heyne, a visiting medical surgeon.[47] The cloth merchants or Nagarths, said Francis Buchanan, advanced money to many different kinds of city weavers, and even weavers as far afield as Doddballapur, for the production of fine and coarse silk and cotton cloth, graded according to quality and use. After 1800 cotton was bought wholesale from the Maratha and Nizam's dominions and retailed to the weavers of the town and the neighbourhood. Indeed, Sarjapur was among the many small towns that were 'dependent' on Bengaluru for supplies of raw materials as well as finished goods. The city's textiles made their way to Srirangapatnam, Gubbi, Nagar, Chennapatna, and Chitradurga. Although trade with the Marathas, the Nizam of Hyderabad and the Company's territories was forbidden during his time, Tipu did much to attract foreign traders to Mysore. In addition, factories were started at Kutch and Muscat during his time to trade in Mysore's products, which included the silk manufactures of Bengaluru.[48]

Three types of textile manufacturing systems were identified by writers such as Buchanan. The first was the production of superior cotton and silk cloths almost entirely for the court or export market. Weavers were advanced raw materials by merchants to whom they gave the finished product, and were among the wealthiest. In the second system, weavers of muslin depended on the moneylender for their advances, and sold most of their goods either to the merchant or at the local market. The poorest of weavers were also low caste and possessed few printing, dyeing, or other skills, and sometimes hired themselves out as agricultural labour. Buchanan provided an elaborate list of the types of cloth produced for specified uses: there was the silk cloth made by the 'Puttuegars' (Pattegars) for saris and dhotis, the muslins of the 'Shaynagaru', 'Padma Shalay', and 'Samay Shalay', and the coarse cottons made by the 'Whalliaru' (Holeyaru), while smaller items, such as handkerchiefs, were made by the 'Togataru'.[49] Similarly, Benjamin Heyne identified at least 18 different types of silk, cotton and woollen manufacture in the area (Fig. 14).[50]

Allied manufactures, such as textile printing and dyeing, gunny manufacture, and oil pressing were also undertaken. No one denied the importance of Bangalore for armament manufacture, especially under Hyder and Tipu: 'they established at this place a Topana Carcana (sic) (or foundry for cannon) in which two cannons were cast every month, also a *bandook karkana* (or foundry for small arms) wherein monthly 35 firelocks of Muskets were made; these two karkanas were continued till the year Sadharana.'[51] Mackenzie confirmed that 'In the *pettah* there was an extensive gunpowder manufactory. Storehouses, foundries, with public buildings of various descriptions, appeared

FIG. 14 *Dyeing unit for artificial silk in the oldest manufacturing zone in the city, Cubbonpet.* (Clare Arni, 2000)

in considerable forwardness at Bangalore, and a machine copied from a French encyclopaedia produced different samples of carbines but very unequal in the bore.'[52]

The advent of British rule in the last decade of the eighteenth century spelt doom for the weaving industry. The number of looms fell from 5,000 in 1805 to about 2,700 in 1850,[53] with the population dropping from 60,000 in 1809 to about 41,289 in 1851–2 as the city was deindustrialized.[54] The demand for Bengaluru's sophisticated silk and cotton textiles diminished with the dismantling of the court, and coarser fabrics were often replaced by mill-made cloth. The city was increasingly turned into an inland entrepôt for

British goods, and its manufacturing capabilities were eclipsed. A revival of silk manufacture occurred in the late nineteenth century, when Bangalore was described as 'the centre of the silk trade where raw silk is prepared in large quantities for the loom and dyed'.[55]

Carpets, which began to be manufactured in the nineteenth century, won high praise 'for their durable quality and for having the same pattern on both sides'. George Birdwood singled out the pile carpets of Bangalore's central jail for special mention.[56] However, neither the 1911 census' claim that nearly a quarter of all weavers in Mysore state resided in the city, nor the considerable fame of the Bangalore drugget gave any indication of the desperate levels to which the city's manufactures had fallen. Only the establishment of two large textile mills in the western part of the city revived the economy in the late nineteenth century. By the early twentieth century, wartime opportunities for the production of horse blankets and parachute silk dramatically improved the fortunes of several medium- and small-scale woollen and silk filature units in the western part of Bangalore. The city once more became a textile centre, while vigorous state support for industry significantly altered an otherwise unexceptional industrial landscape.[57]

There was a stark contrast between the creative energies of the city's eighteenth century economy and the new Bangalore that developed to its east in the early nineteenth century. Like the old city, the Cantonment too had military origins, but remained rather strictly so until Indian independence. In 1807, British troops that were garrisoned at Srirangapatnam were permitted by Krishnaraja Wodeyar III to station themselves at a vacant site near the village of Halsur (later Ulsoor), in Bangalore district.[58] This open scrub forest area which lay to the north-east of the old city was dotted with farms and tanks. Soon private dwellings of European squatters and Indian camp followers from the Madras Presidency sprang up in the 'assigned tract'. Civilian groups from Madras Presidency, notably the 'Labbes, Mudaliars and lower caste menials' were drawn to the Cantonment by the opportunities for public and private employment. The area was also called Cantonment until 1868 when it was officially designated as a Civil and Military Station, an independent area under the control of the Government of India. Separated from the old city by a broad swathe of parkland (Cubbon Park, planted by Sankey in 1864), all facilities in this new city were developed to serve the troops and camp followers.[59] (Refer Map 2.)

Economic activity in the Cantonment area was dominated by trades and services: there were a large numbers of tailors from Maharashtra, for instance,

MAP 2 *Bangalore, c. 1850*

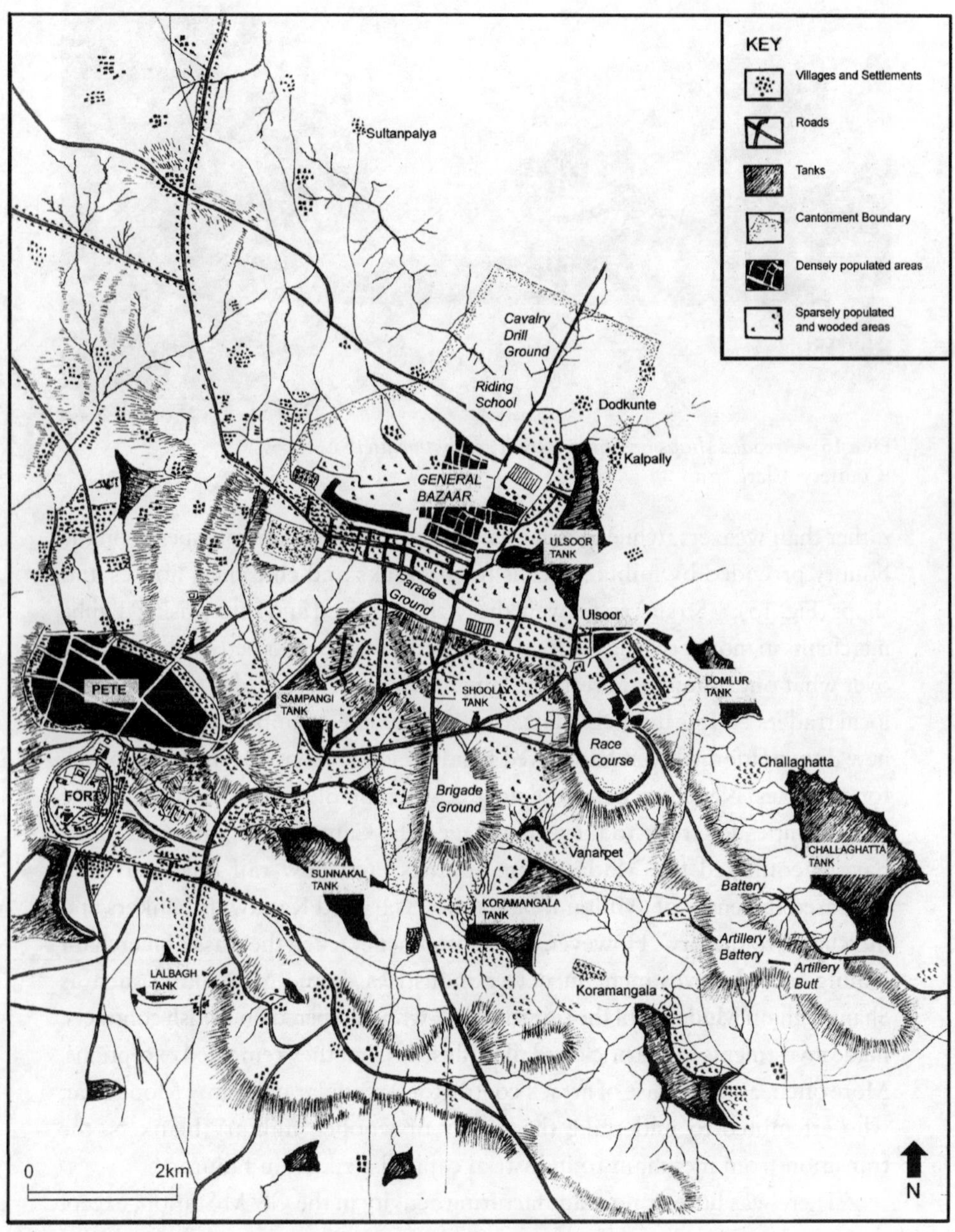

Source: Based on Plan of Bangalore, in *Pharoah's Atlas of Southern India*

FIG. 15 *Arcaded shops on South Parade, early twentieth century.* (Courtesy: Clare Arni)

rather than weavers, while merchants, builders, and bankers prospered on the bounty provided by military needs for barracks and churches, houses and shops (Fig. 15).[60] So successful were the 'well organized and enterprising' Labbe merchants in monopolizing the food grain trade, that they gained easy advantage over what one municipal president lamented were 'caste ridden, conservative local traders'.[61] It is unlikely that caste had become an impediment under the new dispensation when it had served Hindu traders' economic interests so well for centuries. New merchants did no less well than old ones in converting the opportunities for trade to their advantage. The Cantonment authorities may have encouraged the Madras communities, and new rail links certainly increased the entry of 'Multani, Bania, Marwari and Katiawari bankers and merchants to the city'. However, the Cantonment lacked the class of merchant willing to risk investment in newer industries. Some Mudaliars, such as Shanmugham Mudaliar of the Cantonment, who prospered on British contracts, made investments in the brick and tile industries, but they remained exceptions. More often, as in the case of arrack contractor Arcot Narainswamy Moodelliar, who attempted to undertake the supply of woollen military blankets, the transition from merchant to industrial capitalist ended in failure.[62]

There was little or no manufacturing activity in the C&M Station, except that which served the needs of the troops. Taverns supplying beer, and later the Bangalore Brewery, were set up for the European troops, in part to keep them from an excessive consumption of country liquor. A series of tanneries developed in the east towards Devarajeevanhalli on the edge of the Cantonment to meet the growing demand for leather. The only attempt to set up a factory, the Bangalore Steam Woollen Mills established in 1877, languished initially and dramatically improved its fortunes only when it was taken over by managing agents, Binny and Co., and shifted to the western edge of the city in the late 1880s. When the Peninsular Tobacco factory (later Imperial Tobacco Company) was set up in 1913, it formed a small though important enclave of manufacture within the cantonment.

The demographic profile of the two cities reflected the relative decline of the city in comparison with the C&M Station. Both parts suffered a sharp drop in 1898 following the plague epidemic, the station losing 10 per cent of its population and the city 13.5 per cent due to death and desertion. Yet the C&M Station had the edge over the city in terms of population until 1921, when the western part began drawing large numbers to its mills and factories. In 1951, the population of the C&M Station (2,78,191) was far below that of the city (5,00,786). In physical size, the C&M Station remained 13.54 sq. miles until 1941, while the city steadily grew to about 13 sq. miles, at the rate of about 10 per cent per year. Yet the old city retained its distinct form only around the fort, as the grid style of town planning was adopted in all extensions to the city.

Two Modes of City Development

In the old city, the main streets were oriented to the cardinal points, and contained the wholesale and retail shops in Doddpet, Chikpet, Siddikatta, Taragupet, Arlepet, and Nagarthpet. Away from these main thoroughfares was the dense warren of streets, also teeming with economic, religious, and domestic activity. Such a scale allowed for the full interplay of the human senses with the surroundings, although 'the peculiar odours of the Eastern Bazaar' or the 'universal babel which testified to outdoor life' were sensory aspects of the city that were little understood and even less appreciated by colonial authorities. It is likely that these areas were enveloped in a warm, fetid air, rising from both human and animal excrement, mixed in with smells of waste products from the textile and dyeing industries as covered drains were introduced only in the late nineteenth century.

A more intimate relationship between city space and the body was exemplified in the network of *garadimanes*, gymnasiums or body building clubs, which had as their goal the preparation of bodies for warfare, just as marching or polo playing did in the Cantonment. There was equal prowess in training the body to exert its power through restraint and channelized sexual energies, whose goal was the refinement and control of the fluids of the male body. *Garadimanes* were begun as early as 1680, and continued to be established through the 1900s, an equal number based on Hindu and Muslim systems of body building and wrestling.[63] In what was to be long recalled as a warning to the inhabitants of the city, Hyder Ali placed another kind of body on display. Khande Rao, who plotted against Hyder in the early 1760s, was suspended in a cage above the streets of Bengaluru, where he was fed milk and water until he died.

The roads were largely meant for pedestrian traffic, with one or two storeyed buildings opening on to small open spaces. These were zones of domestic and economic activity, where people might gather for talk, work, or repose. Houses were close and generally terrace roofed, 'a style rendered necessary by the army of monkeys which formerly were a most numerous and mischievous portion of the population'.[64] It was more than likely that the street was what was left after the houses had been built, only the main streets bearing the marks of planning. Indeed, the street was an extension of the home, with *jagalis* (raised platforms) flanking the entrance to the house where women often sat and worked or rested. Other homes opened into small private courtyards, a space for domestic chores or sometimes places where skeins of silk were dyed in boiling vats of colour. The large number of temples which studded the living areas provided a sharp visual contrast to the homes, their lavishly embellished portals sometimes opening into the stillness of a courtyard dominated by a peepul tree, with the main temple at a little distance.

Yet it was an urban form with which the British masters had no patience: the old city epitomized the very worst in city planning, and nourished disease and death. Lewis Rice said, 'Owing to the rapid growth of the town, and the various hands through which it has passed, the streets in the old part are often narrow and mostly irregular in appearance' (Fig. 16).[65] While some writers, such as Mark Wilks, claimed that 'the houses of the natives are mean and poor, even those in larger towns such as Bangalore', other observers attributed the comparative lack of large private buildings in Mysore to the uncertainties of life under Tipu.[66] R.K. Narayan was to comment as late as the 1940s, not without impatience, that 'it will be an uphill task for any municipality to push back the projecting façades, straighten the roads which have been wriggling for ages, and clear away choking vermin-breeding buildings'.[67]

Not just the relationship between public space and social life but also private life in the city was redrawn with the development of the Cantonment,

FIG. 16 *Scenes from the bazaar (Avenue Road?), Bangalore, c. 1880.* (From the India Office Library, Photo 447/3b)

itself a new phase in city development. The street was no more what was left after houses were set up, but the vital arteries of the city, built for wheeled vehicles and speed. Roads and open spaces in the cantonment celebrated the body in motion: soldiers on parade, polo playing officers, the rituals of walking the promenade, or cycling around Ulsoor Lake. In striking contrast to the old city area were the broad, straight tree-lined avenues that formed the central axis of the C&M Station, avenues intended for parades of wheeled vehicles or spectacles of military power. 'The parade ground extends two miles east and west and is surrounded by a ride or mall,' said Lewis Rice, in the late nineteenth century, with the Residency occupying a commanding site on its western edge.[68] The tallest structures along the parade ground were the churches of various denominations, such as St Marks' Church on the west and the Trinity Church to the east.

There were well-spaced areas for European bungalows in Richmond and Langford towns, though none were too far from 'native quarters' or lines, which provided vital supplies of domestic and other labour. Those areas which were designated as 'native quarters' included Blackpally (later Shivajinagar) to the north of the parade ground, Ulsoor, and some quarters near Shoolay and the Arab Lines, bore stronger resemblance to the old city area.[69] They

FIG. 17 *A house among the trees: a colonial bungalow in a spacious compound sports several of the classic 'monkey tops' over its windows.*
(Elizabeth Staley, 1980)

remained in sharp contrast to the spacious and well laid-out compounds and gardens of the Cantonment area. These homes were sometimes built on sites as large as two or three acres, emphasizing, as Anthony King suggests, the social distance between ruler and the ruled, and a sense of space largely unhindered by any concern for the economies of land-use (Fig. 17).

The Indian areas within the Cantonment, like the old city area, were oriented towards pedestrian traffic, with narrow streets containing a mix of workshops, dairy farms, manufacturing areas, and residences. Religious structures jostled for space with commercial and workshop spaces, and the links between commerce and religion were never denied. The spacious European style layouts or 'towns' were more strictly 'zoned', so that space was designed and developed for single uses: thus residence, workshop, and religious structure retained their physical autonomy in these parts of the Cantonment (see Map 3). The 'shop-house' was a rarer form, though not unknown even in such central roads as South Parade or Brigade Road (Fig. 18). 'The Cantonment bazaar', said Hayavadana Rao in 1930, 'contains a commodious and well kept market, the Bowring Civil and Lady Curzon Hospitals, numerous imposing stores for the sale of European goods etc., large Indian buildings and also a fine Roman Catholic Church'.[70] St John's Hill was populated with small cottages, giving the impression of a spacious planned area. Before long, the rules

MAP 3 *Bangalore, c. 1897*

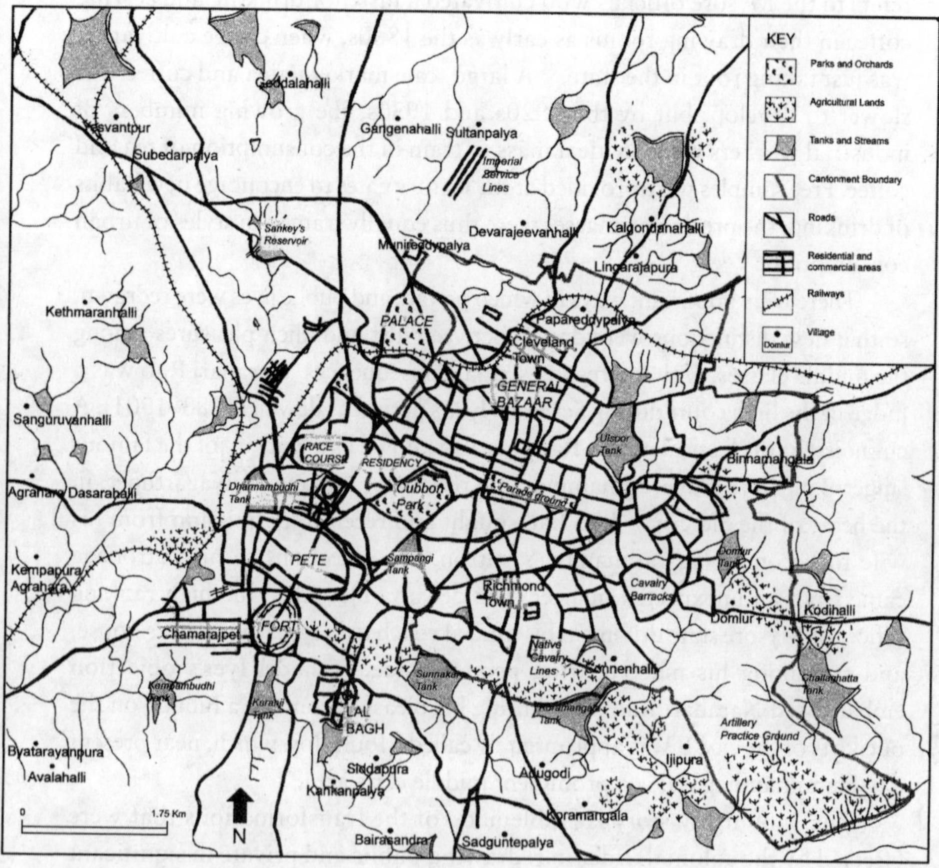

Source: Based on Bangalore City and C&M Station map in B. Lewis Rice, *Mysore: A Gazetter compiled for Government, 1897*

of town planning that emphasized public health and the circulation of light and air were applied to extensions to the city as well. Ovals (such as the Mirza Oval before the City Market), triangles (such as the Hudson Church Triangle), and squares (such as the Mekhri Square) came to represent these new sensibilities.

New Models of Town Planning

After the nineteenth century, all expansions to the city area were inspired by colonial zoning regulations and the strict separation of residence and workplace. For the most part this was a privilege of the newly emerging middle classes, spawned by an expanding bureaucracy. Domestic life was increasingly responsive to and influenced by colonial tastes and desires: Sundara Rao refers to the Mysore officials who cultivated a taste for drinking and serving coffee in their drawing rooms as early as the 1860s, when coffee cultivation was just taking root in the state.[71] A large scale market in tea and coffee was slower to develop, but by the 1920s and 1930s, the growing numbers of industrial workers were an ideal mass to train in the consumption of tea and coffee. Free samples were provided at the factory gates to encourage new habits of drinking: the producing masses were thus equally trained in styles of urban consumption.

There were important ways in which private and public lives were redrawn, so that new distinctions were drawn between licit and illicit pleasures among the middle classes, with interesting spatial consequences. Narahari Rao was a judge in the high court during Seshadri Iyer's period as dewan (1883–1901). A connoisseur of classical music, Rao was also known as a 'patron' of the famous singer Bangalore Nagarathnamma who resided at the time in Nagarthpet, in the heart of the old city.[72] Rao had sought and received permission from his wife to become Nagarathnamma's patron, but objections to his patronage came from an unexpected quarter. The dewan objected to the high ranking officer of Mysore state driving in his official coach to Nagarathnamma's house, and stationing his mace-bearing peon outside. Seshadri Iyer's objection embarrassed Narahari Rao into shifting his pleasure court to a hillock on the outskirts of the city. It was appropriately called Mount Joy, which, near present day Hanumanthagara, is a prominent middle class area.[73]

The Mount Joy story is emblematic of the transformations that were effected by the colonial order in redrawing public and private in significant ways. All extensions and new developments from the late nineteenth century were built strictly according to the 'grid iron or chess plan'. The earliest extensions to the city were Chamrajpet and Seshadripuram, (1892); a city administration shaken by the intensity of the plague epidemic undertook the next series of expansions, in Malleswaram and Basavangudi, which were planned as early as 1892, but executed with some urgency after 1898.[74]

The plague epidemic showed up the insanitary conditions of the city area to the hilt. Standish Lee, the city engineer, proposed the introduction of pit privies, daily conservancy latrines, and conservancy lanes, but as they were too expensive, a series of interim measures were adopted, including 'the removal of rubbish from backyards once a week'.[75] The city required a system of open drains in lanes and alleys and underground pipes for main streets, but that still involved large numbers of scavengers to take excreta out of houses. 'There was no water borne conservancy in the old fashioned town,' the municipal engineer to Bangalore Corporation from 1898 to 1912 J.M. Stephens remarked.[76] Piped water was introduced into the old city just before the plague, but until then was sold by the barrel or supplied from Dharmamabudi tank through troughs and basins called *karanjis*.[77] This was in contrast to the C&M station which had secure supplies of water. Undoubtedly it was anger at the inequities that led to a high incidence of illness in the city and in Blackpally areas, coupled with fear, that prompted some Indians to 'leave plague corpses in European compounds and against officials' doors.'[78]

Basavangudi was the location of the plague camp in the months immediately following the outbreak of the disease in August 1898, but the demand for a permanent exit from the old city area was so great that a layout was planned on 440 acres of dry land. Another 291 acres were acquired for the Malleswaram extension. Both of these were promoted as 'model Hygienic suburbs', well spaced and, most important, so well drained that 'a deluge of six inches would not leave a vestige of standing water in any of the house sites'. The Basavangudi extension appears to have followed the rectangular design, with boundary roads running north–south and east–west, and intermediate roads parallel to them to enable 'houses being built facing the cardinal points in accordance with ancient Hindu usage' (Map 4).[79]

If the concern for public health thus redrew the map of the city, the planning authorities also paid scrupulous attention to the social hierarchies within the city. Within these layouts, hierarchies revolved around caste, and in effect class, so that the largest and best-placed sites were for the Brahmin community. There were villa sites intended for the very rich but most accommodating of social hierarchies were the 'five principal divisions for the different castes, limited by cross roads, Muhammedans, Hindoos, Brahmins, Native Christians and Lingayats'.[80] There was also, 'a block at the north west end set apart for superior house and bungalow sites where no caste distinction is maintained as there is a compound to each house'. Physical distance between homes thus considerably diminished the possibility of undesirable social contact, allowing for a new type of privacy, though not always successfully as we shall see.

Malleswaram similarly had eight blocks, one for each 'particular section of the people'. By 1906, as Mysore Resident Colonel Robertson himself admitted 'hardly any really poor had gone to live in those extensions' unable to afford the move to better locations. Allotting separate areas in each community block for the poor was unworkable in a situation where members of the upper castes raised consistent opposition to their presence in these planned areas. In 1902,

MAP 4 *Plan of Basavangudi, 1894*

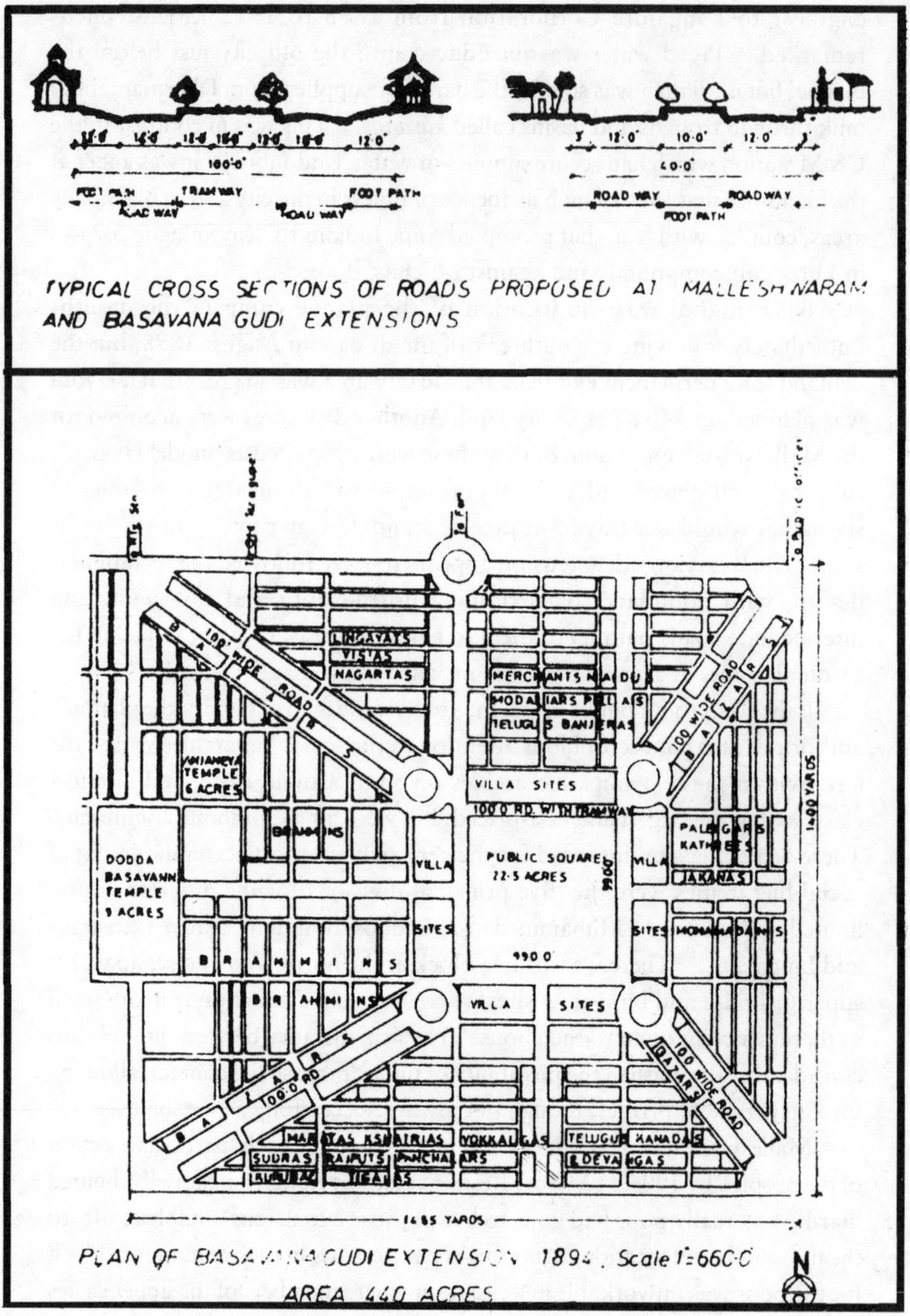

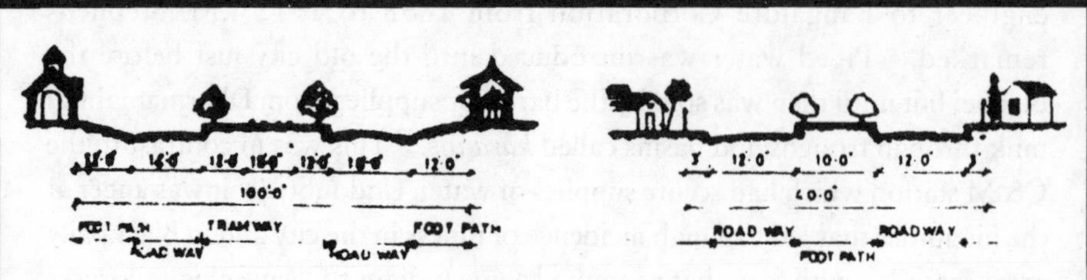

the Brahmins raised vociferous opposition to the grant of building sites to the 'untouchables' of the Queen's Sappers and Miners, forcing municipal authorities to allot new sites well away from Brahmin neighbourhoods.[81]

Yet even when the concerns of the municipality evolved in directions that were somewhat different from those of planners, members of the upper castes did their best to retain a hold on a rapidly secularizing city space by blocking the richer non-Brahman classes from the ownership of large sites. In 1915, the conversion of 24 house sites in Chamrajpet into five 'cottage sites' and their allotment by open auction to non-Brahmins was bitterly resented, not on grounds of equity but on the question of the caste unsuitability.[82] A member of the council had defended the conversion on aesthetic and civic grounds: 'a few decent houses costing from Rs 5000 to Rs 8000 will greatly improve the appearance of the locality', he wrote, while allotting sites ranging from 207 by 105 ft and 236 by 105 ft in size. A resident M.A. Thirumalachar objected strenuously to this proposal, saying that the allotment of cottage sites 'without any class restrictions' opposite Sri Rameswara Temple was a violation of 'the sanctity of the area', and asking that they be allotted only to vegetarians. The better class non-Brahmins, he said, would inevitably bring 'low class non-vegetarian syces and coachmen' in their wake. The Municipal Council briefly wavered, fearing 'objections like these though apparently negligible to start off with often end in riots', but eventually rejected the objection.

In new city areas, caste shaped physical form in very different ways. In the old city, bonds of community and occupation, which may or may not have coincided with caste, formed the basis of separate neighbourhoods. In the newly planned extensions of the colonial period, the laws of town planning, for all their avowed neutrality, in fact reproduced caste hierarchies in a new form, so that the purely residential areas that were zoned into existence now reasserted caste privilege and segregation. In this sense, town planning conceived of space as not merely reflecting social difference but also instituting it, and in the case of working class communities, even promoting social change as we shall see below. In a formal sense, these extensions were also in contrast to both the old city form and the cantonment form. Following the plague, conservancy lanes and well constructed drains ensured hitherto unknown levels of public hygiene and comfort. In old city areas that were reconstructed, such as Tharagupet, a series of measures, including compulsory building codes, fitness certificates for older buildings, as well as outright demolition, allowed for transformations of a city space unsuited to such high densities.

In the C&M Station too, the more congested parts of Blackpally area were demolished, giving way to Fraser Town in 1906, as well as Richards

FIG. 18 *The 'shop-houses' on Commercial Street, allowed merchants to live above their shops, while substantial communities of tailors, jewellers, and bankers occupied the streets leading off this central shopping area in the early twentieth century.*
(Courtesy: Clare Arni)

Town and Cox Town.[83] The provision of 'spaces on the lines of small parks or squares' were central to the new housing areas on the east. Fraser Town, also known as Papareddipalya, was quickly gentrified as 'well to do residents' soon took the place of the poor for whom the areas had been designed. Richards Town which was even better drained than Fraser Town, attracted more middle class residents, as did Cox Town: all the areas had electric lights, wide roads, and conservancy facilities, and were close to Commercial Street (Fig. 18).

A very imaginative case of rebuilding was of the old Knoxpet area which had housed the Chuckliars (leather workers) from 1865 and potters who were evicted from insanitary areas near the Cantonment railway station.[84] The area consisted of poor quality mud houses with thatched roofs. Knoxpet was strongly recommended for evacuation following the plague epidemic of 1898 but rebuilding was finally taken up only in 1923. The municipality applied the rules of town planning to a working class area for the first time. It would raise the area, renamed Murphy Town, to a 'proper social and sanitary standard' for a long time to come. Three defining principles were laid out: the housing, though 'too good for the classes that occupy them' were essential for Panchamas to learn self respect. Second, 'the dull uniformity of barracks' was to be avoided as it hindered social elevation. Thirdly, houses were built with an eye on possible expansion as economic circumstances improved. Substantial

FIG. 19 *Social improvement through planning: open square bordered by working class housing, Murphy Town.*
(Clare Arni, 2000)

improvements were made to their houses in the early 1920s. As many as 108 double and 310 single houses were built, using Mangalore tiles, cement, and bricks, and the area was also provided with schools, temples, churches, a market, and a creche. Houses were grouped around large open quadrangles planted with shady trees, voids which provided a valuable space for social and community events.[85] The planning of open squares and spaces was an attempt to infuse notions of civic or 'community life', and indeed assert new divisions between public and private. It is not uncommon to see these spaces put to unintended uses, sometimes as an extension of private space, so that lines of domestic washing are hung across the squares. Not all these uses are permanent, and the square resumes its public identity at election times or during weddings and feasts (Fig. 19).

By the 1930s, the steady stream of immigrants into the city to work in its mills and workshops was seen as posing a threat to the housing standards of the city. Millhands were crowded into older areas of the city such as Cottonpet, or low-lying lands belonging to the municipality (Pit Colony), or private owners (Anjanappa Gardens), with only a privileged few accommodated in company housing colonies such as Binnypet.[86] Close to 14,000 families were in need of housing at this time. The Srirampuram Labour Housing Colony, inaugurated with much fanfare, was intended as a partial solution to the problem. It became the site, in 1937, of the city's first (and only) rent strike, when the Mass Awakener's Union organized protests against the increase in rent from Rs 1/8 to Rs 2/8.[87]

Decisions regarding facilities for the treatment of the mentally ill, or the location of the Indian Institute of Science alike were determined by the topography of the city: only areas which held the promise of well drained soil were considered suitable. According to Sanjeev Jain et al., informal arrangements for the care of the insane were established in 1848 in the Cantonment area. A separate facility for the mentally ill was later appended to the *pete* hospital, to which the old jail was added in 1850. The asylum was at an elevation and close enough to Dharmambudhi tank to ensure adequate water supply and dry earth conservancy. Despite the addition of new buildings, which were described as being 'simple, but airy', the first location, on present day Kempegowda Road, could not contain the growing numbers who were diagnosed as mentally ill. The move to a more spacious site became imperative. A location in Basavangudi was rejected in favour of 'the second highest hillock in Bangalore (the first having been previously sanctioned to the Indian Institute of Science)'. The new sprawling asylum built in 1920 on well drained soil housed 400–500 patients from all parts of Mysore state, as well as Armenians, European Catholics, Italians, Irish, English, and people from all parts of India.[88] The landscape was thus re-inscribed in terms that privileged conditions of good health rather than production. Furthermore, the productive landscape took on new meanings within a social order that privileged outdoor leisure activities for the military and bureaucratic élite, and an Indian aristocracy that was gradually acquiring the tastes of the British landed gentry.

A Redefined Landscape

British descriptions of the Bangalore countryside, and visual representations in particular, as revealed in the artistic commissions of Robert Home[89] and James Hunter,[90] for instance, were largely commemorative of the British military triumph, paying less attention to the vibrant social and economic life of the region. The territory that had been newly annexed to the British Crown was picturesque, and largely bereft of a population, marked instead by natural features and certain monuments, notably the fort and the palace.

The fort, which was rebuilt to the south of the walled city by Chikkadevaraja Wodeyar in the seventeenth century, fell into disuse after nearly 200 years as a

FIG. 20 *Shoolay, early twentieth century. Once a village populated by those who served the British army, Shoolay was transformed by the appearance of churches, (the spires of the St Patrick's Cathedral are seen in the background) shops and police stations. Today, the area, called Ashoknagar, bristles with exclusive boutique shops and restaurants, gradually transforming the lower middle class area into a gentrified 'boutique' zone.*
(Courtesy: Clare Arni)

military bastion under diverse rulers as the new colonial masters found no strategic use for these structures. The mud fort was substantially improved 'with great strength of stone and fine chunam work' during the time of Hyder Ali (1761–82) by his *killedar* Ibrahim Saheb, with plentifully available granite taking the place of the mud walls, and newly cast cannons to strengthen its defence.[91] The British army was located in the fort only in the early stages of British rule, after which it was used to house the administration until the Attara Kacheri was built in 1868. The handsome granite structure was finally dismantled in stages from the mid-nineteenth right into the early twentieth century.[92] Over time, according to Sundara Rao, Banappa Park in Cubbonpet, the Kalasipalya, area, the Vokkaligara Sangha site, and Pampa Mahakavi Road buildings took the place of the fort walls.[93] By this time, the British army had been stationed in the area adjoining the old city, a new military encampment defined according to a different spatial and strategic logic (Fig. 20).

Interspersed with the military grass farms (for the cavalry), the artillery ranges, the barracks, and cottages in the late nineteenth century were the villages and horticultural farms that continued to thrive in the midst of this new urban order, stubbornly retaining their spatial form as new residential layouts sprang

MAP 5 *Bangalore 1924*

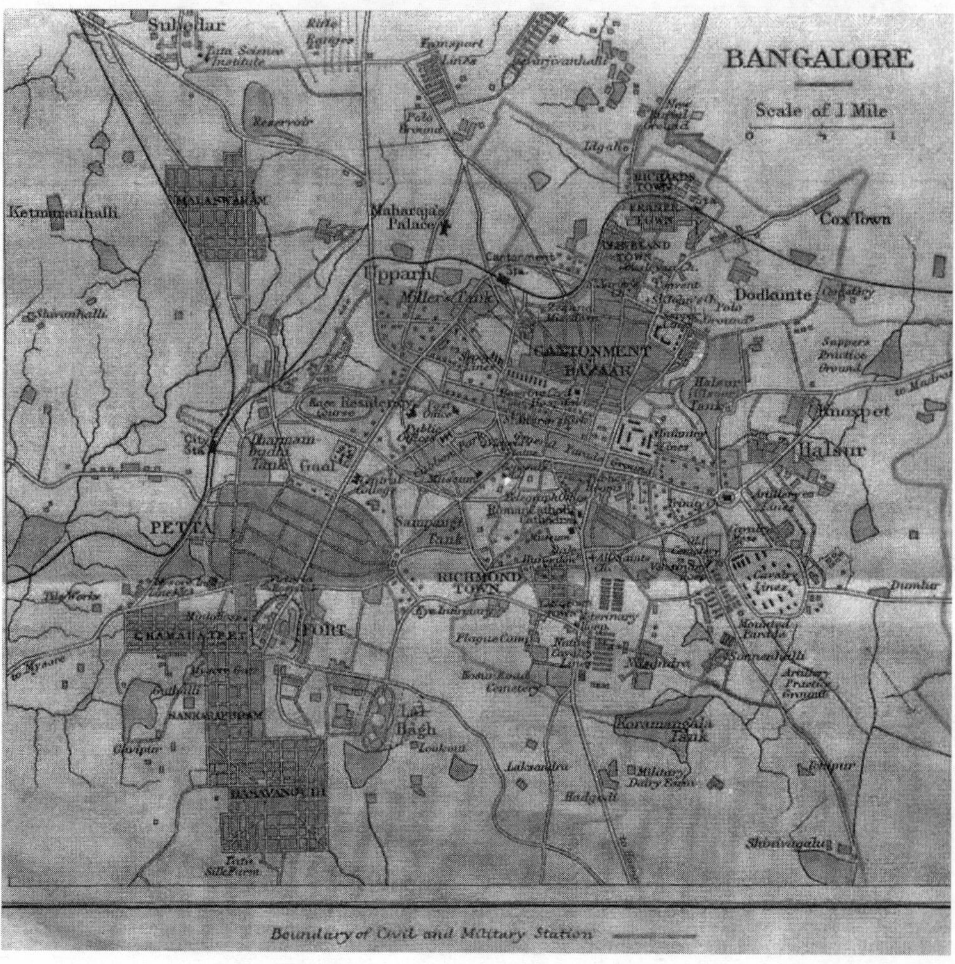

Source: Murray's 1924 Handbook.

up around them. The scrub-covered areas of the thinly populated Cantonment supported the cultivation of leisure activities more appropriate to the English countryside. There were five polo grounds at the turn of the twentieth century: Sampangi tank bed was briefly used as a polo ground, before turning into a slum in the mid twentieth century and then a sports complex. (See Maps 2, 3, and 5.)

The open areas were even more conducive to the pursuit of hunting. The Bangalore Hunt was an annual event that continued well into the 1930s and 1940s, drawing European and Anglo-Indian participants with a taste for the

FIG. 21 *Colonial pastimes: thirty pairs of hounds, trained to pick up the scent of a hare, fox or antelope, readied for the Bangalore Hunt, 1930s.*
(Arthur Hughes Collection, New York)

pleasures of chasing and trapping small animals. The hunt was the re-creation of an English pastime, and required the import of the English fox hound, housed in special kennels and cared for by trained Indian keepers. The Bangalore Hunt was begun in 1924 with Bert Buckley's Hounds, which were owned and hunted by him until 1930. The Hunt Club bought the 30 pairs of hounds in 1930 and the Bangalore Hunt took its place alongside other famous hunts in India, from Peshawar and Murree to MHOW and Ooty (Fig. 21).[94] Members of the Hunt gathered at Queen's Road attired in scarlet and white; hunting was done in the areas around that have now given way to the airport to the east of the city. The season, which began in January and ended in June, found enthusiastic participants from the army, the civil service, and royal Indian families, accompanied by women who were not allowed to hunt. Special events organized for occasional visitors won praise for faithfully imitating the English original.[95]

Yet Bangalore was after all not England. As the Bangalore Hunt recast the countryside in strictly hunting terms, it actually and metaphorically effaced the productive countryside. Thus, guidebooks intended for the British visitor throughout the early twentieth century focused chiefly on areas in and around Bangalore that afforded the visiting Englishman the pleasures of an easy hunt. Of Magadi, it was said, 'an occasional good bag can be made along this route: antelope, bustard and florican can be had about 10 miles from Bangalore, and bears and cheetahs are sometimes to be met with at Savandroog'. There was 'plentiful hare' on the Agram plains, and 'good sniping ground' around Krishnarajpuram.[96] An agricultural topography was recast from the singular perspective of pleasure, and sometimes with disastrous consequences, of which we have only a hint. The 'scent of the fox' drove hounds and horses through various types of country, woodland, grassland, and cropped land, and the hunters were often unmindful of the crops they trampled. Bangalore's 'alien corn' was groundnut, a prime cash crop, and as Simmons, who was master of the hunt from 1932–4, recalled, there were 'over keen gents' who rode roughshod over crops, disregarding warnings and caring little for the groundnuts and chillies, sugar and young casuarinas that were another person's livelihood.[97]

At other levels, the relationship of the farmer to the colonial master was more cordial. Though Bangalore was for long distinguished by its innumerable private and public ornamental gardens, it was horticultural gardens that had the edge. These gardens produced flowers, fruits, and vegetables for the colonial table, and were an additional reason for the city's reputation as a 'garden city'. Apple cultivation was known in the farms around Bangalore, with 'Rome Beauty' among the more prized species: over 450 acres were under apple in the early years of the twentieth century.[98] Vineyards cultivating the Bangalore Blue grape were widespread, though the grape was then considered unsuitable for wine. Many areas of the city recall this earlier history, in names such as Khader Sharief Gardens, Pillana Gardens, and Chinnappa gardens. The gardens may have yielded space either to the slum, or middle class housing area, and sometimes both in quick succession.

The distinct relationship to space developed in each half of the city may also be observed from the relation between courtyard and house. The figure–ground relationship, in which open to sky areas were internal to the structure of the older city homes, was reversed in the colonial period when homes were set in the midst of large compounds (Fig. 22). There were striking distinctions between the two major parks of the city, Lalbagh and Cubbon Park. Lalbagh, first planted by Hyder Ali and expanded by both Tipu and the British, was a horticultural garden which encouraged the growth and propagation of exotic plants, flowers, and fruits, which were widely disseminated in the regions of Mysore and beyond. The cypress garden, as the British found it, was impressive and symmetrically laid out. Plants were procured from as far afield as Kabul, Mauritius, and Turkey. The British, in turn, constituted an Agri–Horticultural

FIG. 22 *Enclosed open spaces: a doorway opens onto a courtyard in Palace Guttahalli* (Clare Arni, 2000)

society at Lalbagh in 1839, which continued the task of disseminating flowering plants and seeds from North and South America, the Cape of Good Hope, South Sea Islands, Australia, China, Great Britain and Mexico, all 'grown in Lal Bagh without any protection whatever'. Consequently, 'a profitable means of livelihood was thus opened to native gardeners [Tigalas], some of whom have set up as florists and seedmen, replenishing their stocks direct from England', transforming the city landscape in enduring ways.[99]

Cubbon Park, on the other hand, was created in 1864 out of a little more than a hundred acres of farmland. It was envisaged as rolling parkland dotted with trees, quite different from the plotted botanical order of Lal Bagh and did not engender quite the same economy of farms and seed banks and nurseries. If anything, as Cubbon Park was expanded through the nineteenth and early twentieth centuries, more and more agricultural land, particularly in the Sampigehalli area, was annexed to its territories.

Cubbon Park was also a swathe of parkland that separated city from cantonment, keeping the two areas and their respective cultures apart well into the twentieth century. The location of the Queen Victoria statue at the southern edge of Cubbon Park in 1906 was a symbolic proclamation of the station's gratitude to the colonial regime, as many Indian, European, and Eurasian groups contributed to its installation.[100] This was the time when the public life of the old city was being shaped quite differently, and expressions of opposition to British rule were far from uncommon in the clubs, associations, hotels, and meeting halls that were slowly coming to life. No wonder that the Queen's statue, which stood at the border between city and cantonment, was the butt of 'mischief mongers' who were probably from the city. Their attacks on this symbol of imperial power in 1917 called for redoubled surveillance of the statue and its surroundings.[101]

Urban Identities and Images

The period of colonial rule saw the introduction of not just different principles of town planning, but a new relationship to space. The distinction between the naming of streets and areas in the old city, as opposed to the C&M Station, makes this clear. The old city areas were recognized by the names of occupations (eg. Arlepet), inhabitants (eg. Nagarthpet) and uses of areas (eg. Taramandalpet which was named after the 'constellation' of factories set up in Tipu Sultan's time) with occasional references to the people who may have endowed a tank or a temple (eg. Siddikatta). The newly developed Cantonment areas were named after individuals, administrators, soldiers, and merchants who lived in the city giving such names a commemorative function. This colonial tradition has, as Narayani Gupta has pointed out, continued to the present day, with municipal authorities and social groups alike obliterating and rewriting local histories through the invocation of nationalist or regional heroes.[102] Thus, if Fraser Town, so named after a Resident of the C&M Station, superseded Papareddipalya, the village on whose lands the new extension was built, the renaming of the area today as Pulakesinagar continues the modalities of a colonial naming procedure instead of redefining it. It, therefore, neither retains its descriptive uses, nor does it represent a shared linguistic cosmos.

So too, the memorial or statue, often of someone who may have had no part in city development (eg. Queen Victoria), marks city space in ways that speak of authority and power, matched only by the temples and their majesty in the pre-colonial period. Not surprisingly, the naming of streets and the installation of statues has become increasingly contentious in contemporary Bangalore.

Colonial rule inaugurated a cosmopolitanism of a different order from that which had been nurtured in the old city area. The composite linguistic culture of the old city was dominated by Kannada but accommodated other languages of the north as well as the south: Pushtu, Punjabi, Gujarati, Rajasthani, and Persian mingled with the sounds of Kannada, Telugu, and Tamil. The new linguistic bridge between north and south was Rekhta, later called Dakhni, which served both Kannada and Marathi, on the one hand, and Persian and Arabic, on the other.[103] Such mingling must not be mistaken for harmony, for we know that with the first stirrings of nationalism, languages could be aligned with other social identities to produce bitter and sometimes irreconcilable divisions, particularly in the city area. The identification of Kannada and Urdu with particular religious groups, though slower to take root, could come to the surface as nationalism mobilized new identities but did not always triumph over other local loyalties, as we shall see below. The best known case of conflict between Hindu and Muslim groups, called the Bangalore Disturbances, occurred in 1928, when a small shrine of Ganesha at Sultanpet situated within a school compound became the rallying point for a bitter and violent protest. The incident refashioned the social and political space of the city in profound ways that we shall consider below. The temple is still popularly referred to as the 'Galate Ganesha' in memory of this conflict.[104]

In the old city area, successive waves of immigrants from diverse language and ethnic backgrounds, had settled into a more or less composite culture dominated by Kannada, and in much smaller part, Urdu speakers. In the Cantonment, to which large numbers migrated from Madras Presidency in response to the burgeoning opportunities for employment and trade, a new division of labour between languages was achieved under the dominance of English, an administrative language and the language of power. The immigrant majority of Tamil speakers retained their language for domestic and cultural uses. There was widespread use of Telugu and Urdu as well, though the language of the region, Kannada, was rarely heard in the Cantonment area, as labour was drawn exclusively from the regions beyond Mysore.

The self-conscious propagation of the Kannada language, particularly as it was materialized in institutions such as the Kannada Sahitya Parishat (1915), or in the debates over the language of instruction in schools, was itself a response to a transformed linguistic market. The vastly expanded use of English soon became the means by which new subjectivities were sculpted as the language of rights, citizenship, and political freedom were debated and discussed with extraordinary vigour, often in ways that questioned the hegemony of English. Older identities were questioned, if not altogether abandoned, as a new public life took root in the old city area.

A New Public Life

D.V. Gundappa (DVG) recalls in his memoirs the forbidden pleasures of eating in 'one of Bangalore city's oldest hotels'. Venkanna's Hotel was on Arcot Srinivasachar street, an establishment run by and for Brahmins.[105] It required patrons not only to 'register' beforehand so that their place was secured, but also pronounce their Brahmin-ness, providing 'vibhuti' (sacred ash) at the entrance to those, like DVG, on whom the city may have left the sign of the secular, in the form of an unmarked forehead.[106] Eating at hotels was taboo, a lower class practice meant only for students from elsewhere who could find no high caste family with whom to board. However, hotels became a necessity for Brahmins, says DVG, following the late nineteenth century plague epidemic when many sent their wives and children away from the city.[107] K.T. Appanna's was one such establishment, begun in his large home in the Chikpet–Tharagupet area after his father died during the plague. The women of the family cooked for those single Brahmin men who were compelled to eat out.

Yet the attractions of such hotels were many and not confined to the pleasures of eating out alone. When Appanna's establishment expanded and shifted to Chikpet, and was called the Hindu Coffee Club, it became a 'cultural centre frequented by teachers, performers, officials'. Combined with the widespread availability of newspapers and other forms of mass communication, such clubs became a crucial site for the circulation of other longings and imaginings. Sangeeta Vidwan Dakshinacharya named it the 'Independent Board' which he defined as 'Freedom! There are no restraints on the tongue. If you talk, it is speech, if you shout, it is music'. By 1907, its Brahmin patrons were discussing the split between the Moderates and Extremists of the Surat Congress, as well as 'news of the Mysore administration, the conflicts in the city, debates about music, and contests over the sastras'.[108]

This did not necessarily inaugurate a democratic mode of expression or an inclusive membership. Older styles of deference persisted among a clientele that was discovering not only a new language but new forms of speech. DVG recalls being profusely apologetic for having breached the protocols of seniority when he inadvertently insulted Guruswami Iyer, a visiting Madras Brahmin, by correcting his English: 'I was not yet 20 and he was over 50.' Moreover, Hindu Coffee Club, and later Modern Hindu Hotel, were resolutely male and Brahmin establishments, modes of exclusion that the innumerable liberal civic institutions that sprang to life in the early twentieth century did nothing to challenge. Even more radical associations, such as the Mass Awakener's Union in the 1930s and 1940s, were not exempt from this exclusiveness.[109] Yet, such hotels and meeting places were crucial to the circulation of ideas of the nation-space, and, therefore, in building up a sense of citizenship. The artist K. Venkatappa, who moved to the city from Mysore in 1940 when the patronage of the Mysore Palace was rudely severed, suspended his famed austerity once a year to celebrate his birthday with friends at Modern Hindu Hotel.[110] It was a time when his own studio had become a place of 'pilgrimage' for cultural nationalists, gradually building up the notion of a 'Kannada modern' in literary and other spheres.[111] The People's Protection League was set up to 'protect property of the city against rowdies and anti-social elements' during World War II when there was an influx of people from the neighbouring Madras Presidency, and Bangalore itself was on the list of Japanese targets.[112] Nittoor Srinivasa Rao remembers the time when these vigilance committees gathered at Mavalli Tiffin Rooms to apportion duties and share information on the day's events in their jurisdictions.[113]

The hotels and clubs of the C&M Station performed a different role, catering as they did to an European and Anglo-Indian clientele, and providing more strictly leisure time activities. To many from the old city area, they spelt an unmatched social freedom. Ramachandra Sharma recalls the 'thrill of the first foray into the forbidden areas of the Cantonment' which surely included hotels and cinemas frequented by men and women. Hotels and coffee clubs in the Cantonment served alcohol and meat and also provided the excitement of the chance, if sometimes unpleasant, encounter with strange men and women in these public spaces. Blighty's (after *vilayati* or foreign) Tea Rooms catered to a European church crowd, other hostels and hotels were meant for foreign visitors. But the Cantonment was also a truly urbane space that allowed young visitors from the city the advantage of anonymity. Thus, M. Shivaram recalls one uncomfortable moment when he visited Spencer's lounge at the City railway station for a drink with the famous playwright T.P. Kailasam: predictably he was spotted by relatives and teachers who did not fail to admonish him.[114] For those such as Shivaram who lived in the city area, there was no escape from the claustrophobic hypocrisies of his upper caste 'tribe', who monitored the movements and friendships of its younger members. Only the Cantonment lay beyond their surveillance: indeed 'Cantonment was alright and the people we met there understood us'.

Yet the City could spell freedom of a different kind to the subalterns of the British army who were morally a class apart from the ruling élite. Soldiers seeking an alternative to the expensive Columbo arrack, the only spirit that was permitted to be sold in the C&M Station, regularly visited the City for supplies of cheap country liquor.[115] Smugglers of country liquor into the Station were undeterred by the punitive measures designed to keep them out. The Bangalore Brewery was started to quench the thirsts of subalterns by providing safe and cheap supplies of milder liquor. Far more vexing were the sexual appetites of these men, for whom the military authorities made no special provisions, forcing them to seek casual liaisons with women in the city, beyond the reach of the Station's surveillance measures. The alarming spread of venereal disease among these soldiers troubled the military and health authorities well into the twentieth century.[116]

Some tea rooms and coffee clubs took on a self-consciously pedagogic role, run by churchwomen who were anxious to keep the flock—poorer Europeans and Eurasians—from the powerful attraction of bars. The Shoolay Coffee Room only thinly disguised its Christian temperance mission by claiming to 'provide cheap meals to poor Eurasians of the place and at the same time keep them away from evil influences'.[117] In the City area, the working classes were the focus of temperance activity, and by the 1930s and 1940s this combined with Gandhian self-restraint initiatives to make games, drama, literary events, and even morally appropriate cinema an attractive substitute to drinking. Among the working classes of western Bangalore then, Christian women on temperance missions and upper caste nationalist reformers, for whom drink was culturally tabooed, were able to join forces in a programme of reform and upliftment.[118] These efforts intersected with the wider mobilization of Bangalore's residents in the name of an imagined nation.

Public life and Patronage

The political redefinition of caste occurred in the early twentieth century as the dominant castes of the countryside, notably the Lingayats and Vokkaligas, sought a place in the prestigious bureaucratic order of the Mysore state, until then the monopoly of Brahmins. Between the 1920s and 1940s, there was a steady rise of caste associations based in Bangalore. These caste groups and associations had long recognized the value of bonding together to secure state benefits, but were also critical in redefining caste as a route to urban social mobility.[119]

Caste associations defined a style of politics but also a tradition of philanthropy in the city. The opportunities for higher education in the city were clearly unmatched in the mofussil areas, but how were middle or lower caste people to enjoy this privilege without assistance from the caste association hostels and fellowships? The upper castes were better provided for by institutions such as *vara anna,* which allowed single male students to eat in a fellow caste person's house in return for sharing chores. Emerging new hostel facilities within the city too primarily met the needs of men from these dominant castes. The B.K. Mariappa's Charities, set up in 1914, were the bequest of a prosperous Nagarth Lingayet merchant who set up a boarding and lodging hostel for boys of the 'three prominent communities in equal number, Brahmin, Nagarth Lingayet and Vokkaliga communities, each with their own kitchen and dining hall in Chamrajpet of the city.'[120] But other castes were not far behind: the Sri Lakshmi Narasimha Charities otherwise known as Janopakari Doddanna's Charities were founded in 1905 to enable young Vysya boys to live and study in the city, by providing free boarding and lodging, clothing and text books as well.[121] By the early 1930s, a number of such hostels had been set up for students of different communities, including one for the Depressed Classes: the Vysya and Virasaiva hostels were housed in 'fine piles of buildings' on Seshadri Road.[122]

The city could also become the launching pad for those, such as the Vokkaliga student B. Puttaiya, who received a training in printing technology in England. Puttaiya topped the lists at the St Bride's Printing School in London, and came home to supervise the work of the Government Press.[123] But he also shared his privileges by serving institutions such as the Mysore Civic and Social Progress Association, as well as remaining a member of the arcane Non-Entities Club, which specifically sought to liberate those who sought a foreign degree from the deadening bond of government service.[124] In the cantonment area, the charities associated with the Rai Bahadur Annaswamy Mudaliar were among the most prominent, especially as they funded schools and other educational activities. It was he, along with other notables of the C&M Station such as Khan Bahadur Hajee Ismail Sait, Rutna Singh, Rao Bahadur Maigandeva Mudaliar, and Kunnaswamy Naidu who put forward the money to build Fraser Town at the turn of the century.[125] With the wealthier Muslims and Parsis who had prospered in the cantonment, the Tamils formed an important class of merchants and contractors who accumulated cultural capital by making such donations.

There were other merchants of the city area, such as the silk merchant Magaji Dhondusa, who rose from humble origins to enormous wealth as a consequence of the demand for parachute silk. Their modes of charity were more closely linked to funds for temples and associated *chatrams*. Dhondusa's pledge of support for the Harihareswara temple, near the Gavi Gangadhareswara temple, and for a *chatram* in the area recalled earlier modes of philanthropy.[126] Such philanthropy was not averse to refashioning the customary symbols of Shiva to include an aeroplane motif on the dome of the temple. The plane thus interrupts the conventions of temple adornment, and visually narrativizes gratitude for the unexpected economic prosperity resulting from war.

If caste and community defined modes of philanthropy, and even determined who the beneficiaries would be, other modes of public involvement sought to disavow caste and community as markers of social status or identity. This was not without its ironies, for the newly evolving public life was restricted to certain castes and classes in ways that would fashion the very content of the imagined democratic nation. Indeed, participation itself was clearly linked to the privileges of caste and class in the city. It is no coincidence that those who passionately embraced a liberal ideal of citizenship were exclusive in ways that were rarely voiced or even acknowledged.

Perhaps no institution in the city aspired to the ideals of secular citizenship as consistently and with such perseverance as the Gokhale Institute of Public Affairs (GIPA). Yet its membership, and indeed its concerns over the years, revealed a firmly Brahminical and even conservative approach to the emerging social order, and the immediate post-Independence years were years of accumulating dismay at the unexpected shape of Indian democracy.

GIPA had its origins in the liberal phase of Indian nationalism. At a public meeting after Gokhale's death, several young Brahmin men, such as DVG himself, formed the Mysore Social Service League.[127] The League largely spent time in social work among factory workers and providing relief during the influenza epidemic of 1918, but was defunct for years after, and revived in 1930 through DVG's efforts. DVG was convinced that a useful role could be played by

> a body of independent citizens who, untrammeled by party attachments and class loyalties, would keep a critical watch over the country's affairs and inform the public from time to time of the possible results of measures carried out or contemplated by the state or other institutions.

Such citizens would smooth the path of democracy and act as a counter to the voices of 'division and confusion'. By 1945, under the able leadership of DVG, GIPA formalized its existence with a membership of 'non-partisan, non-communal, and independent citizens'. Its efforts were largely pedagogic, with the establishment of study circles and lectures: citizenship was defined as that which would efface such divisive issues as caste and language, and effectively distance itself from party politics. Membership of GIPA, though almost exclusively Brahmin and male, was predicated on the subordination of such identities to the proper functioning of liberal nationalism. This liberal agenda would come to grief as democracy was increasingly defined in unexpected ways, setting serious limits to the role of leaders from the middle class, and also emphasizing caste and language as the very ground of Indian democracy. As early as 1928, there were signs that mobilization along the lines of ethnicity and language were not incompatible with a new nationalist politics with DVG himself participating in efforts to draw the city into the nation-space.

The City and the Nation-Space

The choice of Cottonpet in the 1920s for the Congress office could not have been accidental, for close at hand, on the western edge, were the large-scale textile mills. Moreover, not far from Mysore Bank Square were the colleges and their students, masses waiting to be called to action. In addition, an increasing number of printing presses were set up within the old city area and in nearby Chamrajpet and provided ample opportunities for the dissemination of ideas which stretched beyond direct experience or knowledge. Finally, the migration of people from the neighbouring Madras Presidency—workers in the British owned Binny Mills for instance—brought news of the heady success of mass actions.

By 1921, the Khilafat movement found widespread support among the Muslims and Hindus of both city and cantonment areas, and a hartal in support of jailed Malabar Khilafatists was a total success.[128] If the mobs in the city's modern history had threatened to gather due to food shortages following high post-war grain prices, sending city authorities into high alert, they now quickly gathered in noisy protest against the visit of the Prince of Wales.[129]

The gradually emerging forces of nationalism in the early twentieth century re-inscribed the space of the city in specific social and ideological ways. Once more, the city and the C&M Station were marked in very different ways as, for the most part, nationalist activity was confined to the western and northern parts of the city, where the experience of indirect (colonial) rule made for a nationalism that was only weakly articulated until the 1930s.

The discontents of labour in the textile mills yielded much for nationalist newspapers seeking to establish their reading publics. K. Narayanswami Iyer, editor of *Truth* (a local weekly), and Thi Tha Sharma, editor of *Vishwakarnataka* (a nationalist weekly), took on the twin tasks of reporting on labour struggles and assuming the role of labour representative to officials who welcomed the mediation of the middle class.[130] The Binny Mills' strike of 1926, in which four workers were killed due to police firing, and several others were injured, was investigated in extraordinary detail by *Vishwakarnataka,* as was the strike of 1931. The strategy did pay, if the high levels of labour participation in the major nationalist upsurge of 1942 are an indication.

Those who were not reached through the newspaper or broadsheet were gathered, throughout the 1920s and 1930s, into meetings and discussions with nationalists from other provinces. These meetings were organized in several places bordering the old city area: Banappa Park to the south-west of Cubbon Park, was a favoured location, as was Tulsi Thota (later Chik Lalbagh) on the edge of Dharmambudhi Tank. Mysore Bank Square was the starting point of many processions and protests: from these locations, both students and workers could be easily reached and moved to action. It is this geography of the remembered city, as it bore the fleeting imprints of nationalist activity, that K.S. Kumaran recalls. A left wing labour leader who organized the memorable 1941 strike in Binny's, Kumaran connects memory not only with spaces but with the movement of people, whether on processions or rallies. This was a temporary occupation of the street by crowds who rallied around new ideologies of nationalism or trade unionism, rather than religious belief (Refer Map 6).[131]

Among the early events that brought together the politics of space and communalism in a pattern of violence that endures up to the present day were the Bangalore Disturbances of 1928. The Bangalore Disturbances are most commonly referred to as the 'Ganapati Galabhe' (Ganapati Disturbances) or 'Hindu–Muslim Gharshane' (Hindu–Muslim conflict) in Kannada accounts. These nomenclatural differences are of some account, with the former privileging the location (the city of Bangalore) while the latter emphasized extra-local or supra-local identities (Hinduism or the Nation). A small idol of Ganesha in the compound of a Hindu Anglo-Vernacular School on Arcot Srinivasachar Street in Sultanpet became the centre of a confrontation between upper caste Hindus and Muslims of the area, mirroring conflicts that were occurring elsewhere in India. Schoolboys, who used to empty their ink bottles on to the head of the image to propitiate the deity before their examinations, were encouraged to build a small shelter by a stirring editorial in *Veerakesari*, the paper edited by Sitarama Sastry, a right wing nationalist.[132] The idol was not reinstalled following the building of the shelter. The school was situated in front of a house belonging to the municipal president, Abbas Khan, and it

MAP 6 *Bangalore, 1935*

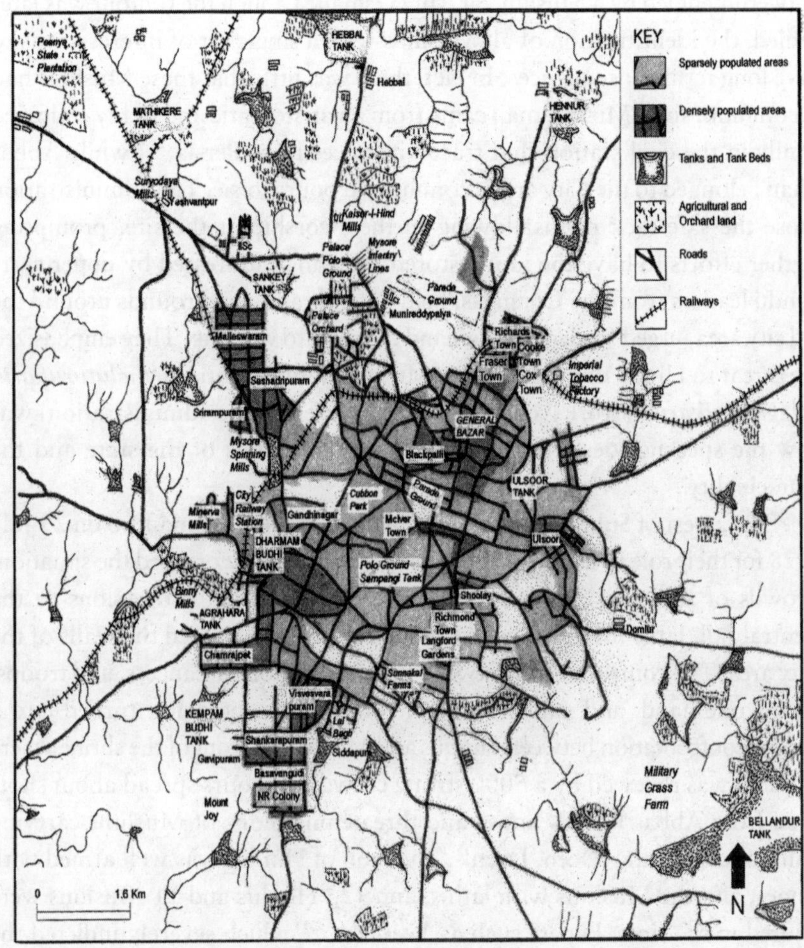

Source: Based on Bangalore Guide Map, surveyed 1935–36, Second Edition 1938.

was rumoured that Khan considered the sudden rehabilitation and worship of the neglected idol a deliberate provocation to the Muslims of the area, who had to file past the spot on the way to their mosque. The schoolboys' affair soon turned into a major confrontation between right wing Congressman such as Ramlal Tiwari, Jamkandi Bhima Rao, and H.V. Subrahmanyam, and the Muslims led by Abbas Khan.[133] On 30 July 1928, disturbances spread over a wide area of the old city.[134]

In all this, the local press, and Sitarama Sastry's *Veerakesari* in particular, played a very major role in exaggerating rumours about Muslim intransigence on the issue. On 27 June 1928, it carried the rumour that the Muslims were led by the municipal president Abbas Khan, who in turn had the support of a government led by a Muslim, Sir Mirza Ismail. Though the rumour was later denied, the identification of all Muslims with a single set of interests was to have long term consequences. In fact, there was little that these Muslims had in common, since Mirza Ismail came from an aristocratic and richly endowed family in the civil station that traced its ancestry to Persia,[135] while Abbas Khan belonged to the City area's commercial bourgeoisie. The administration chose the safe tack of disallowing further worship at the site, prompting further efforts to have the idol restored. Meetings addressed by upper caste Hindu leaders from the Congress, held in fields and playgrounds around the old city area, urged students to demand the right to worship. They emphasized the threat to Hindu dharma from a 'Muslim' administration: '*meluturukaru, kelaguturukaru*!' ('Turks' or Muslims at all levels of the administration) was how the speeches described the twin administrations of the state and the municipality.

The arrest of Subrahmanyam, Ramlal Tiwari, and Bhima Rao on 29 July 1928 for their role in inciting the students dramatically worsened the situation. Crowds of students, demanding their release, took out processions to the Central Jail, large meetings were called, and posters covered the walls of the City area. The confrontation between the Mysore police, Lancers, and troops, on the one hand, and students, on the other, soon thereafter turned into a violent confrontation between Hindus and Muslims in front of the shrine where worship was renewed by a 5000 strong crowd. Rumours spread about shots fired from Abbas Khan's house and threatening mobs of Muslims carrying lathis and shouting 'Deen, Deen!'. The mob of Hindus was well armed with stones, and the Muslims with lathis, and 123 Hindus and 11 Muslims were injured in the riots. Papers such as *Veerakesari*, which severely indicted the government, were shut down under the sedition laws in operation.[136]

The Bangalore Disturbances were a turning point in the city's history for a number of reasons. For the first time, the narrow twisted alleys of the old city area rang with threatening slogans while roving mobs of youngsters threatened residents. Such scenes were far removed from those during the Karaga festival where amiable crowds thronged the lanes, or coursed through the area on their daily work: the political mob was capable of collective action that individuals could not have dreamt of. Moreover, they revealed the fragility of the ritual ties that bound communities together as during the Karaga performance.

Narratives of the Bangalore Disturbances have varied in their interpretations of how the space of the old city was recast as a zone of contention between two communities. Was the communal conflict already foretold in Abbas Khan's alleged opposition to a shrine appearing right in front of his house, as DVG has suggested? Were his road widening measures merely the acts of an inspired Municipal President, or an attempt to remove all religious markers from roads? Or alternatively, did the events take a communal turn only when triumphant Hindus, who managed to overcome official opposition to worship at the disputed shrine, were set upon by angry Muslim mobs, as claimed by Sundara Rao and V.S. Narayana Rao? Or was the Miller Committee report of 1918 'the apple of discord', as the Enquiry Committee had it?[137] At least one Muslim, Abdul Rahman, testified before the Committee that the disturbances were a violent culmination of the simmering resentment of Mysore Brahmins against the new administrative system from which they had been displaced since 1918.[138] Ganesha was deliberately chosen as a symbol 'universally respected and worshipped by all Hindu Communities' to cement these cracks. Certainly, the material gathered by the committee pointed to a rift between Brahmins and Muslims, which surfaced in various petitions to the Government itself.[139]

The Committee to enquire into the disturbances was headed by M. Visvesvaraya, the former dewan and technocrat. He had no patience for such public rallying around religious symbols, and called for a conscious secularization of public life as a lasting remedy.[140] Neither long standing communal differences nor communal conspiracies were discovered. Yet the convulsions in the city revealed the operation of a symbolic economy rooted in space that would resonate well into the late twentieth century when the spheres of state and market, at least, were well established secular entities. Reconfiguring the city within the nation-space could bring to the surface real and imagined antagonisms, and communalize a social space that had long tolerated difference.

Although the differences—socio-economic and cultural—between the City and the Cantonment Muslims were well known, the discourse on the Bangalore Disturbances cast them as unified by religion with profound consequences for years to come. Cantonment Muslims were prevented at the Queen's statue from entering the city during the disturbances, by an administration that feared a religious mob.[141] A few years later, in 1931, when the second round of Bangalore Disturbances broke out, this time in the C&M Station, Muslims and Hindus were portrayed as irreconcilably different. The occasion for the fresh disturbances was a football match between two teams in the Cantonment, one a Hindu team led by a Muslim, Baba, and the other a Muslim team. When Baba's side won the match, the Muslim team objected to one of their co-religionists playing against them and violence broke out. The disturbances were quickly brought under control. However, an important way of belonging to the city, through the formation of local teams that routinely gathered to play football, a sport whose popularity was high in the C&M Station, stood transformed by communal rifts emerging elsewhere.[142]

The high visibility of Brahmins during the disturbances, and indeed in public life in general, realigned castes and communities, and may even have brought the Muslims closer to the non-Brahmin movement. Conspicuously absent in all these events, whether as participants or witnesses, were the women of the city; their reactions to this cataclysmic event are unknown. The public life of the city was thus divided, not only in a spatial sense, between east and west, but also on the lines of caste and gender, though these divisions remained less visible.

Conclusion

By the early twentieth century the two cities had developed as independent entities, with their own central markets, railways stations, hospitals, and wholesale and retail areas. If the city was determined in form and function as a commercial and industrial space, the expansive cantonment was structured around the presence of the military. Beyond this was an expanding edge of industries to the north and west, nurtured and protected by the state. The two distinct nodes of City and C&M Station were separated by a 'trough' of sparsely populated parkland. Yet traffic between the two areas was regulated as strictly as ideas between them. Thus, nationalism could flourish only in the city area; not infrequently, local nationalists escaped the long arm of the law by taking cover in the C&M station. The C&M station, and its all too evident provision of facilities for the European resident, was always cited in nationalist speeches as clear proof of what the independent nation-state could achieve for its citizens: tree-lined streets, large compounds, faces that reflected prosperity, and a heightened respect for privacy.[143]

Certainly, the municipality of the C&M Station took better care of its well off residents than the city municipality, so loyalties to that administration were not unfounded. The Bangalore City Municipality was established in 1862, nine years before its equivalent in the C&M station in 1871. As a post-Independence survey by P.S. Narayana Rao put it 'The City Municipality had made relatively better progress in underground drainage and street lighting, whereas the C&M unit was ahead in housing schemes and welfare centres.'[144] The disparity persisted in several crucial areas of city life: per capita expenditures on public health were significantly higher in the C&M Station compared with the City, as were expenditures on parks and playgrounds. Between 1930–9 and 1947–8, expenditures on construction and maintenance of roads expanded by 300 per cent in the station in contrast to a 50 per cent decline in the City. Furthermore, the Civil Station was much better served by metalled roads than the city, where 33 per cent of the roads were unmetalled. Overall, the influx of people into Bangalore in the war years strained municipal resources to the limits as the less well defined City area absorbed the intensified migration from the neighbouring Madras Presidency.

Indeed, the cantonment was peopled by those for whom British rule had spelt not just political certainty but unbridled economic opportunity. The plan for retrocession (or the return of the C&M Station to Mysore state) in 1935 drew alarmed responses from the Anglo-Indians, Muslims, and commercial Hindu groups of the Cantonment who had for long loyally served the colonial masters. Ratepayers, domiciled Europeans, tradespeople, and religious minorities recoiled with horror from the threatened assimilation of their territory with Mysore. The Catholics sought various safeguards under the new dispensation, including the assurance that their educational institutions could continue under the University of Madras. The Bangalore Trades Association feared the 'detrimental effect on the value of land' if the C&M Station became part of Mysore.[145] However, the retrocession plan also brought to the surface a difference that had nearly been forgotten in the wave of communal feelings following the Bangalore Disturbances of 1928 and 1931. There were important cleavages between the local, Kannada speaking, Muslim of the City and the Muslims from the Station. The C&M Station Muslims feared that the status of their counterparts in the city would be thrust upon them, and had no wish to be 'politically merged with the non-Brahmins'. Abbas Khan from the city and other Muslims from rural Karnataka had made impassioned pleas in Kannada in the Representative Assembly against the allegation that the Mysore state did not safeguard Muslim interests. It was however the threat of assimilation with the politics and culture of the City that most alarmed the C&M Muslims who raised the cry of Muslim culture in danger, and pointed to the declining status of Urdu as a case in point.[146]

Though the retrocession plan was finally dropped, and the C&M Station retained its independence until 1949, even today it is not a moment that is remembered without rancour by those fiercely loyal to the British. Kora Chandy, an old and loyal resident of the C&M Station, recalls the lowering of the British flag as a 'shock' and 'not a very happy occasion'. Clearly, the

C&M Station produced a totally different set of political loyalties, which echoes, as we shall see, in some discussions even to the present day. On the eve of Independence, then, the city of Bangalore retained its divided character, with the two halves only weakly joined in the social, political, or economic spheres. Consternation on the part of the Civil Station's residents about the prospect of unity gave way to a resigned pragmatism. In the immediate post-Independence years, the task of strengthening these bonds was left more or less entirely to administrative compulsions, with significant consequences for the contemporary design and social life of the city.

TWO

Remembered and Imagined Cities

The beauty of the city is already becoming a thing of the past, due to continued neglect. Because of the huge growth of population and the Government's failure to take necessary measures in time to meet the city's growing needs, new slums have sprung up to add to the growing squalor. Lack of proper planning and lax supervision over building activity have resulted in haphazard growth on every side and the emergence of ugly structures all over the city. The miserable condition of the roads, their poor lighting, the sad state of the parks, once the pride of the city, and the general appearance of neglect and disrepair which the city wears have their own sad story to tell.

Deccan Herald, 4 Dec. 1961.

Our city has a date with the future. And a dream which is the mandate of the Bangalore Agenda Task Force (BATF)—making Bangalore a world-class city by 2004–2005 AD.

www.blrforward.org

In 1949, the twin municipalities of Bangalore City and Cantonment were brought together in the Bangalore City Corporation. A *pete* founded in the sixteenth century and a Cantonment established in the nineteenth century were administratively united in the twentieth century. Bangalore was wrenched out of its existence as a divided town to become a big city in the 1970s, then startled into the recognition that it was already a metropolis by the 1980s, hurtling towards a destiny it only reluctantly acknowledges, and for which it

MAP 7 *Bangalore, c. 1960*

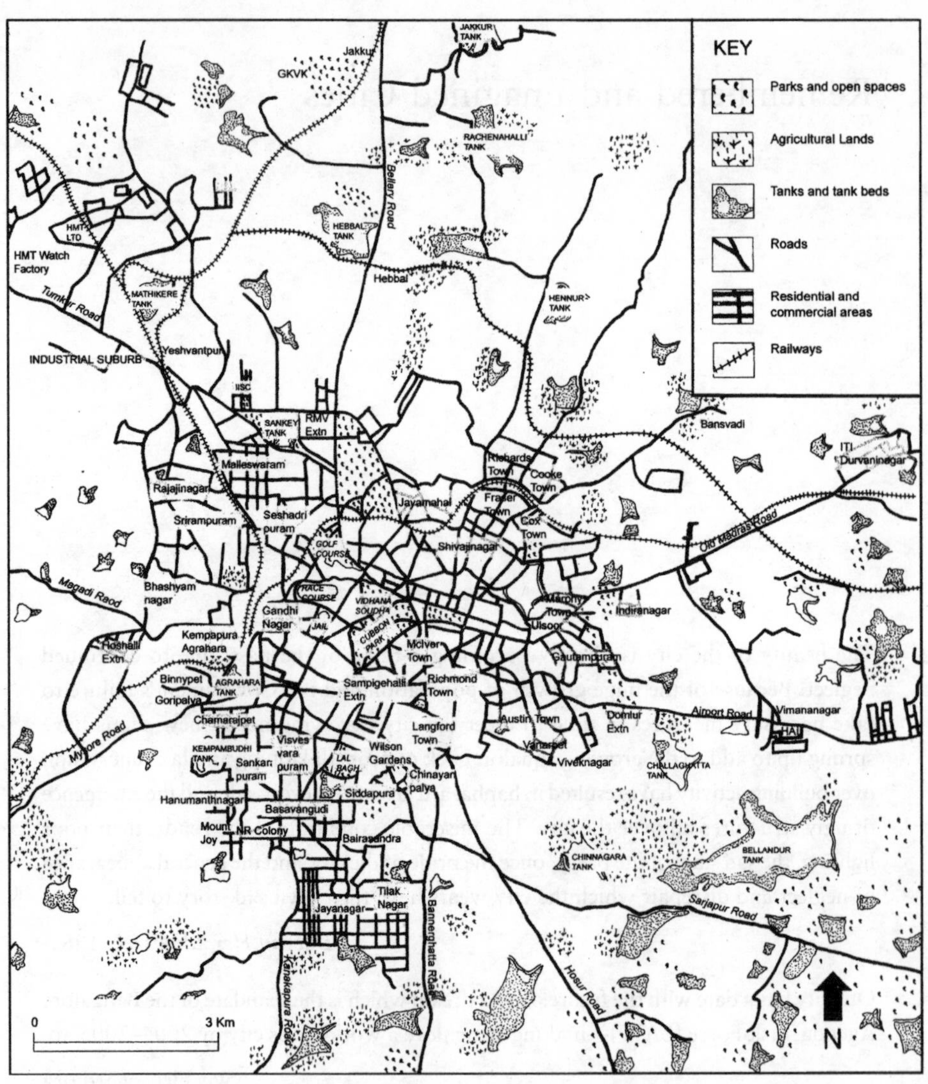

Source: Based on Bangalore Guide Map, Surveyed 1960–61, First Edition, 1969

is largely unprepared. Between 1941 and 2001, the population of the urban agglomeration of Bangalore grew from 410, 967 persons to 5,686,844, the city itself expanding far beyond the 66 sq. km. of that time to a become an urban agglomeration of 531 sq. km (refer Map 7).[1]

Demographic and spatial evidence notwithstanding, the residents and administrators of the city have been slow to respond to its new metropolitan status. It is nostalgia as a structure of feeling that has marked many responses to its phenomenal growth. The editorial comment from the 1960s, with which this chapter begins, has been the unvarying chant of those who long for a mythicized past, right up to the present day.[2] Those who are dismayed by, and are perhaps fearful of, the baffling directions taken by urban democracy, seek comfort in a far more placid and restrained past, and strive to recreate this moment not just at the ideological level but through new institutional mechanisms that are discussed elsewhere in the book.

More recently, there has been a futuristic vision of the metropolis as conforming to international standards, for which Singapore has been the single most important model. This received its most forceful articulation in the actions of S.M. Krishna, chief minister of Karnataka from 1999, who insisted not only on a vision of Bangalore that physically mirrors the island nation (an elevated railway and international airport included), but one in which 'the value systems adopted by the citizens of Singapore like accountability, civic sense and respect for law gets spread to Bangalore and other cities of Karnataka'.[3] Towards this end, the chief minister enlisted the support of the leaders of the new economy, brought together in a forum called the Bangalore Agenda Task Force (BATF), headed by the CEO of Infosys Technologies, Nandan Nilekani, and including several nominated members drawn primarily from the corporate world.

Between the longing for a Bangalore of a bygone era and the futuristic visions of the Singapore-in-the-making through a unique 'private–public partnership' lies a complex history of a city that has been marked by national, regional, and global forces and interests in its passage to metropolitan status. In the five decades since Independence, a small and unremarkable town was transformed into an internationally known metropolis (see Table 2.1). The increase of the built-up area of the city between 1945 and 1973 was three times that of the previous 33 years (1912–45), doubling in the seven years between 1973 and 1980.[4] The transformation of Bangalore has thus been crowded into a short span that affords none of the advantages of gradual growth, as may have happened in, say, Presidency cities such as Bombay, Madras, or

FIG. 23 *The persistence of older uses of space in the city centre: a view, looking west, of Mahatma Gandhi Road, where a row of shops faces the vast Parade Ground.* (Department of Information and Publicity, Karnataka, 1980)

Calcutta. No single metaphor adequately describes the new metropolitan experience, for Bangalore is not quite the industrial district,[5] the technopole,[6] the informational city,[7] nor the 'silicon valley' of Asia[8] that have been used to describe processes elsewhere. Yet the historical emergence of the city as the *urbs prima* of the Karnataka region, accounting for close to 30 per cent of the state's urban population, is undoubted (Fig. 23).

No other contemporary Indian city allows us to track the passage from small town to metropolitan status within a few decades as well as does Bangalore. We may begin by tracing the successive economic phases through which the city has passed, while simultaneously plotting the consequences for its spatial form, its social and public life, and its associational cultures. These maps may not always be congruent, but will provide the coordinates within which we may understand how this space has been produced in the fullest sense of the term. This will lead to a discussion of the new institutional mechanisms that are being forged in a period of globalization and its consequences for notions of citizenship and democracy. These questions, schematically set out in this chapter on the post-Independence history of the city, will be further elaborated throughout the book.

A Space of Production

Bangalore is at once the capital of Karnataka state, the home of several large scale public sector industries and their ancillaries, and more recently private electronic, infotech and garment industries. It is, importantly, an internationally recognized gateway to styles of globalized consumption. Between the time when it was a nondescript small town that boasted a few large industries to its emergence as a premier metropolis in India, the city of Bangalore has passed through at least three recognizable stages in its industrial history. Each of these phases also corresponds to changes in the significance of the state as the prime mobilizer and distributor of resources, as the increasing command of the market eclipses the developmentalist state and its apparatuses.

In the first part of the twentieth century, the city was a centre of textile production. The clack of looms in the old city today is a reminder of the oldest manufacturing zone of the city. By the early twentieth century, three large textile mills that sprang up to the west of this zone located themselves close to the railhead. Bangalore Woollen, Silk and Cotton (Binny) Mills (1884) was followed by Maharaja of Mysore Mills (1887), and Minerva Mills (1920). The inter-war period led to the mushrooming of a large number of smaller woollen, cotton, and silk textile units, clustered on the western edge of the city. Mill workers were scattered among far more diverse populations of the labouring poor, including head load workers and *jutka wallah*s in older city areas such as Akkipet, Ranasingpet, Kurubarpet, and Arlepet. They also colonized new areas such as Pit Colony, Anjanappa Gardens, and Srirampuram.[9] In his demarcation of the 'factory zone' in the 1950s, K.N. Venkatrayappa included six areas on the western side of the city, an industrial landscape where brick and tile factories nestled in the shadow of textile mills and government run porcelain and electrical factories. Only one of the early factory areas was located in the east, around Imperial Tobacco Factory, which was close to the large number of tanneries.[10]

A policy of state-led industrialization in the inter-war period, as we have seen, transformed the rather sluggish profile of the deindustrialized city. However, the city gained its image as a public sector city par excellence in the 1940s and 1950s with the establishment of the Big Four public sector units, Hindusthan Aircraft Factory (1940, later Hindusthan Aeronautics Limited), Indian Telephone Industries (1948), Hindusthan Machine Tools (1955), and Bharat Electronics Limited (1956). All these units were located on the eastern and northern outskirts, separated from the city by vast tracts of

FIG. 24 *Pride in patriotic production: export orders on display in Hindustan Machine Tools.* (T.L. Ramaswamy, 3.3.1972)

agricultural land. By the 1970s, Bangalore was the acknowledged centre of the public sector, and new state run units such as New Government Electric Factory (1961), HMT Watch Factory (1972), and Bharat Heavy Electricals Limited, were added to the existing structure. Clustered around the public sector giants were the giant national laboratories, such as the National Aeronautical Laboratory (NAL), Defence Research and Development Organization (DRDO), and Electronic Research and Development Establishment (LRDE) to the east, and the Indian Space Research Organization (ISRO) and Central Power Research Institute (CPRI) to the north-west. In addition to these factory–lab complexes were the research and development wings internal to every public sector unit. Bangalore could thus stake a stronger claim to being a Science City than the time when the Indian Institute of Science (1909) existed in somewhat splendid isolation.

Yet, throughout the 1950s and 1960s the city clung to its image as a mixed economy, so that the Model Dairy Farm in Madhavnagar in the prestigious High Grounds, which proudly announced the arrival of pasteurized milk comfortably shared advertisement space with REMCO's radio receivers, ITI's telephones, and HAL's HT-2, the first Indian aircraft.[11] Agriculture, or more correctly horticulture, remained part of the city landscape. Speaking of the area west of Brigade Road in the late 1950s, R.L.Singh remarked that the landscape, dominated by the military, was interspersed by large tanks such as Halsur (Ulsoor), Koramangala, and Challaghatta, the latter two 'lined with market gardens'.[12]

Until the late 1950s, no other Indian city had such wide open areas as the city of Bangalore. The agricultural zone within and on the periphery of Bangalore was largely dependent on the demand of the city, but the demand for housing sites was even greater, so the large market garden of Dodda Bylakhana area, comprising 428 acres in the south-west of the city, was increasingly settled with houses by the late 1950s.[13] Similarly, Sunnakal tank, into which the *pete* area was drained, was a sewage and market garden before turning into a residential area.[14]

By the early 1980s, the public sector industries, including the HMT watch factory and BHEL accounted for over 80,000 jobs: well into the 1990s, HAL alone accounted for more than 42,000 jobs (Fig. 24). Several large private sector units matched the public sector in size and employment: Motor Industries Company Limited, International Instruments, and Amco Batteries, as well as Kirloskar Electric, to name a few, were new signs of a town that had blossomed into an industrial city. Yet even such private investment in the city (and we may note here that a regional bourgeoisie was only weakly present),[15] did nothing to dim the presence of the state as the prime mover of industrial production within the city (see Map 8).

The number of industrial units, classified under large, medium, and small scale, burgeoned to 5641 in 1981 compared with the more modest 283 units of the early 1950s. The growth of workers in the city was comparable, rising from 45, 878 to 212, 506 in the same period.[16] Combined with the service sector workers in 1971, the total workforce of the city was 576, 531.[17] A high proportion of textile, automobile, electrical, and electronic units were based in the city, and nearly all the state's workers in these industries were located in Bangalore. Over 73 per cent of the private sector workers were in these industries.[18] By the 1990s, electronics and electrical industries alone accounted for over 114,000 jobs in the city, with engineering and manufacturing firms, not including textiles, employing 55,000. At this time, Bangalore district had 3,437 factories employing 365,000 people, 13 industrial estates, and 20,400 small scale units employing 194,000 people. As much as 63 per cent of these organized sector jobs were in the public sector.[19]

These statistics did not usually reveal the numbers working for the large

MAP 8 *Bangalore, c. 1980*

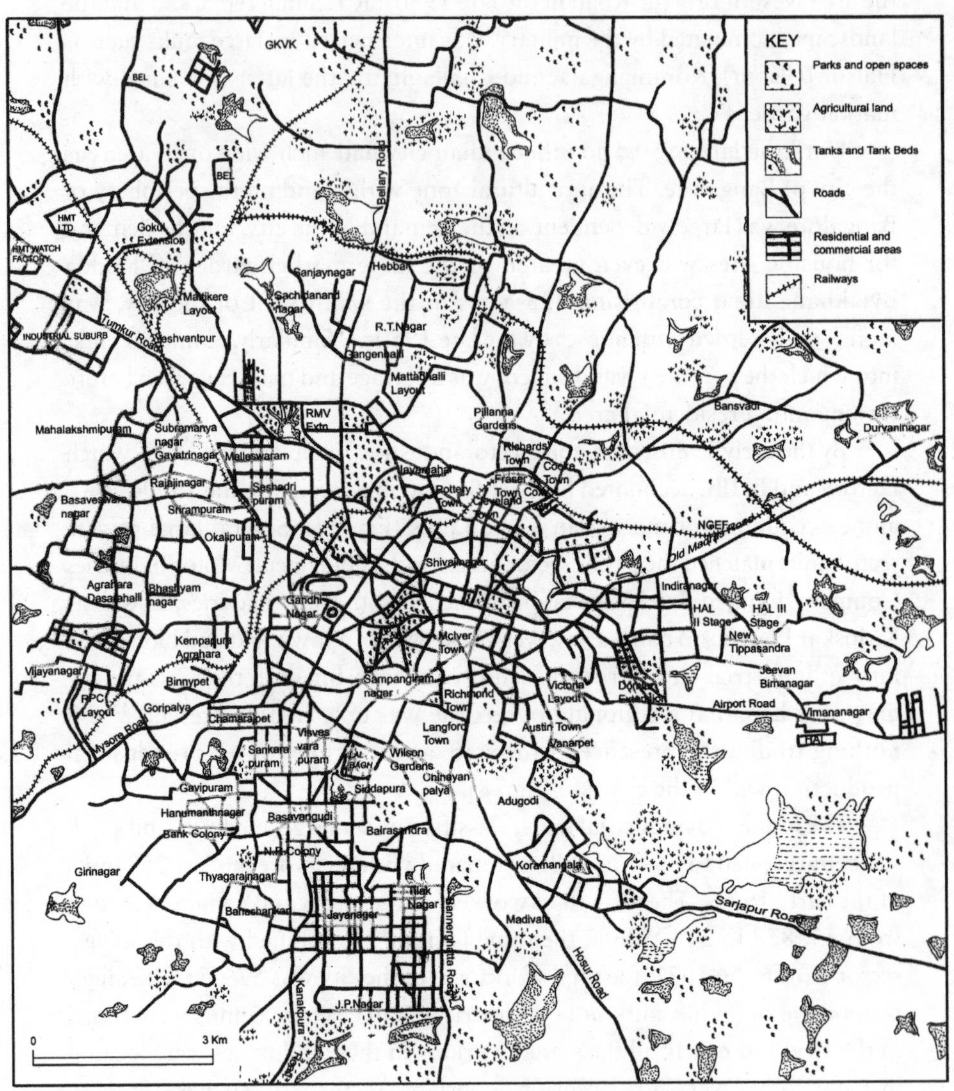

Source: Based on Bangalore Guide Map, Surveyed 1979–80, Second Edition 1983.

and growing informal sector in the city. As early as the 1950s Noel Gist had pointed out that 'a number of machine shops including those with lathes and grinding equipment have sprung up in the vicinity of Binny Mills';[20] this was a pattern repeated many times over as the large industries were established. As P. Thippaiah's more recent work on the informal sector has shown, workers in this sector accounted for 69.16 per cent of the total workforce in 1991, up from 55.25 per cent in 1971. The annual average compound growth rate of the informal sector, he claimed, was more than 5 per cent in 1981–91, 'substantially higher compared to the growth rate of the formal sector' which was just 2 per cent during the same period.[21] Migrants to the city, attracted by employment opportunities, his sample proved, were able to find work within two months, with very high mobility between jobs. The real estate boom, the development of large scale middle-class housing, and new infrastructure projects in the city during the 1990s have vastly expanded opportunities for skilled and unskilled workers in the building industry.

Importantly, Thippaiah's work pointed out that the informal sector was 'not necessarily a training ground for the formal sector, instead it provides training for the informal sector itself'.[22] Dilip Subramanian similarly notes that the 88 day strike by 7000 workers in MICO in 1980 affected the fortunes of '8000 permanent and 35,000 temporary workers' in 260 ancillary units across the city.[23] The reliance of large organized units on the unorganized sector was undeniable, but the divisions between these sectors would remain. Through the 1990s, however, there were clear signs that large state run units were no longer the preferred mode of industrialization, and the ranks of the informal sector would only be strengthened by new economic developments. Holmstrom shows that organized public sector employment fell 1.8 per cent in 1991–2, at a time when organized private sector jobs increased by 7.4 per cent.[24]

Since the 1980s, the size and visibility of the public sector has been overshadowed by the private sector, beginning with the proliferation of the garment units in every part of the city—employing nearly 70,000 workers by the late 1990s—and including several units producing electronic consumer goods. With the arrival Texas Instruments in the city in the early 1980s, the city's attraction as a centre for computer software and hardware development dramatically increased, and the concentration of skilled labour in the public sector units and laboratories, as well as the graduates of the various engineering colleges in the region made Bangalore an attractive destination for Indian and multinational firms engaged in software development.[25] According to James Heitzman, the city's visibility as a 'Silicon Valley' was slow to reveal itself in the figures, as only a small number of people (2,619) of over 3,80,000 workers

FIG. 25 *Coralled in comfort, at the IT enabled services workplace, where work is defined as lifestyle: Health Scribe offices.*
(Clare Arni, 2000)

in 1991 were reported as employed in the hardware and software fields.[26] In the mid-nineties, Bangalore had 109 firms, including multinationals such as TI, Verifone, and Digital which drew on the software designing capabilities of local engineers.[27] This was to change drastically in the very next decade as IT and IT-enabled services accounted for close to 60,000 jobs distributed over 1,400 firms by the late 1990s.[28] At the beginning of the new millennium, the demand for associated services has swelled the sphere of the IT and IT-enabled service industry to include nearly 3000 firms, expanded with the arrival of medical transcription, back office operations, and call centre work (Fig. 25).[29]

The map of the city reflects the three phases of development that shaped its industrial structure and led to a burgeoning informal economy. If the early focus of industrial activity was to the west of the old city area, the public sector units leapfrogged the boundaries of the city to occupy sites along highways to the north and east. Before long, a process of residential in-filling made it a contiguous tract of the city and its industrial suburbs. New greenfield sites for industries at Veerasandra, Bommasandra, and Electronic City, according to A. Ravindra, did 'not seem to be guided by rational considerations, except availability of land'.[30] The consolidation of the new economies between International Tech Park in Whitefield (where more than 14,000 people were employed in 2003) and Electronic City to the south-east (where more than 12,000 people were employed) in what has been designated as the 'IT corridor' was matched by the far more tenuous existence of the small scale sector, which relinquished its hold on Peenya industrial estate to the north-west while thriving in the interstices of the planned city. The new economy shows scant regard for zoning laws, with software firms spilling out of the 'IT corridor' and garment units sprouting in nearly all residential areas of the city, while the small scale informal economy, as Solomon Benjamin and Bhuvaneswari Raman have shown in their study of Azadnagar, thrives on informal and perhaps even illegal land regimes in numerous parts of the city.

Each of the phases of economic growth have spawned spatial practices that have shaped the urban form of Bangalore in specific ways (Map 9). As we shall see in Chapter 3, in the decade after Independence it was the industrial worker who dominated the planning imaginary. This visibility was, however, brief. Since the 1970s, production itself, and the industrial worker in particular have been invisibilized, with interesting consequences for the image of the city. The invisibilization of production has occurred at a number of material and ideological levels. For one, Bangalore largely bypassed the smoke stack stage of industrialization, leapfrogging straight into 'cleaner' forms of industrial production. The result is the absence of a proletarian culture in the city, since industrial labour has not carved out a distinct space for itself. Two, the location of the public sector units in planned enclaves on the outskirts of the city physically isolated these centres of production from the rest of the city. This despite the fact that the majority of public sector workers lived in mixed localities and commuted to their jobs from residences in the city.[31] However, perhaps the most important reason for the invisibility of work, and indeed the worker, in the city, is the ideological definition of the public sector worker as middle class. The public sector has produced an enclave of privilege in which workers, notwithstanding a strong tradition of collective action, have adopted the lifestyles and aspirations of the middle class. Prakasa Rao and Tewari were among the earliest scholars to point to the overwhelmingly middle-class profile of the city, even in the mid 1970s.[32] The income distribution of the middle income group in zones which had public sector industries, said Tewari, ranged from 78 to 92 per cent, higher than most other working class areas of the city.[33] The work culture of the new economy has strengthened the middle-class link, to foster a self image that is far removed from any concept of a labouring self, emphasizing work as a lifestyle whose goal is enhanced consumption. Notwithstanding the massive presence of workers, and informal workers in particular within the metropolis, labour is thus invisibilized and subordinated

MAP 9 *Growth of Industries in Bangalore, 1940–90s*

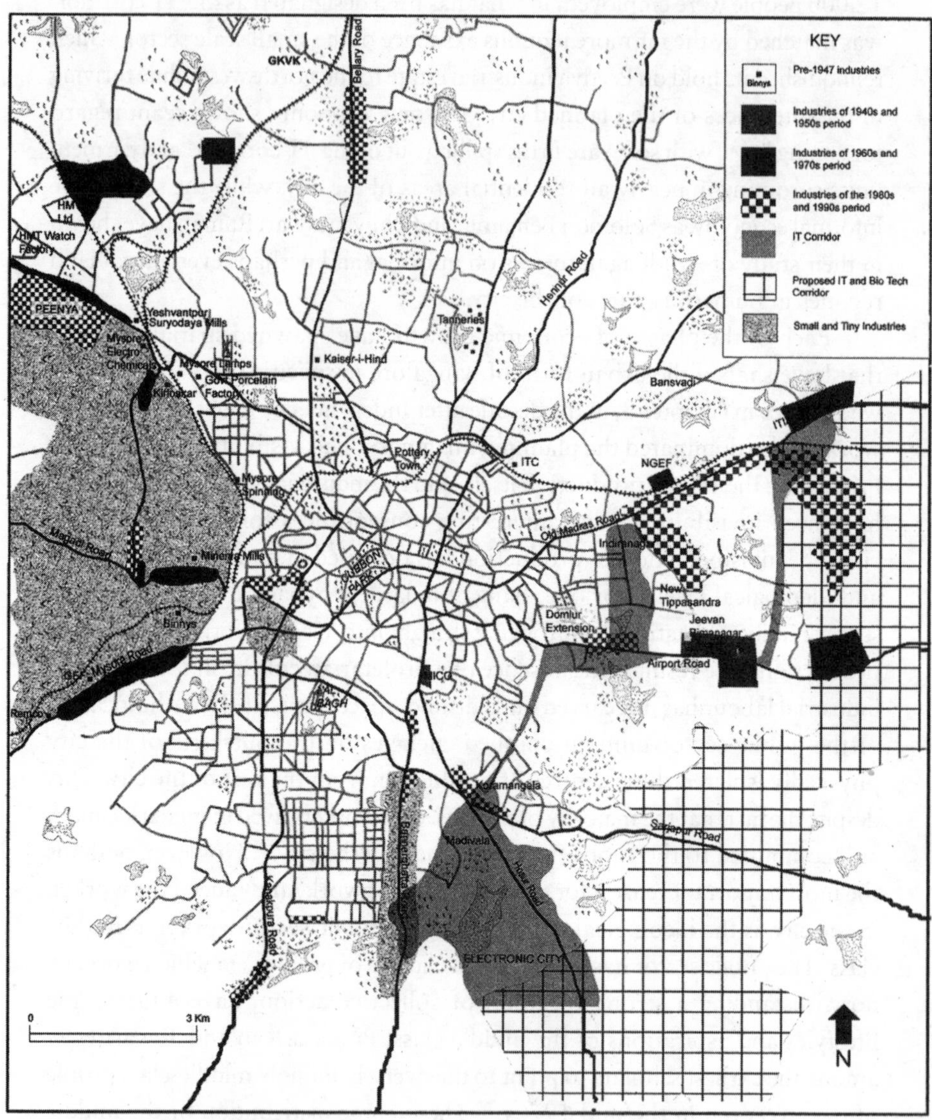

Source: Noel Gist 'The Ecology of Bangalore' (1952); K.S. Rame Gowda *Urban and Regional Planning* (1986), A Ravindra *Metropolitan Bangalore* (1992); *Bangalore Existing Land Use Revised Comprehensive Development Plan* (1995); Business World (2001); Millenium Biotech Policy (2000)

Industrial areas marked are only indicative and not to scale.

to the image of the city as a residential zone. This becomes clearer when we look closely at the modes of consumption of space for residential purposes.

Housing and the Consumption of Space

When the Rajajinagar extension was built to the north-west of the city in the early 1960s, it was partly envisaged as an 'industrial suburb', the first of its kind that would permit city-based industries to move to the edge of the city, and enable labourers to reside nearby.[34] The suburb recreated the housing form that would characterize Bangalore's residential development well into the 1990s: an independent house within a modestly proportioned site. This was a far cry from the generously proportioned bungalows and compounds that were the preferred building styles of the colonial middle classes, and yet the idea of a dense high rise complex held little appeal.[35] Rajajinagar became the preferred residential area for government servants, particularly in the years following state reunification. To the north-west, industrial activity thickened on both sides of the Tumkur Road, making it the most densely industrialized area of Bangalore in the mid 1970s.[36] Yet so abundant was land within and beyond the city, that it was possible to waive the acquisition of land in such central areas as Austin Town even in the 1960s on grounds that 'the owners [of the acquired land] are mostly persons belonging to the Economically Weaker Sections, having small fragments of land and growing vegetables for their livelihood'.[37]

With the establishment of the large public sector units at the edge of the city, the model of the low-rise spacious township gathered support, and housing styles became the basis for instituting new modes of citizenship, as workers produced for the nation. The township would reflect the pride of production as in 'Durvaninagar', or Telephone city, of ITI or 'Vimananagar', the Aircraft Township of HAL.[38] By the 1970s, the industrial townships and outgrowths occupied vast tracts of land: HAL had 2847 acres, HMT 635 acres, BEL 640 acres, and ITI 367 acres. As such, they were the epitome of good planning, generously provided with facilities for recreation, education, and shopping. No wonder then that even as late as 1981, when the census report noted that 'underground drainage facilities and sewerage systems were only available in 7 out of the 27 towns in the Bangalore district', all the towns so identified were industrial townships.[39] The townships were a deliberate effort to contain large-scale industrial production in ways that would not strain the city's resources. But before long the spaces between the township and corporation area filled up with settlements that were variously referred to as extensions, or outgrowths.[40]

So strongly grounded in the ownership of a site was the 'ideal home' in Bangalore, that numerous House Building Co-operative Societies, which mushroomed in the 1980s, joined the Bangalore Development Authority (which in 1976 replaced the City Improvement Trust Board) in offering sites-and-services schemes to their members. The site was attractive even to those of modest means in the city, and it became an attainable ideal for many among the lower middle classes as the city steadily incorporated marginal areas of villages. Although high rise living was richly recommended to others, particularly by those dismayed by the expansion of the city,[41] the conditions were not ripe for the middle and upper classes to accept this style of living until the entrance of the professional builder. Single male, and sometimes female, workers were first housed in hostels as the public sector expanded in the city: by the 1970s the state itself made provisions for satellite townships and working women's condominiums, signalling a recognition of new standards of privacy, space, and comfort for a wide range of people, especially the industrial worker.[42]

The dramatic transformation of the low rise, expansive city occurred only with the emergence of the real estate developer, who emphasized the attractions of apartment-style living in terms of a centralized location and enhanced safety. The apartments that soared in the small by-lanes of the C&M Station and other older areas of the city such as Basavangudi and Malleswaram thus recast the concept of the 'ideal home' as a stand-alone house on a site. The ideology of the owner-occupied home, more often than not built by the contractor in consultation with the builder, gave way to a real estate ideology, with apartments increasingly sought as an investment by many who saw Bangalore as a possible refuge from the pressures of metropolitan life elsewhere in the country, or sometimes as a second home. Housing by this time had become a means for the display of newly acquired notions of taste and of unrestrained consumption, both in the design of residential, commercial and recreational space, and in the choice of building materials.

Architectural Styles and Reformed Taste

The choice of architectural styles and building materials used in private or public and commercial construction makes the shifts in the economic structure of the city abundantly clear. The authority of the solid granite structure, which was the most distinctive feature of the colonial and immediate post-colonial public architecture in Bangalore, quickly gave way to a Nehruvian fascination with reinforced cement concrete. Public and private buildings alike bore the traces of a new austerity. The military barracks ironically powered the democratic imagination: barracks style hostels, offices, hotels, schools, and shops allowed for repetition on several floors. Sometimes, even such austerity could be made to stand out in the city's landscape: the Visveswaraya Towers, built in a brutalist style is strikingly different from the excessively ornamental public buildings with which it shares space in the central administrative area.

Granite, abundantly available in Mysore, was for very long freely used in building anything from pump house or textile mill to private home or castle in the state capital. The rough hewn surfaces of granite blocks lent permanence and grandeur to the functional buildings of the colonial order, since the pump house, railway station, or electrical sub station also made free use of wrought iron, structural materials of an industrial age that were sometimes bent into delicate tendrils in an imitation of nature. These ghosts still haunt the city landscape. Long after the looms and winding machines of Binny Mills were stilled and reduced in number, and the steps of hundreds of workers on the flagstones became faint, these acres of granite in western Bangalore are reminders of the plenitude of a different era, when both land and building materials were for the taking.

After the late 1980s, privately built shopping and 'new economy' workplaces, hospitals, schools, and apartment buildings displayed a new aesthetic. The rough hewn granite gave way to dressed granite, and by the late twentieth century there were few buildings that did not sport polished granite on façade or floor. The most distinctive feature of the last decade's architectural style is the spacious atrium, an enclosure of carefully tended 'nature' which provides an illusion of outdoors with none of its discomforts. Cocooned from noise, heat, and dust in polished granite, it is as 'urban still life' of sorts, one that allows only a distilled air of privilege to circulate. Hailed for the opportunities it provided to architects to imagine space 'free of context', shopping malls sport a hushed interior, with atriums that keep out the public life of the street, with its unexpected and perhaps unpleasant encounters of plebeian crowds.

In its latest phase, the phase when the IT, and more recently the biotech companies have seen an enormous expansion within the city, a heroic style of architecture has been inaugurated in the new steel and glass structures that adorn the techparks, such as the Whitefield International Tech Park and the Electronic City. Yet, significantly, large numbers of smaller firms have adapted themselves to the low rise structures in residential localities, often in violation of zoning and building laws. Only partially has the new economy restructured the landscape of the city: like economies that have gone before, the IT revolution is occurring within enclaves across the city, spilling beyond the designated IT corridor.[43] (See Map 11.)

Since the 1990s, the demand for international architectural styles has led to the widespread use of steel and glass, resulting in a shiny skin that celebrates the surface. The most recognizable image of Bangalore city, the dressed granite structure of Vidhana Soudha, with its flourishes derived from history, now joins the glass towers of the International Tech Park to represent the real and imagined cities of Bangalore.com. Reflecting on the 'glass curtain wall' that has become the supreme symbol of an internationalized corporate identity, Vandana Baweja suggests that a previous obsession with transparency has been reversed as opacity takes its place, offering furthermore a surface that is 'opaque and reflective during the day' and luminous at night.[44] The fleeting, momentary quality of the images has, she says, a 'cinematic quality'. Seen against the totality of the urban landscape, the 'theft of the image', to borrow Umberto Eco's phrase from a discussion of the mirror,[45] is somewhat inappropriate when the stolen image is not a restful but an already busy street, crowding it further with multiple visions of the sound and fury of the city. In Bangalore, narrow one way streets appear to converge and clash when glass or polished granite is freely used on both sides, adding to the visual disorder of the streets of a small town turned into a big city (Fig. 26).

Visual and aesthetic considerations apart, the choice of glass in construction which has become so widespread in Bangalore, can have its share of perils: it is extremely vulnerable to the kind of urban furies that periodically erupt. On occasion, the glass structure's heightened visibility, its proclamation of privilege, invites anger which leaves an easy mark in the form of broken window panes, as in the violence that broke out after the kidnapping of the actor Rajkumar in August 2000. The city's Diamond District was defiantly defaced, and its smooth skin for long bore the interruptions of paper panes. A decent interval had to elapse, and certainly the celebrated hostage had to be released from bondage before the owners of the building could dare any replacements.

The transformations of residential architectural styles are equally striking. The colonial bungalow for long epitomized the city's historical image, a low pitched-roof structure set amidst acres of land. The sudden revival of the regency style in the 1980s was a result of the entry of the professional architect as a decisive figure in residential construction. The development of housing in the city was led by the market after the 1980s, bringing the architect to a new and more prominent position in construction. 'Everybody,' says Sharad Padalkar, 'was working overtime. The architect's job was mainly to provide a colonial elevation or a façade from any European period.'[46] Although there

FIG. 26 *The 'theft of the image' in glass construction: Diamond District, Airport Road.* (Clare Arni, 2003)

were many people looking for simpler housing styles, he continues, 'no developer understood this demand. All of them were rediscovering the colonial past of Bangalore through the palaces, mansions, arcades and other such noble structures they were building for rich investors.' Pesi Thacker, co-founder of the oldest architectural firm in the city, Chandavarkar & Thacker, thus referred to Bangalore as a 'cluttered museum of buildings'. Speaking of the obsession with the neocolonial among architects, Thacker attributed the obsession to fear of the new and unfamiliar.[47]

For a long while, the architect had been no more than a marginal presence, designing commercial buildings perhaps, but not so often the individual home.[48] More often than not, according to Sathya Prakash Varanashi, the few architectural firms in existence were subordinated to owners and engineers who required no more than drawings or elevations.[49] Most homes followed predictable plan forms with rooms opening on to the long rectangular hall, while 'external compositions were ... bookish'. Describing developments since the 1990s, following the arrival of the architect into her own, Varanashi notes three kinds of trends. In a notable break from the past, the homeowner enjoys freedom to choose materials of construction, leading to 'chaotic designs' which vary from site to site 'at the cost of city aesthetics'. Second, revivalism has taken new shape in the use of open skylights, stone arches, and old pillars, striking a different note from the regency revivalism that was equally common. Finally, the gradual hold of the architect over housing styles has been eroded by the emergence of another specialist, the *vaastu* consultant.

An expression of the sudden upsurge in popular religion in contemporary India is the rise to importance of the *vaastu* consultant, who offers protection from unknown aspects of the future through the deployment of skills quite different from those of the architect. The coding of homes according to cardinal directions was well known in Indian residential architecture and usually respected through minimal or token investment in buildings. The boom in the construction industry since the 1980s has brought new parameters of designing space to the foreground. By conforming to cosmological principles, such architectural practices can frequently be at dissonance with the practical uses of residential or commercial space and with the aesthetic principles of architecture. As a guarantee of well-being and wealth, the principles of *vaastu* are invoked in ways that are quite different from earlier codes of auspicious directions, and involves expenditure of a distinctly higher order.[50]

It would be tempting to see the increased invocation of *vaastu* in house construction as an indication of the fear of forces over which one has no control. It is in part an aversion to risk in a time of relative freedom from the privations imposed by the state, when both market restrictions on goods and services and societal norms which spurned conspicuous consumption may have prevailed. The practitioners of *vaastu* have benefited from the boom in construction since the 1980s, and display a remarkable agility in adapting to a range of budgets.[51] They have, moreover, adapted principles to cover different kinds of house and building design, from the relatively inflexible apartment space to the more malleable individual home.[52]

Yet this account provides no explanations for the reasons why *vaastu* continues to have appeal among those to whom it may represent an additional financial burden and perhaps even physical and aesthetic discomfort. It is not uncommon for people to transact losses on homes that they discover to be unsuitable because of poor *vaastu* orientations. The extraordinary appeal of *vaastu* may be understood in terms of its capacity to provide solace in a context where the new norms of urban social security are as yet undetermined, particularly in an economic system, namely capitalism, that does not prepare one for failure.[53] The 1990s have witnessed a surge in popular religion, and its spatial manifestation in the city is most striking, an aspect to which we shall return later. The 1990s have also been a time of enormous physical mobility, within and between jobs, homes, and households, when the certainties of an earlier time, such as lifelong job security, work satisfaction, and the comforts of retirement are everywhere under threat, yielding place to riskier and shorter term commitments both at the workplace and within the home.

Privilege in the city, on the other hand, wears a more guarded look, so that a new architecture of fear is materialized in the gated, high-security enclaves which guarantee its occupants a life safe from the disorders of the streets. The colonial masters used a mixture of force and persuasion to keep democracy at bay. In the post-colonial period, this enclave is more nakedly forceful, as in the 24-hour security systems, and high and impenetrable walls with only one point of entry, once more reducing the occupants' encounters with the unexpected.[54] This 'city of fear' nevertheless flaunts its new found wealth in a number of ways: polished granite clads many buildings, and castellated walls and pitched roofs abound.

Increasingly, the space within the home emphasizes the homeowner as consumer, who collects and displays 'modern conveniences' more often as a badge of honour or as an announcement of status. Technologies within the home may have reinscribed the meaning of domesticity, but have equally tended to turn homes into a museumized space for inhabitants who are dazzled by technology. In the 1960s, one of the most popular sections of the Visvesvaraya Industrial and Technological Museum was the 'room of the future', a dream space with voice-activated doors and lights, and 'remote controlled' radios. The rest of the museum emphasized the ways in which technology harnessed water, channeled electricity, connected people across vast distances through telephony and thus produced a vision of National Progress. The attractions of the little room were not only the more human scale into which this technocratic vision was translated, but the intensely privatized experience of technological modernity that it seemed to offer. The dream space has been realized in many homes across the city as forms of consumption have been internationalized; only rarely has technology emerged as a response to societal changes or the travails of life in a third world city.

The Space of Consumption

Within the space of their small one bedroom quarters at Durvaninagar, V. Babu and his wife, both employees of ITI, had crammed most of the 'Eight Bigs': television, refrigerator, stereo, water purifier, motorcycle, furniture set, washing machine, and electric fan.[55] Of these, one may take the example of the private water purifier alone as a gadget that responds to the local need for safe drinking water that public water systems do not guarantee. In other cases, the internationalization of consumption has been achieved through the white goods revolution. If workers had marched in thousands against the unprecedented rise in prices of essential commodities in 1973, by the 1990s they gathered as part of a huge and growing consumer market in supermarkets, malls, and consumer fairs. A history of the BEL trade union lamented that 'so many workers have been recklessly taking loans to buy all kinds of consumer goods which they can ill afford'. In public sector companies such as BEL, this had led to a widespread phenomenon of 'Rs 10 monthly wage earners' as most of the salary was attached by credit companies.[56]

The Congress exhibition held on the grounds of the dried up Dharmambudhi tank throughout the 1960s was a celebration of production, a proud display of what the state had produced, from soaps to lamps and machine tools (Figs 27 and 31). This has gradually yielded space to annual Consumex exhibitions which offer commodities, sometimes entire kitchens and drawing rooms, for sale. The invitation to intensified consumption is equally an invitation to redefine notions of public and private. New zones of intimacy and privacy have been produced within the home. However, equally, new styles of consumption have reorganized private space so that it is no longer uncommon for middle-class

FIG. 27 *Dharmambudhi Tank Bed, renamed Subhashnagar, was the site of the annual Congress exhibition. The Mysore State Road Transport Corporation pavilion's motif was the Gandabherunda, the double headed eagle emblem of the Mysore Wodeyars.*
(T.L. Ramaswamy, early 1960s)

homes to sport two living areas and two kitchens, one that is actually used for daily cooking (usually by paid domestic labour) and one that displays gadgets such as oven, microwave or blender (usually by the owner).[57]

The happy commingling of traffic and commerce on the street has increasingly been abandoned, especially by the upper classes, who prefer shopping in the supermarket or mall, which has retreated into enclosed but well-lit spaces. Gone are the adventures of bargaining: fixed prices and other middle class customers and salespersons alike keep the uncertainties of the bazaar away from the mall. The streets are left to a different class of loiterer, usually male, who is actively discouraged from disrupting the flow of pedestrian traffic by the uncomfortable grills that have replaced the rounded bars on the kerb, as on Bangalore's central Brigade Road. Still, there are crowds who throng the city's Commercial Street, undaunted by the heightened noise and light. If the gigantic stores produce a new kind of consuming subject, a new man-in-the-mass, there is a growing demand for specialty stores, which are discreet and charming, with well crafted goods lit up in a warm glow. The stores stock a wide variety of commodities, which may, as Walter Benjamin remarked, be entirely 'freed from the drudgery of being useful'. However, such signs of urbanity are not without their ironies, for the self service supermarket is rarely a response to the scarcity of domestic help, and serves to enhance the pleasures of shopping.

Bangalore's culture of eating out has a long and interesting history, as we have seen from DVG's account of the first Brahmin hotels. Not infrequently, visits to some hotels, like Mavalli Tiffin Rooms near Lalbagh, were lessons in citizenship, with detailed instructions provided on ways of enhancing public hygiene and order. It also became the location, as we have seen, for discussions on the vigilance of citizens in times of crisis.

However, consumption was far from conspicuous at least until the 1970s, although the severe restrictions imposed during the Emergency years may have signalled the death-throes of state imposed restraints. There was a wartime ban on serving rice based foods in hotels in the late 1940s; the idli vanished, under protest, from the menu. 'The food scenes in the streets of Bangalore', wrote DVG to C. Rajagopalachari, 'are pitiful .... my hardship is nothing when compared to what thousands are passing through in endless queues from 6 am to long after 6 in the evening.'[58] Wheat (and the 'north Indian' chapati) made a hesitant entry into Bangalore diets in the sixties, once more as a result of food shortage and rationing. During the Emergency in the 1970s, guest control orders were the norm at weddings, and the Janata Meal was introduced by Labour Minister Sriramulu. The 'Sriramulu' meals and snacks specified the quantity and cost of meals in average restaurants frequented by the lower classes. Some restaurants staged their compliance in a dramatic fashion, placing a pair of scales on the front counter for those who doubted the proportions of what they served.

Today the increasingly common '*darshini*' embodies the logic of the market in prepared food: it is not merely, as in the Udipi style restaurants, production of food at high speed, but a form of high speed consumption that is also encouraged. Costs are minimized by the standardized menu and the complete absence of seating. This compels people to gobble their food and move on, rather than linger, stripping the meal of all but the ingestion of nutrients.

New internationalized styles of eating, moreover, have called for unusual protection measures. Since the 1980s, Bangalore has been the launching pad for a number of American style food chains, notably Pizza Hut, Domino's, and Kentucky Fried Chicken. Such foods were hardly absent from restaurants in Bangalore before this time, but the food chains proclaimed a new ideology of consumption that emphasized its international character. Repeated attacks were made on the Kentucky Fried Chicken premises in the city's central Brigade Road by the Karnataka Rajya Raitha Sangha in 1996, to protest the possible changes in the agricultural sector that would ensue. As a result, the KFC restaurant was guarded by a van full of police, inaugurating a new role for

FIG. 28 *Against new regimes of consumption: Karnataka Rajya Raitha Sangha activists attack the Kentucky Fried Chicken outlet on Brigade Road.*
(The New Indian Express, Bangalore, K. Bhagya Prakash, 30.1.1996)

custodians of law and order. If a number of governmental interventions had once restrained consumption in the city right into the late 1970s, in keeping with the developmental role of the state, in the 1990s, state apparatuses were not unwilling to protect the rights of those who wished to consume brand name chicken (Fig. 28).

The new use of glass in restaurants signals a departure from earlier modes of restraint as eating itself becomes a spectacle, the glass serving simultaneously as 'invitation and denial'[59] to those in the street. Glass is also used in quite different ways, sometimes up to the third floor, so that buildings appear to have a wall cut away, turning all passers by into witnesses to the theatre of consumption. Overstuffed (and unoccupied) armchairs, entire living rooms, lights, and washing machines may suddenly loom out of a darkened street as phantoms in the night. Art here enters the service of the merchant to build new and entrancing sets which define and arouse desire. Glass that is used in shop windows could foster other kinds of spectatorship as well, and the throngs outside a TV store during a cricket match well illustrate this.

If Bangalore is today seen as the ideal gateway of consumption, and the launching pad for innumerable national and international brands of goods, services, and more recently, events,[60] it has found active support from a state government which is keen to exploit the spatial spread of Bangalore and the new access to the outskirts that has been enabled by the ring roads. Goods might once have made their way to the doorstep of the consumer, as a number of vegetables and fruits still do. In a rapidly automobilized society, the consumer herself is placed in circulation and urged to go further afield to malls and supermarkets. The new sign of the metropolis is the road that is dedicated to the flow of motorized vehicles.

The Space of Circulation

Nothing has drawn as much attention to the poor administration of the Bangalore metropolis as the condition of its roads. Roads in the city appear to have taken on a scandalous life of their own, stubbornly resisting repair efforts and impeding mobility rather than enhancing it. Bad roads have become a metaphor for corruption, for the impossibility of being 'modern', and for the intractable problems posed by legal claims over land use in the city. Amply supported by the press, which has prominently featured the grievances of vehicle owners on the bad road surfaces, there is a growing belief among vehicle-owning sections of the public that improving and increasing the road surface will increase mobility, improve traffic conditions, and reduce accident rates.

Some have gone to court, others have taken up their shovels in symbolic protest, and yet others have staged their concern by measuring the size of potholes on prominent thoroughfares such as the Hosur Road.[61] What remains largely unquestioned is the need for intense privatized *automobilization* of a largely poor society, and where the majority of road users are pedestrians, cyclists, and bus riders. Pleas that focus on the *road* as primary make *road users* into a secondary concern. This development, which is no more than two decades old, has atrophied the imaginations of planners, bus corporation executives, and the vehicle-owning public alike.

In part, the demographic expansion of the city occurred alongside a nationwide boom in private vehicle ownership, beginning in the mid 1970s, and intensifying in the 1990s. This expansion has been amply aided by the fact, as we shall see, that the city is poorly served by a public transport system. In the early decades after Independence, the town of Bangalore, as K.N. Venkatrayappa's study in the 1950s mentioned, was compact and required only a minimal transport infrastructure since 'a large number of persons wishing to go from place to place in the city either walk or go on bicycles.'[62] 'Unscrupulous jutkawalas' met the need of outsiders to the city since the bus service was skeletal. Walking was the fastest way of getting around, and most distances were measured in terms of walking time.[63]

By the 1970s, the planning apparatuses recognized the problem of an expanded vehicle population, especially as it was expressed in terms of higher accident rates in the city. By September 1975, there were 93,388 registered vehicles on the road, of which four-wheelers were 21,974, and two-wheelers 47,027, followed by buses and other vehicles.[64] However, the 2,00,000 bicycles still had the edge, constituting 71 per cent of passenger carrying vehicles, and hence 'design of a set of cycle tracks was found necessary' (though never implemented). Between 1971 and 1982, motorized vehicles increased by 222 per cent, and streets were flooded with 1,20,0334 motorcycles and 33,566 cars, while buses were a paltry 1,760.[65] The concerns of planners were no longer the accommodation of non-motorized forms of transport but their eviction from city roads to enhance traffic flows.[66] Despite a detailed traffic survey in the mid 1970s, which mentioned ring rails and other forms of mass transport as vital to the city, ambitious plans were laid for ring roads and one way streets, while cyclists and pedestrians dropped from public view. A new problem, that of parking in the central areas of the city, was recognized, and solutions to this problem first resulted in the narrowing or abolition of footpaths.

The city's automobile population exploded in the 1990s, so that by the year 2000 the city had a registered vehicle population of 14,18,361, which

TABLE 2.1: Growth of Population in Bangalore 1941–2001

Name of the city	Census year	Area (sq. kms.)	Persons	Males	Females	Percentage increase in population
Bangalore urban agglomeration @	1941	NA	410,967	216,340	194,627	32.66
”	1951	65.86*	786,343	417,706	368,637	91.34
”	1961	113.31#	1,206,961	644,047	562,914	53.49
”	1971	177.30	1,664,208	887,782	776,426	37.88
”	1981	365.65	2,921,751	1,541,397	1,380,354	75.56
”	1991	445.91	4,130,288	2,170,985	1,959,303	41.36
”	2001	531.00	5,686,844	2,983,926	2,702,918	37.69

* For the Bangalore City Corporation area. *Report of the Bangalore Development Committee*, 1954.
# For Urban and Suburban Bangalore, including Bangalore City Corporation area. *The Outline Development Plan for the Bangalore Metropolitan Region*, 1963.
@ The concept of Urban Agglomeration was introduced in 1971. For comparative purposes the aggregate population of the towns included in the UA are given for various censuses even before 1971.

SOURCE: *Census of India, 2001*. Series 30, Karnataka. Provisional Population Totals, Paper 2 of 2001.

was dominated by two-wheelers (Table 2.2). What Bangalore has experienced in the past two decades is neither unique nor exceptional in the history of automobilization. Even the solutions seem to follow routes that are well tried elsewhere. If roads are too narrow to accommodate private car traffic, the sidewalk is removed. The footpath could also be used for parking, particularly with the burgeoning two-wheeler population. Too much traffic on certain routes at peak hours is solved through one way systems. Grade separators and ring roads relieve the pressure of good vehicles crossing an expanding city. Finally, slow moving, non-motorized vehicles are banned from using certain roads.

TABLE 2.2: Registered Vehicles in Bangalore, year 2000

Two-wheelers	10,53,007
Cars	1,98,004
Jeeps	6,822
Autos	60,750
KSRTC	7,367
Private Buses	1,509
Goods vehicles	41,244
Contract Carriages	768
Maxi Cabs	4143
TOTAL	14,18,361

SOURCE: Sanjeev Aundhe '*A Comparative Study of Three models for evaluating Urban Infrastructure Projects*' (Phd Thesis, IIM Bangalore, 2001), p. 41.

Dreams of a Mass Rapid Transit system yielded the Elevated Light Rail Transport System (ELRTS), which was seen as the answer to the woes of commuters. The Infrastructure Leasing and Financial Services study of 1994 suggested that the ELRTS at a cost of Rs 4000 crores, (later downsized to Rs 2600 crores) was the 'least cost solution' to the city's transport needs in comparison to installing a metro.[67] By 1999, World Bank experts, invited to assess the feasibility of the project, declared it 'economically unviable' as it would lead to hurdles even in execution; examples from other parts of the world had, with few exceptions, 'failed to deliver results.'[68] The authority of the World Bank changed the tone of the discourse on the ELRTS, leading to pleas that the state government give up this project in favour of suburban or circular railways.[69] The large tracts of land thrown in as an incentive for those likely to undertake the project, in this case the UB consortium, did not sustain interest, and the project was abandoned in 2002.[70]

The discourse on new mass rapid transit systems produced unanimity among planners, corporate groups, and private vehicle-owning citizens on at least one ground. They concur that an increasing number of roads and highways must be single purpose routes, thereby reducing multiple uses that allowed for non-motorized traffic or pedestrians. Not only is there money to be made, but prestige and short term political mileage to be gained from such infrastructure schemes. Critics of such schemes are dismissed as those who are bent on preventing the Singaporization of Bangalore.

The irrelevance of Singapore to the Bangalore case, however, may be judged by a look at the transportation system in the city state. The development of a mass rapid transit system in Singapore has been combined with severe disincentives to private car ownership and usage. Car populations are controlled by issuing certificates of entitlement, which are prohibitively expensive for luxury vehicles, by imposing 150 per cent import duties on cars, and through road taxes which are equally high. There are restrictions on access to the roads in the central business district during certain times of the day. Over 80 per cent of the population is thus forced to rely on the public transport system.[71]

In contrast, the automobilization of Bangalore city is already complete, with citizens seeking increasingly privatized solutions to public problems, and the ring roads will only accentuate the process. A study by Sanjeev Aundhe demonstrates that MRTS will not make a significant difference to the number of vehicles on the roads. Indeed, 'some vehicle owners who did not use their vehicles earlier will use them after MRTS is built, leading to congestion again ... the efficacy of any form of MRTS in reducing the congestion problem is debatable'.[72] In Bangalore, nearly 60 per cent of passenger trips are made on buses which account for less than 2 per cent of the vehicles on the road: the ELRTS is priced at 2.2 times the BMTC bus fare and would probably exclude such users.[73]

As a sign of the new focus on the image of the city, the red and silver bus system, which earned affection if not admiration, was changed to blue, on grounds that red was a 'harsh' colour and should no longer be used. The association of the colour red with popular anger and perhaps even the organized Left movement may have prompted the petitioner M.A. Parthasarathy, chairman of the Urban Arts Commission, who suggested 'shades of green' as more appropriate to the image of Karnataka.[74] The activist judge, M.F. Saldanha mandated a new colour code through his disposal of this public interest petition. He also mandated a radio taxi service into existence.[75] Activism of a different kind furthered the concern for the city's image: the police commissioner H.T. Sangliana banned cyclists from the M.G. Road on grounds that they were unsightly to foreign visitors, despite the fact that cycles account for as much as 18 per cent of passenger trips in the city.

The cost effectiveness and wisdom of metro rail and elevated rail projects have been repeatedly questioned, and it has been demonstrated that they do not relieve congestion or decrease private car usage. Nonetheless, 'infrastructure' is the keyword in the city today as dreams of a network society take command. Bangalore received as many as eleven mega-city projects announced in 1997. Of these, only two have seen completion; others are mired in legal and financial problems.[76] The two flyovers and one grade separator have certainly put the gleam back in the eyes of those who dream of corridors of speed. Such projects have also succeeded in keeping at bay any surprising or uncomfortable encounter with the realities of urban poverty and survival. The flyover at KR Market, for instance, has demonstrably affected the economies of those who live and work below, particularly women retailers. Temporary business losses when such projects are underway thus often turn into more permanent business losses.

Associational Spaces

The passage of the city from a space of patriotic production to a space of globalized consumption has altered the meaning and content of democracy itself. The wide range of associational forms that have been fostered in the city have been shaped by the national, regional, and global forces that have produced the space of the city. Though Bangalore's associations may not trace the same trajectories as that of the economy, their modes of addressing and forming a public make them important sites for the redefinition of citizenship and democracy.

In the early post-Independence years, the task of nation-building and grooming a responsible citizenry formed the basis for at least some of the types of associations that flourished in a city like Bangalore. Disillusionment was however quick to set in as democracy, by its liberal definition, appeared to lose its transformatory promise. Other groups were formed, particularly in the 1970s, around alternative notions of citizenship that arose from disappointments about the unkept promises of the nation state. The task that the associations set themselves was largely pedagogical.[77] By the 1980s, the identities of caste and language formed the basis for new organizations that forged yet another version of citizenship based in the neighbourhood. Almost simultaneously, the neighbourhood was being defined as a strictly residential space by the emergence of neighbourhood associations, which inaugurated a new phase of civic activism by mobilizing an altogether different social class.

I will briefly consider these fairly disparate forms of association in the city in the two sections that follow to establish the career of the idea of citizenship in this fifty year period. Examples that are provided elsewhere in this book will further bear out the schematic thesis developed here. I begin with a discussion of the Gokhale Institute of Public Affairs, then discuss the emergence of a cultural movement, Samudaya, and end with an account of the Kannada Shakti Kendra, on the one hand, and the Swabhimana movement, on the other. These organizations are by no means an exhaustive typology, and all continue to survive up to the present day. Rather, the examples reveal the conditions for the possibility of conceptualizing the urban 'citizen' in a variety of ways and with different degrees of success.

Looking back in 1965 on the fifty year history of the Gokhale Institute of Public Affairs (GIPA), the well known writer and publicist D.V.Gundappa said, 'The GIPA is an altogether new type of institution in India. While the concept of democracy is itself new to this country, the concept of a non-party organization as an instrument of it is a more unfamiliar one to the general public ... the future of the institution depends upon our being able to find a body of men of such disinterested public spirit and active concern for duties and felicities of good citizenship.'[78] Toward the construction of this new citizen, the GIPA, founded on the liberal ideals of Gopal Krishna Gokhale, organized study groups on the classic liberal texts of John Stuart Mill such as *On Liberty* and *Representative Government*, and Plato's *Republic,* as well as some Sanskrit and Kannada works. It also organized public lectures and meetings, started a journal called *Public Affairs,* and ran a reading room.

However, perhaps one of its earliest activities which has had a resonance in the 'social municipalism' of the more recent kind, which I shall consider below, were the 'civic surveys' undertaken by members of the study circle. Starting in 1948 and continuing well into the 1970s, GIPA members, such as S.V. Seshadri and A.R. Subbanarasimhaiya, visited particular localities of the city and undertook a comprehensive survey of sanitary conditions, public amenities, roads, lights, water supply; grievances were forwarded to the government.[79] The call was made to set up ratepayers' associations in all localities, and exert pressure on an unresponsive local government to improve conditions in the city. More important were the schemes to educate the new legislators themselves, on the evolution of parliamentary institutions, role of the opposition, and rules and procedures in legislation, and the like.[80]

In its aspiration to be the 'Belfry Tower of Civic Conscience',[81] the GIPA hoped to stir the public through the power of speech, which would in turn serve as an incitement to talk: '... the speeches here will first provoke talk, talk based on knowledge and talk informed by conscience. When such talk comes

FIG. 29 *Earlier modes of civic protest: Poura Samiti members, K.M. Naganna, T.R. Shamanna, A. Lakshmisagar and Rangappa in a demonstration against corruption.* (T.L. Ramaswamy, 18.5.1970)

to be heard in clubs, and in friendly gatherings, in the streets and in buses, our legislators and party leaders will find a new force to reckon with. They will ignore the talk at peril to their own future.'[82] Such correctives were necessary, said DVG, as, 'Our public life today is politics and not citizenship: the devices of democracy tempt one with promises of an easy road to a career not only gainful, but also exciting'.[83] The suspension of democratic institutions, such as the Bangalore City Corporation, was thus welcomed even when popular correctives to the decisions of these institutions appeared to be making headway. The Poura Samiti, a non-party forum, was proving successful in mobilizing citizens against corrupt city leaders: its leader K.M. Naganna was briefly mayor in 1965 (Fig. 29). Along with T.R. Shamanna, the Samiti organized city-wide protests against the withdrawal of free water supplies in 1966, leading to a peaceful bundh in the city. Yet the then Nijalingappa-led Congress government decided to supercede the corporation, principally to stifle non-Congress dissent.[84] *Public Affairs* commented: 'The whole of India will be a gainer for a decade or two of clean and correct bureaucracy', suggesting that the country itself was as yet unfit for democracy.[85]

The training in good citizenship appeared to be increasingly irrelevant as events that unfolded in the city and beyond revealed a very different democracy at work.[86] As newer groups made their voices heard in the city, there was even more liberal hand-wringing at the fate of democracy among those unaccustomed to it. When the students of Bangalore University resorted to extreme violence to protest against the many undeserving students who were chosen to go to the Expo 70 in Japan, *Public Affairs* commented, 'The problem is to bring democracy to realize that to weaken the aristocracy of culture and character is to impoverish its own sources of strength and vitality'.[87]

By this time, institutions such as the GIPA were far less relevant to the emerging order, particularly since, for all its sense of purpose, it had failed to evolve a more inclusive definition of citizenship. Even as its membership and study circle participation grew steadily from year to year, it remained resolutely male and upper caste, indeed, almost overwhelmingly Brahmanical.[88] Not surprisingly, there was bitterness if not resentment at the rise of lower caste identities that did not conform to, and even questioned, modes of liberal citizenship. When Minister B. Basavalingappa famously described Kannada literature as *busa* (cattle-feed) in the early 1970s, large numbers of upper castes

FIG. 30 *A carnival of protest: students rise up in defence of Kannada literature during the* busa *agitation.*
(T.L. Ramaswamy, 1973)

took to the streets in violent protest. Yet *Public Affairs* chose to comment on the inappropriate gestures of the minister, showing great uneasiness about what was clearly a challenge to the caste order. 'Mr Basavalingappa, the minister under reference, is a member of the Harijan Community,' it said, 'and he should have had the self-restraint to know his place ... no one publicly objects to him as a Harijan, but privately his manner would have been objectionable to many.' Furthermore, 'the Panchama problem is not an insoluble one if Harijans set limits to their ambition. They will be regarded by the Hindu community as another caste group, fifth or sixth or seventh added to the four caste groups of the orthodox sastras.' (Fig. 30.)[89]

DVG recognized that the styles and modes of civil disobedience that had been well learned within the national movement stood distorted in the age of Independence. He remarked, 'The Mahatma had hoped that his twin Talismanic words of Truth and non-violence could save the civil character of the disobedience movement from the risks of perversion into criminality. But the talismans have evaporated into thin air and Disobedience has stayed a solid fact in the life of the country.'[90] The restrictive brand of liberalism that the GIPA espoused did not allow its members to see the developments of the post-1970s period as anything but symptoms of a democracy gone awry. Although the portrait of Gokhale continued to adorn the walls of the GIPA building, flanked on either side by Locke, Bentham, Mill, and Shakespeare, and Dadabhai Naoroji, Tilak, and Vivekananda, these frail heroes of the liberal movement have been rendered irrelevant by post-Independence developments. Its meetings, seminars and talks did not resound with the same conviction as they did in the 1950s and 1960s. An institution which prided itself on criticizing what it perceived were the assaults on democracy remained strangely paralysed during the crucial period of the Emergency (1975–7). A member, K. Gangaram, 'expressed disappointment that *Public Affairs,* the organ of the institute has not proved equal to the task of mobilization of public opinion in the 1975–78 crisis'. On the whole, said another member, 'the institute had in 1975–76 reduced itself to the status of a conservative cultural organization.'[91]

Other groups were galvanized into action by the Emergency and developed new and striking styles of cultural disobedience. The cultural movement, Samudaya, saw the turbulent years of the 1970s from a different perspective, and called for vigilance of a different kind from those interested in extending the meaning of democracy. The cultural critique of the social order provided a new language for those who were citizens-in-the-making, those who were finding a voice in the urban milieu. Yet the kind of activities Samudaya undertook also emphasized the largely pedagogic role it would play.

For a state that had no robust Left tradition, the emergence of Samudaya in the mid-70s was an expression of an unexpected moment when cultural, literary, and social movements found a common cultural platform (Fig. 31). Samudaya was a unique arts collaboration of left wing theatre people, writers, poets, and artists that sprang to life during the Emergency. Following the tradition of the Indian People's Theatre Association elsewhere, leftists such as Prasanna, Viranna, Ki Ram Nagaraj, Shudra Srinivas, K.V. Narayana, D.R. Nagaraj, C.G. Krishnaswamy, Janardhan, Hasakru, S. Siddalingaiah, Bargur Ramachandrappa, and B.V. Karanth, among others, evolved a style of theatre that would comment on contemporary themes and issues relating to bonded labour, untouchability, corruption in the political order, and the cultural remnants of feudalism.[92] Departing from the norms of proscenium theatre (Fig. 31), Samudaya's first play was an adaptation of Samsa's play *Vigada Vikramaraya*, called *Huthava Badidare*, which experimented with Brechtian styles adapted to a company theatre tradition.[93] Other successes soon followed, with *Thayi, Mareechana Bandhugalu* and *Kuri,* which deployed the talents of musicians and artists as well as theatre personalities. Many of these shows ran to packed houses in the city.

FIG. 31 *Traditional proscenium theatre performance sponsored by Mysore Soaps and Detergents at the Congress exhibition.*
(T.L. Ramaswamy, early 1960s)

Samudaya was thus unique for a number of reasons: it drew on the resources and creative energies of a number of new movements that were emerging in Karnataka, and it thrived on the energies of the city. The Dalit Sangarsh Samiti had its origins as a cultural movement at about the same time, questioning established caste orders in remote villages of Karnataka, and providing the numbers critical to the transformation of Samudaya from theatre group to cultural movement. The evolution of the Bandaya or revolutionary literary movement provided many innovative approaches to the Kannada language that could be adapted to the stage. The political crisis of the Emergency and the emergence of a radical farmers' movement brought a certain urgency to the dramatic communications of Samudaya and its comments on emerging class tensions in the countryside. For instance, if C.G. Krishnaswamy's *Belchi* and *May Day* effectively used poet Siddalingaiah's poems in stunning performances through the slums of Bangalore, they resonated with meaning among rural audiences as well.[94] There were attempts at adapting theatre to the shifting economic scenario within the city itself: the play *Horata* directed by Laxmi Chandrasekhar and M.C. Anand involved workers themselves in dramatic performances based on the seven month strike in the Metal Lamp Caps factory in 1978.[95]

Above all, the group recognized the necessity of reaching beyond its urban audience to the villages of Karnataka. During the Chikamagalur election of 1978, when Indira Gandhi chose to contest from the safer political environs of Karnataka following her 1977 debacle, Samudaya took on itself the role of educating people about the excesses of the Emeregency.[96] It put up over 250 shows criticizing authoritarianism throughout the constituency. The very next year, Samudaya evolved a mode of communicating with the state's people in a unique series of *jatha*s. Starting simultaneously at KGF in south and Bidar in north Karnataka in October 1979, the month long *jatha* included street side performances, songs, and sale of books and pamphlets.[97] Several other *jatha*s followed over the years, staging plays in all parts of Karnataka while *mofussil* branches of Samudaya took root and expanded.

To be sure, the Samudaya movement, which spread out to the villages from the city, did view villages as places to which enlightened urban people could bring their messages of salvation, rescuing some from the clutches of rampant superstition, and training others in the language of democratic rights. The pedagogic approach was however tempered by the links that the movement had with the organized left movement. Though many of those who participated in Samudaya's programmes were only tenuously linked to the left parties, the movement had its uses for both the CPI and CPM, many of whose members enthusiastically threw themselves into the sale of theatre tickets or books, or even productions such as the *Life of Galileo*.[98] However, this vibrant and inclusive movement, with its critical style of theatre activity in Kannada faded into relative insignificance by the early 1980s, when language ceased to be the medium through which claims to a more democratic polity could be made. Instead, language became the identity around which the beleagured Kannadigas rallied, making it a contentious and divisive issue. The Gokak agitation of 1982 crystallized an identity based on language for the first time, and territorialized it, demanding that the state define educational and work opportunities within the Karnataka region according to linguistic and ethnic markers.

In the early 1980s, Kannada nationalism adopted a more militant and exclusive emphasis following the massive mobilization of people across Karnataka during the Gokak movement. If the Gokak agitation united the litterateurs and artists, workers and intellectuals, upper and lower castes, men and women in a cry of anguish about the predicament of Kannada in the state, it soon deteriorated into an exclusivist 'fear-centred nationalism', which identified its enemies among the subaltern classes. Most closely identified with such a linguistic nationalism is the Kannada Shakti Kendra, which had its origins in the Kannada Writers' and Artists' Guild, with the noted intellectual Chidanandamurthy as its convenor. For the first time in 1984, the demand was made for a committee to study the employment opportunities for Kannadigas in the public sector undertakings of the state. Moving away from the cultural concerns of the earlier period, it was Kannada as the language of employment that took centre stage. With the appointment of the Sarojini Mahishi Committee in 1983, this link was cemented. In its report in 1986, the Committee recommended that 100 per cent of Class IV jobs and between 65 and 80 per cent other posts be reserved for Kannadigas.[99]

The Shakti Kendra was started in 1988, and soon had about 1200 members from all castes and classes. It began as a moderate group but adopted a more virulent tone following its active involvement in a number of local issues relating to work opportunities for Kannadigas in public sector units, the language of liturgy in churches, and even such symbolic issues as the unveiling of the Thiruvalluvar statue in Bangalore.[100] It joined forces with such groups as Rajkumar Abhimanigala Sangha and Karnataka Ranadheera Padhe in defining Kannadiga identity in ways that began to exclude Tamil and Muslim residents of the city. Shakthi Kendra's focus on the employment of Kannadigas in state-run units was quite distinct from older collective identities such as the trade union, despite the fact that unions were the sites where language identities first crystallized. The claim on the city was emphatically a claim to jobs that were secure, well paid, and relatively less demanding.

By resorting to violence as soon as it entered the Gokak agitation, the Rajkumar Abhimanigala Sangha took the language question to a level that specifically targetted the subaltern classes. By the time of the Cauvery riots of 1991 and the anti-Urdu agitations of 1994, attacks on the lives and properties of those considered a threat to the Kannada sons-of-the-soil were becoming routine. The question of language defined the parameters of such associational politics, and residential neighbourhoods, rather than the workplace, formed the locus of mobilization. Since the 1980s, the neighbourhood has also become the site of a new kind of organization that emphasized the city as a residential space. This new form of civic activism defined a new activist citizen, who looked for ways of participating in the administration of the city in ways that went beyond the protest mode.

In terms of styles of political participation, membership, and ideals of democracy that were held dear, there was little that organizations such as the GIPA had in common with either Kannada Shakti Kendra or Samudaya. By the 1990s, both liberal and the Left forms of mobilizing people in the city were transformed, in part by the valorization of the 'local' in the construction of political activism, and in equal part by the heightened role played by violence in making claims upon and within the space of the city. The next section will consider each of these moments as they have constructed new relationships between citizenship and the space of the city.

Refashioning the 'Local'

The neighbourhood has long been the site of a range of activities and provides some clues to the transformations in public life that have been enabled by the city's rise to metropolitan status. Going against the grain of using neighbourhoods to address residential concerns was the use of the neighbourhood as a site for contacting workers about workplace concerns, especially when the factory could not serve as a meeting place during strikes. When the trade union movement was flourishing, and organizations at the workplace had gained a certain visibility, particularly in the 1960s and the 1970s, working class neighbourhoods were a crucial point of contact between the leaders and the rank and file. During the public sector strike of 1980–1 the neighbourhood took on a new meaning when, for the first time in the trade union history of the city, area committees were formed to serve as means of mobilizing and communicating with workers. In all, there were an estimated 30–40 committees all over the city,[101] which served as conduits for information between the rank and file and the leadership while also attempting to solve local problems. A new leadership emerged as a consequence from among those who were engaged in the symbolic actions and negotiations.[102] Militant workers were chosen to initiate these committees in localities which had a large concentration of working-class residences. Thus 'HAL and BEML along with ITI took charge of east Bangalore while BEL, and to some extent HMT took charge of west Bangalore.'[103] Dilip Subramanian traced the process by which the area committees served the strike: they distributed handbills, 'countered rumours and generally boosted the morale of workers;' they also became the most important means of mobilizing workers for the many rallies, jail *bharo*s and other symbolic protests in the city during the 77 day strike. However, Subramanian suggests that the success of the area committees was severely limited and perhaps even discouraged by the strike leadership, as they did not want the emergence of an alternative locus of power, be it during or after the strike. Indeed, the committees, which could have served as powerful organs for sustained mass actions, were not deployed to their fullest capability.

The success in using working class neighbourhoods to rally workers on workplace concerns ironically led to changes in recruitment policies. Initially, garment and electronics factories found it advantageous to be located near the sources of labour as young unmarried women were the preferred employees. This policy was changed when it was discovered that unions, banned from organizing workers within the units, could successfully regroup them in the neighbourhood. During the five month strike at BPL in Bangalore in 1998–9, which affected 6336 employees in 14 units in and around Bangalore, nearly 80 per cent of whom were single young women, the union attempted to organize meetings in the residential neighbourhoods.[104] Yet this was a difficult task since, as Theresa, secretary of the union at the Arikere Unit that produces the television monitor, said, 'BPL does not employ people from around the unit'. The potential threat posed by an organized workforce was reduced through long distance mobilization of women from areas around Bangalore: thus nearly all workers at the Doddballapur units were from Bangalore city, and were bussed to their jobs.

A redefinition of the 'local', and the neighbourhood as the site of such redefinition, has occurred as a result of two separate processes which correspond to distinct class groups in the city. On the one hand, identities based on caste or language, which have strengthened since the early 1980s, proclaim a right to the 'local' and a sense of belonging to a wider identity through such physical markers as the establishment of flagpoles and statues, usually enabled through contributions from local sources. Kannada Sanghas, fan clubs of film stars, and Ambedkar Sanghas, whose insignia crowd the entrance to many slums and villages in the city are a visible sign of how poor and lower middle class young men in particular assert a new identity. An older social order did not successfully efface but only suppressed class and caste markers in the city. The new movements make confident claims on street space, and proclaim new urban identities. Other more temporary claims on the city by such groups are the frequent high decibel celebrations of local festivals (*ur habba*s), political events (*Rajyothsava*) and national religious festivals (Ganesh Chathurthi).

On the other hand, the idea of the neighbourhood as a site from which to address strictly municipal concerns took shape as far-flung areas were annexed to the city as middle-class layouts. The flowering of associations based in the neighbourhood, particularly since the early 1990s, has occurred at a time when concerns about service delivery in the city have crowded out any other definition of political involvement particularly by the middle classes. This form of political activism privileges the private home owner (namely the taxpayer) as the quintessential citizen, and energizes hitherto apolitical sections of the city, women and retired people in particular, to take an interest in maintaining a vigil over the problems of the neighbourhood. Such associations were formed in newer middle-class localities, and numbered about 150 at the end of the 1990s.

Swabhimana, 'a citizen-Local Government initiative for a cleaner, greener and safer Bangalore', was launched by the proactive bureaucrat A. Ravindra in 1995 in collaboration with the Bangalore Development Authority, the Bangalore City Corporation, NGOs, as well as resident's associations with the specific brief of strengthening community participation in the provision of civic services.[105] Following Ravindra's appeal as BMP commissioner in the early 1990s, several neighbourhood associations were set up to monitor garbage collection, maintain parks, and supervise the installation of electric lights.[106] They were hailed as proof of a new and vibrant form of citizenship organized against the failures of local government. This notion of the 'local' was further strengthened by the emergence of weekly English language tabloids in several areas that reported on municipal problems and the efforts of local activists to solve them.

The emphasis of these groups has been to make municipal officials more responsive to the needs of residents. The government initiative was moreover an attempt to invite corporate groups to share in the maintenance of the city, through the sponsorship of parks, circles, light fixtures, etc., and thereby redress 'the steady deterioration in the quality of life which is proving to be a traumatic experience for citizens'.[107] Identification with the 'local' was increasingly sought to be redefined to correspond to the administrative division of the city into wards. In particular, the enabling provisions of the law, especially the 74th Amendment which strengthened urban local bodies and called ward committees into existence, were invoked to expand the meaning of the term local.

Such definitions also brought the identity of the middle-class neighbourhoods into direct conflict with the notion of the local that was marking city space in ways I earlier outlined. Thus, Subbarayan Prasanna, in a detailed discussion of the role of neighbourhood associations and ward committees, said of the 'huge number of welfare associations' in cities like Bangalore that 'their main activity seems to be the celebration of an annual or seasonal ethnic festival in a major way'.[108] The celebrations disrupted the normal functioning of the neighbourhood, its traffic and tranquillity, he said, as they focused on 'the number of roads and streets they can block out of traffic for the duration of the festival, the wattage in the high volume public address system they can blare their music and noise through'. Such a concept of 'welfare' was questionable and therefore best discouraged as an instance of 'ethnocentric parochialism': Prasanna suggested that the young workers and volunteers of such associations be weaned 'into more secular items and activities of urban co-operation'. Finally, he said, collectivities that embraced the urban poor were either nonexistent or unviable, and therefore necessitated thinking afresh the modalities by which they would be drawn into this kind of civic activism. What is attempted in the definition of the new collectivity is a more rigorously middle-class notion of city governance that attempts to correct modes of political association and activism favoured by other sections of people in the city. The middle class has thus been urged to turn its management and housekeeping skills to the neighbourhood, in an extension of the private; this call to action also redefines the idea of citizenship in the contemporary city.

Citizens and Stakeholders

Although Bangalore's passage through the historical transformations organized by informational technologies are as yet hazy, there is at least one semantic shift that denotes the ways in which the notion of citizen has been redefined. The concept of Employees' Stock Options, which has excited the imaginations of those seeking not just jobs but stakes in the IT workplace, has paralleled the emergence of new modes of public participation in city life. Not just the agencies that provide the infrastructural services to the city are now increasingly referred to as 'stakeholders' but citizens' groups themselves have turned into owners of rights.

The term 'stakeholder' has its origins in corporate management, and refers to managerial practices that identify 'persons or groups with legitimate interests in procedural and/or substantive aspects of corporate activity'.[109] The 'stakeholder' concept gained currency in the 1990s when the problems of rapidly urbanizing societies, particularly in the Third World, began to engage international agencies interested in the 'management' of cities. A forum like Citizen's Voluntary Initiative for the City (CIVIC), which evolved in the early 1990s, is a response both to the 74th Constitutional Amendment which mandated the gradual devolution of funds to urban local bodies, and to the enormous interest of international agencies such as UN–ESCAP in promoting the ideology of 'good governance' in cities across Asia.[110] As more and more international funding agencies—ADB, ESCAP, and the World Bank to name a few—have turned their attention to cities in general and cities in Asia in particular, notions of good governance have succeeded in reducing the role of the state to the status of organized and well managed service providers. The mandate of the Public Affairs Centre (PAC), formed in 1994 by Samuel Paul, a former director of the Institute of Management Ahmedabad, was described by one of its coordinators as posing a '"market force" alternative to bureaucratic monopolies and also to provide necessary advisory services to bilateral funding agencies.' Thus the PAC has produced a series of well-researched 'report cards' on services in Bangalore and some other cities to assess the money and time spent on accessing public services, in order to make the broader argument for a market driven and, therefore, efficient provision of services to the city dweller.[111] Considerable effort also goes into providing information on the assets and records of candidates for local elections.

In Bangalore, the term 'stakeholder', whether taken to mean service providers or residents' associations, has come to replace the notion of the citizen as a *rights bearing individual subject*, with one who enjoys *an ownership of rights* to the city. Central to the use of this concept in the urban context is the notion of partnership, an equalization of abilities and entitlements through which a new kind of civic activism is encouraged in order to serve as a corrective of electoral politics. CIVIC, an NGO which was formed in 1992 by a group of concerned citizens who had been regularly meeting to discuss city problems and analyse the Corporation budget, had as its stated intention 'increasing people's participation in the city and civic affairs'. This was in contrast to civic activism which was more closely tied to electoral politics: indeed the NGO eschewed any such association by describing its work as 'apolitical'. It thus distanced itself from the more contentious issues among the urban poor that might have deployed electoral politics to its advantage, and also from modes of civic mobilization in the past that involved modes of mass agitation. Vinay Baindur, the coordinator of CIVIC described the reasons why stakeholder is the preferred term in the discourse on managing the city:

The citizen has a very weak definition of responsibility and ... citizen led demand ... which is resulting in responsiveness in urban governments hasn't been enough ... so the stakeholder is a stronger definition of the word. And it is dependent on more transparency and complete openness and collaborative efforts between the government and the community as well as to see the role of private sector participation.[112]

To the extent that the 'stakeholder' represents a pre-existing interest group which is concerned with the city as a space of residence, it is middle-class by definition. Other classes are collectively represented by 'the trade union, the student union and the slum dwellers' associations'. The 1990s forums and organizations represent efforts at forging new institutional forms which will replace or at least supplement the overwhelmingly state-run modes of mobilizing and distributing resources.

The contrast with previous modes of public activism is well illustrated by the work of the Poura Samithi in the 1960s, which included political stalwarts such as K.M. Naganna and T.R. Shamanna who represented a non-party effort at entering and running the council. As mayor in 1965 Naganna had abolished the unpopular cycle tax, but it was restored by the subsequent Congress-led Council. He led struggles to restore free water supply to ratepayers', organizing rallies, dharnas, and hunger strikes against the Nijalingappa government. Above all, he called for an accountability among corporators from within the world of electoral politics. Although most issues for which Poura Samithi gained visibility were middle-class ones, the strategy of working within, rather than outside elected bodies distinguished it from forms of civic activism that followed.

Circumstances in the 1990s have been vastly transformed due to the expansion of the city and its economy. The attractions of local body elections are undiminished by the activities of PAC or CIVIC. The reasons are not far to seek: the BMP council has expanded from 63 (up from 50 wards after independence) to 87 (in the early 1980s), and now 100 wards(since 1996), with populations between 35,000 and 50,000 residents. Its budget runs into 938 crores (according to the 2002–3 figures), and the attractions of large infrastructure projects for the accumulation of both money and prestige are considerable. They cannot easily be replaced by non-elected or parallel supervisory bodies, although the Congress' record of periodically superceding the corporations continues to animate chief ministerial pronouncements to this day.

In 2002, the launching of a programme called Janaagraha by Ramesh Ramanathan, a member of the BATF, was an invitation to residents' groups, numbering over 150 throughout the city, to participate in governance through ownership. The programme, tried for the first time in early 2002, was intended to prioritize local area needs, and prepare budgets on the basis of ward allocations which would persuade corporators to 'include some of the real needs of the people'.

The operational effects of this scheme are as yet uncertain, but the general effort of the BATF has been to forge a new relationship between private and public, between unelected residents' associations and elected representatives, and transfer the goals and methods of corporate governance to the management of the city. These efforts have been aided by the emergence of forums such as PAC and CIVIC which share a concern for the management of the city. Combined with the legal activism of the 1990s, which literally dragged a reluctant city into a metropolitan existence, placed controls on agitational modes of seeking redress, and recast the meaning of urban citizen, these new institutional structures represent a step towards asserting a place for the middle-class resident in governmental discourse. Urban renewal is thus understood in terms of highly visible infrastructure projects and flyovers, and the ease with which the industries in the new economy are able to take root. Good governance, as Ramesh Ramanathan defined it, 'eliminates much of the political noise that now occupies the airwaves'.[113]

It would be tempting, but an unduly narrow reading of current events, to see the new mechanisms that have been brought into being as translating into direct benefits for the IT sector alone. The title of a brief diary in *Outlook* magazine in November 2001 produced a skein of relations and relationships around the central figure of the CM S.M. Krishna.[114] Certainly, the number of corporate icons—Nandan Nilekani, Kiran Mazumdar, Narayana Murthy, et al.—who have been drawn into cooperating with emerging bureaucratic icons—K. Jairaj, Vivek Kulkarni, Jayakar Jerome et al.—reveals a tight network of people working to overcome political and legal hurdles to the realization of the vision of a bright new metropolis. The chief minister did not hesitate to deploy the image of the most important icon, Narayana Murthy, in the run up to the prestigious Kanakapura by-election, which was, however, won by the H.D. Deve Gowda in early 2002. Such overwhelming evidence of the material underpinnings of links between government and the new economy notwithstanding, the new institutional mechanisms are still in flux, and as the pitched opposition to the location of the new biotech park in the UAS campus demonstrated, they will have to contend with a range of other interests in the city.

Conclusion

The transition of the city from small town to metropolis is being fitfully managed at a number of levels. The fact that an estimated 20 per cent of its population resides in slums, that close to 70 per cent of its employment is in the unorganized sector, and that 60 per cent of its population is ill served by a public transport network challenges any proud claim that Bangalore is well on the way to becoming a network society. The new economies contend not only with fragments of the traditions and formative cultures of the past, but with new definitions and styles of democracy from below that do not comprise a 'consensus' on the image of the city.

The history of electoral politics in the city reveals an interesting shift in the way constituencies, and indeed ideological strengths, are constructed. Throughout the 1970s and 1980s, it was possible for left wing trade unionists such as M.S. Krishnan (CPI MLA, Rajajinagar and Malleswaram, 1967, 1972, 1978, and 1983)[115] or Suryanarayana Rao (CPM MLA, Varthur 1983) to win seats to the legislature by relying on the sectional strength of workers in the city. Today, labour representatives have become rarer in a city that is more hospitable to those who have founded their careers in the real estate business: the recent election of 'Layout' Krishnappa to the Karnataka Legislature is a case in point.

Bangalore's transition to metropolitan status has also paralleled a shift in the character of the state. The developmentalist phase of the state was evident in the preponderance of the public sector, controls on consumption, and redistributive mechanisms that it instituted. Institutional arrangements in these enclaves as well as in civil society reflect optimism about fashioning a public that could function as a responsible citizenry. Yet, if the middle-class locality once wore the proud badge of the public sector company (e.g. HAL Second Stage), today the dream of dollars lends its name to entire colonies (e.g. Dollars Colony). The interim period has been characterized not only by the growing preponderance of the market, and a decline in the largely pedagogic role of civil social institutions, but equally has seen the rise of social movements which imagine democracy quite differently. If there once were areas of the city where Kannada was rarely heard, (e.g. Fraser Town) as the city is re-territorialized today, a more assertive voice of the region is heard, not through a return to the name of an older settlement that was displaced as the city grew (i.e.

Papareddipalya) but through the production of a new linguistic cosmos of names drawn from history (i.e. Pulakesinagar). In its latest, metropolitan phase, therefore, the city has become the ground on which broadly two contending forces stake their claim: on the one hand are the newly renovated citizens, who are amply aided by a technocratic vision of change offered by the leaders of the new economy. On the other hand are those for whom democracy has come to have a different meaning in the urban setting.

The metropolis is, therefore, a restless territory and a disturbed zone that rarely conforms to the planners' map or the administrator's designs. Between the technocratic imaginations of planners, leaders of the new economy, and the bureaucrats, on the one hand, and the social life of various groups, on the other, lies a very wide and contested range of meanings of urban space. This gulf may not be bridged by a revolution powered only by information technologies. It is to the uneven careers of planning, law, and urban aesthetics in Bangalore city that the next three chapters turn.

THREE

Conceiving the City: Master Planning and Informal Power

It is the ultimate aim of every Bangalorean to own a house. It is virtually impossible for a person who does not own a site in Bangalore to approach an authority, agency, developer or dealer and purchase a site across the counter by paying its price .... the lower middle class or weaker sections part with their hard earned money in the hope of owning a piece of land ... The numbers of public who have resorted to such illegal purchases and unauthorised constructions and the sheer number of public involved in such acts has virtually converted what will be a law and order situation into a human social problem.

K.C. Raju Reddy v. *Commissioner BDA*, Karnataka Law Journal 1995 (4)

In October 1996, 400 'suit-clad executives' from Bangalore's Electronic City quit their desks and picked up shovels to register their protest against the appalling state of the roads that connected the city to the premier industrial park. The symbolic protest duly received the attention of the press, and the opportunity was put to good use: it emphasized the crores that were lost due to thousands of workers and vehicles affected by the indifferent state of the city roads.[1] The warmth and even admiration for this protest were missing in similar reports on the protests of the Raitha Horata Jagrithi Committee. Farmers, whose land was acquired for the 12.2 km stretch of the proposed Outer Ring Road, were outraged when part of the acquired land was offered to private developers by the Bangalore Development Authority.[2] Since the late 1990s, Bangalore's high visibility as the capital of India's Information

Technology sector has tipped the balance of forces in favour of the needs of private industry for 'infrastructure', for conceiving the city as a space for the unimpeded flow of commodities, people and information. The city thus increasingly becomes a space 'to move through' rather than 'be in'. Those who are materially and symbolically affected by such progress, such as farmers, are usually considered no more than a frustrating ideological drag.

In the five decades since independence, there have been important shifts in the conception of the city within the ideology of planning. Planning as ideology, says Henri Lefebvre, 'formulates all the problems of society into questions of space and transposes all that comes from history and consciousness into spatial terms. It is an ideology which immediately divides up'. It is, moreover, an attempt to subordinate history and consciousness to the singular logic of geometric (physical) space, which is normalized by institutions such as the law.[3] In the case of cities like Bangalore, whose rise to metropolitan status has been telescoped into less than three decades, such ideologies do not enjoy unqualified success. If anything, the multiplicity of spatial practices that constitute the urban fabric are engendered by such rapid and uneven urbanization.

In these decades, the image of the city of Bangalore has also been wrenched from its regional moorings to the status of an international IT capital. The concentration of scientific research and development institutions, electronics and software firms in the city has earned it the reputation of 'Asia's Silicon Valley'. Bangalore has joined the race in which cities vie with each other to be 'national champions', for advanced investment and infrastructural facilities.[4] In the era of globalization, said Dinesh Mehta, secretary of the Urban Management Programme of South Asia, multinational corporations were looking not to countries but to cities as critical locations.[5] Increasingly claimed as independent spaces, there are attempts to integrate them into national and international circuits that are unconstrained by geography. In this context, previously expressed concerns about 'restricting' city growth have increasingly yielded to concerns about 'managing' the city. Since coming of age in the 1990s as the capital of the nation's information technology industry,[6] there were fears that the city's lead was slipping. This led to a demand for emergency measures as 'Bangalore by default became the Silicon Valley of India' and could secure its future only through planned effort.[7] As a high-tech enclave that competes with cities such as Hyderabad, Pune, and Chennai for foreign and domestic investment, Bangalore must strive to conform to internationally acceptable standards.

Yet what has the experience of planning been in these last few decades? This chapter begins with the history of how the city has been imagined in official discourse and realized in planning. What are the existing critiques of planning in the Bangalore context and why are they inadequate in explaining the predicament of planning today? By way of an answer, I suggest a critique of the ideology of planning itself, by tracing the imaginary that is at the heart of successive plans for the city, and how it has been transformed as the city has developed into a metropolitan centre. Under what circumstances does planning succeed in enclaves, thereby engendering the unplanned city? What are the social uses of space that were unanticipated by planners and yet have significantly altered urban form? Finally, what are the circumstances under which planning takes on *exchange value*, so that it is planning itself, rather than housing, that is offered for sale in the real estate market today? The discussion of these questions proceeds by analysing specific elements of the cityscape of Bangalore such as the township, the slum, the village, the developer's enclave, or the green belt.

Visions of Singapore

Soon after the new Congress Government was sworn to power in 1999, Karnataka's chief minister S.M. Krishna declared his intention of turning Bangalore into another Singapore.[8] The BATF, set up in November 1999, was to be the vehicle of this transformation.[9] The first public display of the corporate will to power came during the Bangalore Summit on 24 January 2000, where many new plans for the coordinated development of the city were unveiled, promises extracted from the seven 'stakeholders' (largely service providers) of the city, and pledges secured from new economy corporate houses.[10] At the Bangalore Summit, the corporates were in command: the elected corporators, all of whom showed up, were mere witnesses to the spectacle of power.

The Bangalore Summit represented a new stage in the public life of the city, bringing the private sector to the foreground in a place which has long been envisaged and promoted as the public sector city par excellence. Shedding its more timid presence in a city where the state has long been prime mover, the new corporate culture attributes the city's problems to inefficient management, while envisaging realizable plans that made a Singapore possible. This is a fresh attempt at moving to centre stage the economic and technological aspects of planning which may be at odds with social, community, and ecological uses of city land.

Singapore has long dominated as the ideal of town planning: in this sense, the Krishna government was only echoing a desire expressed by predecessors, as well as mayors, bureaucrats, and planners dazzled by the importance of that island nation, not least for its physical planning successes. Moving away from the ideals of the pioneering technocrat Dewan M. Visvesvaraya in the colonial period, which were usually London, Paris, or sometimes Tokyo, Chief Minister Veerendra Patil was the first to make a strong plea for a fresh vertical orientation for the city after a visit to Singapore in 1970.[12] Mayor J. Lingaiah, in the same period, was bowled over by Eastern European town planning models, suggesting in his enthusiasm that perhaps democracy was a dispensable ideal, and civil liberties were an appropriate sacrifice in achieving a beggarless, tree lined city.[13] By early 1981, leading architects like P.M. Thacker were citing Singapore as an instance of successful town planning,[14] and since then, dreams of Singapore have dominated the vision of Bangalore's future: even A. Ravindra claimed that 'With imaginative planning and foresight, Bangalore can be developed as the Singapore of South India.'[15]

Singapore, with its broad clean streets, its elevated Mass Rapid Transit System, its sleek downtown skyline, and theme park tourism, therefore, exerts a powerful hold on the imagination of town planner, CEO, politician, and citizen alike.[16] The reasons are not far to seek. Singapore is an achievable ideal, a realizable utopia as the city-state shares the common legacy of colonial rule with Bangalore, is an Asian society with some common social features, and above all, has transformed its spatial and economic identity in less than 40 years. Yet, no analogy could be less appropriate for the Indian context.[17] Despite its superficial similarities, there is little in the economic, social, or political history of the city-state that compares with the deeply segmented social body, complex economies, and distinct democratic cultures of Bangalore. Most important, the field of power in the Bangalore context is, unlike Singapore, composed of a range of forces over which the state has but a tenuous hold. The informal sharing of power with other forces defines and shapes the city in ways that planners rarely acknowledge. Others hope that the influence of such forces will disappear in time.

Critiques of Planning

The optimism about the 'future-as-Singapore' is less a critique of existing modes of town planning than a reassertion of faith *in the ideologies of planning*. Master plans exist only for 32 per cent of urban agglomerations/towns in India; only 27 per cent of Karnataka's Urban Agglomerations or towns have a master plan.[18] It is now widely acknowledged that master-planned areas account for only a small part of the city, with the rest given over to unauthorized (middle class) constructions, revenue layouts, *gramthana* sites, and slums.

There is less unanimity about the exact proportion of planned to unplanned city.[19] The gap between the intention of the state and the ground reality is usually explained in terms of the *failure of planning*, an inability of the technocratic planning apparatuses to manage or cope with bewildering demographic growth. In an early and optimistic reading of the possibilities of planning for an exploding city, K.S. Rame Gowda called for stricter enforcement of zoning regulations and building by-laws to curb unwieldy growth: more, rather than less planning was the answer.[20] Further, it is suggested that the planning mechanisms are subverted by forces, political or economic, that technocratic processes are either unable or unwilling to overturn. Thus, one scholar asserted that 'urban planning peters out (sic) to be a political administrative ritual' as a result of 'politician's indifference' and 'socio-economic forces, primarily of the countryside'; he concluded that transformations in the countryside alone would control and manage city growth.[21] In a stricter and more exhaustive assessment of the objectives, strategies, and effectiveness of various planning documents until the early 1980s, Subbarayan Prasanna and V.S. Vathsala faulted the modalities of planning, as planning apparatuses base decisions 'mostly on authority and less on objective forms of rationality' keeping both the public and 'locally relevant' groups away from the planning process.[22] Here, the belief was that planning could shape and direct city growth with local participation.[23] The failure to build a consensus was remarked on once more by the Bangalore Urban Management Committee, pointing to the purely formal modes of formulating a Comprehensive Development Plan which make no reference to the relative successes or failures of previous plans.[24]

In the 1990s, there has been growing concern about the management of the burgeoning city that has led to calls for more efficient land and infrastructure policies. The need for an enabling fit between economic and spatial planning lay at the heart of A. Ravindra's critique of the management of the city. Recognizing that the (physical) planning process has been hampered by a multiplicity of laws, he suggested '... the Comprehensive Development Plan approach has become irrelevant for dealing with the complex problems of metropolitan growth in Bangalore'. He argued for a wider perspective that takes the region and the economic role of the city in state and nation more seriously.[25] The regional economy assumed importance here as a means of reversing the attractiveness of the city to migrants, a point to which I shall return below. Thus, strategic planning, indeed four interlinked plans of various temporal lengths, were seen as a way of redressing the failures of one shot planning.[26]

There were other critiques of the 'heroic' mode of planning from within the bureaucracy: Lakshmi Venkatachalam, one time commissioner of the Bangalore Development Authority, spoke of a form of 'social planning' which places greater emphasis on practical wisdom to access 'other ways of knowing such as intuitive and experiential knowledge of communities' though the modalities of such a process remained unspecified.[27] Most recently, James Heitzman has suggested that not even the immense possibilities of information technologies have triumphed over 'profoundly local patterns of political authority'.[28]

Nearly all these critics seek more rather than less planning even if different routes are suggested for a planning process that involves public participation. In contrast, Solomon Benjamin argues against the concept of master planning itself. He suggests that 'local economies', namely tiny and small enterprises that thrive in unplanned or even illegal layouts, account for a substantial portion of the city's economy and are directly affected by master-planning processes: 'master planning promotes dualistic structures of (legal/illegal) tenures, forcing the relocation of industries and placing such economies at a disadvantage'.[29] Indeed, in a study which examines several locations in contemporary Bangalore, Benjamin and Bhuvaneswari suggest '... the planned environs of South Bangalore ... form more fragile situations for poor groups largely influenced by Master Planning. Master Planning, we argued, opens up institutional space for higher income groups and corporate economies, while closing options for poorer ones and economies that support them.'[30] In short, in the current socio–economic order, less planning (and the multiplicity of tenures that it fosters), has usually worked to the advantage of the poor. According to this analysis, the city may be read as a dichotomous space, with master-planned areas corresponding to the needs of the corporate/middle class élite for single use zones, clarity of land titles, and the like, while the mixed economic uses, weak titles, and 'unplanned' life allow the poor to survive and even thrive in the city.[31]

Apart from Benjamin, most critics assume that planning provides a neutral framework for the exercise of power, given 'the necessary political will'.[32] Further, all the critics view town planning as unquestionably determined by economic or technological considerations. While following Benjamin up to a point, I suggest that the 'divided city' concept is limited in laying bare the heterogeneous composition of the field of power. This field is shared by forces that one may distinguish as formal, informal, and illegal. These forces result in arrangements that do not strictly conform to élite/subaltern needs and interests in any simple dichotomous sense, and may even be mutually constitutive. Rather than opposing community to state, as Benjamin et al. appear to do, it may be more important to reveal how the *ideology of planning* negotiates this complex field of forces. The restricted sphere within which planning takes effect is thus taken as a symptom of the organic structure of (state) power and its accommodations with other (non-state) forces.

Housing the Worker

Over the past fifty years, the small town of Bangalore has recast itself as a metropolis. There was a period when top–down technocratic planning was a realizable ideal, compared with a later period when planning processes came to grief, undermined by developments from below. Several dramatic spatial and demographic changes occurred in less than half a century of development, with important social and economic consequences for existing and immigrant populations alike. Two maps of the late 1880s and the 1980s provide important visual clues to this brief century of change (compare Maps 3 and 8). The dense blue network of lakes, tanks, and channels interspersed with green vineyards and gardens, which was the dominant feature of the settlement called Bangalore in the 1880s, has progressively yielded to a dense network of roads and highways, black lines which carve up, define, and contain the metropolis in new ways. The two maps signal a shift away from the meaning of land as a *productive agricultural resource* to land as blocks of *real estate*, but also testify to changing images of the city. It is no coincidence that the drying tank-bed has been one of the most contested sites in post-Independence city history, sealing the fate of erstwhile market gardening communities while opening up opportunities for new middle-class and working class immigrants alike.

Between 1949 and 1999, there were two periods of striking demographic growth that irrevocably altered the face of Bangalore. Vastly expanded wartime production in the city and the establishment of the two large public sector units, Hindustan Aircraft (1940) and Indian Telephone Industries (1948) accounted for the first demographic leap of 91 per cent between 1941–51. By the mid-fifties, not only had HAL and ITI trebled and quadrupled in size respectively, two other public sector giants, HMT (1955) and BEL (1956), were established. Together with the ancillary industries they fostered, these industries accounted for over 110,000 jobs by 1961.[33] Even in 1991, when retrenchment was well underway, the national public sector units accounted for about 81,414 jobs.[34]

The industrial worker therefore loomed large in the imaginary of urban planning and government policy alike. If urban planning had its roots in historical concerns about the threat posed by the labouring classes,[35] a late developer like Bangalore proved no exception. The state redoubled its efforts to house the new working class. The Mysore Labour Housing Act 1949 brought the Mysore Labour Housing Corporation into existence. The City Improvement Trust Board undertook to build some (240) workers' housing by the early 1950s; the suburb of Rajajinagar was planned for housing industrial labour and workshops, and finally, public sector units developed separate townships for the immense numbers they were mobilizing for production.[36]

In the first document on planning in the city, the Bangalore Development Committee of 1953 devoted a chapter of its report to the imperatives of providing 'industrial housing'. It noted the 'wholly inadequate' attempts to provide housing for workers in the major industries in Bangalore: textile mills and new public sector industries provided less than 1500 houses for a workforce of over 50,000.[37] Indian Telephone Industries had only just embarked on a housing programme, and HAL housed a mere 400 of its 6,000 workers. Three of the five 'satellite towns' proposed by this committee were therefore for each of the major clusters of new industrial activity, HAL and ITI in the east and HMT in the north,[38] with suggestions that the older (textile) workforce be housed in the north-western quadrant of Bangalore.[39] In its early years, the focus of the City Improvement Trust Board was on housing two classes of new entrants to the city, namely the public sector worker and the government servant.[40]

From the late 1950s, 'unauthorized construction' compensated for woefully poor public provision of housing for workers since only 5,500 of 35,000 public sector workers had homes in industrial townships by 1961. At a rough estimate, there were 23,000 such structures on agricultural land in and around the city. Unauthorised layouts emerged as a category in the reports of the Bangalore City Corporation in the 1950s; by 1960, they had already become a cause for anxiety.[41] Workers spilled over into neighbouring villages, revenue and *gramthana* sites where land was available at affordable prices. In order to regularize their illegal status, revenue site-holders formed themselves into associations beginning in the 1960s.[42] The four new townships that came into being by 1971—the HAL township, the HMT, ITI Notified Area, and BEL township—and the HMT watch factory township in 1981 did nothing to stem the tide.[43]

For several decades the public sector and government occupied centre stage: there were twice as many public service workers than private ones even in 1988.[44] In the 1970s, the provision of industrial housing by the government and private employers alike was made mandatory, with the requirement that a minimum of 50 per cent of workers be housed to prevent 'pressure on housing

TABLE 3.1: Land Use Analysis in Various Planning Documents for Bangalore City, 1952–90
(area in hectares)

	1952(1)	1961(2)		1974(3)		1983(4)		1990(5)	
			Percentages		Percentages		Percentages		Percentages
Residential		4262.3	37.50	9670.00	60.00*	5777.65	28.48	9877.65	34.78
Commercial		276.5	2.55	460.00	2.80	634.07	3.13	675.07	2.38
Industrial		1242.5	10.57	1805.00	11.10	1956.61	9.65	2038.61	7.18
Public & semi-public		850.2	7.60	2156.00	13.40	2533.64	12.49	2615.64	9.21
Transport				401.00	2.40	5216.81	25.72	8946.63	31.49
Parks, play-grounds, etc.		893.0	7.98	1656.00	10.30	2050.16	10.11	2132.16	7.51
Defence land / UC		2621.0	23.20	2114.24	10.42	2114.24	7.45		
Agriculture		1190.0	10.60						
Total	16,336 acres	11,335.5	100	16,148	100	20,283.18	100	28,400	100
Bangalore City Corporation	65.86 sq.kms	113.35 sq.kms		161.48 sq.kms		202.83 sq.kms		284 sq.kms	
Bangalore Metropolitan Area				500 sq.kms		1279 sq.kms		1279 sq.kms	

SOURCES:
(1) Zoning categories developed in Report of the Bangalore Development Committee (Bangalore, 1954) were: administrative, commercial, industrial, residential, and agricultural, of which the last comprised, (a) all agricultural lands within the limits of Greater Bangalore beyond the Corporation Boundary and, (b) an area of about 2000 acres of revenue land situated within the Corporation limits, pp. 104–7.
(2) The Outline Development Plan for Bangalore Metropolitan Region (Bangalore, 1963), p. 9. Area includes urban and suburban areas of the city.
(3) Report on the Comprehensive Development Plan of Bangalore (Bangalore, 1976), p. 56.
*area under residential includes defence land / unclassified and agricultural land.
(4) Comprehensive Development Plan Report (Bangalore, 1985), p. 24.
(5) Comprehensive Development Plan (Revised) Bangalore—Report, Volume I & II (Bangalore, 1995), p. 74.

and traffic congestion'.[45] There was also the suggestion that some townships be started to 'absorb and provide employment for a proportion of the people who would otherwise drift into the city ...' By this time, 36 villages that were part of what was called the 'rural tract' were dominated by non-agriculturists (97.87 per cent) leaving hardly any cultivable land.[46]

Despite the poor translation into practice of policy suggestions for limiting city growth, there was continuing optimism about the state's ability to make additions to the housing stock. More important, the planning imaginary was now dominated by the figure of the middle-class citizen, a category which began to include the public sector worker. The substitution of the term 'residence' with 'housing' is, as Lefebvre points out, a minimalist and purely functional abstraction, shorn of the trappings of comfort or pleasure.[47] In Bangalore, however, planning agencies and the law in Bangalore were being forced to contend with an urban form that privileged sites on which the middle class could build individual homes.

The Dominance of the Middle-Class

By the mid 1970s, city planners were haunted by the spectre of a metropolitan disaster on the scale then experienced by Calcutta. The Comprehensive Development Plan called for urgent pre-emptive measures, including the immediate reduction of the number of industries. The planning focus was shifted to improving services and amenities for the existing population.[48] In the second surge after Independence, the population of the Urban Agglomeration increased by 76 per cent to 2.9 million in the decade 1971–81, belying earlier estimates that Bangalore would reach the 2 million mark only in 2001, or at worst by 1991. The industrial complex, which brought migrant populations and unplanned growth in its wake, was classed along with slums as a 'problem' for the city.[49] Ten years earlier, planners had suggested that developments should take place only on one side of radial roads.[50] Now, planners looked beyond the city boundaries to the region, advocating 'ring towns' within a 50 mile radius to reduce pressure on the metropolis.[51] Self-contained industrial townships and satellite towns were considered preferable as a way of containing the influx of migrants, but suggestions for stemming the tide included the erection of barriers between satellite towns and the mother city.[52]

There were signs that the contours of the big city were being rethought. Concerns were expressed about recreational facilities in the city as the work week shortened.[53] New drama and cinema halls on the fringes[54] and the construction of 'fashionable shopping complexes' were recommended as an alternative to the concentration of cinema halls near Kempegowda Road.[55] The Bangalore City Corporation declaring its willingness to recast the largely horizontal lay of the city in vertical terms by sanctioning the 24-storey Public Utility Building.[56] Even so, vertical development was only acknowledged as an answer to the housing needs of the poor, with the Slum Clearance Board setting up multi-storeyed complexes for those evicted from central parts of the city. The automobile was not yet 'king', and cycle tracks were considered as important as inner, intermediate, and outer ring roads to relieve traffic congestion.[57]

The figure of the industrial worker was becoming blurred in the planning imaginary, and his place taken by the individual homeowner and, much less visible, the slum dweller and those from the 'economically weaker sections'. Meanwhile, people coped with the serious housing shortage by occupying agricultural land within and beyond the corporation limits.[58] The ideal of a 'site', and I would argue, lingering nostalgia for the bungalow and the compound, aided by the discourse on city beauty,[59] maintained its hold on the imagination of the middle-class. The mid-1970s study by Prakasa Rao and Tewari found that the city was characterized by low density, low profile housing. Forty seven per cent of their 1745 household sample had compounds, 61 per cent were main houses, and 55 per cent were separate houses. 'Of the total dwelling units, 88 per cent were on ground floor ... Thus Bangalore is still an individual space oriented and low rise city'.[60]

Prakasa Rao and Tewari believed that the efforts of a central planning agency such as the BDA would put an end to haphazard growth. The twin processes of leap-frogging and infilling by residential, industrial and institutional land uses showed, among other things,

> a preference for location near the outward moving edge of the city to avoid congestion, and the very availability of space at the city's edge. The one common denominator in the spread of the city was the haphazard growth of the land used in spite of the City Master Plan. This is attributed to the multiplicity of jurisdictions involved in city development, and the uncoordinated and individual decisions of the private developers.[61]

The public provisioners of housing sites barely succeeded in keeping pace with the increased demand. The CITB distributed about 64,656 sites between 1945 and 1976, and the BDA distributed about 63,062 sites between 1976 and 1988,[62] and a total of 71, 483 by 1991. The Karnataka Housing Board built 5506 houses in Yelahanka, and 15,000 on the outskirts. The Karnataka Slum Clearance Board had built a mere 2125 houses up to 1989.

The dream of an independent house could still be realized through the revenue layout, and housing cooperative societies. The state agencies rewarded those who were more patient. House-building cooperative societies (HBCSs) vied with the BDA in their enrolment of members, formation of layouts, and distribution of sites. A record 353 were in existence by the mid-1990s, with 230,586 members, 'formed mostly by employees in Government and quasi government undertakings, industrial workers'. As many as 182 layouts were formed and 12,000 sites distributed in the two decades from the mid-seventies to the mid-nineties. The HBCSs shot into public view when the illegalities to which they were drawn, through inflated membership records, appointment of agents, and acquisition of lands beyond their jurisdiction, came under governmental and judicial scrutiny.[63]

With the entry of the private builder into the housing market by the late 1970s, the image of the city was redefined in at least two ways. One, the 'layout' yielded some space to the 'apartment complex'. The relentless march of the horizontal grid over farm and tank bed was now matched by the vertical one, as apartments became a desirable dwelling for even the upper classes.[64] The pressure on the central areas of the city demanded more intensive use of the land and by the early 1980s as many as 50–60 licenses were being granted to multi-storeyed constructions on sites which had previously housed large bungalows.[65] There was active encouragement of an alternative vision of city growth and, indeed, housing.[66] Secondly, group housing schemes/office blocks and the private builder moved centre stage. There was widespread violation of building by-laws in the corporation area by 1981, where the population increase was greater than the metropolitan area.[67]

The BDA was meanwhile faced with a crippling scale of litigation in acquiring land for new layouts and other public purposes. This was largely because, Lakshmi Venkatachalam observed, acquisition was seen not 'as sort of subordinate to the scheme or rather as a step in the implementation of the scheme' but as 'an end in itself', stifling the planners' freedom to decide against acquiring all the land. Not surprisingly, recognition of previous transactions on land was piecemeal, though quickened by political intervention. 'Reconveyance' and 'regularization' through government orders and legislation have become the twin modes of recognizing existing land use. This did little to resolve the problems of planning since, as Venkatachalam pointed out, BDA never planned city-level infrastructure projects: 'whatever infrastructure we developed [w]as part of the township scheme, never stand alone infrastructure and really as a developer and planner for the Bangalore area we should have been [doing that]'.[68] The scarcity of serviced sites with public agencies made private options even more attractive, particularly as the latter offered dedicated and uninterrupted services which the rest of the city often had to forgo.

Global Citizens and Globalized Spaces

The shift in middle-class preference from plotted development of the BDA kind to the more stylish housing offered by the private builder became sharply evident from the early 1980s. In addition to providing a complete product rather than just a site, the private builder was able to negotiate multiple claims and authorities far more successfully than the public agency. Furthermore, private builders met the demand for lifestyles, indulging customers in the very choice of building materials—mosaic tiled floors, for instance, yielded way to marble—so that the home was as much a space for consumption as it was a consumption of space.

Speaking of the suburbanization of Paris, Henri Lefebvre draws the distinction between the fullness of 'inhabiting', i.e. 'the plasticity which allows for modifications and appropriations even if it is within the space of the house', to the concept of 'habitat', 'where growth has only one law—speculation on plots and property'.[69] Between the 1970s and 1990s, those who speculated in housing gained new visibility. The surge in real estate prices in the mid-1990s was an indication of this transition: referring to the frenzied apartment construction of that period, James Heitzman says, 'in a healthy market, 60 to 70 per cent of flats should have been purchased by end users, but instead 80 per cent were going to land speculators'.[70]

The non-resident Indian became a welcome if legally less well-defined figure in the metropolis, assured of sites and services that the general population had been urged to give up. Entire areas were now designated by the mode of payment: the Dollars Colony of north Bangalore is a case in point. Note here the distance the city travelled from the time in the 1960s when even the middle-class locality testified to the overwhelming presence of the public sector. HAL, First, Second, and Third stages, East of NGEF layout, and so on, were important examples of a time when industrial production was the key feature of the city's landscape. The term Dollars Colony raised expectations of a whole new style of consumption, replete with shopping malls, swimming pools, golf courses, and gymnasiums. Aided by rapid automobilization, these areas promised a suburban American dream.[71]

The NRI, and by the late 1990s the itinerant IT worker, were actively associated with the dream of nature and wealth set apart from a deteriorating city. Most important, what was offered to this 'citizen' was what was denied to the residents of the city, namely *planning itself*. What is new and different about developers is that they no longer sell housing or buildings but planning; indeed, planning itself takes on exchange value. The new housing colonies promised enclaves of privileged consumption of public and private goods, while offering to eliminate all aspects of urban reality by turning away from the street, the square, or other public meeting place. An exaggerated privacy and social homogeneity succeeded in keeping plebeian democracy and its discontents at bay.[72]

At the end of the century, the concept of regional planning has gained ground as the only way of sharing the fruits of development and thus reducing the pressure on the metropolis. The Southern Karnataka Region (SKR) Concept Plan and the Bangalore Metropolitan Region (BMR) Structure Plan were primarily suggestive exercises that aimed at redressing both market and policy failures, and transforming the investment climate of southern Karnataka.[73] The SKR plan carried forward earlier proposals for dispersal by developing rings of towns—counter magnets, growth centres, and satellite towns—which would attract new populations and cater to their economic needs. The BMR structure plan sought a reorientation of the older pattern of industrial location within the metropolitan area, so that the historical clustering of industries in the north and east, and the continued preference for the eastern segment, could now be reoriented to favour the south-west, better placed in terms of water access. Also, concern for the environment was writ large, competing with an enhanced concern for infrastructure: predictably, tourism and recreation gained new visibility in this plan.

What this plan shared with all previous planning efforts was the conviction that absolute power vests in state planning apparatuses, and could be redirected in ways that will benefit economic growth and attract foreign capital investment. In such a view, planning was reduced to a technocratic exercise. It echoed the vision of Infosys Technologies Chairman N.R. Narayana Murthy who called for the use of foreign expertise if necessary to set the city on course, and an 'extended time horizon allied to effective budgetary and executive powers' to build up the infrastructure.[74] From this optic, the move to 'decentralize planning' (in accordance with the 74th Constitutional Amendment which envisaged devolution of finances to urban local bodies) appeared particularly attractive.

In fact, 'devolution' of an altogether unexpected and less desirable kind has already taken place, so that state power has continually made its accommodations with informal and sometimes illegal power networks, resulting in an urban form where planned layouts, unplanned enclaves, and illegal squatter settlements, whether by the rich or the poor, are uneasily aligned. For instance, the IT industry has seen zoning norms as a needless restraint on the growth of the city economy. In the early 1980s, a USAID team specifically recommended the 'possibility of allowing small scale and good neighbour high tech activities into residentially zoned areas'.[75] It suggested that 'unless high tech activities are permitted within the city centre or in residential zones it seems likely that they will not easily find locations nearer than 10 kms or so from city centre'. The demand of high-tech industries for 'easy in, easy out terms' and the attractiveness of Bangalore as a location for appropriate 'footloose enterprise' was emphasized.[76]

By the late 1990s, such a suggestion had been translated into practice, though less as a result of policy decisions and more as a result of the need for affordable commercial space. Hundreds of IT firms are tenants of residential buildings. A survey by the BDA in 2001 of an important zone in the IT corridor, Koramangala (see Maps 9 and 11), found that IT companies accounted for 70 of 132 violations, in which 'neither the owner nor the tenant had applied for change in land use all of which violated the rules governing the CDP'. In at least one case, indya.com had usurped BDA property 'which amounts to encroaching Government land'.[77]

Bangalore has thus been produced by the nation, the region and globalized capital in specific but not always predictable ways. The Indian nation-state, through the establishment of giant public sector enterprises and industrial townships, laid claim to the city throughout the 1940s and the 1950s. Bangalore's expanded administrative role as the capital of the unified Karnataka state occurred only in 1956, when this defining feature of the physical–material city was already in place. When Kannada nationalism did make its presence felt by the 1960s, as we shall see later, it laid claim to the mental–imaginative realms of space. Today, a muscular, and internationalized real estate market attempts to produce what Mike Davis has called the 'archisemiotics of class war'. Disclosing plans for an IT township on 500 acres close to Electronic City, IT Secretary Sanjoy Dasgupta said in November 1998 that he envisaged a 'new republic'. 'The concept is a cross between San Jose and Santa Clara' 'a slice of the US in Bangalore',[78] where the CEO will be mayor. The 1990s desire to make Bangalore an internationally acceptable destination not just for global capital but for a globalized workforce has eclipsed other images of the city, yet neither planning nor legality so far dominate the heterogeneous field of power relations in the Bangalore metropolis. An analyses of specific sites, institutions, and practices in Bangalore today, to which the rest of the chapter turns, will bring clarity to this field.

Planning for Patriotic Production[79]

Bangalore was chosen as the most suitable location for the national public sector in recognition of the Mysore state's long history of state-aided industrial development.[80] The second of the 'four bigs' after Hindusthan Aircraft, Indian Telephone Industries, (ITI) was set up in 1948 in the eastern part of the city close to the road- and railhead at Krishnarajpuram. At its height, ITI employed 18,000 workers, and in 1995 still maintained a workforce of 11,000 at two locations in the city. In addition, it spawned, like its other public sector counterparts, excellent opportunities for subcontracting firms.

Vast tracts of land were acquired for building industrial townships.[81] ITI acquired a total of 368 acres and 12 *gunta*s in two plots, dispossessing nearly 100 owners of small plots of land in the villages of Krishnarajapuram, Vijnapura, Byatarayanapura, and Kowdenahalli on the Old Madras Trunk Road. The dispossessed were given priority in employment at the unit even though their land was classified as 'dry land where no regular irrigation facilities were available [though] dry crops like ragi, jowar pulses ... were grown'.[82] Despite this, the landowners sought enhanced compensation from 597 to 1700 per acre; of the land that was acquired, a mere 66 acres was actually used by the factory and the remaining 302 acres was in most cases returned to the owners for cultivation until further use.[83]

Subsidized industrial housing schemes introduced by the Government of India in 1952 offered up to 25 per cent of the costs of construction through the ministry of works and housing.[84] In Bangalore, five experimental houses were constructed by ITI in 1952 when there were 1690 workers;[85] by 1964, this had expanded to1524 houses for a workforce of 10,316, making subsidized housing available to 17 per cent of the workers. By the time of the second phase of construction, the scheme was decentralized and administered by the Mysore Housing Board.

A certain prodigality in the use of space was recommended by the Committee on Plan Projects. There was a need to go beyond providing mere residences for workers, it said, in order to plan a whole lifestyle which included 'hospitals, parks, recreation places, schools, shopping centres etc'. Indeed, planning would enhance patriotic production.

A properly planned town should stimulate community life and feeling of belonging and pride among the inhabitants. This can be achieved by dividing the town into planning units small enough to create neighbourliness. The smallest unit of organization of the community is a neighbourhood ... Such a neighbourhood is planned around a primary school and a local convenience shop.[86]

This, it was believed, would evolve a 'socially balanced and integrated community'.[87] A healthy civic consciousness was promoted 'through the mixture of all classes of employees'.[88]

In practice, the design and allotment of quarters at Durvaninagar conformed strictly to the hierarchy of the shop floor. Homes ranged from the smallest (E-type) quarter of 232 sq. ft, which consisted of a living room, a multi-purpose room with bath and lavatory as well as space in front of the house, to a more spacious 425 sq. ft of space with at least 3–400 sq. ft of space in front and at the back of the house. By 1996, there were 946 E-type quarters, 505 D-type quarters, 154 C-type quarters, 113 B-type, and seven management bungalows.

The Durvaninagar Township is a planning showpiece. Well-laid roads are lined with imaginatively constructed houses of all types. The best located and landscaped are the managers' homes or A-type quarters, replete with servants' quarters and garage. Even smaller types of houses are thoughtfully and even tastefully designed. In particular, the B-type houses are placed on three sides of a large tree-shaded quadrangle, a 'void', which is useful for play, general recreation, and special events such as weddings.[89] Other types of houses, though proportionately smaller, are all provided with yards. The area is furnished with open fields and playgrounds; gardens and temples have sprung up at some spots. A full-fledged hospital and high school, as well as banks and post offices, complete the range of services on campus. Hostels cater to the needs of bachelors, 'spinsters', and trainees from other parts of the country.

The spaciousness of the township (with densities ranging from 20–5 to 60 persons per acre), and its proximity to the workplace made it an attractive proposition to a wide variety of workers.[90] The colony was attractive as it also provided opportunities for supplementing incomes in new and unanticipated ways. As many families ran small scale dairy and poultry farms in their yards, the company was forced to intervene and reassert the purely residential uses to which the quarters could be put.[91] There were however other more acceptable economic uses of residential space, such as home-based manufacture by women. The township council contracted small assembly jobs from the factory and

FIG. 32 *Beyond the imagination of planners: an Adi Parashakti Shrine that has sprung up in the midst of official ITI workers' housing.*
(Janaki Nair, 1999)

distributed raw materials to employees' wives who earned Rs 15–25 a day. The Mahila Udyog Sahakara Sangha was formed in 1965 to gather women together at a central location, and paid daily wages upwards of Rs 75.[92]

A tightly administered township catering to a regular turnover of employees was equally a training ground for 'good citizenship'. Grooming in nationalism and citizenship was repeated at all public sector townships and factories across Bangalore: as BEL's B.R. Sharma put it '[BEL] was not like a factory. I felt we were in a University, learning new things. It was a process of education'.[93] So homogenous was the ITI township and so strongly unifying the experience of its work ethic that the local village panchayat's influence was believed to have only negative effects. The worker-identity was stressed in 1959 when the neighbouring KR Puram panchayat wanted to exercise its jurisdiction over the new enclave in order to levy tax on buildings built by the company.[94] ITI made a plea for a separate sanitary board on the lines of the HAL Sanitary Board, which would serve as an exemplar to the surrounding villages. What followed was a period of growing tension between a group village panchayat wanting to reap some of the benefits of the planned area and a township administration that jealously guarded its autonomy in order to arrest the growth of 'slums in the area'.[95]

Yet there were many benefits that ITI derived from the villages as 600 to 800 ITI employees lived in the KR Puram area and regularly used weekly markets, burial and cremation grounds.[96] Still, both the company and the government believed that the formation of a combined sanitary board for HAL and ITI was a better arrangement by which the 'company can give some money ... to villagers without allowing them to interfere in the administration of the Township'.[97] ITI refused to be clubbed with HAL, and finally, with the passage of the Mysore Municipalities Act of 1964, it was declared as a notified area run by a committee of three to five members. In 1970, when the Government of Mysore proposed the 'Hoskote Decree' which would allow provisions of the Hoskote Town Municipality to be applied to the area, this too was resolutely resisted.

Such autonomy was only sustainable so long as the township and village panchayat populations were kept apart. By the early 1970s, the promiscuous mingling of worker and peasant had gone too far, and the villages that had so strenuously been kept out of this well administered area demanded affiliation to the notified area.[98] This was a sure sign that ITI employees themselves were trying to improve the quality of services in the surrounding villages where they resided. In 1973, 120 families comprising about 800 people were living in KR Puram and 50 families (300 people) were in B. Narayanpur panchayat. The union representatives declared that if the ITI notified area was included in the KR Puram panchayat areas, 'the difficulties in getting building licences and no-objection certificates for ITI employees keen on building houses around ITI' would be eased, and layouts could be formed and distributed to needy employees and villagers.[99] Another group of workers however saw no advantage in this amalgamation, arguing that 'if two blocks of heterogeneous composition of population [workers and agricultural workers] are forced for amalgamation ... there would be ... clashes and disharmony in the entire area which ... will retard the physical production of the Company which will be a great national loss.' Nevertheless, the trend was inexorably towards integration: Ramamurthynagar, a new layout outside Durvaninagar, was after all catering entirely to the needs of working and retired ITI employees. By March 1984, the Notified Area Committee was reconstituted and representatives from the new areas were brought in, thus signalling the triumph of the unplanned areas over the planned township.[100]

The responsibility of the two premier industries in eastern Bangalore, ITI and HAL, to the areas around became cause for pitched battles between elected representatives and the company management. In 1984, Varthur MLA Suryanarayana Rao forcefully argued that ITI and HAL had developed at the expense of surrounding villages. These villages were still badly in need of basic facilities, and demanded a compensation of Rs 10 lakh from each unit. Meanwhile, the Notified Area Committee itself was making demands for the payment of tax liabilities from ITI for the provision of drinking water to the Ramamurthynagar and KR Puram areas which were throttled with unauthorized constructions.[101] The question of tax liability of ITI to the Notified Area Committee was finally settled in 1991, but not before the ITI Notified Area Committee and the HAL Sanitary Board were merged with the Bangalore City Corporation.[102]

The struggle between the planned area (ITI township) and the unplanned developments that it had spawned (the areas around, notably Ramamurthynagar) resulted in 'haphazard and uncoordinated developments of the fringe areas of the city'.[103] Enclaves of planned privilege had little power to control or limit the kinds of changes that were wrought on the agricultural areas around. Indeed, until the newly constituted notified area made its forceful demands, the ITI township benefited from informal arrangements that serviced the factory and built up a community of ex-ITI employees without cost to the company.

The public sector worker was the labour aristocracy of the city, closely identified with middle-class needs and aspirations. The fate of the two satellite towns which were developed in the 1960s to ease the pressure on the core areas of the city emphasizes this. Kengeri Satellite Town in Bangalore South-West and Yelahanka New Town to the north were built with a view to 'set up ancillaries in the metropolis and thereby to provide employment opportunities'.[104] Instead, they have turned into middle-class townships or dormitory towns for the city. Residents consist largely of outsiders looking for subsidized housing opportunities.[105] While many residents of Yelahanka work in the Escorts factory or Wheel and Axle Plant nearby, most of the residents of Kengeri are in administrative jobs. As Lakshman Rau has pointed out, the satellite towns became suburbs of the city instead of drawing people away from it as 'the economic base is Bangalore itself'.[106] The areas which lay beyond planning were far messier. Those who were involuntarily relocated to areas on the edge of the city received only the formal, token benefits of city-wide planning.

Beyond Planning

The temporary nature of the slum, and the involuntary resettlement of its occupants, reveals a certain powerlessness on the part of the inhabitants who constitute the bulk of the informal labour market. These are areas that, above all, provide essential services to the city economy at little or no cost. In many cases, slums are also important centres of production and distribution.[107] The economic vitality of slums has been recognized in studies which distinguish between manufacturing and non-manufacturing slums. In Bangalore, manufacturing is a characteristic of one-fifth of all slums.[108]

Official discourse, however, distinguishes between slums on strictly legal terms: thus they may be 'unmarked', 'notified', or 'declared'. Only the 'declared' slum successfully resists relocation; conversely, a slum may be demolished only after it is notified. Below the 'notified' slum is a range of informal arrangements which render the poor invisible in a city like Bangalore, and make a precise calculation of slum populations very difficult. Estimates of the number and growth of slums in the city have ranged from Prakasa Rao and Tewari's early assessment that 10 per cent of the city population lived in 159 slums,[109] to H. Ramachandra's suggestion that 287 declared slums accounted for 13 per cent of the city's population.[110] The more recent STEM report of 1991 says that 464 slums account for 19 per cent of the population.[111] In the late 1990s, there were at least one million people (20 per cent of the city population) living in slums which numbered anywhere from 450 and 472.[112] Slums, thus, have a clandestine presence in planning documents, their dubious legal status sometimes inviting 'clearance' as an official response.[113]

Lower-class migrants into the city move into the hollows and pits, railway sidings, and tank beds which are usually considered the lowest, most worthless, or unusable sites in a city. This is however never a permanent abode. The relocation of populations usually occurs as a consequence of the changing meaning and value of these marginal areas of a city, redefined over time as valuable real estate. Surging land values, particularly in central areas of the city, bring even the most undesirable land into the real estate market (Fig. 33). Yet economic reasons do not account for all relocations. The manipulation and management of linguistic identities through the politics of relocation are not unknown, and may even account for illegal settlements in the first place.[114] In Bangalore, even the ideology of beauty has played a role in determining the relocation of slums. As Lakshman Rau claimed 'The effect of ... amenities like gardens is completely neutralized if slums are allowed to develop and sufficient attention is not paid to general sanitation'.[115] Recalling the relocation of people who were residing on the edge of Ulsoor Lake, and the subsequent establishment of a garden in its place, Rau said, 'I had to work quickly, very early in the morning to prevent a stay on eviction. In spite of that there was a stay on grounds that people had lived there for 20 years. But the stay was infructuous

FIG. 33 *Sampangi Tank Bed served variously as polo ground, slum area and even hosted a cattle fair before it was transformed into a sports complex.*
(T.L. Ramaswamy, early 1960s)

since people had already shifted'.[116] The relocation of people from the Ulsoor Lake area and Jakkarayanakere (where a stadium was planned) in 1977–8 ended on a relatively happier note as Rau established a layout in Viveknagar for the ousted.[117]

Rosita Mertens' study claims that although at least two-thirds of all slums are on private land, relocation from government lands is far brisker and more frequent.[118] Most relocations are more like violent dislocations to the edge of the master-planned city, where the only marks of planning are the demarcations of sites. The history of Tilaknagar bears this out.

> They [the government] brought us in a lorry [to] that well, there beside the tank, [we] took water from that well and tasted the water. Said the water is good, we won't get any disease. And they left, they left us in this slum by measuring 20 ft per head, and left us here. They only gave us wood and things to build the house.

The settlement of Tilaknagar in southern Bangalore some time in the mid 1950s is remembered this way by 65 year old Parvathiamma.[119] Her small red-tiled hut, where one can barely stand upright or stretch out, is a stark and increasingly lonely reminder of the early settlement. A few doors away is K. Veera Sundariamma who invoked a telling metaphor to describe resettlement: 'They dumped us here like rubbish.' She now lives in a two-storied cement concrete house built just ten years ago.[120] The widely different statuses of these two women speaks of the unevenness of changes in the economic life of the area during the past fifty years.

Parvathiamma had been a resident of Sampangi Tank (Gopalappa Gardens) area slum for a brief while when she worked with hundreds of others on the building of Vidhana Soudha. In the mid fifties, residents of this slum were relocated by the City Improvement Trust Board, along with those from JC Road, Patalamma Garden at South End, and Lalbagh Siddapura to the area around Byrasandra Tank Bed or the BTB area.[121] At that time, the area was dotted with vineyards and *ragi* fields, and there were few roads connecting with the newly developing Jayanagar extension. The area to the south of the BTB area, across the east–west Tilaknagar Main Road, which became Tilaknagar per se, was occupied in 1961 when people from Parvathypuram, the Vijaya College area, and Gangamma Chery ('people from 8–10 areas') were brought to this location.[122]

Tilaknagar today consists of four areas: Tilaknagar, BTB area, the multi-storied housing scheme, and Tilaknagar Hutment colony (Swagath slum). The Tilaknagar Main Road running east–west divides the Tilaknagar area, which is predominantly Muslim, from the BTB area which is a mixed Muslim/Tamil Dalit area. To the north-east of the BTB area are the KHB flats which, though unfinished, are partially occupied. The Byrasandra public housing is to the west, as is the Swagath slum on private land. The population is estimated to be about 10,000.

A heterogeneous mix of buildings speaks of very uneven economic fortunes within this relatively well serviced area. Structures along the main road are all pucca constructions given over entirely to commercial uses, including mutton and fish stalls, tea shops, and restaurants. Two- or three-storied cement concrete buildings with narrow staircases crowd out the handful of small tiled-roof structures, which today belong largely to the Tamils. There are also asbestos roofed intermediate structures built of plastered brick. Most homes today have access to water from a tap that is attached to the main at the doorstep. Sewage lines too have been laid. The roads are well paved, and most houses open directly on to them, so that private and domestic tasks such as washing and bathing are performed in this extended space.

However, it is not just privacy that is redefined in this area. Although designated a slum, Tilaknagar boasts of a vibrant economy. In 1988, Peter Giessen found a varied economic base, though one which concentrated largely on providing services such as carpentry, tailoring, and smithy work.[123] The economy has expanded vastly in the last decade, to combine manufacture (eg. of steel cupboards), repair shops (eg. autorickshaws and stoves), recycling (eg. of waste paper and plastic) bulk retailing (eg. of low end aluminium ware and plastic goods), fabrication (eg. wire bending factories) in addition to various services such as saree 'polishing' (i.e. cleaning and starching of sarees, or 'dry cleaning') and tailoring. The area defies all zoning categories by combining housing with manufacture, and household industries employing women and children (eg. *agarbatti* manufacture) also thrive in the area. More recently, a garment unit has begun employing large numbers of young women. A few other trades, such as the hiring of vessels and *shamiana*s for social occasions, have gradually shrunk in importance.[124]

This economic activity has not always depended on recognizable rights to land. 'When we came here in the 50s we were given *patta*s to the sites and these were later on converted into *khata*s.' There were 301 sites in the BTB area, about 120 in the Tilaknagar area, and seventy sites in the Swagath slum area. Today, much subdivision of small sites has occurred and there are at least 800 families in the BTB area alone, while 140 families live in Swagath slum.[125] About 120 KHB flats built under the Ashraya scheme about 4–5 years ago have yet to be provided with water, sewage and electricity connections. Nevertheless, some people occupy these shells or put the area between the flats to good use, as a group of saree polishers have done (Fig. 34). Burials continue to take place at the edge of the tank bed although 'there is no scope here for getting a corporation death certificate, so most people have to go to Wilson Gardens, the nearest official burial ground.'[126]

If the first move into the area was purely involuntary ('we were dumped here like rubbish'), ownership rights in the area have been transformed through the operation of the market in land, as the area has gradually formed the margin of Jayanagar, a well planned area of Bangalore. As a consequence, voluntary migration out of the area has occurred.[127] According to Veera Sundariamma whose prospects brightened through contact with a local NGO, 'three quarters [of the Tamils] have moved out, mostly outsiders have come and bought the sites for as little as Rs 500. Muslims came and improved the area.' There has been a pronounced demographic shift away from a mixed slum area to one dominated by economically more successful Muslims. Tamil men, in whose names *patta*s and *khata*s were issued, were eager to take advantage of the market opportunity, sometimes moving to take up residence with a second wife elsewhere.[128]

There is room for about 300 small homes on the dried up tank bed which has predictably become the site of a pitched legal battle between contending

FIG. 34 *Unpredictable uses of lower class residential areas: sarees that have been 'polished' left to dry between blocks of unfinished Karnataka Housing Board Tenements, Byrasandra Tank Bed.*
(G. Raghav, 1999)

groups. Members of the Slum Dwellers' Association led by N. Kannan have argued in their writ petition that they must be shown priority in these allotments over the 500 'Gulbarga migrants' near the Mental Hospital who are slated to occupy the place.[129] There is more than a hint here that the linguistic composition of the area may thus be administratively manipulated to yield political gains.

A combination of aesthetic and commercial concerns determined the fate of those people who had laboured to build up the central administrative area of the city near the Vidhana Soudha. According to a study by P. Sudarshan, over 50 per cent of those who were relocated in the early 1980s to Laggere in western Bangalore had been involved in the construction of Vidhana Soudha.[130]

From a prime location in a well serviced area, the population was shifted to agricultural scrub land which had none of the services that had been promised by the Government. This brought the slum dwellers into conflict with those of the local village (Laggere) whose water resources were severely strained.

By far the most serious consequence of dislocation was its effect on work opportunities. 'Since the relocated area was on the outer fringe of the city, job opportunities were almost absent. The opportunities ... in the industrial estate [nearby, Peenya] needed competence and training which the slum dwellers lacked.'[131] Women were disproportionately affected by the relocation, since the distance between work and home severely discouraged them from taking up paid work.[132] Those who had usually walked to work in KR Market or Majestic from their previous location, tended to drop out of work. There were appreciable differences in the number of days employed per month: while 61 per cent of the women and 58 per cent of the men had work for 25 days a month before relocation, a mere 5.88 females and 30.52 males were similarly employed after relocation.[133] This more than offset the higher wages they received at the new location.[134]

The Laggere Project, consisting of 1,818 houses with basic amenities, was officially sanctioned in 1987, long after relocation to the area had already begun.[135] The housing programme at Sanjay Gandhinagar took shape only after huts were burnt down during the Cauvery riots of 1991. In other words, more than ten years had lapsed between relocation and construction.[136] But the riots brought home the importance of politics in both relocation and reconstruction efforts, which more or less determined the fate of these slum dwellers in the absence of other resources.

Of the three structures of power that impinge on the lives of the urban poor, with varying results—policies and planning, the judiciary and local politics—the poor are ill-served by planning processes and policy decisions. The law can, and often does, become a means of delaying, though less often reversing, decisions of the Karnataka State Slum Clearance Board to clear the slum.[137] By comparison, local political structures become the only resource for poor citizens fighting for a claim to the city.[138] Benjamin and Bhuvaneswari have also pointed out that the mosaic of settlement patterns and hierarchy of land rights reduces, or even negates, the meaning of planning in poorer areas. They say 'The land supply system in Azadnagar comprises a variety of subsystems: free sites formed by state agencies, and distributed to poor groups, revenue plots, *gramthana* or layouts on village land, and squatter settlement' (sic).[139] This multiplicity of tenures has of course been interpreted as unambiguously benefiting the urban poor. Certainly, planning proceeds by this double movement, dispossessing some and benefiting others, though not always in any symmetrical fashion. Yet planning, and clarity of land titles, offers advantages to the poor as well, especially when it becomes a stable resource for bargaining between sections of the poor, as the example of women in Tilaknagar demonstrates.

The fate of slums which emerge as largely unplanned areas in the city is thus not always uniform, and some, like Tilaknagar, could be transformed through the operations of the market into lower middle-class areas. Other sites in the city however, may turn into settlements that are increasingly identified as 'slums' as they retain a physical form or economic life which is increasingly made irrelevant by the urban setting. The numerous villages that are absorbed within the city are visible instances of why the grid of the planned city is difficult if not impossible to impose.

The Urban Village

The planning grid comes to grief in the middle of the city when it is unable to impose its order on the village form. Over the past five decades, the city of Bangalore has expanded and taken over agricultural lands for the creation of layouts, so that literally hundreds of villages have technically ceased to exist. The village is effaced in many ways, and the mutation of its name into an urbanized form is just one indication: Gangenahalli thus became Ganganagar, and Binnamangala yielded place to Indiranagar. In addition to the '100 villages' absorbed between 1901 and1970, say Prakasa Rao and Tewari, were the '218 villages located within the metropolitan area, providing space for the future city.'[140] The 1981 census lists nearly 180 villages that have been absorbed into the Bangalore Urban Agglomeration.[141] Rame Gowda provides a history of this absorption:

> The Municipal Limits of the city covered about 68 sq.kms. upto 1964, with 36 villages merging with the city. In 1964, the municipal limits were extended to cover 115 sq.kms, thus engulfing another 36 villages. There is a proposal to increase the limits of the City corporation to about 250 sq.kms with another 110 villages being incorporated into the urban mass. Thus the city will take within its fold nearly 200 villages apart from the influence on the neighbouring tract.[142]

By 1991, 189 villages in Bangalore North and South were incorporated in the Bangalore Urban Agglomeration, signalling that there was no halt to the process of absorption.[143]

Individual village homes rarely retain their original shape, as tiled roofs and *jagalis* (platforms in front of the homes) have yielded place to the modern reinforced cement concrete structure. Yet street patterns continue to survive as stubborn clots in the middle of a grid, where scenes of the rural appear unexpectedly off a main road. The physical features that remain make the original village settlement instantly recognizable. The temple of the village goddess opens on to a small village square, dominated by the peepul tree with its generous platform or *katte* where panchayats may have been held. The integration of this form into the city layout has usually never been attempted, as the principles of layout development are rigidly geometric, and make no allowance for undulations in the topography or changing landscape. Apart from the obvious charms of occasionally picturesque settings, these villages are a sign of how certain practices survive in the heart of the metropolis. With roads too narrow to sustain anything more than an occasional two-wheeler, the villages support activities such as cattle rearing and nursery gardens.

Reflecting on the process by which lands of a village are annexed by the formation of layouts, BDA Commissioner Lakshmi Venkatachalam admitted in 1999 'I don't think in a single BDA scheme we have attempted to rehabilitate the village ... this transition has never been properly addressed'.[144] If the physical layout of the village reflects this lack of integration, the older settlement is forced to come to terms with the city in many other ways. There is no idyllic resistance to the urban in these villages overwhelmed by the city, for the cultures, lifestyles, and economic activities of the village in the city are easily eroded or subordinated to a different spatial logic. When the city's new Ring Road, for instance, separated the *hebbagilu* (ceremonial gateway) at Byatarayanapura in north Bangalore from the village, the structure came to be an isolated cultural relic straddling the median. Within the urban setting, the *urhabba* (village festival) gains volume and brightness, and in many cases honours the *gramadevatha* or female village deity. In other instances, as an early study of an urban village Garudapura in eastern Bangalore showed, older religious forms yield room to newer urban deities who espouse notions of social equality rather than hierarchy.[145]

Village lives are recast in far more profound ways at the level of politics and the economy. Although, until the early 1960s, political institutions such as village panchayats still survived alongside newer structures of urban governance, Garudapura, says Mark Holmstrom, was no isolated pocket. Caste could not retain the same meaning in the urban village as new solidarities and political allegiances were forged, especially as 'the village attracted immigrant workers, some of them skilled, to work in the newer factories making aircraft, machine tools, telephones, car parts, electronic equipment etc.' Holmstrom's analysis of the municipal election reveals a fairly close involvement of the village in city-wide politics, though mediated through the traditional power groups. 'Garudapura, like other urban villages, has a political influence out of proportion to its population' not least because of the contacts of the 'big men' who own many houses in the surrounding suburbs.[146] A similar process by which the village is incorporated into urban political networks has been traced by Alan Beals. Ideals of democracy and social equality, he says, 'were derived from Government schools, from experience in the nearby military camp during World War II, and from their knowledge of the urban culture of the city'.[147]

The process of 'becoming urban' had different connotations for the state and those who actually made the transition on the city. The priority of migrants looking for a foothold in the city was easy access to land and housing, and outlying villages were rapidly transformed into revenue 'pockets.' Questions of legality or of access to municipal amenities were thus of secondary importance in the early stages. To the state authorities, especially in the 1950s, such haphazard settlements were seen as an alarming aberration which placed intolerable strains on the municipality. But there was confidence that they would disappear once the supply of residential land and housing was made more plentiful. In 1964, however, when 36 new villages were absorbed by the city corporation, the municipality declared that the 'Layout Range,' a temporary department created for the purpose of regularizing unauthorized settlements in and around erstwhile villages, had to be given a more permanent basis.[148] The process of regularization implied huge outlays for the corporation, which were in part offset by the increased collection of house tax and betterment charges, which new homeowners were loath to pay. This called for coercive steps to collect the improvement expenses from six of the 24 layouts identified for regularization in 1968–9, and the crisis deepened when residents of as many as ten layouts contested the rates by taking their challenge to the courts.[149]

In the 1960s, the ideology of urban community development went beyond the municipal concerns of the local government to add a new dimension to the debate on housing in the city. The existence of these poorly serviced pockets were thus a blot not just on the city and its environs, but on national pride and notions of citizenship itself. In the late 1960s, the Government of Mysore chose a newly urbanized area in south western Bangalore to inculcate new civic values and an enhanced national consciousness. Among its stated objectives was the desire to 'chang[e] skills and attitudes of the people from the traditional and static to the progressive and national.' Following in the steps of those who envisaged public sector townships as places to nurture patriotic workers, the urban community development programme saw improved living conditions as a means of educating people in citizenship rather than as a fulfillment of citizenship itself. This, in addition to preparing the communities for democracy, a richer civic life, and greater self reliance, constituted a new road map for social change.

Though Padarayanpura, Binnypet and Azadnagar were chosen for this pilot project, Binnypet was dropped when it was discovered that, as a labour housing colony of the nearby Binny Mills, it had long enjoyed 'excellent welfare measures' and 'above average civic amenities.' Moreover, the presence of a single labour union was perceived as a positive unifying element in the colony. On the other hand, Padarayanapura, formerly known as Padarayanagutta, was brought into the corporation in 1958–9, and had burgeoned into a settlement of 23,000 people and 3700 households, since 'houses sprang up occupying every bit of land.'[150] Along with Azadnagar, a newly settled and compact area, the region was considered fit for a development programme.

Predictably, a sample survey taken before the launch of the programme identified those elements that would hinder a programme for producing responsible citizens. As much as 57 per cent of the population, it was found, were recent migrants into the area, having moved into Padarayanpura in the last five years. This along with the heterogeneity of castes (19 castes) and religious affiliations (32 per cent Muslims, 6.5 per cent Christians, and 60 per cent Hindu) made for a community that bore little relationship to the rural community which was at its core. Indeed, a good 27.5 per cent of its workers were in factories, while another 6.5 per cent were in government service. The continued existence of weaving among 12 per cent of the inhabitants was taken as a sign of the rural, although, along with the 23 per cent employed in agarbathi and beedi manufacture, these were signs of an urbanized economy. Despite these obvious impediments to community building however, it was noted that the relationship among the castes and religious group was cordial. Indeed, 'The outlook of this heterogenous community is progressive and nationalistic as can be seen from the behaviour pattern. Though the caste system is practiced and it is in vogue, it is not explicitly expressed.'

If such tolerant heterogeneity was taken as the sign of the urban, the survey report also evoked images that were a positive sign of homogeneity. Of the residents of Karithimannahalli, part of the Azadnagar site chosen for the programme, it was said that they 'display[ed] sentiments of rural people more than the men and women of the area for self help and self reliant community activities.' The programmes that were initiated worked towards the fulfillment of an ideal citizenship, which was deferred to the future. Despite a detailed account of the exploitative basis on which women and children worked in the agarbathi industry, for instance programmes were initiated only to fill in the leisure hours of the women.[151] The economic importance of home-based manufacture was thus effectively ignored in the community development programme. Even the existing leadership within in the area, which consisted of ex-panchayat leaders and ex-corporation officials, in the case of Padarayanpura, as well as some local notables, was found unsuited to the task of producing the ideal citizen.

Yet, nearly 30 years later, Padarayanapura was increasingly recognized as an ethnically polarized community poised on the brink of riots, including divisions based on language. Economically, however, it was a vibrant manufacturing slum which frustrated the desires of those who looked for a separation of manufacturing from residential zones.[152] Padarayanapura had become a vast manufacturing slum, although the comparison with Shivajinagar was not intended as a mark of appreciation for such economic vibrancy.

Smaller pockets have fewer resources to resist a complete takeover, and may only briefly resist being overwhelmed by the logic of layout formation. In the heart of the Kalyanagara Layout (HRBR Layout) in eastern Bangalore, is a small part of the village that originally belonged to Kacharakanhalli. A group of seven Handijogi families continues to run a piggery, much to the consternation of the overwhelmingly middle-class residents who have built homes in the area. The area was acquired by the BDA in the late 1970s, and the layout was formed in 1985. The piggery now sits squarely in the middle of the Second Block of the new layout, the grazing pigs, the squeals and the smells an offensive reminder of times past. The Handijogis have resisted eviction, arguing that they know no other trade and must be relocated close to their customers. According to Annaiah, a member of this group, the Handijogis were both cultivators and pig rearers but when the lands were lost [to the BDA], 'more turned to pig rearing.' Today, it is a thriving business, and to leave the area is to place the business at risk. Such defiance of local residential norms can continue only until the area is joined to the corporation, when municipal by-laws will automatically prohibit such practices. The village people cling to this occupation as a bargaining chip which some young men believe could be successfully traded for a government job.

Other people whose villages have been swallowed by the city have been less fortunate, giving up their lands and livelihoods, and occasionally seeking more by way of compensation.[153] However, the relentless drive to bulldoze the village into the city soil is far more violent when it recasts meanings and memories, particularly the memory of ancestors. After all, in the history of the city, as Lewis Mumford has pointed out, 'the dead were the first to have a permanent dwelling'.[154] A city must therefore prepare as much for the death of its citizens as it does for their lives and livelihood. The relentless growth of the city of Bangalore into all available spaces has threatened the resting places of the dead, dishonouring several community graveyards of the village. As Kannan of the BTB area pointed out, even when such graveyards are not physically displaced, secular town planning deprives the community graveyard of meaning when the requirement of a death certificate transforms a sacred space to a space attested by state power.

Strategies for recovering these spaces may be seen as instances of a claim on what Richard Sennett calls 'narrative time' in a city wholly given over to processes of 'compulsive neutralization', which empty place in order to create 'spaces of negation which seem the promise of freedom'.[155] These claims intersect with political developments in contemporary Indian cities to produce an urban landscape that once more lies beyond the imagination of planners and city administrators. The growing phenomenon of shrines that have occupied public space in defiance of the modalities of law and planning illustrates this best.

An Assertion of Narrative Time

The desacralizing of space by secular planning apparatuses has been mirrored in the past few decades by a phenomenon from below. The appropriation of land by the law of Eminent Domain is resisted in ways that subvert this logic: space is thus sacralized as a way of either grabbing land or resisting its takeover by the agencies of the state.[156] Landowners whose property has been notified for acquisition and those wishing to lay fresh claim to city property, frequently resort to a strategy of attaching extra-economic meaning to space. Antiquity, religious sentiment, or respect for the resting place of their ancestors are variously claimed by people as reasons for exempting land from acquisition. The owners of a small two and a half acre plot in Banaswadi village (which was notified for the formation of the Hennur Road–Banaswadi Road layout in 1980) challenged the decision on the grounds that they wanted sites for their own use. A long drawn case followed, with the high court finally deciding in favour of the BDA. When the land was inspected 'it was found that there were eleven AC sheet houses, two RCC houses, ... and 18 *samadhi*s in this survey number, hence this land could not be taken possession of'.[157] Predictably, the samadhis proved more difficult to evict than the houses or sheds, and what the family had lost in the law court was won through other strategies.[158]

The unauthorized construction of temples on disputed or public properties, especially since the early 1980s, on first sight appears to confirm this process. A 30 year long court case was won by the BDA in September 2000: the owners of land in Binnamangala village (who had already transacted on the land with private parties) contested the acquisition afresh with a stay on the BDA.[159] Within days, they built a small temple to Kaveryamma (a benign version of the village goddess Kaateriamma), which deliberately extended on to the proposed BDA road. Inside this temple, a freshly laid granite slab proclaimed that it was established in 1977 by Ramaswamy Reddy, the father of the present contestant. Regular worship at the place has ensured its survival, and will no doubt complicate the process of BDA takeover even if the agency eventually wins the case.

If many of these occupations of land occur well away from the public eye, and on private property, there are far more public occupations of space by religious structures. Shrines, and related profitable ventures such as Kalyana Mantapas, have unhesitatingly occupied streets, Civic Amenity (CA) sites, and disputed properties. One of the most striking instances of this spatial strategy occurred in the 1990s and on a scale that dwarfs the more common occupation of footpaths by shrines. A large 65-foot statue of Shiva was installed on revenue land near the airport by a leading entrepreneur Ravi Melwani, who wished to build a temple on the spot.[160] Melwani declared his intention of making religion more exciting by turning the site into a major tourist attraction for those arriving by air from the city, 'a temple-amusement park–showroom complex with Om Namah Shivayah Towels and Raincoats'.[161] The statue, amply visible from the airport road, attracted hundreds of devotees, and regular worship was begun.

Before long, a structure came up at the site which blocked the view of the statue from the road. It was a vast toy showroom named Kemp Fort, in a playful pun on both the city's hero Kempegowda and the historic Red Fort. The architectural reference is, however, to the fort-like structures of mammoth American toy stores. Those who had developed a ride-by relation to the deity objected to the building that obscured their view, but Melwani countered this objection by claiming that the temple was meant for his employees and not as a 'drive in God' for all Bangaloreans. The temple has invented newer more commercialized modes of worship, particularly during the Shivaratri festival (Fig. 35).[162] The entrepreneur's violation of several aspects of the city's building bye-laws was given governmental clearance in 1999 on grounds that it has the potential of becoming a major tourist attraction.

Melwani's strategy of occupying the property with a temple, and then developing commercial uses of the site, is one that city administrations find increasingly hard to contest. Likewise, innumerable religious structures which

FIG. 35 *From 'drive by' God to religion in the service of commerce: devotees throng the massive Shiva Statue behind mega store Kemp Fort, on Mahashivarathri.*
(The Printers Mysore, Private Limited, Leonard Aarons, 25.2.1998)

have come up on public land—streets and pavements, civic amenity sites, and disputed property—have skilfully exploited the growing cleavage between law and order in the city. Especially since the 1980s, an increasingly contentious and communalized public sphere has developed alongside an upsurge in popular religious practices. The state, which fears 'interference' with the 'religious sentiments' of the people, frequently permits the violation of the *law* in the interests of *order*.[163] The cleavage between law and order has repeatedly been upheld by city authorities as a way of lowering the risk of disruption. A multiplicity of interests in land has exploited the cleavage to advantage.

City authorities, the press, and the public in the city alike have viewed with growing dismay the encroachments of footpaths by shrines of all descriptions. Pedestrians have, at least since the 1970s, shared footpaths with small commercial activities such as cycle repair shops, cobblers' shops, and retail shops. More recently, there has been more permanent occupation of the streets by extended shop awnings, automobile repair shops, and, most permanent of all, roadside shrines of all denominations. In 2001, local dailies *Deccan Herald* and *Prajavani* invited readers to participate in reporting on such buildings in their neighbourhood.[164] The response was overwhelming, and the column on unauthorized Hindu, Christian, and Muslim shrines ran for 89 days.

This occupation has usually been understood as another expression of commercial interests in public land that exploit the state's timidity in the face of the threat of disorder. There are instances of shrines that spring up on footpaths, in traffic islands, abut homes, extend on to the road, and come up around trees. Furthermore, as the *Deccan Herald/Prajavani* series strove to prove, there is growing consensus among vocal sections of the Bangalore public that they are an untidy manifestation of disrespect for municipal order, disrupting public life in ways that impede and even endanger the rights of passage through the city. Reports emphasized the 'unauthorized' status of a shrine in a number of ways: a photograph accompanying the story on a shrine in Kumara Krupa showed pedestrians who were forced to step off the footpath due to the obstruction.[165] Also emphasized in these reports was the helplessness, and perhaps connivance, of municipal authorities in allowing these shrines to exist and expand. Thus, the official home of the chief minister opened on to a road that sports an illegal shrine, while other shrines flourished in the shadow of municipal offices (Fig. 36).[166]

FIG. 36 *The Siddi Vinayaka temple is part of a three temple complex that has sprung up on the city's premier commercial thoroughfare, Residency Road, and opposite the municipal court and offices.*
(Janaki Nair, 1999)

To consider all these activities solely from the point of view of their illegality, and to read their meaning as tied closely to material interests in property is to refuse to acknowledge what is clearly a very important aspect of contemporary urban cultures. To be sure, there are many instances where material interests determine the use of public space, but the meanings of such activities are far from exhausted by the languages of municipalism or economism. Lakshmi Venkatachalam spoke of the frustrations of highway laying when it ripped apart villages and small towns. When the freshly laid Ring Road from Old Madras Road to Bellary Road passed through Babasanpalya, a small shrine to Highway Anjaneya was installed at the crossroads as high speed traffic had killed several people.

> One day I see this huge Anjaneya's stone with Anjaneya on the Ring Road, so I asked how they [BDA engineers] allowed this. I got furious, threatened dire consequences. The next day ... this sub inspector comes in and says, Okay it was taken out, and to my [bad] luck about a week later there was another accident so all these 200 ... residents of that erstwhile village gathered together and they asked me to put the statue back. There was a law and order problem .... what I took out was mild in comparison to what they planted, concrete and tiles around, and an even more colourful picture of

FIG. 37 *Propitiated to stave off hit and run accidents: the Highway Anjaneya at Babasanpalya, Ring Road.*
(Janaki Nair, 1999)

Anjaneya Swamy. My engineer says 'I can't [remove] it, if I go there they will beat me up,' I mean we need the police force to ... you know maintain law and put *some fear of god*.[167]

Venkatachalam's invocation of the law was in fact unsustainable in direct opposition to 'the fear of god', and the unintended phrase is revealing. She was able however, in retrospect, to recognize peoples' need for other kinds of attachment to space than those dictated by plans and infrastructure schemes: 'It's not a question of going and breaking something, but also incurring their wrath .... Why do we see a profusion of temples and ... places of worship? It is basically this insecurity psyche ... which is coming up, and you know "our village deity".' (Fig. 37.)

The claim on city space by diverse religious groups may well be a way of correcting a long existing bias in the planning process, one that consistently ignored how the urban area constructs and reconstructs social lives of people, emptying it of meanings, often without offering the neutrality of urban space as compensation. The mental–imaginative meanings of space are rarely recognized in the planning document or its maps, so that the uses of space are frequently at odds with the intentions of planning authorities. Recent work by Annapurna Garimella on roadside shrines in Bangalore has uncovered a host of reasons for their emergence and existence: as a focal point of activity for youth clubs, as a gift of erstwhile civil engineers to the city, as a yearning of small immigrant or artisanal groups to assert a cultural presence in the city and as fulfilling the need for a quick prayer during passage through the city.[168] Even the 'unauthorized shrine' has its authors, though its signatures and its marks of identity may often not bear the authority of the state.

If, abstract *space* in an era of capitalism subordinates *time*, then the roadside shrine must be seen as an instance of a narrative claim on the city. The reassertion of narrative time, to adopt Sennett, interrupts the subordination of time and space in both form and function to purely economic uses, and in contemporary Indian cities serves as a disturbing reminder of the limits of the ideology of planning itself. We might well ask, for instance, how many 'authorized' temples, churches and mosques have come up in the same decades when the population expanded by over 136 per cent (1981–2001)? Whose needs or interests do these authorized shrines serve? Nothing demonstrates the different constituencies of new religiosities in the city as clearly as the small decorated anthill, and now shrine, of Adi Parashakthi that has sprung up on the footpath adjoining the popular Sri Krishna Temple in the prosperous layout of Indiranagar. The Sanskritic modes of worship at the Sri Krishna Temple do not appeal to all communities that inhabit a middle-class area such as Indiranagar. It is faulty logic to argue that such popular religiosity must be zoned out of existence. Shrines that have sprung up on Field Marshall Cariappa Road, described as 'the most important street in a prosperous neighbourhood of the garden city of Bangalore, the home of national and international commercial firms' were seen as illegitimate since this is 'an area which does not require religious places'.[169] If anything it is the linear use of space that is challenged in such untidy occupations of public space. Some, though certainly not all, 'unauthorized' shrines therefore assert a narrative, producing a renewed 'sense of place'. Consider a pamphlet issued in the early 1980s by the Sri Varasiddhi Vinayaka Temple Building Committee to Hindus of areas around the city's central Brigade Road:

> There is only one lack in the area around Brigade Road which has wonderful cinemas, large shops, and hotels which serve appetizing food. Have you noticed? There are enough Christian and Muslim places of worship, but you will find not a single temple where Hindus may worship ... without any fuss and noise, Vinayaka has come and established himself in the environs of the KEB office since Ganesh Chathurthi last year.[170]

This pamphlet spoke of a desire to mark the city's business district through the invention of new narratives.

At times, the gap between map and territory occurs as a consequence of conflicting understandings of space. At other times, and more visibly so, the gap between planning intention and use of the land is revealed in more direct tussles between state and market. The fate of the city's green belt demonstrates that the interest in the conversion of all kinds of land and property into real estate may render the state incapable of asserting its authority in deciding land use in the city.

The Wavering Frontier of the Green Belt

The relationship between town and country has historically been a problematic one and the medieval city often jealously guarded its frontiers from marauders through fortifications. Yet the modern city also grows and develops by absorbing villages, placing the idea of 'fortifications' at odds with city growth. The concept of the green belt attempts to solve this apparent paradox. Derived directly from the visions of British planners such as Patrick Geddes and Patrick Abercrombie, it deploys open space as a structuring element in city planning.[171]

About 80 per cent of the city consisted of open spaces in 1925, when the built up area was only 6.4 sq. km out of an area of 35 sq. km, with recreational spaces such as parks, water bodies, and playgrounds accounting for 15 per cent of land area.[172] By 1980, the open spaces had dwindled to 40 per cent, in inverse proportion to the built up area of 72 sq. km, with recreational spaces dropping to a mere 5 per cent. In 1952, the Bangalore Development Committee noted that 'uninhabited areas alone [agricultural lands and other open spaces] ... take up altogether 6.62 sq. miles out of a total of 25.56 sq. miles'.[173] It made a strong plea for the retention of an agricultural zone. This zone would consist of both agricultural lands beyond the Corporation boundary and '2000 acres of revenue land situated within the Corporation limits'.[174] As 'the principal source of supply of some of the essential requirements of the city population such as fruit, fresh vegetables, milk and cattle fodder'[175] these lands could become '"a continuous green background of open country" all around the city together with the strips of green patches of varying sizes within the city limits.'[176] Yet the same report also observed that the City Improvement Trust Board was 'unable to acquire virgin land in the neighbourhood of the city and develop it ... at sufficiently low cost'.[177] The creation of a green belt or the retention of agricultural land in the city was contingent on sternly administered planning regulations which, the committee strongly hinted, was impossible until 'public opinion' became a viable alternative to political interference.[178]

Since the Bangalore Development Committee lacked legal authority, its recommendations were unenforceable.[179] It is however striking that the Committee argued for a preservation of essential features and, one might say, associated livelihoods of the people of the area, rather than suggesting new zones or changed uses. Also, the use of Abercrombie's green belt idea as an element of urban design defied economic considerations alone, and provided a visually distinctive edge to a city which was relatively formless. K.N. Venkatarayappa's division of the city into seven zones similarly acknowledged the existence of an 'agriculture zone' which was further classified into four areas, each distinguished by different modes of cultivation and products.[180] In addition to the garden lands in parts of southern and western Bangalore, where a variety of vegetable and fruit crops were grown, were the dry land based *ragi*, *avare* and *togari* farms of the north and the east. Indeed, 'unbuilt areas and open fields have added to the beauty of the city and well-being of citizens'. The green belt once more appears as an element that provides visual relief.[181]

Successive plans attempted to prescribe land use on similar lines. The Outline Development Plan prepared under the Karnataka Town and Country Planning Act 1961, was to cover a 15 year period until 1976 and was the first step towards land use planning and zoning in the city. It was approved with minor changes only in 1972, a few years before the plan period was to end. By this time, the city form was rapidly changing, with the new public sector units located on the outskirts of the city engendering 'ribbon developments' along the highways, and 'unregulated developments' in the villages around.[182] The growing demand for land made the green belt which separated City and Cantonment a thing of the past and the document noted that even 'the area of lands cultivated with fruit and garden crops is shrinking and Bangalore has ceased to be a Garden City as it was known for many years'. Moreover, the report noted a distinct shift in occupations of areas around the city from 'cultivation of land to industry as a means of livelihood'.[183] In any case, the productive agricultural tracts within the city, for whose retention the Bangalore Development Committee had so passionately argued, were gradually banished to the edges, as urban farms were increasingly seen as a threat to the health and sanitation of the inhabitants.[184]

The green belt, first zoned into existence in the CDP of 1985, was wholly outside the city. About 840 sq. km was set aside as the green belt area out of a total metropolitan area of 1279 sq. km. The land so designated accounted for 65 per cent of the Amalgamated Planning area, which covered a total of 543 villages and Bangalore city.[185] This plan too drew from British town planning patterns 'according to which the green belt protrudes into the built up area in the form of wedges'.[186] By this time, however the green belt functioned less as a visual element and more as an urban fence. A significant attrition of this area had taken place by 1995, the green wedges having turned decidedly brown, so the green belt was reduced to a more realistic 714.35 sq. km.,[187] though the concept of the green belt itself was not overturned. This, despite serious questioning of the value of the green belt as a zone which would restrict urban development, on the basis of the experience of places such as London and Singapore.[188] Certain kinds of low intensity institutional activities, which were already encroaching on green belt space, it was argued, could be encouraged in order to lend permanence to land use patterns.[189]

By 1997, the court-appointed commissioner investigating a public interest petition filed against the BDA found a green belt full of security gated, stone-wall compounds, enclosing potential cities. There were 336 layouts, 13 resorts, and 42 crushers and quarries.[190] Only 120 villages of the 392 villages that constituted the green belt area, seemed to have escaped the speculative gaze of the real estate developer. Most of the land was barren and well on the way to becoming developed real estate. The lands that had been built up comprised in many cases *gomala* land that had previously been allotted to the poor or Scheduled Castes and Tribes as in Tavarekere Hobli, Yeshwantpur Hobli, and Jigani. The developments ranged from Sanjay Khan's international resort in

Nagarur/Heggadadevanapura to a Nature Cure Hospital with jogging tracks and swimming pools in Thalagatpura. An enclosed 300 acre Sai City was being developed at Hommadevahalli in Begur Hobli replete with a watchtower, while Delhi builders, the Ansals, were planning a layout in Varthur including schools, community centres, club houses, swimming pools, children's play areas, parks, gardens, and jogging tracks: indeed a whole lifestyle behind protected walls. Some local builders, such as the Prestige Group and Adarsh Developers, had substantial interests in these areas, although land was also earmarked for HBCSs.

To the extent that the green belt existed at all, it was in privatized forms: Sun Valleys, Tulip Resorts, and Laughing Waters were nearly all exclusive housing developments or farm-houses which doubled as restaurants or clubs. Devaraj Urs' prescience in this regard appears almost uncanny: when sites close to Bangalore were allotted to thousands of poor lower castes in the early 1970s, he had warned against such sites making their way into the real estate market.[191] In the late 1990s, the other girdle that had been thrown around the city, the Ring Road, has enabled even more rapid occupation of lands within the green belt. Indeed, the rapid automobilization of the city since the late 1970s has enabled greater occupation of lands which provide enclaves of privilege and shelter from the sheer unpredictability of contemporary urban Indian life. It is to this aspect of the transformed metropolis that the last section turns.

The Promise of Eden: Planning as Exchange Value

In a judgement suffused with nostalgia, Justice Chinappa Reddy deliberated on the finality of the Outline Development Plan of 1972 by saying, 'Gone are the flowers, Gone are the trees, Gone are the spaces' of Bangalore. Instead, 'we are now greeted with puffing chimneys and high rise buildings both designed to hurt the eye and the environment and the Man.' The judgement predated the dramatic transformation of the city skyline, and Justice Reddy's words were a premature reaction to developments of the 1970s. By the early 1990s, such premonitions had come true, at least as far as it concerned the ferocious automobilization which resulted in pot-holed roads and a severely strained infrastructure. Moreover, there were few signs that the unwelcome flow of large numbers of casual and skilled workers could be stopped except at the expense of affecting the more welcome influx of corporate headquarters, banks, and the IT and electronics industry. Migrants who were the mainstay of the boom in housing construction and infrastructure development were a necessary complement to the general expansion of the city economy.

The expansion and extraordinary growth of the real estate market, which attracted national level builders such as the Rahejas and Ansals to the city, has in fact resulted in the widespread cultivation of middle-class tastes in apartment living. Builders now offer privatized luxury and a satisfactory negotiation of scarce public goods in the city, such as power or water supply, while guaranteeing new standards of safety. Every builder of upper middle-class housing in Bangalore promotes the idea that what he is offering on sale is not mere housing but a 'lifestyle'. In a city like Bangalore, which lacks several kinds of infrastructural facilities, what builders place on offer is the dream of successful planning itself. A brochure of the Prestige Group advertises its Greenwoods project in this way:

> *Welcome to guaranteed power, water and communications*
>
> Considering the infrastructural reality of Bangalore, we've ensured that electricity will come home to you in concealed conduits with copper wires. Backed by one generator in each block for common service. Assured water supply comes from underground and overhead storage tanks of suitable capacity supported by an auxiliary borewell. You connect to the outside world through a telephone connection in the hall with a parallel point in the master bedroom.

What is on offer in these new real estate deals is also the promise of arcadia. Real estate brochures urge you to 'get away from it all' and yet remain in the city. The Purvankara group offered duplex villas in the Whitefield area using these terms:

> Laid amidst nearly three acres of classic English countryside. Exposed brick exteriors with overhanging creepers. Picket fences. Wicket gates. And the fragrance of flowers.

In short, this was a peaceful haven which combined '19th century simplicity' with '20th century conveniences', such as a fitness centre, gymnasium, swimming pool, jogging track and 'standby generators in case of power breakdowns, Satellite TV and intercom connections'. Finally, the builders offered 'round the clock security'.

The conveniences and luxury services offered by builders evoke a variety of images that would appeal to the city élite. First, there is the invocation of a pastoral idyll in such names as 'Whispering Meadows', 'Whitefield Bougainvillea', 'Laughing Waters', or 'Nisarga'. These estates evoke images of lush green meadows, babbling brooks, and nature apart from toil in the city. Second, there is the invocation of European history, in such names as 'Belvedere', 'Windermere', or the classic 'Prestige Acropolis'.[192] Finally, there is the evocation of sentiments of peace and tranquillity.

Beneath the list that bundles several services and conveniences together are the unspoken advantages of paying up for these gated cities.[193] They are an escape from the travails and sheer unpredictability of plebeian democracy, and provide for new modes of sociality centred on the clubhouse, gym, swimming pool, and shops where there is a guarantee of homogenous social class and undisturbed enjoyment of privilege. Banished from these locations are the footpath encroachments, the occasional intrusive noises of street festivals or protests, and the untidy life of the street corner. The 'archisemiotics of class war' Mike Davis says, keeps out the masses by a number of visual, legal, and physical signs. Protected by an architecture of fear—high walled compounds, 24-hour security, and restricted single point access—occupants find a refuge from the hurly-burly of political or social life, and a retreat into uninterrupted consumption.

Already the annexation of large swathes of agricultural land for clubs and resorts, as well as farmhouses has offered large sections of the burgeoning middle-class population an escape from the city. The attrition of the green belt has happened as a result of the vast appetite of the middle-class for new and more exclusive lifestyles. As many as 52 clubs and resorts were identified as violating land laws, whether in their use of non-converted private land or in encroaching on government land.[194] These are symptoms of the retreat from the mixed public political sphere. Appropriately, the Sobha group has advertised itself as providing 'Relief, at last', the unspoken promise of serenity and 'fresh open spaces' that successfully conceals the violence of acquisition. Planning is therefore offered here as a further item of consumption, relieving the middle-class buyer from the tedium of seeking permissions, negotiating bribes, or securing licences. A visual relief is also assured in the form of aesthetic homogeneity, namely uniformly built, furnished, and maintained homes, as opposed to the scandalous profusion of architectural styles that marks most middle-class layouts. The image of the white middle-class person is conspicuous in the lavish real estate brochures, at once the ideal consumer of these living pleasures and a reminder of the ideal towards which successful planning must strive.

These enclaves are therefore a retreat from politics itself. The unwillingness to participate in the uncertainties of politics, and to secure oneself from such contamination in *physical* ways, is also a sign of how beleaguered such an existence may be, and how they represent at best privatized solutions to intractable social/public problems. Therefore, these dreams are always haunted by the fear that the future may not be Singapore, as what lies beyond these walls is the same deeply segmented social and economic life from which one may have temporarily escaped. The limits of the real estate dream are immediately evident in the poor state of the infrastructure that neither the air-conditioned car nor the home can avoid. The late1990s dream of Bangalore as Singapore therefore turns on the 'six lane roads, flyovers, ring roads, municipal bond roads and many more projects'.[195] These are ways of extending the privileges of the enclave beyond the edge of the condominium. No real estate developer, not even architects or state planners, has dared to dream of the heroic scale of public housing for which Singapore is equally well known.[196]

Conclusion

In their critique of financial planning, Partha Chatterjee and Asok Sen fault the critics of state planning who praise the 'progressive content' of Nehruvian planning while lamenting its leaks and inefficiencies. Thus, 'the innate political consistency of the logic of state supervision of the economy in the entire period is missed'.[197] I find an interesting corollary in their analysis to the critiques of city planning with which this chapter began. Arguing for a different perspective on planning procedures and the 'diverse system of "leakages" in the entire structure of public expenditure', Chatterjee and Sen suggest this is 'not simply a matter of bureaucratic inefficiency or corruption'. It is rather, 'an elaborate mechanism of marginal transfers from the core to the periphery—fragmented, molecular, politically supervised, designed to create opportunities for conceding sectional demands and yet producing the ideological effect of a regime of power which is responsive to the popular will.' In many ways, this assessment appears to hold true for the heterogeneous composition of power in the context of the city. A close examination of the specific instances which represent the success or failure of planning, reveals that city development and expansion consists of three broad processes which may be broadly classified as the legal, the illegal, and the informal, each of which signifies an accommodation of older and newer interests in the city which share power with the state apparatuses. The bourgeoisie struggles with and even adopts the older aristocratic order while its new enemy, the working classes and the urban poor, make their appearance on the city horizon. A detailed examination of the processes of the law and its operations in Bangalore city will bear this out even more clearly, but it is amply evident that planning's success will depend on how state apparatuses arrest or transform the 'fragmented, molecular and politically supervised transfers' which are nevertheless ideologically produced as 'responsive to popular will'. How might such processes be made responsive to popular aspirations for a life and livelihood in the city? As the examples discussed above indicate, it may be necessary to rethink the ritual obeisance to the Master Plan which by its very rigidity invites and engenders countless illegalities.

There has not been an adequate response to the problems of planning metropolitan cities, except in the timid sense of borrowing ideals from other cultures. The obsession of the technocrats, media, and the ideologues of the state in Bangalore with the image of Singapore is a symptom of this bankruptcy. Increasing economic activity in an area may mean building up a meaningful planning mechanism that takes account of the diversity of city economies and respects the multiplicity of claims to the city. Meanwhile, the institution of the law, far from acting as a corrective to the distortions of planning, largely functions as a way of normalizing the processes by which abstract space is produced, revealing even more sharply the gap between an officially conceived map, and the territory over which it expects to establish its hold.

FOUR

The Map is not the Territory: Law and the Production of Space

It was only through the illegal actions of land seizure that many migrants had access to lots—access that in most cases was eventually authorised. Moreover it was only through rebellious associations that they could undertake organised political action. Thus paradoxically, it was the illegality of their land seizures that permitted access both to property rights and new political identities.

Holston, *The Modernist City*

The expropriation of land for the Bangalore Cantonment was enabled, in its founding moment, by acts of force untempered by the instruments of the law. Even so, control of city territory was predicated on fixed and stable uses of land, and relied on identifiable boundaries. During negotiations with Krishnaraja Wodeyar III in 1814 on the jurisdiction of military authorities in the newly established Cantonment, the commanding officer suggested that its limits should be well-defined by 'high roads, bunds, impassable ravines, etc.' 'The boundaries that I propose', he continued, 'are those of *nature*, [so] that the whole cantonment forms a kind of elevated island during many months of the year'.[1] The resident, A.H. Cole, however, had some difficulty in convincing the 'Rajah' of 'the use of an imaginary line'. The 'Rajah' refused to permit any boundaries, while readily agreeing to give spots of land for houses or barracks when the need arose.[2] The negotiations were prompted in the decades after 1809 by the large number of European 'squatters' in the areas around who preferred military authority to indigenous rule. Since 'Bangalore as a military station has no fixed limits', the land made over to the Commanding Officer was chequered and intersected by other areas which were not given over by the Mysore authorities, making 'British residents of Bangalore ... merely denizens of Mysore State'.[3]

Intervening 43 years later at the height of the Rebellion of 1857, Commissioner Mark Cubbon argued for the advantages of continuing civil rather than military authority, but his views clearly lost the day when the Civil and Military Station was established and its boundaries clearly marked, on ground as on the map.[4] Until the formation of the Corporation of the City of Bangalore in 1949, which united the city and cantonment municipalities, yellowing granite stones inscribed with Roman numerals marked the boundaries of the C&M Station.

The alleged reluctance of the Mysore 'Rajah' to accept the finality of a map marked by 'imaginary' yellow lines, serves as parable for our times: if the British sought boundaries and maps as a way of fixing jurisdictions and legal rights of British inhabitants, the monarch preferred a more porous arrangement which retained his authority and from which his subjects stood to gain. Maps were, and continue to be, a way of laying claim to territory, and are texts of power which bear the intentionality of the state. Today, over 150 years later, although expropriation of land is enabled by law, the porous boundaries and competing legal jurisdictions in Bangalore have produced a whole range of illegalities that have decisively shaped the city and are periodically a source of anguish to town planners and development authorities alike. The map can, therefore, never be an authoritative version of the territory: below its well defined features and lines, indeed its claim to truth, lies a tangled skein of negotiations between politics and the law, between court and legislature, which render no territory absolutely inviolate, and constitute the city as a far more disturbed zone than that envisaged by its planners.[5]

Negotiations therefore contribute to the production of space in the city and any understanding of changes in the urban morphology goes well beyond, or below, the two dimensionality of the map. While distinguishing between the *city,* 'a present and immediate reality, a practico–material and architectural fact', and the *urban,* 'a social reality made up of relations which are conceived of constructed and reconstructed by thought', Lefebvre has cautioned against reifying the urban by emphasizing that it 'cannot go without a practico–material base, a morphology'.[6] Nevertheless, if we are to render space visible as a social product, rather than a product of nature, the specific operations of the economic, politico–juridical, and ideological apparatuses of a city's social formation must be laid bare.[7] The only way to penetrate the 'mystical form of the commodity' called real estate in the urban context[8] is to denaturalize the production of space through attention to its specific social settings, which the science of space, partial and fragmentary by definition, may not address at all.[9]

In Bangalore, whose morphology has been fundamentally transformed and vastly extended since 1949, both the legal and planning apparatuses of the state have attempted to impose some order on the unruly growth. The demarcation of a 'green belt', a girdle of agricultural land and forest surrounding the expanding metropolis, was an attempt in this direction, although this new 'imaginary boundary', as we have seen, has continually been breached by illegalities of state and citizen alike. That other more pragmatic girdle being thrown around the city, the Ring Road, too has been severely clotted by legal claims and illegal squatters. These are exemplary signs of a planning mechanism that has been undermined by the operations of the law or the designs of politics, with their continual redefinition of what is right, just, or appropriate for the production of space in a burgeoning regional metropolis. The law here performs a normalizing role, rarely questioning the ideology of urban development as it is predicated on the expropriation of one set of owners, and therefore their rights as owners, in order to create and sustain a new ownership of rights over space in the city.

This chapter will chart those features of the production of space in Bangalore city that have been enabled by the instrumentalities of the law. More correctly, it explores the fit between politics and the law in this production process, institutions that may sometimes retain their relative autonomy or at other times intersect and combine, but always to protect, preserve, and extend the ideology of private property in land and a market for housing. The oft expressed hope of a tighter fit between map and territory is in fact an expression of the desire for a more complete economic domination of the production of space, a declaration of the sovereignty of the market. The clearest expression of this, both in judicial and administrative discourse since the 1980s, is the persistent demand for a drastic reduction in the multiplicity of laws that breed illegalities in their interstices. This, it is claimed, will bring a greater clarity to the real estate market.[10]

On the other hand, the multiple levels at which a vigorous market in illegalities is sustained, and not least the illegalities of the state itself, points to the impossibility of a perfect market in land/housing in a society that is so deeply stratified and segmented. In effect, the state, as we have previously seen, remains only one of the forces that shapes urban territory.[11] It alternately acquiesces to the growing demands of a developer-dominated market in land, on the one hand, and, on the other, to pressures from below, as some sections of society use a mixture of illegal or informal measures to remain outside the domain of the market. This chapter will briefly outline the legislative mechanisms of successive political regimes as they have responded to the pressure for urbanizable land, before considering the ways in which a market in illegalities has been nourished by both public (e.g. BDA) and private (e.g. House Building Co-operative Societies) provisioners of land and housing. The next section explores the scale and significance of the illegalities of the state as they shape and define the city. How successfully does judicial discourse serve as a check on these illegalities, whether in its definition of 'public purpose' or in its generation of new modes of citizenship through a definition of 'public interest'? And finally, what are the strategies for survival in the city developed by those whom legal forms of citizenship largely exclude, or are abandoned by the state at a time of generalized real estate (commodity) production?

The Region, Politics, and the City

Early signs of a reorganized market in land, in a city severely strained by demographic growth, were evident in two quite disparate events of the early 1970s. About 150 Dalit families of Mariyappanapalya, a slum between Rajajinagar and Srirampuram, were rendered homeless in a fire which reduced their thatched huts to cinders in less than an hour. Residents testified to women and children being beaten by the police before the arson began.[12] A case was registered against the landlord and his family who had chosen arson as a way of evicting recalcitrant tenants who had yielded neither to threats nor persuasion.[13] The incident drew attention to the problems of migration, and the illegalities it engendered, and the modes of clearing populations off land that was increasingly gaining value. 'In the 20 years since 1951', an editorial on 'Our City' said, 'vast throngs of migrant labourers poured into the city from arid tracts of Tamil Nadu', thereby adding to the number of slums in the city.[14]

A few months later came an admission of near bankruptcy by the City Improvement Trust Board for whom 'the payment of enhanced compensation to landowners as decreed by the court' had raised the costs of acquiring the Vyalikaval area from Rs 4 lakhs to Rs 45 lakhs.[15] If the CITB had constructed housing for the poor in its early stages, there was little scope for such activity now as funds were low and 'slum dwellers were on the increase'. Even franker was the admission of defeat by the CITB regarding multiple, informal transactions on the land it acquired. 'Houses had been constructed on over 50 per cent of the sites in the newly announced Gokul Layout' the CITB admitted, which could not be demolished due to stiff resistance from the residents. The CITB therefore asked the applicants themselves 'to ascertain whether any construction existed on the site they intended to apply for.'

Both these developments were symptoms of a land market which was taking shape in response to the growing clamour for sites and housing. (See Tables 4.1 and 4.2). The 1970s was the defining decade in which planning apparatuses recognized that the city may be growing in ways far beyond their ability to control, calling for political intervention from above. In the early 1970s, a series of decisions was taken to secure and enable the production of space in the city within the legal framework of a regulated market in land and private property. The state remained the prime mover on the question of housing, attempting to voice some concern for social justice in the city and, the housing needs of the poor and economically weaker sections, without challenging the ideology of private property or the real estate market. 'Clearance, rehabilitation, conservation' which were declared the key concepts of planning in the 1960s, continued to define the initiatives of this period. There was considerable optimism about the effectiveness of top–down planning processes, and indeed

TABLE 4.1: Housing Units and Estimates of Housing Shortages in Bangalore

Year	Population (in lakhs)	Houses	Increase (Regd. No. of Houses)	Provision (Additional Input)	Shortage
1951	9.81	84,549	—	—	—
1961	12.07	1,42,300 (2,15,363)	57,751	—	(26,037)
1971	16.54	2,45,057 (2,62,926)	1,02,757	—	47,000 (67,874)
1981	29.13	4,71,573 (5,15,599)	2,26,516	1,75,000	51,516 (67,001)
1991	40.86	6,93,000 (824,022)	2,21,427	2,00,000	46,127 (83,978)
2001	70.00* (58.00)	10,25,000 (11,22,155)	3,32,000	2,25,000	1,07,000 (1,66,736)
2011	95.00* (70.00)	13,80,000 (14,20,285)	3,35,000	2,50,000	2,70,000 (1,35,271)

* Estimated population, 1985
Figures in brackets are revisions made in 1995

SOURCES: *Comprehensive Development Plan Report* (Bangalore, 1985).
Comprehensive Development Plan (Revised) Bangalore: Report (Bangalore, 1995)

TABLE 4.2: Growth of Population in Bangalore City and Metropolitan Area, 1901–2001, and Projected Population Growth (in lakhs)

	Metropolitan Area		City Corporation		Projected Population				
Year	Population	Percentage increase	Population	Percentage increase	in 1954	in 1963	in 1976	in 1985	in 1995
1901	2.28	—	1.61	—	—	—	—	—	—
1911	2.60	14.50	1.92	19.20	—	—	—	—	—
1921	3.11	19.20	2.40	25.40	—	—	—	—	—
1931	3.96	27.50	3.08	29.10	—	—	—	—	—
1941	5.10	28.90	4.07	32.60	—	—	—	—	—
1951	9.91	94.90	7.79	91.60	—	—	—	—	—
1961	12.07	21.80	9.06	16.70	9.00	—	—	—	—
1971	16.64	37.00	14.22	56.90	10.11	16.62	—	—	—
1981	29.13	76.72	24.82	74.57	11.40	21.62	22	—	—
1991	40.86	40.27	26.50	6.77	12.80	—	29	45	—
2001	56.86	37.69			14.40	—	38	70	58

SOURCES:

Report of the Bangalore Development Committee (Bangalore, 1954).

Outline Development Plan for Bangalore Metropolitan Region (Bangalore, 1963).

Report on the Comprehensive Development Plan of Bangalore (Bangalore, 1976).

Comprehensive Development Plan Report (Bangalore, 1985).

Comprehensive Development Plan (Revised) Bangalore: Report (Bangalore, 1995).

planners today would acknowledge that the CITB was more successful than its successor the BDA in fulfilling its planning obligations.[16]

Successive regimes since the 1970s have recognized that the unwieldy growth of cities calls for policy and legislative measures that limit, if not actually direct, these changes. The regime of Chief Minister Devaraj Urs, 1972–80, has been described as 'the most promising non-Communist regional experiment'[17] and with good reason, if one considers the range of measures that were taken to secure a new coalition of forces in the countryside. In the urban areas, Urs' regime coincided with several initiatives that were taken (within Karnataka and at the Centre) to regulate and centralize transactions on land. The state declared its desire to lay claim to and control the unwieldy revenue site phenomenon by setting up a planning body, the BDA in 1976 which had wider jurisdiction than the CITB.[18] It aimed to regulate and limit private access to urban land by introducing the Urban Land (Ceiling and Regulation) Act 1976;[19] to control the reckless conversion of agricultural to non-agricultural purposes by fresh provisions in the Karnataka Land Reforms Act (1974); to boldly recover properties belonging to the state, and finally, to install a mechanism to deal with the burgeoning slum population, the Karnataka Slum Areas (Improvement and Clearance) Act, 1973. The first attempt was also made, through the institution of the Urban Art Commission, to preserve and promote an urban aesthetic.[20] On the face of it, many of these legislative or governmental measures were echoes of central policies, forged during the troubling period of the Emergency. Yet Urs' autonomy from the Centre ensured that these measures were informed by principles of distributive justice, even as the state was insulated from some of the worst excesses of the Emergency.

These were the signs of the developmentalist state par excellence. By no means did Urs remain untouched by the handsome financial rewards of being in office, but there is no doubt that a new alignment of rural political forces was attempted with success. This was less true of the urban areas in general, although the chief minister attended with vigour to the symbolic as well as the actual political gains of providing housing to the urban poor. The residents of Mariyappanapalya, for instance, were given titles to sites in the same area and in nearby layouts at subsidized rates: new schemes for sites for slum dwellers, Economically Weaker Sections, and SCs and STs were announced with great fanfare.[21] The newly formed Karnataka Slum Clearance Board was headed by G. Basavanappa, who announced ambitious programmes for slum redevelopment and clearance.[22] Above all, as the chief minister himself recognized, the newly constituted BDA would be empowered to combine the role of developer and planner, authorized to prevent private layouts, and 'permi[t] housing co-ops of industrial labour only' instead of running into the same problems as the CITB which allotted 'one site to six people'.[23]

Before long, these state controls themselves led to a vast market in illegalities, as the actual operations of the acts were quick to reveal. By the mid 1980s, the BDA was mired in litigation, unable to function well either as the service provider it was intended to be, or effectively develop and implement plans for the city. The ULCRA yielded paltry returns: a mere 0.57 per cent of land that was identified as exceeding the ceiling was actually handed over to the state.[24] The national record was no better, as little land was recovered and even less distributed: as the Government itself declared in 1987–8, ten years after the passage of the act, 'less than one half per cent of the land declared surplus has been used for construction'.[25] Unauthorized revenue sites proliferated, forcing the state to periodically 'regularize' illegal structures. Conversion of agricultural land for non-agricultural purposes was briefly permitted on the payment of a fine, and although it was suspended, continues apace.

Nevertheless, in retrospect, the Devaraj Urs regime has been considered the period when a number of checks on land use were instituted, and the availability of urbanizable land restricted. The city did not occupy the same centrality in the political imagination as it did in the 1980s and 1990s. If the decade of the 1970s was the one when the state made an attempt to define and control the development of the city and put a lid, however partial, on conspicuous consumption,[26] by the 1980s it was clear that the law proved no impediment to the designs and aspirations of the private builder. The figure of the developer, who represented wholly urban and unmistakably speculative interests, was on the ascendant, and found willing accomplices among political representatives who were prepared to bend the law through administrative intervention. Ramakrishna Hegde's regime, 1983–88, was a period when the illegalities of the state became amply visible, outstripping the scale of illegalities by, say, housing cooperative societies, or individual citizens. Indeed, for the first time, the chief minister of the state functioned directly as a real estate agent, as we shall see below, inviting non-resident interest in urban property, encouraging private developers, and meanwhile authorizing some of the most ruthless slum clearance measures in the history of Bangalore.[27] The legal apparatus functioned only as a partial check on the political arms of government, and a telling sign of the times was the increasing frankness with which the judiciary admitted the role of politics in subverting the law to facilitate housing and real estate development. For instance, despite the withdrawal of permission in the early 1980s for the conversion of land from agricultural to non-agricultural uses on the payment of fines, conversion proceeded on an ad hoc basis.[28]

By 1986, the administration was compelled to take fresh stock of the growing field of illegalities. The first steps were taken to review unauthorized constructions, and a committee set up by the government recommended regularization subject to certain procedures and principles.[29] Rather than resulting in a judicious process of selection, however, it opened a new space for parties to argue against demolition, and even courts agreed that demolition might deprive the litigant of possible regularization. Not much later, in 1990, this was taken as a policy statement, and the cut-off date of 1986 for unauthorized buildings was revised to 31 March 1990. This gave rise to fresh expectations that the cut-off date for unauthorized structures would be periodically extended and no demolitions would take place. Indeed, this hope has been honoured as recently as 1995.[30] The court, which inveighed against the decisions of the government to strengthen the power of governmental agencies such as the BDA, was quick to recognize that the boundary between legality and illegality could be continually manipulated. Thus, 'the several orders issued by the Government from time to time providing for regularization of constructions have come in handy to the unscrupulous dealers to persuade the purchasers that they will also get regularization and title ... the layout itself is imaginary and exists only on paper'.[31]

Activist judges who initiated a series of measures to protect the city environment and staunch the wounds inflicted on formal, legal processes were sometimes directly locked in combat with the legislature. Justice Michael Saldanha of the Karnataka High Court gained extraordinary visibility in the late 1990s for his outspoken espousal of the middle-class urban consumer looking for sound legal investments in property. Thanks to political manoeuvring by successive governments, he said,

> The courts were choked with thousands of cases wherein it is demonstrated that after the process of acquisition is complete even in those cases where the lands are free of encroachers, a large number of unauthorized persons thereafter occupy the land, trade in it, and sell it along with immovable structures of various buildings ... This the court can only observe with a degree of distress that all these activities bear the unmistakable stamp of not only collusion but active partnership of the authorities concerned.[32]

The hope of regularization therefore sustained and promoted defiance of the law, or 'speculative aggression', to use the BDA Chairman Basavaiah's apposite phrase in the early 1980s.[33] This was equally true of building violations within the corporation limits: a Supreme Court verdict that ordered the demolition of floors in excess of the 55 ft height limit in two blocks of apartments at RMV

Stage II was flouted with impunity. The buildings still stand, with the BCC continuing to weakly claim that 'it does not have the requisite equipment'.[34] Another 47 buildings that were notified as having exceeded the 55 ft limit were, several years later, still awaiting the BCC demolition order.[35] In response to the Supreme Court order, M. Chandrasekhar, then minister of urban development declared in the Legislative Assembly that the government would consider a revision of by-laws that concerned multi-storeyed buildings and regularize construction activities in this area. The Bangalore City Planning Area Zonal Regulations (Amendment and Validation) Bill of 1996, passed during Deve Gowda's term as chief minister (1994–6), thus circumvented the court decision and the contempt petition, and benefited at least 45 apartment blocks in the city.[36]

The discourses of politics and the law therefore often intersected but sometimes diverged, with one subverting the pronouncements of the other. Political decisions periodically brought legality to acknowledged illegalities of the past, while the judiciary often held that what had been thought procedurally legal was in fact questionable. The claim by a group of 57 revenue site holders of the Mount Joy area that it was promised regularization in 1961 by the then minister for local self-government was struck down by the court.[37] By the 1990s, competing interests on land in the city were willing to adopt a more muscular form of legal activism. Beginning with the agricultural landowner who challenged the relentless manner in which the city acquired lands by the acre to be sold by the square foot, there were revenue site owners, slum dwellers, members of cooperative societies, frustrated BDA site applicants, and finally the citizen acting 'in public interest' who took on the institutions of the state on a number of grounds. Builders and real estate agents gave stronger voice to the demand to limit the interventionary role of the state, to ease conversion of agricultural to non-agricultural land, and to go beyond the confines of the ULCRA act.

By the 1990s, state apparatuses were more than willing to introduce legislative change as well as reinterpret the statutes of public bodies to suit new needs, and subvert court judgements. Since the early nineties, and particularly during the Janata regime, 1994–9, the city has come full circle. Several legal blocks to the mode of production of space in the city have been swept away. The Land Reforms Act has been amended to make conversion of agricultural land easier and declare housing an industry;[38] the ULCRA has repealed;[39] unauthorized constructions have been regularized;[40] and most recently, amendments to the Karnataka Town and Country Planning Act have defined afresh, and regularized deviations from building laws.[41] Land that has been acquired may be reconveyed to original owners,[42] land that is built up is denotified, and amendments to the Town and Country Planning Act will permit more 'realistic' building norms.

The provisions of the Karnataka Town and Country Planning (Amendment) Bill, 1998, laid bare the efforts of the legislature to trump judicial decisions and planning policy in order to normalize and even engender illegalities, by sacrificing planning norms in a city where building violations are rife. The newly crafted Section 76ff of the act sought to regularize all buildings constructed in violation of building norms if the offender paid a penalty of not less than market value. In the event of the offender not being able to pay such penalties, the provision allowed any person interested in the deviant building to pay twice the current market value and save it from forfeiture. In an even more blatant concession to the burgeoning luxury hotel industry, Section 14b (2) entitled starred hotels to construct up to twice the normal permissible area in the relevant zone.[43] Such measures came at a time when an average of 50–60 licences for high rises were annually issued, leading to excess capacity in the luxury housing market.[44]

Efforts to swiftly regain control of properties belonging to public agencies such as the BMP and BDA have redoubled with the establishment of the Bangalore Metropolitan Task Force (BMTF) in 1995. Following state elections in 1999, when the S.M. Krishna-led Congress government was installed, the BMTF has gained new visibility for its actions against informal and illegal occupations of public land, usually by smaller commercial interests, sometimes in swift response to court orders and other times to nip informal occupations in their early stages. The chief minister has restored the BDA to its role of service provider: an estimated 30,000 sites were distributed between 1999–2002 alone.[45]

Both the judicial and legislative spheres of activity, however, despite their apparent contradictions, were intended to bring a closer fit between map and territory, and greater clarity to the operations of a real estate market. Meanwhile, courts often declared that what was 'authorized' (by officials of the corporation or the BDA) was procedurally illegal but violators were increasingly confident that political intervention would overide the illegality. There is increasingly the willingness to assert the law not as a corrective to illegalities but as a post hoc recognition of them. In this process, what is achieved is a redefinition of 'public purpose' and a fresh definition of 'public interest' which asserts the rights of the citizen as a consumer of city space and services.[46] This also radically alters the contract between state and citizen to correspond to that of service provider and customer, with an increasing role played by market forces in defining the relationship.[47]

BDA and the Traffic in Illegalities

The map is not the territory. Indeed, knowledge of the gulf between the map and the territory has become a form of property itself, exploited by the rent-seeking intermediary within the government apparatuses, and especially since the 1990s, extra-legal extortionists. There may be no accurate cartographic representation of a complicated social and political process in which knowledge itself is power. For the social historian of contemporary Bangalore, it is the document generated by these illegalities that provides an optic on the limits of the law in shaping the city. Simply put, the expectation of enormous profit from transactions on land produces illegalities variously initiated by the state, the builder/developer or richer class of citizen. The illegalities of the poor alone, which are prompted by the need to find a foothold in the city, are repeatedly and more easily rectified, not necessarily through means that are strictly legal.

The complex economy that develops in the interstices of the state apparatuses is well illustrated in an institution like the BDA. Set up in 1976, the BDA has a jurisdiction over 1279 sq. km, of which the Bangalore conurbation of 449 sq. km includes the BMP areas, with the green belt beyond.[48] By 1999, the BDA had implemented 206 developments, including several large layouts.[49] Historically, the first signal for clandestine land deals was the announcement of population projections for 1991 (45 lakhs) in the year 1981 itself, when it was acknowledged that the city had almost doubled in size. In an often reproduced, and somewhat ambiguous table (see Table 4.1) showing the number of registered houses, provisions for housing, and shortfalls based on population projections, estimated shortage nearly equalled the estimated excess capacity in the housing market.[50] Land acquisition by the BDA was hampered from the start by litigation and unplanned occupation. An estimated forty-one layouts were formed between 1976 and 1991, for which only 10,458 out of 19,054 acres, or half the original planned area, was notified for acquisition. Of this, a mere 5750 acres were used for actual sites, as 1,636 acres had already been built up, 1123 acres were under litigation, and 1670 acres were bulk allotted and reconveyed. (See Table 4.3.)

The policy of reconveyance is peculiar to Bangalore and not practised in any other city in India.[51] The gaps between notification and acquisition, between acquisition and actual site formation, and even after the sites were

TABLE 4.3: Extent of Area Acquired and Utilized in 41 BDA Layouts between 1.1.1976 and 31.3.1990

(Acres-*guntas*)*

Sl. No.	Year	Area acquired	No. of sites formed	Area used for formation of sites	Area under UAC (built up)	Area under litigation	Ring road	Area bulk allotted & reconveyed	Area not utilizable
1	Prior to 1976	2823–34	6785	481–26					
2	1976–77	214–10	1764	153–14½					
3	1977–78	98–06	10	0–28					
4	1978–79	361–00	4271	297–16					
5	1979–80	238–22	1009	70–32					
6	1980–81	787–34¾	675	49–32					
7	1981–82	596–26½	1223	87–16					
8	1982–83	1143–26¾	5759	419–36					
9	1983–84	647–22	3284	242–39	1636–01¼	1122–35¼	235–21	1690–38¾	115–03
10	1984–85	255–38	1965	142–30					
11	1985–86	403–15	6531	547–20					
12	1986–87	1146–10¾	5931	451–20					
13	1987–88	1140–37	11021	941–16					
14	1988–89	485–13	7070	632–18					
15	1989–90	108–37	2449	222–27					
16	1990–91	03–02	471	32–32					
Total		10454–17½	60,218	4775–16					
Ten Layouts of East Division			11,265	975–14¾					
Total			71,483	5750–30¾					

SOURCE: Bangalore Development Authority

*One acre equals approximately 40 *guntas*.

FIG. 38 *Veneration of found objects among the records at the BDA legal offices.* (Janaki Nair, 1999)

formed, the 'disappearance' of sites from the registers of the BDA were signs not so much of inefficiency as of a brisk black market in that much desired commodity, namely land (Fig. 38). Indeed, it is clear from court records and official documents that the preliminary notification acted as a sort of signal to owners to begin building on their properties. In high income areas like RMV II Stage, for instance, up to 75 per cent of the land was built over, and impossible to recover; the figures in the case of BTM layout are even more striking. (See Table 4.4.)

Transactions on BDA land, especially since the early 1980s, increasingly became clandestine, leading legislative committees,[52] special commissions, and court-appointed commissioners[53] to routinely complain that there were no accurate records, and that maps and site registers were unreliable. There was, and indeed continues to be, no agreement on the number of layouts, sites, or vacant lands in the jurisdiction of the BDA.[54] It may be no coincidence that one of the first tasks the Bangalore Agenda Task Force set for itself was a full-fledged mapping of the city. What does become clear from the enquiries into specific contraventions of the law is that the confusion and lack of clarity disappear when the need arises. The White Paper on the BDA in 1984 gave

TABLE 4.4: Land Utility Study of Five Layouts, 1991
in Acres/*Guntas*

Sl. no.	Name of layout	Area to engg. section (A-G)	Area under litigation (A-G)	Area under unauthorized constructions (built-up)	Area bulk allotted (A-G)	Area re-conveyed (A-G)	Total (4) to (7) (A-G)	Percentage unutilizable by BDA (8) to (3)
(1)	(2)	(3)	(4)	(5)	(6)	(7)	(8)	(9)
1	BTM Layout	824–03½	83–37	273–36	200–13½	30–07	586–13½	68.10
2	Nagarbhavi II Stage	517–28	119–27	14–07	—	—	133–34	25.85
3	Koramangala	870–17½	31–33½	18–38	305–13½	—	356–10½	40.91
4	Rajmahal Vilas II & further extn of RMV II	689–27	108–10	204–09	209–31	—	522–10	75.72
5	Hosur Road/ Sarjapur Road	867–35½	76–22	22–20	29–0	—	128–03	14.69

SOURCE: Bangalore Development Authority

innumerable examples of the instantaneous allotment, at the urging of certain politicians, of 'stray sites' in prime localities, especially in RMV Stage II, to persons who were not normally eligible for them. Sites were identified and allotted within hours of any governmental decision.[55]

In a severe indictment of the functioning of the law department of the BDA, a three man committee appointed in 1991 revealed that 'lack of system' and 'negligence' were inadequate to describe the way in which cases were dealt with. Between 1980 and 1990, for instance, there were 2382 cases against the BDA of which 465 had been pending for over 5 years. These included stay orders and temporary injunctions which were issued against the BDA as early as 1980 and remained unattended. Written statements were filed in as few as 513 cases, while the BDA itself declared a lack of information in the file in as many as 83 cases. By 1 January 1999 the number of pending cases had reached a stupendous 5660, with only 132 disposed of in December 1998.[56]

In many of the nearly 900 cases that were decided in favour of the BDA between 1986 and 1990, the agency simply failed to take action in time, leading to the rapid growth of 'unauthorized constructions' between the issuance of an eviction order and its execution. For instance, when more than 17 months lapsed between 1989 and 1990 on an eviction order, the BDA found that in addition to the original occupier, more than '180 members of a Wandering Tribe' were able to colonize the place, requiring the deployment of enforcement agencies. The timing of action was crucial in this business; thus the committee reported:

> The interests of the BDA are permanently damaged perhaps on the first few days or weeks of the operation of a stay order because during those crucial periods, the land under litigation will have been turned into plots, buildings built overnight, false documents created and the sites sold to site hungry people or clever middle men. The BDA when it finally wakes up, on getting a stay order vacated is faced with a *fait accompli*. It will have lost the land even if it wins the case!

So baneful was the use of the individual writ petition in stalling the work of the development authority that the committee was willing to question the wisdom of exercising individual rights. It said, 'It is difficult to say to what extent courts should keep their eyes squarely on the main issue and the public good and not allow a large public good to be held up on the ground of a minor remediable damage to an individual.' At the same time, the committee noted that the judiciary was not an immovable object: housing societies briskly vacated stay orders against them, and were quick in deploying the right resources to procure clear and unencumbered titles to land.

'Public Purpose' Redefined

There were more than ample signs that the person most adversely affected by the law of eminent domain, the landowner, was no longer willing to plead only for higher levels of compensation, as had happened through the sixties and even seventies.[57] He could question the legality of the planning mechanism itself. In many cases, the landowner, who possessed anything from a few *guntas* of land to a few acres in villages around Bangalore, challenged the notification for acquisition under the Land Acquisition Act of 1894, either on procedural grounds or on grounds that compensation was inadequate.[58] The law of Eminent Domain deprived the landowner of the value of her assets as a productive resource, so that wells or vineyards of Bangalore Blue grapes were rarely reckoned in the compensation.[59] Fewer landowners were paid in anticipation of the uses to which the urban land would be put.[60] The court repeatedly revealed a willingness to enhance the quantum of compensation: 'It is clear', said the court, 'that potential value is a necessary element in the assessment of compensation.'[61] Thus, in *Union of India and Others* v. *Narsappa and Others,* 56 people whose land had been acquired for the Bharat Electronics Ltd demanded higher compensation of Rs 8000 per acre, instead of the meagre Rs 3500 offered; the court enhanced the quantum to Rs 5000.[62]

The planning apparatus meanwhile annexed more and more territories to its map. Forced into the recognition that the population of the city had nearly doubled in the previous decade, and the area of the Urban agglomeration was close to 449 sq. km, the Comprehensive Development Plan of 1985 expanded the Local Planning Area of Bangalore from 500 sq. km to 1279 in 1995, which brought an additional 779 sq. kms. and 326 villages into its jurisdiction. As the one who faced the surest prospect of expropriation and the least benefit, as holder of what might either be a 'parcel of hope' or a 'parcel of despair',[63] the landowner showed new willingness to question the validity of state actions. In *Subbanna* v. *State of Karnataka,* representatives of Doddabommasandra Jalahalli in Bangalore North sought the court's intervention in striking down the amalgamation of the area to green belt as it placed restrictions on the uses to which the land could be put.[64] The court however upheld the authority of the revised development plan, saying 'that the CDP is an integrated [plan] and either it must exist as a whole or fall through as a whole. It cannot be sub-divided or truncated as it would amount to redrafting of the CDP'. The court did admit, however, that the state had permitted several BDA schemes (amounting to 7419 acres) housing societies (200 acres) and new industrial uses (610 acres) within the green belt area, but believed that these developments served a public purpose. In the tautological reasoning of the court, 'The expansion of a city and its improvement are purposes from which flows a direct public benefit and a purpose which is productive of results so advantageous to the public is a clear public purpose'.[65] Though the challenge to the modalities of planning itself did not succeed, there were signs that the courts were increasingly pressed into adjudicating on the meaning of 'public purpose' in order to protect the landowner's rights to the city.

By the mid-1980s it was amply clear that the house-building co-operative societies were functioning as major players in the real estate market by securing land at low rates through state acquisition procedures, and selling them to the public at higher prices. The G.V.K. Rao Committee Report of 1988, which looked into the functioning of 98 societies established after 1984, uncovered a wide range of illegalities. The submission of bogus lists of members, acquisition of lands which were beyond their jurisdiction, and most telling, the appointment of agents who would undertake acquisition of land and negotiation with the government were some of the more striking illegalities.[66] The report established that a range of intermediaries had become important to the functioning of the real estate market.

> On the whole, the practice of these societies going through estate agents for acquiring the land under Land Acquisition Act appears to be totally unwarranted and in the process substantial amounts collected from gullible members have been deployed in these dubious activities.
>
> The sole beneficiaries of this practice appear to be the estate agents. In the entire transactions neither the land owners nor the members of the societies are getting as much benefit as the estate agents.[67]

In the case of Vishwabharati House Building Co-operative Society Ltd, Rao noted that there were agreements with five agents, including the Executive Director of the Society B. Krishna Bhat himself, to procure land under the Land Acquisition Act, even though the act did not empower such middlemen.[68]

Public purpose had come to mean the 'BDA exercising their special powers to deprive one section of the public to favour another section of the public'.[69] In BTM layout alone, for instance, where more than half the acquired land could not be acquired, the housing cooperatives and other private parties laid claim to 388 acres, leaving the BDA with a paltry 212 acres (one-eighth the notified area and a quarter of the acquired area). The court expressed astonishment at the scale of informal monetary transactions: SR Constructions had collected as much as Rs 1 crore even before the housing society was approved by the government. There were landmark judgements that declared that the acquisition of property for cooperative housing societies was not for a public purpose when the prior permission of the government had not been obtained.[70] The bench quashed the notifications of lands for Vyalikaval House Building Society, Amarjyothi House Building Society, and the Bangalore City Chikpet House Building Society Ltd, and REMCO–BHEL House Building Society on these grounds.

Once the floodgates had been opened in the 1980s, repeated court judgements and government orders did little to stem the growth of house-building cooperative societies, and they swelled to 353 by 1995. The courts were therefore repeatedly pointing to the ways in which an institution such as the BDA, set up for the formation of residential layouts in the Bangalore Metropolitan Area, was abdicating its responsibility by making over large chunks of its lands to housing cooperative societies. The court argued that

> Acquisition of large extent of land in the area for which the BDA is established in favour of so many housing societies renders the establishment of BDA under a special law futile ... whereas the power conferred under the Land Acquisition Act is for acquiring lands for carrying out housing schemes by a housing society, in each of the cases the acquisitions of lands is not for a *bona fide* housing scheme but is substantially for the purpose of enabling the concerned office bearers of respondent societies and their agents to indulge in sale of sites ... and to make money ... therefore it is a clear case of the colourable exercise of power.[71]

Insisting that the BDA stake sole claim to land acquisition in the city, the court declared

> Therefore the formation of layouts for housing within the Bangalore Metropolitan Area as a rule must be undertaken by the Bangalore Development Authority and the acquisition of land in favour of any society if considered feasible, must only be an exception.

Further, the court was far stricter in asserting that BDA had no powers to make such allotments,[72] in contrast to the government's recognition that bulk allotment was necessary.[73] The court inveighed against the increasing tendency to reconvey land that had been acquired. In practice, these judicial pronouncements were ignored, if the wide range of societies to which BDA gave its approval is an indication. Between 1989 and 1998, for instance, 134 private layouts were sanctioned, largely to house-building societies, upon agreement that 25 per cent of housing or sites would be given to lower income groups and middle income groups.[74]

In the 1980s, however, the tussle between the BDA and the housing cooperatives over the right to acquire land was heightened with the court upholding the power of the BDA to acquire land on which cooperative societies may already have transacted.[75] At the same time, the court struck down the BDA's deployment of the ULCRA.[76] The court, similarly, did not hesitate to uphold the interests of the BDA when the public interest to be served was greater than the individual rights of people, refusing to overturn large schemes in favour of individual owners.[77]

The public renunciation of the role of the state as the principal provisioner of housing, expressed in the Hegde government's interest in promoting privately developed 'group housing' made room for those wishing to build housing for profit.[78] However, there was also a growing demand for land for new infrastructural facilities, such as airports, roads, and industrial estates, entailing appropriation of land from the agriculturist. Attempts to challenge these acquisitions usually did not succeed. Land acquisitions for purposes such as airports[79] and golf courses[80] and technology parks, even within designated green belt areas, were declared as falling within the definition of 'public purpose'. In *S.S. Darshan* v. *State of Karnataka* the court concurred with the change in the land use decreed by government, by once more resorting to its tautological reasoning:

> It is no doubt true that when an area is earmarked as coming under the green belt area, it may not be possible for utilization of such land for any industrial purpose. But in the present case part of the land has been allowed to be converted for an industrial purpose and therefore it obviously shows that the authorities concerned were not averse to allowing coming up of industries in the area.[81]

This was in striking contrast to the willingness of judiciary to declare acquisitions invalid when they were for housing cooperatives. When it came to large and prestigious projects which involved international capital flows, or more generally the scope and direction of economic development, the judiciary was unwilling to contradict the wisdom of government decisions. Large establishments that sought exemption from the provisions of the Urban Land (Ceiling and Regulation) Act were similarly exempted by the court.[82]

Clearly, the judicial apparatus was committed to extending and deepening the scope of the market in land rather than confining it to specific enclaves. Central to these cases, therefore, was the definition of 'public good' or 'public purpose'. If largely middle-class housing cooperative societies had succeeded, with a few exceptions, in asserting that their operations constituted 'public purpose' could the private developer be far behind?[83] As the stakes were much higher, the anonymity of the governmental power which was referred to in many judgements was difficult to maintain. In the eighties, the faces behind what the courts called the 'colourable exercise of power' were coming into focus. The illegalities of the state gained greater visibility when compared with the puny illegalities of revenue site holders or even housing cooperative societies.

State Illegalities and Real Estate Production

The growing attractions of Bangalore city as a site for altogether new kinds of industry, such as the leisure industry, and the urgency of building up facilities to meet new international standards called for land acquisition on a large scale. This time, however, acquisition was not ideologically defined as fulfilling a 'national purpose', as in the case of the public sector industries. The state forged new links with private developers. Rapidly drying tank beds, once acceptable to none but the marginal populations of the city, became the most contentious sites, gradually undergoing a process of 'gentrification' as they came within the ambit of the urban. Most recently, a Karnataka State Tourism Development Corporation (KSTDC) golf course has come up on Challaghata tank bed,[84] and the National Games Complex on the Koramangala tank bed.[85]

The links between the private developer and the state, on the one hand, and negotiations between individual landowners and developers, on the other, were laid bare in certain court judgements. Individual landholders went to court challenging the acquisition of their properties in Kodihalli and Challaghata area which were notified for the 'public purpose, to wit, for golf course cum hotel resort near Bangalore Airport'. The area was notified in 1982 and the award approved in 1986, well within the statutory period.[86] However, the court unveiled the ways in which political power was deployed to benefit individual builders in the name of the larger public good. At a meeting with various officials in Vidhana Soudha in January 1987, a prominent builder Dayanand Pai, claiming to be the representative of various landholders, insisted that land amounting to 12 acres 34 *gunta*s be released to him out of the 39 acres on the Challaghatta tank bed area notified for the KSTDC. He claimed that

> he has got a firm commitment for putting up a group housing scheme on this land. These built units would be given only for Central public sector, State Public Sector, and the State Government Employees in equal proportions. However, if there is no adequate demand from any of these sectors within six months after the builder/developer has notified in prominent local newspapers such residual accommodation may be offered to the general public.[87]

The KSTDC conceded his request, not having the finances for the acquisition of the land for the golf course, and agreed to allow Dayanand Pai to put up the money as a loan. Pai's role was to ensure the smooth transfer of lands from landowners, including those who contested the quantum of compensation. By September 1988, Pai claimed his 12.31 acres though he had not arranged the transfer of land to the KSTDC. In the meantime, 8 acres were released to Bangalore International Centre, and a further 5 acres to C.K. Baljee of Universal Resorts Ltd. The court observed that 'it appears to us this is nothing more than a conspiracy to deprive the owners of the lands by use of the power of Eminent Domain which is to be used for an avowedly public purpose and for strong compelling reasons and not whimsically or to satisfy the private needs of an individual'.

We may note here that the court did not question the validity of the acquisition of land for a golf course and hotel as defeating public purpose. Indeed, the court's critique of the scandalous use of power for private gain did not stretch to suggestions for stopping acquisitions. Thus, despite periodic references in BDA documents that the policy of land acquisition must give way to a policy of land purchase, compensating the landowner in adequate measure for yielding her land to the city, only small moves were made in this direction.

Private interests in land were ably aided not by provisions of the existing law, or even the rules of a real estate market, but by the active intervention of the state apparatuses in contravening the legal framework. It was no longer a case of a faceless estate agent colluding with equally faceless bureaucrats and officials to exploit the need for housing, but important political figures and administrative personnel who colluded with builders and their agents. An even more vivid example of the misuse of power came to light when investigations were begun in 1988 on the Hegde regime's proposal for an NRI housing scheme on a 110 acre plot taken out of the Hosur–Sarjapur Road Layout Scheme.[88] Here too, the illegalities of the state were laid bare. The chief minister himself played the role of real estate agent in promoting the scheme, choosing a private developer with whom his son-in-law had close links, and making land speedily available for the NRIHA (K) with the active assistance of BDA officials. Hegde's interest in promoting Bangalore among NRIs of Karnataka origin was first evident in mid-1986. In May 1987, he went on a foreign tour with a brochure inviting NRIs of Karnataka origin to buy sites in the city. The BDA was instructed to take 110 acres out of its Hosur–Sarjapur Road Layout for this development. On his return he directed that a special cell be set up to monitor the progress of NRI applications for Dollar sites, headed by a retired IAS officer, H.G.V. Reddy. By July 1987, the transfer of 110 acres by the BDA to the NRIHA (K) was approved, even before rules relating to the allotment of land for NRI housing associations were framed in January 1988.

There were several reasons why such moves were illegal: the Justice Kuldip Singh Commission of Inquiry, instituted after the Hegde government resigned from power, pointed out that the action of the BDA in taking land from a sanctioned development scheme of 12,000 sites to benefit a group of NRIs was illegal. Moreover, 40 of these 110 acres fell in the green belt area. Also, the government had erred in making bulk allotments to associations which were not eligible, such as NRIHA (K). Furthermore, the commission found that the NRIHA (K) was a non-existent front for a Bombay builder Siraj Lokhandawala who was closely associated with Manoharlal Nichani, Hegde's son-in-law, and therefore did not represent 'established groups of NRIs' as the government had claimed. Lokhandawala invited people to 'come and settle in idyllic Bangalore' through the publication of colourful brochures promising 'garden villas, cosy homes and lakeside mansions etc.'

A quick succession of events eventually thwarted plans for the idyllic resort in Bangalore following the exit of the Hegde government from power. Government permission for the scheme was denied, public interest petitions filed by B. Krishna Bhat questioned bulk allotment and permission to build in the green belt, and enquiries were initiated by the Enforcement Directorate into deposits of Rs 55 lakhs from Dubai. By March 1989, the NRIHA (K) had peacefully handed back the property to the BDA.[89]

The investigations into the NRI housing scandal revealed the 'colourable exercise of power' by the Hegde government. More important, it revealed the impossibility of envisaging such ambitious schemes within the bounds of legality.[90] By no means was it possible for the Hegde government to assert that the NRI scheme was meeting the housing needs of the general Bangalore public. This reason was given by the government in another case for which exemptions to the ULCRA act were sought. The Revajeetu land scam revealed that large scale developments could make no progress without large scale violations of prevailing laws.[91] Public purpose once more came in handy. In March and April 1987, the government passed two orders exempting M/s Narayanaswamy & Sons, owners of vacant property in Dasarahalli (VI Block Jayanagar) from the provisions of the ULCRA. It permitted the sale of this to M/s Revajeethu for Rs 90 lakhs on the grounds that the landowners were indebted, and, more important, public interest would be served as 600 dwelling units would be constructed on the site.[92]

The government drew pointed reference to the acute shortage of housing in the city: 'a shortage of 75,000 dwelling units per year' necessitated a 'crash programme' for which the government might grant exemptions to individuals, firms, and companies. The court struck down the exemption as violating public interest.[93] What is striking is the role of the government in enabling large scale illegalities in an economic setting which called for new laws. An insistence that the state uphold the law, meanwhile, led to the emergence of the legal citizen acting in 'public interest'.

'Public Interest' and the Legal Citizen

Even when the law challenged the power of the government in determining the public good or public purpose, it was within a framework that acknowledged that both court and legislature should serve the needs of the market. However, it was really in the 1990s, when new modes of legal citizenship came into circulation, that the middle-class public began to play a role in determining the shape of the city, largely as it enhanced and deepened the rights of ownership in the city. A review of the many public interest petitions that have succeeded yields interesting insights. Public interest petitions are frequently linked to the protection of private interest, or more correctly, the value of private property. Petitions that seek to prevent civic amenity sites from being allotted to noisy *kalyana mantapas*,[94] protect public parks from multiple users, or reassert middle-class zoning wherever it has suffered attrition[95] must be viewed as actions that succeed in enhancing the 'quality of life' in an area, with important economic consequences. The claim of the legal citizen to rights within the city has passed through a number of stages, which we shall consider below.

Since the late 1980s and throughout the 1990s, the state has been increasingly perceived as a service provider, one from whom the consumer–citizen can demand his or her dues against payment. Residents of Kalyani Gardens in South Bangalore were able to successfully resist attempts to run industries in the area, and reassert the right to a purely residential zone.[96] Groups of citizens began to demand that land be offered to them at rates that had long been exceeded in the open market.[97] Others demanded that the BDA fulfill its promise of providing services even when the layout was subject to dispute,[98] and some were able to successfully claim the right not to pay taxes.[99]

The dawn of this form of legal activism makes it possible for the same figure who has been a prime violator of the law to turn into its prime defender. A striking example is the case of B. Krishna Bhat, who has initiated over 125 cases against public bodies, and in the process brings his own long engagement with illegalities out of the shadow.[100] In 1989, he even filed a case demanding the abolition of the BDA, which, although it was dismissed, brought the failures of the public agency into focus.[101] Over the years, he has questioned the actions of public agencies, challenged its right to collect taxes, and forced the BDA to publicly admit its lapses and failures. Concerned citizen's actions can also set limits to the sovereignty of the market in the name of the environment or aesthetics. Thus, owners of garden land near Siddapura were prevented from building on their land on the grounds that it would destroy the beauty of the area. A group of important south Bangalore citizens had filed an objection petition against exemptions granted under ULCRA to these owners.[102] Citizens of the Indiranagar/Defence Colony area who filed a public interest litigation against the growing trend of erecting apartments on properties designed for individual homes received the full sympathy of the court.[103] However, sometimes the concern for environmental and aesthetic harmony was quickly overshadowed by the attractions of the real estate market.[104]

More recent styles of legal activism have included cases filed by agencies such as CIVIC against the former BCC (now BMP) for the poor state of Bangalore's roads, or private citizens against the use of the Cubbon Park for building purposes. These are public goods, whose improvement is made to confer equivalent benefits on all users. An improved road, a beautified park, or a nicely maintained monument, however, are valued only by those sections for whom city life is less uncertain. Those for whom the city is a space of toil, and for whom the rights of residence are far more precarious will attach a different meaning to urban space.

The Illegalities of the Poor

The law has usually had only a negative presence in the lives of the urban poor. If the court and legislature work in their own independent ways to extend the market in urban land, protect private property and exchange value, there is little room for the protection of those who lie outside the market, and are reliant entirely on the state for such a basic need as housing. The enforced illegalities of the planning process, legal action, and political power often violently define the horizon of the poor. In most cases, a change of home among the poor is involuntary, executed by the state in ways that disrupt access to work as well as the modes of sociality and notions of territoriality. Often lacking the resources to contest the actions of the state, the illegalities of the poor are the most visible and therefore the most easily undone, often through a denial of legal remedies.[105]

Rosita Mertens' study of the CSI slum in Bangalore reveals that the law can at best delay relocation decisions, but not reverse them. Over a 20 year period, a slum that took root on private land belonging to the Church of South India grew to a colony of about 340 huts. When notified in 1987 under Sections 3 (as a slum) and 11 (as a slum to be cleared), the slum-dwellers began a legal battle against relocation, with support from local organizations such as Karnataka Kolageri Nivasigala Samyuktha Sanghatane and Women's Voice. When relocation was ordered by the high court in 1989, a fresh writ was filed by Women's Voice. When this too did not stand, the case went all the way up to the Supreme Court, on grounds that the area to which people would be relocated was very poorly serviced. This too was struck down, and clearance on the scheduled date of 15 April 1993 was only averted through the intervention of the local MLA. However, neither a fresh petition filed in the Supreme Court nor political intervention were able to eventually avert eviction: 'Relocation was inescapable this time; the MLA was out of town and the only person who could be asked for help was the lawyer [who was arrested while the clearance happened]. The next morning, 29 July 1993, at 5 am, the whole slum was surrounded by police cars and policemen with *lathis*. Everybody was ordered to leave their huts immediately and to take their belongings with them.'[106] Neither the legal nor the political route appears to have sustained the slum-dwellers in their hour of need. However, when legal clearance of slums is not possible, as we have already seen, it is not unusual to resort to arson.[107]

Government agencies themselves confess to a certain laxity in provisioning for the poor: the Karnataka Housing Board constructed houses in Bangalore on a limited scale, but by 1991, the BDA was no longer giving it any land.[108] The White Paper on the BDA in 1984 claimed that though 1268 sites were distributed to the poor under the 20 point programme in 1982, only *hakku patras* (letters of entitlement) without site numbers or layouts were given rather than proper possession certificates.[109] The BR Ambedkar Birthday Scheme for Scheduled Castes and Scheduled Tribes announced in December 1988 received 5145 applications but no sites had been allotted until 12 December 1995.[110] Many commented on the deplorable contribution of government agencies to the addition of housing stock for the poor or economically disadvantaged. The Karnataka Slum (Improvement and Clearance) Board built a mere 1908 houses in the city between 1976 and 1989; BDA constructed 5290 out of a planned 7296 homes until the 1990s; while KHB had since 1974 constructed about 15000 houses on the outskirts of the city and 5506 houses in Yelahanka.[111] These fell far short of the requirements of the poor. Solutions to this crisis were always envisaged as measures that would encourage private builders to play a part,[112] despite widespread acknowledgement of the many ways in which provisions to benefit the poor are circumvented.

The tank bed has always been the space to which new immigrants flocked, as they were areas considered undesirable at a certain stage in the city's development. The residents of Sampangi tank, many of whom were allowed to settle there when Vidhana Soudha was under construction, were evicted in the mid-1950s and relocated near another tank bed, the Byrasandra Tank Bed area and given small 20 by 30 sites for their use.[113] The Sampangi tank area became a stadium complex. The residents of Pit Colony in Malleswaram were relocated in Rajajinagar, with great fanfare, but such celebrated relocations have been few and far between, dwindling as the premium on space in the city has appreciated.[114] The residents of Miller's Tank were summarily evicted in the early 1970s and sent off to Bagalur slum: today Miller's Tank bed is a thriving piece of real estate.[115] Slums near Vidhana Soudha were cleared and the workers who had built the multi-storeyed buildings were relocated in the 1980s to Laggere.[116]

A more recent example of the balance of forces between the illegalities of the state and those of the urban poor arose during the construction of the National Games Complex and associated facilities. The eviction of 218 families from Ashoknagar slum adjoining the football stadium occurred on aesthetic grounds; the eviction of slum dwellers from Koramangala tank bed area, it was claimed, was done for the 'public purpose' of building 5000 flats. Despite stiff resistance, the eviction of the Ashoknagar slum dwellers was effected without too much delay or disruption. The slum, which had existed for 30 years, was notified for evacuation as early as 1991. Nothing actually happened until the National Games was scheduled to be held in Bangalore, and a contempt of court notice was issued on the slum dwellers for not having vacated the land as held in court. Between 15 and 20 May 1993, news of the eviction led to organized resistance in the form of dharnas, demonstrations, and occupations of the footpath, but had no effect.[117] The people were all shifted to Ullal, 20 km from the city, where basic services were non-existent (Fig. 39).[118]

Those evicted from the Koramangala area secured some compensation as a result of the legal action initiated by some citizen's groups, but they did not succeed in stalling the clearance and construction of the National Games Complex. The illegalities of the state, on the other hand, were difficult to challenge, and even more difficult to overturn. The government had directed the KHB to undertake the building of MIG and HIG housing to be sold at a profit after the games. This was in clear violation of the KHB mandate which required it to construct only low income, non-profit housing. The government

FIG. 39 *A contentious eviction: a thirty year old settlement adjoining the Football Stadium was demolished before the Fourth National Games, 1997.*
(The Printers Mysore, Private Limited, P. Samson Victor, 1997)

also violated the CDP by building in the green belt area.[119] The flats, meanwhile, continue to remain unsold, forcing the KHB to offer them to the public at lower than market rates.

Indeed, in the past few decades, the state has seriously defaulted on its commitment to the urban poor. A 1995 GO which insisted that builders give 25 per cent of their flats/sites to Economically Weaker Sections and the poor has been honoured only in the breach and proved unworkable.[120] The scheme was a 'non-starter' as the BDA 'have no way of really ensuring that [the builder] does it. He may show a plan with two small flats of one bedroom each, [but] when he actually constructs he will combine the two ... and sell it off ... Who can follow it up, who can police all this?'[121] Only rarely have the urban poor had recourse to the courts, and actually advanced their interests through long and tedious battles.[122] For the most part, the urban poor rely on the help of NGOs[123] and readily embrace the power of political parties in order to stake their claim to the city.[124]

The real dilemma of the urban poor, whether they are people who are fresh immigrants to the city or those who have been embraced by it, lies in the conflict between the way in which urban space is perceived among various classes. There are those whose decisions are driven by considerations of *use value* as opposed to those concerned about *the exchange value* of the site/ home. For the urban poor, the neighbourhood is a space of work, a node of sociality, as well as a place of dwelling, unlike the middle-class persons' more diversified spatial identity. The neighbourhood rarely fulfils all the needs of a middle-class resident, and is therefore ideologically zoned as exclusively residential. An open or unoccupied space may thus represent very different values to different social groups, and such differences are exaggerated at moments which bring these two notions of value into conflict.

The multiple and often ambiguous claims to property in the city are best illustrated in conflicts over the tank beds of the city. The tank's economic value as a water body or resource for agriculture has been entirely transformed by the development of the city. The Byrasandra Tank Bed area, as already mentioned above, is one to which over 1000 poor Tamil speaking and Muslim families were relocated beginning in the 1950s. Today, many residents value this open space for a number of reasons. For one, given the failure of the state to provide these residents with adequate sanitation facilities, it is used as an open air toilet, especially by women and children whose movements are often confined to the area. Secondly, bordering the squalid remains of a tank is a graveyard that is still in use marked by *mantapa*s and stones. Finally, the slum residents have demanded that a part of the area be developed as sites to meet the needs of the expanding slum population. These residents have therefore asserted customary rights to the tank bed area, and asked that the graveyard be certified by the municipality.[125] Although the high court stayed the allotment of sites in the tank bed area, nearly 38 sites were allotted by 1994 under the Ashraya scheme to people from elsewhere, in what might be an attempt to alter the ethnic profile of the area as well.

Other legal claims to the sprawling 15 acre tank bed include that of RBI Colony Welfare Association of Jayanagar Third Block which has secured an order against the filling up of the tank bed and any construction whatsoever.[126] They have claimed that the area must be kept open and free, divested of those who 'commit nuisance', while the 'disused' graveyard be recovered as open space for the residents of the colony 'in public interest'.[127] Meanwhile, H. Subrahmanyam, an individual, has claimed the place as his ancestral private property.[128] These three claimants in fact represent only two competing claims: those who claim the BTB area for its use value (the slum dwellers) and those who lay claim to its exchange value (the residents' association and private owner). Indeed, the value of the area has been estimated at Rs 30 crores.[129] In this contest between groups with unequal resources, it is not surprising that the slum dwellers were least likely to be heard. In 2000, the high court decided in favour of the RBI Colony Welfare association, and the area will finally become a park.[130] This example makes the normalizing function of the law much clearer, especially as it upholds and enhances the rights of middle-class apartment owners to a 'lung space', an environmental good which will enhance the economic value of their property.

In making the map correspond more closely to the territory, the formation of the Bangalore Metropolitan Task Force has been useful, particularly in reclaiming properties on behalf of BDA and BMP. In just three years between 1995–8, properties occupied by the poor, such as the footpath, the tank bed, small informal commercial and retailing bunks, and so on have faced the wreckers' ball.[131] In the 1999–2002 period, the BDA has been conspicuously reclaiming commercial properties on which encroachments have occurred.

If citizenship in its legal sense still eludes the urban poor, the legality of property ownership does not always confer the legitimacy of citizenship. Legal citizenship may be bound up with ethnicity, producing contradictory effects on the claims to space within the city. The production of abstract space, aided by the normalizing functions of the law, falters in its encounter with certain social identities which make spatial claims. Far from effacing (social) difference in its production of a property owning subject, the law could become the ground for claiming or denying ethnically specific property rights. This account of the legal production of space within the city concludes with a consideration of such an anomaly.

Ethnicity, Space, and the Uses of the Law

On 4 September 1982, the BDA was engaged in the demolition of a temporary thatched structure on a site marked for development as a children's park. This structure had been used by the Muslim community of Viveknagar for prayers. Large numbers of Muslims therefore gathered to protest the demolition, and in the violence that ensued, police opened fire, resulting in the death of Mohammed Abrar and injuries to four others.

In the course of an enquiry into this incident, the communal ramifications of this confrontation became clearer.[132] In July 1981, the Muslim Welfare Association of the area had applied to the BDA for permission to use the site for Ramzan prayers, but did not vacate it when the temporary permit expired. Instead, the association filed a suit (No 1042 of 1981) seeking to restrain the BDA from demolishing the structure, which was dismissed by the court. Meanwhile, other residents of the area filed a writ petition in which the BDA was asked to clear the site and desist from allotting it to anyone else.[133] In compliance with an interim order of the court, the BDA went ahead with demolition.

The confrontation between the police and the Muslims of the area was the culmination of a period of growing tensions between the Muslims and those who were variously identified in the inquiry commission report as 'Malayalis of Austin Town' or 'residents of Austin Town'. The Muslim Welfare Association laid claim to the area as Wakf property on the ground that the Wakf is also created by usage, 'even by prayer offered by one member of the Muslim public'. The commission decided that such a claim was invalid, and upheld the right of the BDA to demolish the structure. The Muslim Welfare Association linked up the local hostility to its occupation of the site to a wider history of hostility to Muslims in other parts of the city. The installation of an idol of Ganesha close to a dargah in Chamrajpet was cited as an attempt to incite communal violence.

The alacrity with which the BDA demolished the structure using police assistance was rarely matched in subsequent decades. As we have seen in the previous chapter, the cleavage between law and order has revealed itself most clearly in the reluctance of city authorities to remove religious structures from public properties. Commissioner of the BCC A. Ravindra was abruptly shifted from his post when he took steps to remove a Hindu shrine from a footpath in Jayanagar in 1997, even though there was a high court ruling on a PIL filed by Citizen's Action Group, Bangalore Environment Trust, CIVIC and Nagarik.[134]

The city has become an increasingly contentious territory to which rival religious and ethnic groups lay claim. The reluctance of the state to interfere with such claims has its uses for those challenging the rights of legitimate claimants. Communities of citizens-in-the-making, such as Muslims, who bear the burden of excessive identity, have been particularly vulnerable in such moments of crisis. The bitter struggle between a section of Muslim and other (largely Hindu) residents over the ownership of an Idgah maidan in Jayanagar demonstrates these strategies quite well. The persistent attempt to question the legal status of this site by city authorities have resulted in a dispute over property that had long been in the possession of the Basavangudi Muslims.

In 1935, the Muslims of Basavangudi were given a site of 5.35 acres by the Maharaja of Mysore in Byrasandra village for use as a burial ground. At this time, Jayanagar was not even a gleam in the planners' eye, but by 1970, when this edge of the city became the heart of a densely populated extension, burials were given up at the site.[135] Meanwhile, the site was declared Wakf property in 1965, and confirmed in a government order of 1976, after giving due allowance for the widening of the road adjoining a major bus depot in the area. The Basavangudi Masjid Committee, now in charge of the property, agreed to grant land for road expansion if it was given permission to build a community hall, a Madrassa and a commercial complex on the site.

Repeated efforts of the BCC to exploit the distinction between *possession* and *ownership* of the site and reclaim it as its own were struck down by the court. Moreover, a committee formed by the government in 1985 to suggest a solution to the wrangle between the corporation and the Basavangudi Masjid Committee recommended acquisition of a portion of the property for a fair market rate while granting permission to the Masjid Committee to build on its property in return for surrender of some land for the road.

When these instructions were ignored, Jayanagar Muslims built a mosque and regular prayers were begun on the site, which resulted in some friction between Basavangudi and Jayanagar Muslims. However, the main battles were still against the 'encroachments' of the BCC. When the Wakf Board obtained a stay against the attempts of the BCC to occupy a part of the disputed space, it was met with equal determination by the Jayanagar Nagarika Committee, a resident's association which declared its opposition to any building on the land. Though the high court confirmed possession of the land by the Masjid Committee and directed the BCC to file a suit in a civil court for a decision on ownership, the BCC chose not to act legally. Before long, a fresh attempt was made by the state government to resolve the issue when the commissioner of the Corporation was directed to issue the *khata* (and thus ownership rights) on the Wakf Board. In return, the Board would concede land for the road widening.

An uncleared pile of rubble soon became a bone of contention between the community of Muslims and the corporation. The long drawn out legal battle over the Idgah Maidan also resulted in an unexpected clash on 17 September 1997 between two groups of Muslims, one group fearing that the other group was entering into a secret deal with the corporation. The conflict erupted into a riot, in which four people, including a constable, lost their lives: of these, two people died in police firing.[136] Far from remaining a local affair, riots spread through areas in south Bangalore with large Muslim populations, such as Jayanagar, Tilaknagar, Bismillahnagar, and Gurappanapalya, and spread further afield to areas of Muslim concentration such as Madivala, Koramangala, MICO Layout, D.J. Halli, K.G. Halli, and Bharatinagar, as well as Goripalya.[137]

Not much progress was made on settling the question of ownership until 1999, when a road accident resulting in the death of a young woman near the bus stand led to a fresh demands for road widening using a portion of the contested land.

The road was widened under high security, and a strictly municipal crisis thus resolved a bitter dispute which had called the ownership of a religious site into question. In exchange, the Wakf Board received a *khata* in its name, and its ownership of the site was finally settled. Yet this has not cleared the air of communal tensions, with the Jayanagar Nagarika Samithi threatening further acts of violence over the grant of the *khata* by the government. The hyper-visibility of the Muslim resident thus makes the claim of legal citizenship recede from view.

Conclusion

Has the role of the BDA as a provisioner of sites and services become redundant at a time when the market has clearly taken the upper hand, increasing the percentage of homeownership from a mere 25 per cent in the early 1990s to over 60 per cent in under a decade? Successive committees had argued for limiting the BDA to its role as planner. However, the first few years of the new millennium have revived the visibility of the BDA as a public provisioner of housing, and indeed the ideal of a middle-class home on a site appears to have regained lost ground.

However, 'the housing question' says Manuel Castells, 'is above all that of its crisis'.[138] The radical gulf between demand and supply of this basic need is itself determined by the social conditions of production of this commodity, which is fuelled by speculation for profit, pure and simple. The identification of an undifferentiated shortage (see Table 4.2) is therefore misleading insofar as it suggests that the problem is one of simple demand and supply. If anything there is a paradox in the relation between a growing demand for, and excess supply of, housing. Private developers focus exclusively on the needs of the urban élite. As we have seen, the problems arising from an exploding urban population are insoluble by the operation of market forces alone, and indeed there is no known historical example of the private sector meeting the demand for 'social housing'. Many have, predictably, suggested a cap on the demand itself by restricting the flow of immigrants who 'lower the standards of the city'. If there is one point on which judicial, municipal–administrative and legislative discourses converge, it is in bringing a greater clarity to the role of the market, and in increasing the sovereignty of the market on the question of urbanizable land. The confidence with which land laws are transgressed depends on access to political power and successful legitimization of these transgressions. Thus developers, house building societies, corporations, and even slum dwellers are not averse to using this route to legalize their informal or illegal occupations of space. Transgressions of the law on such a scale speak of the nature of state power itself, which far from being absolute, shares space with a range of informal and illegal forces. Until the present time, therefore, the market determines without dominating, production of space in the city; the state on the other hand, dominates, without determining the legalities of urban space production. Nevertheless, the demand for a unified legal regime is growing, and the new economy's appetite for greenfield sites is being gradually met by legislative change and by the intensified use of agencies such as BMTF. But there are other spheres where the middle-class has been more assertive of its rights, as in the sphere of city aesthetics, and in the uses of public space. It is to this aspect of the city's public life that I now turn.

FIVE

Past Perfect: Architecture and Public Life

In the city ... the truth of industrial and commercial society had to be screened in the decent draperies of pre industrial artistic styles. Science and Law were modern truth but beauty came from history.

Carl Schorske, *Fin de Siecle Vienna*

When Bangalore came into its own as a regional capital in the years after Indian independence, the question of defining its new architectural profile was among the concerns of the new state leadership. Brimming with optimism about the potential of democracy, the new leadership could make choices ranging from a frank borrowing of the American style of public architecture, as a tribute to the model of democracy, or stage a return to the Indian past, the pre-colonial heritage, as it were. These decisions were, moreover, not merely about the authenticity of architectural styles, but about the forms of public life that such spatial arrangements could foster.

Architectural quotations from the past were the mark equally of styles that were forged in colonial and post-colonial societies, as history became a resource for defining new ideals of beauty. If the retreat into (classical European) history generously mixed in with the Indo–Saracenic was a striking feature of public architecture in colonial India,[1] an attempt to command a long and respectable lineage of authority equally marked the Indian nationalist response in the early post-Independence period. How better to proclaim a shift in power from a colonial regime to a nationalist government, to redraw the compact between the nation and its people, than in a recast public architecture? Yet the grammar of the evolving discourse on public architecture was 'past perfect', a marked nostalgia for the forms of the past which drew from or preserved styles of a bygone era as the most appropriate and authentic in a nation emerging from colonialism. The appeal to history for ideals of beauty, as Carl Schorske's observation bears out, was hardly novel. It is to the specific relationship between architecture and public life that this chapter turns, particularly as it defined the space of democracy and of a national–modern image that yearned to be authentically Indian.

In the city of Bangalore, a stretch of parkland called Cubbon Park, which lies between the old sixteenth century settlement and the cantonment established in the nineteenth century, became the location of many offices of state during the colonial period. Additions to this clutch of buildings have occurred since Independence, when the city became the capital of the expanded state of Karnataka in southern India.[2] Yet the array of monumental buildings on the edge of Cubbon Park, strung along Ambedkar (previously Vidhana) Veedhi in Bangalore lacks visual unity. The short corridor of the apparatuses of state power (the legislature, judiciary and administrative buildings) does not reveal any single ideological project (as does, for instance, the imperial construction of New Delhi).[3] The buildings instead exist as multiple signs of a post-independent aesthetic struggling to take shape. A markedly nationalist aesthetic (represented by the Vidhana Soudha or Legislative Building), has over time given way to an aesthetic founded on an ideal of beauty which nostalgically recalls the colonial period (i.e. the extension to the high court and the General Post Office buildings), and finally yields space to a starkly modern monumentalism (Visvesvaraya Towers). As such, there is no single notion of power or authority that is communicated in this strip, and there is no easy redrawing of a 'public space'.[4]

Such visual disarray, however, must not be mistaken for the indifference of state authorities to the redefinition of public life in the city. Rather, the deployment of specific aspects of the Karnataka past in mortar and stone is equally matched by the construction of the citizen–subject in specific ways, by attempting to define the meaning and content of public life in a democracy. In turn, the public space has been put to varied and sometimes unanticipated uses. In this sense, the structures and their forms must be read in conjunction with their changing uses, the flow and control of people becoming as crucial as the mass and volume of the buildings.[5] As Kevin Lynch suggests, 'Moving elements in the city, and in particular the people and their activities, are as important as the stationary physical parts'.[6] Far from being cast in stone as lonely 'texts of power', the motley collection of buildings in Bangalore has been defined by the shifting relationship between the state and its citizens, or more correctly between the intentions of the state and the citizen's desire for democracy. Through a discussion of the design and social life of Vidhana Veedhi and of Cubbon Park in various historical phases, I hope to reflect on contemporary Indian urban culture, in particular on those aspects that relate to the aesthetic practices and definitions of public space and democracy in the post-Independence period. I realize that the term 'public' cannot be used lightly in the Indian context. Sudipta Kaviraj has drawn attention to the meanings of the term 'public' (and even 'private') in Indian, as opposed to Western European, discourse, in his discussion of how these conceptual categories mapped on to a distinctly different and deeply segmented social domain.[7] This chapter will take forward the effort to specify the meanings of the term while defining a rather different trajectory from the one he has outlined for Calcutta, where, he argues, there have been increasingly plebeian uses of public space over the years.

To a large extent, the public architecture of Ambedkar Veedhi recalls the past in decidedly nostalgic ways. Nostalgia as a structure of feeling about the present harks back to an idyllic, imagined historical past. Fundamentally, it is associated with alienation from the present, a longing for the stability and order of a mythicized past to cope with the alienating effects of contemporary democracy. Less often, nostalgia as a structure of feeling seeks continuity with another organic, social order as a way of redressing the inequities of the present. Nostalgia is marked by the persistent illusion that the past was more just or humane than the present.[8]

However, as Raymond Williams points out, 'The structure of feeling [nostalgia] within which this backward reference is to be understood is then not primarily a matter of historical explanation and analysis. What is really significant is this particular kind of reaction to the fact of change and this has more real and more interesting social causes.'[9] What interests or anxieties concerning developments in Bangalore since the 1950s have led to a singling out of architectural motifs from the past in the structuring of the central administrative space of the city? What are the uses of nostalgia in imagining this space? Also, how successfully does an architecture which is free of such nostalgia, namely Visvesvaraya Towers, recast the relationship between the rulers and the ruled, the meaning and content of democratic authority? Finally, what are the kinds of contests over the public space that reflect a recast field of forces in the city? In particular, I discuss the debate around the design and construction of Vidhana Soudha, the extension of the high court and General Post Office (GPO) and Visvesvaraya Towers, within the broader context of debates over the control and use of Cubbon Park itself.

Nostalgia and Monarchical Modes of Power

A keen need for a new and more permanent legislative assembly and council building for Mysore was felt on the eve of the first Indian elections in 1951 (Fig. 40). What were the sentiments that such a structure would communicate to the newly independent Mysore public? 'Power of rule now vests with the people and therefore the design of the House of legislature should be such as to convey this idea of power and dignity, the style being Indian, particularly of Mysore and not purely Western.'[10] These were Mysore Chief Minister Kengal Hanumanthaiya's instructions to a committee he set up in 1952 to design afresh the proposed house of legislature. In 1951, Prime Minister Jawaharlal Nehru had laid the foundation stone for a more modest structure at Bangalore, when K.C. Reddy was the chief minister. Yet the Vidhana Soudha, the legislature

FIG. 40 *Inauguration of the Mysore Assembly at the Town Hall, by Governor of Mysore Jayachamaraja Wodeyar. Also seen in this photograph from left are G.S. Venkataraman Iyer, (Secretary, Legislature), K.T. Bhashyam (Chairman, Legislative Council) and H. Siddaiah (Speaker of Legislative Assembly).*
(T.L. Ramaswamy, 1953)

cum administrative office building that has come to dominate both the Bangalore skyline and the Karnataka imagination, reaches back to a very particular historical legacy in order to claim an authenticity and an authority that was markedly different from the symbols of colonial power. It sought this authenticity by quoting from the magnificent stone edifices of a distinctly Hindu past, recklessly selecting motifs from a range of dynastic styles, from the Chalukya (sixth to twelfth centuries) or Hoysala (twelfth to fourteenth centuries) periods to the Vijayanagara Empire (fourteenth to sixteenth centuries).

Hanumanthaiya was Congress president when plans for the new structure were made in 1951. He expressed his displeasure over the proposed structure that followed 'the plain and simple type of American architecture'. Therefore, when he won the election and assumed the chief minister's office in 1952, he lost no time in revising the more modest plans to produce 'a work of art in keeping with the tradition of Mysore State'.[11] The earlier plans, which were estimated to cost Rs 33 lakh, were for a modest two-storeyed structure which would permanently accommodate the expanded legislature and council following the 1951 elections.[12] Hanumanthaiya's grandiose structure, which was to include the government offices, archives, library complex, and banquet hall, cost the state exchequer a massive Rs 180 lakh when it was completed in 1956.

It was an experience of colonialism as humiliation, rather than as oppression[13] that marked the new aesthetic of public architecture in Karnataka (then Mysore) in its early phases.[14] Several writers have asserted that Hanumanthaiya felt as his own the humiliation of M.K. Gandhi when Winston Churchill disparagingly referred to him as a 'half naked fakir' who climbed the viceregal steps at Delhi to meet Lord Irwin in 1930. Hanumanthaiya had long resolved to build an even grander flight of steps worthy of Gandhi's memory, and thus undo the humiliation.[15] Hanumanthaiya's insistence on a Dravidian style and his nostalgia for the Hindu monarchical order may seem at variance with his oral instructions to the committee:

> ... the new building should be the biggest and the most beautiful in the Mysore State and even if the cost went up to 30 or 40 lakhs of rupees it would not matter provided their [the members'] intentions and purposes were fulfilled. All the members should pay particular attention and assist in evolving a suitable plan for the building which would stand as a beautiful stately structure and be a permanent building for all time to come.

Then, almost anticipating his critics, Hanumanthaiya continued:

> Sovereignty has been shifted from the palace to the legislature and it was therefore imperative that the building should depict this transfer of power and reflect the power and dignity of the people. That should be the main characteristic of the building.[16]

By this act, the newly constituted state hoped to culturally reconnect with a princely Mysore social order that was rudely interrupted by colonialism. Other pre-colonial Mysore legacies were resolutely ignored in this choice of building styles: the grandeur of the Islamic architecture of the Bijapur sultans, or even the buildings of Tipu Sultan's time, for instance, was passed over in favour of a specifically Hindu past.[17] Vidhana Soudha, therefore, evoked an earlier social order of a very specific kind, namely the majesty and awe of the Hindu princely state, although this time buttressed by the sovereign power of the electorate.[18] This reassertion of a monarchical style envisaged the public space around it as subservient to the structure, a space from which the people could pay homage to authority, instead of becoming a site of collective civic action.[19]

Yet Hanumanthaiya was unblinking in his repeated assertion that his intention was not to recreate the ambience of a palace.[20] Rather, as he told Ba Na Sundara Rao who asked why he simply did not recreate the Amba Vilas Palace of Mysore in Bangalore, the Vidhana Soudha 'must be a place which people can enter fearlessly', a people's palace as distinct from the exclusive royal enclosure.[21] The simpler plans made by the K.C. Reddy government were nevertheless rejected in 1952 in favour of a far more lavish and elaborately embellished legislature cum government department complex. This, despite the suggestion from the government architect B. Manickam, while submitting a fresh design: 'On the whole, the elevation is almost Dravidian in characteristics with the absence of carvings by a sculptor, who is no more required to either tell the story or define the function.'[22] In other words, the sculptor had no narrative function in a structure which was designed for the exercise of democratic power and not to overawe or impress a subject population.

Also ignored were suggestions that the location of the Vidhana Soudha be further to the north of its present location, which would have saved lakhs of rupees in levelling the natural incline.[23] With an urgency prompted by the briefness of his authority, as the uncertainties of parliamentary politics and imminent reunification of the Mysore state would soon put him out of office, Hanumanthaiya decided against open competition for the design. The resulting structure wore the 'illusion of permanence' and served to dazzle the people, as much as it stood, measure for measure, in triumph over the colonial Attara Kacheri (the former government offices, and the building which today houses the high court). By this, Hanumanthaiya also produced the illusion of overarching unity within an emerging system of fractious Congress party politics.[24]

The Vidhana Soudha, which houses the legislative assembly and council, the legislature library, the secretariat offices, state archives, the banquet hall, and most of the ministerial chambers and offices, measures 700 feet north–south and 350 east–west, with two inner open quadrangles measuring 250 by 230 ft. It is the largest legislature cum office complex in India. The northern wing consists of a ground floor and three upper floors, while the southern wing also includes a basement. The auspiciously east-facing front elevation combines with a central dome to make a height of 175 feet. It, therefore, soars above the Pompeiian red Attara Kacheri, and dwarfs it in the sheer scale of ornamentation, while its twelve pillars above the grand flight of steps which lead to the legislature match the number of the Attara Kacheri. The main structure is of granite, with selected use of red porphyry for decorative work.

The entire architecture of the building combines richly ornamented bases and capitals for pillars, deep friezes, cornices, arches, heavy pediments, ornamental ceilings, teakwood panelling, sandalwood doors, and the like with modern structural materials such as reinforced cement concrete, glass, and plastic. Built at the dawn of the Nehruvian political order, such scandalous indulgence was just cause for censure of a democratically elected chief minister who had grossly abused his power. A three-person committee, headed by retired Nagpur High Court judge P.P. Deo, was appointed by the Kadidal Manjappa government in July 1956 to look into allegations of an extravagant squandering of state finances on Vidhana Soudha. The committee was also asked to effect some economies in the ongoing construction. In a way, the indictment of the chief minister was already foretold: a head of government who dared to ignore architectural and administrative norms, squandered governmental funds with impunity, and personally supervised the building on a day to day basis, was far too preoccupied with the image of the new state to escape censure.

Most objectionable of all was Hanumanthaiya's singular obsession with the embellishment of the legislative assembly building, through excessive borrowings from the iconography of a monarchical Hindu past. In his discussion of Indian architecture, Romi Khosla suggests that the basis of Indian aesthetics is iconographical, resulting in a saturated visual field as evident in many aspects of everyday life in India.[25] Yet Khosla remains alert as an architect to the dangers of simply lifting elements from the past: 'architecture is not a structural form modified by the application of iconography. On the contrary, it is iconographic form made out of structure ....'[26] In his choices, however, the Mysore chief minister was guided by frankly revivalist intentions, and remained largely unmindful of the eclecticism of his choices. He chose to ignore the norms established by the committee he himself had appointed, providing day to day instructions on what was to be added or altered as the construction wore on. Indeed 'The Chief Minister constituted himself the final authority in the matter of architectural features', claimed the Deo Enquiry Committee. A sample of his instructions regarding special architectural features bears this out:

26 September 1954: The design of the pillars in the Palace, Amba Vilas Hall [in Mysore] together with the details of decorations made on the arch joining two pillars may be adopted with suitable modifications for the pillars in the Dining Hall.

5/7 October 1955: The Kotethene [merlon as on top of a fort] on the south side being too plain carving may be done in the same manner as is done in the Subrahmanya Swamy temple.

9 November 1955: The circular pillars at the entrance of the Dining Hall which are slender may be finished with step design as has been done at the Mysore Palace

30 November 1955: The entrance into the Council Hall may be provided with ornamental wooden doors sufficiently wide and high, of the type of the temple Mahadwara.[27]

Drawn from further afield were the audience balconies or *jharoka*s recalling Rajasthani fort palaces, 'purely decorative', but nevertheless unmistakably feudal in appearance. Nor were all the embellishments drawn from the temple/palace complex: sometimes the grandeur evoked secular, though equally imposing structures. Thus, the northern portico was amended to look like the gateway entrance to Krishnarajasagar dam.[28] In other cases, the monarchical flourish was adapted from a more mediated image of popular culture: 'the capitals as provided in the Drama scenes of Lakshmi Theatre [in Bangalore]', Hanumanthaiya instructed, 'may be copied for circular pillars in the western vestibule'.[29]

Hanumanthaiaya did hope to communicate the pride and importance of nation building in a structure such as Vidhana Soudha, despite its nostalgic evocation of the monarchical past. It was to serve as a memory of the nationalist struggle while communicating certain imperatives to the citizens of a newly independent state. Thus he ordered:

31 January, 1956: The saying 'Government work is God's Work' may be carved with large size letters on the entemblature [sic] slab over the eastern entrance over the grand staircase. The same may be fixed with neon lights also in order that the same could be read during nights.[30]

In addition to portrayals of the Congress volunteers marching with their flags, were scenes celebrating the work of a new nation struggling to take shape. His vision of the new Mysore state, as indicated in his order for 208 paintings (most of which were later cancelled in the interests of economy) included pictorial representations of the legislative assembly at Jagan Mohan Palace, the famous parts of Mysore, 'Scenic beauties', Irrigation, and Hydroelectric plants, men at work and women in native costumes. There was an inescapable gendering of these representations so that while the worker/citizen was male, the woman embodied the (diversity of the) Kannada nation:

21 May 1956: Replacing the painting originally proposed for the Assembly Hall panels by one plough, man with plough and bullocks, and another industrial scene may be examined as they represent main subjects of national development. Garments worn by women in different parts of Mysore State vary in custom and fashions: good photos of the same may be obtained and represented by painting.[31]

The chief minister's assumption of the role of builder–statesman was severely constrained by threats to his tenure and it is possible that the deployment of prison labour, the introduction of night work, and departmental execution of all work were all choices dictated by these circumstances. Even while under such pressure, Hanumanthaiya took care to commission a record of the construction, whether in photographs, paintings, or film.[32] Although he was never destined to set foot in the Vidhana Soudha as chief minister, Hanumanthaiya, in the style of a potentate builder, commissioned this record with an eye on the future. He has himself been photographed beforethis magnificent edifice, looking off the camera into the distance, in the style of a Nehruvian 'visionary' (Fig. 41). Also, as we shall see, the critical comments of his contemporaries did little to diminish Hanumanthaiya's place as a builder of an enduring image for the city as well as the state, and only added to the admiration with which he has been remembered in several historical accounts.

Censure and Democratic Recovery

In his quest for a refashioned idiom of power, Hanumanthaiya overruled pragmatic architectural advice. Chief Architect Manickam claimed before the Deo Committee that although he had argued that 'architecture should be suitable to the functions of the Houses of Legislature and should not look like a temple', the chief minister overruled him.[33] Striking down the decision of the committee to omit domes on top of the structure, four side domes and a central dome were added. Hanumanthaiya flouted emerging conventions of architectural practice and ignored the weight of public opinion. Thus, B.V. Narayana Reddy, general manager of Bank of Mysore, protested before the Deo Committee 'This heavy expenditure on ornamentation of the building

FIG. 41 *The Nehruvian style for the 'architect' and the medieval Karnataka style for the building: Kengal Hanumanthaiya poses before the Vidhana Soudha.*
(From T.P. Issar, *The City Beautiful*, 1956)

is a criminal waste of money and besides is quite out of place in an office'. Finally, Hanumanthaiya also violated emerging canons of good taste among the community of architects: *The Indian Builder* minced no words in its criticism of the structure.[34]

The Deo Committee's findings of 'extravagant expenditure, avoidable waste, questionable transactions, inefficient execution, unsatisfactory statement of accounts, indifferent supervision, constant interference of the Chief Minister' and so on, were the words of a self-righteous citizenry functioning as watchdog.[35] The committee pointed out that neither Bombay nor Madras had such ostentatious legislature buildings, and tried to establish that funds for developmental projects (irrigation) had been diverted for the building.[36] The big gap between an earlier estimate of Rs 50 lakh, and the revised estimate of Rs 130 lakh (itself lower than the final figures of over Rs 180 lakh) was accounted for in part by architectural features and embellishments costing Rs 46 lakh. The enquiry committee deduced that although Kengal Hanumanthaiya disclaimed all intentions of making a palace, he was driven primarily by his desire to visually vanquish the Attara Kacheri building, a symbol of imperial power, in length, height, and majesty.[37]

These indictments came too late to stall the building itself, which was more or less complete, and left little room for the exercise of economy.[38] As such, the committee's stern tones could only serve as a warning to future governments. 'It is not necessary to impress on the people *their own sovereignty* with such display of wealth (emphasis added)', the committee concluded, explaining that 'ostentatious architecture and embellishments reminiscent of the Princely order' were a flagrant defiance of democratic ideals which should be 'dignified and austere'.[39]

Hanumanthaiya defended his decisions by claiming in response to the question 'how was the transfer of power from Palace to Legislature to be depicted in this Building?':

> The size, the architecture and the beauty of the Building. Buildings have their own characteristics and convey ideas to the onlooker. Buildings have their individuality. I remember the debates that used to take place in the old Central Legislative Assembly at Delhi. Leaders like Shri Motilal Nehru, Shri Malaviya and others ... used to say that the Parliament building must be more prominent than the secretariat building.[40]

This appreciation of symbolic power and authority, as embodied in stone, was not shared by his critics in the legislature who included the outspoken socialist Gopala Gowda. Gowda deplored the idea of Vidhana Soudha as a spectacle for the masses, even if it was a 'people's palace'. The ostentatious sentiments

MAP 10 *Cubbon Park and its Environs*

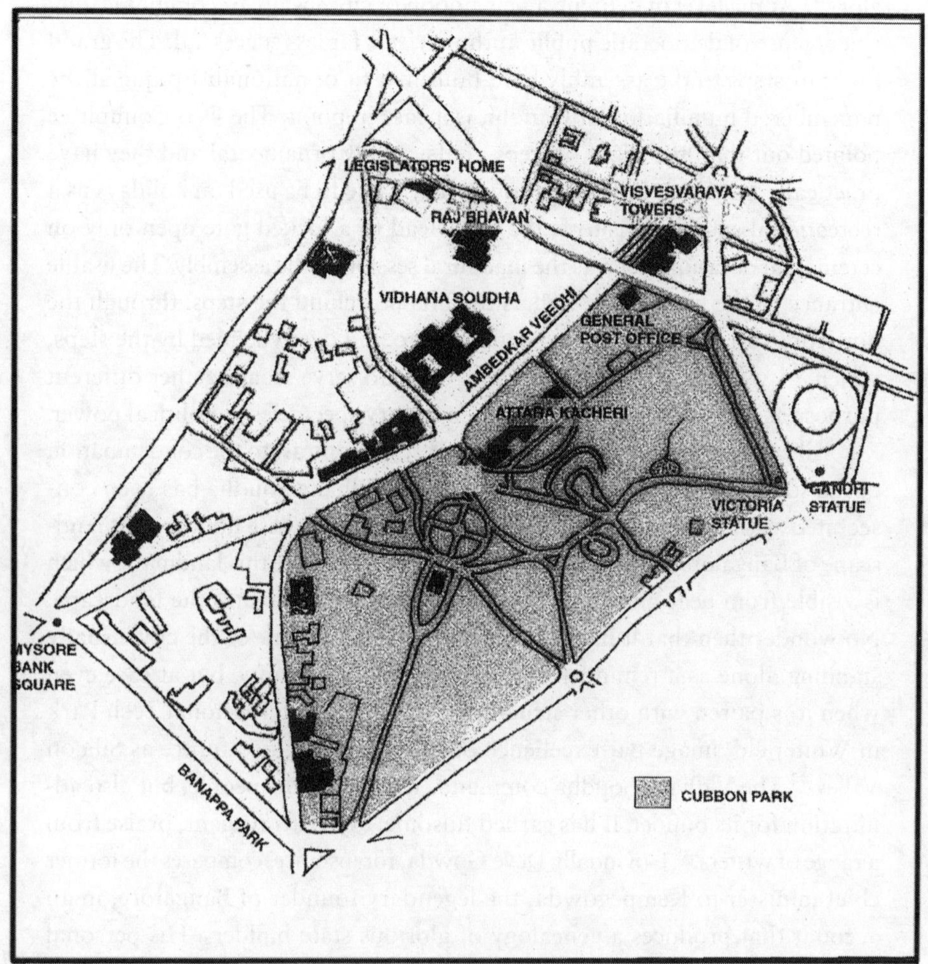

inscribed above the eastern entrance ('Government Work is God's Work') were condemned as a mocking travesty of democratic justice, as the work of government did not usually get done even with a bribe. The architectural majesty of a princely order were entirely inappropriate in the time of democracy.[41]

Still, history appears to have avenged Hanumanthaiya's stress on the importance of symbols of power and authority. Indeed, we might go so far as to say, if such structures at all play a role in communicating national independence, it is primarily at the level of the symbolic. Vidhana Soudha successfully functions as a distilled essence of Kannada pride, an eclectic mix of elements from all over the state: even the domes have been reinterpreted as referring to the classical Islamic heritage, long neglected in narratives of Karnataka glory.[42] At the level of defining a new notion of citizenship, or communicating a new sense of democratic public authority, it is far less successful. The grand flight of steps to the assembly hall, built in a fit of nationalist pique at the remembered humiliation of Gandhi, is a case in point. The Deo Committee pointed out that 'the flight of steps are [sic] only ornamental and they have practically no use'.[43] Indeed, although they came to be used on holidays as a recreational space by visitors, the steps lead to a locked gate open only on ceremonial occasions such as the inaugural session of the assembly. The usable entrance to the building as well as the lifts lie behind the steps, through the portico: as an entrance, it is subordinated to and overwhelmed by the steps, which, as we shall see, have gradually come to serve an altogether different purpose as a space for launching contemporary spectacles of political power.

All criticisms notwithstanding, and in stark contrast to the condemnation of the structure as an example of bad taste, Vidhana Soudha has been consecrated as the most important landmark in the otherwise nondescript landscape of Bangalore. It is difficult to imagine a time before this landmark which is visible from near and far, by day or night, and dominates the landscape. No wonder then that it has become the prime landmark of the city, usually standing alone as a reminder of historical princely beauty, but at ease even when it is paired with other structures such as the International Tech Park in Whitefield, image par excellence of the city's imagined future as Silicon Valley.[44] The Vidhana Soudha commands the awe of the people, but also admiration for its builder. It has earned fulsome, even extravagant, praise from a range of writers.[45] Govindally Deve Gowda, for instance, compares the former chief minister to Kempegowda, the legendary founder of Bangalore, in an account that produces a genealogy of glorious state builders. His personal supervision of the edifice is praised, rather than reviled as 'interference', while the words enshrined at the main entrance ('Government work is God's Work') are seen as setting an exemplary ideal for a new work culture.[46] Most important, popular accounts of Hanumanthaiya and his achievements uphold without contest the relationship that casts people as *subjects* rather than *citizens* of a new nation state. More recent developments which have resulted in the gradually restrictive and rather ritualized uses of public space around Vidhana Soudha appear to confirm the fear of plebeian democracy that has developed among the ruling classes in the immediate post-Independence decades. The historical uses of the Cubbon Park area as a whole and its centrality to the civic culture of the city have been transformed by the fears that haunt the elected representatives and the middle-classes alike: an increasing fear of plebeian democracy. A discussion of this transformation goes beyond monumental architecture to the making and meaning of public space in this central administrative area.

Democracy and the Uses of Public Space

Throughout the period of the freedom struggle in Bangalore, the areas around Cubbon Park, which properly belonged to the city municipality, were those from which rallies and demonstrations were launched. Shankarappa Banappa Park to the north east of the old city area bordering the south-western edge of Cubbon Park was frequently used by Congress workers and unionists alike from the 1930s.[47] Another favoured meeting place of the nationalists was Tulsi Thota (today called Chik Lal Bagh) which bordered the old city area, in the neighbourhood of the Congress office at Cottonpet. Mysore Bank Square, to which several major roads of the city debouched, was the site of both peaceful demonstrations and pitched battles as we have seen in Chapter 1.

After the unification of the two parts of the city in 1949, namely the western old city area and the cantonment to the east, Mysore Bank Square became a popular node from which a variety of struggles were launched. In 1956, the newly unified state of Mysore included vastly extended areas, from Hyderabad and Bombay Karnatakas to the north, as well as Coorg and parts of Madras Presidency. The establishment of the Ambedkar Veedhi in front of Vidhana Soudha that very year provided a new route through which groups of workers, peasants, students, and others coursed, sometimes to squarely confront their elected representatives within the imposing building. Since the late 1960s, discontented groups, whether from within or outside Bangalore, had developed a more direct and entrenched mode of address to the state legislature from a corner of Cubbon Park that faced the main (eastern) entrance of Vidhana Soudha. Right through the sixties, seventies, and the early eighties, many memorable struggles, such as the anti price-rise stir,[48] the Non-Gazetted Officers' (NGO) Forum strike of 1965,[49] the struggle against water tax in 1966,[50] the Public Sector Strike of 1981,[51] the farmer's *jatha* (march) during the agitations in Nargund–Navalgund,[52] and rallies of the Dalit Sangarsh Samiti, to name a few, converged on this strategic corner opposite the state legislature. Other annual events, such as the May Day rallies of the late 1970s and 1980s, laid claim to the park itself. Also, in 1979, Karnataka Dalits urged the government to rename Ambedkar Veedhi after the great architect of the constitution, B.R.

Ambedkar.[53] In addition to all this, the park has remained a popular haunt of unemployed youth, while providing a hospitable resting ground for workers from many government offices and courts bordering the park.

These plebeian rights to the park and its environs have, however, been gradually eroded through the late 1980s and in the 1990s on a variety of aesthetic and environmental grounds, with the clamour over the environment reaching its peak in the late 1990s. The call for 'beauty by banning' was frequently made after the late 1970s, when the Bangalore Urban Arts Commission (BUAC) was set up.[54] The middle-class citizenry focussed its ire on organized political movements and their use of the park. Since at least the early 1980s, there has been noticeable reluctance to give police permission for meetings in the park. During the memorable public sector strike of 1981, workers' marches were routed from Shivajinagar Stadium to Silver Jubilee Park, possibly as the stadium made surveillance easier and kept workers away from the more central Vidhana Soudha area (Fig. 42).[55] The campaign to 'Bring Back Beauty to Bangalore' made a further assault on those who lacked the power and the resources to resist involuntary dislocation. Those who had toiled to build these central administrative structures were regarded as a blot on the landscape: in the early 1980s three hundred families of construction workers near Vidhana Soudha were therefore evacuated to Laggere on the western edge of the city.[56]

By far the most forceful plea to ban rallies and demonstrations in Cubbon

FIG. 42 *Rally by workers of Bharat Electronics Limited, on Ambedkar Veedhi during the Public Sector Strike of 1981.*
(T.L. Ramaswamy, 1981)

Park was made by the committee to beautify Bangalore. Set up in 1993 to formulate 'a time bound plan for restoring the beauty of Bangalore and removing the numerous hazards which are looming large and threatening the deservedly admired ambience of the city', the committee called for the 'banning of public rallies and political or labour demonstrations in public parks'.[57] An example of the more objectionable uses of the park, in this account, were the gatherings at the corner near the high court, called Gopala Gowda Vritta after the socialist leader and member of the legislature. The report cited a 1993 rally by farmers who 'ran all over the place and destroyed the greenery within a few hours' as an example of reckless unconcern for the environment, and argued that there would 'be no denial of freedom of expression if such misuse of park areas is prevented'.[58] There were other proposals as well, all of which were intended to curtail or make more manageable the use of the park. There was one to introduce an entrance fee to discourage vandals,[59] and another to design 'aesthetically pleasing railings and barricades where necessary'.[60]

In 1995, the high court admitted a public interest writ petition filed by N.H. Desai against debris from construction in the park and directed the government to ban rallies. In 1997, regular middle-class users of the park successfully secured a ban on public rallies in the park.[61] The familiar corner at which hunger strikes, protests and *dharna*s were held was sealed off, and protestors were forced to seek other locations which did not have such direct access to the legislature. These included areas on the periphery of the park, such as the space opposite Visvesvaraya statue, the park before the Gandhi statue on Mahatma Gandhi Road, and, more recently, the area around Queen Victoria's statue at the junction of Kasturba Gandhi and Mahatma Gandhi Road. Meanwhile, now that the uses of Cubbon Park are more firmly individual rather than collective, and a certain kind of privatizing of the park is under way, some officials have found it possible to imagine more restrained and dignified forms of protest by responsible citizens. Thus, the secretary of the Department of Environment in 1997 proposed a Hyde Park, a 'speakers' corner' reserved only for 'green speakers': the idea was warmly welcomed by Hotel Windsor Manor which agreed to serve tea on such occasions.

Although no such speakers' corner has been established, the agitation to 'save and protect Cubbon Park' in September and October 1998 was a significant sign of the success with which the changed uses of the park were firmly anchored in the new confidence of the city bourgeoisie.[62] Conducted in full public view in the area just below the Queen Victoria's statue, which has been refurbished and maintained by the prominent Bombay builders, Raheja's, the protest had its back to the apparatuses of the state, thereby preferring to address the media and perhaps a section of the commuters at the fairly major intersection. This restrained and largely silent action by a large number of middle-class protestors was organized in relays and was so highly publicized that most newspapers began a regular column to track its progress for nearly two months. A middle-class whose enjoyment of this public facility had been diminished by the more plebeian democratic occupations of the 1970s and 1980s, thus publicly staked fresh claim to the park, though largely on grounds of concern for the environment.

Clearly, the process of plebeianization that Sudipta Kaviraj outlines for most post-colonial societies has had a different trajectory in places like Bangalore, where changes have neither been unilinear nor uniform. If anything, the success and visibility of the middle-class in re-establishing its claims to the park, and the involvement of the corporate sector in sponsoring such efforts, comes at a time when the city government itself increasingly seeks the latter's partnership in running the city. An older social order placed Cubbon Park and its surroundings well within the control of the middle-class; though it was gradually transformed by the everyday occupations of the lower classes, the park has once more reverted to being a place of leisure. The latest stage has been ensured by a mixture of legal controls and physical barriers. Robert Sommer's words are worth recalling in this context: 'the deterioration of dominance

FIG. 43 *An increasingly restricted space: Cubbon Park with newly installed gates, which are locked at fixed times of the day to prevent drive through traffic.*
(G. Raghav, 1999)

relationships within a social system leads to a greater reliance on territorial rights. A society compensates for blurred social distinctions by clear spatial ones—physical barriers, keep out signs and property restrictions'.[63] By 1998, this public utility had been more or less 'privatized' or made an 'elite space'[64] with the installation of chain link fences and large gates which, though 'aesthetically pleasing', kept all except the jogger or walker from the use of the park at certain hours.[65] Not only have rallies been banned, points of access to or entry into the park have been drastically reduced (Fig. 43).

Meanwhile, the eastern lawns of Vidhana Soudha have also seen occupation of another kind: statues of national heroes have been installed on these lawns. The one of B.R. Ambedkar was unveiled with great fanfare in 1981 by the then chief minister Gundu Rao.[66] Ambedkar was soon joined by the quintessential national hero, Jawaharlal Nehru. This pantheon of national heroes has most recently been expanded to include Subhas Chandra Bose. In an interesting semiotic distinction between the nation and the region, Karnataka heroes such as former Chief Ministers Kengal Hanumanthaiya and Devaraj Urs have been assigned to the western lawns.

Statues rarely stand out in a city like Bangalore since the visual field is already saturated with signs and advertisements and obscured by an extensive tree cover. Statues, therefore, serve more as a symbolic means of rallying specific political identities. In turn, the skilful deployment of the semiotics of statuary and road renaming fulfils the need of successive political regimes to simultaneously possess and disavow the heroes of different constituencies. Such active social movements as those of the Dalits have thus been accommodated in this public realm. There are however also gestures towards other histories: the circle near the high court, named after Gopala Gowda who was involved in the memorable Kagodu Satyagraha of 1950–1, is a symbolic recognition of Karnataka's radical past,[67] though the new restrictions on public life seal the place from all but the rush of traffic.

Restrictions on the uses of these public spaces around Vidhana Soudha were accompanied by another significant trend in the mid-1980s. The imposing façade of Vidhana Soudha was increasingly put to a new use by which the elected representatives, usually the Chief Minister, addresses the masses as 'spectators'. In a mode that mimicked the royal darshan, Chief Minister Hegde was sworn in on the steps of the Vidhana Soudha before a crowd of admirers in 1985. Since then, it has remained the preferred location for the swearing in, displacing Raj Bhavan (or governor's residence) which had hitherto served as the place for such ceremony. This decision to relocate the swearing-in to a more public place, especially one which had as its backdrop

FIG. 44 *Chief Minister S. Bangarappa launches a rally from the steps of the Vidhana Soudha, whose lawns are filled with supporters and cut outs of party leaders.* (*The Hindu*, Chennai, T.A. Hafeez, 1992)

the prime symbol of post-colonial Karnataka, allowed large numbers of political supporters to declare their loyalties to their elected leader. It was Chief Minister Bangarappa, (1991–3) who took these monarchical gestures to new heights when he launched campaigns from the steps of Vidhana Soudha, replete with larger than life cut-outs that proclaimed his closeness, even gratitude, to the party high command (Fig. 44).

The ritualized use of the steps of Vidhana Soudha apart, the gates installed at the entrances to Cubbon Park and other legal restrictions speak of the middle-class citizenry's success in preserving this area from the uncertainties of plebeian democracy. The fencing of an area that once was open parkland amounts to a privatization of a public space that bestows 'user rights' on the individual pleasures of joggers, walkers, or those on a family picnic. This 'ownership of rights' over a public space replaces all public collective uses with strictly privatized ones, and represents a triumph of the discourse on the environment. In such discourse, the environment is defined as a general public good, indiscriminately benefiting rich and poor alike. The recurrent emphasis on the environment and the need for its protection in the city is, as Manuel Castells points out, a specific ideological construction that posits human society as eternal and undifferentiated, technological progress as a 'blind and ineluctable force', and nature as a set of resources existing prior to human intervention.[68] In the context of Bangalore, however, the environmental concern is a re-articulation of the 'ideologies of beauty' that have long been tied to every discussion of city development. Indeed, though many other cities in post-independence India may assert the image of a 'clean and green city', Bangalore has throughout the twentieth century been promoted as a uniquely greened and planned space. This notion of beauty combines natural elements such as tree cover with the ambience of the low rise, generously spaced colonial bungalow as the defining elements of a new aesthetic, an aesthetic of conservation, as it were. An aesthetic which places an overwhelming stress on beauty in its sternly conservationist sense predictably comes into conflict with other notions of what an authentic post-Independence aesthetic should be. The former notion, therefore, has been contested and even largely ignored by the interests that actually shape the aesthetics of the city skyline whether by design or default. The ideology of beauty, nevertheless, enjoys high visibility in the discourse on the city's aesthetics, even if it has been overwhelmed by the logic of the real estate market.

The Ideology of Beauty in City Development

For a long time, planners and senior citizens alike have been committed to an ideology of city beauty, marked by a nostalgic longing for a time of fewer people and, therefore, much less pressure on the resources of the city. Too frequently, it is not redevelopment, or even reconstruction, but beauty that is emphasized in the writings of those concerned about the festering slums of the city. The reference to Bangalore as a 'Garden City' rarely refers to the substantial part of the city that was given over to the cultivation of fruits, flowers, and vegetables right up to the 1960s, even in such areas as Jayachamarajendra Road. Instead, 'Garden City' has come to refer to the compounds and gardens in which the private residence or the public building was set.[69] Yet I believe it is possible to speak of the 'Garden City' as a metaphor that emphasizes the long history of simultaneous displacement and containment of communities old and new. Market gardens and agriculture accounted for over 10 per cent of the land even in the 1960s but were increazingly annexed as real estate as the city expanded (See Table 3.1). Combined with tanks which dotted the city, this rich mix of farms, vineyards, and housing gave Bangalore its special character.[70] The tank's own career in the history of the city has gone from valuable resource (in productive terms) to least desirable land in the city (marshy areas settled with slums) to prime real estate in contemporary Bangalore. All these uses compete with the ideology of beauty, which is today signified by the semantic shift from 'tank' to 'lake', indicating the transformation of a water body from being a working entity to an aspect of the picturesque landscape. Since the late 1980s, the call for the revival of city beauty has included a forceful plea to retain tanks as leisure spots, even as the entire economy of market farming has been thoroughly recast.[71]

At least since the dewanship of Mirza Ismail (1926–42), beauty (signified by tree cover, landscaped gardens, and large circle gardens) has been consecrated as a city planning ideal that must be pursued even if it is at odds with contemporary life. Thus, Jawaharlal Nehru, addressing the members of Bangalore Municipal Corporation in 1962 described Bangalore as the city of the future, particularly as it did not carry the burden of history as did the Presidency cities:

> Most of the cities of India remind one certainly of the present, certainly of the future, but essentially of the past. But Bangalore, as I said, more than any other great cities of India, is a picture of India of the future, more specifically because of the concentration of science, technology and industries in the public sector here ... Most of the old cities represent ... history whereas your great city represents the future we are moulding ... in addition to its representation of the future [it] is also one of the most beautiful cities of India.[72]

He however added that 'It is scandalous that a city like Bangalore should have slums. Don't allow them to grow up here. Root them out. Once they grow they have a tendency to stay.'[73] Although he urged the adoption of urban planning as the answer to such problems, the pointed reference to the ideal of beauty was not lost. The theme of 'City Beautiful' was nurtured throughout the 1960s even when the problem of housing posed a formidable challenge to planning capabilities. As governor of Mysore in the 1960s, V.V. Giri made a ritualized spectacle of his weekly cleaning campaigns and expressed frequent shock at the persistence of slums in the middle of well planned layouts. 'Asia's most well planned extension, Jayanagar', he complained, wore telltale evidence of its rustic ancestry in the stubborn resilience of Kankanpalya village whose 100 odd huts could be 'cleared and converted into a park'.[74] Chief Minister Nijalingappa declared the public water tap a visual blot on the city's image, with overflowing water adding to the dirty image of the city.[75]

A seminar on city architecture held in 1966 repeatedly emphasized the importance of beauty. Its deliberations on the 'Creation of the City Beautiful' suggested standardized building norms to enhance the beauty of the city and a master plan which would help oversee and monitor the city's architecture. At a time when the role of the professional architect was just being recognized and elaborated, such suggestions firmly rooted the architect in town planning and design. Aesthetic sensibilities, and indeed the development of *taste* in building, were made into formally learned skills which reposed only in the professional architect rather than the modest contractor or builder: if need be, the authority to decide on city aesthetics should be bestowed only on these architects through rules and regulations. This aesthetic ideal had little in common with the conservationist lobby, and emphasized order and uniformity rather than a preservation of the building styles of the past.

There are some other [buildings] which though conforming to the building bye laws are not in harmony with the neighbouring buildings. This condition has arisen as the building designs are not prepared by architect–engineers but many a time by owners themselves or by unqualified people not having the necessary aesthetic feeling. If all the buildings in the city should be architecturally so composed that the overall aesthetics of the city can be achieved it is quite necessary *that some kind of regulation is necessary* [sic] *as to who should prepare the plans who should build them and so on.* The consensus was that all structures of the city should be designed by architects who should be registered in the various local bodies such as the corporation, City Improvement Trust Board etc.[76]

Taste itself was defined as a quality or skill possessed by this guild of professionals who would arbitrate on the city's urban form. Yet violations of building by-laws were a sign that the emerging housing market would strive to maximize the exchange value of a given plot of land.[77] By making good taste a product of specialized training however, the architect–planner was able to insert himself (and at this time, the profession was largely gendered male) in the emerging market for housing. Thus, 'Slums were a blot on the architecture of the city' rather than being a symptom of growing housing shortages and economic inequality in the city.[78] Such control over the city's aesthetics was, however, slow to be established, and frequently clashed with the cherished ideals of bodies such as the Bangalore Urban Art Commission, which assiduously cultivated an aesthetic rooted in a nostalgically remembered colonial social order.

Nostalgia for a Colonial Social Order

Perhaps no single statutory body exemplified the will to arbitrate on the aesthetics of the city as the Bangalore Urban Art Commission (BUAC). Set up in 1976, with former chief secretary T.P. Issar as Chairman, the BUAC's mandate was to preserve and develop the city aesthetics, in effect to serve as a watchdog against the unrestrained operation of political or market forces in transforming or altering the heritage of the city. In its 25-year existence, the commission knew only two chairmen, Issar and M.A. Parthasarathy. As guardians of the 'future development of the City Beautiful', the commission was set up during the fateful decade when the population increased by nearly 76 per cent, in response to which a city that had 'been planned and developed on spacious lines' witnessed 'certain ugly appearances on the Bangalore skyline'.[79] Among one of its early achievements was the imposition of the 80 foot maximum height for commercial buildings in the city. By this time, the Public Utility Building on Mahatma Gandhi Road (built by the city corporation in 1978) and Visvesvaraya Towers on Ambedkar Veedhi (built in 1983), condemned as 'structures which offended the eye with their abruptness and incongruity and which were obviously not dictated by any civic need', had already exceeded this limit.[80] The clearance of the BUAC had to be obtained for all buildings coming up in 11 specified spaces (largely in the central administrative area) and 21 roads, as well as for all towering structures such as TV towers, flyovers, bridges, statues, and the like.

From the outset it seemed that the BUAC was waging a losing battle against the more muscular logic of the real estate market. It yielded ground on the contentious issue of the floor area ratio (FAR) fixed for the city as a whole, making it more generous in the area which was to become the central business district, Mahatma Gandhi (MG) Road and Brigade Road.[81] While successful in restricting the plans for a commercial building on M.G. Road,[82] it was unable to prevent the construction of several other buildings in the same area.[83] Indeed, it was also clear that the BUAC's campaign against the 'big time builder from Bombay' was undermined by the willingness of the government to clear high rise projects 'ignoring the existence of Bangalore Urban Art Commission and agreements earlier reached'.[84]

The BUAC defined for itself a notion of beauty that nostalgically recalled another social order, namely colonial Indian society. It is not surprising that its chosen emblem was the 'monkey top', a distinct feature of colonial buildings designed to keep simian invaders at bay in what some described as a 'metropolis of monkeys'. This openly expressed nostalgia is for a socio–spatial structure in which homes and gardens were built and maintained by the colonial ruling classes, unrestrained by a 'rule of law' or a developed market in the acquisition and use of land. As Anthony King, among others, has demonstrated, the colonial urban form showed no need for spatial economy: if anything, the 'generous provision of residential space well above the norms obtaining for persons of similar status in the metropolitan society [Britain] was one of the major compensations for a life spent largely in exile'.[85] Furthermore, colonial built forms were designed with an eye on defining and maintaining social distance and separation between the ruler and the ruled.[86] Bangalore cantonment subordinated all economic activities to its primary military purposes. The vastly transformed social circumstances in which Bangalore develops—a political framework of democracy, a market in land, and the compulsions of housing large masses of urban workers in an industrial city and regional capital city—no longer permit such prodigality of spatial use. What BUAC supports as part of its aesthetic agenda are quotations from a more leisurely, spacious, and decidedly undemocratic past. Peter Hall points out that the 'City Beautiful' movement, whether in Chicago, London, or New Delhi, was conceived by those who were unmistakably authoritarian: Herbert Baker's 'Hurrah for despotism!' was an exuberant expression of the freedom he relished as the architect of empire, when with Edwin Lutyens, he designed the new capital in Delhi.[87]

Far from being an irrelevant institution, BUAC frequently intervened to save heritage buildings from the wreckers' ball. It was less successful in preventing the large-scale conversion of medium and large bungalow sites from being turned into apartment blocks for residential or commercial purposes. Blinded by nostalgia, the BUAC lists amongst its handful of triumphs Hotel Windsor Manor on Sankey Road, a building which reflected more than longing for a bygone age. The hotel was unveiled in 1982, with words that reinvented colonial history: 'a magnificent recreation of imperial grace and elegance' to recall 'earlier, more gracious times ...'.[88] This was held up by the BUAC as 'an eloquent tribute to the residency style of architecture which characterizes many buildings of Bangalore built during the last 100 or 150 years'.[89]

Another victory claimed by the BUAC was the design for the new General Post Office building on Ambedkar Veedhi. The original European classical style building, a modest structure, was clearly inadequate for the burgeoning city in the late 1970s. It was finally pulled down in 1977, but not before consultations with the BUAC had yielded a design that was acceptably aligned with the structures on Ambedkar Veedhi, namely Attara Kacheri and Vidhana Soudha. A structure in reinforced cement concrete, it has stone facing, a flight of grand steps that leads to a high porch with pillars adorned by Chalukyan capitals, and is topped by a dome.[90]

The then BUAC Chairman, T.P. Issar defended his decision to sanction plans for the building, suggesting it 'softened the shock of the Charles Correa

Tower' which was inappropriate for a street like Ambedkar Veedhi.[91] Such aesthetic decisions were, however, keenly contested by the growing band of city architects more committed to an idiom of modernism: some of BUAC's shrillest battles have been with practicing architects who have forged a different vision of beauty for the city. In a scathing attack on the aesthetic criteria that were upheld by BUAC in the General Post Office design, P.M. Thacker, who is among the earliest professional architects in the city and an uncompromising modernist, said:

> How the General Post Office can be called a graceful and dignified building is beyond comprehension. I can best describe it as a painful carbuncle in Cubbon Park. Its grotesque detailing and other features which are quite out of proportion cannot certainly fit with the landscape of Bangalore.[92]

In reply, Issar ruled out a role for architects in 'urban aesthetics', citing the example of untidy modernism on Kempegowda Road as a rash of 'ugliness'.[93] The battle between architects/designers and the BUAC was not just between alternative conceptions of beauty in aesthetics but between the possibility of a professional practice and a rigidly defined opposition to certain kinds of built forms more appropriate to a growing city. 'The idea that everything old is beautiful', said Shivadatta Sharma, chief architect of the Indian Space Research Organization, 'and everything modern is ugly is unacceptable', adding however that problems arose from engineers operating as architects.[94] Thacker asserted that high rise buildings were inevitable: 'The baby has grown up and must acquire adult clothing so let's rip off the nappies and give Bangalore a new look.'[95] Other architects who joined the fray included S.K. Karekar who exclaimed against 'too much adoration for the old'.[96] In turn, the BUAC portrayed itself as resisting the incursion of the big builder, who served only the new rich, defending, in the name of 'grace and charm', a built form that was unmistakably aristocratic.[97]

Yet the BUAC was far from unequivocal on the question of preservation of building styles, which was the most prominent aspect of its ideal of beauty. The fate of the other public building on Ambedkar Veedhi, namely Attara Kacheri (Eighteen Offices), the old public offices which housed the high court is a case in point. Attara Kacheri was threatened with demolition in 1982, when the state government gave its approval for the construction of a new high court building on that site in its order of 24 March 1982.[98] In a writ petition filed in the high court against the state government as well as the Bangalore Urban Art Commission, some concerned citizens sought to prevent demolition of this 'protected monument'. The petitioners claimed that 'as respected citizens of Bangalore and men of eminence' they were acting with the 'highest of motives and in public interest'. The petition pleaded that the beautiful landmark in the city of Bangalore was a 'precious cultural heritage and a part of *an ancient legacy* which any city would treasure', further adding that the 116-year-old structure was 'a symbolic connecting chord for the future, and its destruction snaps an emotional experience vital to a sense of belonging to this beautiful city'.[99]

The state government argued that the structurally weak building could be reinforced only by spending Rs 75 lakh, and would still be inadequate for the expanded uses, although admitting that the proposed new structure was expected to cost Rs 11 crore. The Urban Art Commission initially suggested that Attara Kacheri could be put to lighter uses, by shifting the high traffic high court to another location.[100] However, later it bowed to government pressure for more space adjoining the old public office, by according a conditional permission to build, namely that 'the existing style and façade' be 'repeated without any change whatsoever while providing for the required levels within the proposed additional height of 10 feet'.[101] In other words, the concern for preserving the architectural form of a bygone era (and thereby maintaining a dubious visual unity) overshadowed the BUAC's concern for preservation of a piece of Bangalore heritage. The writ petition against all the agencies which agreed to the demolition, including the BUAC, was struck down on grounds that the judiciary could not alter the existing law on the protection of endangered buildings.[102] On appeal to the Supreme Court, however, the state government was ordered to consider afresh its decision to demolish this structure; the decision was reversed in 1985 and repairs to and the extension of Attara Kacheri were begun.

The BUAC's insistence that the extensions to Attara Kacheri be an echo of the classical buildings in the front was criticized on two quite different grounds, both of which addressed the question of an appropriate aesthetic for the city. The BUAC's vision of Bangalore aesthetics drew disproportionate inspiration from long irrelevant architectural forms. This has been severely challenged by the professional architects who seek to define a contemporary practice of architecture, and believe that quotations from the past negate 'the existence of half a century of architectural development', as a leading city architect Edgar D'Mello put it. He argued instead for a 'flexible strategy that could be challenging, experimental, confrontational or even provocative'. This aesthetic strategy shared none of the concerns for a notion of beauty drawn from history, or even mindless conservation; instead, a distinction was made between degrees of skill and elegance in architectural design (Fig. 45).

FIG. 45 *The old Attara Kacheri Building has been doubled to make more space for the Karnataka High Court.*
(Clare Arni, 2000)

There were also those who upheld stricter rules of conservation that would deflect mass public occupations of space. No extension to Attara Kacheri should have been allowed, said the principle campaigner M. Bhaktavatsala, since it would soon become 'a dangerous pollutant of Cubbon Park' as 'the heart of the Park is likely to be run over by an heterogenous crowd which inevitably hovers around the court building'. The court, he suggested, should ensure that there was no park access for the people who daily thronged its halls.[103] The 'heterogenous crowd', it feared, would show scant respect for notions of elegance and beauty which could not be guaranteed in an age of mass consumption.

The field of urban aesthetics, then, is crowded with competing ideologies. Nor is there a consensus on the ideal of city beauty. The ideology of beauty is brought into direct conflict with the democracy of the market and the cultures of mass consumption, whether of space or other commodities. With mass culture as its enemy, the ideology of beauty has many easy targets in a vastly transformed commodity culture. Not just the builder who seeks to meet a growing need for housing, but the multiple uses of public space for communicative purposes were reviled by the BUAC. The commission consistently voiced its opposition to the visual expressions of democracy or the market, namely the advertising and wall writing practices of the city. It indicted the 'political parties, besides trade unions and cinema exhibitors' for not adhering to a code of conduct in the use of public spaces in the city.[104] 'The residents of Bangalore, the City Beautiful, must set an example to the rest of the country by effectively preventing such a rash of ugliness.' Such a call to arms clearly restricts the definition of the resident, and indeed the citizen, to one who shares these ideals of the BUAC, in effect, a minority of concerned elite citizens against the practices of the majority.

This received fuller articulation in the report of the high powered committee in which 'visual pollution' was identified with 'mindless scrawling of political and other slogans and messages on walls and buildings' as well as 'multiplicity of name boards'.[105] Among other popular practices that the ideology of beauty tries to prevent is the growing symbolic political practice of installing, honouring, and protecting statues of political heroes. 'Bangalore must not go the way of Madras ... where it is difficult to take a few steps without bumping into a statue', warned BUAC in its report.[106] This was the basis for its opposition to the decision to install a statue of former chief minister Nijalingappa near Vidhana Soudha. Closer scrutiny however reveals that opposition is not in fact against statuary as visual embellishments for the city, but only against the politicization of statue installations, especially as the symbolic occupation of public space by various political formations has gathered momentum since the 1980s. The high power committee on Bangalore's 'beautification' in fact suggested in 1993 that 'pleasing statuary—not of important personages only—but of common folks such as a street vendor of dolls, a girl running to school with the school bag, a typical housewife, a postman, a police constable, etc.' may be installed and protected from vandals.[107] No wonder then that such agencies as the BUAC, while expressing helplessness over political processes it cannot control,[108] wholeheartedly participates in the aestheticization of urban practices that are designed to restrict public life and access to public spaces, willingly designing gates for Cubbon Park and grills for Vidhana Soudha.[109] In the name of the aesthetic then, a range of plebeian practices was rendered unacceptable, namely the wall poster, cinema culture, or the manifestation of the political (e.g. the trade union) itself.

If public life must be redefined, zoned, and confined as it were, how has this been achieved through architecture, particularly on a street such as Ambedkar Veedhi? Perhaps the fate of the grand steps that lead to the high entrance of the General Post Office is a sign of the limits of (historic) beauty as a defining ideal in public architecture. For the steps of this building are in fact an unusable space as they lead up from a patch of lawn and a side of the road that has been completely surrounded by a fence, with a small turnstile entrance. Far from presenting a more welcoming face to the Bangalore public, the General Post Office functions as a forbidding, out-of-bounds structure which is used only minimally, a restricted space in a public administrative area. The movement of people into the building is hurried, even furtive, in the transaction of business, so that the grand wide staircase remains merely a passage and not a space for social interaction.

The Bangalore Urban Art Commission, the 'custodian of beauty', was abruptly 'dissolved in its present form' in April 2001.[110] 'Our aim was to minimize commercial activities around the State capital [building] and to preserve old buildings in the area', said M.A. Parthasarathy, the outgoing chairman. In its 25 year tenure, BUAC made an enduring, if somewhat controversial, contribution to the public debate on city aesthetics. Yet the battle over city aesthetics and the redefinition of public life in post-Independence Bangalore is not easily resolved even by structures which have broken free from the constant references to a glorious Indian or colonial past. The very modernism of Visvesvaraya Towers at the corner of Ambedkar Veedhi invites critical comments; furthermore, as a structure, it has come to be used in ways that were unintended in its design, and once more fails to redefine the meaning and content of social life on this central strip.

Against Nostalgia: The Celebration of Function

By a quirk of administrative fate, the offices of the rather conservative BUAC were housed in the belly of the beast, namely Visvesvaraya Towers. Long reviled by the BUAC as a structure which has ignored all acceptable aesthetic norms for that central corridor, the towers were completed for the use of the Life Insurance Corporation in 1983 with Charles Correa as the consulting architect. Far from being nostalgic in orientation, or even appealing to some mythic past, its sullen phallic presence is rather like, to adapt the words of a nineteenth century architect cited by Schorske, 'an architecture of Adam, naked and strong',[111] sharply contrasting with the softer rounded contours of the other public buildings. Its cement concrete structure is a celebration of function, and is a definite attempt at redefining the Bangalore skyline. Built at a time in the early 1980s when the vertical was only hesitantly accepted as a vision for the city's skyline, it is stark, even brutalist in style, defiantly unadorned and a grey celebration of concrete itself. It has today been bought over by the state to house government offices in its two towers, of 23 and 13 floors each, connected by a podium on the fourth floor.[112] The commercial uses for which the space was designed have been subverted by the needs of government, and the predictable dullness of bureaucracies.

Nevertheless, one might still ask how such a modernist structure succeeds in redrawing the compact between government and people. What new notion of authority does the structure command or communicate? Here too, the intention of the architect appears to have reached an impasse, dictated by the uses to which the building has been adapted. There is no doubt that the building enhances the legibility of the Bangalore skyline as a modernist monument in a city that is largely characterized by low rise buildings. It also offers a refreshingly democratic, and less imposing, relationship to the public, as the west-facing main entrances to the buildings are at the ground level rather than relying on the grandeur of a flight of stairs. Even the brisk design of the flight of stairs that ascend to the left of the main entrance could have envisaged a space for gathering, conversing, or simply resting. Yet the stairs are relatively unused in these ways by the people who may approach the office of the rent controller at the top, and the enclosed open space in front of it is vacated of all but the anxious shuffles of house hunters. At lunch time and in the evenings, the ground level spaces are crowded with people seeking post-lunch fruit or drink. At other times, the place has not been able to shake free of its official functions, with large numbers of people, heads bent, hurrying in and out of the lobbies, to offices on various floors. The large number of official white cars parked in front of the building not only impede pedestrian traffic, but block an appreciative view of the structure itself (Fig. 46).

Like its counterpart, the General Post Office building, Visvesvaraya Towers fails to stimulate a new inclusive public culture, or communicate a new sense of authority, though in this case a striking architectural design has been betrayed by the uses to which it has been put. The podium which might have been intended as an off-street location of social interaction has remained doomed from the start. In part, this area lacks vitality as commercial retailing activity is disallowed. Perhaps the design is a miscalculation of the predilections of people who function only uneasily within a multi-storey office culture and wish to join the stream of ground level life and traffic in their breaks. The monumental cement concrete structure persistently referred to as 'modernist' or 'cubist' art by the BUAC does not develop a different relationship to the street from any of the other public structures. Although designed for purposes that are distinctly more accessible to the public, its yearning to be monumental forecloses the option of addressing the vital horizontality of the street. A street level public life that is vibrant and interactive occurs in spite of it, rather than as a result of conscious design.

FIG. 46 *Visvesvaraya Towers, with the statue of B.R. Ambedkar in the foreground. Also visible is the dome of the new General Post Office building.*
(Clare Arni, 2000)

Full Circle

The decision by the S.M. Krishna government in 2001 to build an annex to Vidhana Soudha brings the architectural history of the Ambedkar Veedhi full circle. Once more, the state declares its allegiance to a remembered regional architectural form as the most authentic expression of the national–modern. While many may agree that the original structure 'has become synonymous with Bangalore' despite being ill suited to the needs of contemporary governance, the decision to replicate the structure has invited more stringent comment. Architectural comparisons have been drawn with more imaginative designs in other state capitals.

> Recent attempts at designing Legislative Assembly [sic] have resulted in generating a totally new vocabulary of public architecture for example at Bhopal and Panaji. The approach has been to use abstract rather than literal symbolism as a reference to the past ... further the concept of public space has changed from mere visual experience to one of actual participation. The need for monumentality as a proxy for power is irrelevant today.[113]

Yet the state government decision to build a 'twin for the Vidhana Soudha' is in clear defiance of such architectural ideals. The planned annex or south block of the Vidhana Soudha will be a 'blend of modern and old architecture' and will be an echo of the original structure. Nearly forty years after the controversies that surrounded the decision to build the Vidhana Soudha, Chief Minister S.M. Krishna models his contribution to the Bangalore skyline on the adaptation of an original that has endured despite its critics.[114] Indeed, even the stone for the building is being quarried from the same sites as was done in the 1950s—Hesarghatta, Mallasandra, and Avalahalli—and the PWD department, for long marginalized by government decisions to award contracts to private architects and builders, has been chosen to design the new structure.

The Chief Architect Shankar has defended the return to 'history' with these words: 'Many tall buildings with attractive glass window panes have come up in Bangalore including the IT park. But these fail to hold the attention of tourists. It is not so in the case of historical buildings'.[115] The regional historical legacy that is claimed is an adaptation of multiply mediated forms, as we have seen, and is yet chosen as most appropriate to the image of city, disregarding any arguments about the link between form and democratic function. A quotation from history becomes history itself, valorized as the most authentic expression of modern Indian identity, as distinguished from the steel and glass international styles that have become the norm. Moreover, as James

Holston explains in the context of Brasilia, the 'simple and legible architectural convention' which sets public buildings off from the private is used to heightened effect. As a public building, Vidhana Soudha is a sculptural figure set in a void or green ground 'heavily ornamental, sculpturally massed and massively scaled' to emphasize monumentality.[116]

Meanwhile, other decisions relating to the security needs of the elected have made Ambedkar Veedhi and Vidhana Soudha in particular a far more restricted zone for the ordinary citizen. An area which is the location of prime administrative/public buildings of the state is thus a space which is increasingly defined in ways that are largely opposed to democratic citizenship through a mixture of architectural choices, physical barriers, prohibitions on movement, and, not least, unintended uses. The fear of democracy, as it re-inscribes the city in unpredictable ways has periodically been resisted by those who argue for the aesthetically more unified forms of the time before democracy. Senior citizens and leading intellectuals of the city, dismayed by the combination of political and market forces that were redrawing the city landscape, made anguished pleas to 'leave old Bangalore alone' and urged that development be achieved 'through the creation of townships and satellite towns'.[117] Leading sociologist M.N. Srinivas went on to say 'I would say that although I believe in democracy and Panchayati Raj, what we really need [for the city] is men with the zeal and vision of dictators'.[118] Only rarely does the vision of a new public life that is not founded on prohibitions find expression, as in architect Karekar's suggestion:

> Bangalore does not have a real prominent mall, shopping arcade, or public plaza ... the public plaza in front of Vidhana Soudha comprising Attara Kacheri, General Post Office and LIC building with Central Park (sic) could be developed into such a dynamic space. The space that buzzes with activities during the day should be made a completely vehicle free plaza during evenings with park parlours and music.[119]

However, here too the vision of a public life remains restricted to modes of consumption that have been nurtured in the advanced capitalist world rather than the untidy democratic occupations of space that are a hallmark of Indian public life.

Conclusion

By largely featuring emblems from the past, Ambedkar Veedhi invokes awe for the power of the state in its remembered monarchical or colonial form. Even when the styles are more contemporary, e.g. Visvesvaraya Towers, the strip as a whole does not succeed in redefining a public life appropriate to a post-colonial democracy. That which infuses democracy into the space, albeit of a very unexpected and unplanned kind, is the horizontal movement of the people and traffic on the street itself, which is today a major thoroughfare for those moving across the city. Ambedkar Veedhi, which sweeps past the front of Vidhana Soudha rather than leading up to it, is often used as a space for demonstrations, for tourist traffic, or simply daily commuting, and restores a certain vitality to the area. It is movement then, rather than volume and mass, 'the clash and roar of traffic', not the rootedness of stone, that opens up and defines the space. At the same time, the chaotic disorders of the street and the anxieties of passage have removed the possibility of awe or appreciation for public architecture to such an extent that most structures may even be ignored.

This democracy too is endangered: the gates around Cubbon Park, barricades around Vidhana Soudha, and the unused stairs of the General Post Office which are blocked off from use, are portents of a controlled public life, to be zoned perhaps as traffic free in the near future. Until then, however, a democratic public asserts itself against a vigilant 'citizenry', often in ways that violate notions of order, quiet, and good taste.

If the controls on the use of public space have been most effective in areas around the control administrative district, and if plebeian occupations have been removed from the space, other modes of territorializing the city have been established. The mental-imaginative map of the city produces symbolic meanings of place that may go against the designs of urban planners. It is to these processes that the next two chapters turn.

SIX

Language and the Right to the City

Kavery neeru kudiyuva munna Kannada kali!

Sign on the back of an autorickshaw, 2002

For three days between 30 July and 2 August 2000, a pall of silence fell upon the city of Bangalore, when its streets were emptied of noise, traffic, and frenetic crowds.[1] Not even the 'virtual' city entirely escaped this spell of silence as many homes lost their cable connections and the busy hum of the Internet parlour was stilled. The abrupt shutdown of city life was informally imposed by a set of forces that had gained increasing visibility in the city for at least two decades. This display of anger was against the kidnapping of the leading cultural icon of the Kannadigas, Rajkumar, by the notorious forest brigand Veerappan in the early hours of 30 July 2000. The helpless anger of a wide range of Rajkumar fan clubs and Kannada associations that spread across the city and the state was only heightened by the fact that the film star, who had come to represent pride in the Kannada language itself, was kidnapped by a man who shed his image as a sandalwood and ivory poacher to take up the cause of Tamil nationalism.

Right across the city, the violence took the form of bringing public transport to a halt, forcing people to abandon their private vehicles and walk home as a mark of solidarity with the abducted hero.[2] More important, it was a moment when, by his very absence, the entire city was made aware of Rajkumar's larger than life presence within the world of Kannada, his place in a cultural universe that had thus far embraced only a section of people in the city (Fig. 47). Not always was this a voluntary recognition of his fame. When roving bands of young men vented their anger and grief on new glass and steel structures that have an insistent presence in commercial areas of the city, vulnerable business establishments and car owners quickly declared their allegiance to the Kannada hero by pasting his picture on the glass. Violence against property and people was low key—though one person was stabbed to death for not complying with those who ruled the streets that day—but there was a menacing threat from those who brought the city temporarily under their rule.

The unity of silence that was thrust on Bangalore by the roving bands and the police alike, briefly made for a withdrawn and watchful space of the city.[3] Industry analysts and others were quick to calculate the economic costs of such disruption,[4] while the film industry imposed a *bandh* on itself, refusing to open theatres, undertake production, or release new films until the star was released.[5] Yet throughout Rajkumar's tedious 108 day captivity the fan clubs, Kannada organizations, film institutions, and the 'first family' (as Rajkumar's wife and children were referred to in the press) retained a focus on the predicament of the star by organizing rallies, bandhs, *urulu seve*s, pujas, meetings, and days of prayer.[6] In this, they were amply aided by the taped messages and news reports of Rajkumar's life in the jungle at the mercy of his abductor Veerappan. The star's eventual release from captivity on 15 November 2000 brought relief to a capital city that had been precariously poised on the edge of full-scale riots.[7] Yet, not even Rajkumar's release from captivity, which happened only after repeated rebuffs by Veerappan of the Tamil journalist and emissary Gopal, and after several reversals in the court, resulted in anything more than a carnival of joy.

The abduction of Rajkumar was not just a criminal act of a forest brigand, but was staged as a dramatic encounter between two nationalisms, Kannada and Tamil, that had over the past two decades come into violent conflict over issues relating to land, jobs, and water in the southern regions of Karnataka and particularly Bangalore city. It was striking then that the Tamils and other citizens of Bangalore more generally were not exposed to violence that conformed to these established patterns. The restraint was all the more significant given the provocations of Rajkumar's captors, who bargained with state authorities in both Karnataka and Tamil Nadu on issues concerning the fate of Tamils in Karnataka and of some Tamils in Tamil Nadu itself. In his list of ten demands that was handed over at the time of abduction, Veerappan and his new found allies in the forest, the Tamil National Liberation Front (TNLF),

FIG. 47 *The reigning cultural hero of the Kannadigas: Rajkumar's cutout dominates the front of the Kapali Theatre at the screening of the film Shabdavedi.*
(Clare Arni, 2000)

included several that were previously the cause of violent clashes between the two linguistic groups. Among those that concerned Karnataka in particular, he included: a permanent solution to the Cauvery water dispute, adequate compensation to all Tamil victims of the Cauvery riots of 1991, the inclusion of Tamil as an administrative language in Karnataka, the installation of the Thiruvalluvar statue in Bangalore, and a vacation of the stay on the Sadashiva committee which investigated atrocities of the Special Task Force in the forest.[8] The demands included several that addressed both sides of the border at once: thus both states were asked to implement minimum daily wages of Rs 150 for plantation workers.

This mixture of economic and cultural demands blurred the battle lines between the two linguistic groups, and in many ways diffused the tension, producing new loyalties and alliances. Bangalore Tamils were quick to distance themselves from the actions of a forest brigand, refusing to acknowledge that he represented their interests. There was even some bitterness at how readily the state government was prepared to acquiesce to Veerappan's demands: R.S. Maran of the Tamil Sangham said it was an insult that government was heeding Veerappan's demands rather than the petitions of Tamil organizations in Bangalore. Nearly all the issues that were raised in the demands of Karnataka state had left their scars on a city that was deeply divided on the question of language and its implications for a right to the city. Veerappan and his allies chose to address the state on issues that had long slipped out of its grasp, and had become the battleground of groups and associations in Karnataka. Maran's plea was that the state reassert its power and rein in these non-state organizations.

For those long involved in the Kannada movement, the predicament of Rajkumar was in fact the predicament of Kannada itself, held hostage to what was perceived as the more robust nationalism of the Tamils. Clearly, the triumphant march of computer languages such as Java and C++ through every neighbourhood of Bangalore, and some other parts of Karnataka, had done nothing to resolve or render irrelevant the crisis within which the Kannada language and the state found itself, and may only have accentuated it. Indeed, 'When the capitalists give Kannada a sidelong glance [*kadeganninda noduthiruvaga*], Kannada itself becomes capital to some', said the Kannada Development Authority chairman Bargur Ramachandrappa, in his plea for recasting Kannada pride.[9] A similar anguish marks the speech of nearly all those who have been involved in the Kannada movement over the past few decades.

This chapter traces some of the ways in which Bangalore has been re-territorialized by those who lay increasing claim to the city as a regional, rather than a national or international metropolis. It develops a framework for understanding language issues in the city by tracing the broader contours of the language question as it emerged in pre-Independence and immediate post-Independence years. It then traces the successive stages through which the Kannada movement has passed, particularly as it has reconfigured specific domains of life in the city, such as work opportunities, access to land, or governmental power. Finally, there is a consideration of the prospects of Kannada nationalism in a time of rapid but uneven capitalist development.

Conceiving the Kannada Nation

From its tentative start during the colonial period, Kannada nationalism measured itself and its inadequacies not against the overarching triumphs of the imperial power, but against the more modest successes of other linguistic nationalisms within India itself.[10] Alura Venkat Rao's anguished response in 1917 to the nationalist imperative, 'We don't have a history! We must have a history!!'[11] recognized that it was only through a recast history of the Kannada people that the Indian nation could be imagined. Even more important, he deplored the fact that his effort came a full 40 or 50 years after his Bengali, Marathi, and Telugu counterparts had made their heroes and historic triumphs part of the nationalist common sense.[12] The absence of a unified administration under which the Kannada people could develop continues to haunt even contemporary historical accounts.[13]

Since the narrativization of Kannada's modern identity had been somewhat overwhelmed by the sense that it is unoriginal, weak, and even imitative,[14] the massive and indisputable presence of the state in envisioning modernity, particularly the old Mysore state, has been overlooked. By the late nineteenth century, the bureaucracy of the princely state forged a paradigm of development which, while unmistakably nationalist, strove to usher in a legal and economic modernity through the instrumentalities of the state.[15] The state thus absorbed the nationalist agenda and restricted the conditions of possibility for the development of a public sphere, tending, as Sudipta Kaviraj says, 'to suffocate non-state institutions of civil society by theoretically equating the principle of public good with the institutional form of state control'.[16] There were, for instance, a number of caste associations whose scope remained limited until at least the 1930s.[17]

For a long time in Mysore, the state loomed large in the imagination of cultural nationalists searching for patrons and sponsors of a rejuvenated Kannada: thus B.M. Srikantia (B.M. Sri) made the plea in 1915 at the Mysore Economic Conference that

> Governments concerned with Kannada areas will, as they have been doing already, encourage writers systematically and on settled principles, and may even see the way to establish a sort of academy with power to lay down general principles to map out a course of production and to reward any work that is done in an excellent manner and to print and distribute it if necessary among the people at large.[18]

It is no surprise then that the Kannada Sahitya Parishat was set up in 1915 as a part of Dewan Visvesvaraya's overall vision of Mysore's material progress and welfare.[19] B.M. Sri's was among the many voices that argued for a Kannada adequate to the tasks of modern industrial and scientific life.[20] Yet he too made the point feebly, acknowledging instead the sphere within which Kannada was condemned to circulate, envisaging a division of labour where English 'our cultural and political language' Sanskrit 'our spiritual and classical language', and Kannada 'our native and speaking language' could coexist.[21] It is striking that the language of the economy did not figure in the division of labour envisaged by B.M. Sri, who attached cultural and political rather than economic dominance to a language like English. This was to change dramatically in the post-Independence years, when the international hegemony of English only increased. The division of labour between languages which B.M. Sri envisaged was untenable in a situation which strongly tied English to the historic emergence and expansion of capitalism itself in a country like India. With the market strongly on its side and the growing demands of the new economy, English medium schools have burgeoned in a city like Bangalore: attempts to stall this march have usually been through an appeal for state intervention.[22]

Kannada protagonists have attempted to forge stronger links with the cultural world through private and state bodies such as the Kannada and Culture Department. We shall consider in some more detail the consequences of this for the field of culture, and the contests it has generated in the Bangalore context. Notwithstanding widespread acknowledgement of its dominated status, there has never been, in the past or today, a widespread movement to promote literacy or encourage reading, as happened in the library movements of Kerala and the Andhra Mahasabha during the colonial period.[23] The obvious limits of promoting the growth of a language through its literary texts have been recognized by several Kannada intellectuals,[24] and even the leadership by a renowned writer, Bargur Ramachandrappa, of the Kannada Development Authority in 2000–2 did little to recast this link.

If, like all Indian languages under colonialism, Kannada bore the burden of domination, it sometimes translated into a very material marginalization. Despite its wry humour, B.G.L. Swamy's description of the Kannada Department as it was when it first took shape in 1917 in Central College, Bangalore, suggests that self-effacement was thrust upon the language:

> Unlike the other departments, the Kannada department had no architectural pretensions. Neither a house nor a stable, nor a block, nor a hut, it was unique in its own way. Two rooms of the building in the northern corner with an adjoining one to the west constituted the department.
>
> There were doors, one on the western wall of the twin rooms and one on the

eastern wall. The door on the western wall was used by the other language departments for entry and exit. The door on the eastern wall was used by the Kannada department.

It is my hunch that this decision was taken because the road in front of the western wall was used by most of the people coming into or going out of the college and by customers of Narayan's hotel. Or because of a sense of humility the Kannada people with its ideal of living one's life as a forest bloom away from the pomp and people's gaze.[25]

The Kannada teacher had a comparatively lower status, for as N. Lakshman Rau recalled of the time when he was student of Central College in the 1930s, 'Kannada professors were big men but their salaries were so low they were looked down upon. Their position was not so good. The Kannada scholars were given poorer chambers ... students failed in Kannada and passed in other subjects'.[26] The dominated status of the language had its effects on the psychology of its speakers too, as Nittoor Srinivas Rao, former chief judge of the high court, and one of the pioneers of the publishing trade in Bangalore remembered:

... we had pundits in Maharaja's college in Mysore and in Bangalore, not only in schools and colleges, [but] elsewhere, very great scholars in Kannada, but they were all called Munshis and their salary was 40 rupees and 50 rupees while a man like me passed B.Sc. and [when I] was appointed as demonstrator in Central College, I got 75 rupees. That was the position of our Kannada ...

The domination of Kannada within the colonial order had much to do with the emerging division of labour between languages as English occupied a hegemonic presence as the language of science, technology, and indeed capitalism, while Kannada strove to make its presence felt in the politico–cultural sphere. Yet it was still a time when English was only one among the languages that the nationalist intelligentsia knew and used, although it had already made inroads into the spheres of intimacy and private life. Nittoor Srinivasa Rao, who came to Bangalore in 1919 for higher studies, captures the gradual growth of English hegemony in private life:

In regard to what we consider to be sophisticated important ideas we think in English. And I used to write letters to my father [in Kannada] and he would write back to me in English, writing in Kannada was considered a departure. I may tell you that even as high school students we used to talk to each other mainly in English and even if we spoke in Kannada there was a large mixture of English words. Very important operative words were taken from English and as a matter of fact, [when we became] part and parcel of the Kannada movement, now we had sort of evolved a rule amongst ourselves that we would pay a fine of one paise for the use of English words in the course of our conversations.[27]

In fact, the debate about whether Kannada should be the medium of instruction was still raging, and was far from settled until at least 1940. Kannada high schools preparing students for the upper secondary examination at the turn of the twentieth century 'did not flourish in competition with English' and were therefore abolished in 1935 although Kannada was made the medium of instruction that year.[28] Only in 1919 were girls' schools reluctantly made bilingual from the middle grade on, despite the belief that English was 'intrinsically bound up with information offensive to native tradition'.[29]

The few isolated efforts made by nationalist intellectuals did little to change the restricted domains of Kannada as a literary or domestic language: Nittoor's decision to teach both mathematics and physics in Kannada 'which I regarded as a great departure from what was happening all over' was indeed a refreshing attempt to reverse the downslide. This was however a losing battle as English began invading the private sphere as well, sometimes restructuring the self, at other times appearing as a means to address the nation in the making. It sculpted new subjectivities that allowed for a confident use of the new language even to record one's own life history: the accomplished Karnataka painter, K. Venkatappa, who maintained diaries from as early as 1913, chose to keep them largely in English.[30] However, the need to command the language of the masters often overshadowed other concerns: Nittoor Srinivasa Rao remembers his disappointment when, at their first meeting, the great B.M. Sri spoke to him in English.[31]

Nevertheless, in the period before Independence, the language question was figured more in terms of the political and literary successes of languages such as Marathi, Telugu, and Bengali: Tamil and Urdu were barely visible on this horizon. At least two other elements made their appearance only in the decades after Independence: the increasing recognition that the hegemony of English cannot be easily challenged led to a displacement of demands on to the political cultural sphere, that called for the intervention of the agencies of the state which at this time was a far from insignificant distributor of resources. Second, questions of demography and geography became central to the imaginary of Kannada nationalism, which ranged itself against subaltern groups in southern Karnataka, particularly in its chief metropolis, Bangalore. After all, as Partha Chatterjee points out, following Foucault, the concept of population, 'differentiated but classifiable, describable and enumerable', has been crucial to the emergence of modern governmental technologies.[32] Census data of the state and of the city reveal much that could become the basis for rallying people to the cause of language, on both sides of the language divide: it has been one of the major bases for seeking state intervention to alter terms which are determined by an emerging linguistic market.[33]

Language and Power and the Reorganization of States

If, following Pierre Bourdieu,[34] we adopt the notion of a 'linguistic market', an economy within which particular language competencies take on value, we may discern the deeply segmented and far from unified linguistic market which has developed in Karnataka through the twentieth century. It is a linguistic market that sustains a division of labour between different languages and language competencies, defining a very restricted sphere within which Kannada may circulate. The restrictions imposed by such objective factors as geography and demography appear then as far less crucial in defining the predicament of Kannada than those imposed by the economy or the organization of the political sphere. The overwhelming dominance of English as an internationally hegemonic language, in the commercial, financial, scientific, or IT fields, or the dominance of Hindi and Tamil in the cultural spheres (e.g. TV and cinema) leaves Kannada to its lonely reign over the literary sphere, or within the space of domesticity. Strenuous attempts to make Kannada the administrative language of the region have done little to recast the segmented linguistic market or compensate for the division of labour between languages that has emerged.

FIG. 48 *Reterritorializing the city: Kannada signs being added to the popular Lakeview Coffee Bar and Icecream parlour on Mahatma Gandhi Road.*
(T.L. Ramaswamy, 15.5.1970)

Although Kannada has been the official language of the state since 1963, and is by and large the language of governance, this does not sufficiently remedy its dominated status, particularly in the erstwhile cantonment areas (Fig. 48).

The overwhelming success of economic nationalism in the colonial period compared with the more modest gains of cultural nationalism is crucial to any discussion of the predicament of Kannada today. Rather than being a latecomer to linguistic and communal identities, Karnataka has fashioned a different path to modernity, fraught with anxieties that have violently manifested themselves in the past two decades. This violent renegotiation of the terrain of development occurs between those who are poised to benefit most from Karnataka's new economies, particularly in the field of information technology, and those who seek a stake in it. Moreover, the post-Independence years have been marked by a diglossia in crisis,[35] where a nationalist élite which was thoroughly bilingual (moving between English and the regional language) has yielded space to two or more resolutely unilingual groups.

One of the earliest attacks on Tamils in the city followed the Talwadi incident, when Kannada Chaluvali leader Vatal Nagaraj was arrested for demanding that a part of Tamil Nadu be joined to Karnataka. 'Leaderless, disorganized mobs' stoned several cinema houses, shops, and buses including one belonging to Tamil Nadu in protest and an effigy of the Tamil Nadu chief minister, M. Karunanidhi was carried in a mammoth procession to the Gandhi statue.[36] The main areas to be affected were the older Tamil areas of the city such as Laxmipuram, Okalipuram, and Magadi Road. By the late 1990s, Mysore's unique multilingual character was seen as a burden, and mild disturbances of the 1970s gave way to city-wide upheavals and unprecedented acts of violence against the lives and properties of linguistic minorities.

Has the early nationalist *vision* of Karnataka come to grief, close to turning into a *nightmare* in the hands of some groups in the 1980s and 1990s? This was D.R. Nagaraj's chief concern in an article that discussed the emergence of a more strident Kannada nationalism, particularly in the last two decades of the twentieth century. He distinguished between a 'fear-centred nationalism' as represented by the writings of M. Chidanandamurthy (and the activity of Kannada Shakti Kendra) and the 'spiritual nationalism' of earlier writers such as Alura Venkata Rao. Consider Alura Venkata Rao's message on the occasion of Karnataka unification in 1956:

In short, we should not forget that Karnataka is a much broader entity than Kannada. Not only the speakers of dialects, we should also not forget the minorities who speak other (neighbouring) languages—in the construction of united Karnataka this is a principle to be kept in mind. In other words, Kannada has the dominant status. But knowledge is welcome from all sides. As someone who keenly conducted the Karnataka movement, I never forget this. Thus, once when the Marathi library in Dharwar was facing closure, I took it over, added the collection to my own Bharata Pustakalaya, ran it for some years and when the Marathis here came forward to manage it, I handed it over to them.[37]

Chidanandamurthy's activist prose, and the copious outpourings of Kannada Shakthi Kendra, on the other hand, are marked not just by fear but by envy of the more muscular Tamil nationalism.[38] Indeed, the self-confidence of Venkat Rao in the early twentieth century was largely replaced by an aggressively defensive stand by the end of the century, allowing a more fragile presence for a writer like P. Lankesh who occupied a 'secular socio–political' space. This 'secular socio–political space', which values the multiple strands that make up contemporary Karnataka, has consistently opposed the 'language of violence and militancy' as a solution to the predicament of Kannada, and indeed Karnataka itself.[39] It was sorely tested on more than one occasion over the last two decades, and in particular in 1991 and 1994 when two different minorities, Tamils and Muslims, were singled out for attack. One might however go further to suggest that the identity of Karnataka itself is endangered when its constituent elements are threatened, for who will hesitate to acknowledge Karnataka's debt to the literature and labour of Marathi, Urdu, Telugu, and Tamil speakers?

It is impossible to understand the predicament of Kannada without an understanding of the language's dominated status within Karnataka. This, the votaries of Kannada Shakti Kendra would have us believe, is to be understood in demographic terms. We may note here that the experience of 'wounds inflicted by geography' (especially the experience of Kannada speakers remaining fragmented under different administrative authorities in the colonial period) gives way to a reckoning of citizenship by numbers. Commenting on D.R. Nagaraj's critique of his activism as a Kannada supporter, Chidanandamurthy was reported to have defended his own position by claiming that his position 'stems from very real memories as well as contemporary realities. He was only trying to point out that in two or three decades there would be no Kannada left in Bangalore. Soon Kannada would [be evicted from] other parts of Karnataka as well.'[40]

Not a small part of the effort of Kannada Shakthi Kendra, headed by Chidanandamurthy, has gone into a careful charting of demographic imbalances within the city of Bangalore. Such an understanding is seriously flawed as it is translated into a programme for redressal that turns against minorities in the state. In demographic terms, after all, the estimated 20 per cent of Bihari Hindi speakers in Calcutta[41] or the substantial number of Malayalam and Telugu speakers in Chennai has done nothing to challenge the hegemony of Bengali or Tamil respectively in Bengal and Tamil Nadu. Clearly, something other than mere demography or geography is necessary to come to terms with the present crisis. An exclusive focus on demography thus avoids engagement with the most important factors which have resulted in Kannada's dominated status, which is largely due to the structuring of opportunities by the market, rather than the state, and in the consequent privileging of English over other languages.

Domination and its Effects

'The name is Karnataka, now let the breath be Kannada' (*hesaraayithu Karnataka, usiraagali Kannada*) was the rallying call of poet Chennavira Kanavi, who recognized that neither the linguistic reorganization of states in 1956, nor Kannada literary achievements had translated into linguistic dominance (Fig. 49). Clearly, the state machinery has a large role to play in making this a reality, and as Sumathi Ramaswamy's recent work has shown, even such a robust nationalism as that of Tamil could not do without the state's support in making Tamil the de facto language of the state.[42] Karnataka is unusually rich in the number of languages that are spoken within its borders. While Kannada is spoken by about 65 per cent of its inhabitants, languages such as Konkani, Tulu, and Kodagu (which are identified with sub-regions of Karnataka), and Marathi, Telugu, and Tamil (identified with other linguistic states), are among the important minorities. During the four significant moments in the history of language politics in the past two decades, i.e. the Gokak agitation (1982), the Cauvery agitation (1991), the anti-Urdu telecast agitation (1994), and finally the crisis produced by Rajkumar's kidnapping (2000), the geographical spread of the movement has narrowed to become more closely identified with southern Karnataka, and Bangalore in particular. An impressive all-Karnataka affair in 1982 (Gokak) with an organizing nucleus based in Hubli–Dharwad, was restricted, during the Cauvery agitation, to a struggle over jobs, land, and water in southern Karnataka.[43] Indeed, the Cauvery agitation shifted from the Cauvery basin to the city of Bangalore within a few days, becoming virulently anti-Tamil in ways that were unforeseen and unprepared for.[44] The anti-Urdu agitation which revolved around the question of Kannada's visibility as an official language, was more or less confined to Bangalore and Mysore.

Associations such as Vatal Nagaraj's Kannada Chaluvaligaru, Kannada

FIG. 49 *Asserting linguistic pride: Kuvempu's* Ramayana Darshanam *being taken in procession on an elephant from the Kempegowda Statue.*
(T.L. Ramaswamy, 8.1.1969)

Shakthi Kendra, or Rajkumar Abhimanigala Sangha, to name a few, maintain a vigil against real and perceived threats to the language in its home state. The city of Bangalore has become emblematic of the dominated status of Kannada: by the 1991 census only 35 per cent of the people declared Kannada as their mother tongue, followed by Tamil (25 per cent), Urdu (19 per cent), and Telugu (17 per cent). This demographic deficit is produced as humiliation in nationalist discourse. Thus, Chidanandamurthy recalls asking for a ticket in Kannada in a cantonment cinema theatre and being threatened by the manager: more humiliating than the threat was the fact that other 'Kannadigas were [reduced to] mute witnesses'.[45] The Kannadiga is here a 'local refugee', said Ra Nam Chandrasekhar, an HAL employee who has produced some of the most detailed analyses of the demographic data to prove that Kannada has only a marginal presence in the state capital.[46] This is both a result of, and a cause for, the 'Kannadiga's lack of self respect and the limitless tolerance of others' needs' which have been represented as 'positive' attributes (the 'large heartedness of the Kannadiga' or the 'civilized Kannadiga') to trick the guileless Kannadiga into a state of contentment.[47]

The 'cosmopolitanism' which is hailed by the city's bourgeoisie and the English press in particular thus takes on a pejorative meaning in Kannada writings: says G. Narayana, former mayor of Bangalore, 'Bangalore is today a "cosmopolitan city". If this situation continues [the whole of] Karnataka itself may become "cosmopolitan"'.[48] The demographic lack, these writers suggest, may be redressed in a number of ways: by encouraging migration into the city from north Karnataka,[49] for instance. This has, however, already been enabled by the new modes of labour mobilization, particularly in the construction industry. By the 1950s, inter-state migration was overshadowed by intra-state migration, and the trend has not been reversed. Nevertheless, the protagonists of Kannada suggest that the wounds inflicted by geography must be redressed in other ways.[50] Since Bangalore is located near the borders of two other states, Andhra Pradesh and Tamil Nadu, it attracts many of their workers. This situation can only be avoided, Sa Ra Govindu, the President of the Rajkumar Abhimanigala Sangha declared, by banning new industries in Bangalore.[51] During the Cauvery agitation Siddaiah Puranik, a litterateur, who feared 'losing Bangalore to outsiders' suggested that Bangalore should be made a 'Kannadiga city'.[52]

The use of demographic data is an attractive stratagem as it abundantly lays bare the dominated status of Kannada in Karnataka and particularly Bangalore, compared with other state capitals such as Chennai, Trivandrum, or Hyderabad.[53] However, the Kannada movement did not owe its origins to the activities of the Shakti Kendra (begun in 1988), nor the Rajkumar Abhimanigala Sanghas (begun in 1982). Nor do these groups today monopolize the struggle to build a new identity for Kannada. What then were the Kannada movements' early forms after state reorganization and how have these been transformed since the 1980s to raise not only new demands but adopt new strategies in the achievement of its goals? How do other groups, such as Karnataka Vimochana Ranga for instance, envisage and work towards *another Kannada nation* and with what success? The rest of this discussion will focus on specific sites where Kannada's dominated status is revealed in recent struggles over space in Bangalore. Contentious struggles have occurred in a variety of sites, over the language of liturgy, work opportunities in the formal and informal economies, or access to power in the city.

Language and Culture

In the early 1960s, the Kannada movement in Bangalore had two principal aims: to build up cultural resources that drew on and strengthened the Kannada language, and to secure jobs for sons-of-the-soil. As old Mysore and particularly Bangalore withdrew from its cultural dependence on Madras Presidency,[54] there was a vigorous call to support indigenous (Karnataka) cultural productions (Fig. 50). Aa Na Krishna Rao (Aa Na Kru) and Ma Ramamurthy of the Karnataka Samyuktha Ranga were among those who demanded that Kannada singers be given a place in the annual Ramotsava cultural festivals, then dominated by artistes from Tamil Nadu.[55]

Cinema too emerged as a site of struggle from the 1960s. At one level, leaders of the Kannada movement objected to representations of Karnataka

FIG. 50 *Asserting linguistic pride: writer Aa Na Kru (in dark glasses) and others take the Kannada Bhuvaneswari in a motorcade.*
(T.L. Ramaswamy, 1970s)

in Tamil films. In *Kanchi Thalaivan* (1963), a Tamil film, the humiliation of Mayurvarman, the Kadamba king, at the court of the Pallavas at Kanchi was taken as a humiliation of the entire Kannada nation, and the movie was withdrawn from circulation.[56] At another level, there were growing demands that more Kannada films be screened in the city. At the start of his political career, Vatal Nagaraj threatened to shut down, through violence if necessary, the theatres where Tamil films were being shown, particularly in the Majestic area of Bangalore city.[57] Finally, in order to stress the separation of the new linguistic state from its earlier cultural moorings in Madras Presidency, there were appeals to actors such as Kalyan Kumar to restrict themselves to acting in Kannada language films.

The quest for a way to dominate the sphere of culture has passed through many phases, though by no means is culture the unalloyed domain of Kannada. The struggle over films that are screened in the city is illustrative of the dominated status of the language. A national culture, which has been purveyed throughout the country via the medium of Hindi, has rarely been questioned and has even been strengthened through the wide spread of the televisual medium. In fact, tolerance of Hindi is a badge of honour, compared with the virulent opposition to the language in Tamil Nadu. Mahadev Banakar cited the Tamil objection to the use of the term 'Akashvani' as a symptom of its anti-national stance, a position from which he was anxious to distance Kannada.[58] Even the demand to replace the broadcast of Hindi news with Kannada at prime time was raised by the regional Tamil AIDMK party in Bangalore.[59] Instead, when there were protests against Hindi tele-serials such as Sanjay Khan's *The Sword of Tippu Sultan*[60] or Ramanand Sagar's *Ramayana*,[61] it was because the dubbing of such films, rather than their remake, reduced opportunities for jobs in the film industry.

Even when Kannada films have a more assured presence in the city, periodic protests against the dubbing of other language films or 'remakes' have continued. Dubbed films are the lowest in a hierarchy which places films originally made in Kannada at the top; 'remakes' continue to maintain a substantial hold along with original films and dubbed ones as there is an acknowledged 'lack of story lines and even directors'. In a mid-1990s recurrence of this crisis, the Karnataka Film Producers' Association and Karnataka Film Directors' Association under the leadership of the Rajkumar Abhimanigala Sangha demanded that Bangalore exhibitors reduce theatre rent for Kannada films and show Kannada films for at least six months in a year. It also asked the government to impose a 12 month ban on the release of non-Kannada films.[62] Exhibitors however claimed that it was difficult enough to run Kannada films for more than two to three weeks. The self-imposed shutdown of the film industry during the kidnapping crisis dealt a body blow to an industry already in decline. Neighbouring states such as Tamil Nadu and Andhra Pradesh were at an advantage as they 'had a huge ready viewership outside their respective states', assuring them of audiences (and therefore film budgets) that Kannada could only dream about.[63]

Notwithstanding a measure of pride in the fact that 'films in six languages are shown in the state', the insistence, particularly during moments of crisis, that only Kannada films be seen in theatres in Bangalore and that DD1 and DD9 telecast only Kannada at peak times are a sign of Kannada's limited reign over the field of culture. During the debates in the legislature, Chief Minister J.H. Patel jocularly declared that it was not the job of the government to teach film artistes to sing and dance as well as their Hindi or Tamil counterparts.[64] In other words, no government action could compensate for the preference of cinema viewers for Hindi or Tamil films: that was to enter the thickets of taste, a point to which I shall return below.

Kannada seeks to monopolize the state channels knowing that it is powerless against the myriad private channels that beam programmes in English, Hindi, and Tamil throughout the day. The aspiration to monopolize the official channel is part of a wider effort to acquire legitimacy in a situation where dominance has been denied: there were times, as in 1976, when suggestions were made for the nationalization of theatres to promote the Kannada industry.[65] Thus, the violent agitation which broke out against the introduction of Urdu news at prime time was a consequence of the desire to monopolize, by force if necessary, the symbolic face of the state on television. From its early days, Kannnada programmes on the national channel had been a contentious issue, many preferring programmes from Madras and resentful of the subtle imposition of Hindi.[66] The periodic protests also point to a very specific relationship between religion and language that has been a part of the Kannada movement to this day. Most recently, the renewed conflict over water-sharing in a distress year, which led to fresh hostilities between the two states in September 2002, was immediately effected as a ban on Tamil movies and television channels in Karnataka's capital city.

Religious and Linguistic Spaces

Elsewhere I have discussed the way in which the dominated status of Kannada has been narrativized by early nationalists: the epistemological violence of colonialism in the nineteenth and twentieth centuries in these accounts is considered less important than the waning fortunes of the Vijayanagara empire and the rise of the Muslim sultanates in the sixteenth century.[67] The commonsensical link between Karnatakatva and Hindutva was most evident during the outbreak of violence against Muslims during the agitation against the Urdu news telecast in 1994. Once more, Kannada protagonists in Bangalore and Mysore acted on a version of history which identified Urdu speakers in Karnataka as Muslims, choosing to ignore Kannada's links with Urdu, and indeed Karnataka's historic encounter with Islam. If the Tamil speaker is envied for an extraterritorial loyalty, for an allegiance to the politics of a neighbouring state, the Urdu speaker is feared for her excessive identity which guarantees the language a space in governmental discourse despite its lack of a territorial location. Both these languages thus survive and even flourish without an official political structure to patronize their community of speakers.

Envy and fear of the languages of minorities, and usually subaltern minorities such as Tamil and Urdu speakers, often, though not always, devolves on the question of jobs created for people within the space that is officially Karnataka. The pattern of such demands in Bangalore has followed well-established patterns set by groups in Bombay and Madras through the 1960s and 1970s. Susan Lewandowski has analysed the riots against Malayalis in Madras and several cities of Tamil Nadu during 1974: Malayali establishments were attacked and even cinema houses were not spared. This was followed by a state government effort to reserve up to 80 per cent of jobs for Tamils and domiciled Tamils. Importantly, however, she points out that Madras remained relatively free of bitter ethnic conflict due to the long history of Malayali involvement in the non-brahmin movement, and the numerical dominance of Tamils in Madras.[68]

The case of Bombay bears closer parallels to the history of Bangalore. Thomas Hansen's recent study shows that although Marathi speakers were far from reduced to minority status, 'sharpened competition over middle class, white collar jobs' in the 1970s paved the way for the rise of a sons-of-the-soil movement led by the Shiv Sena that targeted south Indians.[69] Indeed, the self-perception of Marathi language speakers as a dominated 'minority' bore a close resemblance to the emerging identity of Kannada speakers as a similar minority. Moreover, the tussle over government jobs, and public sector jobs in particular, were the breeding ground of Kannada nationalists through the 1960s and 1970s.

When the Ramakrishna Hegde government relaxed the compulsory Kannada examination for Class III and IV employees in 1984, as a concession to Muslim government servants, the Rajkumar Abhimanigala Sangha demanded a restoration of the compulsory examination.[70] Despite government explanations for the decision, the Sangha organized a city-wide *bandh* which turned violent, and there were attacks on the property of Tamils and Muslims in the western part of Bangalore, as well as on government property.[71] Yet it was a moment when the government succeeded in sticking to its decision: the more virulent attacks on Tamils and Muslims, respectively, were the 1991 and 1994 attacks when the Rajkumar Abhimanigala Sangha had the tacit support of the state government (1991) and of groups such as the Kannada Shakti Kendra and the Hindu Jagarana Vedike in 1994.

In October 1994, the telecast of a ten minute Urdu news bulletin at prime time (7:45 to 7:55 p.m.) was taken as a direct provocation to those committed to deepening the presence of Kannada. It was viewed as being just as a step away from 'making Urdu the second language of the State'.[72] It was the public face of Urdu on the state run TV channels that was most resented. Thus Chidanandamurthy, in an interview with the People's Democratic Forum declared: 'Let there be Urdu news on Doordarshan (DD) 2 but not on DD1 or DD9.'[73] Indeed, 'there are enough Urdu programmes on TV' but Chidanandamurthy's primary objection was to the timing: 'why should Urdu news be telecast only during the prime time from 7:30 p.m. onwards?' Although the programme was not the result of a popular Muslim demand, riots that followed targetted Muslim-owned homes, businesses, and shops.

The identification of Muslims with Urdu is achieved with greater ease than the identification of Christianity with any one language. The Kannada movement's focus on Christians has therefore taken the form of asserting a Kannada presence in a Tamil-dominated church. The substantial presence of the Christian church in Bangalore, and its role as distributor of charity and resources, has been well recognized both within and beyond the church. Throughout the nineteenth century, as the Protestant church gained ground, the flock in Bangalore and nearby Kolar Gold Fields was composed largely of lower caste Tamil speakers who moved to the more profitable Bangalore region.[74] The language of liturgy of many churches, particularly in the Cantonment area, was Tamil, though industrial workers settled to the west of the city were quicker to assimilate the local language for worship.[75] A similar linguistic preference is true of the Catholic church in the city, with some congregations remaining wholly or predominantly Tamil while others were more mixed.

The predominance of Tamils in both the Protestant and Catholic churches has made for a very great source of tension in the past few decades. If the

Protestant church has been free of the acrimonious exchanges between church functionaries and congregations, it is a result of an informal arrangement that appoints a Kannada-speaking bishop for each of its dioceses in the State. The principal focus of Kannada nationalist attention has therefore been the Catholic church. In the early 1980s, the Karnataka Catholic Christhara Sangha became a significant presence, as it was felt that there were not enough Kannada catechists or even priests to meet the needs of the minority.[76] Writers and other intellectuals who jumped into the fray, such as V.K. Gokak, commented on the way the Catholic church was imposing Tamil on Kannada Catholics, often by simply not providing services in Kannada. Indeed, there was growing resentment that there were Kannada services only in 12 of 23 parishes in the Bangalore metropolitan area, while daily services in Tamil and English were most common. One aspiring priest, Thomas Puttaswamy, said that 'The Karnataka youths that are barred from priesthood had to go to Mysore Diocese to fulfill their vows and Karnataka women are blocked from nunneries'.

Such openly voiced resentment found supporters among the more strident sections of the Kannada movement who based their objections to the language of liturgy, especially during major festivals. Begun as a movement to declare the Bangalore diocese as a Kannada diocese, members of Christhara Sangha attempted to stop the Latin Special (Easter) Mass at St Xaviers' Cathedral in Bangalore east in 1981 and assaulted (the Tamil) Reverend Arokiaswamy. The demand for a mass in Kannada infuriated the Tamil majority congregation.[77] There was another attack on the church in Briand Square to the west of the city to demand that Kannada and not Tamil be adopted as the language of the high mass, despite the fact that the congregation was mostly Tamil.[78]

Kannada writers who threw themselves into the agitation declared that it was a problem of culture and language and not religion. 'The fact that Tamil songs and liturgies were being printed in Kannada and imposed on Kannadigas showed that the Church was trying to create a mini-Tamil Nadu.'[79] Once more, the protagonists resorted to the use of numbers to make their respective claims: Kannadigas wanted the Bangalore diocese to be declared a Kannada diocese, while Tamils did not want even a single Tamil mass to be reduced, and even asked for an increase of masses where the majority were Tamils. After all, of the 200,000 Catholics in Bangalore, 75 to 80 per cent were Tamils.[80]

In 1988, the church issued a special circular 2188 declaring a three language formula of Kannada, Tamil, and English services which the Kannada Catholics refused to accept.[81] As a result, almost every year, protests are organized during Easter against the language of liturgy.[82] Writers and artistes participated in these protests out of concern not only for the language but for its speakers 'since the use of Tamil or any language other than Kannada ... meant that all the jobs in the churches and various related offices would not go to Kannadigas'.[83] In some ways symbolic victories have been won, as the Archbishop is now chosen from within Karnataka.

The controversy over the language of liturgy cannot be reduced to concern over the power and opportunities for advancement that are offered by the church. Nevertheless the access of the Kannada Christian to opportunities for work in the church has fuelled many such interventions. For the right to the city has been materialized in its most important sense as a right to jobs in the city. It is in this domain that the Kannada movement may have recorded its most important successes.

Realm of Work in the City

If the protests against the status of Kannada in the cultural sphere and as the language of liturgy have made largely symbolic gains, there is another sphere in which the Kannada movement has been relatively more successful. This is in the realm of public sector jobs, which were important entitlements not only to a salary but a whole new way of life in the city (Fig. 51). Public sector

FIG. 51 *Not just jobs for the 'sons-of-the-soil': women on the assembly line at the HMT watch factory.*
(T.L. Ramaswamy, 28.10.1971)

companies paid good wages for fairly undemanding work. The perquisites are equally important, and include housing, transport, subsidized canteens, etc, all of which were gains consolidated by a left wing trade union movement. The Big Four units, HAL, BEL, HMT and ITI, employed largely Malayali and Tamilian workers: the Kannadiga presence was rather muted until the 1960s when a combination of demographic shifts, management policies and new cultural politics began to gain ground. The public sector units were also important locations of well-funded cultural and fine arts groups, initially monopolized by Malayalis and Tamils. One might even say that these were the languages of cultural organizations and trade unions well into the 1970s.[84] The Tamil Mandram, Kerala Samajam, and Telugu Mithrulu registered their presence well before the Kannada Sanghas were started. Many realized the limits of such activism: as industries minister in 1973, S.M. Krishna urged Kannadigas not to remain content with cultural troupes and instead start industries.[85]

Since the formation of the linguistic states, migration from erstwhile Presidency areas into Bangalore has been gradually overtaken by flows from areas of rural Karnataka. As the new linguistic state consolidates its resources, simultaneously redrawing and restricting the sphere of influence of the Presidencies, labour mobility (of the Tamil versus the Kannadiga labourer for instance) has been transformed, slowing down inter-state and enhancing intra-state migration.[86] The state has, however, been a net gainer from immigration in comparison with the other three southern states which are net losers of population. These migration patterns were offset by recruitment policies: in BEL, for example, the strength of the AITUC was challenged in 1967 by the Workers' Unity Forum, which consisted primarily of new Kannadiga (middle peasant caste) migrants, who were encouraged by a management anxious to curb left wing militancy.[87]

At the height of the 77 day public sector strike, when workers of seven public sector units decided to stay off work in March 1981, posters appeared under the signature of INTUC threatening to 'socially boycott Tamilians and Keralites' if they were not expelled from the state in a week: the implication was that as strike organizers, they were keeping hard-working Kannadigas from rejoining work.[88] The letter from the National Student's Union of India, which was reproduced in the INTUC posters, threatened to cut off water and electricity in workers' colonies, as 'the heritage of our beloved Karnataka is at stake ... the Employee's State Insurance Scheme is being misused by Keralites and Tamilians in large numbers'.[89] The 'treacherous' Tamil or Malayali was thus pitted against 'peace-loving, loyal' Kannadigas, whose desire to work was being thwarted by the outsiders.

Though this had no strike-breaking impact, and even embarassed the Congress government into disavowing the offensive posters, it had important effects on the psyche of the leadership. Michael Fernandes, a member of the Joint Action Front heading the strike declared that this was a ploy of the state to divide the working class on lines of language and regionalism where it had failed to divide it on the grounds of caste and religion as had been tried in BEL and HMT.[90] Yet the poster incident forced Fernandes to defensively declare that 'four of the joint convenors of the JAF were Kannadigas'.

Fernandes' response was an acknowledgement of the scrupulous attention that Kannada groups were paying to the recruitment policies of institutions and agencies within the city. The audit of institutions from the perspective of language had begun as early as 1973, when it was discovered that the newly started Indian Institute of Management, which had procured land and other resources from the state government, was not employing a fair proportion of Kannadigas.[91] The real battleground continued to remain the public sector units, although by the mid-1980s it was clear that Kannada speakers easily formed the majority.

The large number of Kannada Sanghas which participated in the Gokak Chaluvali of 1982 was ample indication that the tide had turned in favour of the Kannadigas. Indeed, the decision of the Devaraj Urs government to make the Kannada test compulsory for Class 2, 3, and 4 employees in government even led to a temporary decline in the activities of the Chaluvaligars.[92] So much so, that the Sarojini Mahishi Committee report which recommended that 100 per cent of the Group D jobs, with proportionately lower percentages for the other categories, be reserved for Kannadigas, came just when the Kannada speakers were a growing majority in nearly all public sector units. The statistics submitted to the Sarojini Mahishi Committee were revealing, though they failed to satisfy Kannada organizations (Table 6.1).[93]

The Hegde government's decision to reverse the policy of a compulsory Kannada test in 1984 led to the first agitation on the question of jobs headed

TABLE 6.1: Language Spoken in Public Sector Units, 1984

Unit	Kannada speakers	Other language speakers
ITI	13,826	4,418
HAL	16,670	1,848
HMT	8,858	2,800
BEML	9,622	3,622
BHEL	2,539	150

SOURCE: *Deccan Herald*, 16 May 1984.

by the Rajkumar Abhimanigala Sangha.[94] The Gokak Chaluvali of 1982, initially a movement of litterateurs, artists, and academics, centred in the Hubli–Dharwar region, which also included significant numbers of women, brought a fresh and positive unity to the Kannada movement, while drawing a whole range of new groups to its fold of which Rajkumar Abhimanigala Sangha was the most important. The entry of Rajkumar into the Gokak Chaluvali truly made it a mass movement, with the actor addressing meetings all over the state.[95] In turn, the emergence of Rajkumar Abhimanigala Sangha signalled a new stage in the movement, with the unhesitating use of violence against public property.[96]

By the time the Wheel and Axle plant was set up in Yelahanka in the early 1980s, '50,000 from all over Karnataka took out a procession' under the leadership of the Rajkumar Abhimanigala Sangha to complain against the injustice done to the Kannadigas in recruitment. The Sarojini Mahishi Committee was a result of this agitation, so that, as Sa Ra Govindu asserted, it soon became a unit that employed 60 per cent Kannadigas. Thus, the local language speaker became a forceful presence in the organized sector, and was willing to assert his claim to the privileges of blue collar work. The 'sons-of-the-soil' policy was deliberately gendered male, since women did not form a part of the Kannada imaginary at any level as we shall see below. Yet such triumphs occurred just when the public sector itself was shrinking, and major changes in the economic profile of the city were underway.

Informal Economies and 'Politics in a New Key'

Two simultaneous processes in the 1980s altered the composition, course, and strategies of the Kannada movement: the marginalization of the public sector and its (usually left wing) trade unions, and the increasing privatization and informalization of the economy. When the long and bitter public sector strike ended in 1981, the eclipse of this sector as prime employer was already under way. Only sporadic protests could take place on the question of jobs, for after all, how could the same pressure be put on the private or largely informal sector? The 1984 agitation against the Hegde government order on Kannada tests for government jobs, and the later demand for the Wheel and Axle Plant or the Railway headquarters in Bangalore were protests largely aimed at the government. Yet, the gradual eclipse of well-established arenas of working class action, such as trade unions, made the informal networks (neighbourhood youth groups, Kannada Sanghas and Abhimanigala Sanghas in particular) even more important sites of political activity. Large numbers of those who belong to Abhimanigala Sanghas for instance are service providers in the city: autorickshaw drivers, tempo drivers and mechanics, recycling job workers, petty shopkeepers, and KEB or BWSSB employees.[97] Not surprisingly the more important arena of action in the 1980s was the symbolic reterritorialization of the city: red and yellow Kannada flag poles that mushroomed all over the city after 1982 were compensating *visually* for what was an *audible* absence. This will be considered at length in the next chapter.

Even so, the contentious question of language in the city was not serious enough to warrant the attention of the state apparatuses. The deputy commissioner of police (intelligence) confessed before the N.D. Venkatesh Commission inquiring into the violence against Tamils in 1991, that 'for purposes of collection of intelligence he had made some classification such as labour problems, communal problems, etc but he is certain that *linguistic relationships with the City population* was not a subject for gathering information.'[98] The violence against Tamils in the old Mysore region, and particularly in Bangalore in 1991, was indeed unprecedented and, further, came at a time when the issue of jobs for Kannadigas was less important than the questions of rights to the land and water. Steen Folke's study of the agricultural uses of the Cauvery river in both Karnataka and Tamil Nadu points to a wide range of bitter disputes over water rights, usually between head- and tail-end users within the same village and between villages, with caste and class (rather than language) playing an important role in deciding water allocations.[99] Nevertheless, the Cauvery water dispute has since the 1980s increasingly been staged as a dispute between two linguistic regions and nationalisms.[100] The centrality of land and water rights both within and beyond the city thus became crucial to the way in which the language question was framed in the 1990s.

The historical conjuncture at which the violence against Tamils occurred in 1991 is of some importance: it was a time when the right to land within the city and beyond had become more uncertain and yet more critical as a resource in an informal economy. Conflicts over land rights within the city had heightened in the decade when the population increased by a massive 76 per cent (1971–81). The geographies of violence, both during the riots of 1991, and 1994 against Urdu speaking Muslims reveal a very interesting congruence. They were both concentrated in the western parts of the city, where land rights were most precarious, a terrain that was fully occupied by illegal constructions, and further, hilly ground that made surveillance difficult. The riots did not affect older settlements of Tamils to the east of the city. The Venkatesh Commission noted that the 1991 violence was confined to 13 police station limits, all of which were contiguous and in the western part of the city.[101] In the 20 sq. km falling to the Basaveshwaranagar and Kamakshipalaya police stations, 'there existed several revenue pockets and slums mostly inhabited by labour class and migrant poor people considerable number of whom were linguistic minorities'.[102] In the anti-Urdu telecast riots of 1994, the properties and businesses of Muslims were singled out for attack in the same western divisions of the city off Mysore Road.[103]

This area, as Benjamin and Bhuvaneswari's work has shown, boasts of one of the most vibrant informal economies in Bangalore city, but ironically in an area which has the most tenuous of rights to property, and where ownership is constantly in a state of flux.[104] The authors say of Azadnagar, near the KR Market,

> The land supply system in Azadnagar comprises of a variety of subsystems—free sites formed by state agencies and distributed to poor groups, revenue plots, Gramthana or layouts on village land and squatter settlement. Valmikinagar one of the largest layouts in the ward for example was developed partly by the State for free sites and partly by private developers. Azadnagar, another large layout in the ward evolved on gramthana land. In addition, there are a large number of smaller private revenue layouts in the ward—Markandeya layout, Vittal nagar layout, Adarshnagar, Rudrappa garden etc. Besides, the Bande Squatter settlement emerged on 'marginal' land in the abandoned quarry area, low lying land in the ward. The different land settings encompass the variety of economic activities and its actors.

Property here has economic value not merely as housing but also as a source of livelihood. Further, as locations outside the master planning area, 'claims are established not only via markets, but also [via] ethnic and political routes'. Such fragile and complex economies have been most vulnerable during the riots of the 1990s (Fig. 52).

Both in 1991 and in 1994, the property and livelihoods of Tamils and Muslims respectively were subjected to far more sustained attack than the bodies of these inhabitants. Of the 23 deaths that are believed to have occurred in 1991, 17 were due to police firing and six due to mob violence.[105] Property loss in these riots was put at Rs 17 crores in both Tamil Nadu and Karnataka by the Indian Peoples' Human Rights Tribunal.[106] The Venkatesh Commission put the estimate of losses variously at Rs 3 crores (state and central government losses) at Rs 15.5 crores (according to Department of Commerce and Industries) and Rs 20.5 crores (according to police estimates).[107] In the anti-Urdu riots, 25 were killed, an equal number dying as a result of police firing and stabbing injuries. These are shocking statistics for a city that had no previous history of such deadly violence. However, the statistics relating to the loss of private

FIG. 52 *A steadily growing informal economy: roadside welding shop in Tilakanagar.* (G. Raghav, 1999)

property and livelihoods and the threat to certain social groups in the western part of the city were indicative of more enduring strategies by which claims to an area or neighbourhood were altered.[108]

Kannada speakers are preponderant in north-west and west Bangalore, according to recent analyses of slum populations, indicating that the migration of people from other districts of Karnataka has been most sustained in these areas.[109] This contrasts with successive waves of migration to the city of Bangalore from areas in Tamil Nadu. Tamil migrants, despite their substantial contribution to the economic profile of the city, particularly in the informal sector, are culturally viewed as inhabiting slums, a visible blot on the city landscape. Mahadev Banakar, at the height of the Gokak agitation, said that a disproportionate number of Tamils live in the slums of Bangalore: 'they seem to be happier in Karnataka than Tamil Nadu'.[110] Even less charitable were the versions of Tamil migration that were attributed to Tamil Nadu's prohibition policy.[111] Town planners and officials, who may not share this hostility to Tamilians, nevertheless reinforce the idea that migration is the cause of the city's problems, as the 'bulk of the migrants are illiterate and would accept substandard existence in the city'.[112]

As suppliers of goods and especially services that are vital to the survival of the city, slums render the boundaries of linguistic states irrelevant. Bangalore is the preferred destination of migrants from Tamil Nadu, particularly from the districts of North Arcot and Chingleput: Gertrude Woodruffe's 1959 study of migrants to a segregated slum of 207 Adi Dravida families in Bangalore showed that though the city was 125 miles away from the migrating village, and Madras only 75 miles away, 'no one in either cheri has ever gone to Madras except en route to Penang'.[113] This, she explains, is a 'self reinforcing process which is both the result of and results in villagers going to places they have heard about often in detail or where they have relatives'.

More recent studies also confirm that the attractions of Bangalore as a destination for migrants have not been tarnished by the episodes of violence directed against Tamils. A majority of the hawkers at KR Market are migrants from villages in South Arcot: Kattupaiyur has sent many of its families to work in Bangalore. Benjamin and Bhuvaneswari found that

> families prefer to go to Bangalore because of the diversity of employment opportunities enable them to generate greater surplus. Those who have moved to Madras can find only low grade work as coolies in the airport or as unskilled industrial workers in North Madras. They have less mobility as compared to employment in Bangalore. Also in Madras, women do not find much opportunity to earn an income, and have to usually work as domestic servants with a low pay and less upward mobility. In

Bangalore, in contrast, both men and women are involved in hawking and are able to generate enough surplus to send remittances and also make investments back home.[114]

Jobs within the organized sector may be shrinking, but the burgeoning opportunities of the informal sector are an attraction enough for new migrants who find the city a source for capital accumulation, even when the cultural conditions may not be as hospitable as they may have been. The population of the slums in Bangalore is changing, as more intra-state migrants enter the city competing for the opportunities offered at the lower end of the scale for economic mobility and accumulation. This has produced politics in a new key, and the dangers of equating the urban poor with certain linguistic groups (Tamil or Urdu) poses political perils that are only gradually being recognized. A 'rather grand scale' government policy of slum improvement in the early 1990s fixed a cut-off point which qualified older slums for 'improvement' and younger slums for 'clearance'. The programme was called off when it was discovered that it would have led to the improvement of predominantly Tamil slums and the clearance of more recent Kannada ones.[115]

The definite link between the growing violence of language politics in the past two decades (particularly in the 1990s) and transformations within the economic sphere, however, must not obscure the work of ideologically constituting, and mobilizing, the Kannada people in the name of linguistic nationalism. An account of the role of language politics in defining the right to the city in economic terms alone would clearly be inadequate in understanding the meaning and scope of politics in the new key since the 1980s.

Modes of Mobilization

It would be tempting to see in the actions of Kannada activists since the 1980s a mimicry of the styles and strategies of Tamil nationalism. Yet not always was the image of nationalism in Karnataka one that was subordinated to language. At a mammoth rally in Shivajinagar on the occasion of Annadurai's birthday addressed by the then Tamil Nadu chief minister M. Karunanidhi, the CM asked the DMK (Dravida Munnetra Kazhagam) state unit to 'identify with Karnataka and fight for the supremacy of Kannada'.[116] A similar sentiment had earlier been voiced by the ideologue of the Dravidian movement, E.V. Ramawamy Naickar, on a visit to Bangalore, when he called on Tamilians 'to live as Kannadigas' in Karnataka.[117]

In the 1960s, the relative political quiescence of the Kannadiga was deplored by those Bangalore Tamils who threw themselves into the anti-Hindi protests:[118] there is an apocryphal tale of Tamils sending the shaming 'gift of bangles' to their Kannadiga counterparts to goad them into opposing Hindi. The 'emasculated Kannadiga' here is contrasted with the 'virile Tamil', and structures the response of the Kannadiga, leaving language conflicts gendered on both sides of the border.

For language itself is 'feminized,' personified as Kannada Bhuvaneswari/ Tamilttay, while her supplicants, devotees, and protectors are overwhelmingly male.[119] Mobilization on the question of language and state identity has remained resolutely and aggressively male: not only has participation in fan clubs or language associations been male, the female has been mobilized within this discourse as a revered but weak personification of language itself, calling for the constant vigilance of her protectors.[120] Tejaswini Niranjana's scrutiny of the cultural productions—cassettes, tabloids, and the like—focused on the kidnapping of Rajkumar by Veerappan reveals an overwhelmingly masculinized discourse, which called on Kannada *abhimani*s to shed their historic timidity. The new masculinity, nevertheless, valorized Rajkumar as a cultured and urbane figure compared with Veerappan. The two men and their respective linguistic nationalisms were made to stand for the dichotomy between village, or more correctly forest and city/state (*kaadu* and *naadu*). Most of the cultural productions and periodic public utterances of the first family therefore urged the *abhimani* to exercise self-restraint, in what Niranjana calls a 'double performance' which was 'necessary for the preservation of Kannada pride'.[121]

The woman is figured not as 'citizen' in this discourse, but an embodiment of regional/linguistic honour. Neither Chidanandamurthy nor Sa Ra Govindu recognized the need to draw more women into their organizations, still less recast this profoundly gendered discourse. On his part, D.R. Nagaraj, while characterizing 'virile politics' as entirely a modern invention, a weapon of the Hindu nationalists, falls back on valorizing Gandhi as the embodiment of an Indian ideal of '*ardhanareeswara*'.

The commonalities between the gendered discourses of both Kannada and Tamil may be understood within the broader context of nineteenth century nationalist mobilizations that strove to correct the colonial stereotype of the emasculated Indian male. Rather than the Kannada linguistic movement being simply imitative of the Tamil model, there are quite often common sources for modalities of mobilization, as Niranjana has shown in her discussion of the construction of masculinity following Rajkumar's abduction. There are, however, other discernable debts to the political energies of Tamil activists. S. Siddalingaiah, Dalit poet, teacher, and former MLC, recalls his early tutelage by RPI activists from Tamil Nadu (who were also vehemently anti-DMK) and the support of the Tamil Dalits during the *busa* agitation of 1973 when he was himself under attack.[122] This was a time when Dalit or trade union politics was unmarked by an exclusivist emphasis on language. The gradual evolution of a stress on (exclusivist) pride in the Kannada language has thus had serious repercussions on the tolerance for minorities. Suggesting that multilingualism was a 'mistake' rather than a virtue, Chidanandamurthy says, 'at the same time we too have erred, we know it, we have been too good, we have been addressing Tamilians in Tamil, Malayalees in Malayalam, without initiating them into our language.'[123]

Fortunately, even the Rajkumar abduction crisis did not dim the pride that many people of Karnataka took in their multilingualism: Deputy Chief Minister Mallikarjun Kharge spoke in the chaste Urdu of his native Gulbarga to his NDTV interlocutors; Rajkumar and his family themselves did not hesitate to use the language of the captors in their appeals. This is why the politics that brandishes numbers in its support may be somewhat misleading, since, as K.S. Singh's *Peoples of India* project has shown, there is overwhelming indication of the multilingualism of many Indians (as much as 66 per cent in that sample). Knowledge of Kannada in Bangalore may be far more widespread than is admitted in mother tongue counts; the only sections who may afford the luxury of ignorance may be the English speakers.

However, while it is quite possible to legislate on the language of administration, employment, or education, there remains the stubborn question of taste. D.V. Gundappa, writing to R.R. Diwakar in 1950, despaired over the relative unpopularity of Kannada songs:

> We are now supposed to have as many as five AIR centres for Karnataka. But there is not even one among them which is doing what is necessary to encourage the singing of Kannada songs. Even the Mysore station prefers to provide Tamil and Telugu pieces as recorded music and the Mysore Palace artist T. Chowdiah prefers to render a Tamil Pallavi rather than a Kannada or a Sanskrit one.[124]

More recently, Radhakrishna, president of the Jaga Mechida Maga Dr Rajkumar Abhimanigala Sangha, expressed similar dismay over the preference of Kannada speakers for the more lavish productions of the Tamil or Hindi film industry. For the price of a cinema ticket, the audience is transported to Simla, Kashmir, or Washington, whereas the Kannada film shows 'the same Nagarhole, the same Bandipura, the same Mysore Palace'.[125] Nor ιs tnis merely a consequence of the smaller population of Kannadigas in the country. What cannot be achieved through the mechanisms of persuasion is therefore achieved through the modalities of compulsion: the compulsory screening of Kannada films in all theatres for a fixed number of weeks per year has thus been a repeated demand of the Kannada movement.[126]

Events of the last two decades have hardened the position of both Kannadigas and Tamils who may formerly have been political allies within the trade union, the Dalit movement, or even the linguistic movement. Let us recall, for instance, that many left wing groups in the public sector responded in the early 1960s to the contentious issue of language by promoting Kannada literature and celebrating Kannada's ascendence. Forced to respond to the mobilization of workers on linguistic lines in BEL during the late 1960s, the AITUC devised programmes for the sale of books by Kannada writers, talks, and other cultural programmes in Kannada as a means of playing down the management emphasis on the regional origins of left wing trade union organizers. Celebrations of Karnataka's Rajyotsava, meanwhile, were increasingly resembling large-scale Ayudha pujas, forcing work stoppages and promoting the worship of Kannada Bhuvaneswari at factory locations.

The defensive Tamil response to the relentless campaign against migration into the city has been to produce a mythicized past that speaks of Tamils as the 'original inhabitants' of the Bangalore and Kolar districts. Even Kempegowda, the founder of the city, it is claimed, 'was a Tigala who belonged to the Tamil Vanniyar caste'.[127] Many solidarities were broken, says the Tamil Sangham report, citing attacks by Dalits in Siluvepura as a sign that in addition to myths of Hindu, Dravidian, or class identity, even a 'caste based unity of Dalits' has begun evaporating in the minds of Tamils.[128] This, despite the fact that there were many voices raised against the ferocious attacks on Tamils and Tamil properties by a range of organizations and individuals in Karnataka—Karnataka Rajya Raitha Sangha, Karnataka Vimochana Ranga, women's groups in Bangalore such as Vimochana, and sections of Rajkumar Abhimanigala Sangha themselves. Could these alternative positions, no matter how weak, be taken as resources for a envisaging another Kannada nation?

Another Kannada Nation

Never before in Karnataka's history has the economic value of English education been as visible as in the opportunities offered by the new economy. Infosys Chairman N.R. Narayana Murthy's plea for a massive expansion of English education to wrest the opportunities offered by the global market for software production has been matched by an equal and opposite response among Kannada protagonists. U.R. Ananthamurthy's inaugural address at the 69th Kannada Sahitya Sammelan in February 2002 remarked on the imbalance which keeps Kannada as a language 'confined to the kitchen':

> Children who attend the modern schools in Bangalore do not know the work of DVG, Kuvempu, Bendre, Kumara Vyasa, Karanth. If caste was the most unequal division of our society in the past, today it is the possession of English that produces inequalities.[129]

Ananthamurthy inveighed against the 'mindboggling tolerance' of Kannadigas, and called for 'meaningful resistance' to protect the language, culture and civilization of Karnataka.[130] The identification of the hegemony of English as resulting in Kannada's beleaguered status was evident in the statement of those Kannada intellectuals who were pained by the anti-minority direction in which the 1982 Gokak agitation was developing: if English was the 'prestigious enchantress', Kannada was the 'sobbing mother'.[131] The state, meanwhile, elides the issue by citing the exigencies of law which have interfered with implementing its policy of compulsory education in Kannada from standard 1–5.[132]

At the height of the Gokak agitation, K.N. Harikumar, the young editor of the *Deccan Herald,* himself under siege for having criticized the 'conservative integrationism' of the pro-Kannada movement, produced a lengthy critique of the movement in his own newspaper. In his analysis of the language agitation, its protagonists and beneficiaries, from a strictly Marxist perspective, Harikumar made a useful observation:

> Because the Kannada intellectual tradition is largely literary, the role of Kannada in particular and languages in general is highly overplayed. The role and meaning of non-linguistic identities, modes of perception and expression, and of wider social and political forces, is neglected or at best seen as subservient to the role of language, i.e. Kannada.

Furthermore, the obsession of the Kannada intelligentsia with language—be it Kannada, English, or Sanskrit—forces them to view everything from this perspective so that 'they are unable to ... see that in certain areas of intellectual activity, e.g. in music, painting, mathematics, modern science etc. and of life itself, e.g. Harijan oppression, marriage, untouchability, trade union struggles etc., language or the differences between language has no role or plays a very different role'.[133] Throughout this article, Harikumar was careful to distinguish between different phases and sections of the language agitation, although his critique pointed to the impossibility of conceiving a democratic culture founded only on the ethnocultural unities of language. Nevertheless, the real link between language and democracy was ignored, the fact that language is not a neutral medium, and that access to the very instruments of democracy—the law or education, for instance—was enabled in and through language.

In an important study of the historical cleavage between patriotism and nationalism as it developed in Europe, Maurizio Viroli suggests that though 'patriotism' and 'nationalism' compete on the same terrain, they are antithetical to each other.[134] Identifying the former with republican ideals and fights for freedom rather than a singular language or ethnicity he says, 'properly understood, the language of republican patriotism could serve as a powerful antidote to nationalism'. However,

> the ethnocultural unity [of nationalism without a republican liberty] may translate into civic solidarity, if a culture of citizenship is erected on it; or better, if the sense of belonging based on common culture and common ethnic descent is translated into a culture of citizenship. Without a political culture of liberty, ethnocultural unity generates love of one's cultural uniqueness (if not superiority) and a desire to keep it pure from external contamination and intrusion. We would have the nation but it would not be a nation of citizens ... Democratic polities do not need ethnocultural unity; they need citizens committed to the way of life of the republic.[135]

Such an opposition between the sites of patriotic (democratic) actions and (modern) nationalisms (and sub-nationalisms are hardly exempt from the monstrosities of the full-fledged nationalisms, as we well know) may be relevant in delineating the strands of the Kannada movement. At the present time, there is no doubt that the dominant strand is one that calls for the kind of ethnocultural unity that Viroli warns against. There are however many signs of political activities in Karnataka that complicate the picture of a resolutely ethnocultural nationalism.

Even such an apparently unified movement as Rajkumar Abhimanigala Sangha was composed of multiple strands. Until 1987, said Radhakrishna, president of Jaga Mechchida Maga Dr. Rajkumar Abhimanigala Sangha, the Sanghas were intolerant, particularly of the large minority of Tamils.

> After 1987, we realized we were wrong. By this time, a lot of gaps had grown between Kannada and Tamil brothers. After 1987, our viewpoint changed. People who live in Karnataka are called Kannadigas. Kannadiga is not the one who knows Kannada ... Those who live here, who migrated for the sake of livelihood ... they also are the people of the state.

He urged that 'Both [Kannada and Tamil speakers] should join our movement [which opposed the rapacious forces of the market in globalized consumption—e.g. the struggle against Kentucky Fried Chicken—and the appropriation of livelihood resources in return for only an image—e.g. the ongoing struggle against the Bangalore–Mysore Infrastructure Corridor.'[136]

There is recognition among such groups as Karnataka Vimochana Ranga (KVR) that the only language that the Karnataka state is actively promoting is the language of capitalism, and resistance to that calls for a critique of the development paradigm itself: to what use must the resources of Karnataka be put? to benefit which people? The KVR, as Ramesh Bairy's research has pointed out, is possessed of a different vision of Karnataka, one that questions and restructures the frames within which the language question may be posed.[137] The current campaign to halt work on the massive acquisition of land for the Bangalore–Mysore infrastructure project has been joined by respected Gandhians such as H.S. Doreswamy, environmental activists, KVR, Dalit groups, and branches of the Rajkumar Abhimanigala Sangha.

Other critiques of the dominant voices on the predicament of Kannada have come from unexpected quarters, and adopt alternative strategies of mobilization. Karnataka Rajya Raitha Sangha, though not unambiguous in its agenda, has consistently questioned the emerging 'sovereignty of the market' which has begun to reduce the role of the state to that of 'service provider'. Further, its critique of the absorption of rural resources by cities has sometimes led to untenable demands that no more Cauvery water should be allowed to flow into the city of Bangalore. A strong feminist critique of the gendered discourse of linguistic politics has laid bare the inadequacies of norming the subject of the Kannada nation as male. Also, although Karnataka's Dalit groups have wavered more recently on whether they must support the strident calls to defend Kannada identity, they remain only uneasily aligned with the clearly pro-Hindutva version of Kannada nationalism. Thus, Karnataka Samata Sainik Dal, at the height of the protests against the unveiling of the Thiruvalluvar statue, detected an upper caste plot to keep a Dalit hero (Thiruvalluvar) from occupying public space in the city.[138]

Indeed, Rajkumar himself has remained loyal to another nation in his increasing distance from the activities of the majority of his fans' associations. In 1978, he went into hiding to avoid being dragged into standing for elections against Indira Gandhi in Chikmagalur. In 1984, he condemned the violence during the bandh, and refused to serve on the government panel which the Hegde government set up to solve the issue of Kannada examinations for Class III and IV jobs, though he declared the cause just. By the late 1980s, the activities of 'fan clubs' were a positive embarrassment to him when they took to violent road and rail *rokos*: the 1987 rail *roko* campaign which was meticulously organized to press for a Southern Railway Centre in Karnataka, led him to publicly stage a break, saying that he was in no way related to fans' associations. It was at that moment that many Abhimanigala Sanghas publicly declared *their* autonomy. 'It is like, in a poster somewhere, a beedi is kept in [Rajkumar's] mouth,' explains Radhakrishna. 'Does that mean he is smoking a beedi? No. So like that we will keep his name, we have that right. *When he has come into public life we have the right to use him.*' Thus, the man who wished to represent the aspirations of '3 crore Kannadigas' in 1982 has been increasingly distanced from the very organizations that invoke his name.

Conclusion

Between June and November 2002, the districts of southern Karnataka were once more convulsed when the failure of the south-west monsoon resulted in a crisis of water-sharing between Karnataka and Tamil Nadu. Karnataka's reluctance to comply with the Supreme Court order to release at least 8000 cusecs per day to Tamil Nadu, following the death of a farmer in the Kabini reservoir, invited the charge that Karnaṭaka CM S.M. Krishna had committed contempt of court. Meanwhile, Veerappan struck once more, taking as hostage a former MLA Nagappa who tragically died in captivity. The conjunction of events once more raised the spectre of a confrontation between two irreconcilable nationalisms, which, however, spared the city of Bangalore from violence. Antagonism against Tamil Nadu instead took the form of shutting down Tamil TV channels, thus banning the screening of Tamil films. Once more the conflict over scarce water resources was mapped on to a linguistic difference with important consequences for the relationship between the two communities.

Undoubtedly there was widespread support for the programmes and activities of the more extreme linguistic nationalisms, especially during the Rajkumar abduction which was increasingly (and dangerously) read as an 'encounter between two nationalisms'. Such readings sweep complex histories out of sight, leaving the borders of the administrative state as the final space within which such identities may unfold. Nothing could be further from the fanciful wish of the advertisement for BPL mobiles which proclaims 'Geography is history'. Yet it is possible, even in these globalizing times, to detect the anguish about the destiny of a language threatened by the votaries of globalization in Bangalore. Karnataka's unique state formation, geography, and history may be the starting point for conceiving a different kind of nation, one that grasps both ends of a slippery pole to 'achieve universality through being specific', as D.R. Nagaraj has suggested, by placing these gathering passions at the service of a new democratic citizenship. Meanwhile, the contest over territories, and the territories of Bangalore in particular, continue to mark a range of struggles and contests of the last few decades. This becomes clearer when we turn to the many contests over symbolic spaces, as the city is reterritorialized in ways that bring many mental–imaginative maps to life.

SEVEN

Battles for Bangalore: Reterritorializing the City

Streets are the dwelling place of the collective. The collective is an eternally wakeful, eternally agitated being that—in the space between the building fronts—lives, experiences, understands, and invents as much as individuals do within the privacy of their own four walls.

Walter Benjamin, *The Arcades Project*

In May 1999, Ramesh Kalkur, a Bangalore-based artist, seated all the major statues of the city down to a meal in Kannada Bhavan.[1] The central figure in this tableau, entitled *Royal Feast*, was the statue of Queen Victoria, flanked on either side by 12 colonial, national, and regional heroes who are part of the iconography of the city.[2] A tablecloth spread with banana leaves, imprinted with the motif of fork and knife, formed the foreground of the work, and playfully evoked the mood of an Indian feast. The painting mimicked the pictorial arrangement of Leonardo da Vinci's *Last Supper*, while its unifying architectural backdrop was drawn from a minor Italian painting of the fifteenth century depicting the *Feast in the House of Levi*.[3] If he deliberately deployed the skills of the banner painter in producing this work, Kalkur also called attention to, and questioned, the importance of symbols and images within contemporary Indian culture.

By bringing such diverse political figures as Queen Victoria and Krishnaraja Wodeyar, Mahatma Gandhi, Edward VII, Mark Cubbon, and

B.R Ambedkar into posthumous dialogue, the artist doubled the symbolic space of the city. In the representational space of the painting, he paid tribute to a system of signs that mark the city, often in visually unobtrusive ways, but frequently becoming the rallying point for expressions of urban democracy or its discontents. In his own representation of these symbolic spaces, the artist only hinted at the increasingly contentious struggles over symbolic space in the city. The imperial finger of Queen Victoria, which has been broken, was the theme of several other works, entitled *Finger from the Queen's Museum* or *The Growing Finger*. However, Kalkur's intention of installing a site-specific work in the space around the Victoria statue was thwarted by procedural delays and bureaucratic refusals, forcing the artist to scale down his work to fit the more conventional space of the gallery at Kannada Bhavan.

Although Bangalore has not seen political movements demanding a symbolic stake in the city on quite the same scale as the cities of Chennai and Hyderabad, the iconography of the city has increasingly come under scrutiny. It is sometimes the state that promotes, lays claim or yields to a particular strand of Karnataka or Indian history to call recalcitrant constituencies to order. At other times, public spaces in the city are the focus of groups interested in making new meaning within an urban context, and may variously question a semiotics that privileges the histories of colonial subjugation, national dominance, or regional cultural and political interests. Kalkur's work was an ironic comment on the range of conflicting memories evoked by these monuments in the city. Yet by bringing them together, he symbolically erased the ideological baggage attached to each of these statues and spaces, equalizing them and exaggerating the unity of the mental–imaginative universe to which they belong.

In fact, the economy of symbols and symbolic spaces in the city is far from unified or equally valued. The commemoration of heroes or events in the statuary or street furniture of the city is far from being a mere reflection of the economic, social, or cultural order, and many mental–imaginative maps of the city jostle for power. The sphere of the symbolic is thus the sphere within which accumulation of a different kind occurs, an accumulation of symbolic capital, often among those denied other forms of capital accumulation. The street or street corner may thus take on different meanings, temporarily suspending its primary identity as the space of 'trade and traffic', an artery for the flow of people and vehicles, to become a far more contested space inviting temporary and permanent occupations by those who wish to express their pride, anger, or anguish about developments within the city or the region. They may, in short, be taken as signs of a democratic order asserting itself in very visual ways, and the conflicts a sign of the lack of consensus among the citizens.

This chapter will examine the question of how symbolic space in Bangalore city has been appropriated, deployed, or controlled by competing interests and ideologies over the five decades since 1949. Specifically, the chapter turns to the symbolic spatial strategies of dominated and ascendant cultural or economic groups, strategies that link in everyday practice the physical–material and mental–imaginative aspects of social space.[4] What emblems of the colonial past, for instance, have been replaced or found a fresh lease of life within the newly dominant corporate cultural order? What nationalist fictions have found symbolic expression in the city? How has the increasing dominance of global capital, on the one hand, or older cultural formations, on the other, been challenged by the spatial strategies of relatively newer claims on the city? How do the frequent symbolic occupations of city space, though sometimes temporary, re-articulate notions of 'citizenship' or acknowledge the marks of caste, ethnicity, and gender in ways that were unanticipated within the moral cultural ground of modernity, and indeed 'civil' society, as Partha Chatterjee has suggested?

New political and social forces that have laid claim to the city in order to make it their own have evolved varied and incommensurate strategies: invoking the language of rights to the city, contesting uses of the city's past, deploying images that recast power in the city or aggressively asserting a vision of the city in the 'new economy'. If Bangalore has, especially in the last two decades, come to exemplify both 'consumption of space as well as a space of consumption',[5] these competing claims on city space achieve a number of goals. They set limits to the consumption of the city's colonial and monarchic past, as exemplified in campaigns to 'Bring Back Beauty to Bangalore';[6] they also question a long history of city development that has kept production and the labouring classes invisible. Bangalore's class, caste, and ethnic fractions occupy, control, or deploy space in ways that recover visibility, so that the city is a far more disturbed zone than what is valorized in technocratized planning.[7] These processes not only express the uneven development of capitalist relations in the city, but pose challenges to the 'universals' (and their exclusions) on which Indian modernity is founded.

The Legacies of a Divided City

Some of the battles for Bangalore recall the city's unique divided legacy, and serve as a useful starting point for the consideration of symbolic spaces within the city. Despite the administrative unity of the city that was declared in 1949, the city's east–west zonation continues to persist, and the uncomfortable question of 'independence',[8] or at least administrative freedom of the erstwhile Cantonment has often been reiterated.[9] Such battles sharpened after the city of Bangalore became the capital of the unified state of Karnataka in 1956, and a premier metropolis of the southern region. Today, the dream of turning Bangalore into a 'city-state' is shared by the corporate sector, amidst forlorn hopes of keeping at bay those political forces that impede the information technology industry's visions of 'spaceless' production.[10]

In Chapter One, I discussed at length how the eastern and western zones of Bangalore developed along distinct historical, demographic, economic, and spatial trajectories. For a while after the formation of the single corporation of Bangalore, the divided city heritage was acknowledged in the choice of mayor and deputy mayor, who represented the city and the cantonment in turns.[11] Oath-taking was in three languages, English, Kannada, and Tamil, though it came increasingly under protest.[12] The demand to acknowledge these spatial and cultural divisions was repeated even as recently as 1998, when the DMK corporator refused to vote for the deputy mayor unless the post went to a person from the erstwhile cantonment.[13] The city itself continues to bear the signs of its divided past, with two densely populated commercial areas served by their own bus and train depots and markets.[14] While the spacious lines of the former cantonment have today become the core of the unified city—a blend of business space with the residential that has appealed to national and multinational capital—the two old city cores remain important production and commercial centres.

More striking in previous times were the linguistic and cultural distinctions between the zones, since the cantonment had attracted a large number of camp followers from Tamil-speaking areas of the neighbouring Madras Presidency.[15] Consequently, as we have seen in the previous chapter, the Kannada language's restricted presence in the city was only altered in two decades of somewhat spectacular demographic growth, the decade of 1941–51 when the population almost doubled, and the decade of 1971–81 when the city grew by 76 per cent. The city drew more migrants from districts within the state after the 1950s, significantly altering the linguistic map of the city.[16]

If Bangalore has enjoyed the reputation of a 'clean' city that is 'cosmopolitan' in character, and 'tolerant of income disparities'[17] it is not merely the topography that is being described. True, the strongly middle-class demographic profile and the relative invisibility of the labouring poor contributes to such an image. Yet such descriptions ideologically privilege an absence, the relatively weak and delayed emergence of nationalist politics in the city and the severely restricted career of the Left, which in the post-Independence years was founded on the (overwhelmingly male) trade unionism of the privileged public sector and large private units, such as MICO. Over the past two decades, however, the city's claim on 'tolerance' has weakened, such attributes even taking on a pejorative meaning among those arguing for a more assertive linguistic presence, marking a break from earlier efforts at redefining the city's colonial past.

Pasts in the City

Which of the city's many histories would the new masters evoke in their monuments, spaces and architecture? Here was a city marked more strongly by its colonial and monarchical legacies than by participation in national or other movements for social change. Nationalist ideologies were late to develop, and were always somewhat overshadowed by the monarchical culture of old Mysore. Predictably, the imperial and indigenous royal legacy is writ large in the erstwhile cantonment area, in the form of place names, parks, and statues, and architectural features that the newly migrant multinational houses have found uniquely allied with the styles of consumption they wish to promote.[18] Pride in, and nostalgia for, this aristocratic past has clearly marked conservation efforts, architectural imaginations and literary genres alike.[19]

It took another nationalism, the linguistic nationalism of Kannada which flowered after reorganization of the Indian states in 1956, to challenge and transform some symbolic legacies of the colonial period, and to carry out one of the earliest decisions of the corporation of Bangalore. As early as 1949, the Corporation decided to demolish a cenotaph honouring British soldiers who had died during the battle for Bangalore in 1791–2.[20] The monument, established some time in the nineteenth century in memory of those who died in the battle, was located at the site that where the new municipal offices—today's corporation building—were built in 1935. The Corporation decision to demolish the monument was a way of erasing the memory of historic humiliation, and its place was to be taken by a symbol of national pride and glorious Indian antiquity, the Asoka pillar.[21]

Yet nothing came of this decision until a new battle for Bangalore began more than a decade later, when the movement to enshrine Kannada as the state's official language began to reach beyond the restricted realms of protests and activities of the literary élite.[22] By this time, Mysore state, and more properly Bangalore, was moving out of the cultural shadow of Madras Presidency. It was Madras that had supplied generations of bureaucrats and workers, and even performing artistes for the annual music and dance season in Bangalore. It was to Madras city that generations of aspiring Bangalore officials had travelled for their higher education; even the fledgling Kannada film industry found its feet in that Presidency city.

The nascent Kannada movement's battle for Bangalore was to wrest linguistic control or at least dominance in a city that was at once state capital, industrial metropolis, and gateway to new and intensified forms of consumption. Anti-imperial protests were therefore merely a prelude to asserting the Kannadiga as the true son-of-the-city-soil, whether in jobs or educational opportunities. Producing a new linguistic cosmos[23] of Kannada cultural heroes—figures from history, intellectuals, or artistes and politicians—could become possible only when the supporters of Kannada and Karnataka found a mass base in Bangalore and seats in the municipal corporation.

In 1962, leading litterateur Aa Na Krishna Rao launched a protest against a concert by the famous classical singer, M.S. Subbalakshmi, during the Ramanavami festival in Bangalore. His objection was to the monopoly of Tamil musicians and dancers over the Kannada cultural domain. Decrying the neglect of Kannada artistes, he said *Idu Ramotsava alla, Tamilotsava* ('This is not a festival for Rama, but of Tamils')[24] Aa Na Kru's campaign was successful in turning attention to the plight of Kannada in its home state, a region which was only gradually coming into being. His protest coincided with the period when the Kannada film industry, so crucial to the development of linguistic identity, was seeking to relocate in the state capital of the unified Mysore. By this time, as the previous chapter has shown, employment in the Bangalore-based public sector industries began attracting Kannada speaking migrants, to whom the city offered new possibilities for economic, cultural, and political redefinition, just as it had for their Tamil and Malayalam speaking forerunners.[25]

Even as protests against the perceived cultural hegemony of Tamil/Tamilians in Bangalore were beginning, the consensus on installing the Asoka pillar had yielded place to a new initiative in 1959 to commemorate the life of Kempegowda, the founder of Bangalore. The absence of a reliable visual record of the legendary hero delayed work on the statue for five years.[26] When plans were finally made to install it on 1 November 1964, to commemorate the day on which a unified Karnataka came into being,[27] the long forgotten call to remove the humiliating cenotaph in the area was revived.[28] In September 1964, following several assaults on the cenotaph by groups of Kannada Chaluvali volunteers who threatened to destroy it,[29] Corporation authorities sought permission from the chief minister to demolish the British war

FIG. 53 *Protecting the colonial heritage: police guard the cenotaph (since demolished) from possible attack by the Kannada Chaluvaligars.*
(T.L. Ramaswamy, 1964)

memorial (Fig. 53).[30] Today, Kempegowda's statue presides over Narasimharaja Square in front of the City Corporation offices, while Cenotaph Road has been renamed after the Kannada poet Nrupathunga. In his speech at the unveiling, G. Narayana said 'In the 1791 battle fought by Col. Moorhouse, 600 were killed and killed cruelly. More cruel than Jallianwala Bagh! So this monument is an insult to all Indians, and especially all Kannadigas. Gone is the time when the citizens of Bangalore hung their heads in shame before a cenotaph to British victory in the city centre; in its place is the statue of Kempegowda, an achievement which has brought pride and joy.'[31]

The image of the city as a refuge for the hard working son-of-the-soil was soon deployed in one of the early Rajkumar films *Mayor Muthanna*. Cast out of his village because he was falsely implicated in a temple theft, Muthanna (Rajkumar) arrives in the bewildering city of Bangalore, and falls asleep at the foot of Kempegowda's statue. Not surprisingly, his first encounter in the city is with the state's emissary, the policeman on night beat, who rudely evicts him from the spot. Muthanna, appeals to Kempegowda's bronze visage, 'O Kempegowda! You built this city for people to survive and live in, but if there is no space for an orphan like me to lie down, what kind of city is this?' Of course, Muthanna, goes on to triumph in the city of Bangalore, and eventually himself becomes the mayor:[32] the rural migrant finds not only a job, a home, and a wife in the city, but political power by rescuing the institutions of the newly independent state from venal politicians.

The erasure of a colonial memory was thus accompanied by an assertion of regional pride, which in turn was swiftly deployed against other linguistic groups in the city. The shift in attention to the dominance of Tamil in parts of Bangalore has therefore muted protests against the symbols of colonial rule: the tarring of Queen Victoria's statue during the protest against the Dunkel Draft in 1994 by the GATT Virodhi Okkuta was an exception rather than the rule.[33] In part this is due to the zealous protection of this heritage by new corporate sponsors, the Bombay builders, Rahejas,[34] but more important it is because the focus of at least some sections of the Kannada movement is on keeping other linguistic and cultural heroes away from the public spaces of the city.

The Territories of Linguistic Nationalism

Muthanna's filmic fortunes were not usually matched by other new migrants into the Bangalore of the 1960s. The sense of being a 'local refugee' haunted the Kannadiga migrant, in a city, or more properly a Cantonment area that was awash with English and, perhaps even more distressing, Tamil popular culture. As I have already noted above, M. Chidanandamurthy's small town origins did not prepare him for the humiliations of the Cantonment.[35] The city of Bangalore, and more properly the Cantonment, was alien not simply because it was a zone where Kannada was rarely heard but one where Tamil enjoyed a dominance, although largely among the working classes. 'In every public sector unit', according to Ra Nam Chandrasekhar, a worker at Hindustan Aeronautics Limited (HAL) and activist of Kannada Shakti Kendra, 'we only saw groups of workers reading Tamil newspapers, not Kannada ones'.[36] Underlying the anxiety about the visibility, or more correctly audibility of Kannada, was the concern about jobs in the prestigious public sector, whose workers were the labour aristocracy of Bangalore. They earned good wages, enjoyed relatively undemanding work routines, with all the perquisites of housing and transport and subsidized canteens. Much of this had been enabled by the efforts of strong, centralized, usually left wing, unions. Not surprisingly, unions, as well as the ebullient workers' cultural troupes and organizations that sprang up at these units, soon became the battleground of new Kannada entrants.[37] Kannada sanghas in turn received a shot in the arm from those managements that were anxious to curb the growing influence of left wing unions in the public sector.[38]

In the previous chapter, I have suggested that in its early stages, the political models of the Kannada movement were those of Tamil nationalism. Many Kannada activists cut their political teeth within the Dravida Kazhagam (DK) movement. Rifts that emerged within the early Kannada movement were marked by the politics of non-Brahmanism, with Vatal Nagaraj's Kannada Chaluvali Paksha splitting away from Ma Ramamurthy's more Brahminic Kannada Paksha.[39] The Kannada flag designed by Ma Ramamurthy in 1968 may have been an attempt at reconciliation, and bore more than a striking resemblance to the flamboyant colours of the Dravida Munnetra Kazhagam flag, black and red. Not unwittingly, moreover, the new red and yellow flag evoked associations with the sacral colours of Hinduism.[40] The colours were supposed to symbolize 'peace, co-operation and struggle' within the confines of a newly defined Kannada nation. Yet this symbolic identification of language with a dominant religious identity was of some consequence, as we shall see later.

Kannada activists were not slow in seeking an end to Hindi domination, following the lead set by Tamilians in Karnataka, but they also sought a reduced Tamil presence, demanding a larger number of films in their own language.[41] The link between linguistic and cultural dominance was most visible in the realm of cinema, for the Tamil film held its own against Hollywood and Hindi films in the city. Kannada films were a distant fourth or even fifth in this hierarchy. The same groups led by Vatal Nagaraj's Kannada Chaluvaligaru, which had staged their protest against the cenotaph, threatened to close down theatres where Tamil films were being shown.[42]

Although, by 1973, the anti-Hindi agitation was more firmly in the hands of Kannada activists, they could not quite overcome the charge of being poor imitators, and of leaning too heavily on the state to take initiatives which Tamil nationalists had won on the streets. Indeed, when the Karnataka government made the unexpected announcement in 1977 that it would shift the 'statues of three foreigners' out of Cubbon Park (the statues of Victoria, Edward VII, and Mark Cubbon), the English-speaking middle-class voiced its protest, opposing the erasure of what they believed was a precious aesthetic legacy. They insisted that there had been no popular or vociferous demand for such a shift.[43] Bangalore was described as remarkably free from what has been described as the 'statue culture' a highly politicized phenomenon in Tamil Nadu.[44] The state has not been overly active in commemorating its cultural past, at least until the 1980s. There is a massing of statues on the eastern and western lawns of Vidhana Soudha, as we have seen, but not on the same scale as on Marina Beach in Chennai or Tank bund in Hyderabad.

By the time of the agitation in 1982, which demanded sole first language status for Kannada,[45] the Kannada movement was supported not just by the intelligentsia but by Kannada sanghas in various industrial units, Dalit organizations, and professional groups. The movement had found a new and confident voice.[46] If anything, the Kannada movement in Bangalore gained disproportionately from statewide mobilizations centred in Hubli–Dharwar, historically the cultural centre of Bombay Karnataka and home of the Karnataka Ekikarana movement. The Gokak agitation coincided with Kannada matinee idol Rajkumar's decision to move his work and residence from Madras to Bangalore. The popularity of the Gokak movement coupled with a growing fan culture were signs that 1982 was a far more appropriate historical conjuncture for such an entry into politics. As seen above, it was the entry of Rajkumar and the Rajkumar Abhimanigala Sangha (Rajkumar Fans' Association) into the Gokak movement that decisively altered the nature of its mass appeal.

A new and more belligerent face of Kannada activism soon became evident in the occupation of public spaces both in a temporary and more permanent sense. If newer Tamil-dominated slum areas have been the target of rioters, older and more established Tamil localities have been the site of symbolic occupations. Poles sporting the Kannada flag mounted on tiled platforms that figure Kannada Bhuvaneswari have proliferated across the city in the years since 1982, at street corners and in circles, sometimes functioning as road dividers. They are signs of the efforts of small neighbourhood youth groups and Kannada sanghas at mobilizing local support. The president of the Rajkumar Abhimanigala Sangha, Sa Ra Govindu, claims that more than 40 per cent of the flagposts that dot the city were inaugurated by him.[47] Flags in front of major public sector units proclaim the pride of Kannada sons-of-the-soil, leaving no doubt as to the markedly (male) gendered politics of language. The Kannada Rajyothsava day on 1 November has become an annual occasion for young Kannadiga males to occupy street corners, in a gesture that celebrates the unification of Karnataka but also emphasizes defiance of notions of good citizenship among other class fractions and linguistic groups.

Yet if red and yellow flags are particularly numerous in areas which are dominated by Tamilians, such as Ulsoor or Murphy Town, they do not symbolize linguistic dominance: rather they serve to visually compensate for what is plainly an auditory absence (Fig. 54). Thus, it was plaintively remarked

FIG. 54 *Redefining the locality through celebrations of Rajyothsava day: Kannada flag being hoisted, with freshly drawn map of Karnataka in state colours in foreground.* (G. Raghav, 1999)

at the height of the opposition to the Thiruvalluvar statue that the change of street and area names did nothing to alter the popular references to older coordinates. Neither is Fraser Town known as Pulakesinagar nor has Benson Town switched to Kadambanagar.[48] The attempt to produce a new linguistic cosmos that reflects the fullness of Kannada literary culture is defeated by familiar historical associations with place, and the sheer weight of habit.

However, the Kannada movement does not speak in one voice, nor does it reduce its yearnings to the mere realization of this linguistic cosmos. Groups such as KVR have rallied cultural workers and intellectuals to challenge the state's development strategies. Yet, though KVR narrativizes Karnataka history differently and questions the dominant paradigms of economic development,[49] it is those who are seeking a stake within this paradigm that have become the dominant voice of the movement. Their claims to land, labour, or water are based on the exclusive identities of language. Sa Ra Govindu claimed 'It was to realize the aspirations of Kannadigas that the state was formed'.[50] In 1984, Rajkumar's call for a Bangalore bandh that shut down the city proved deeply unpopular. It did little to compel the state to reintroduce Kannada examinations for Class III and IV employees,[51] but it did establish the more strident face of Kannada nationalism in the city. Sa Ra Govindu identified this as a turning point: 'People say "they caused riots, looted", but without riots and loot government would have assumed that we are all dead ... when we are dominated there are always limits to this toleration'.[52] The battle took on a new form, tilting against the languages of subaltern minorities such as Tamil, and the prominence of its cultural heroes on the city landscape.

The Politics of Compensation

So respectful are the people of Bangalore city of the English language, said H. Narasimhaiah, that they 'even converse with their dogs in English medium. I have not come across a single Kannada medium dog all these [30] years'. Narasimhaiah's humourous narrative of encounters on his daily walks through Lalbagh does nothing to disguise the anguish of one who has served as vice chancellor of Bangalore University and chairman of the Kannada Development Authority.[53] The language that had served the noted chemist C.N.R. Rao so well during his childhood, and did not hinder his passage to a career in science, Narasimhaiah noted, was now overthrown by the craze for English medium schools.[54]

The submission to the elevated status of English is not paralleled in the attitude to other languages. The relative invisibility of Kannada and Kannadigas within Karnataka is emphasized in language activists' analyses of demographic change in Bangalore city. Not only are Kannada speakers a minority in Bangalore, but non-Kannadigas such as 'north Indians' dominate the business world, while Tamils and Malayalis dominate the privileged enclaves of industrial work, and even trade union leadership.[55] Statistics are used to prove that Tamils constitute the most numerous body of migrants into the city after Kannadigas. In the view of groups such as Shakthi Kendra, Tamils are the stubbornly unassimilated minority in the city, flaunting their language, cultural symbols, and heroes unlike Telugu or Malayalam speakers.[56]

The longer history of Tamil residence in the erstwhile cantonment has certainly produced a well developed identity that newer Tamil migrants, particularly from non-upper castes, have found easy to identify with. The Bangalore Tamil Sangam has played an important role in enabling such assimilation, promoting Tamil literary and cultural programmes since 1950, as well as organizing Kannada classes (since 1962) popular among government employees seeking promotions.[57] Notwithstanding this record, it was the Sangam's effort to install a statue of its cultural hero, Thiruvalluvar, that led to a bitter and prolonged controversy that remains unresolved.

Statues of Thiruvalluvar, a Sangam poet, are common in many parts of Tamil Nadu and in Tamil-dominated areas of Karnataka such as Kolar Gold Field. A proposal to install one in the lake opposite the Tamil Sangam was sanctioned by Chief Minister S. Nijalingappa in 1967,[58] although the revived proposal was turned down by the Bangalore Urban Arts Commission in the late 1970s on aesthetic grounds.[59] Following the allotment of a small park bordering the lake in 1989, the Tamil Sangam began a collection drive from members and sympathizers in early 1991.[60] Hundred of subscribers contributed to the statue which was commissioned.

Plans were made to unveil the statue on 1 September 1991 after the Corporation commissioner's permission was obtained.[61] By late August, when some Kannada organizations led by Kannada Shakti Kendra and Kannada Pulakesi Sangha got wind of the plans, the statue had already been installed. The Kannada groups sought a stay on the unveiling function, questioning the authority of the commissioner to give permission without a debate in the Corporation Council.[62] Meanwhile, dharnas and protests grew steadily more violent until the commissioner withdrew his permission.[63]

There were a number of registers on which the protests were pitched. For one, the installation of the statue was seen as a deliberate re-territorialization of the Ulsoor area. The Bangalore Tamil Sangam president's unwitting remark that the statue could not be offensive as it was in a Tamil-dominated area served to further provoke those who had desired that Bangalore city should reflect 'Kannada culture and civilization'.[64] One objection was to the statue's location on public ground, rather than at the Sangam's own premises.[65] Also, Kannada Pulakesi Sangha leader Pramila Nesargi and others claimed that the alacrity with which the commissioner had agreed to the statue was in conspicuous contrast to his lukewarm attitude to similar demands from Kannadigas.[66] Betraying both envy and fear of the more robust Tamil nationalism, activists bargained for equivalent compensation, certain that the Tamil Nadu government would never agree to a demand for a statue of a Kannada hero in Chennai.[67]

Kannada activists had had a full dress rehearsal in the late 1980s when they opposed the installation of the statue of Shivaji in Sadashivnagar on similar

FIG. 55 *Threatened by the prospect of a less homogenous linguistic cosmos: armed policemen stand guard before the veiled statue of Shivaji at Sadashivnagar, following threats from pro-Kannada activists.*
(*The New Indian Express*, S. Ramaswamy, 9.1.1994)

grounds.[68] Demands were made for the installation of a statue of Kittur Rani Chennama in Mumbai, but they came to nothing when the Shivaji statue was installed and unveiled after a brief period under wraps (Fig. 55). Its existence is seen as a serious failure of the Kannada movement to act in time.[69] Yet at the time, the protest against the Shivaji statue was also joined by those from among the Left who viewed this installation with alarm. To them, Shivaji statues belonged to the semiotics of a militant Hindu revivalism, which had had considerable success in occupying public space in Bombay.[70]

The vociferous protests against the Tamil Sangam had unintended consequences, as pictures of a fully wrapped statue of Thiruvalluvar served to rally Tamilians in other parts of Karnataka and all over Tamil Nadu (Fig. 56).[71] The Tamil Sangam in particular, and Tamilians in general, have also been at pains to point out that Thiruvalluvar cannot be strictly called a Tamil national hero as his Kural does not mention Tamil or Tamil Nadu as a region and that his poetry has universal appeal as a code of ethics and morality.[72] Even the politics of compensation deployed by the Kannada activists was quickly turned to the advantage of the Tamils. Did not the Tamil Nadu government honour the Kannada technocrat Sir M. Visvesvaraya with a tower and a park in his name?[73] Had not a large number of Tamilians made vital contributions to Kannada literature?[74] Had not the Indian state itself conceded that Thiruvalluvar belonged to the pantheon of Indian heroes by honouring the poet in Delhi?[75] Was not the opposition to the Thiruvalluvar statue a sign then of working against national integration?[76] All Tamil organizations understood the demonstration against the statue as 'unnecessarily creating problems for Tamils in Karnataka'.[77] Finally, the move towards conciliation was made by the Bangalore Tamil Sangam and the Chennai Kannada Balaga by seeking permission for a statue of the seventeenth century Kannada poet, Sarvagna in Chennai.[78] This attempt to equalize honour for cultural heroes of two linguistic groups has yet to be fulfilled.

FIG. 56 *Thiruvalluvar statue, scheduled for unveiling in 1991, remains under wraps following massive protests by assorted pro-Kannada political groups.*
(*Deccan Herald*, 1991; inset: Janaki Nair, 1999)

By no means did those who raised virulent opposition to the Thiruvalluvar statue speak for all Kannada intellectuals and social groups. A large group of Kannada intellectuals publicly condemned this stand as trivializing the cause of Kannada, and undoing a unique heritage that had been enriched by several languages.[79] Leading Kannada writers, such as U.R. Ananthamurthy, Ramachandra Sharma, P. Lankesh, S. Siddalingaiah, Bargur Ramachandrappa, D.R. Nagaraj, Ki Ram Nagaraj, and Chandrasekhar Patil declared that 'this kind of destructive opposition has become part of the hallmark of fundamental groups like Shiva Sena (sic) and is opposed to all that is humane and civilized'.[80] Many of them had consistently opposed the more belligerent, and anti-minority, turn that the Kannada movement had taken in Bangalore since the Gokak agitation.[81] Another critic of Kannada chauvinism, Karnataka Rajya Ratha Sangha (KRRS) chief Nanjundaswamy said both Tamils and Kannadigas should make common cause as Dravidians.[82] Opposition to the Kannada protagonists was framed quite differently by the Karnataka Samata Sainik Dal which laid claim to Thiruvalluvar as a Dalit poet, and read the opposition of upper caste Kannadigas as another move to deny Dalits any visibility.[83]

These dissenting voices were overwhelmed by the strident tone of groups such as the Kannada Shakti Kendra and the Rajkumar Abhimanigala Sangha against Tamil cultural assertion, a tone that became more menacing in the days leading up to the Cauvery agitation and anti-Tamil riots of December 1991 following a central directive regarding the sharing of the Cauvery river waters.[84] Many Kannada leaders emphasized that the people of Karnataka were paying the price for their historic tolerance of other communities. 'We are ... opposed to the influx of non-Kannadigas who are usurping jobs, business, agricultural lands and sites meant for Kannadigas,' said a group of leading litterateurs during the Thiruvalluvar protests.[85] The obduracy of the non-Kannadiga who did not heed such warnings was met with a language that they would understand: the language of violence.

No wonder then that the Tamil groups resorted to a defensive reinterpretation of Bangalore's history, suggesting through an analysis of place names and temples that the region had been a Tamil stronghold since the time of the Cholas. 'In fact', said the Tamil Sangam pamphlet *A Mute Genocide*, 'Tamils of Bangalore and Kolar are the original inhabitants and these areas were gradually colonized'.[86] The alleged arrogance of former Tamil Sangam President Maran in saying 'I was born in Bangalore, not in Karnataka' echoed demands for Bangalore's 'autonomy' from the region.[87] Meanwhile, a more opportunistic politics became apparent, when support for the Tamils at one point was transformed into virulent opposition at other times. Karnataka Chief Minister S. Bangarappa, for instance, who had first decided to unveil the Thiruvalluvar statue withdrew after protests began, and found it politically expedient to embrace an anti-Tamil stance during the Cauvery riots.

Though the Thiruvalluvar statue continues to remain under wraps, the walls of the area around spring to life every January sporting demands in Tamil and English that it be unveiled. The abduction of Rajkumar by Veerappan once more raised the pitch of the confrontation about this symbol of Dravidian culture, but failed to resolve it. Yet it is a symbol of not just Tamil cultural pride, but of citizens' participation in defining public spaces. It is important to note that the Thiruvalluvar statue is fully funded by public subscription, in striking contrast to most other statues in the city. Only the colonial icons such as Queen Victoria and Edward VII were similarly funded by the 'public' in the C&M Station, in a show of gratitude to the colonial masters. The Thiruvalluvar statue is a reminder of the unified effort of the ordinary citizens of Bangalore to mark the public space of the city in their own way. The only parallels in a landscape of such symbolic occupations are the flag-poles and Ambedkar statues that dot the city.

The attempt to forge a unity of all Kannada speakers was not unmarked by caste as we have noted above: in 1967, the Worker's Unity Forum at BEL was seen not only as a Kannada sangha but more correctly, a sangha of newly urbanising agricultural castes with no experience of factory life.[88] Non-upper caste Kannada and Tamil workers were therefore warned against the possible reassertion of upper caste hegemony by the leaders of the Kannada movement.[89] Given the growing claims on the city's economic, political, and cultural spaces, both in a physical–material and a mental–ideological sense, the state too deployed public spaces within Bangalore in accordance with emerging political alignments, sometimes on an avowedly caste basis. By the late 1980s, when new ways of marking the locality or of deploying space to proclaim identities were becoming common, the state maintained no neutrality. For instance, state as well as popular initiative combined to provide Dalits in the city with a new visibility, but it was equally crucial that state apparatuses remained alert about continuing protection for these symbols of power.

Geographies of Caste

More than two lakh Dalits from all corners of the state descended on the state capital on 19 August 1981 during the regime of Congress I Chief Minister M. Gundu Rao, to attend the unveiling of a bronze statue of Babasaheb

Ambedkar, national hero and chief architect of the Indian constitution.[90] Ambedkar's emphatically national status was proclaimed by the fact that the unquestionable hero of the new Indian nation, Jawaharlal Nehru, was eventually placed opposite him. However, a different Ambedkar was beginning to be deployed in city and village spaces to become the proud symbol of self-assertion on the part of Dalits. The extraordinary spatial congruence between caste and class, for long disavowed by technocratized town planning, was thereby made visible, this time not as a sign of a place within a caste hierarchy but as a mark of a new political identity.

A flurry of activity relating to the installation of Ambedkar statues was taken up in various localities (Tilaknagar and Kadugondahalli to name just two areas), though only sometimes by Dalits themselves: such symbolic spatial strategies were equally deployed by local MLAS or council representatives seeking the support and sympathy of the Dalits. Before long, the Ambedkar statue had become a new deity on the city horizon, attacks on which were as routine as attacks and violations of Dalits themselves.[91] Semantic shifts in news reports of such attacks reflected the gradually evolving status of these symbols: beginning with the use of the word 'defaced' or even 'defiled', such vandalism has more recently always been described as 'desecration'.[92]

The primacy of class over caste in the ideologies of city planning has obscured from view the very real ways in which upper castes have historically appropriated and controlled space in the city. In the colonial period, it was caste and community that dominated the vision of town planners, as was evident in plans for the two new extensions of Basavangudi and Malleswaram, but also in the arrangements that were made in other areas of the town such as Knoxpet or Murphy Town.[93] In the post-Independence period, the class-based ordering of space has repressed, not effaced, the operations of caste, with lower castes more or less exclusively being confined to the burgeoning slums and poorer areas of Bangalore.[94]

The emergence in the 1970s of a Dalit movement primarily led by Dalit Sangarsh Samiti (DSS), and the policy of reservations have combined to provide new avenues of improvement for Dalits in the city. The state, meanwhile, has been quick to respond to or even pre-empt Dalit anger on questions relating to symbols of assertion, thereby seeking to hold in check a radical challenge to the caste order. Indeed, as Mangaluru Vijaya, long time activist of the DSS pointed out, the DSS has never made statue building a programme, but has always reacted strongly to cases of vandalism, largely to counter the placatory role played by the state.[95]

Emerging job and educational opportunities have produced a layer of

FIG. 57 *Members of Praja Vimochana Chaluvali demand the resignation of Minister for Kannada and Culture B.T. Lalitha Naik, for her son's alleged role in the desecration of Ambedkar's statue.*
(The Printers Mysore, Private Limited, P. Samson Victor, 23.11.1995)

Dalits whose class position has distanced them from the symbols and structures so dear to other Dalits. For instance, the name of Ambedkar has been used to set up a private medical college, ostensibly to serve the needs of Dalits for higher education, although such private colleges are guided more by financial concerns. This became clear in December 1995, when a group of 7 inebriated students at Ambedkar Medical College, including three Dalits, vandalized the bust of Ambedkar in front of the college, and offered liquour and meat to the statue.[96] Violent statewide protests followed for ten days, with various Dalit groups, particularly the DSS, calling for stern action against the culprits, and demanding the resignation of Kannada and Culture Minister Lalitha Naik, herself a Dalit, for her son's involvement in the incident (Fig. 57).[97] The protests targeted state property through rail *roko*s, road blocks, burning of buses, and demonstrations, particularly in district headquarters, and in Dalit-dominated areas of Bangalore.[98] Despite her resolve, Lalitha Naik was forced to resign her ministerial post.

The scale of Dalit protests was quite unprecedented and overwhelmed the government's feeble claims that opposition was primarily focused against a Dalit woman in power.[99] The government in turn claimed credit for its contribution to building a positive Dalit identity: translating Ambedkar's work into Kannada and building Ambedkar Bhavans in the state. The desecration was no simple case of upper caste contempt for Dalit symbols: if anything, the politics of class and gender seemed to blunt the force of an exclusively caste argument. The People's Democratic Front report revealed that all the seven students involved in the vandalism had bought seats for a capitation fee, and that a culture of asserting class privilege had already set in even among Dalit students.[100] The Ambedkar Medical College incident cast new light on the problems generated by the increased privatization of higher education in the state,[101] and the creation of new economic élites. Ambedkar Medical College was no exception: it could not claim to represent the desire of many poor or marginalized Dalits for high quality education.[102]

Even so, the massive Dalit response speaks of an emerging economy of symbols in the process of self-definition in the city. Space that has been 'de-territorialized' by the operations of the real estate market or the town planning process is being 're-territorialized' in new ways. Protests over perceived insults to symbols of caste or ethnic assertion have increased at a time when there has been an intensified consumption of (particularly urban) space. In such a process, dominated communities in particular gain sudden and violent visibility in a city that may long have treated them as not-yet-citizens. These protests testify to several changes in the urban public sphere, where representations of particular communities, even when they may not be the visible representations discussed so far, are taken as a slight against an entire religious or linguistic minority.

Not-yet-citizens: Muslims and the Public Space

The occupation of the street and other public spaces during regional or religious festivals and locality-wide celebrations adds to the fullness of life in cities. Yet they do not, in cities such as Bangalore, belong to a shared universe of meanings, and the disruption of the tenor of everyday life, particularly for the middle classes, could even become intolerable. Even more unpredictable are the swift occupations of the street during moments of protest, whether in the form of rallies or peaceful protests. The altered street furniture in the form of statues or flagpoles which are installed by groups wishing to mark the territory of the city in particular ways, can be made invisible and even ignored by those who find them a visual strain, unlike disruptions of traffic or of peace in the neighbourhood. Yet, for many groups who have neither the means nor the power to shape the space of the city in positive ways, the moment of crisis provides occasion for political visibility.

The burden of identity continues to be borne disproportionately in the city by such minorities as Tamils, Dalits, and Muslims. The excessive identity of the Muslim does not however make its claims on the city's symbolic space in the same manner as the Dalit or linguistic identities do. Instead, the sudden explosions which bring visibility to the Muslim man-in-the-mass succeed in casting a shadow on the excessive force of the state against these citizens. As a sizeable minority in the city, the Muslim community flares into public view when they are called into action as a 'mob', or as an inarticulate 'community' resisting the efforts of a state striving to produce consensus and order.[103] In the city's history, there are many moments—and we have considered at least two of these above—when the contests over symbolic representations and symbolic occupations of space, in turn, stage the excess of identity as a reminder that many people are not-yet-citizens. At these moments the lanes and by-lanes of Muslim dominated areas appear as always readied for battle, a dense territory too dangerous for unarmed policemen to enter.[104]

The narrative of Muslims' ability to act in unison—and only at the behest of politicians—in defence of real or imagined slights and indignities to their identity renders them as less-than-citizens though perhaps in not quite the same way as other dominated groups in the city. Yet there are moments when the excess of identity that is attributed to the Muslim may also be staged to its advantage. Such a moment arose when sections of Muslims protested against a contentious representation of Prophet Mohammed. A short story inadvertently published in the city's leading English newspaper, *Deccan Herald*, on 7 December 1986, led to a series of protests by Muslims both in Bangalore and Mysore. They objected most strongly to the offensive title of the story, and to its contents which maligned the name of the Prophet. Muslim residential areas, particularly around Shivajinagar, were abuzz with what was seen as an insult to all Muslims.[105]

The promise of police actions against the newspaper and the apology from the newspaper itself failed to satisfy the Muslims groups that wanted to demonstrate before the newspaper office on the city's central Mahatma Gandhi Road.[106] They gathered with sticks, stones and other crude weapons, fully prepared to demand an apology. The demonstration on M.G. Road also became an opportunity to publicly stage the excess of identity, when the crowd that was gathered chose to complete its evening prayer on the cordoned off road.[107] Even as the editor prepared to print an apology, some missiles flew into the air sparking off a full-scale riot that spread into neighbouring areas, leading to the police firing that killed 11 in Bangalore alone. Riots spread to Mysore as well, where another five were killed in police firing.

The press was at pains to point out that politicians such as C.M. Ibrahim were seen 'instigating' the crowd; this interpretation was borne out by claims that 'all the people who died in police firings are virtual illiterates' and could not have understood 'a word of English'.[108] Other interpretations were more willing to consider that the events were triggered by more than 'a handful of agent provocateurs', although here too there was agreement that the episode itself was 'trivial'.[109] Such interpretations failed to come to terms with the knowledge that rumour had long played a role in mobilizing people into action. More important, the perceived offence to the identity of the Muslim did not require literacy as the expanded public sphere had ensured such representations a sphere of circulation that went far beyond any individual comprehension of the text.

Muslim groups chose the moment to draw attention to their dominated status as a group, and staged their victimhood in a way quite different from the groups that had symbolically re-territorialized the city. The actions of the Muslim groups were therefore acts that reaffirmed their identity through temporary occupations of public space normally given over to 'traffic and trade': Russell Market Square and Mahatma Gandhi Road thus became the space of meetings and prayers. Yet such assertions of identity, in what was becoming a well-established pattern in the city, met with excessively violent responses from the police.

The instance cited above emphasizes the distinction not only between two types of citizenship—the active citizen-subject versus the passive citizen-in-the-making—but also emphasises the difference between dominated groups themselves as they lay claim to symbols, symbolic spaces, and as they support or oppose representations of collective identity. The increasing fragmentation of social space in the city reveals once more the failure of the state to produce shared and binding social meanings, often taken as a failure of legitimacy itself. Thus, its claim of a consensus on the meaning of public life in India remains meaningless when it is the terms of the consensus itself that are challenged, contested, or sought to be transformed.

Nevertheless, certain actions of citizen subjects in the city in the recent past have recreated the illusion of a consensus on the making and meaning of public space. In contrast to the move to replace place names that are reminiscent of the colonial master with those that resonate with Kannada cultural pride, newer corporate groups and old élites have more than amply declared their interest in protecting and nurturing some of the more elegant architectural and spatial legacies of central Bangalore, via the agency of the Bangalore Urban Arts Commission and the corporate 'sponsorship' of colonial, historical monuments. This has not been without a complementary definition of the meaning of responsible citizenship, and its preferred modes of protest.

The Citizen's Initiative

The proliferation of symbols of linguistic and caste identities in-the-making, and the symbolic occupation of space by ethnic minorities calls attention to the multiple meanings of citizenship in the city. In equal measure, if one considers the universe of symbols, there has been a renewed interest and even pride in the colonial street and street furniture heritage. The statue of Queen Victoria has since its installation proved irresistable to vandals. Periodically it has been the target of anti-imperialist anger, especially in the 1990s. It is now patronized by the well-known Bombay building firm, Rahejas. However, it has also been, at least since 1993, the rallying point for the citizens of Bangalore, although larger numbers also rally around Gandhi's statue just across the road. The most important use of the Victoria statue as the site of public protest occurred in 1998, over the issue of the newly fixed boundaries of Cubbon Park.

On 30 July 1998 the government of Karnataka specified new boundaries for Cubbon Park, removing about 32 acres from its legal limits in order 'to legally correct' the status of the land upon which the annex to the Legislators' Home was being built since 1996.[110] Cubbon Park first took shape when Mark Cubbon purchased 91 acres of land in 1836 to build a residency for himself (the current Raj Bhavan, built in 1849). The sprawling park of 100 acres was laid out before the residency as a tribute to Cubbon in 1864 by Richard Sankey before Attara Kacheri was built. The park was expanded in 1910, 1917, and 1930, and although many buildings were added to it, it still occupied some 192 acres in 1967.[111] In 1983, several institutional areas, such as Raj Bhavan, Vidhana Soudha, the LRDE compound, and the Legislators' Home, amounting to 76 acres, were included in the area of the park. It was a denotification of a portion of these newly added areas that led to the public outcry, court case, and eventual campaign to protect the park.

For six full weeks in September and October 1998, the Victoria statue became the rallying point for middle-class citizens seeking to protect Cubbon Park from the slow process of attrition that had reduced its original size.[112] For the first time in the city's history, there were daily gatherings of women, children, and men at this important road junction, silently expressing anger over the decision of the state government to 'denotify' parts of the park.[113]

In a series of pamphlets, a women's organization called Sanmathi urged the citizens of Bangalore to save Cubbon Park by sending letters of protest to the government. Soon the campaign snowballed to include a variety of actions that were organized in relays but centred on the statue of Victoria 'so that', as one pamphlet put it, 'she can be reminded that her prestigious place is under threat'.[114] They included handholding on the perimeter of the park, *urulu seve*s, silent marches, silent demonstrations by women and children with placards in their hands, and the like.

The arguments against the proposed buildings were many and ranged from strictly ecological concerns to concerns about citizenship itself. An interest in protecting the park as an important ecological niche[115] followed a census of trees and butterflies that was conducted during the protests.[116] However, the dominant mood was that of indignation at the 'unaccountable actions' of politicians and anger at the deteriorating condition of public services in the city.[117] Alleging that the construction of the Legislators' Home was begun when the area was still legally a part of Cubbon park, the Save Cubbon Park Campaign announced that it represented 'the collective will of the people of Bangalore from every shade of life and section or society' to ensure that the lawmakers were not lawbreakers.[118]

The Cubbon Park protest was widely covered in the press, leading to the deliberate deployment of a range of local personalities. Nearly 30,000 women and children signed protest letters. Civic and corporate groups were mobilized for the protest in addition to writers, artists, animal welfare groups, environment groups, and resident's groups. Notably absent from these protests was the BUAC, despite its history of participation in moves to restrict park access. Indeed, the Save Cubbon Park Campaign came at a moment when the plurality of public uses of the park had already been severely restricted, as I have shown in Chapter 5. Protestors have now moved to the edges of the park, most favouring the statue of Mahatma Gandhi and another major road junction near Visvesvaraya's statue as their new rallying points.

At the time of its installation in 1906, the Victoria statue was a sign of the loyalty and gratitude of her subjects to the colonial order. The site bordered the C&M Station and marked the boundary of the city area: the statue came to signify the union of the residents of the C&M Station with their city counterparts. In his address at the unveiling of the statue in 1906, the Dewan emphasized:

> ... The Maharaja and people of this country had the privilege of contributing largely towards the national Victoria Memorial of Calcutta, ... they also together with the

> residents of the C&M station eagerly desired to commemorate the name and virtues of the Empress by an enduring local monument that would hand down to posterity a visible memorial of their veneration for her majesty and her glorious reign. Men in all walks of life vied with one another in associating themselves with this movement.[119]

The statues of Victoria, Edward VII, and Sir Mark Cubbon have stayed on in the environs of Cubbon Park, leading the humourist A.N. Murthy Rao to remark in his reminiscences that they served as sentinels of the British Empire and were more forbidding than patrols by actual soldiers. Their continued existence today, he suggests, is a sign of the largeheartedness of Kannadigas.[120]

The choice of the Victoria statue as the location for a protest to save the park therefore sought to empty the site of its historic meanings and deploy it as a sign of an aesthetics under siege. Indeed, the protest itself was aesthetic in its mobilization of the middle-class. In addition to the choice of this site, the aesthetics of this mobilization further involved vintage car rallies,[121] protests by former beauty queens, actions by artists,[122] and such remarkably arcane groups as the Hash House Harriers.[123] This did not preclude the use of conventional strategies such as appeals to the law,[124] the invocation of science, and a marshalling of people's support through 'opinion polls' led by the

FIG. 58 *Protecting the city's 'public goods': members of Compassion Unlimited Plus Action stage a protest against the denotification of land belonging to Cubbon Park for the Legislators' Home.*
(The Printers Mysore, Private Limited, Sanath Kumar, 1998)

mouthpiece of the new urban élite, the *Times of India*.[125] The groundswell of opinion against the 'venal politician' was deployed not only by the press but by the judiciary as well, led by the activist judge Michael Saldanha.

The Cubbon Park protests foregrounded the willingness of several fractions of the city's middle class to confront the ambitions of the politicians, not all of whom were from Bangalore itself, while redefining the strategies of the less privileged groups against whom the park had already, and more easily, been 'protected'. This protest was framed in terms of general environmental benefits that would accrue to the population at large, and thus an attempt was made to recast a fragile consensus of citizens whose quality of life was threatened. Here too the emphasis was not on the radical ways in which the market has transfigured the topography of the city; a great deal of anxiety was focused on the image of the city among potential global investors. Hence, one of the slogans which said 'Don't drive the birds to Hyderabad' reminded the political masters of the flight of capital to more attractive destinations in the south.[126]

Among the more remarkable aspects of the Cubbon Park protests was its large-scale mobilization of women,[127] in striking contrast to the (male) gendered sphere that has long characterized linguistic or caste movements, fan club, or trade union activity in the city. Clearly, the organizers succeeded in gaining a high degree of visibility for this 'part-time' protest, which easily fitted into otherwise busy official or domestic schedules. The active mobilization of women and children (as well as the handicapped)[128] gave the protest its 'universal' appeal.[129]

The location also ensured that the protest, which was not addressed to the elected representatives sitting in Vidhana Soudha but against them, was more directly addressed to the media. Thus, groups gathered at the base of the statue every morning to register a token protest, while ensuring that they were photographed below the regal Victoria, now a sign of all that the city stood to lose. In addition, the visually pleasing and dignified protest attracted public and media attention for conforming to rapidly vanishing norms of liberal–democratic discourse, compared with the traffic-disrupting, slogan-shouting counterparts of political society. In that sense, the Cubbon Park protests were the most sustained public display of a new kind of civic activism of the 1990s, aimed at preserving an uninhabited space that was increasingly under siege. It was pitted not merely against professional politicians but against the new, unrecognizable forms that politics itself had taken. It reasserted the value of restraint while producing a new consensus which had been severely fractured in other spheres of city life.[130]

In its judgement which considered several pending cases filed on the uses of the park, the court upheld the denotification of the government as valid, and said that no blanket ban on constructions was possible. Sharing, however, 'the concern of the petitioners for as much open space as possible' it held that no further construction be undertaken without obtaining the clearance of the court.[131] The court, however, remained silent on the petitions of the six hawkers that it had included in its ambit, who complained of police harassment.[132]

Conclusion

I began this discussion of struggles over symbolic spaces by citing the destruction of a colonial symbol in the years shortly after Independence, and concluded with an example that speaks of the fearless confidence with which colonial symbols have been protected in an era of globalization. Yet what becomes clear in this discussion of strategies to occupy or deploy public space in Bangalore city is the question of who speaks for the city's pasts, and possible futures. Politicized linguistic, caste, or ethnic groups frequently frustrate the ideologies of (corporate) beauty by expressing their 'desire for democracy', thereby disrupting the rational visions of the town planners and citizens who cherish the image of a city that will take its proud place in a global capitalist order. At a time when the instrumentalities of the state (the judicial or the planning apparatuses) are skilfully deployed by those possessed of a vision of modernity, the untidy often violent spatial strategies of political society may well 're-territorialize' space that has been 'de-territorialized' by the globalization of capital.

I would like to end this account with a symbolic and very temporary occupation of city space of a different order, in which dissent was expressed using a very different aesthetic, and the city itself was visualized in imaginative terms strikingly different from those of the groups cited above. In January 2001, the Bangalore based artist Sheela Gowda produced an art work on the campus of the University of Agricultural Sciences in northern Bangalore, in which nature was 'recast' using found objects. A carefully laid trail took the visitor from the edge of a rough road a few yards inside the UAS campus, marked by the all too familiar super sized cable bobbin, over the detritus of the city: building materials including tar and broken brick and tile, the clayey yellow useless soil that is churned up every time a borewell is drilled, and the stubbornly unassimilable plastic, thickly wedged between layers of soil.

The staging of this encounter with the creation of urban 'nature' was enabled by the careful way in which the eye was trained to look at the work of art. The eye was first focused downwards, on the path as it picks its way over the rubble. The walk through the trench, recalling both an archaeological dig and a trench for warfare, refocused the eye so that it was on level with the impacted layers of soil, the plastic, and bits of rubber. The stepped rise yielded a hollow which drew the eyes upwards to the wall that loomed overhead; a wall previously used for artillery practice and today topped by leafy growth. The trees that stood behind the wall were gently emphasized by the lines scored by the artist on the wall itself. The eye was further drawn to the small gap in the wall, the focus enhanced by the smoked passage, darkly setting off the green beyond.

The work of art made only a temporary claim on the city, before it was 'dismantled' and the site restored to its previous state. In its found stillness, and in its very transitory claim on the site, it brought control of the territory (by the bureaucracy, the army, or the disposers of municipal garbage) face to face with an artists' yearning to conceive a new relationship between an urban topography and the human senses, without implying or deploying control or possession. Its symbolic re-territorialization of the city was intensely personal, becoming a communication rather than striving to become a more permanent sign of social identity.

EIGHT

The 'Body Politic': Gender and the Practise of Power

Women coming from joint families have to fulfil their duties before coming to the council. If the daughter becomes a councillor, parents adjust very well. But a daughter is a daughter and daughter-in-law is a daughter-in-law. Ayyo! I have seen it all.

Padmavathi Gangadhara Gowda, former mayor of Bangalore Mahanagara Palike.

It is tempting, on the basis of what I have said so far, to conclude that the city determines, but is not determined by the spatial practice of women. In this separate consideration of gender and the space of the city, however, I continue the task of defamiliarizing categories of planning, public life, and the law, that I have undertaken throughout this work. The separate consideration is imperative in order to speak productively of gender, and especially of women, and the practise of power in the city.

The city of Bangalore was founded on the vision of a military chief. It was also founded on the sacrifice of a woman. Lakshmamma sacrificed her life, and that of her unborn child, in order to stop the city edifice from crumbling. This tale is often recounted without question as a noble, though not founding, act. Ba Na Sundara Rao gives the fullest account of this sacrifice, and also gives Lakshmamma a voice as the dutiful daughter-in-law of an ambitious chieftain, Kempegowda, who realizes the necessity of taking her own life in order to secure the gate to the city. Thereby she performs a double duty: she ensures that the gates of a city, threatened by mysterious and repeated collapse, stand firm, and also relieves the patriarch, for whom the sacrifice of a pregnant woman is a repugnant imperative, of a moral dilemma.[1] 'Why not I be the one to sacrifice my life for the establishment of this fort?' she says, 'Let my sacrifice be counted too'.

This richly ambiguous account celebrates the volition of the woman who makes her own decisions, but according to the needs of the feudal family order.[2] The body of the woman is thus inscribed into the stones of the city in a way that naturalizes sacrifice. What is memorialized in this account of the city's founding moment is the disturbing violence that occurs at the heart of the family. Lakshmamma's sacrifice may be taken as a starting point for a consideration of gender and the practice of power in the contemporary city.

Memorialized in a small and neglected grave at Koramangala, some distance from the old city area, Lakshmamma has once more retreated into silence, largely excluded from the map of celebrated historical sites. The woman is thus made invisible in the very space that she helped to found. The problem of visibility continues for women in the city to this day, for the conventional colours of a zoning map—yellow (residential), blue (commercial), purple (industrial), green (parks and open spaces), red (public and semi-public), white (transportation), and orange (unclassified)—signify nothing when the lens of gender is used to analyse the meanings of urban space. One may mark an industrial district,[3] a lower caste area,[4] a largely 'retired people's zone',[5] an Infotech or Biotech corridor on a map,[6] but the design and use of city space is 'gender neutral'. In their pioneering study, Prakasa Rao and Tewari were scrupulously attentive to caste, income and ethnicity markers, but gender remained only a marginal concern.[7] In fact, only when women's bodies posed a moral or medical threat to the city was their presence spatially noted. The hypervisibility of a 'red light' district in most Presidency towns was an exceptional spatial representation of 'public women' whose work could be territorially defined as no other sphere of women's work could be. In contrast, a new and heightened visibility affirms their role as consuming subjects in the present. In the late 1990s, it is the new female consumer who is hypervisible, invited to transgress social norms and perhaps temporarily suspend her identity as a sexed being in the night city.

Rethinking Space and Gender

The general absence of women in most spatial representations is insufficiently explained by the conventional distinction between 'private' and 'public' city space. Neither is the private merely a woman's domain nor are men the exclusive users of public space. The rules of gender, nevertheless, do operate in assigning physical, social, and political space to men and women, although only for women is temporality so crucial a determinant. The zones of women's visibility and power, for instance, are coded according to a temporal as well as a spatial logic, and their mobility—whether the movement of a woman's body through the space of the city or their circulation as commodities—is governed by a set of rules that is neither forged nor consulted by the town planner.[8] To the extent that the town planner or even real estate developer considers only the physical attributes of space, the spatial practice of women remains invisible. The 'temporal neutrality' of the town planning apparatus, moreover, is a form of gender neutrality and does not reveal the operations of gendered power in the city.

Doreen Massey has underlined the importance of both space and time in revealing the meaning of gender in geography.[9] Her critique of the conventional dichotomy between male and female spaces points to the ways in which 'space' implies 'the lack of politics'. Against this, she proposes the unified concept of space/time which should serve as a necessary corrective although, '[t]he point ... is not to argue for an upgrading of the status of space within the terms of the old dualism ... but to argue that what must be overcome is the very formulation of space/time in terms of this kind of dichotomy'.[10]

My own use of the space/time concept is somewhat distinct from one that wishes to challenge the dichotomy of stasis/agency as it corresponds to space/time (and thus female/male). If temporality is a crucial element in the city space, then any attempt to map the gendered practice of power in the city must code space according to times of day and stages in the woman's life cycle. Space thus has no stable or fixed uses that cannot be undone at different times of the day or in different stages of a woman's life. Indeed, it is only by mapping the varying relationship between 'flesh and stone' that the civic life of woman may become visible, for the 'body politic' practices power by circumscribing, using, or invoking bodies in specific ways that may include or exclude men and women.[11]

Yet narratives of 'exclusion' or 'absence' do not exhaust the experience of women in the city. One may begin outlining women's spatial practice by asking 'how bodies—particularly female bodies—inhabit and negotiate space ...'[12] In her study of women in a village setting, Seemanthini Niranjana argues, 'the body is the central material anchor for the discourse on gender and sexuality', and notions of femininity are implicated in the socio–spatial, as gender is constructed in and through physical, social, and cultural space. Niranjana's observations arise from the narrower space of village society, and need to be revised in the urban setting.

In the city, the practice of power may be different. The everyday lives of women, especially those who are poor and underprivileged, are guided by strict 'zoning laws'.[13] A complex matrix of gestures, markings, bodily controls, and language enables the safe passage of the woman through the urban space. Sometimes, when her movement is purposive—to the water pump, near the temple, or with children in tow—she becomes safe as well as invisible. At other times, or in other spaces—lingering at the street corner, in a restaurant, or on the streets at night—her visibility as a sexual being is heightened. Male control of the street is established through cat-calls, unwelcome gestures and contact, or more brutal molestations:[14] thus the privileges of the flaneur, or one who strolls the city streets, are uniquely male.[15]

Conversely, the space of the home is neither sacrosanct nor inviolable, as is always assumed, as it is founded on everyday and episodic violence against women. The sexual control of women in the Indian context is direct and unmediated in both rural and urban settings so that opportunities and restrictions on women's participation in the world of work arise from the control of sexuality. Secluded home-based production, for instance, accentuates the invisibility of women within the workforce. At the same time, it is in the city that the woman's role as consumer is amply visible, within and outside the home. The twin processes of producing woman as a consuming subject and as object to be consumed are aided, in this time of globalization, by the sexualization of the visual field.[16]

By no means are women totally deprived of power in the city, condemned to lives wholly determined by spatial arrangements that are not of their own making. The history of the female body in the space of the city, how it is deployed, restrained, circumscribed, or invoked in city space will be critical in unmasking the gender neutrality of the city. This in turn will reveal that dichotomies—such as presence/absence, visibility/invisibility, inclusion/exclusion, private/public—are only of limited use.[17] It will also reveal that the city constitutes woman in ways that mark her off from the 'citizen' who is normed as male.[18]

In this last chapter, I will discuss the practice of political power in Bangalore city through a specific consideration of how gender relations are constituted and define a role for women. I begin with an account of an individual working woman's life, which serves as the social biography of a caste/class. It points to the general invisibility of women's labour in the city, even within organizations that represent the political interests of the worker–citizen such as the trade union or the caste organization. Only episodically was the norming of the worker-citizen as 'male' challenged, sometimes by the heroic and exceptional leadership of women, as the case of Mary Davasia will demonstrate. Since the early 1980s, however, the visibility of women within the political sphere has increased as a consequence of a number of developments. For one, their presence in civic bodies has been mandated by law. For another, women have been called to action within an emerging sphere of 'social municipalism'. These modes of political engagement have, however, been radically redefined by the emergence of a specifically feminist politics, which intervenes and makes visible the pervasive and iterative violence against women within the family, but also questions and opposes the heightened visibility of the sexualized female body, as in the opposition to the Miss World contest of 1996. Taken together, these multiple levels will outline the practice of power in the city from an optic that is quite different from practices outlined elsewhere in this book.

Citizenship and the Labouring Woman

'Stadt Luft Macht Frei' ('The city air makes [you] free') is only a partial promise to women in the city since citizenship, as J.G.A. Pocock reminds us in his discussion of Aristotlean notions of the term, 'is not just a means to being free, it is the way of being free itself'.[19] If citizenship is bound up with a legal notion of owning property, women may often lay claim to it against the corporate interests of the family. The complex relationship between property ownership, the ownership of women's labour, and citizenship becomes clearer from a discussion of the life of Lakshmi Devamma, a long time resident of Bangalore. In her unmarried years, as the daughter of a market gardener for whom the village 'survived' in the city, Lakshmi Devamma's labour enabled production for the table of the colonial master.[20] Her father's market garden, on half an acre of leased-in land a short distance from Lalbagh, produced English vegetables (celery, leeks, lettuce, red radish) using seeds imported from America. The produce was then taken to Russell Market for sale.

Married at the age of 15 in 1939, Lakshmi Devamma's labour services were in effect transferred to the family of her husband who lived in Sarakki, a village to the south of Bangalore. It was mobility of a different order, as she left the city for the countryside though the area bordered the city itself. 'Here', she recalls 'it was a different type of work, we never grew English vegetables, we grew beans, cabbage, beetroot, cauliflower, and carrot', or vegetables for which the middle-class Indian had developed a taste. This produce was sold at KR market.[21]

By the seventies, the city engulfed the four acres that belonged to Lakshmi Devamma's husband as the BDA acquired productive lands in Puttenahalli and Jaraganahalli for the development of a middle-class layout (Sarakki) and the 100 foot road. For this, the family received compensation, which was slightly enhanced after a contest. This left only a strip of land on which the houses of her children stood, escaping acquisition. Yet land had long since stopped being a productive resource and had become a piece of real estate well before that acquisition. Forced to depend on her labour in the informal economy for an income, Lakshmi Devamma began threading flowers for sale in south Bangalore. From 1960 to 1995 she purchased flowers from KR Market with small loans obtained from her clients to thread and sell for a profit, and thus put her family through school and college. This female-headed household, even when the husband was alive, thus came into being when the land settings on which the family relied (i.e. agriculture in the city) were no longer economically viable. Lakshmi Devamma was thus transformed from being a landowning person, who produced vegetables and fruit, like hundreds of other Bangaloreans, to one who made a living from retail trade. Like hundreds of women, of both local and migrant origin, who find a foothold in the city by retailing fruit, flowers, and vegetables, Lakshmi Devamma too became a link in the chain of supply from central markets to outlying zones in the city.[22]

The dispossession of the Tigalas throughout successive periods of city growth has been described by Smriti Srinivas, who suggests that the Karaga performance today memorializes the remembered city of market gardeners. Yet, despite their fullness, neither the ritualized performance, nor the civic activities associated with this politically resurgent Backward Caste group in the city include or represent women in any significant measure.[23] Within the wider story of the marginalization of the Tigalas as a landowning and productive community in the city is embedded a story of female labour that is largely rendered invisible. Within the family too, despite the long years of labour, first on her father's land and then on her husband's, Lakshmi Devamma's is only a partial claim on land as a productive resource. Today, all that survives in her name is a small patch of guava garden left by her father.

Even property which is merely residential (and therefore not agriculturally productive) is critical to the lives of women in the city. Nevertheless, women's *access to property* in the city, the woman as a legal citizen, is still intimately bound up with her *status as property*. We may see this in the transfer of Lakshmi Devamma's labour from father to husband, and her narrow rights to property. In Lakshmi Devamma's case, the gendered division of labour ensured that she had primary responsibility for the daily reproduction of her family, and yet was largely excluded from all transactions with the apparatuses of the state, especially those dealing with compensation for lands that were annexed to the city.

The paths traced by Lakshmi Devamma through the city, at first from farm to Russell Market, and later (after marriage) to and from KR Market, were purposive, and hence invisible. Other women engaged with the world of work from the space of their own homes, remaining invisible in quite another sense. Yet to both these types of working women, the city held its attractions as the space of opportunity, even accumulation, on a scale that they may not have envisaged in rural settings.

If the 'home of one's own' is critical, particularly for home-based manufacturing, the very survival of the female-headed household in an urban setting is dependent on a title to land. The acknowledgment of women as the primary care-givers among the urban poor has sometimes led to the announcement of government policies which favour woman on the question of land rights.[24] However, programmes that target women could also place an undue burden on those who are already heads of households.[25] Prakasa Rao and Tewari noted that household character 'associated with females per thousand males, household size, resident migrant ratios, and per cent women workers' had high positive scores in Broadway, Shivajinagar, and Maharaja Mills, all of which were poorer working class areas.[26] Among household heads, the authors found only 5 per cent were women, although nearly 44 per cent of these women were in the low income group, compared with 23 per cent of the men.

The preponderance of female headed households among the poor has been noted in several more recent studies, emphasizing the centrality of women's work to the sustenance and reproduction of the lower classes. Thus, the STEM survey of Slums in Bangalore confirmed that women formed the heads of household in 22 per cent of the families, with the number rising to 36 per cent in the lowest income group.[27] Other researchers have confirmed the high proportion of female-headed households among the poor: in a sample of 50 families, according to Mirjam Letsch, 12 (or about 25 per cent) had females as the sole breadwinners.[28] In yet another sample of communities in Laggere, female-headed households constituted 12 per cent of the total.[29] According to H. Ramachandran and Daljeet Singh, women formed 98 per cent of the labour force in the house-based manufacturing slums, which were intimately linked to large informal economies.[30] Even when women were not acknowledged as household heads, they played a crucial role in the slum economy in comparison to their male counterparts. In many locations, household and wage labour together constituted at least 11 hours of work per day.[31]

In most cases, there is no consensual family strategy which equally distributes the securities of property ownership to all members of the household. Many women in Tilaknagar slum, for instance, have become the de facto heads of household due to the widespread prevalence of 'the absent male' phenomenon (resulting from the death of the husband, desertion, multiple marriages, or failure of the husband to support the family). They spend an extraordinary amount of time and energy in securing the title to land on which their house stands, often in opposition to male rights. Velliamma spent eight years in struggle with the BDA to transfer the ownership of her small house, measuring 14 by 25 feet, from her unemployed husband, fearing that he would simply sell it at the first opportunity to the Muslim neighbours who were already encroaching from both sides.[32] Finally, although nearly Rs 3000 was paid in bribes, the transfer was enabled only through the intervention of the MLA, Ramalinga Reddy.

A similar set of claims on residential property in the south Bangalore squatter settlement is discussed by Benjamin and Bhuvaneswari. Putturoja, a woman whose father gave her a hut to live in, was deserted by her husband for another woman: she herself subsequently remarried. The Bangalore Urban Poverty Programme, which attempted to procure titles to that land, in its insistence on identifying the 'head of household' produced three claimants, none of whom corresponded to the woman-occupant: the three-cornered battle between her brother, her former and her present husband left her out of the picture.[33]

Far from being a non-issue, the clear title to urban property helps women to deploy it in ways that will provide security, and perhaps even an income. The possession of clear titles, moreover, helps the urban poor make a legitimate claim for improved local services. In his detailed analysis of 12 slums in Bangalore, Michael de Wit notes, 'The granting of pattas was persistently mentioned as the *sine qua non* condition for further improvements. Contrary to planners who tended to conceive the problems of slums in terms of infrastructure, particularly in terms of a sites and services scheme, the dwellers absolutely prioritized the dwelling itself'.[34]

Beyond the realm of city-based agricultural workers and home-based manufacture, women in Bangalore have enjoyed a presence in the organized workforce which is rarely acknowledged in the organizational strategies of the trade union. In the phase of the public sector, women were largely employed in those sections of the industry, such as watch manufacture, or electronics assembly, considered most suitable to the woman's capacity for repetitive, monotonous tasks requiring fine motor skills. Special efforts were made by BEL in the mid-1950s to recruit engineering graduates from women's colleges for the new electronics industry: radio wiring continued to be a women's job right into the 1980s.[35] Similarly, telephone assembly was entirely undertaken by women in ITI, as was watch assembly in HMT Watch factory. Not surprisingly, the predominance of women in electronics assembly continued well into the phase of private industry in the 1980s, when the face behind the television monitor was that of a woman. Meanwhile, in its latest phase as the centre of microprocessor-based, information technology industries, as much as 21 per cent of the workforce is female.[36] If women took advantage in the past of the gendered division of labour in the workplace to avoid night shifts,[37] the new IT-enabled industries in particular thrive on an ideology of making few gender based distinctions on the shop floor.[38]

Even the robust trade union movement of the public sector, however, did little to draw women into the unions and address and acknowledge their specific roles. Indeed, the woman worker embodied the notion of sacrifice and good conduct, even during moments of strike,[39] when the more militant actions of the unions were undertaken by men. In industries such as electronics and garments, where young women have been recruited in large numbers, unionism involving women has had to develop new styles and modes of engaging with the state and the employers. It is to the new embodied politics of the woman worker that we now turn.

Embodying Politics: The Woman Worker

There is a long tradition, from the period of the nationalist movement, of using the bodies of women to stave off actions of the police. Women have been deployed in processions, or during demolition drives to prevent or delay repressive actions. These calculated deployments of the woman's body could go awry when the logic of 'respect for women' deteriorates into violence. Thus, women workers of the pharmaceutical firm, J.L. Morrison, who joined a spontaneous strike in 1986 at Peenya, were, according to Babu Mathew, pushed to the front in order to prevent a police attack on the procession. Yet the women were brutally hit with no consideration whatsoever for their vulnerability.

> When the police blocked the procession, somebody in the crowd said, 'Let the women workers go in front'. So the assumption was that the police will not stop women workers. Therefore the procession parted and allowed the women workers to go forward. And the women got the worst bashing of the lot as a result of it. The calculation that they would not be beaten up was completely wrong and they got the worst beating.[40]

Such calculated deployments of working woman by no means imply that women have played only symbolic roles in trade union activity. Indeed, there have been occasions when the planned or spontaneous participation of women in labour agitation recasts the meaning of trade unionism and mass action. Two recent examples of women's involvement in strikes illustrate the new relationship that has developed between the trade union, the state, and its women workers, whether during long strike actions, such as the five month long BPL strike of 1998–9 or in wildcat actions, such as the flash strike in Peenya in July 2001.[41]

The BPL strike was a culmination of efforts by over 6336 first generation women employees to organize a CITU-led union in 1998 demanding minimum wages and certain basic facilities in 14 units in and around Bangalore. The electronics major had a turnover of Rs 2400 crore, and over 30 per cent of the colour TV market. In 1997–8, the company introduced Total Quality Management and Kanban (just-in-time) processes which increased the uncertainty of permanent employees and pointed to a possible casualization of the workforce. Predictably, the union had its first success among a small group of retrenched workers. At least two previous efforts to begin unions in the 1980s had failed, and in 1998 too, the management withheld recognition of the union, though they immediately raised wages to minimum levels. Meanwhile, the management did everything in its power, using the police and the courts, to derecognize BPL Karmikara Sangha and suspended up to 800 members and sympathizers.

Despite these difficulties, the increased wages had the unexpected effect of drawing more women into the union, and membership soared. When the union announced a strike in November 1998, its female members were ready to deploy the familiar repertoire of actions that had been tried by male trade unionists over the years: dharnas, *urulu seves*, gate meetings, neighbourhood meetings, and the like. The unexpected resolve of the women workers was opposed by the company, the government, and the labour commissioner alike. Meanwhile, reports of violence were mounting as the company attempted to employ blacklegs to carry on production. This pointed to the ease with which labour supplies could be guaranteed. The strike carried on for five months, and was only called off when a bus of 'blackleg' workers (many of whom were also women) was burnt 26 March 1999, resulting in the death of one young woman.

The BPL strike was a rare example of a long drawn out strike sustained by the hope that union recognition would win enduring benefits for a young and overwhelmingly female workforce. Young women were once chosen for their docility and their historically acknowledged aversion to prolonged union action, but the BPL strike proved that women had unexpected resources to sustain long periods off work, and were far from unwilling to undertake militant actions. The electronics industry brought legions of young unmarried women out of villages and slums in Bangalore into the factory premises, for whom the job was a means of accumulating a dowry in the interim period before marriage. The BPL strike proved that these women were quick to develop a taste for, and pride in, factory work, and an unexpected commitment to work that they would defend through a prolonged strike.

At the opposite end of the spectrum are those female workers who may be more resigned to the uncertainties of long term employment in the city, are usually unexposed to organizational efforts by trade unions, but could still resort to 'wildcat' strikes. Nearly 10,000 garment workers, most of whom were women, took to the streets in the Peenya industrial area in north-west Bangalore on 24 July 2001.[42] Workers who poured out of one factory (Apex Garments) called out those from other factories in protest against a rumour that a new rule would make it impossible to withdraw their provident fund until they were 45 years old. None of these units appear to have had unions. This leaderless strike action was predictably brief and lasted only for a day.

The garment industry has employed women in large numbers in the 1980s and 1990s (Fig. 59). The number of garment workers in a city like Bangalore has been estimated at 70,000, of which over 70 per cent are women.[43] The garment industry has approximately 445 units in Bangalore district alone. These may range from the more informal unit which employs a few dozen women in a slum like Tilaknagar, to a large unit employing over 500 workers as in the Gokaldas Exports Factory, Peenya.[44] Recruitment is quite casual, with even established companies placing a board outside the unit until vacancies are filled.

It needed no union to teach these legions of workers that their labour was not justly rewarded. Indeed, garment unit owners took great pains to keep away the trade unionist by firing potential organizers. However, the Peenya incidents showed that repression does not guarantee peace. When two units of JB Exports closed down in 2001, the 1,400 workers began thronging the PF office to settle their dues. An overworked PF official appears to have sparked the unrest by saying that dues would not be settled before they turned 45. Harassment at the PF office was common, with claim forms being sold for up to Rs 250, and further bribes being paid when dues were settled. The wild cat strike brought long standing humiliations and new resentments to the foreground.

FIG. 59 *The new informal sector: young women at a garment unit in Agarahara Layout.* (The Printers Mysore, Private Limited, 1991)

What was unsettling to the police and media, as well as the established trade unions was the anonymity of the mob, which refused to identify its leaders. The women who marched to the PF office and were told that the rumour was false refused to believe the officials and wanted a clarification from the highest authority in the state, the chief minister himself. They refused to name any leader and were single minded in their effort to establish the truth of whether their PF would be paid to them when they needed it. In an industry that thrives on women who save for their weddings, and which ensures that married women have only a tenuous hold on the jobs, the PF assumes unusual importance. The poignancy of the rumour and its widespread effect on this population of garment workers was that few, perhaps none, of these women expected to continue working until the age of 45. There was perhaps no more eloquent statement on their working conditions than this sudden outcry from the garment worker, which baffled the authorities and the unions alike.

The two instances of collective action described above came at a time when trade unionism of the older kind was on the decline. The relative anonymity of the woman worker, and especially the woman leader during these strike actions was in striking contrast to the heroic styles of leadership that had previously prevailed. Women's participation in unions had been rare, and their leadership even rarer, but within the restricted realm of trade union leadership there were exceptions. The heroic leadership of Mary Davasia is one such exception in the history of public life in Bangalore, especially as she dominated the field at a time when women workers were fewer and less visible.

Davasia, who came from her native Kerala in 1950 to find a job in the then Mysore secretariat, gave a new lease of life to the languishing non-gazetted officers' union. Begun as early the 1920s, the organization was moribund when Mary Davasia entered the secretariat. By the 1960s, she had earned such titles as 'tigress from Kerala' and 'a spark that refuses to be extinguished'.[45] With indefatigable energy, she worked in the late 1950s to infuse a militant spirit into the union, pedalling around the city on her bicycle to enroll new members and often travelling ticketless to other cities in Mysore on organizational work.[46] By the early 1960s her efforts paid off, and the NGO union was a large and powerful organization, no longer content to present petitions to the chief ministers and await a favourable response.

As secretary, and later president, of the non-gazetted officers' association, Davasia fought for parity in wages with the central government employees, and also for parity between various parts of the newly unified Karnataka.[47] She led major joint actions, culminating in a mammoth NGO rally in 1960.[48] Her leadership of the historic NGO strike in 1965 overcame every effort of the state to suppress her in direct and indirect ways.[49] At the height of the inflationary 1960s period, she asked all state government employees to reject the paltry government offer of a Rs 5 Dearness Allowance, and soon Chief Minister Nijalingappa's chambers were flooded with thousands of money orders from those returning the amount.[50] The government was looking for ways to put an end to this massive upsurge among its employees, and Davasia provided an opportunity when, in opposing the private contracts given for cycle stand and canteen operations in the secretariat, she called the Nijalingappa regime a government of 'contractors' socialism'. Davasia was compulsorily retired from government service in 1965 for her defiance; it was a sign of her success as a leader that massive rallies of NGOs demanded her reinstatement.[51] For a long while, the NGO association continued to raise this demand, and in 1969, she won the case against her 'compulsory retirement'.[52]

Throughout her career, Davasia faced systematic campaigns against her leadership. Most of them relied on the tactic of maligning her character, branding her a communist for her unorthodox leadership, and claiming she 'smoked, drank and went to late cinema shows'.[53] Her common law marriage to a press worker was taken as a further sign of her depravity. Over the years, she also coped with opposition from within the union that she had founded. In a moving defence entitled 'I Speak', written in 1968, Davasia answered her critics. She defended her actions as president, and spelt out the kinds of sacrifices she had made throughout her leadership of the union, including her refusal to give in to government's tempting offers in the mid-1960s.[54] It was also a strident critique of the new leadership for succumbing to the pressures of state authorities and ministers:

> I reliably learnt that frequently the authorities used to tempt our heroes with certain remarks. 'Why do you have a woman as your leader? Are you men not capable of leading the NGOs movement? Are you not ashamed to work under a woman? Secondly, could you not find a Kannada Puthra to lead your struggle? Why a Keralite should come and lead you? Are you not the heroic sons of Karnataka?' Thirdly, religion. All these venomous thoughts were being injected to the minds of these heroes ...

In response to charges that she had embezzled funds, Davasia asked 'Did I ever say [sic] that Malayalee (Keralite) NGOs should only be paid DA? Or did I ever say that the additional DA received by NGOs should be sent to Kerala? Have I ever said that because I am a woman, my leadership is to be accepted by all?'[55]

Predictably Davasia has been neglected in conventional trade union histories.[56] She developed a style of trade union leadership that was unusually charismatic and difficult for other women to emulate. Indeed, when occasion demanded, Davasia was not above using 'masquerade' in ways that were strikingly different from the deployment of women as surrogates in political life. The success of women political leaders is conditional on their wearing conspicuous marks of a respectable femininity. Davasia both complied with and transgressed these prescribed roles. She evaded arrest in 1965 for a long while by going underground, but kept up her visits to offices through the adoption of a variety of disguises. The climax was when she appeared on the steps of Vidhana Soudha dressed as a man in trousers and a turban, audaciously removing the headgear to reveal her identity. This provocative act, which amounted to a staging of masculinity, was a fitting reply to those who, decrying her life as an austere trade unionist—she wore no jewellery and always dressed in simple white sarees—faulted her leadership for being too masculine.

The heroic and exceptional efforts of such women as Davasia in the 1960s have been transformed since the 1980s for a number of reasons. More women are drawn into active political careers, partly as a response to government mandates, as well as in response to the pressures from below for a new style of engagement with municipal maintenance. The engagement of women in these realms of city politics, while remaining distinct from feminist modes of engagement, has exceeded the expectations of what constitutes appropriate political activity for urban women.

The 'Body Politic' and Local Governance

In a remarkable vignette of political transactions in slum areas of Bangalore, Benjamin and Bhuvaneswari recount the role played by one Ghousie, a resident of Azadnagar and a Congress supporter, in the councillor's by-elections of 1998, in campaigning for the 'independent' candidate. Among the tactics he used was the deployment of young men in purdah:

> On the day of the elections, my gang caught hold of the 15-year-olds in the settlement and dressed them in purdah and asked them to vote for all the absentee votes. It is not that the opposition party did not know it ... they also did it. All the parties have an understanding on this .... If the booth officer objects we will threaten him altogether and he cannot do anything ...[57]

Despite this use of surrogate women, the contestant Sardar lost the election. Perhaps because, as another contestant confessed, it was the counter strategy that succeeded: 'We knew that they being Muslims would send up people dressed as women in *burkhas*, so we decided to lengthen the process of genuine voting for as long as possible'.[58] In this well worn tactic of electoral politics, the sign of female ethnic identity was exploited by the very patriarchal forces that might have kept real women away from the public sphere.

Where the presence of women is mandated by law, as in the reservation of seats for women in the local bodies, a different kind of surrogate politics is engendered. In the operation of this level of politics, we may find the clearest example of the value of the concept of space/time. Women had been a token presence in the municipality after 1949, rarely numbering more than 10 per cent in the council. Between 1954 and 1963, however, women found a space within the double member wards, in which one of the two seats was reserved for the 'weaker' sections. Between 1949 and 1996, there had been only one woman mayor, Indiramma, although women were sometimes chosen as deputy mayors in council. In 1983, the Karnataka government raised the level of women's reservations to 20 per cent in municipal wards thereby transforming city level campaigns and elections.[59] The 74th amendment to the Constitution in 1991 extended these benefits nationwide and provided for the reservation of one-third seats for women in urban local bodies.[60]

Since the early 1980s, the enhanced system of reservations dramatically altered the previous picture of poor female representation in the council. In the two rounds of elections held under the new law, 1996 and 2001, a large number of women corporators have gained visibility, enjoying the posts of mayor and deputy mayor, as well as membership of important standing committees. These women corporators have largely been seen, particularly in the media, as mere surrogates for other males in their family—usually husbands, but also fathers and sons. Sometimes this is with good reason. Padmini Reddy, corporator, Pulakeshinagara from 1996–2001, confessed that she was only the de jure councillor, while her husband was the real corporator. 'I had no intention of entering into politics. When my ward was chosen as a women's reserved ward, my husband was the real functionary. Therefore he gave me a chance to enter politics'.[61] Nalini Basavaraj, who represented Pattabhiramanagara ward in 1996, admitted that her husband's influence in the Janata Dal party won her the seat and got her the prestigious chair of the Appeals Committee.

Similar statements have often been taken as the truth of the experience of all women in urban politics. Certainly, many women candidates were supported by their husbands, sons, and fathers when the reservation of wards for women was first announced in 1983 and then in 1996. A substantial number of women do restrict their public appearance to the council and committee meetings which require their physical presence. The daily work of the ward which often spans day and night, is sometimes the full time responsibility of the male for whom the woman councillor functions as a proxy.

The semiotics of campaigns in women's wards is richly suggestive of this dependence: posters for Vijaya D. Muniraju, a Janata Dal (S) candidate from Chandra Layout featured her husband looming over her shoulder, while an audio cassette laid ample stress on the woman's surname. Thus the voter was not allowed to forget that the previous corporator was really being 'represented' by his wife. The publicity campaign of Pratima Raghu, corporator since 2001 of C.V. Raman Nagar, similarly advertised the achievements of the previous corporator who was her husband, and his links with the central party leadership. A young unmarried woman, J.N. Nirmala, who represents Subrahmanyanagar ward (2001) allowed her father, an active BJP worker, to launch and run her campaign: he still performs the role of corporator as she is a student. So widespread is the phenomenon of de facto power being wielded by some men that they are referred to as the 'general power of attorney' or GPA holders of the women concerned. These men make promises to voters, complete ward works on hand, and generally remain most visible as the corporator, on behalf of, and less frequently, along with the elected woman.

However, by no means do these examples complete the picture of women in urban local bodies. A recent investigation of the success of women in ward politics reveals a far more complex picture. Of the 29 women who were interviewed as part of the sample of 59 corporators, less than a third conformed to the political experience exemplified by Padmini Reddy or Prathima Raghu. There were at least two other identifiable modes of engagement with ward level politics. There were those who saw the advantage of being identified as family women, and therefore worked alongside their men in the political sphere. Padmavathi Gangadhara Gowda, who served three terms as a corporator, actively sought the support of her husband as a way of learning the ropes of ward politics. By the end of three or four years, she was quite adept at handling issues on her own. Seeking the support and help of the husband (or other male) is seen as an added advantage as that provides the ward members with two people whom they can approach with their problems.

Indeed, keeping the post of councillor within the family is considered as important as winning the seat for the first time. Mahadevamma, corporator of Kamalanagar in 1996, took the support of her son in her work, and he went on to triumph in the 2001 election, keeping the ward in the family. Moreover, even when the husband is involved, he need not always be the dominant partner. Lalitha Srinivas Gowda, corporator since 2001 of Srinagar ward, holds a royal court in her house which doubles as office, flanked by her husband who occasionally assists her. Her political career draws on, but is not founded on, the husband's support, and her proximity to Chief Minister S.M. Krishna is well known. Similarly, Ratna Gopal Reddy, corporator of Jeevan Bima Nagar (1996), struck an independent path and developed a credible relationship with her constituency: it was she, rather than her husband who was put up as a candidate when the ward was declared a general ward in 2001.

It is revealing that many of the women interviewed did so in the presence of their spouses: the constant use of the plural 'we', however, indicated that ward work was considered a joint political responsibility. As Mahadevamma put it, it didn't matter whether she or her son won, as 'ultimately it is in the family'. However, as the recent results of the Bangalore Corporation elections held in 2001 showed, fielding a wife or daughter is no guarantee of re-election to the same ward. Only two of the 36 women who won the elections were, in fact, related to sitting or former corporators.

In contrast to the women who are proxies and those who seek their family's help are the significant number of women who function independently. G. Padmavathi won the 1996 election from the Sriramamandira ward: her reputation as a councillor in this ward enabled her to stand for and win the 2001 election from the neighbouring ward, Prakashnagar, when it was reserved for women. The former corporator of Shivanagar, Y.G. Vydehi, relied on her long years as a teacher and as a member of the Rashtriya Sevika Samithi to get elected and serve as a corporator. There were further instances of women converting power of an informal kind into electoral power. The case of Mari Muttu Adimoolam is an indication of the possibilities of the reservation process for both men and women. Mari Muttu was implicated in the liquor scam of 1981, which led to the deaths of over 330 people. She has since been acquitted of all charges in 21 cases, and although she is a local 'rowdy sheeter', she went on to become a corporator for the Sagayapuram ward in 2001.

The support of the party was critical to the success of both men and women candidates. In the 1983 elections, independents (men and women) who constituted nearly 59 per cent of those who contested, were barely able to win two per cent of the seats.[62] Many women corporators, such as Ratna Gopal Reddy, Bharati Shivaram, and Nalini Basavaraj, admitted that their campaigns succeeded because of the support of the party and in particular the MLAs: the word 'godfather' was often used by both men and women to describe the senior politician in question.

Nevertheless, there is no doubt that the support of the family was crucial to the success of women. Freedom from child care and other household responsibilities was vital to the participation of women in politics. This freedom could come from having an extended family,[63] from having grown up children,[64] and from having a daughter-in-law in the family.[65] On rarer occasions, women corporators relied on paid domestic labour.

The demands of ward work forced women to rely on the support of men in the family on a regular basis. There were occasions when women felt neither comfortable or safe at local festivals or late night programmes. Many women expressed their distaste for the hurly-burly of ward politics, which involved aggressive dealings with contractors and officials. Existing codes of public behaviour placed a greater strain on women than men: women corporators in the council preferred to sit together, according to their party position, rather than freely move around the council. Travelling through the ward on daily rounds and attending late evening sessions threw women into contact with male colleagues that many were socially unprepared for. Women who were not sexually neutralized by age or marital status were vulnerable to unsavoury speculations. Padmavathi Gangadhara Gowda spelt out what it meant to conduct oneself in public: 'there are some women who stay in the corporation from morning till evening. They make the mistake of getting into vehicles of all those who offer, go for meals and coffee with all those who invite her. The woman may have good intentions, but others think she is "social".'

These were important reasons why women had to mark themselves as 'family women' in order to remain visible and succeed in the field of politics. Indeed, the most successful way of maligning women candidates has been to suggest that they owe their seats to important males in the party. N. Shantakumari of Mudalapalya ward in west Bangalore, who won the election in 1996 to a reserved ward, managed to retain her ward even after it was converted to a general seat. Her rival suggested in public that only her relationship to Congress leaders V. Somanna and D.K. Shivakumar secured her the nomination.

Opposition to women candidates from the community often challenged the support of the party or other local associations. Mamtaz Begum, a Congress I corporator from Shivajinagar, has won three elections in 1983, 1990, and 2001, and has been an active member of the Meat, Beef and Poultry [sellers'] Associations in the Shivajinagar area. Nevertheless, she had to contend with the former corporator who legally challenged the reservation of the ward for women in 2001. Arguing that representation by a woman in a Muslim-dominated ward was inappropriate, his campaign drew support from local religious leaders, who discouraged others from filing nominations in an attempt to render the election invalid.

In addition to being discriminated against on grounds of gender, women were not immune from the difficulties posed by the politics of caste in the city. P.N. Chandrakala, who represented Peenya in 1996, was harassed because she was poor and came from a Backward Class (BC-A category) in an area dominated by Vokkaligas. On the other hand, being from the regionally dominant Vokkaliga caste was cited as a definite advantage by Padmavathi Vijaykumar of Malleswaram ward. In a ward that had a large Brahmin population, her loyalty to the ideology of the BJP also helped her win with ease by using the RSS, the network of temples and other local religious organizations. Membership of local organizations, particularly the Kannada sanghas and the Ganesha associations, and occasionally the RSS or the caste organization, was crucial to the success of the corporator although most women lacked access to these modes of political engagement before they won the election.

Women have thus not only gained visibility but power within the local body politic. To a considerable extent their careers have been determined by the policy of reservations, and the consequent compulsion on parties to field female candidates. However, women have belied predictions that they will remain tied to male political representatives, although the policy of reservations which was adopted by Karnataka in 1983 was not the result of a sustained campaign by women's groups for greater power in elected bodies. If anything, a new role for women in urban civic life has been defined outside the realm of electoral politics, as a consequence of the growth of the city and its redefinition as a vast residential space.

Since the 1980s, women have been warmly welcomed into certain other kinds of civic activism, particularly after the emergence of residents' associations. These associations were a continuation of the old rate-payers' associations in many ways, though their concerns and membership are strikingly different. The associations became a way for far-flung layouts to seek and secure basic city services such as water supply, electricity, or bus services. By the mid-1990s, the nascent activism received a further boost following a state-sponsored initiative, called Swabhimana. This initiative was an effort to develop new non-governmental institutional forms to enhance citizens' participation in ward level politics. One of the earliest groups existed in Malleswaram, and the idea of building up a city-wide forum came up in conversations between UN–ESCAP representatives and the then corporation administrator, A. Ravindra.[66] In 1995, Chief Minister Deve Gowda officially launched the Swabhimana forum, which was to be co-ordinated by the Public Affairs Centre of Bangalore. The Malleswaram and Bangalore East Swabhimana forums were among the earliest to succeed, but they paved the way for nearly 150 such organizations by the late 1990s.

Middle-class women have been noticeably active in these forums. Much of the work is seen as an extension of their role as housekeepers to the neighbourhood as a whole, as this form of activism is associated with garbage clearance, park maintenance, and community activities in middle-class residential localities. Women have also been remarkably successful in entering the sphere of civic activism by actively intervening in maintaining the strictly residential profile of the neighbourhood. Women of Lal Bahadur Shastri Nagar, for instance, took the law into their own hands by closing down a liquor shop following the suicide of a young woman, and were applauded for their act.[67] This engagement with 'social municipalism' is quite different from the presence of women in urban local bodies, especially as it draws on and redefines gender specific tasks within the city space.

In contrast, the reception of the feminist movement has been mixed. The spectacular growth of the women's movement since the 1980s has recast women's roles in public life, buttressed in part by state policies which have made women more visible. This level of activism questions and challenges the exclusion of women from formal structures of power, particularly as they have remained largely marginal to the labour, the left, the Kannada, and the Dalit movements. In Bangalore, there has been a close link between the emergence of women's activism and the growing presence of the non-governmental sector in the pedagogical and organizational life of the city. The history of Vimochana, the women's group that has enjoyed a long and active existence for over two decades, brings this relationship into focus. The issues that Vimochana has chosen to focus on and its style of functioning are instructive especially as they contrast with feminist groups in several other metropolitan cities.[68]

Body Politics: Violence in the Family

Begun in 1979 as part of an NGO called the Centre for Informal Education and Development Studies, Vimochana has worked for over 20 years on women's issues, with a focus on domestic violence and sexual harassment at the workplace.[69] In the absence of a wider movement for women's rights in Karnataka, and Bangalore in particular, the link with the NGO has proved crucial for the survival of the group.[70] Initially, Vimochana operated as an office based counselling organization, but has over the years taken up sustained and painstaking case work investigating unnatural deaths of young married women in the city of Bangalore. These investigations serve as an important reminder of how precarious the bodily safety of women in the city maybe, even within the space/time of the home.

Feminist activism and scholarship since the 1980s had brought the widespread phenomenon of wife battering to the forefront. Battering takes the form of routine assaults on women in their homes, sometimes until they die either through an act of suicide or murder. These deaths, recorded as 'unnatural deaths' by the police, were relatively unnoticed until a national campaign in the early 1980s paid closer attention to the ways in which young brides were falling victim to 'stove bursts'. Like its counterparts in several other Indian cities at the time, Vimochana undertook years of activism and protest against individual cases of 'dowry deaths'. Unlike its counterparts in other cities, however, Vimochana has not only persisted with detailed case work, but has organized periodic Truth Commissions in Karnataka, and Bangalore city in particular, while beginning a systematic study of such deaths from 1997. Vimochana has thus sustained and broadened its campaign against dowry murders long after other urban women's groups had moved on or felt incapable of dealing with the intensity of case work.

The death of the woman, and in particular the young married woman, is a symptom, not just of how the family economy is organized around the life, labour, and sexuality of a woman, but also the kind of systematic violence against women that is naturalized in urban society. The transformations in the urban family and its effects on women are only beginning to be recognized and studied. Older studies of the urban family in Bangalore make passing mention of the violence against women as resulting from rigidly defined antagonisms between a woman and her daughter-in-law.[71] The Vimochana study, however, which took researchers into the marital homes of brides, raised a number of new questions. By collecting information from the police, the courts and hospital authorities, Vimochana raised a number of questions about contemporary urban life and family forms that were emerging. Why was it that young brides were affected in the stove bursts as were no other female members of the family? Why were less than 10 per cent of such cases registered? What role did family courts play in the perpetuation of violence against women?[72] and why were the natal families of the harassed young wife unwilling to take her pain seriously until she was silenced by death?[73]

Investigations into dowry murders generated new insights on the form of the urban family and the place of women in these settings. Several studies have revealed that familial migration is the norm in Bangalore city.[74] Migration of women to the city through marriage accounts for higher female in-migration from within the district.[75] Nevertheless, the sex ratio has been adverse, with only marginal improvements since the 1981 census (see Table 8.1). However, violence against women within marriage shows no discrimination: women who have settled in the city for long period are as vulnerable as first generation migrants.

It would be easy to see the growing phenomenon of dowry murder as a sign of the 'commercialization' of the marriage transaction, particularly in urban areas, or even as the means for a primitive accumulation of capital in the nuclear family. M.N. Srinivas distinguished 'modern dowry' which is 'entirely the product of forces let loose by British rule such as monetisation,

TABLE 8.1: Sex Ratio in Bangalore 1941–2001

Year	Sex ratio (females per thousand males)
1941	900
1951	883
1961	874
1971	875
1981	896
1991	902
2001	906

SOURCE:
Census of India, 2001, Provisional Population Totals, Series 30, Paper 2 of 2001, p. 22.

education and the introduction of the modern sector', from its predecessor. He suggested that dowry, unanchored from its previous symbolic moorings, was increasingly characterized by 'asymmetry, uncertainty and unpredictability'.[76] Most feminists favour this economistic reading of the phenomenon. However, as Mary John has pointed out, there has been a close and unquestioned fit between the (feminists') politically strategic need to view dowry as a commercial transaction and sociological understandings of the phenomenon which have pushed social and cultural dimensions to the background.[77] A closer look at the cases which have been recorded by Vimochana and its Truth Commissions challenges the singular economistic reading of the phenomenon.

Although the phenomenon of accidental deaths involving women was noted at least since the early 1970s in Bangalore, poorly designed and unsafe stoves were blamed more than the systematic patterns of violence within the family.[78] Of the 280 people who died in the five years from 1977–82, 88–90 per cent were women and 30 per cent in the 20–30 year age group, and as many as 70 per cent of these women were married. The unusual link between kitchen accidents and young brides remained understated in reports that nevertheless admitted the evils of dowry. In the 1970s, dowry was widely acknowledged as a 'social evil', and wedding gifts were even prohibited by law.[79] A door-to-door campaign against dowry conducted by students of NMKRV college for women, for instance, targeted middle-class homes in an effort to educate those who may have been ignorant of the law.

A very different focus relating to domestic violence and dowry murders emerged in the Indian women's movement in the late 1970s. The repertoire of actions was also strikingly different from the more pedagogic campaigns of the past.[80] In the eighties and nineties, women's groups actively participated, as part of a nationwide wave of anger and concern for young brides, in protest against those who had participated in these criminal acts. The neighbourhood was the site of many such symbolic actions,[81] and the principal tactic was to publicize what was considered a very private matter. A noisy protest was a show of concern by people from other parts of the city, and served the purpose of 'shaming' the perpetrators of the crime in the heart of their respectable neighbourhoods. Not infrequently, the tactic of shame was used in front of the workplace of the husband too,[82] and sometimes against the police.[83]

From the mid-1980s on, the action moved into the courtroom, when groups like Vimochana worked to book culprits under amended laws.[84] Yet over the years, the experience of repeated delays, dismissals, and acquittals of accused families in the courts has produced a situation where, as Gowramma put it 'there are too many rights for women, but no justice'. The focus has thus shifted to a programme of 'try[ing to] save more women, rather than protest after their deaths'.[85]

The dialectic of action and analysis exemplified in Vimochana's strategy over a twenty year period has emphasized the need for a hard look at the structure of the urban family and the way it naturalized violence against women. Their study of 'unnatural deaths' of young women aged between 18–40 years in Bangalore district over a four year period from 1997–2000 revealed that the incidence of such deaths had reached alarming proportions: from 714 and 713 deaths respectively in 1997 and 1998, the numbers mounted to 768 in 1999, and 860 in 2000.[86] On an average, about 100 women per month died 'unnatural deaths' in the city of Bangalore alone.[87]

In the majority of the cases, women died between three months and three years after their weddings. In 1997–8, as many as 446 out of 703 unnatural deaths were of women in the 18–30 age group.[88] The victim of such violence was usually a young woman from the lower middle-class, who was consistently harassed for more dowry from the date of the wedding.[89] In many cases these were garment or construction workers, and in rarer cases, professional women. The harassment noticeably increased, often leading to death, when the young woman returned from her natal family after a festival visit.[90]

The link between marriage as a strategy for capital accumulation, and the consequent harassment of the bride as the bearer of such capital is too obvious and perhaps even facile to bear repetition.[91] The Vimochana study, however, revealed the disturbing and irreducible grammar of this violence: namely, that it was critical to the construction of masculinity. Testifying before the legislative committee to look into atrocities against women in 1999, M.C. Gowri of Jayanagar said that she 'gave up her job as newsreader in Doordarshan',[92] while Rekha, a 20-year-old software engineer, complained 'that she was harassed therefore she left the job'.[93] Geeta, a pharmacist from Girinagar who earned Rs 3000 per month, and who died within two years of marriage in 1999, was 'stopped from going to work' by her husband Chandrasekhar, a private driver whose own work was somewhat erratic: the husband complained to the father that 'your daughter goes to work and comes home late, I can't cook'.[94] Bhanumathi, a garment worker who 'lived life to the full' was wooed by Murthy, but within six months of the wedding in 1998, was asked to give up her job and 'perform her wifely duties of looking after the house and his comforts'.[95] The reduction of the woman to the status of non-earner did not ease the demands for money from the family.[96]

The working woman who is defining a new productive identity for herself beyond the family, is frequently forced to resume a dependent role in an urban

TABLE 8.2: Stated Reasons for Unnatural Death of Newly Married Women 1997–2000

Year	Dowry	Suspected infidelity	306 IPC (forced to commit suicide)	Stove burst	Others (including 302 IPC 'Unnatural death')	Total
1997	62	22	32	15	585	714
1998	45	34	34	6	592	711
1999	61	62	63	74	540	800

SOURCE: Vimochana.

sexual economy that strives to retain its feudal face. It is striking that a large number of cases studied by Vimochana pertained to garment workers, the most visible group of working women since the 1980s. As we have seen above, the garment industry has provided women with economic independence and an opportunity for sculpting new subjectivities, not least of which is the ease of passage through the city. The city itself, and the workplace in particular, thus emerge as sites of potential pleasure and danger, at once offering a woman a right to new self-definition while setting limits to the possibility of achieving this within marriage. Integral to the masculinity of the partner, and to the institution of marriage itself, was the fidelity of the working woman.[97] Suspicions of infidelity and consequent marital violence account for a high proportion of deaths, sometimes even exceeding the number of dowry related deaths according to the study by Vimochana (see Table 8.2).

Husbands who all too frequently procure an acquittal (as the conviction rate is only about 6 per cent) are also quick to remarry. This is often taken as a further sign of the family's desire to begin another cycle of accumulation. This may however be too reductive a reading of the phenomenon. Forms of marriage which allowed multiple wives were widely accepted in the past, and continue to this day, but have largely yielded to a form of serial monogamy, in the absence of a strong tradition of divorce by mutual consent. In other words, the 'accidental death' of a wife who stood in the way of serial monogamy was a possible way of dealing with the intransigence of the wife. Jayalakshmi who was burnt to death was the third wife of Kannan, an ITI employee whose two previous wives had died of burns.[98] In another case an ITI driver was sentenced to life for brutally murdering his wife, Lokanayaki, in 1987, and setting fire to her body to make it appear like suicide (see Table 8.3). The court noted:

All the material shows that although the elders reunited the accused and the deceased and advised them to live happily, the accused continued to ill treat the deceased by

TABLE 8.3: Mode of Unnatural Death of Newly Married Women 1997–2000

Year	Burning	Hanging	Poison	Drowning	Murder	Others	Total
1997	455	119	66	13	23	38	714
1998	454	99	59	15	34	50	711
1999	443	84	60	9	60	35	768 (137 regd)
2000	317	41	86	51	8	37	540*

*The figures for this year were incomplete.

SOURCE: Vimochana.

making certain demands and these demands were made only to see that he is relieved of the deceased so he can live happily with Laxmamma [the mistress]. This was the real reason for the accused to demand money long after marriage.[99]

To deny the importance of material demands would be a serious error: the burden of providing funds for contingencies and daily needs alike were squarely placed on women and their natal families. This could range from money required for the crippling one year of rental advance for a home in the city, capital for running petty businesses, or even funds for everyday needs. The intensified harassment of women who returned empty-handed after a celebration of the important festival at her natal home is an important feature of the pattern of violence.

The understanding that all unnatural deaths of women in the city result from harassment relating to dowry demands appears ironically to spring from the 'script of the law'. The institutions of the law admit that women are victims of dowry demands, but rarely place such demands within the context of the continuous harassment of women. Indeed, some studies have shown the difficulties of prosecution under Section 498 A (harassment of women) of the IPC. There is, to begin with, 'lack of proof' of harassment throughout the marriage. More often, the court normalizes the violence within the home and does not treat it as anything that violates the integrity of women. Violence is treated as episodic, rather than being central to the masculinity of the husband.[100] There are innumerable instances of women who are repeatedly asked by their natal families, and by the family court, to 'adjust' even when they complain of harassment.[101] In this sense, state institutions support the very structure against which the voice of the woman is raised.

It is even more striking that the harassment of the woman is not taken seriously even by her natal family, which also normalizes this violence. The phenomenon of violence against women in the home thus makes sense only when viewed from the perspective of both the natal and marital abodes. The normalized violence of familial structures is intrinsic to the sustenance of patriarchy and, more properly, masculinity, and is therefore crucial in understanding the phenomenon of dowry murders. Aileen Ross's study of the 1950s gave some indication of harassment that accompanies the demand for material goods after marriage,[102] but there is no doubt that harassment leading to death has become more common since that study. The hierarchy of affective ties between various members of the husband's family provided by Ross is instructive: the love between mother–son and brother–brother top the list compared with the very weakly asserted affective ties between husband–wife.[103]

Within such a framework of acceptable violence against women in the family, the casual and indifferent collection of evidence by the police is not surprising. The need for firm proof of culpability for murder, rather than suicide, accident, or more vaguely, 'unnatural deaths', requires a certain rigour in evidence gathering. The dying declaration was intended to allow the victim's family an opportunity to avenge her murder. However, too many circumstances intervened to prevent even the truth of the dying woman's voice from being heard. In 1986, when the Supreme Court took closer note of offences in the matrimonial home, the Dowry Prohibition act was amended to provide for the 'dying declaration' as 'conclusive piece of evidence' to seal the fate of the accused.[104] However, complications soon set in, for women made two or more declarations, leading to inconsistencies which made a dismissal of the case easy. More than 72 cases investigated by Vimochana showed that the victim rarely implicates her husband even when she suffers 65 per cent burns. In addition to her fear of how her own offspring may be treated, the woman's silence is produced by the fear that she may survive and face even greater hardship in her marital home.[105] Women are, moreover, coerced into 'forgiving the husbands because it was [only] a mistake'[106] or to 'think of the children', leading them to forget or revise the dying declaration.

The household is thus a different private space depending on who is kept from seeing what is happening behind closed doors: the kinds of surveillance or 'eyes' that Jane Jacobs lauded as essential to the safety of the American urban neighbourhood,[107] are thus rendered irrelevant in a situation where the private is defined not in ways that shut off vision, sound or smell, but in a social sense. According to police data, the number of women who are afflicted by 'unbearable stomach pains' leading to death are legion. Through such a misrecognition, the intense female experience of pain remains normalized or inaudible. The kitchen, the home as a whole, and the street can pose equal dangers to the women's body and sense of self, at once making her hypervisible when she transgresses the codes of safe times/spaces, while muffling her pain, misrecognizing it, and allowing the woman to die, even within space/times that are normed as safe.

Over the years, Vimochana's focus on aspects of dowry murder has been framed within the wider context of drawing general attention to the ways in which women are represented or portrayed. By the late 1990s, this form of feminist activism attracted the opprobrium of those who viewed politics itself as an unnecessary interference with the woman's 'right to choose', with the woman here defined as a consumer. The increased sexualization of the visual field has sharpened conflicts between feminists who are opposed to such representations and those who use the language of rights to defend such representations.

Beyond the Spectacle of the Female Body

Feminist activism exceeds what is properly prescribed as the civic role of women as it brings to crisis the portrayal of the city as a site of unrestrained consumption, including the consumption of female images. Since the early 1980s, guerilla actions against film posters that portrayed women as sex objects were widespread. In 1996, an ad campaign that enjoined the public with its text 'If you have a pretty girlfriend, hang her!' evoked feminist outrage at a distasteful example of misogyny, especially considering the very real threat that women faced in the marital home. However, the call for the removal of the offensive advertisement was widely reported as amounting to a restraint on the freedom of expression, a sign of the 'dangerous path that Bangalore is treading'. As one editorial had it, the feminist protest attacked 'several basic freedoms, to work, to create, to do business in India's fastest growing city ... the loser is of course the Bangalorean, the ordinary citizen. His right to eat food that he likes is threatened, his right to see pageants that he cherishes is under attack, and his credentials are being questioned on grounds that can only be considered to be "parochial".'[108]

The 'citizen' here is once more normed as upper-middle class and male. His rights to unrestrained consumption in the city were sometimes questioned by women's groups and other political movements. Protests against increasingly sexualized representations of women through the 1980s and 1990s brought to the foreground the tensions between the woman as a subject of consumption and the female body as an object of consumption. The increasing scale and importance of events which foregrounded the female body were a sign of the growing importance of Bangalore as the new gateway of enhanced consumption, though the new global image of the city in the 1980s and 1990s has not gone unchallenged.

The large-scale controversies and protests against the Miss World contest in 1996 underlined the tension in the most dramatic way. What was called into question in this debate was the image of the city itself, as it was telecast worldwide, and the need for spectacles such as the Miss World contest to sustain that image. The use and display of the female body by the international beauty industry was critiqued on a number of counts, of which the feminist critique was only one. The unexpected alignments between various segments of a heterogeneous political field, the ready invocation of the language of rights over the question of deploying women's bodies, and the internationalization of the protest made 1996 a crucial year in the history of the city.

The Miss World competition of 1996, in which women from 89 countries participated, got off to a high security start in November, with hundreds of armed policemen lining the 3 km route from the official hotel to the Air Force Parade grounds.[109] Threatened at the outset by a wide range of groups in Karnataka, the competition was rescheduled to minimize public confrontations. The swimsuit round of the contest was held in the more remote Seychelles islands, away from the politically alert city. Three of the events, Ms Photogenic, Ms Personality, and the Coronation Ball, were held on the Air Force Parade Grounds on the outskirts of the city, to avoid possible disruptions from activist groups.[110] In all, over 10,000 policemen, including three companies of the Central Reserve Police Force (CRPF), two companies of specially trained CRPF women, three companies of the élite Rapid Action Force, and two companies of the Border Security Force, as well as a sniffer dog team, were deployed for the final event. This ensured the rights of some citizens, local and global, to enjoy without unseemly interruption a spectacle focused entirely on the female body.[111]

The benefits to the city of such an extravaganza were emphasized. In his 'case for the defence' of the beauty contest, journalist Dilip Thakore wrote '... the garden city will look good on television (however bad it is in reality)' and provide a boost to the local hospitality industry.[112] 'Bangalore', said Amitabh Bachchan, the chief Indian promoter of the contest, representing Amitabh Bachchan Corporation Limited, 'is known all over the world for its hi-tech capabilities ... This is where the MNCs are heading. I think the pageant will put Bangalore once and for all on the global map when a 2.5 billion audience spread over 115 countries sits glued as the contest unfolds.'[113] Furthermore, the pro-pageant forces presented a solid phalanx of political, economic, and social interests that were only too willing to resort to the most illiberal means to protect their rights to visual pleasures in the city. A leading English daily, which has carefully produced the 'beautiful people' in Bangalore through a lavish coverage of trivial social events since the mid-1980s, gave more than a hint that the support of non-state vigilantes was not too high a price for the city to pay in ensuring that the 'show must go on':

> It is not enough to ask why Bangalore cannot whirl with Miss World while Mumbai can jive with Jackson. If Bangaloreans want their pretty city rid of the rag-tags that specialize in rabble rousing, they must get down to investing in one 'big boss' who can make sure that crusaders from distant lands do not turn up to spoil the show in town. Indeed, any city which wants its fun and survive too must take a crash course from Mumbai on keeping protestors happy.[114]

Most troubling to the organizers were the spectacles, including self immolation—that the protesting women were willing to stage. This was in direct contrast to the liberal image of the new Indian woman that was being promoted by the beauty industry signifying the transformation of the woman from an object to a subject of sex, and a willing consumer of beauty products. Not surprisingly, organizers skillfully deployed leading female figures of the city to endorse the active sexual agency of women as a way of countering the threat from women activists.[115]

If the contest was billed as an event that would showcase the city worldwide, the controversies and protests brought an unexpected visibility to the contentious traditions of the city and indeed the nation. Opposition to the beauty contest came from a baffling array of political forces, making strange bedfellows of groups from the far left to the far right. Nor were these unified categories: Mahila Sangarsha Okkuta, for instance, was a federation of 15 feminist and other groups that linked the subjugation of women with the new economic policies and the beauty business.[116] The People's Democratic Forum similarly criticized the links between multinationals and the decision to locate the contest in 'virgin' territory which promised high yields from cosmetic sales. The All India League for Revolutionary Culture called the pageant an 'imperialist strategy to target the lucrative consumer market of the Third World'.[117]

These perspectives strongly identified economic reasons for the advantage of siting the contest in locations such as India. In this sense, they were distinct from culturalist objections to the contest which were equally varied. Some groups, such as Kannada Chaluvali Vatal Paksha, objected to the obscene depiction of women: its protest procession included nude cutouts of ABCL chief Amitabh Bachchan and fierce women *rakshasis*, in opposition to those

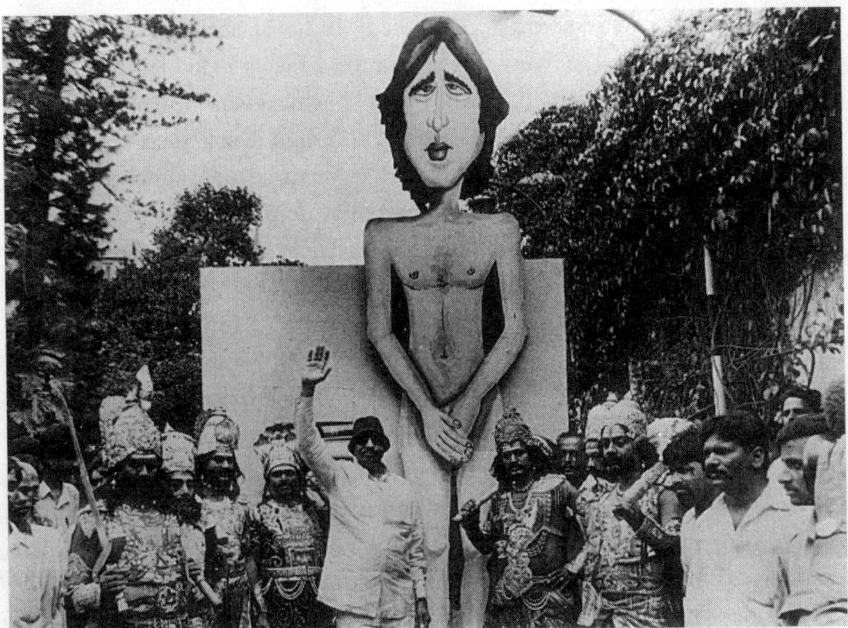

FIG. 60 *Culture under threat: a cutout of ABCL chief Amitabh Bachchan flanked by* rakshasas *forms part of the protests against the 'cultural hegemony of the west' organized by Kannada Chaluvaligars (Vatal faction) during the Miss World contest.*
(The Printers Mysore, Private Limited, M.S. Venkatachallam, 1996)

who placed women's bodies on display (Fig. 60).[118] Such colourful protests apart, M.D. Nanjundaswamy of Karnataka Rajya Raitha Sangha emphasized that the 'beauty pageant is part of a conspiracy against Indians to thrust on them part of the degenerated culture that prevails in the west'.[119] Others saw it as an attack on Kannada culture and people. It was described as a 'cultural onslaught from the west' by several speakers at a convention organized by the All India Mahila Samskrutika Sanghatane.[120] Finally, Mahila Jagran President Shashikala, who made the most dramatic threat that she would immolate herself if the show was held, raised a spectre of moral and medical decay. In her writ petition seeking a stay on the beauty contest, she said 'the contest would bring internationally organized gangs and groups in flesh trade and narcotics, and this would result in sexual exploitation abuse of women and contribute to the spread of the dreaded AIDS ...'.[121]

Despite their differences, left and right wing groups, materialist and culturalist arguments alike, were similar in at least one respect: they were both aligned against the West. The West was seen either as the locus classicus of capitalism and its attendant evils, or as the crucible of permissive cultural practices. Neither of these frameworks, as Mary John points out, is adequate in explaining the widespread acceptance in India of notion of beauty that historically arose in the West nor the myriad levels at which the beauty business has been sedimented.[122] The beauty business was far from unknown in a city like Bangalore even in the 1960s, although it was the Cantonment, with its more permissive gender regimes, that nurtured and launched some of the city's famous female faces. Over the past three decades, however, the beauty business has spread more evenly through the city as the fashion industry has flourished.

More important, though feminist protests had long been organized against beauty contests in terms that were distinct from both the culturalist and materialist arguments, they were either annexed or subordinated to the far more visible and shrill protests of the two camps. Nearly all groups opposed to the beauty contest were brought together in the federation of opponents to the Miss World Contest.[123] Blasts went off at the venue of the contest, the ABCL office was trashed, and at least 15 women threatened to immolate themselves if the contest was held in Bangalore. None of these actions resulted in the cancellation of the contest, nor did it put a damper on the growth of the beauty business, but the image of the city was portrayed, especially on television, as far from consensually derived.

Conclusion

The increased visibility of women in public life is richly ambiguous, signifying new powers as well as new constraints on women in the urban setting. The 'Kineticization' of the city is a case in point. By this I refer to the widespread use of the automatic gear Kinetic Honda scooter, which has become hugely popular among women since the late 1980s, providing them with a new and relatively easy-to-handle means of private transport. In turn, the woman rider was exposed to new and unprecedented forms of violence, often pushed by male motorcyclists from the back while riding, resulting in temporary loss of control and sometimes injury. The sexualization of the visual space, reservations in the political system, or feminist mobilization of women have not been unequivocally empowering, since a complex and multi-layered definition of private/public has still kept many zones of city life 'out of bounds'. The increased visibility has invited newer modes of control on women in the workplace, home, and on the streets. The city has also engendered new forms of political activism, ranging from insouciant graffiti, concerted campaigns, and sometimes violent protest. Women, in this sense, are also 'out of bounds', exceeding the confining boundaries of the space/times that they are allowed to inhabit, sometimes producing intractable problems for the administration, and at other times undermining the power of representational practices in the city. This has led to widespread questioning of the norming of the citizen as male and upper-class.

Local and national movements, state initiatives, and expanding markets in a time of globalization have all altered the practice of power in the city in significant ways. There are signs, however, that the *international* in the political imaginary, which has been thoroughly discredited in the recent past, has by no means exhausted its capacity for rallying people. Since 1992, Vimochana has organized a silent protest on Thursday evenings at various public locations in the city to draw attention to local, national, and international problems. 'Women in Black' is a loose network of women worldwide committed to peace and justice, and actively opposed to war and other forms of violence. It is not an organization, but a means of mobilization and a formula for action. The vigils were started in 1988 by women protesting against Israel's occupation of the West Bank and Gaza, and demanded peace between Israel and Palestine. It has since caught on as a mode of protest in many parts of the world.[124] It draws inspiration from the silent protests of women in Latin America, notably Chile, who mourned the 'disappearance' under various repressive political regimes of their sons, brothers, husbands, and fathers. Vimochana has radically

FIG. 61 *Addressing a commuting public: the Women in Black demonstration focuses attention on the war in Iraq from the steps of the Town Hall.*
(Vimochana, 2003)

redefined the protest while retaining its form.[125] Black is less a sign of mourning in the Indian context, but strikes a contrast to the colour historically associated with the political activism of women, namely white. The sight of these women in black, silently holding aloft posters and placards, and distributing leaflets on issues that range from the local to the international, is a disturbing performance, not least because of its choice of location and its timing. 'Women in Black' has met at the foot of the Victoria statue, at road junctions, edges of parks, and with perhaps most dramatic effect, on the steps of the Town Hall, sometimes late in the evening (Fig. 61). It stages the protest through the symbolic deployment of the female body in ways that depart from other material, social, and symbolic deployments of the female body in the city. It is disturbing for its very silence and stillness, while eloquently drawing attention to the possible practice of political power by women in the city.

CONCLUSION

Is 'Singapore' Bangalore's Destiny?

I say without the slightest remorse, that we wouldn't be here, we would not have made economic progress, if we had not intervened on very personal matters ... who your neighbour is, how you live, the noise you make, how you spit, or what language you use. We decide what is right. Never mind what the people think, that's another problem.'

Lee Kuan Yew in Tremewan, *The Political Economy of Social Control in Singapore.*

Now it is possible to meet metropolitan Indians whose only relation to this world is as landscape, as earth, not as world.

Sudipta Kaviraj, 'The Culture of Representative Democracy', 1998

Jawaharlal Nehru's famous description of Bangalore as the city of the future, unburdened by traces of the past has itself become something of a burden for the city to bear. Heroic dreams of turning the metropolis into a technopole, at least in strips or corridors, continue to dominate the technocratic and political imaginations. Most recently, this has taken the form of a 'glorious master plan' for a 25 km long IT corridor that will connect the Electronic City in the south east to the International Tech Park. In a draft structure plan submitted to the BDA, Jurong Consultants Pvt. Ltd proposed an IT corridor to cater to one million people by 2021, including business parks and a commercial centre, six townships, two universities, three hospitals, six polyclinics, and two golf courses, one at each end of the corridor, to cater to the 'recreation needs of foreign IT expatriates.'[1] The plan envisaged that about 40 per cent of those who flocked to the new town for work would also 'live, work, play and strike business deals' in the corridor bounded by 'two peripheral expressways'. The final plan would lay down what will come where: 'the idea is to prevent encroachments and haphazard development of the area'.

A slice of Santa Clara in India? Clearly, the uneven success of master planning in the metropolis has done little to caution administrators and planners against dreams on this heroic scale. The experience of the city from its public sector phase, beginning in the 1940s, to the latest IT-led industrial phase since the 1990s, has shown that such planning could succeed in enclaves, although its effects on the rest of the city and its economy are far more unpredictable.

Although the industries of the new economy have shown remarkable adaptability to an urban form that preceded the 'knowledge revolution', the need for greenfield sites and assured and uninterrupted public services is growing. In its eagerness to take advantage of the fresh promises held out by biotechnology, moreover, the S.M. Krishna government announced a series of policies in 2001 to attract biotech industries to the metropolitan region. Announcing 'heavy concessions and incentives in taxation, physical infrastructure, registration etc', the policy also included the relaxation of a series of existing regulations relating to locational restrictions, floor area ratio, and labour recruitment and deployment.[2]

In many ways, the Krishna government appears to continue a long Mysore tradition of 'state aid to industries', with one important difference. Such policies come not at a time when the market needs to be coaxed into playing a determining role in industrial and city development, but when it has already gained dominance. At no previous stage in the economic history of the city has industry aspired to redefine the image of the city, manage its services, and streamline its finances with as much confidence as the captains of the new economy, represented by the BATF and its subsidiary Janaagraha. These efforts constitute a sharp departure from at least two previous phases of the city in its post-Independence decades. The state led industrialization of the first phase also coincided with the moment when citizenship was seen as an achievable ideal, through the pedagogical practices of state and non-state institutions alike, such as the planning agencies, the industrial township, or the GIPA. The indifferent careers of such practices and institutions, we have seen, were a sign that these ideals were faltering. Raising questions about earlier ideals of citizenship were new democratic practices and institutions that were anchored in a different vision of the city's responsibility to the region and the many groups that were not-yet-citizens. The gradual abdication by the state of its developmentalist roles, and indeed its redistributive functions, and the ascendance of the market have given rise to a new parastatal managerial élite, embodied in such institutional innovations as the BATF and Janaagraha.

This may appear to suggest, to borrow the phrase made famous by D.D. Kosambi, that the bourgeoisie is finally 'coming of age' in the city.[3] Not quite, for the aspirations of the managerial and technocratic élite have done nothing to displace or even challenge the forces from below that make the city responsive to democratic demands. Nor has the managerial élite been able to translate the opportunities offered by the new technologies into a programme of economic development, one that will homogenize or at least subordinate the heterogeneous composition of power in the city to produce a new urban culture.

The BATF is a 15-member nominated body that consists of professionals from the IT and biotech industries, management and financial experts, and architects. It declared its intentions of making Bangalore properly reflect its status as a site of globalized production: 'The [BATF] mandate is basically to upgrade the infrastructure and systems of Bangalore through Private Public Partnership to enhance the quality of life in the city. The BATF in particular is to recommend specific measures to initiate IT, best practices, innovative management tools, as well as internationalization of norms and tools and to involve corporate bodies and empower citizens and provide for urban advancement.'[4]

The mandate of the BATF also reveals that the government did not stop at envisaging a body that would improve the quality of life in the city through a strengthening and deepening of the public–private partnership. It also entrusted the BATF with 'institutionalizing upgraded service delivery mechanisms by amending the legal framework'. In other words, the BATF was not merely a parastatal agency to which each of the stakeholders would report their progress, but one which would duplicate, or at least shape, the legislative functions of the government. Thus, the BATF claims that one of the lessons it learned was the importance of consensus on its initiatives: it is 'important to seek a balance between the Political system and the Executive. It is essential that the system effectively be in one voice for any legal amendments necessary.' Indeed, if the new and exceptional vigour with which the BDA under its commissioner Jayakar Jerome, has reclaimed disputed properties and distributed sites since 1999 is any indication, there are clear signs that the legal regime may be transformed in ways that bring greater clarity to transactions on land.[5] Moreover, BDA has resumed its role as a sites and services provider with renewed vigour,[6] while seeking international aid and assistance for its planning agenda.[7]

The renewal of the BDA as a service provider seems to conform to the BATF's suggestion that state agencies 'view [the] citizen as "customer".' The notion of the citizen as customer, as I have already shown, has echoed in the conceptual foundations of many civic initiatives. An important indication of this is the definition of city service agencies as 'stakeholders', a term that has been extended to the citizen herself. Implicit in such a vision of urban citizenship is the question of ownership of rights to the city. Janaagraha founder member Ramesh Ramanathan thus invited citizens to participate in governance through ownership: 'We the people will take ownership and get to participate in governance.' The overwhelming emphasis during the last decade, and of the BATF itself, is the city as a space of flows, of uninterrupted traffic and information channels, of continuous power and water supply, and of an untroubled market in commercial and residential properties (Fig. 62). A great deal of attention, as we have seen, has been on the city's infrastructure, and on the tedium of dealing with state agencies. Singapore, as an ideal of city development, has thus inspired dreams of large scale infrastructural projects, rather than the more innovative public housing schemes that mobilized public (provident) funds for construction on a heroic scale.[8] There are no signs yet that a radical reorientation of the city's housing schemes, which have historically favoured independent sites, is being envisaged. If anything, the provision of low rise, low density, and privately owned housing by public agencies such as the BDA has been ramped up in the new millennium.

The BATF's inaugural sampling of the five problems that required immediate attention in the next few years were starkly revealing. The poll found that the five most important public concerns were, in order: the condition of the roads, garbage, mosquitoes, pollution, and public toilets. Roads, rather than public transport; garbage and pollution, rather than public housing; mosquitoes and public toilets rather than public health. The second tier of problems included blocked sewage, poor traffic management, alcohol in residential areas, public safety, and finally bringing up the rear, public transport.

Questionable sampling methods apart, the strongly middle-class profile of the city itself could have accounted for this order of priorities. Other studies that have been undertaken of how different sections of the city prioritize their municipal problems reveal altogether different concerns: they include, importantly, concerns about the availability of water, the existence of job opportunities in poor neighbourhoods, and an overwhelming anxiety to claim citizenship and voting rights by getting on to the voters' lists.[9] The last was

FIG. 62 *Uninterrupted traffic bypasses the city and its architectural heritage: the Sirsi Circle Flyover eclipses the Jamma Masjid at the KR Market.*
(Clare Arni, 2000)

seen in many cases as critical to the survival of poorer groups in the city, as politics is often the only resource in a system which may deny the benefits of policy decisions or legal remedies to the poor.

The state government has suggested that private–public partnerships were imperative in infrastructure building and maintenance.[10] Only token gestures towards the city's maintenance have thus far been made towards the publicized 'public–private' partnership. At the high profile BATF seminar in January 2000, several corporate groups made pledges to do the following: Volvo agreed to upgrade 2.5 km of road near Old Madras Road, Biocon and Coca Cola pledged Rs 1 crore each for parks, BPL agreed to beautify Church Street, ABB and the Prestige Group agreed to improve small sections of Tumkur Road and Infantry Road respectively, the Brigade Group and Aditi Technologies pledged to improve 2.2 and 0.5 km of road, the Infosys Foundation agreed to establish 100 sanitation systems and a private individual, B.V. Jagadeesh, donated $1 million for improving corporation schools.[11] In its sober end-of-the-year review (February 2001), the report card did not include a stocktaking of these promises.[12]

No summit of the BATF has been held since September 2001, at least on the scale on which it began. In its review of the three-year period that it had been in existence, the BATF makes only general and no specific claims, particularly on the publicized commitment of private funds to the city's infrastructure development:

> These funds were indicative and no detailing of project plans was done at that time. The complexities of operationalizing and converting some of these final commitments into projects and hence translate the monies into actuals was not possible due to a variety of reasons. Since the first summit a number of corporates have continued to come forward either through the BATF or directly with the ULB as the faith quotient has increased and the pilots deliver results.[13]

However, the BATF continued its quest for a consensus on its agenda of reform by conducting a citizen's poll on the initiatives of the three-year period. The response, which was largely positive, was taken as a vote on the success of the BATF's initiatives. The three year review, however suggested a reorientation of priorities:

> This is evident from the fact that there is a shift in priorities for the citizen—where cleanliness and roads were a major issue three years ago, the citizen now wants the government to tackle issues like mosquitoes, stray dogs as well as more esoteric issues such as corruption and ease of transacting with the government.

In several of his public pronouncements, the leading icon of Bangalore's Infosys Technologies, Narayana Murthy, has declared that there are two Indias, one rural the other urban, which have recognizably different needs. Only in rural India, where the poor and the underprivileged reside, he claimed, can the state play its redistributive role.[14] Without a timely recognition of this difference, Bangalore's current advantages as an IT capital could evaporate. The suggestion that the state reduce its presence as a regulatory authority within urban areas was a simultaneous plea to encourage private investment in all aspects of the urban economy, from English medium schools and five star hotels to housing and fibre optic cable installation. Freed at last from the sentimentality that pays ritual obeisance to India as the land of villages, which I have discussed at the outset, Murthy seeks a redefined role for the state in urban India. In the process, he homogenizes the space of the city to one that is free of the preoccupations and problems of the Indian village.

The refusal to recognize the city as a deeply divided space, and as a far more disturbed zone than is normally acknowledged, is no indication of wilful ignorance. Rather, it is confident expectation that, given time, the market will manage this space far more efficiently than the state and its political machinery might have previously done. In that sense, the city is envisaged as a space that is free of politics and free of responsibilities to the region. In seeking to circumvent politics itself, new institutional arrangements attempt to develop

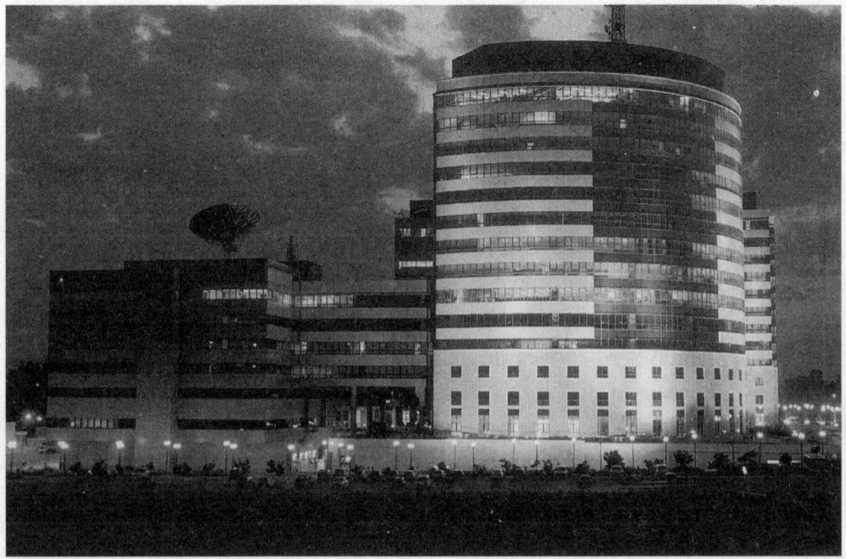

FIG. 63 *From garden city to technopark: globalized architecture of the International Tech Park, Whitefield.*
(Clare Arni, 2004)

a private–public partnership which will fashion city space as neutral and recognizably global (Fig. 63). In this, the corporate groups have been amply aided by the English language press, which routinely derides the politician while applauding the gestures of those who stake a new claim to local civic life.

It was striking that Krishna's announcement of the new biotech policy in 2001 coincided with the sobering review meeting of the BATF, which dressed up the paltry gains of the previous year as significant achievements.[15] Among the most important municipal successes of the first year of the Krishna government and the BATF was the introduction of the self-assessment scheme which allowed home owners to calculate their own property tax dues. Among the most important admissions of failure was the inability of the state to define the protocols within which the companies who were awarded the contracts for Optical Fibre Cables would operate: BATF chairman Nandan Nilekani admitted that 'OFC is the only area lacking inter-stakeholder co-operation'. Perhaps nothing emphasizes the triumph of unbridled market forces as clearly as the impunity with which telephone and cable companies have scarred Bangalore's road surfaces.[16] Perhaps nothing illustrates the limits to the new economy's 'will to power' in the city as the fact that the BATF's news website was not updated for a while after 2001.

Nevertheless, BATF's efforts, however limited and piecemeal, are symptoms of the distinctive aspirations of the new economy. Never before in the city's recent history, and indeed modern Indian history, has the capitalist class achieved such hegemony in the shaping of the urban form. The leaders of industry today attempt to control and manage systems that embrace the entire city, and in technocratic ways that bypass political systems already in place. Certainly, neither the public sector at its height in the 1970s nor the more conventional private sector industries have shared the totalizing ambitions of the knowledge economy. In part, the desire to exercise control over the city must be seen as compulsions produced by the industry itself. In none of the previous phases of economic development has a single industry aspired to recast the image of the city as a whole and redefine it as a 'space of flows'. The emerging hegemony is achieved precisely at a conjuncture where the leading icons of the new infotech industries have gained high visibility in a range of fields, that extend well beyond the boundaries of the purely economic to build up a persuasive ideology of success. Consensus building through interventions in education (as the WIPRO foundation has done), in public health services (as in the setting up of pay-and-use public toilets), budget framing and analyses (as in the Janaagraha initiative), as well as participation in the wider cultural and academic worlds appears to succeed in promoting an ideology of success, and of a movement towards a more efficient urban order.

Bangalore's transition to metropolitan status has clearly paralleled a shift in the character of the state. The developmentalist phase of the state was evident in the preponderance of the public sector, controls on consumption, and the redistributive mechanisms that it instituted. Institutional arrangements in these enclaves as well as in civil society, I have shown, reflected optimism about fashioning a public that could function as a responsible citizenry. The interim period has been characterized not only by the growing preponderance of the market, and a decline in the largely pedagogic role of civil social institutions, but has equally seen the rise of social movements which imagine democracy quite differently.

A few months after the announcement of the biotech policy, the government of Karnataka's attempt to reallocate 100 acres of land belonging to the University of Agricultural Sciences on the GKVK campus to a Biotech Park ran aground amidst protests from the Board of Regents of the University, and student and faculty bodies. Although the negative decision of the Board of Regents was conveyed to the IT department on 14 September 2001, Venkatramanan and Associates, a private architectural firm (whose chief architect Naresh Venkatraman is a member of the BATF), was given the task of marking the layout for a foundation stone laying ceremony on 20 September 2001.[17]

Several eucalyptus trees were felled and attempts made to fence off the land with the aid of the police.[18] Violence broke out on the campus when students and faculty alike prevented the Karnataka Land Army from clearing the proposed site by hugging the trees.[19] The 'police action' drew angry responses from civil rights groups in the city and political parties alike, eventually forcing the government to abandon its plans to occupy that site.[20] The Biotech Park will now be a part of the proposed IT corridor.

The proposed park was envisaged as part of the newly identified Biotech Corridor that stretched between the Indian Institute of Science and the GKVK campus of the UAS to simulate conditions in 'Stanford University and University of California': a close relationship between biology laboratories and production facilities was seen as a boon to the students of agricultural sciences themselves.[21] Student opposition to the initiative was thus seen as squandering the prospect of benefiting from the jobs and opportunities generated by the park. People within the industry are more sceptical of the advantages of this promiscuous mingling of lab and industry: Ramesh Hariharan of Strand Genomics, for instance, has said that although the (scientific) academic community in Bangalore is much larger than elsewhere, it had not yet become a critical mass, and by itself was unlikely in the short run to replicate the conditions that had fostered innovation in other institutional locations worldwide.[22] As the work of Balaji Parthasarathy has shown more generally in the case of the software industry, although Bangalore is the 'one region in India that could have encouraged the development and production of specialized software', the overwhelming dependence of the industry on the global, rather than the domestic market and the fundamental 'lack of domain specific knowledge' set limits to the visions of Bangalore as a 'silicon valley'.[23] It is not likely that in the short run, conditions in the biotech industry will be vastly different from those identified for the software industry as a whole.

Predictably, the media has speculated on the many political reasons for the sudden eruption of resistance to the state government's plans, staging the confrontation as a contest between two sets of private interests. It may well have been that the students and faculty of the UAS reacted to the proposed park for reasons that were not strictly environmental: still, the violent opposition to the biotech park points to the prevailing structure of the field of politics that cannot be wished away in any plans for Bangalore metropolis. Every manifestation of the political in the metropolis in the recent past, ranging from *bandh*s and strikes to riots and demonstrations, has drawn the swift condemnation of the economic press. Such disruptions, by their very frequency and growing appeal among large sections of urban society, no doubt produce

MAP 11 *Location of IT industries in Bangalore*

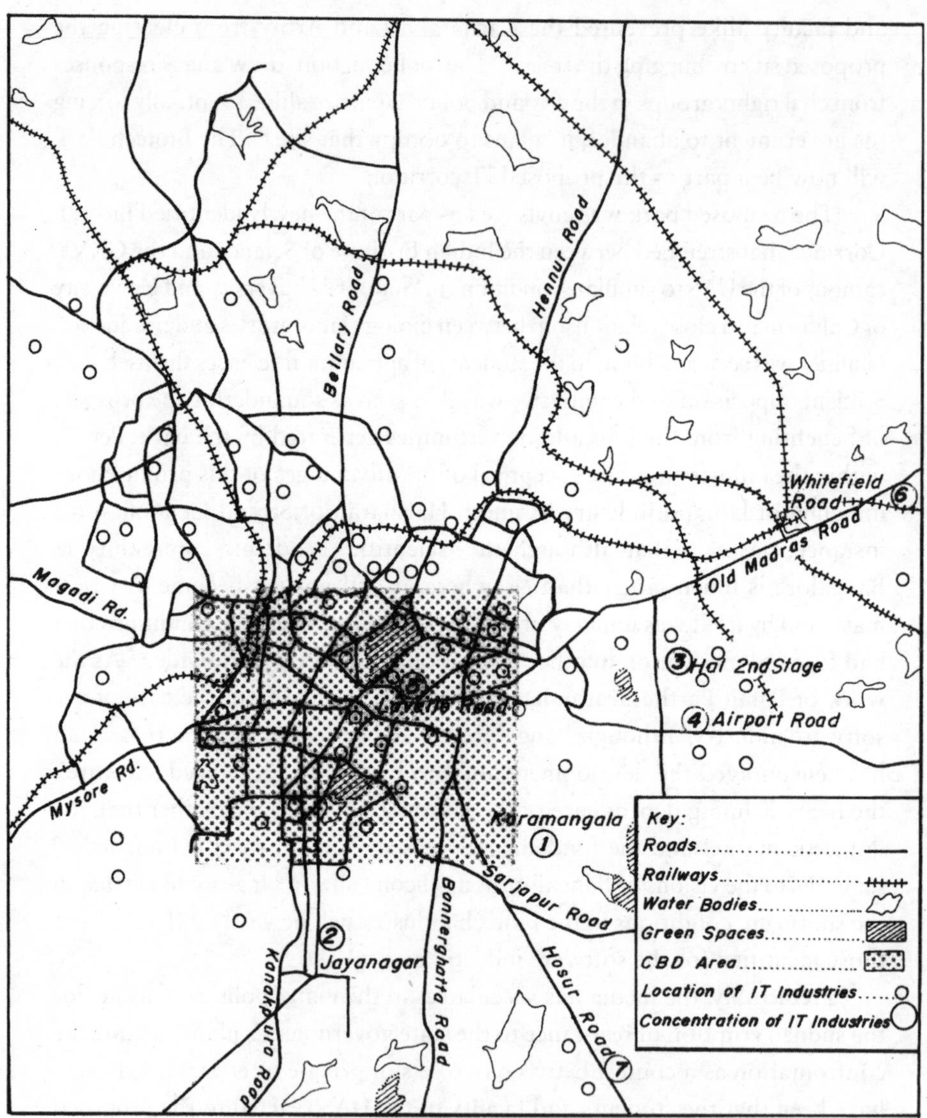

Source: Based on *IT Corridor Bangalore: Structure Plan Final Report*, 2003.

1. Koramangala, 77 units
2. Jayanagar, 45 units
3. HAL 2nd Stage, 20 units
4. Airport Road, 21 units
5. Lavelle Road, 25 units
6. Whitefield Road, 39 units
7. Hosur Road, 36 units

MAP 12 *Proposed IT Corridor*

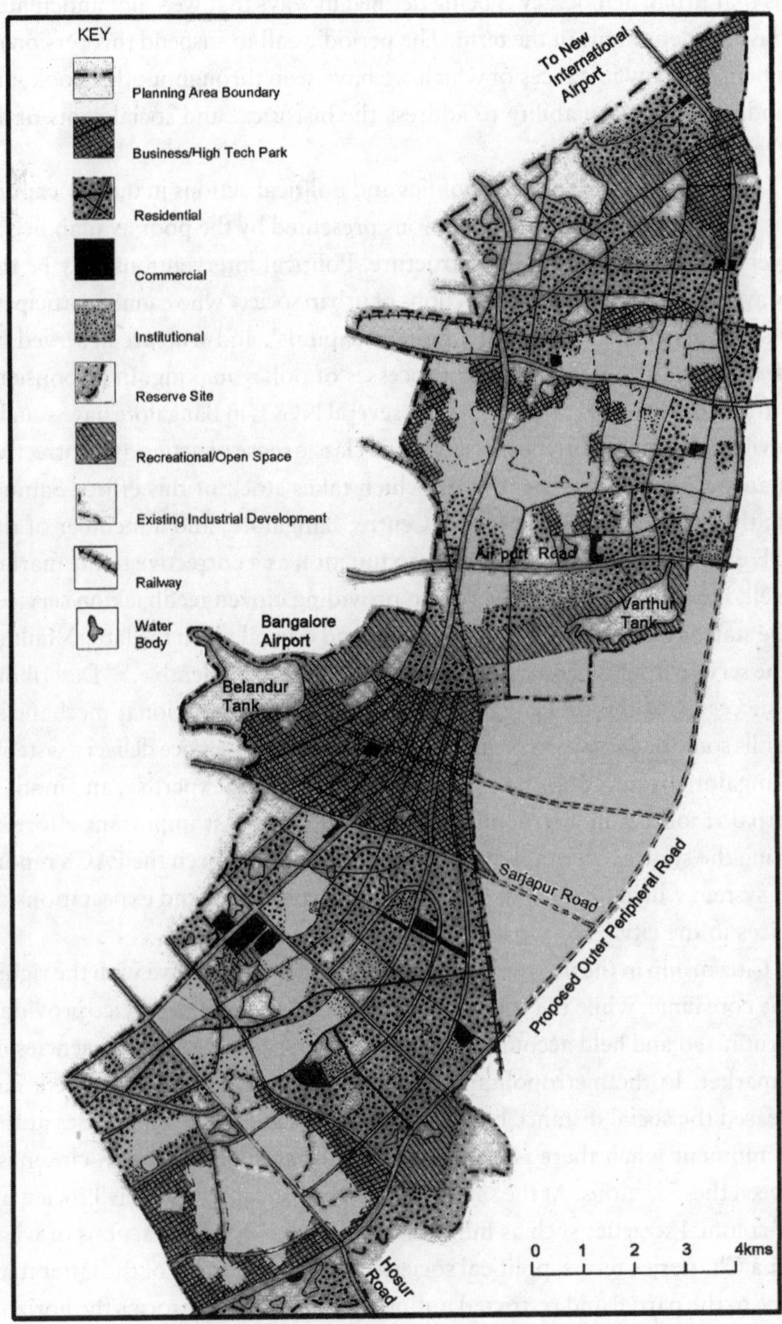

Source: Based on *IT Corridor Bangalore: Structure Plan Final Report*, 2003.

strains on city life, and not just for the captains of industry. Yet they are important signs that urban democracy is being defined in ways that were not anticipated in classical definitions of the term. The periodic call to suspend this version of democracy, many instances of which we have seen throughout this book, are an indication of an inability to address the historical and social roots of an uneven modernity.

The disruptions caused by politics and political actions in the city cannot be as easily overcome as the disruptions presented by the poor availability of power or water, or a poor infrastructure. Political interventions may be the only available recourse for large sections of urban society who cannot participate in visions of 'silicon valleys' and 'biotech capitals', and who are ill served by both the legal machinery and the processes of policy making. In response to the strains of contemporary democracy, several NGOs in Bangalore have sought to revive the meaning of 'civil society' in its classic sense of acting as a corrective to state actions. In his recent book which takes stock of this effort, Samuel Paul, the founder of Public Affairs Centre, Bangalore, and a member of the BATF, extends the use of civil society to function as a corrective to the market as well. He says 'Civil society's role in providing citizen feedback on services to the state is likely to become more active and critical when the latter's failure on the service front is perceived to be inexcusable and intolerable.'[24] Describing the successes of the BATF, Paul says, 'BATF is an institutional mechanism that fills some of the gaps in the urban management and service delivery systems in Bangalore by injecting civil society inputs, technical expertise, and modest external resources in a structured manner'.[25] The most important effort at making the state accountable as a service provider has been the PAC's report card system which documents city dwellers' experiences and expectations of services in the city.

Citizenship in the urban context is thus made co-extensive with the rights of the consumer, while the state itself, reduced to the role of service provider, is scrutinized and held accountable from the perspective of the efficiencies of the market. In the metropolitan context, this market force alternative has increased the social distance between the urban élite and lower classes at the very moment when there is an unavoidable spatial and material closeness between these sections. At the same time, the historical limits of civil society in post-colonial societies such as India have been exposed in the actions of what Partha Chatterjee terms 'political society.' The commitment of the latter may not be to the partial and restricted notion of modernity that forms the horizon of civil society, but to democratization itself.[26] In this process, democracy may not adopt the styles and forms that are familiar to liberal advocates of social change.

As this book has tried to show, the city of Bangalore has, over the past forty years, been swiftly remapped as a territory for accumulation of economic power on an unprecedented scale. It has also served as a site for newly defined notions of citizenship. Only in some instances do these notions of citizenship conform to the liberal desire for peaceful and orderly development. Cities are increasingly the site for the assertion of new and empowering identities, which, in striking contrast to the forms of collective action in the past, re-territorialize urban space in ways that challenge the functional logic of the market or the economic uses of time. These are claims, moreover, on a different kind of city space and express a different kind of attachment to the city. As such, they are not readily neutralized by planning apparatuses nor domesticated by economic interests that are not their own.

For many such groups, the city becomes the theatre on which to stage the claim to a redefined citizenship. For many such groups, moreover, the *local* assumes greater importance than the production of global space in the city. The local, thus, acquires many meanings, as we have seen: the neighbourhood or locality, in the case of women, ethnic and caste minorities, is a space which is staked out and traversed in a variety of daily and occasional transactions, a geography marked and given meaning by older histories as much as by newer uses. This version of the local is now increasingly contested by the more muscular middle-class resident's associations which have arisen in the 1990s. These organizations elevate the rituals and comforts of a middle-class domesticity to city-wide priority, particularly as consumers of goods and services (Figs 64 and 65). The 'local' here takes on administrative meanings, building new responsibilities towards the management of the ward. The efforts of Janaagraha and the PAC to encourage the participation of the middle-classes in the planning of ward finances and to empower residents' associations in many middle-class neighbourhoods may be seen as an important step in this direction.

However, the heterogeneous composition of the metropolitan economy and the equally heterogeneous composition of power, as we have seen, give neither the state nor the market the kind of primacy that is desired. Planning itself generates unplanned neighbourhoods, just as much as the plethora of legal routes to the production of city space engenders new illegalities in its interstices. The organized sector begets and sustains the unorganized sector. The benefits of the new economies have not flowed to all the inhabitants of the

FIG. 64 *A whole new lifestyle defined: coffee and the net at a cyber café in central Bangalore.* (Clare Arni, 2000)

city, and may even have detrimentally affected the lives of large populations. Time in the city, to recall Lefebvre again, has more than one writing system. The metropolis, thus, enjoys only a partial existence, and remains a promise, refracted through many remembered cities and villages, and real and imagined political identities (Fig. 65).

Thus the village of Singapura (population 7149, of which nearly 3000 are SC/ST), to the north-west of Bangalore, has since the 1991 census been classified as an urban outgrowth of the metropolis. Its agriculture has been disrupted by the demand for real estate, its citizens displaced from their conventional occupations. Whether these rural inhabitants are holders of 'parcels of hope' or 'parcels of despair' will depend not only on the success with which they enter into, or resist, the processes of acquisition and conversion of agricultural

FIG. 65 *Invitation and denial: plate glass windows for shops and restaurants.* (Clare Arni, 2004)

space to the city. There are more than ample signs, given the fierce legal and extra-legal battles against acquisition that occur with great frequency, that villages like Singapura will be transformed by their absorption into the metropolis, and not always in ways that impoverish the rural inhabitant. However, Singapura's future will also depend on the hopes that the city will offer its non-landowning inhabitants, and their claims on the city. Whether this transformation will resemble the conceived space of Bangalore-as-Singapore or whether Singapura will fashion its own mode of existence within Bangalore may well depend on the success with which the metropolis embraces and makes 'political society' a part of its fabric.

In its new metropolitan phase, therefore, the city has become the ground on which broadly two contending forces stake their claim: on the one hand are the newly renovated citizens, who are amply aided by a technocratic vision of change offered by the leaders of the new economy. On the other hand are those, including citizens-in-the-making such as women, for whom democracy has come to have a different meaning in the urban setting. There may perhaps be no decisive victory for either of these forces in the short run given the heterogeneous composition of power in the city, although the well planned, legally unambiguous and increasingly legible city will gain visibility in the decades to come.

Notes

Introduction: Where Does the City Begin?

1. Ashis Nandy, *An Ambiguous Journey to the City: The Village and Other Odd Ruins of the Self in the Indian Imagination* (Delhi: Oxford University Press, 2001), p. viii.

2. Ibid., p. ix.

3. Bargur Ramachandrappa, 'Bengaluru nagara enba ondu halli', in B. Srinivasaraju (ed.), *Prabandhagalu* (Bangalore: Kannada Sahitya Akademi, 1992), pp. 65–72 (emphasis added).

4. *Madi panche* refers to the wet dhoti or loincloth that is ritually pure.

5. See for instance Smriti Srinivas's detailed discussion of the Karaga as it has evolved in the recent past to serve as a recollection of older city forms that are encrypted, if only symbolically, in a vastly transformed cityscape. In this account, the city is mapped as an urban performative complex enacting both memories and aspirations of communities of market gardeners (Tigalas) who may have been ruined by the growth of the metropolis. See *Landscapes of Urban Memory: The Sacred and the Civic in India's High Tech City* (Minnesota and London: University of Minnesota Press, 2001).

6. See for instance Erappa M. Kambali, 'Majestic Sutha ...' *Heddarigunta* (Bangalore: 1999), pp. 1–8 which humorously depicts the city as a place of cheats and swindlers. Also, S.G. Sangundayya, 'Bengaluru' (written in 1976) in *Ekantha maththu ithara prabandhagalu* (Bangalore: Kamadhenu Prakashana, 1993), pp. 74–80. See also, A.N. Murthy Rao, 'Bengaluru', *Samagra lalitha prabandhagalu* (Bangalore: Ankita Pustaka, 1999), pp. 217–26.

7. See for instance, S.K.Ramachandra Rao, 'Bengalurina samajika nele', in *Bengaluru nagara corporation bellihabbada sanchike* (Bangalore, 1974), pp. 39–46.

8. As cited in Surinder S. Jodhka, 'Nation and Village: Images of Rural India in Gandhi, Nehru and Ambedkar', *Economic and Political Weekly*, 37:32, (2002), 3343–52.

9. Ibid., p. 3345. See also, Nandy, *An Ambiguous Journey to the City*, p. 16.

10. Several of the contributions to Roy Turner (ed.), *India's Urban Future* (Bombay: Oxford University Press, 1962) predicted a surge in rural–urban migration based on 1941–51 data and foresaw grave strains on the government as a direct consequence.

11. The 'distrust of exploitative urban life', according to Sachin Chaudhuri, also underlay the early emphasis on the rural economy in the five year plans. Chaudhuri, 'Centralization and the Alternative Forms of Decentralization: A Key Issue', in Roy Turner (ed.), *India's Urban Future*, pp. 213–39. Chaudhuri cites Nehru as saying in 1950 that 'When bright people migrated from villages to the city, they did no good to the city but they did a lot of bad to the village by coming away from it. It must be stopped' p. 218.

12. M.S.A. Rao (ed.), *Urban Sociology in India: Reader and Source Book* (Hyderabad: Orient Longman, 1974), p. 1.

13. Surinder Jodhka, 'From "Book View" to "Field View": Social Anthropological Constructions of the Indian Village', *Oxford Development Studies*, 26:3 (1998), 311–31, esp. 314.

14. See M.N. Srinivas (ed.), *India's Villages* (Bombay: Asia Publishing House, 1963).

15. M.N. Srinivas 'Village Studies and their Significance', in D.N. Majumdar (ed.), *Rural Profiles (1)* (Lucknow: Ethnographic and Folk Culture Society, 1955).

16. Jodhka, 'From "Book View" to "Field View"', p. 329.

17. See for instance M.N. Srinivas, 'The Industrialisation and Urbanisation of Rural Areas', in Rao (ed.), *Urban Sociology in India,* pp. 488–99.

18. See, for instance, D.F. Pocock, 'Sociologies: Urban and Rural', in Rao (ed.), *Urban Sociology in India,* pp. 18–39.

19. See, for instance, O.M. Lynch, 'Rural Cities in India: Continuities and Discontinuities', in Rao (ed.), *Urban Sociology in India*, pp. 251–71. Also Richard D. Lambert, 'The Impact of Urban Society upon Village Life', in Turner (ed.), *India's Urban Future,* pp. 117–40.

20. See, for instance, Alan Beals, 'Change in the Leadership of a Mysore Village', in Srinivas (ed.), *India's Villages*, pp. 147–60.

21. Mark Holmstrom, 'Action Sets and Ideology: A Municipal Election in South India', *Contributions to Indian Sociology*, (n.s.), no. II (Dec. 1969), 76–93.

22. Gertrude Woodruffe, 'An Adi-Dravida Settlement in Bangalore: A Case Study in Urbanisation', Ph.D. Thesis, Radcliffe College, Cambridge Mass., 1959.

23. On the city in Indian history, see Dilip Chakrabarti, *The Archaeology of Ancient Indian Cities* (Delhi: Oxford University Press, 1998); R. Champakalakshmi, *Trade*

Ideology and Urbanisation: South India 300 BC to AD 1300, (Delhi: Oxford University Press, 1999); James Heitzman, 'Temple Urbanism', in *Gifts of Power: Lordship in an Early Indian State* (Delhi: Oxford University Press, 2001), pp. 82–120; B.D. Chattopadhyay, 'Urban Centres in Early Medieval India: An Overview', in S. Bhattacharya and R. Thapar (eds), *Situating Indian History* (Delhi: Oxford University Press, 1988), pp. 8–33.

24. Satish Saberwal, 'Indian Urbanism: A Socio-historical Perspective', *Contributions to Indian Sociology* (n.s.) 11:1 (1977).

25. Bert F. Hoselitz, 'A Survey of the Literature on Urbanisation in India,' in Porter (ed.), *India's Urban Future*, pp. 425–43.

26. R. Ramachandran, *Urbanisation and Urban Systems in India* (Delhi: Oxford University Press, 1989), p. 11.

27. R.L. Singh, *Banaras: A Study in Urban Geography* (Banaras: Nand Kishore & Brothers, 1955); also *Bangalore: An Urban Survey* (Varanasi: Tara Publications, 1964).

28. For instance, the two studies that originated as theses submitted to the University of Bombay: K.N.Venkatrayappa, *Bangalore: A Socio–Ecological Study* (Bombay: University of Bombay Press, 1957); A. Bopegamage, *Delhi: A Study in Urban Sociology* (Bombay: University of Bombay Press, 1957).

29. Nirmal Kumar Bose, *Calcutta 1964: A Social Survey* (Bombay: Lalwani Publishing House, 1968), p. 85. Elsewhere, he described the city as a 'premature metropolis': see Nirmal Kumar Bose, 'Calcutta: A Premature Metropolis', *Scientific American* 213:3 (1965), 90–103.

30. Surajit Sinha (ed.), *Cultural Profile of Calcutta* (Calcutta: Indian Anthropological Society, 1972).

31. Pradip Sinha (ed.), *The Urban Experience: Calcutta, Essays in Honour of Prof. Nisith R. Ray* (Calcutta: Riddhi–India, 1987).

32. See for instance Jean Racine et al. (eds), *Calcutta 1981: The City, its Crisis and the Debate on Urban Planning Development* (Delhi: Concept Publishing House, 1990).

33. Sukanta Chaudhuri (ed.), *Calcutta: The Living City Volume I: The Past; Volume II: The Present and Future* (Calcutta: Oxford University Press, 1995).

34. Sujata Patel and Alice Thorner (eds), *Bombay: Metaphor for Modern India; Bombay: Mosaic of Modern Culture* (Delhi: Oxford University Press, 1995).

35. On the city as the space for redefinition of caste/class identity in the early nationalist period see Jim Masselos, *Towards Nationalism: Group Associations and the Politics of Public Associations in Nineteenth Century Western India* (Bombay: Popular Prakashan, 1974).

36. Thomas Blom Hansen, *Urban Violence in India: Identity Politics, 'Mumbai' and the Postcolonial City* (Delhi: Permanent Black, 2001).

37. Ibid., p. 9.

38. Ratna Naidu, *Old Cities, New Predicaments: A Study of Hyderabad* (Delhi: Sage, 1990). The original report is *Inner City of Hyderabad: A Study Sponsored by*

Planning Commission, Government of India Prepared by Ratna Naidu and others (1986).

39. Naidu, *Old Cities, New Predicaments*, p. 87.

40. Ibid., pp. 168–75.

41. Ibid., pp. 188–217. Even Ashutosh Varshney's recent comparative study of six Indian cities, which attempts to provide a taxonomy of urban communal violence by using indices of civil social institutions, only marginally takes the physical–material dimensions of city life into consideration. Varshney, *Ethnic Conflict and Civic Life: Hindus and Muslims in India* (Delhi: Oxford University Press, 2002).

42. As cited in Madhu Sarin, *Urban Planning in the Third World: The Chandigarh Experience* (London: Mansell Publishing Ltd, 1982), p. 26. For an interesting account of the processes by which the early planning decisions about Chandigarh were made, see Kalia, *Chandigarh: The Making of an Indian City* (Delhi: Oxford University Press, 1988).

43. Sarin, *Urban Planning in the Third World*, p. 26.

44. A strikingly similar, though theoretically more rigorous account of the fascination with and failures of modernist town planning is in James Holston's monograph on Brasilia. *The Modernist City: An Anthropological Critique of Brasilia* (University of California Press, 1989).

45. Narayani Gupta, *Delhi Between Two Empires: 1803–1931: Society, Government and Urban Growth* (Delhi: Oxford University Press, 1998). See, also, R.E. Frykenberg (ed.), *Delhi Through the Ages: Essays in Urban History, Culture and Society* (Delhi: Oxford University Press, 1986). See, also, on the building of New Delhi, R.G. Irving, *Indian Summer: Lutyens, Baker and Imperial Delhi* (New Haven: Yale University Press, 1981).

46. Veena Talwar Oldenburg *The Making of Colonial Lucknow: 1856–1877* (Princeton: Princeton University Press, 1984). Col. Robert Napier was the engineer entrusted with the task of demolition and rebuilding, the colonial equivalent of Baron Hausmann of 1870s Paris. See, esp., pp. 29–42. See also Violette Graf (ed.), *Lucknow: Memories of a City* (Delhi: Oxford University Press, 1997).

47. For Singapore, see Brenda S.A. Yeoh, 'Municipal Sanitary Ideology and the Control of the Environment in Colonial Singapore', in Alan H. Baker and Gideon Biger (eds), *Ideology and Landscape in Historical Perspective: Essays in the Meanings of Some Places in the Past*, pp. 148–72.

48. Mariam Dossal, *Imperial Designs and Indian Realities: The Planning of Bombay City, 1845–1875* (Delhi: Oxford University Press, 1996).

49. Gupta, *Delhi Between Two Empires*, pp. 72–6.

50. Monographs on the Bombay working class in the colonial period, in particular, have variously discussed the spatiality of caste, the role of the neighbourhood in building and sustaining worker solidarity, the gendered relationship of work and domesticity, the problems and possibilities of collective action, and the active links between formal and informal labour markets in neighbourhoods. See, for instance,

Morris D. Morris, *The Emergence of an Industrial Labour Force in India: A Study of the Bombay Cotton Mills, 1854–1947* (Bombay: Vikas Publishing House, 1965); Radha Kumar 'City Lives: Workers' Housing and Rent in Bombay, 1911–1947', *Indian Economic and Social History Review* 22 (1987), 47–56; Shashi Bhushan Upadhyaya, 'Cotton Mill Workers in Bombay, 1875–1918: Conditions of Work and Life', *Economic and Political Weekly* 25.30 (28 July 1990), PE 87–99. Rajnarayan Chandavarkar maps the worlds of middlemen and *badli* workers, trade unionists, and blacklegs, and their negotiations of industrial life and urban leisure providing the basis for constructing a history of the city from below. Chandavarkar, *The Origins of Industrial Capitalism in India: Business Strategies and the Working Classes in Bombay 1900–1940* (Cambridge: Cambridge University Press, 1994). More recent studies of the textile strike of 1980–1, reveal not only how the city provided resources for economic and social redefinition, but also drew on the workers' village link as a means of coping with economic distress. See Hubert Van Wersch, *The Bombay Textile Strike: 1982–3* (Bombay: Oxford University Press, 1992).

51. Darryl D'Monte, *Ripping the Fabric: The Decline of Mumbai and its Mills* (Delhi: Oxford University Press, 2002). The gradual transition of a city long considered a lively working class one to one in which workers have a marginal or a largely informal and somewhat disempowered existence is discussed in Chitra Joshi's work on Kanpur. Joshi, *Lost Worlds: Indian Labour and Its Forgotton Histories* (Delhi: Permanent Black, 2003).

52. Nita Kumar, *Artisans of Benares: Popular Culture and Identity 1880–1986* (Calcutta: Orient Longman, 1988). A more ambitious study attempts to provide insights on strategies for survival, modes of politics, and neighbourhoods as a space where solidarities and cleavages were forged on class, caste, or ethnic lines. Nandini Gooptu, *The Politics of the Labouring Poor in Early 20*th *Century India* (Cambridge: Cambridge University Press, 2001).

53. Rao (ed.), *Urban Sociology in India*, p. 1.

54. See Gyan Prakash, 'The Urban Turn', in *Sarai Reader 02: The Cities of Everyday Life* (Delhi: CSDS, 2002), pp. 2–7.

55. The three recent Sarai readers are a case in point. *Sarai Reader 01: The Public Domain* (Delhi: CSDS, 2001); *Sarai Reader 02: Cities of Everyday Life*; *Sarai Reader 03: Shaping Technologies* (Delhi: CSDS, 2003)

56. Michael Johns, *The City of Mexico in the Age of Diaz* (Austin: University of Texas, 1997).

57. Carl Schorske, *Fin de Siecle Vienna: Politics and Culture* (New York: Vintage Books, 1981).

58. See, for instance, Chua Beng Huat, *Political Legitimacy and Housing: Stakeholding in Singapore* (London and New York: Routledge, 1997); also 'Singapore: Management of a City State in South East Asia', in Jurgen Ruland (ed.), *The Dynamics of Metropolitan Management in South East Asia* (ISEAS, 1997), pp. 207–24.

59. Beng Huat, *Political Legitimacy and Housing: Stakeholding in Singapore*, p.

115 ff. Also, Robbie Goh, 'Things to A Void: Utopian Discourse, Communality, and Constructed Interstices in Singapore Public Housing', Paper presented at 'City as Text: Urban Topographies and Critical Interventions', Singapore, Sept. 1999.

60. Holston, *The Modernist City*, p. 101.

61. Lewis Mumford, *The City in History: Its Origins, Its Transformations and Its Prospects* (New York: MJF Books, 1989).

62. Jane Jacobs, *The Death and Life of Great American Cities* (New York: Vintage Books, 1992).

63. For a succinct summary of the interventions of the Chicago school, see Peter Hall, *Cities of Tomorrow: An Intellectual History of Urban Planning and Design in the Twentieth Century* (Oxford and Cambridge Mass: Blackwell Publishers, 1995), esp. pp. 360–86.

64. Mike Davis, *City of Quartz: Excavating the Future in Los Angeles* (New York: Vintage Books, 1992). See also *Ecology of Fear: Los Angeles and the Imagination of Disaster* (New York: Vintage Books, 1999).

65. Notably, Manual Castells' *The Urban Question: A Marxist Approach*, trans. Alan Sheridan (Edward Arnold, 1977); Henri Lefebvre, *The Production of Space*, trans. Donald Nicholson Smith (Oxford: Blackwell Publishers, 1991); David Harvey, *Social Justice and the City* (Baltimore: Johns Hopkins University Press, 1973); Doreen Massey, *Space, Place and Gender* (Cambridge: Polity Press, 1994).

66. Manuel Castells, *The Information Age: Economy, Society and Culture: The Rise of Network Society*, vol. I (2001); *The Power of Identity*, vol. II (2000); *End of Millenium* vol. III (2000) (London: Blackwell Publishers).

67. Castells, *The Rise of Network Society*, pp. 408–9.

68. See, for instance, an evaluation of the twenty-first century industrial complexes, from the better known Silicon Valley and Route 128 in the US to the Siberian, Korean, and Japanese efforts to incubate an information technology powered revolution through the construction of techno cities. Manuel Castells and Peter Hall, *Technopoles of the World: The Making of 21st Century Industrial Complexes* (London and New York: Routledge, 1994).

69. Saskia Sassen, *The Global City: New York, London, Tokyo* (Princeton: Princeton University Press, 1991), pp. 3–4. In particular, financial market control and the enormous growth of 'producer services' accounts for the scale of accumulation that is possible in these metropolitan centres. Producer services refer to an intermediary economy that 'cover[s] financial, legal and general management matters, innovation, development, design, administration, personnel, production, technology, maintenance, transport, communications wholesale distribution, advertising, cleaning services, for firms security and storage.' P. 90. Sassen is careful to insist on the continuance of a largely informal labour market and economy within these globalized spaces.

An interesting consideration of New York's emerging culture industries is in Sharon Zukin's *The Cultures of Cities* (London: Blackwell Publishers, 1996).

70. For a programmatic statement, see James Holston and Arjun Appadurai, 'Cities and Citizenship', *Public Culture* 1996: 8, 187–204.

71. Brenda Yeoh and Lily Kong (eds), *Portraits of Places: History, Community, and Identity in Singapore* (Singapore: Times Editions, 1995). See also, Christopher Tremewan, *The Political Economy of Social Control in Singapore* (New York: St Martin's Press, 1996).

72. Chua Beng Huat, *Communitarian Ideology and Democracy in Singapore* (London and New York: Routledge, 1995), pp. 192–200.

73. Ibid., pp. 166, 210.

74. Consider, for instance, the articles in Edesio Fernandes and Ann Varley (eds), *Illegal Cities: Law and Urban Change in Developing Countries* (London and New York: Zed Books 1998).

75. For a critique of the Singapore fixation among Bangalore administrators, see Nair, 'Singapore is not Bangalore's Destiny', *Economic and Political Weekly* 35: 18 (29 April 2000), 1512–14.

76. See, in particular, *The Uses of Disorder: Personal Identity and City Life* (New York and London: W.W. Norton and Co., 1992); *The Fall of Public Man* (London and Boston: Faber & Faber, 1993); *The Conscience of the Eye: The Design and Social Life of Cities* (New York and London: W.W. Norton and Co., 1992).

77. In an extended discussion of three sets of workers, their encounters with opportunity and failure, and through his skillful deployment of historical reflections on the meaning of work, trust, and discipline, Sennett speaks of failure as the fate of ever larger numbers of people under capitalism. Though what is required is a larger sense of community, a fuller sense of character, it is precisely that sense of community which is disallowed, so that 'we' becomes a dangerous pronoun. Here the author is careful to distinguish this sense of community from communitarianism: there is no community that does not acknowledge difference. 'Teamwork for instance does not acknowledge differences in privilege and power, and so is a weak form of community ...' P. 143.

78. Walter Benjamin, *The Arcades Project,* trans. Howard Eiland and Kevin McLaughlin (Cambridge Mass. and London: Belknap Press of Harvard University Press, 1999).

79. M. Visvesvaraya, *The Bangalore City and Its Future*. Address at the Bangalore Literary Union. (Bangalore: Bangalore Press, 1953), p. 13.

80. 'Janaagraha: Team up for a Better Bangalore', pamphlet (n.d.).

81. On the question of 'right' as a claim upon, rather than as a possession held against the world, see Holston and Appadurai, 'Cities and Citizenship', p. 197. On the ways in which illegalities are the mark of Third World cities, see Fernandes and Varley, *Illegal Cities*.

82. 'Store up food', he suggested to those in his audience, '[in order to] avoid some of the suffering of which the public had bitter experience in recent years.' Visvesvaraya, *The Bangalore City and Its Future,* p. 12.

83. Noel Gist, 'The Ecology of Bangalore, India: An East West Comparison', in V.K. Tewari et al. (eds), *Indian Cities: Ecological Perspectives* (Delhi: Concept Publishers, 1986), pp. 15–32.

84. Venkatrayappa, *Bangalore: A Socio-Ecological Study*.

85. Singh, *Bangalore: An Urban Survey*.

86. Ibid., pp. 82 ff.

87. Ibid., p. 121.

88. V.L.S. Prakasa Rao and V.K. Tewari, *The Structure of an Indian Metropolis* (Bombay: Allied Publishers, 1979).

89. Vinod Vyasulu and A.K.N. Reddy (convenors), *Essays on Bangalore*, vols. I–IV, (KSCST, 1983); see especially vol. I.

90. See, for instance, A. Ravindra, *Metropolitan Bangalore: A Management Perspective*, (Bangalore: Times Research Foundation, 1992).

91. James Manor, *Power, Poverty and Poison: Disaster and Response in an Indian City* (Delhi: Sage Publications, 1993).

92. See Balaji Parthasarathy, 'Globalisation and Agglomeration in Newly Industrialising countries: The State and the Information Technology Industry in Bangalore, India', Ph.D. dissertation, University of California, Berkeley, 2000.

93. See Jane Millar, 'Sustaining Software Teletrade in Bangalore: Fostering Market Agility through Economic Competence', *Economic and Political Weekly* 35.26 (24–30 June 2000) 2253–62.

94. See for instance, Shirin Madon, 'Information-Based Global Economy and Socio–Economic Development: The Case of Bangalore', *The Information Society* 13 (1997), 227–43.

95. James Heitzman, *Network City: Planning the Information Society in Bangalore* (New Delhi: Oxford University Press, 2004). Although I had seen many of the chapters of this book in draft form, the published text is too recent to receive adequate attention in this work.

96. H. Ramachandran, 'Slumming of a Metropolis', in Vyasulu and Reddy (eds), *Essays on Bangalore*, vol. II. Hans Schenk and Michael De Wit (eds), *Living in India's Slums: A Case Study of Bangalore* (Delhi: Manohar and Indo-Dutch Programme for Alternatives in Development, 2000).

97. P. Thippaiah, 'Informal Sector and the Urban Poor in a Metropolitan Area: A Case Study of Bangalore', Ph.D. thesis, Institute for Social and Economic Change, Bangalore, 1994.

98. Solomon Benjamin, Bhuvaneswari Raman, et al., 'Urban Poverty and Governance in Bangalore', mimeo, 2000. This document has since appeared in an amended, longer version as Benjamin and Bhuvaneswari, 'Democracy, Inclusive Governance and Poverty in Bangalore' (University of Birmingham: Urban Governance, Partnership and Poverty, Working Paper, 26 May 2001). See also Rosita Mertens, 'Forced Relocation of Slum Dwellers in Bangalore, India: Slum Dwellers, Landlords and the Government', MA thesis: Vrije Universiteit, Amsterdam, 1996.

99. Dilip Subramanian is the only scholar who has worked on the contemporary trade union movement, particularly within the large public sector. See 'The MICO Strike: A Retrospective', *Economic and Political Weekly* 15: 22 (31 May 1980); 'Bangalore Public Sector Strike: A Critical Appraisal', *Economic and Political Weekly* 32: 15–16 (12 and 19 April 1997); 'Bangalore Public Sector: The Unofficial Strike, 1981', *South Indian Studies,* 3 (Jan.–June 1997). His full length monograph on the ITI labour movement is awaited. See also, for a perspective on labour in pre-independence Bangalore, Janaki Nair, *Miners and Millhands: Work, Culture and Politics in Princely Mysore* (Delhi: Sage, 1998).

100. T.M. Joseph, 'Politics of Recruitment in Public Sector Undertakings: A Study of the Nativist Movement in Bangalore', Phd thesis, Institute for Social and Economic Change, 1994; T.S. Ramesh Bairy, 'Competing Constructions of Kannada Identity: A Study of Two Organisations', MPhil thesis, University of Hyderabad, 1996.

101. A recent attempt to theorize the relationship between space and gender has once more chosen the rural as its ground. See Seemanthini Niranjana, *Gender and Space: Femininity, Sexualisation and the Female Body* (Delhi: Sage Publications, 2001).

Chapter One: Bengaluru/Bangalore: The Presence of the Past

1. The arrest in Bangalore of K.F. Nariman, a former Congress mayor of Bombay, led to widespread protests in the city: police firing on a mob of 5000 led to the death of six men. See James Manor, *Political Change in an Indian State: Mysore, 1917–1955* (Delhi: South Asia Books, 1978), p. 105.

2. In this historical account, I retain both these spellings in order to distinguish the pre-British settlement from the colonial and post-colonial cities of Bangalore.

3. In this sense, Bangalore reflects the experience of many other colonial cities, with the structure, function, and form of one part bearing the marks of a European presence, while another part reflects an altogether different spatial logic. In colonial cities such as Calcutta, the 'native town' and 'white town' were contemporaneous: see Pradip Sinha, 'Calcutta and the Currents of History' in Chaudhuri (ed.), *Calcutta: the Living City*, vol. I, *The Present*, pp. 33–4. For an account of the morphology of the Presidency cities of Madras, Calcutta, and Bombay, see Norma Evenson, *The Indian Metropolis: A View Toward the West* (New Haven: Yale University Press, 1989), esp. pp. 1–112. On Singapore's growth and divided city status, see Yeoh and Kong (eds), *Portraits of Places*, pp. 29–33. Bombay's European quarter was transformed into a business district as a result of mid-nineteenth century movements into the 'suburbs'. The new suburbs, moreover, were home also to the rich class of Indians. See Dossal, *Imperial Designs and Indian Realities*, esp. pp. 16–20.

4. The most important historical narratives are Fazlul Hasan, *Bangalore Through the Centuries* (Bangalore: Historical Publications, 1970) and Ba Na Sundara Rao, *Bengalurina itihasa: sthapaneyinda hididhu swarajya labhisuvavarege* (Bangalore: Vasanth Sahitya Granthalaya, 1985).

5. See for instance, Maya Jayapal, *Bangalore: The Story of a City* (Chennai: East West Books, 1997); N. Jagadeesh, *Our Bangalore: A Journey Through Time* (Bangalore: Sapna Book House, 1999); Romola Chatterjee, *Courtyards of My Childhood: A Memoir* (Delhi: Kali for Women, 1996); Paul Byron Norris, *Follow My Bangalorey Man* (London: BACSA, 1996).

6. Heitzman, *Network City*, p. 24.

7. There is a popular tale about an old woman who served boiled beans to Veera Ballala, the Hoysala king, some time in the twelfth century: her grateful and illustrious guest then named the region after his frugal meal of *bendakaalu*. See Lewis Rice, *Mysore: A Gazetteer Compiled for Government* (rev. edn), vol. II (London: Archibald Constable & Co., 1897), p. 43. With the discovery of the ninth century Begur inscription in 1915, which included the name Bengaluru, we know this is no more than a charming story. Sundara Rao, *Bengalurina itihasa*, pp. 2–3. Other historians suggest that Kempegowda named the new settlement after the hamlet Hale Bengaluru near Kodigehalli to the north of the city; Hasan, *Bangalore Through the Centuries*, pp. 1–2. This has not put an end to speculations about the name: some suggest that Bengaluru is a corruption of *bendakaadu-ooru* recalling the forests that were burned to build the city. Sundara Rao, *Bengalurina itihasa*, pp. 5–7 There are also those who propose the city's name must derive from the type of granitic gneiss that is common in the region, hence *benachukalluru*. The settlement itself is popularly referred to as *belladaachhu Bengaluru* or the city shaped like a cube of jaggery. However, Na Geethacharya 'Bengaluru—Sthalanama ondu Tippani', *Rajdhani*, suggests that the original name was Devarayapatna. Though none of these usages and origins are related to the current name with any certainty, it is clear that though the name may have existed before Kempegowda, the settlement we recognize as the city today took shape during his time. C. Hayavadana Rao, *Mysore Gazetteer*; 'Historical Memoir of Bangalore, Communicated to and Translated by Soobba Row, Brahmin at Bangalore, April 1807' (hereafter, 'Historical Memoir of Bangalore'). B. Puttaiah Private Papers, Karnataka State Archives (KSA). This is most probably a translated manuscript from the Mackenzie Collection, which has been partially copied by Puttaiah; I have been unable to consult the original.

8. 'Historical Memoir of Bangalore.'

9. S.K. Narasimhaiah, *The Founder of Bangalore or Magadi Kempe Gowda and His Ancestors, Successors and Collaterals* (Bangalore Vokkaligara Sangha Press, 1924), p. 1.

10. Singh, *Bangalore: An Urban Survey*, p. 4.

11. Prakasa Rao and Tewari, *Structure of an Indian Metropolis*, pp. 175–6.

12. 'Historical Memoir of Bangalore.'

13. D. Ferroli, *The Jesuits in Mysore* (Kozhikode: Xavier Press, 1955), p. 159.

14. Burton Stein, 'Towns and Cities: the Far South', in Tapan Raychaudhuri and Irfan Habib (eds), *The Cambridge Economic History of India*, vol. 1, c. 1200–1750 (Hyderabad: Orient Longman, 1984), pp. 452–8.

15. 'Historical Memoir of Bangalore'; also Hasan, *Bangalore Through the Centuries,* pp. 16–17.

16. Stein, 'Towns and Cities', p. 454.

17. The beneficiaries included one who attained the 'highest consciousness' ('turyiya jati') and triumphed at a disputation at Srirangapatnam. Sundara Rao, *Bengalurina Itihasa*, pp. 33, 192–6.

18. Kakolu Raghavendra, *Shri kadu malleswara kshetra* (Bangalore: Murali Prakashana, 1997), p. 13. The word *kalyani* refers more properly to the temple tank, rather than an irrigation tank or *kere.*

19. Hasan, *Bangalore Through the Centuries*, p. 14.

20. Narasimhaiah, *The Founder of Bangalore*, p.16.

21. *A Guide to Bangalore and Mysore Directories,* 1905, p. 47.

22. Rice, *Mysore: A Gazetteer,* pp. 52–3.

23. M.P. Somasekhara Rau, *Growth of Local Self Government in Bangalore City* (GIPA, Bangalore, 1964), p. 25.

24. K.V. Iyer, 'Deyada Mane', trans. by Ramachandra Sharma, *Sunday Herald*, 13 May 1990.

25. Richard Sennett, *Flesh and Stone: The Body and the City in Western Civilisation* (London: Faber & Faber, 1996), p. 188.

26. Stein, 'Towns and Cities'.

27. See Smriti Srinivas, *Landscapes of Urban Memory*, p. 41.

28. Kakolu Raghavendra, *Shri kadu malleswara kshetra;* Hasan, *Bangalore Through the Centuries,* p. 46. For an account which says that the temple was founded by Venkaji, see Ba Na Sundara Rao, *Bengalurina itihasa,* p. 97.

29. An incomplete listing of temples in the old city area is in *Karnataka State Gazetteer: Bangalore District* (Bangalore: Government of Karnataka, 1990), pp. 932–5. See, also, Su Rangaswami (ed.), *Karnatakada devalayagalu*, (Bangalore: 1994).

30. 'Historical Memoir of Bangalore.'

31. Ibid.

32. Iyer, 'Deyada mane'.

33. *Karnataka State Gazetteer: Bangalore District.*

34. Pani, Anand and Vyasulu, 'Impact of Colonialism on Bangalore', in Vyasulu and Reddy (Convenors) *Essays on Bangalore*, vol. I, pp. 11, 17.

35. Swami D.I. Anthappa, *Britisharu baruvudakku munche bengaluru maththu suththamuththalalli kristadharmada ugama* (Catholic Kristhara Sahitya Sangha, 2000), p. 128.

36. This marked a new phase in patronage, for it was not just the adherents of a particular religion or authorities of state that supported religious buildings. Thus, K.N. Guruswamy, a leading excise contractor who was to become the owner of the most influential English and Kannada dailies in Karnataka until the 1980s, donated the tower with the cross on top, while Sir Mirza Ismail, Mysore's celebrated dewan from 1926–42, offered a Lord's table in mahogany. J.R. Henry, 'A History of Tamil

Churches in Mysore Diocese', Thesis submitted as part of the requirement for College Diploma of United Theological College, 1962, p. 18.

37. Bishop Brenton T. Bradley, *Visions and Victories in Hindustan: A Story of the Mission Stations of the Methodist Episcopal Church in Southern Asia* (Madras: Methodist Publishing House, 1931), p. 298. Madras was a poor second with an 8 per cent Christian population.

38. Henry, *A History of Tamil Churches in Mysore Diocese*, p. 29.

39. Srinivas, *Landscapes of Urban Memory*.

40. *Karnataka State Gazetteer: Bangalore District*, pp. 194–7.

41. Ibid.

42. Narayani Gupta, 'Urbanism in South India: Eighteenth/ Nineteenth Centuries', in Indu Banga (ed.), *The City in Indian History* (Delhi: Manohar, 1994), pp. 120–47, esp 125.

43. Rice, *Mysore: A Gazetteer*, p. 44.

44. 'Memoir of Bangalore.'

45. Sundara Rao, *Bengalurina itihasa*, pp. 88–95; Hasan *Bangalore Through the Centuries*, pp. 54–5.

46. Hasan, *Bangalore Through the Centuries*, p. 28.

47. Benjamin Heyne, *Statistical Fragments of Mysore* (London: 1805), p. 37.

48. Francis Buchanan, *A Journey through Madras Through the Countries of Mysore, Canara and Malabar*, vol. I (Originally published London: 1807; Reprint Asian Educational Services, 1998), p. 198–207.

49. Ibid., pp. 220–1.

50. Heyne, *Statistical Fragments*, p. 52.

51. 'Historical Memoir of Bangalore.'

52. Mackenzie, *Sketch of a War with Tippoo Sultan*, p. 46.

53. Pani et al., 'Impact of Colonialism', p. 13.

54. Walter Hamilton, *Geographical, Statistical and Historical Description of Hindustan and the Adjacent Countries*, vol. 2 (London: 1820), p. 376.

55. Rice, *Mysore: A Gazetteer*, vol. I, Mysore in General (London: 1897), p. 538

56. Ibid., p. 537.

57. This growth is considered at length in Janaki Nair, 'The Emergence of Labor Politics in South India: Bangalore, 1898–1947', PhD dissertation, Syracuse University, 1991, esp Ch. 2. Among the important joint stock companies that were established in the early twentieth century were the Government Soap Factory (1917), Mysore Chrome Tanning Factory (1913), Mysore Industrial and Testing Laboratory (1931), Government Porcelain Factory (1932), Government Electric Factory (1933), Mysore Lamps Factory (1936). Other factories that started in this period included Kaiser I Hind Mills and Mahalaxmi Woollen Mills (1922), Bangalore Silk Filature (1923), AMCO (1934), Mysore Stoneware Pipes and Potteries (1937), Mysore Plywood Corporation, Mysore Leather and Industrial Products, Vellum Parachute Silk Co (1943). Hindusthan Aircraft Limited was begun in 1940 by Walchand Hirachand and taken

over by the Mysore State in 1942. At the time of Independence there were 278 firms employing a total of 39,613 workers in Bangalore district.

58. *A Brief Note on the Origin and Development of the Assigned Tract of Bangalore* (n.d.), KSA.

59. See also Elizabeth Staley, *Monkey Tops* (Bangalore: Tara Publications, 1981).

60. On bankers in the Cantonment, it was said that they were a numerous community and dealt with large sums of Government money, *A Guide to Bangalore*, p. 121.

61. B.K. Garudachar, 'Bangalore Past and Present', *Mysore Economic Journal*, May 1915.

62. I have discussed these efforts in some detail in 'The Emergence of Labor Politics in South India'.

63. Harihara Srinivasa Rao, 'Bengaluru haleya peteya garadigalu', *Itihasa darshana*.

64. *A Guide to Bangalore and Mysore Directory*, p. 50.

65. Rice, *Mysore: A Gazetteer*, vol. II, p. 44.

66. Major Dirom, *A Narrative of the Campaign in India, which terminated with the war with Tippoo Sultan in 1792* (London: 1793), p. 249.

67. R.K. Narayan, *Mysore* (Mysore: 1944), p. 70.

68. Rice, *Mysore: A Gazetter*, vol. II, p. 51.

69. A study by Jaspreet Kaur on Ashoknagar (formerly Shoolay) documents a relationship between private and public space that was more intimate, less well defined, and encouraged social interactions of a different kind from the wealthier bungalow/compounds that lay in the immediate vicinity. Kaur, *Ashok Nagar, Bangalore: Habitat, Documentation, Urban Design*, Unpublished paper: School of Architecture, Ahmedabad, 1993.

70. C. Hayavadana Rao, *Mysore Gazetteer*, vol. v, (Bangalore, 1932), p. 125.

71. Sundara Rao, *Bengalurina itihasa*, p. 362.

72. D.V. Gundappa, himself a connoisseur of music, reconstructs a dialogue between Narahari Rao and his wife, in which the wife gives him 'permission' to become Bangalore Nagarathnamma's patron. I have discussed this in 'The Devadasi, Dharma and the State', in *Economic and Political Weekly* 29:50 (1994), 3157–67.

73. Sundara Rao, *Bengalurina itihasa*, p. 420. It is also referred to as Naraharirayanagudda.

74. C. Hayavadana Rao, *Mysore Gazetteer*, vol. v (Bangalore, 1931), p.112.

75. File no. 10–98, no. 1–5; Improvements of the Bangalore City, Oct. 1898, Municipal, KSA.

76. J.M. Stephens, *Plague Proof Town Planning in Bangalore, South India* (Madras Methodist Publishing House, 1914), p. 29.

77. Somasekhara Rau, *Growth of Local Self Government in Bangalore*, p. 11.

78. Stephens, *Plague Proof Planning*, p. 30.

79. *A Guide to Bangalore and Mysore Directory*, 1905, p. 53.

80. Ibid., p. 53.

81. File no. 134 of 1902, sl. no. 1–2, Municipal, KSA.

82. File no. 256–14, sl. no. 1–3, Municipal 1915, KSA.

83. *Campbell's Directory for Mysore and Bangalore*, 1920, p. 91.

84. Hayavadana Rao, *Mysore Gazetteer*, vol. v, p. 12.

85. MSS Eur: New model housing erected at Knoxpet by the municipal commission, 1923, India Office Library (henceforth IOL).

86. R.K. Srinivasan and C. Narasimha Moorty, *Labour and Housing in Bangalore City* (Bangalore: Bangalore Press, 1935), pp. 20, 22, 31.

87. See Nair 'Contending Ideologies: The Mass Awakener's Union and Congress in Mysore, 1936–42', *Social Scientist* 22: 7–8 (1994), 42–63.

88. Sanjeev Jain, Pratima Murthy, and Vivek Benegal '150 years Young: The Mental Hospital in Bangalore', *Sunday Herald*, 1 Nov. 1999.

89. *Select Views in Mysore, The Country of Tipu Sultan, From Drawings Taken on the Spot by Mr Home with Historical Descriptions* (Delhi: Asian Education Services [1808] 2000).

90. Some of James Hunter's drawings have been reproduced in Hasan, *Bangalore Through the Centuries*, between pp. 64–5.

91. 'Historical memoir of Bangalore.'

92. The municipality made plans for the use of the stone as jelly in road building, a suggestion that was not carried through. The fort stone was recycled, though it is not quite clear in what fashion. File no. 228–18, sl. no. 1,3,4,5,7, Chief Engineer Mysore to Chief Secretary Mysore, 2 July 1919, General Misc., KSA.

93. Sundara Rao, *Bengalurina itihasa*, p. 362.

94. 'Good Masters Make Good Hunting', *Illustrated Weekly of India*, 20 Jan. 1935. From the Collection of Arthur Hughes, New York.

95. Philip Chetwoode to Captain Simmons, Master Huntsman of the Bangalore Hunt, 2 Aug. 1934. From the Collection of Arthur Hughes, New York.

96. *A Guide to Bangalore and Mysore Directory*, 1905, p. 136–7.

97. 'Happy Hunting Days in Bangalore', *Madras Mail*, 26 Aug. 1933. From the Collection of Arthur Hughes, New York.

98. M. Subbaiah, 'Apple Cultivation in Bangalore', *Mysore Economic Journal* (June 1915).

99. Rice, *Mysore: A Gazetteer*, vol. II, p. 14

100. File no. 510–05, sl. no. 1–17, General & Miscellaneous Files, KSA.

101. File no. 202–16, sl. no. 1–9, Police (July 1917), KSA.

102. Narayani Gupta, 'Urban Form and Meaning in South Asia: Perspectives from the Modern Era', in Howard Spodek and Doris Meith Srinivasan, *Urban Form and Meaning in South Asia: The Shaping of Cities from Pre-Historic to Pre-Colonial Times* (Hanover and London: University Press of New England, 1993), pp. 243–52.

103. Hasan, *Bangalore Through the Centuries*, p. 56.

104. Sundara Rao, *Bengalurina itihasa*, pp. 535–64.

105. 'Hotel' here refers to restaurant.

106. D.V. Gundappa, 'Bengalurinalli hotel udhyamada praramba', *Jnapaka Chitrashale*, vol. 7, (Bangalore, 1974), pp. 114–21.

107. Ibid., 'K.T. Appannanavaru', p, 123.

108. Ibid.

109. See Nair, 'Contending Ideologies?'

110. See Nair, 'Drawing a Line: K.Venkatappa and His Publics', *Indian Economic and Social History Review* 35:2, (1998), 179–210.

111. Nair, 'Palace/Gallery/Museum: The Importance of Being "National"', MIDS Working Paper 149, MIDS, Madras, 1997.

112. D.V. Gundappa, 'The Gokhale Institute of Public Affairs: Its Birth, Growth, Prospects and Ideals', *Gokhale Institute of Public Affairs 1915–1945–1965* (Bangalore, 1965), pp. 55–84, esp. 63.

113. Interview with Nittoor Srinivasa Rao, 15 May 1998 and 14 July 1998.

114. M. Shivaram, 'Kailasam and I,' *Sunday Herald*, 13 May 1990.

115. *Select Papers from the Old Records of the Mysore Government Secretariat* (1832–67), KSA.

116. See Nair, 'From Devadasi Reform to SITA: Reforming Sex-work in Mysore, 1892–1937', *National Law School Journal: Feminism and Law*, vol. I (1993), pp. 82–94.

117. *A Guide to Bangalore and Mysore Directory*, p. 67.

118. A more detailed account is in Nair, 'The Emergence of Labor Politics in South India', pp. 243–51.

119. See G. Thimmaiah, *Power, Politics and Social Justice: Backward Castes in Karnataka* (Delhi: Sage Publications, 1993), pp. 70–1.

120. 'The Late Sahukar Mr B.K. Mariappa Charities: Administration Report for 1914–1935', B. Puttaiya Papers, KSA.

121. *City of Bangalore Municipal Handbook* (1931), p. 21.

122. Ibid., p. 23.

123. *Karnataka*, 18.9.1915, B. Puttaiya Papers, KSA.

124. Private and Confidential Note on Non-Entities Club, B. Puttaiya Papers, KSA.

125. Stephens, *Plague Proof Planning In Bangalore*, p. 107.

126. 'Magaji dhondusa avaru', *Kempegowdanagara darshana* (Bengaluru, 1980), pp. 46–7.

127. K.S. Krishna Iyer, A.R. Nageswara Iyer, N. Narasimha Murthy, M.G. Varadachari, Anantha Padmanabha Iyer, S. Surya Prakash, Mokshgundam Krishnamurthi, Belur Srinivasa Iyengar, B.V. Subba Rao, and Bhima Rao were among the founders, Gundappa 'GIPA', p. 47.

128. File no. 235–20, sl. no. 1–2, CB, KSA.

129. *Hindu*, 25 Nov. 1921.

130. More detailed accounts of labour in Bangalore are in Nair, 'Emergence of Labor Politics in South India'.

131. K.S. Kumaran, 'Bengalurinalli swatantrya samarada smaraneeya sthalagalu', in *Bengaluru Nagara Corporation*, p. 47–54.

132. *Report of the Committee of Enquiry Appointed by the Government of Mysore on Disturbances at Bangalore City, July 1928*, vol. I (Bangalore Government Press, 1929); hereafter *Report on Bangalore Disturbances*, p. 7. See also Sundara Rao, *Bengalurina itihasa*, pp. 535–64.

133. Interview with Nittoor Srinivasa Rao, 15 May 1998.

134. *Report on Bangalore Disturbances*, p. 10.

135. Jayapal, *Bangalore: The Story of a City*, 229–34.

136. Bangalore's first sedition case was against Surya Narayan Rao and Sitarama Sastry following this event. Nittoor Srinivasa Rao defended the two in this case. Interview with Srinivasa Rao, 15 May 1998.

137. *Report on Bangalore Disturbances*, p. 55.

138. This is how Nittoor Srinivasa Rao recalled the government response: 'Government issued a communication giving their version which was not only contrary to what people believed to be the real course of events, it also developed side by side a theory of the conspiracy which went several years back to dethrone the Maharaja, to destabilize the government and that the events of the previous day were part and parcel of a conspiracy which had been going on for many years.' Interview with Srinivasa Rao, 15 May 1998.

139. For instance, the data appended to the report pointed to a growing disparity between the communities. *Report on Bangalore Disturbances*, App. iii, p 115. See also the 'Memorial of the Muslims of the City to the Government of Mysore', File no 37–26, sl. no. 69, 89, 90, 97, 106, 113, Confidential Branch, KSA.

140. *Report on Bangalore Disturbances*, pp. 82 ff.

141. Ibid., p. 7.

142. L/P&S/13/1308, IOL.

143. In several of his speeches, the Congress leader K.T.Bhashyam promised his audience 'Cantonment like faces, houses and wealth'. *Political and Private Meetings Held by the Congress Party, Bangalore City, Vol. II, 9.8.1937–29.12.1937*, Confidential Branch, KSA.

144. P.S. Narayana Rao, *The Bangalore Municipal Corporation: Problems and Finances* (Corporation of the city of Bangalore, 1970), p. 13.

145. *Papers Relating to the Restoration of Jurisdiction over the Assigned Tract of Bangalore to the Mysore State* and *Memoranda of Several Associations on the Retrocession of the Civil and Military Station of Bangalore to the Mysore State*, KSA.

146. Ibid., 'Rejoinder from the Musalmans of the C&M Station to the Memorial Submitted by the Central Mohomeddan Association on the 12th December 1934', KSA.

Chapter Two: Remembered and Imagined Cities

1. *Census of India, 2001*, Series 30, Karnataka, Provisional Population Tables, Paper 2 of 2001.

2. See, for instance, the statement of several senior citizens of the city including Raja Ramanna and M.N. Srinivas, 'It is of utmost importance to preserve Bangalore's old charm. Development and growth is fine, but it can also be achieved through the creation of townships and satellite towns.' *Times of India*, 22 Feb. 1997.

3. Interview in the *Economic Times*, 19 March 2000.

4. G. Behera et al., 'Growth of Bangalore City Since 1900 Based on Maps and Satellite Imagery', unpublished paper, ISRO, Bangalore, 1986?

5. See Mark Holmstrom *Bangalore as an Industrial District: Flexible Specialisation in a Labour Surplus Economy?* Pondy Papers in Social Sciences, 14 (Pondicherry: Institut Français de Pondichery, 1994).

6. See Heitzman, *Network City*, pp. 166–217.

7. Madon, 'Information-Based Global Economy and Socio-Economic Development'. Heitzman, *Network City*, pp. 69–122.

8. Parthasarathy 'Globalisation and Agglomeration in Newly Industrialising Countries'.

9. A fuller discussion of the growth of industry and, of working class zones in this period may be found in Nair 'The Emergence of Labor Politics in South India'.

10. Venkatrayappa, *Bangalore: a Socio–Ecological Study*, pp. 127–30.

11. See *Mysore Dasara Exhibition Handbook, 1953*. There was moreover a link between these two sites as the most important clients of the Dairy were the large public sector companies. See Singh *Bangalore: An Urban Survey*, p. 85.

12. Singh, *Bangalore: An Urban Survey*, p. 25.

13. Ibid., p. 79.

14. Ibid., p. 2.

15. Mark Holmstrom notes that though the city had a number of organizations that provided technical support for the medium and small scale electronic engineering industry, none of them, not even the voluntary Nettur Technical Training Foundation, were of local origin. Holmstrom, *Bangalore as an Industrial District*, p. 69.

16. K.S. Rame Gowda, *Urban and Regional Planning: Principles and Case Studies* (Mysore: Prasaranga, 1986), p. 131.

17. M. Bhaskara Rao and M. Johnson Samuel, 'Growth of Bangalore: Population and Industrialisation', ISEC Working Paper, IPD 368, Bangalore, p. 15.

18. *Outline Development Plan for the Bangalore Metropolitan Region*, vol. II, p. 36.

19. Holmstrom, *Bangalore as an Industrial District*, p. 19.

20. Gist, 'The Ecology of Bangalore', 21.

21. P. Thippaiah, 'Informal Sector and the Urban Poor in a Metropolitan Area: A Case Study of Bangalore', PhD thesis, ISEC, Bangalore, pp. 108, 128–9.

22. Ibid., p. 261.

23. Dilip Subramanian, 'The MICO Strike: A Retrospective', *EPW*, vol. 15:22 (31 May 1980), M59–68, esp. M67.

24. Holmstrom, *Bangalore as an Industrial District*, p. 21.

25. The direct ways in which the nascent IT industry drew on and benefited from the R&D units of state enterprises is rarely acknowledged. Balaji Parthasarathy claims that both BEL and ITI were hard hit when most of their integrated circuit designers left to join companies such as TI or Motorola or migrate to Singapore; as a consequence, BEL was forced to contract out design. Parthasarathy, 'Globalisation and Agglomeration in Newly Industrialising Countries', p. 354.

26. James Heitzman, 'Becoming Silicon Valley', 43.

27. Parthasarathy, 'Globalisation and Agglomeration in Newly Industrialising Countries', pp. 352–3.

28. *IT Profile at Bangalore*, Centre for the Symbiosis of Technology, Environment and Management, Bangalore, 1999, p. 93.

29. John Stallmeyer, 'Redefining Bangalore? Architecture and Urbanism in India's Silicon Valley', Paper presented at the City One Conference, SARAI, Delhi, (8–10 Jan. 2003). The estimates vary quite dramatically; in plans for the new IT corridor, Jurong Consultants mention 'more than a 1000' IT companies operating in Bangalore City. *IT corridor, Bangalore India: Structure Plan Final Report*, 2003, p. 3–4. See Maps 11 and 12.

30. Ravindra, *Metropolitan Bangalore*, p. 57.

31. V.K. Tewari, 'A Model of Bangalore Metropolis', Institute for Social and Economic Change, 1978, p. 70.

32. Prakasa Rao and Tewari, *The Structure of an Indian Metropolis*, pp. 319–20.

33. Tewari, 'A Model of Bangalore Metropolis', p. 65.

34. A number of industries, such as the Mysore Electric Chemical Works, Government Soap Factory, and Kirloskar Electric Company shifted to the area from their city bases. *Annual Administration Report of the City Improvement Trust Board, 1956–7,* p. 15.

35. Ibid., p. 16. A total of 3,200 sites were formed in one of the industrial housing areas adjoining Rajajinagar by CITB; other areas too were designed around the concept of individual site ownership.

36. *Report on the Comprehensive Development Plan of Bangalore,* 1976, p. 57.

37. *Activities and Achievements of CITB Since its Inception i.e. from 26-1-1945 to 6-6-1973*, p. 25.

38. *Mysore Dasara Exhibition Handbook*, 1953, p. 69.

39. BEL, HA (Sanitary Board), HAL (township), HMT, HMT Watch Factory Township, and ITI Notified Area were independent towns, in a class of their own. *Census of India, 1981*, Bangalore District Handbook, p. lxviii.

40. The territorial and jurisdictional changes in Bangalore city have been tracked by Bhaskara Rao and Johnson Samuel, 'Growth of Bangalore' which may be summarized as follows: While the 1961 census included all villages within a five mile radius of the city as falling within the jurisdiction of the Bangalore Metropolitan Area, of which CITB was a part, this was not acceptable to the 1971 census which transferred 171 localities of the Trust Board area to rural areas. Some localities, including Jodikempapura, Kethmaranhalli, and Yeshwantpur, were then joined to the city. In 1981, three more villages were joined to the city corporation. Meanwhile, the extensions to the city were growing, and were added to the Bangalore Urban Agglomeration in censuses after 1971. By 1981, there were 47 'outgrowths' to main localities which were considered as part of the urban agglomeration, including outgrowths adjoining BEL, B.M. Kaval, HAL, ITI, Kengeri, Krishnarajpuram, and Yelahanka. Some of these were managed by city municipal councils, notified area committees, or sanitary boards. By the 1990s, the Bangalore urban conurbation was the sum of the city, the urbanized outgrowths, and villages earmarked for urbanization, totalling 449 sq km.

41. See, for instance, K.S.Rame Gowda, *Urban and Regional Planning*: pointing to the increasing burden of servicing far flung areas, and the rising costs of urbanizable land, Gowda suggested, 'vertical growth of the city has to be gradually encouraged to prevent these defects, both from the point of view of land economy and city architecture', p. 149.

42. V. Keerthi Shekar, 'Rapid Urbanisation and Satellite Townships: A Study in Urban Sociology', (Ph.D. Thesis, Bangalore University, 1992), pp. 34, 53.

43. Stallmeyer notes that in the Indiranagar/Airport Road area alone, 117 of 229 establishments occupy former residences. 'Redefining Bangalore?'.

44. Vandana Baweja, 'Through the Looking Glass', *Architecture and Design* 27: 3 (May–June 2000).

45. As cited in Baweja, 'Through the Looking Glass'.

46. Sharad Padalkar, 'Housing Development', *Architecture and Design*, Special Issue: Bangalore Profile 14: 2 (1999).

47. Edgar D'Mello, 'Sentinels of the South', *Architecture and Design* (July–Aug. 1987).

48. Ibid.

49. Sathya Prakash Varanashi, 'Continuities vs. Discontinuities: An Overview of Bangalore Residences', *Architecture and Design* (May–June 2000), 90–2. See, also his 'Shifting Images of Bangalore: Pubs Clubs and Darshinis', *Architecture and Design* (March–April 1999), 38–40.

50. Here it must be emphasised that *vaastu* consultants usually insist on characterizing its modalities as 'science'. See, for instance, N.S. Murthy, 'A Brief Introduction to Vaastu Science' (Bangalore: Centre for Research and Application of Vaastu Science, 1994). Others do try and retain the mystique of *vaastu* by insisting that the conditions of its successful working are faith and trust. It is this insistence on its mystique, M.A. Parthasarathi, a *vaastu* consultant said at a public lecture, that led

many of his educated clients to consult him in utmost secrecy. Lecture given at the Institute of Engineers, August 1994. Hardpressed to provide consistent evidence of the efficacy of the method to the doubting client, *vaastu* consultants may also use the exception to advantage: thus, said Parthasarathi, the people of the Sankey Tank area are wealthy and powerful despite the location of the water body in the wrong direction as external powers operated to make them wealthy before they got there.

51. Parthasarathi mentioned that he offered his clients a range of solutions that were similar to inexpensive and expensive ways of dealing with illness or disease.

52. There have even been attempts to apply the principles to the city as a whole, in order to diagnose why the 'north–east quadrant', where the small scale industrial estate of Peenya is located, is currently in decline: it is losing the benefits of cosmic energy as its water bodies are drying up. This was a the diagnosis of K.V.Raja Rao, former Urban Development Scientist at ISRO, Bangalore. 'Vaastu cures for Bangalore's ills!', *Indian Express*, 15 July 1996.

53. On the effects of the new economies on the moulding of character, and particularly as they do not prepare people for retrenchment or failure, see Sennett, *The Corrosion of Character*.

54. The mode of residing in enclaves of privilege is by no means restricted to the Indian city. See, for instance, Caldeira, 'Fortified Enclaves'; see, also Michael Southworth and Balaji Parthasarathy, 'The Suburban Public Realm: Its Emergence, Growth and Transformation in the American Metropolis', *Journal of Urban Design*, vol. I, no. 3, 1996, pp. 245–63, and vol. II, no. 1, 1997, pp. 9–34.

55. The term 'Eight Bigs' was a playful allusion in post-reform People's Republic of China to the 'Four Musts' of the Mao era: the latter included a bicycle, a radio, a watch, and a sewing machine. Jonathan Spence, *The Search for Modern China* (New York and London: WW Norton & Co., 1990), p. 733.

56. In BEL, 3000 workers, close to half the workforce, were Rs 10 earners in the early nineties. *History of the Bharat Electronic Employee's Union and Bharat Electronics* (BEEU, 1993), p. 44.

57. For a discussion of the use of domestic space in the colonial bungalow, especially as it sometimes included as many as three separate kitchens, see Janet Pott, *Old Bungalows in Bangalore* (London: Published by the author, 1977), esp. pp. 15–16.

58. DVG to C. Rajagopalachari, 23 Oct. 1964, DVG Private Papers, KSA.

59. Sudipta Kaviraj, 'The Culture of Representative Democracy', in Partha Chatterjee (ed.), *Wages of Freedom* (Delhi: Oxford University Press, 1998), pp. 147–75, esp. p. 163.

60. In the 1990s, Bangalore has been the preferred, and sometimes the sole, choice of those who organized events featuring Western rock and pop stars.

61. Mr and Mrs Verghese measured potholes on a 2.8 km. stretch of road between Elgin mills and Koramangala, a residential area. 'Bumpy Rides on Highways Too', *Hindu*, 31 Aug. 1998.

62. Venkatrayappa, *Bangalore: A Socio-Ecological Study*, p. 113.

63. Ibid., See, also, Singh, *Bangalore: An Urban Survey*, p. 46.

64. *Report on the Comprehensive Development Plan of Bangalore*, 1976, pp. 30, 33–4.

65. *Comprehensive Development Plan Report* (Bangalore, 1985), p. 17.

66. 'Ee bandiya sancharakke nirbandha: sahebana paadenu?', *Prajavani*, 14 July 1998, drew attention to the fact that the banning of animal-drawn vehicles on 100 Bangalore roads affected 15,000 drivers, a disproportionate number of whom were poor Muslims.

67. 'ELRTS is a better option than metro rail: experts', *Indian Express*, 2 Aug. 1998.

68. 'ELRTS economically unviable: WB', *Deccan Herald*, 29 May 1999.

69. 'Time to scrap', *Deccan Herald*, 31 May 1999.

70. Heitzman, *Network City*, p. 88.

71. Chua Beng-Huat, 'Singapore: Management of a City State in South East Asia', in Ruland (ed.), *The Dynamics of Metropolitan Management in South East Asia*, pp. 207–24; V. Setty Pendakur, 'Elaboration of the Transport System', in Kernial Singh Sandhu and Paul Wheatleaf (eds), *Management of Success: The Moulding of Modern Singapore* (ISEAS, 1989), pp. 399–419.

72. Aundhe, 'A Comparative Study of Three models for Evaluating Urban Infrastructure Projects', p. 66.

73. Ibid., p. 76.

74. 'Paint the buses green', *Times of India*, 6 Aug. 1998.

75. 'Court Stay stalls radio cabs hitting Bangalore roads', *Deccan Herald*, 22 Oct. 1998.

76. 'Bangalore lags behind in implementation', *Hindu*, 21 June 1999.

77. The term 'pedagogical' is used in the sense developed by Partha Chatterjee, 'Beyond the Nation? Or Within?' to mean the role performed by civil society, functioning within a narrow definition of modernity.

78. *Gokhale Institute of Public Affairs Souvenir, 1915–1945–1965*, p. 82.

79. Ibid., p. 74.

80. *Public Affairs*, vol. XI, 8 Aug. 1967, p. 184.

81. *Conspectus of the GIPA, 1956.*

82. *Public Affairs*, vol. VI–I (Jan.–Feb. 1959), p. 6.

83. *Public Affairs*, vol. IV–5, (Sept.–Oct. 1955), p. 113.

84. *Deccan Herald*, 2 Feb. 1966; 23 April 1966; 25 Dec. 1966.

85. *Public Affairs*, vol. IX–2 (Feb. 1967).

86. No wonder that DVG approved of those moments when democracy was suspended. Welcoming President's rule in Kerala in 1959, DVG wrote: 'It is a superstition to regard democracy as something more than an instrument to ensure good government. It is equally superstitious to think that democracy can grow unperverted without certain pre-conditions of soil and climate.' *Public Affairs*, vol. VI–4 (July–Aug. 1959).

87. *Public Affairs*, vol. XIV–10, (Oct. 1970).

88. As revealed in the lists of names of members, *Annual Reports of the GIPA*, 1948–1983.

89. *Public Affairs*, vol. XVIII–12 (Dec.1973), p. 233.

90. Ibid., vol. XI–8, Aug. 1967, pp. 174–5.

91. *Supplement to Public Affairs*, March 1978, pp. 1–2.

92. M.G. Venkatesh and C.R. Bhat, 'Samudaya nadedhu bandha dari', *Samudaya 25: Samskritika Jatha Utsavagalu* (Hubli Dharwad: Samudaya, 2000), p. 11.

93. Narendar Pani, *Staging a Change* (Bangalore: Samudaya Prakashana, 1979), p. 45.

94. Ibid.

95. Ibid.

96. It must be emphasized here that the Devaraj Urs government protected the state from some of the worst excesses of the Emergency. See James Manor, 'Pragmatic Progressives in Regional Politics: The case of Devaraj Urs', *Economic and Political Weekly* (Feb. 1980), pp. 201–13.

97. C.K.Gundanna, 'Samudaayada odanaatadalli', pp. 54–5.

98. Laxmi Chandrasekhar, 'Brihat samskrithika aandolana', p. 25.

99. Joseph, 'Politics of Recruitment in Public Sector Undertakings, pp. 76–7.

100. Ibid., p. 111.

101. Subramanian, 'Bangalore Public Sector Strike 1980–81', p. 844. The BEEU pamphlet however suggests that there were 80 area committees. *History of the Bharat Electronics Employee's Union*, pp. 40–1.

102. *History of the Bharat Electronics Employee's Union*, pp. 40–1.

103. Subramanian, 'Bangalore Public Sector Strike', p. 844.

104. Janaki Nair, 'Finding a new voice', *Deccan Herald*, 30 April 1999.

105. Swabhimana pamphlet (no date).

106. The Beautify Lavelle Road Association was among the earliest to respond to the call: see *Times of India*, 3 Dec. 1997. Other Associations in the ISRO Layout, HAL Third Stage, and Hanumanthanagar followed suit. *Times of India*, 9 Sept. 1996; *Deccan Herald*, 21 Nov. 1997.

107. *Swabhimana Initiative and Karnataka Urban Infrastructure Development and Finance Corporation*, 3 Nov. 1998.

108. Subbarayan Prasanna, 'The Role of Ward Committees and Neighbourhood Associations', mimeo, p. 16.

109. Thomas Donaldson and Lee Preston, 'The Stakeholder Theory of the Corporation: Concepts Evidence and implications', *Academy of Management Review* 20:1 (1995), 65–91, esp. 67.

110. See Heitzman, *Network City*, pp. 123–64, p. 5. Interview with Vinay Baindur, 29 Sept. 1999.

111. For instance, Samuel Paul *A Report Card on Public Services in Indian Cities: A View from Below* (Bangalore: Public Affairs Centre (PAC), 1995); using

data from a sampling of citizens in three cities, Bangalore, Pune, and Ahmedabad, Paul argued that citizens were already incurring 'unproductive investments' to compensate for the 'uncertainty and unreliability of the services provided'. Such infructuous investments totalled Rs 1000 crore, demonstrating the ability and willingness of the middle class to pay for more efficient services. Similar Report Cards were produced for Madras and Calcutta,

112. Interview with Vinay Baindur, 29 Sept. 1999.

113. Ramesh Ramanathan 'Can Good Governance be the Answer?' *Janaagraha*, vol. I, Issue 20.

114. 'Does Infy Rule Bangalore?', *Outlook*, Nov. 2001.

115. Babu Mathew however was careful to distinguish Krishnan's first victory, in 1967, from his other victories, saying that 'only his first victory was really a working class supported victory; all other occasions, it was victory through alliances'. Interview with Babu Mathew, former AITUC leader, 8 Oct. 1999. It cannot be denied that Krishnan's Brahmin caste status may have assisted him considerably in constituencies such as Rajajinagar and Malleswaram which are overwhelmingly upper caste. His public persona was, however, that of a Communist trade union leader. Interview with M.S. Krishnan, 8 Aug. 1987.

Chapter Three: Conceiving the City: Master Planning and Informal Power

1. *Indian Express*, 9 Oct. 1996; *Economic Times*, 9 Oct. 1986; *Times of India*, 9 October 1986.

2. *Indian Express*, 16 July 1996; *Times of India*, 24 July 1996.

3. Henri Lefebvre, *Writings on Cities*, trans. and edited by Eleanore Kofman and Elizabeth Lebas (Oxford: Blackwell Publishers, 1996), p. 99.

4. Bob Jessop, 'Cities as the New National Champions in International Competition'; paper presented at 'City State and Region in a Global Order: Towards the 21st Century' conference (Hiroshima, 1998). It is doubtful whether Bangalore can be called a 'global city' in any of the senses developed by Sassen, *Global Cities: London, New York, Tokyo*. Heitzman has rightly called this self-description into question; see *Network City*, pp. 166–217.

5. Dinesh Mehta, 'Introduction to the Urban Management Programme', Consultation Workshop to prepare a Collective Vision and Strategic Action Plan for Bangalore, 21 April 1998. Six cities of South Asia were chosen for this programme of the UNDP/UNHCS; in India they were Bangalore and Surat.

6. An estimated 60,000 people are employed in the IT and IT-enabled sectors of Bangalore's economy, spread over software, hardware, maintenance, distribution, and training facilities. 'IT Profile at Bangalore', STEM study, Bangalore 1999, p. 93. Between 1991–2 and 1997–8 software exports from Bangalore grew from Rs 56m to Rs 17,000m, Millar, 'Sustaining Software Teletrade in Bangalore', 2253–62. Commensurate statistics

for the increase in jobs are not yet available, although N.R. Narayana Murthy, chairman of Infosys Technologies, envisaged that jobs in the IT sector would grow to 100,000 in five years from 1998. Workshop on Infrastructure Project of Bangalore Mysore Corridor, NIAS, 25 Sept. 1998.

7. The words were those of Deepak Mehta, secretary, Electronics City Industries Association, in his representation at the Consultation workshop, UNDP/UNHCS 1998. According to Heitzman, Narayana Murthy suggested in 1997 that 'the metropolitan region had about five years time to turn the situation around, before irremediable shifts in capitalist tactics resulted in the abandonment of Bangalore'. Heitzman, 'Corporate Strategy and Planning in the Science City: Bangalore as 'Silicon Valley', *Economic and Political Weekly* 34.5 (30 Jan. 1999), PE 2–11.

8. 'Singapura maadariyalli bengaluru abhivruddhige krama', *Kannada Prabha*, 13 Dec. 1999; 'CM Issues Order to Improve Market, Roads: Promises to turn Bangalore into Singapore', *Deccan Herald*, 13 Dec. 1999. He has since tempered the growing clamour for turning Bangalore into another Singapore with blameless pragmatism: the state will strive only for 'strips of Singapore', perhaps between Whitefield, the location of the Singapore Technology Park and Hosur Road, home of the stock market frontrunner Infosys.

9. 'Task Force to Convene Meet to Discuss City Improvement Plan', *Deccan Herald*, 4 Jan. 2000.

10. 'Task Force Plans to make Bangalore Best City by 2004', *Deccan Herald*, 25 Jan. 2000. Notably absent were the older, more established corporate houses of the city who prefer to be publicly associated with horse racing, fashion shows, and cultural events.

11. While the maiden Bangalore Summit last year was full of euphoria, the second summit concentrated on reality,' said the *Times of India*, 'BATF: A Small Steady Step for City,' 25 Feb. 2001. 'CM Snubs Politicians for Opposing BATF', *Deccan Herald*, 25 Feb. 2001.

12. *Deccan Herald*, 2 July 1970.

13. *Deccan Herald*, 8 June 1971.

14. 'No Blanket Ban on High Rise Buildings', *Deccan Herald*, 1 March 1981.

15. Ravindra, *Metropolitan Bangalore: A Management Perspective*, p. 6. Ravindra served as commissioner of the Bangalore City Corporation, and Chairman of the Bangalore Metropolitan Region Development Authority.

16. At the first Bangalore Summit, Central Minister for Youth and Culture Ananthkumar, announced plans for the development of a Disneyland theme park that would feature Indian historical figures.

17. A longer critique of the Singapore comparison is in Nair, 'Singapore is not Bangalore's Destiny'. *Economic and Political Weekly* 35:18 (2000), pp. 1512–14.

18. STEM 'An Objective Review on Implementation of Master Plans', vol. I and II (n.d.) as cited in Lakshmi Venkatachalam, 'Urban Planning Processes: A Critique of the Master Plan Concept', mimeo, n.d.

19. Solomon Benjamin, 'Governance, Economic Settings and Poverty in Bangalore', *Environment & Urbanization* 12.1 (April 2000), 47–8, suggests that master-planned areas may account for no more than 20 per cent of the city. This may be an inordinately low estimate, given the high proportion of well spaced out middle-class layouts. The relative importance of unplanned layouts compared with the more modest size of the BDA layouts is acknowledged, without accompanying statistics in A. Ravindra et al., *Report of The Committee on Urban Management of Bangalore City*, November 1997, esp. pp. 94–5.

20. K.S. Rame Gowda, *Urban and Regional Planning: Principles and Case Studies* (Prasaranga, University of Mysore [1972], revised and enlarged, 1986), pp. 109–72.

21. N. Jayaram, 'Sanguine Plans and Stark Realities: Limits to Planned Urban Habitat Change (The Case of Bangalore)', *Nagarlok,* 21.3 (July–Sept. 1989), 36–52, esp. 47.

22. Subbarayan Prasanna and V.S. Vathsala, 'Development Sequences and the Planning Continuum in Bangalore Metropolis', mimeo, 1983.

23. There was renewed optimism that decentralized governance would act as a necessary corrective to top–down planning with the passage of the Nagarpalika Act, 1991. A major advocate of the potential of this layer of government is CIVIC, Bangalore. See 'The Bangalore Comprehensive Development Plan: Philosophy Attitude Process', mimeo, 1997.

24. Ravindra et al., *Report of The Committee on Urban Management of Bangalore City*, p. 132.

25. Ravindra, *Metropolitan Bangalore*, p. 44. A similar plea for regional planning's obvious advantages from an environmental point of view is made by M.N. Buch, *Environmental Consciousness and Urban Planning* (Orient Longman, Hyderabad, 1993).

26. Ravindra et al., *Report of The Committee on Urban Management of Bangalore City*, pp. 89–150.

27. Venkatachalam, 'Urban Planning Processes: A Critique of the Master Plan Concept'.

28. Heitzman, 'Geographic Information Systems in India's "Silicon Valley": The impact of Information Technology on Planning in the 1990s', mimeo, courtesy the author, 2001. Elsewhere, the author suggests that it might be the separation of culture from planning that accounts for the latter's limited success. See 'The Fulfillment of the Planning Model', mimeo, 2001 courtesy the author. The fuller explication of this suggestion is awaited.

29. Benjamin, 'Governance, Economic Settings and Poverty in Bangalore'. Also, Benjamin and Bhuvaneswari, 'Urban Poverty and Governance in Bangalore'.

30. Ibid., p. 195.

31. Madhu Sarin uses the example of Chandigarh for a full length critique of planning as it deprives the urban poor of legal, planned spaces for production. See Sarin, *Urban Planning in the Third World*, p. 133 ff.

32. For a critique of the use of the term 'will' as a pure psychological state in

political discourse, see Sennett, *The Fall of Public Man*, p. 12. 'These words as pure psychological states mislead because they do not explain how a whole society would lose its will altogether, or change its desires. They further mislead in suggesting a therapeutic solution to shake people out of this self absorption, as if the environment which has eroded their social will and transformed their desires might suddenly welcome individuals with open arms.'

33. *The Outline Development Plan (ODP) for the Bangalore Metropolitan Region* (Bangalore, 1963), pp. 16–17.

34. HAL dominated with 42,389 workers, followed by ITI (16448), BEL (13829), HMT (5434), and BHEL (4314). Government of Karnataka, *Bangalore Urban District Industrial Directory* (Bangalore, 1991), as cited in Heitzman, 'Corporate Strategy', PE 11.

35. Hall, *Cities of Tomorrow*, pp. 13–46; Patrick McAuslan, *The Ideology of Planning Law* (London/New York: Pergamon Press, 1980), pp. 2–3. Planning in pre-Independence Bangalore, as I have suggested in chapter one, followed public health concerns. On the imperatives of urban planning to reduce a politically recalcitrant population, see Oldenburg, *The Making of Colonial Lucknow*, pp. 29–41.

36. *Report of the Bangalore Development Committee* (Bangalore 1954), pp. 30–4.

37. Ibid., p. 30.

38. Ibid., p. 107.

39. Ibid., pp. 116–17.

40. Prasanna and Vathsala, 'Development Sequences and the Planning Continuum in Bangalore Metropolis', p. 11, 15. The reorganization of states made Bangalore the capital of an expanded Karnataka state, and 'not less than 30,000 workers' in state and central government offices put further pressure on housing and infrastructure in the city in the late fifties. *The ODP for the Bangalore Metropolitan Region*, p. 6.

41. Administration Report for the year 1957–58, Bangalore City Corporation, p. x; Administration Report for the year 1960–61, Bangalore City Corporation, p. i.

42. An estimated 'one lakh revenue site holders' met at Bangalore city in 1967; this figure may have been somewhat exaggerated. *Deccan Herald*, 15 May 1967; also, *Deccan Herald*, 6 January 1968.

43. Asian Institute of Urban Development, *A Medium Term Development Plan for Bangalore City*, mimeo, Bangalore, 1988, p. 7.

44. Ravindra, *Metropolitan Bangalore: A Management Perspective*, p. 30.

45. *The ODP for the Bangalore Metropolitan Region*, p. 47.

46. Ibid., p. 75.

47. Lefebvre, *The Production of Space*, p. 314.

48. *Report on the Comprehensive Development Plan (CDP) of Bangalore* (Bangalore, 1976), p. 9, 224.

49. See however Venkatrayappa, *Bangalore: A Socio-Ecological Study*, pp. 131–3.

50. For instance, the ODP suggested that 'permission be granted for all new developments in town and villages situated on main roads only on one side even though they might have developed on both sides at present', *ODP for the Bangalore Metropolitan Region*, vol. II, App. C-3, p. 200.

51. The assumption was of course that the maximum number of migrants were from within the state itself; while the earlier trend of inter-state migration was slowing (from 20 to 15 per cent between 1961 and 1981) and even reversing in favour of intra-state migrants, the former still formed a substantial part. See M Johnson Samuel and M. Lingaraju, 'Migrants in Bangalore', Working Paper 13, Institute for Social and Economic Change, Bangalore, 1989.

52. This suggestion was reportedly made by the town planner, K.S. Rame Gowda, 'City Population May Double in 25 Years', *Deccan Herald,* 27 January 1977.

53. *Report on the CDP*, p. 27.

54. For a history of the gradual shift of public interest from drama to cinema, see Venkatrayappa, *Bangalore: A Socio-Ecological Study*, pp. 86–8.

55. *Report on the CDP*, p. 12

56. Ibid., p. 13, 24.

57. *Report on the CDP*, p. 49; also pp. 42–3; the *ODP for the Bangalore Metropolitan Region, Vol. II,* predicted that bicycles would increase to 60,000. As late as 1977, city police suggested separate cycle tracks to cope with the phenomenal increase in traffic. *Deccan Herald,* 8 May 1977.

58. There were 11,000 families on revenue lands in the midst of the city in 1951 (*Report of the Bangalore Development Committee,* p. 25); by 1961 this had increased to 21,000 (*ODP for Bangalore Metropolitan Region, Vol. II*, p. 95). Justifying the supercession of the Corporation in 1966, Chief Minister Nijalingappa said that there were as many as 75,000 unlicenced houses in Bangalore, *Deccan Herald*, 25 Dec. 1966.

59. Minister for Public Works H.K. Veeranna Gowda and B.R. Manickam, chief architect in the 1960s said that the population of Bangalore had to be kept down by discouraging new industries and encouraging 'vertical development', criticizing the uncoordinated housing schemes of the government which kept BEL and HMT townships half a mile apart. *Deccan Herald*, 16 Jan. 1962. Also, there was a call for vertical growth *Deccan Herald*, 26 June 1962. However, just ten years later the chairman of the City Improvement Trust Board, Padmanabha, suggested that 'the city could only become beautiful if individual households paid attention to beauty as they did in the old days, by leaving space around the houses for gardens.' *Deccan Herald*, 3 Oct. 1973.

60. Prakasa Rao and V.K. Tewari, *The Structure of an Indian Metropolis*, p. 329.

61. Ibid., p. 270–1.

62. *Comprehensive Development Plan (Revised) Bangalore—Report*, vol. I and II, (Bangalore, 1995), p. 28.

63. G.V.K. Rao, *Report on an Enquiry Conducted under Section 64 of Karnataka Co-operative Societies Act 1959 into the activities of certain House Building Co-operative Societies of Bangalore City,* 1988 (hereafter *G.V.K. Rao Committee Report*).

64. Ownership flats were first advertised in the early 1970s, though they held only limited appeal until the end of the decade. *Deccan Herald*, 2 Sept. 1973.

65. In 1984, the Bangalore Corporation framed new building by-laws which permitted high rise buildings for commercial use in some areas. Ravindra, *Metropolitan Bangalore: A Management Perspective*, p. 38.

66. Thus the former BCC administrator Lakshman Rau, a vigorous supporter of the 'city beautiful' concept, became an advocate of apartment living: 'Very low density extensions are coming up all around. It is desirable to have a reasonable density so as to reduce the physical area of the city and make it more manageable.' 'High Rise Buildings Apartment Living', Lakshman Rau, Private Papers.

67. *Comprehensive Development Plan (CDP) Report*, 1985, p. 2.

68. Interview with Lakshmi Venkatachalam, 3 March 1999.

69. Lefebvre, 'Right to the City' in *Writings on Cities*, p. 79–80.

70. Heitzman, *Network City*, p. 79.

71. 'Posh Colony in City, for Foreign Returned', *Deccan Herald*, 14 Aug. 1976; 'House Sites for Indians Living Abroad', *Deccan Herald*, 27 Oct. 1977.

72. For a detailed discussion of the suburban public realm which has succeeded in realizing this dream in the US, see Southworth and Parthasarathy, 'The Suburban Public Realm'.

73. Government of Karnataka, KUID Project *Executive Summaries* produced by GHK International Limited UK, in association with TISS and Tata Economic Consultancy Services, July 1998, p. 1.

74. Heitzman, 'Corporate Strategy and Planning', PE 9.

75. Tim Campbell and Bill Wickstead, 'The Spatial Implications of Technology Development in Bangalore' (New Delhi: USAID, 1987), p. 20.

76. Ibid., pp. 23, 42.

77. The companies included such leading corporates as Microland, Eindiabiz.com, Future Techno Design, Tata Infotech, Oracle Solutions, Pentasoft, Samsung, Planetasia, Bharti Telesoft, indya.com, and Aztec, all of whom had occupied unauthorized structures. *Deccan Herald*, 12 March 2001.

78. 'World Class Lifestyle at IT Township', in *Economic Times* feature 'Karnataka IT's Powerhouse', p. 5; also interview 27 March 1999 in which he said 'we would like it to be an independent republic'.

79. Nearly all the material for this section was provided by Dilip Subramanian, to whom I am extremely grateful.

80. Kasturbhai Lalbhai, *Report on the State Owned and State Aided Industrial Concerns in Mysore* Bangalore, 1951.

81. The acquisition of 113 acres 29 *gunta*s of land in Doddabommasandra and Kodigehalli of Yelahanka hobli in Bangalore north for BEL was challenged by 56 owners who demanded higher compensation than Rs 1500 per acre. The arbitrator sanctioned Rs 3500 and the court Rs 5000 on the basis of its proximity to the city. *Union of India v. Narasiyappa and Others*, *MLJ* 1970, (1).

82. *Committee on Public Undertakings* (COPU), 1964.

83. *Committee on Public Undertakings* (COPU), 8th report: Third Lok Sabha on Townships and Factory Buildings of Public Undertakings May 1965 (Lok Sabha Secretariat, Delhi).

84. Internal management note, 21 Nov. 1966.

85. *Bangalore Development Committee Report*, p. 32.

86. *Report on Industrial Townships: Committee on Plan Projects* (Building Projects Team), New Delhi, May 1963), p. 8

87. Ibid., p.42.

88. Ibid., p. 34

89. The provision of a 'void deck' in multi-storied public housing in Singapore is among the most ambitious plans to architecturally reorient social life in a city. Detailed discussions of these spaces are in Chua Beng Huat, *Political Legitimacy and Housing*, and Robbie Goh 'Things to A Void: Utopian Discourse, Communality and Constructed Interstices in Singapore Public Housing'.

90. Government of Mysore: Subsidized Industrial Housing Scheme GO no. LLH 315 Hos 58 dt. 20.11.1959.

91. Management Circulars dated 8 Aug. 1987 and 20 Jan. 1989.

92. Management Document on Welfare Activities, 1967–8.

93. *History of BEEU and Bharat Electronics*, pp. 10, 14.

94. Letter dated 20 Aug. 1961 from N.V. Shenoi, General Manager to T. Subramanyam, Karnataka Minister for Development and Local Self Government.

95. D.V.M. Rao, ITI company secretary to secretary, Ministry of Local Self Government and Public Health Department, 26 April 1961.

96. D.V.M. Rao to B. Venkatramana, deputy secretary, Public Health, Labour and Municipal Administration Department, 6 July 1965.

97. Internal note dated 8 April 1962.

98. GO 359 Gazette Notification no. PLM 64 MNZ65 dt. 15 Feb. 1973 extended the ITI notified area to include B. Narayanapura, Vijinapura, Kowdenahally, Seegehally, Sonnathammanahally, Basavapura, Dyavasandra, and K.R. Puram, in effect integrating the KR Puram village panchayat with the ITI notified Area.

99. Note from T. Ramadasappa, union vice president to Executive Committee.

100. No HUD 5 DML 84.

101. Proceedings of meeting regarding assessment of property tax of ITI Notified Area dt. 27 April 1987.

102. By government notification no. HUD 165 MNY 91 (11) dt 30.6.92 both the areas were absorbed in the Bangalore Corporation, though the factory areas were exempt from the final notification.

103. Ravindra, *Metropolitan Bangalore: A Management Perspective*, p. 132.

104. V. Keerthi Shekhar, 'Sociography of Satellite Towns', in R. Ram Mohan Rao and S. Simhadri (eds), *Indian Cities: Towards the Next Millenium* (Jaipur and Delhi, Rawat Publications, 1999), pp. 49–79, esp. p. 53.

105. Ibid., pp. 68–9, 71.

106. Interview, Lakshman Rau, 22 Aug. 1998.

107. Schenk and De Wit (eds), *Living in India's Slums*, 2000.

108. H. Ramachandran and Daljeet Singh, 'Structures and Correlates of Home Based Manufacturing Activities in Slums', in Schenk and De Wit (eds), *Living in India's Slums*, pp. 217–37.

109. Prakasa Rao and Tewari, *The Structure of an Indian Metropolis*, p. 351.

110. H. Ramachandra, 'Slumming of a Metropolis', in Reddy and Vyasulu, convenors, *Essays on Bangalore*, pp. 37–50.

111. 'Survey of Slums in Bangalore', vol. I Analytical Report, p. 2; M de Wit's study of Bangalore slums in 1992 seems to confirm that there are 411 slums of all descriptions, which accounts for approximately 20 per cent of the city population. M de Wit. 'Geographical Information Systems Remote Sensing in Indian Cities: The Case of Bangalore' (IDPAD Occasional Papers and Reprints, 1992–8), p. 60.

112. Mertens, 'Forced Relocation of Slum Dwellers in Bangalore, p. 14. The official assessment alone gives the extraordinary impression that the number of slums in the city have actually declined in the 1990s, from 401 in 1986–7 to 339 in 1996–7. Karnataka Slum Clearance Board, *Saalina Vaarshika Varadi*, 1996–7, p. 4

113. The *Committee of the Legislators on the Slum Problems in Bangalore City: Interim Report* expressed surprise at the economic life of slums despite their illegality, mimeo, Lakshman Rau Papers, p. 8.

114. Tamils form the largest linguistic community in the slums of Bangalore, and a variety of reasons have been attributed to this. The interim Report of the Committee of Legislators on the Slum Problems of Bangalore, constituted in 1979, had this to say about reasons for the large number of Tamils migrating to the state: 'One other reason for people migrating from Tamil Nadu is due to the prohibition policy of that state.' Mimeo, p. 7. The benefits of NGO activity have largely flowed to Tamil inhabitants of slums, and this is sometimes advanced as a reason for, rather than a consequence of, large Tamil populations. See De Wit, 'Geographical Information Systems', p. 58.

115. N. Lakshman Rau, Bangalore City Corporation Endowment Lecture, 5 April 1989.

116. Interview with N. Lakshman Rau, 29 Sep. 1998.

117. Ibid.

118. Mertens, 'Forced Relocation of Slum Dwellers', p. 17.

119. Interview with Parvathiamma, 26 May 1999.

120. Interview with Veera Sundari Amma, 5 July 1999.

121. Interview with Parvathiamma, 26 May 1999; interview with Veera Sundari Amma, 5 July 1999; WP no. 1778/94 Public Interest Litigation on behalf of 805 families.

122. Interview with Shaikh Pir Sahib, May 1999.

123. Peter Giessen, 'Household Industries and their Market Relations: A Case Study of the Situation of Petty Commodity Producers in Bangalore, South India', mimeo, 1988.

124. Interview with Shaikh Pir Sahib, May 1999.

125. All this information is from WP No. 1778/94, *Slum Dwellers Association* v. *Government of Karnataka and Others.*

126. Communication from N. Kannan.

127. WP 8378 of 1992. *N. Kannan* v. *Government of Karnataka and Others.*

128. It has forced several women of Tilaknagar to assert their rights to a space of their own. Such intra-familial negotiation is discussed in Chapter 8 below.

129. WP 8378 of 1992. *N. Kannan* v. *Government of Karnataka and Others.*

130. P. Sudarshan, 'Relocation of Slum Dwellers: A Case Study of Sanjay Gandhi Nagar in Bangalore', MPhil. dissertation, University of Hyderabad, 1998, p. 96.

131. Ibid., pp. 99–100.

132. Ibid.

133. Ibid., pp. 128, 129.

134. Ibid., p. 117.

135. Mertens, 'Forced Relocation of Slum Dwellers', p. 29.

136. Sudarshan, 'Relocation of Slum Dwellers', p. 106.

137. The two cases cited by Mertens are CSI slum and Shaktivenagar, whose residents delayed relocation for about 6 years in each case. 'Forced Relocation of Slum Dwellers', p. 29.

138. Ibid., p. 81.

139. Benjamin and Bhuvaneswari et al., 'Urban Poverty and Governance in Bangalore', p. 33.

140. Prakasa Rao and Tewari, *The Structure of an Indian Metropolis,* p. 268.

141. *Census of India, 1981*, District Census Handbook, Bangalore. pp. xxix–xxx.

142. K.S. Rame Gowda, 'Fringe Area development in Metropolitan Centres with Special Reference to Bangalore', *National Symposium on Planning and Development of Metropolitan Bangalore* (Bangalore, 1987).

143. The Karnataka Gazetteer lists 131 villages as fully absorbed in the BCC and BDA on the basis of the 1981 census. *Gazetteer of India, Karnataka State, Bangalore District*, 1990, pp. 986–7.

144. Interview with Lakshmi Venkatachalam, 3 March 1999.

145. Holmstrom, 'Religious Change in an Industrial City of South India', pp. 28–40.

146. Ibid., p. 89.

147. Beals, 'Change in the Leadership of a Mysore Village', p. 154.

148. Corporation of the City of Bangalore, Administrative Report for the Year 1964–65, p. 172.

149. Corporation of the City of Bangalore, Administration report for the year 1967–68, p. 67.

150. Corporation of the City of Bangalore, Administration report for the year 1969–70, Appendix A, p. 203.

151. Nearly all 560 people who worked in the agarbathi industry at Padarayanpura were women and chidren. Three systems of manufacture prevailed, ranging from the classic 'putting out' system which was controlled by the merchants and a system which used local agents to support home based manufacture to one which brought workers to workshops for the production of perfumed agarbathis. The latter were marginally better paid than the first two categories of workers, but the report noted the poor conditions of work and standards of payment while feeling unable to intervene.

152. 'This indeed is a haven of all ills', *Deccan Herald*, 30 July 2000.

153. On the efforts of the Tigalas in Bangalore District to retain their horticultural lands, and even demand the allotment of new lands near the city, see Smriti Srinivas, *Landscapes of Urban Memory*, pp. 121–3.

154. Mumford, *The City in History*, p. 7.

155. Sennett, *The Conscience of the Eye*, pp. 172–3.

156. 'If you want to grab a site, build a temple', *Deccan Herald*, 12 Dec. 1994.

157. WP no. 11976/84 for Sy. no. 345 of Banaswadi, Law Department, BDA.

158. In another instance, a landowner pleaded for the denotification of his land acquired by the BDA for Jnanabharati Layout on grounds that his ancestors had been buried there. WP no. 16660/1998. *K.G. Vijayakumar* v. *State of Karnataka and Others*. Law Department, BDA.

159. *Deccan Herald*, 14 March 1997; 18 May 1997; *Indian Express*, 21 July 1997.

160. *Indian Express*, 26 Feb. 1995.

161. *Indian Express*, 21 March 1995.

162. Special 'Shiv Kaun Banega Crorepati' shows were organized on the occasion of Shivarathri in 2001, with a box improvised for letters to God. 'Spirituality Takes a Back Seat', *Hindu*, 22 Feb. 2001.

163. See Clive Bell, 'Ideology and Economic Interests in Indian Land reform', in David Lehman (ed.), *Agrarian Reform and Agrarian Reformism* (London: Faber & Faber, 1974), pp. 190–220, esp. 218. I am grateful to V.K. Natraj for this reference.

164. *Prajavani*, 21 April 2001.

165. 'Krishna kannige beelada "krishna" samipada "naga"', *Prajavani*, 12 June 2001. Another report was illustrated with a photograph that showed the traffic having to split up and flow around an island caused by a temple. 'Yediyurinalli ganapatiya anadhikrita devasthana', *Prajavani*, 20 June 2001.

166. 'Beedigilida bhagavantha, prathishtitha rastheya koduge', *Prajavani*, 15 June 1991 reported on the three illegal shrines that have come up opposite Mayo Hall; 'Shrine under BMP's Shade', *Deccan Herald*, 5 Aug. 2001 noted that a temple that had come up 'bang in front of the ward office of BMP in Vijayanagar'.

167. Interview with Lakshmi Venkatachalam, 3 March 1999.

168. The project entitled 'In the City of God: Contemporary Religious Architecture in Bangalore', is underway; personal communication from Annapurna Garimella.

169. 'Beedigilida bhagavantha'.

170. 'Hindu baandhavaralli manavi', (n.d.) N. Lakshman Rau Private Papers.

171. Peter Hall, *Cities of Tomorrow*, pp. 170–1.

172. H. Ramachandran, 'Greening of a Metropolis: An Analysis of Open Spaces In and Around Bangalore', ISEC Working Paper, p. 22.

173. *Report of the Bangalore Development Committee*, 1954, p. 17.

174. Ibid., p. 107. On p. 69, this same area was calculated at 2500 acres. The other zones were: administrative, commercial, industrial, and residential zones, based on existing land use, p. 104.

175. Ibid., p. 68.

176. Ibid., p. 107. The quotations, though unattributed, were from Abercrombie. See Hall, *Cities of Tomorrow,* p. 171.

177. *Report of the Bangalore Development Committee,* 1954, p. 111.

178. Ibid., p 115.

179. Rame Gowda, *Urban and Regional Planning,* p. 113.

180. This zoning is based on social uses of space, see Venkatrayappa, *Bangalore: A Socio–Ecological Study*. His rather selective zones include, 1. the business zone, 2. the factory zone, 3. the agricultural zone, 4. the culture zone, 5. the middle-class residential zone, 6. the retired people's zone, 7. the military zone. See also, Noel Gist, 'The Ecology of Bangalore, India: An East West Comparison', in *Indian Cities,* pp. 15–33.

181. Venkatrayappa, *Bangalore: A Socio–Ecological Study,* p. 146.

182. *The ODP for the Bangalore Metropolitan Region* (Feb. 1963), p. 5.

183. Ibid., p. 6.

184. Cf *Report of the Bangalore Development Committee* 1954, p. 107 and *Report on the CDP*, 1976, p. 60.

185. *CDP*, 1985, p. 23.

186. *CDP*, 1985 p. 25. The words once more are taken from Abercrombie.

187. *CDP* (revised), 1995, p. 78.

188. L.R. Vagale, 'The Green Belt: Can it Check the Growth of Bangalore?', in *National Symposium on Planning and Development of Metropolitan Bangalore*, pp. 13–14.

189. Ravindra, *Metropolitan Bangalore: A Management Perspective,* p. 64.

190. Report of Court Appointed Commissioner Prabha Murthy on Green Belt Violations: in WP 31562 of 1997, (BDA PIL) *Krishna Bhat* v. *BDA and Others*, p. 2.

191. 'CM Cautions Poor Owners', *Deccan Herald*, 21 March 1976.

192. In a pun that can have only limited appeal, the brochure advertising the Acropolis says 'It's so Greek, that everything else looks Spartan'.

193. The concept of the gated city with respect to Los Angeles and Sao Paulo has been more fully explored in Caldeira 'Fortified Enclaves: The New Urban Segregation'. Mike Davis explores the concept of 'Fortress LA' in his forceful critique of the segregation that architecture has enabled. *The City of Quartz*, pp. 223–4.

194. 'Violation of Land Laws: Action against 52 Clubs, Resorts', *Hindu*, 29 May 2001.

195. 'Bangalore: The Next Singapore?', in *Inside Bangalore: The Ideal Address*, pp. 22–3.

196. See Nair, 'Singapore is not Bangalore's Destiny'.

197. Partha Chatterjee and Asok Sen, 'Planning and the Political Process in India: Duality and Differentiation', in A.K. Bagchi (ed.), *Economy Society Polity: Essays in the Political Economy of Indian Planning: Essays in Honour of Prof Bhabhatosh Dutta* (Calcutta: OUP, 1988), pp. 196–226, esp. p. 216.

Chapter Four: The Map is not the Territory: Law and the Production of Space

1. Extract of a letter from Officer Commanding at Bangalore to the Quarter Master Brigade in Mysore, dated 14 December 1814, *Select Papers relating to the Origin and Administration of the Civil and Military Station, Bangalore, 1807–59*, KSA. Note that the 'road' is referred to as a part of 'nature' in this context.

2. A.H. Cole, Resident to G. Strachey, Chief Secretary to Government, Fort St George, 8 Dec. 1815, ibid.

3. Mark Cubbon to Chief Secretary to Government, Fort St George, 24 Sept. 1857, File no. 1, Sl. 1–8, 1857–58, General Misc., KSA.

4. File no. 259 of 1909–10, sl. no. 1–8, General Misc., KSA.

5. I am aware that my use of the term map here corresponds to the intentionality of the state, and not to mental maps or other imaginings that may and certainly do exist, a point to which I return below. I am grateful to V.K. Natraj for urging me to draw this distinction at a seminar in Chennai, April 2000.

6. Lefebvre, *Writings on Cities*, p. 103.

7. Castells, *The Urban Question*, 129–233.

8. Karl Marx, *Capital*, vol. one, Introduced by Ernest Mandel and translated by Ben Fowkes (New York: Vintage Books, 1977), p. 164.

9. Lefebvre, *Writings on Cities*, p. 195–6.

10. See, for instance, Ravindra *Metropolitan Bangalore: A Management Perspective*, pp. 119–41; *Report of the Committee on Urban Management of Bangalore City*, pp. 100–18.

11. On the imperfect nature of the housing market by definition, see David Harvey, 'Society, the City and the Space Economy of Urbanism', Association of American Geographers, Paper no. 18, 1972, p. 16.

12. *Deccan Herald*, 19 Feb. 1971.

13. *Deccan Herald*, 20 Feb. 1971; 23 Feb. 1971.

14. *Deccan Herald*, 23 Feb. 1971.

15. *Deccan Herald*, 1 June 1971.

16. Interview with Lakshmi Venkatachalam, 13 March 1999.

17. See James Manor, 'Pragmatic Progressives in Regional Politics: The Case of Devaraj Urs', *Economic and Political Weekly*, Annual Number, February 1980, pp.

201–13, esp. p. 201. See also, Manor, 'Structural Changes in Karnataka Politics', *Economic and Political Weekly,* 29 Oct. 1977, pp. 1865–9.

18. 'City Development Authority set up by Ordinance', *Deccan Herald*, 18 Feb. 1975; 'BDA Bill Voted with CPI Amendment', *Deccan Herald*, 13 Feb. 1976.

19. 'Urban Ceiling Act in Force: Curbs on Land Transfer', *Deccan Herald*, 22 Feb. 1976.

20. 'Statutory Art Commission set up for City', *Deccan Herald*, 18 March 1976.

21. *Deccan Herald,* 12 May 1975; 31 May 1975.

22. *Deccan Herald,* 26 July 1975.

23. 'Urs Hopes BDA will make City Beautiful', *Deccan Herald*, 18 Jan. 1976; 'City site owners will have to plant trees', *Deccan Herald,* 12 Feb. 1976.

24. These are statistics from the BDA. However, Ravindra, *Metropolitan Bangalore*, p. 137, suggests that 31 per cent of the area identified as excess until 1987, i.e. 3445 out of 11,321 acres, was acquired under the act.

25. Arun Kumar, 'National Housing Policy: The Implications', *Economic and Political Weekly*, 24.23 (10 June 1989), pp. 1285–94, esp. p. 1285.

26. Curbs on conspicuous consumption implied vigilance by state agencies, including a survey of posh houses in select areas of the city, while the urban poor were protected by checks on prices in hotels and curbs on rents charged to slum dwellers. 'IT Department Survey of Posh Areas in the City', *Deccan Herald*, 3 July 1976.

27. The peak period was May–June 1985. 'Fiat against razing of city slums', *Deccan Herald*, 21 July 1985, 'Slum Clearance with Sops: CM', *Deccan Herald*, 17 July 1985.

28. An ordinance issued by government on 10.9.1980 (Karnataka Ordinance no. 8 of 1980), which amended the Karnataka Land Revenue Act, gave the benefit of conversion as a matter of right, but was quickly withdrawn on 28.4.81, though not before a boom in revenue site holders had already occurred. White Paper on the Bangalore Development Authority, 1980–83 (1984), 26–7. Also, Report submitted by BDA to Ananth Nag, Minister for Bangalore development, Jan. 1997, p. 17.

29. Government letter no HUD 36 MNX 86 12.10.1987.

30. *Times of India*, 3 June 1995.

31. *K.C. Raju Reddy* v. *Commissioner, BDA* 1995 (4) Karnataka Law Journal (KLJ), 475.

32. *Deccan Herald*, 18 July 1997; *Hindu*, 19 July 1997. On Michael Saldanha's role as activist judge in the 1990s, see chapter 2 above.

33. 'Demolition in RMV II stage resisted', *Deccan Herald*, 8 June 1983.

34. Initially the BCC took possession of three floors of Palace Orchard Apartments and Rajmahal Apartments in Raj Mahal Extension as decreed by the Supreme Court. *Deccan Herald*, 6 March 1992. Later, it refused to comply with the Supreme Court orders to demolish them. Permission was granted to Bhaktavar Construction Company in 1980 to build eight floors; 64 residential units were built. 'High Rise Buildings in

RMV Extension: SC declares Corporation Licences illegal', *Economic Times*, 27 Feb. 1996.

35. 'Buying Trouble the Costly Way', *Deccan Herald*, 2 April 1988.

36. *Deccan Herald,* 16 March 1996; *Hindu,* 29 Feb. 1996; *Economic Times*, 21 Feb. 1996.

37. *Narasimha Murthy* v. *State of Mysore,* 1967 (1) Mysore Law Journal (MLJ).

38. See Nair, 'Predatory Capitalism and Legalised Land Grab: Karnataka Land Reforms', *Economic and Political Weekly*, 31.5 (1996), pp. 251–2.

39. 'Land Ceiling Act Scrapped', *Times of India*, 9 July 1999.

40. Karnataka Regularization of Unauthorized Construction Act, 1991.

41. 'Town and Country Planning Bill Passed Amid Protests', *Deccan Herald*, 7 July 1999.

42. Thus, although the high court banned reconveyance by the BDA, the government took the decision to reconvey under Section 38c of the BDA act on 31.3.1994. *Report submitted by BDA to Ananth Nag, Minister for Bangalore Development*, p. 18.

43. Press note by B.K. Chandrasekhar, 29 March 1999; discussion note from CIVIC.

44. The GHK report put the estimate of unoccupied flats at 82,000; builders place the figure at a much higher 200,000. The grotesque inequalities of the market show up in the more or less equal match between the number of those who need homes in the city and the number of houses that await occupation.

45. '30,000 Sites Allotted by BDA', *Hindu*, 5 March 2003.

46. Partial possession was given 'in view of public interest' to the builders of Diamond District, Century Galaxy Development Pvt. Ltd. A fine was collected for an additional eighth floor and basement, which violated the original building plans by as much as 31 per cent. 'Government Ignores Building Plan Violation?' *Hindu*, 11 Nov. 1999.

47. See *Report of The Committee on Urban Management of Bangalore City*, 1997, p. 1 Annex. 1.

48. *CDP (Revised) Report*, 1995, p. 3.

49. This figure is from Heitzman, 'Geographic Information Systems in India's "Silicon Valley", p. 8. However, as we shall see below, this may be partial or inaccurate.

50. See Comprehensive Development Plan Report (Bangalore, 1985), p. 3. Comprehensive Development Plan (Revised) Bangalore, Report (Bangalore, 1995), p. 21. The former has been cited verbatim in Ravindra *Metropolitan Bangalore: A Management Perspective*, p. 81.

51. *Report of the Review Committee on BDA* (Bangalore, BDA, 1991), vol. VI, p. 2.1.

52. *White Paper on the BDA,* 1980–3.

53. *Court appointed commissioner Prabha Murthy on Green Belt violations in response to WP 31562 of 1997, filed by B. Krishna Bhat*, mimeo, BDA.

54. Thus, while an internal committee found that between 1976 and 1990 41 layouts had been formed by the BDA, the legislative assembly was informed in 1997 only about 34 layouts!

55. *White Paper on the BDA*, 1980–3, Annex. I–V (F).

56. Here too, there is a discrepancy as the *Times of India* reported that the BDA was then engaged in 6334 cases 'which include those challenging the acquisition by the BDA in several schemes, suits for permanent injunction and declaration of title, consumer redressal, suits for enhanced compensation etc.' 9 Sept. 1997.

57. *M.S. Narayanappa* v. *Special Land Acquisition Officer, CITB*, Bangalore, AIR 1966, vol. 53; *G. Gurubasappa* v. *SLAO, City Municipality and Others*, AIR 1959, vol. 46; *Special Land Acquisition Officer CITB* v. *Chikkaboranna,* AIR 1968, vol. 55; *Union of India and Others* v. *Narsappa and Others*, MLJ, 1970 (1). Also, *Land Acquisition Officer CITB* v. *Narayanaiah K.*, KLJ, 1976 (2).

58. The pattern of landownership in Bangalore District, shown below, was broad-based. Holdings of less than two hectares, according to the agricultural census of 1976–7, constituted as much as 73.6 per cent of total landholdings, and 34.7 per cent of total land held.

Size of Holding	Percentage	Lands held (percentage)
Less than one hectare:	49.8	14.9
Between 1 and 2 ha:	23.8	19.8
Between 2 and 5 ha:	20.2	35.3
Between 5 and 10 ha:	4.9	18.9
Above 10 ha:	1.3	11.1

SOURCE: *Bangalore District Census Handbook, 1981*, xxxv.

59. *Special Land Acquisition Officer CITB* v. *J.B. Kempanna Setty Charities*, MLJ, 1972 (2)

60. *A.K. Ahmed* v. *Special Land Acquisition Officer*, KLJ, 1974 (2). The court ruled that when land is taken over under Eminent Domain, then vines trees, etc. cannot be separately valued.

61. *Bangalore City Municipality* v. *Sub Division Officer, Bangalore and Others*—MLJ, vol. 27 (1946). Also, *T. Adinarayan Shetty* v. *Special Land Acquisition Officer* AIR 1954, Mys 71, vol. 41; *KGNS Sangha, Avalahalli Bangalore South Taluk* v. *Kota Srinivasa Murthy (since deceased) by LRs and Others* 1998 (1) KLJ, 227 (DB).

62. *Union of India and Others* v. *Narsappa and Others,* MLJ 1970 (1)

63. Ramachandran, 'The Greening of a Metropolis, p.15.

64. *Subbanna* v. *State of Karnataka* 1996 (5) KLJ, 190 (DB*)*

65. *M. Maniklal* v. *State of Mysore*, MLJ, 1968 (1).

66. Forty-three societies had committed serious and grave irregularities, and 15 admitted bogus members. *G.V.K. Rao Committee Report*, 1988.

67. Ibid., p. 4.

68. Ibid., Annex., p. 3.

69. *Report of the Review Committee on BDA* (Bangalore, BDA, 1991), vol. I, p. 11.

70. In their judgement on *HMT House Building Co-operative Society* v. *Syed Khader and Others (1996* (6) KLJ 322 (SC DB), Justices J.S. Verma, N.P. Singh, and S.P. Bharucha upheld the HC verdict that these acquisitions of property were 'not for the purpose of *bona fide* housing schemes'. The expanded view of public purpose in Section 3 (f) (vi), 39, 40 and 44A specified that 'The provision of land for carrying out any housing scheme with prior approval of the state government by a Co-operative society within the meaning of any law relating to Co-operative societies for the time being in force in any state shall be deemed to be "public purpose".'

71. *Narayan Reddy* v. *State of Karnataka,* 1991 (3) KLJ 545 (DB)

72. *Bangalore District Central Bank Employee's Co-operative Society Ltd* v. *BDA and another* KLJ 1989 (1).

73. By Order no. HUD 113 MNX 85 dated 18 June 1985, the government declared that housing cooperatives must approach BDA for acquiring land in Bangalore Metropolitan area.

74. BDA Register of Sites: Approval of Layouts.

75. *Vishwa Bharati House Building Co-operative Society* v. *BDA*, KLJ 1989 (3).

76. *Vishwa Bharati House Building Co-operative Society Limited* v. *Bangalore Development Authority*, KLJ 1990 (1).

77. *Kanthamma and Others* v. *State of Karnataka and another*, KLJ 1984 (2).

78. 'Housing Shortage: Government to Encourage Builders: CM Announces Policy Decision', *Deccan Herald*, 8 July 1987.

79. *H.N. Nanje Gowda and another* v. *State of Karnataka and Others* 1996 (3) KLJ 39 (DB).

80. *Annayya and others* v. *State of Karnataka and Others* 1988 (2) KLJ.

81. *S.S. Darshan* v. *State of Karnataka,* KLJ 1995 (4). (DB).

82. *IBM World Trade Corporation* v. *Assistant Commissioner and Competent authority and another,* KLJ 1979 (2); *Assistant Commissioner and competent authority* v. *IBM World Trade Corporation*, KLJ 1981 (2). See also, *BDA* v. *Dr H.S. Hanumanthappa* in which the exemption granted under ULCRA to M.S. Ramaiah Institutions in north Bangalore was cited as the reason for granting similar exemptions.

83. *Narayan Raju* v. *State of Karnataka and Others,* KLJ 1988 (3): appeals were dismissed against acquisition of lands by the Vijaya Bank House Building Cooperative Society, in which government did not have a share, on grounds that it was indeed acquisition for a public purpose.

84. *Mrs Behroze Ramyar Batha and Others* v. *Special Land Acquisition Office, Bangalore and Others*, KLJ 1992 (1). Also, *Deccan Herald,* 23 May 1989.

85. James Heitzman, 'Sports and Conflict in Urban Planning: The Indian National Games in Bangalore', *Journal of Sport and Social Issues*, vol. 23.1, Feb. 1999. 5–23; Amanda Parry, 'Law and Urban Change in an Indian City', in Fernandes and Varley (eds), *Illegal Cities*.

86. *Mrs Behroze Ramyar Batha and Others* v. *Special Land Acquisition Officer, Bangalore and Others*, KLJ 1992 (1).

87. The meeting held on 13 Janaury 1987 included Dr H.G.V. Reddy, chairman, BDA, Bapu Heddur Shetty, chairman, KSTDC, S.R. Vijay, IAS, commissioner BDA, Sri Sreenivasan, managing director, KSTDC, and Dayanand Pai, agreement holder.

88. All the information that follows, unless otherwise indicated, comes from the *Justice Kuldip Singh Commission of Enquiry, Report*, vol. I (June 1990).

89. 'HC Stays Formation of NRI Layout in City', 1 Feb. 1989; 'Government Rejects Bulk Allotment Proposals' of five NRI schemes, *Deccan Herald*, 19 Feb. 1989.

90. 'Ikkattinalli benami mukhyamantri', *Lankesh Patrike*, 5 Feb. 1989; 'Anivasa bharatiyara hesarinalli hegde reddy kolle', *Lankesh Patrike*, 25 Dec. 1988; 'H.G.V. reddy viruddha criminal mokaddamme agathya', *Lankesh Patrike*, 1 Jan. 1989.

91. 'Ombathu revajeetugala patta', *Lankesh Patrike*, 21 May 1989; also 'Hegde ondu aasthithanikhe', 27 March 1988; 'Revajeetu: ondu pratibhatane', 8 May 1988; and 'Revajeethu filina minchina sanchara', 17 April 1988.

92. The property totalled 5 acres and 5 *gunta*s, which was 3444 sq. metres more than the exempted land.

93. 'Public Interest Used to Promote Private Gain?', *Deccan Herald*, 15 April 1988; 'Sale of Land to CM's Relative', *Deccan Herald*, 14 April 1988.

94. *B.S. Muddappa and Others* v. *State of Karnataka and Others*, KLJ 1989 (2)

95. *Muniswamy Reddy and Ningamma Trust and another* v. *State of Karnataka and Others*, 1995 KLJ (6) 55B (DB); *Residents' of MICO Layout II Stage and Others* v. *JSS Mahavidya Peeta Mysore and Others*, 1997 (4) KLJ 442; *SG Heble and Others* v. *BDA and Others*, 1997 (7) KLJ 352. Other cases include WP no. 12481/93, *Kalyan Cooperative Housing Society* v. *BDA/BCC/Bapujinagar Attiguppe Site Owners' association and 10 Others.*; WP 28241/1995, *Model Housing Co-operative Society Limited* v. *Basaveshwaranagar and BDA*; WP 13148/1998, *Vijayanagar East Tax Payers' Association (regd) RPC Layout Vijayanagar and four others* v. *State of Karnataka and Others.*

96. *V. Lakshmipathy and others* v. *State of Karnataka and Others*, KLJ, 1991 (2) 453.

97. 'Sital Value of Sites: Petitions Dismissed', *Hindu*, 15 Dec. 1998.

98. Residents of Amarjyothi layout, a site of many unresolved contests between the landowners, the army, and the BDA, filed a petition seeking BDA amenities. 'Petition Seeks Amenities in Amarjyothi Layout', *Deccan Herald*, 27 Aug. 1999.

99. *B. Krishna Bhat and Others* v. *BDA*, KLJ, 1988 (2) against BDA levying property tax.

100. 'Girinagarada avantarakari krishna bhatta', *Lankesh Patrike*, 6 May 1990;

'Maththe krishna bhattana avanthara', *Lankesh Patrike*, 8 April 1990; 'Krishna bhatta enba kalla bengalurina mugdarannu vanchisiddu', *Lankesh Patrike*, 26 June 1983.

101. *WP 292/89 Krishna Bhat* v. *Government of Karnataka and BDA*.

102. 'GO Permitting Buildings on Nursery Land Stayed', *Deccan Herald*, 3 Feb. 1998.

103. It concluded, however, that 'the problem and the pain of the residents of Defence Colony are not peculiar to them. Every resident of Bangalore shares their misfortune in equal measure but as long as the builder operates within the framework of the law, this court within its realm can do nothing about it.' *Major General M.K.Paul and Others* v. *Bangalore City Corporation*, KLJ, 1994 (2) 158.

104. By the late 1990s, this petitioner too succumbed to the pressures of the market and allowed construction of an apartment building on his land. Personal communication from M.K. Paul.

105. In April 1969, the CITB evicted 100 slum-dwellers from Palace orchards without notice. *Deccan Herald*, 28 April 1969. In February that year one of the first multi-storeyed buildings on Residency Road, Khivraj Motors, obtained a stay on the demolition although they had not obtained BCC permission for the construction, *Deccan Herald*, 8 Feb. 1969.

106. Mertens, 'Forced Relocation of Slum Dwellers in Bangalore', pp. 58–63.

107. There is a disturbing frequency to the use of the metaphor of fire in the discourse on the slum. See, for instance, *Slum Suddhi* 3.2 (April–June 1999), pp. 4–5, on the use of fire as a device for 'clearance' this time not of forests or shrubs but of people. Also, *Slum Suddhi* 1.1 (Jan. 1998), p. 9; sometimes the targets were individuals. *Slum Suddhi* 2.2 (Feb. 1999), p. 3.

108. Ravindra, *Metropolitan Bangalore: A Management Perspective*, p. 85.

109. White paper on the BDA, p. 14.

110. *Bengaluru abhivruddhi pradhikarakke vasathi mathu nagaraabhivruddhi ilakeya vishaya samitiya maanya ahdyaksharu maththu sadasyara bheti*, 15/12/1995: *prashnothara tippani*, (BDA 1995), p. 24.

111. Ravindra, *Metropolitan Bangalore: A Management Perspective*, p. 85.

112. For instance, Ravindra, *Metropolitan Bangalore: A Management Perspective*, pp. 86–7; Ravindra et al., *Report of the Committee on Urban Management of Bangalore City*, pp. 109–10.

113. Interview with Parvathiamma, 25 May 1999.

114. *Deccan Herald*, 29 Aug. 1961.

115. Ibid., 13 Feb. 1973

116. Sudarshan, 'Relocation of Slum Dwellers'.

117. 'Football stadium pakka football aada jana', *Slum Suddhi*, 2.1 (May 1997), pp. 8–9.

118. 'Slum demolition: ondu anubhava', *Slum Suddhi,* 5.1 (Aug. 1997).

119. Heitzman, 'Sports and Conflict in Urban Planning: The Indian National Games in Bangalore'; Parry 'Law and Urban Change in an Indian City'.

120. Interview with Lakshmi Venkatachalam, 13 Aug. 1999.

121. Ibid.

122. The 153 families of Shaktivelnagara, a slum near Audgodi, were successful in averting eviction through a court order which asked the Slum Clearance Board to notify not only (private) owners of the property but occupants of the area as well, in keeping with the 'principles of natural justice'. However, as the landowner has already paid for relocation, and tenements have been constructed in Laggere to house this community, the judicial victory only delayed relocation. *MS Shakthivelanagara Gudisala Nivasigala Kshemabhivruddhi Sangha* v. *State of Karnataka and Others*, 1997, (2) KLJ. Merten's study has shown that the legal victory was reversed. Mertens, 'Forced relocation of Slum Dwellers', pp. 72–6.

123. A. Ravindra, *Metropolitan Bangalore: A Management Perspective*, p. 83; the Karnataka Kolageri Nivasigala Sangha has been active since the 1980s in opposing summary eviction of slum dwellers. However, reliance on NGOs has not been an unmixed blessing: the residents of the CSI slum seriously doubted the intentions of the leaders of KKNSS and Women's Voice, both of whom had close links to the church, and may have been part of a deal not to resist relocation. See Mertens, 'Forced Relocation of Slum Dwellers', p. 62.

124. Communication from N. Kannan.

125. WP no. 1778/94; WP 8378 of 1992, *N. Kannan* v. *Government of Karnataka, BDA, BCC.*

126. WP no. 11480/1992.

127. 'Court Notice to BMP', *Deccan Herald*, 1 July 1999. A board at the edge of the BTB area says: 'Order of High Court of Karnataka in WP no. 11480/1992 (RBI Colony Welfare Association) 1. No part of Byrasandra Tank in survey number 56 of Byrasandra Village shall be filled up. 2. No dwelling shall be put up in and around the Byrasandra Tank.'

128. A board at the edge of BTB area says 'This property belongs to Sri H. Subramanyam, HC stay order granted in WP nos. 3905/1996 and WP Nos. 4020 to 4023/1996. Action will be taken against trespassers of this property.'

129. 'Court Notice to BMP', *Deccan Herald*, 1 July 1999.

130. 'Byrasandra Tank Bed Craves for Authorities' Attention', *Hindu*, 18 June 2001.

131. Statistics provided by BMTF; see also *Deccan Herald*, 30 August 1997.

132. *Report of Sri R.L. Agnohotri, One man Commission Inquiry to Inquire into the Police Firing on 4/9/82 at Viveknagar, Bangalore City.* What follows is taken from this document.

133. WP no. 21140/81.

134. *Times of India*, 8 July 1997.

135. *Who Owns the Idga Maidan of Jayanagar? A Report of a Fact Finding Committee.* (Bangalore: People's Democratic Forum and People's Union for Civil Liberties, 1999). Unless otherwise indicated, what follows is from this document.

136. *Deccan Herald*, 18 Sept. 1997; *Hindu*, 18 Sept. 1997; *Times of India*, 18 Sept. 1997.

137. *Indian Express*, 19 Sept. 1997.

138. Castells, *The Urban Question*, p. 146.

Chapter Five: Past Perfect: Architecture and Public Life

1. See, for instance, Evenson *The Indian Metropolis*, esp. pp. 99–109.

2. The princely state of Mysore was reorganized on linguistic lines and expanded in 1956 to include areas of Bombay–Karnataka, Hyderabad–Karnataka, Madras and Bombay Presidency, and Coorg; the new state was renamed Karnataka in 1973.

3. Thomas R. Metcalf, 'Architecture and Empire: Sir Herbert Baker and the Buildings of New Delhi', in Robert Frykenberg (ed.), *Delhi Through the Ages*, pp. 391–400; Irving, *Indian Summer*.

4. For an interesting interpretation of public architecture in contemporary Singapore, see Chua Beng Huat, 'Decoding the Political in Civic Spaces: An Interpretive Essay', in Chua Beng Huat and Norman Edwards (eds), *Public Space: Design, Use and Management* (Singapore: Centre for Advanced Studies, National University of Singapore, 1992), pp. 55-68.

5. Lewis Mumford emphasized the interplay between built forms and their social uses in successive historical periods in *The City in History*. Speaking of the medieval European city, Mumford says, 'No sedentary student, viewing this architecture in pictures, no superficial observer, taking up a position and attempting to plot out axes and formal relationships, is in a state to penetrate the urban setting even in its purely formal aesthetic aspect ... the key to the visible city lies in the moving pageant or the processions; above all in the great religious procession that winds about the streets and places before it finally debouches into the church or the cathedral for the great ceremony itself. Here is no static architecture.' Pp. 277–8.

6. Kevin Lynch, *The Image of the City*, (Cambridge, Mass: MIT Press, 1992), p. 2.

7. Sudipta Kaviraj 'Filth and the Public Sphere: Concepts and Practice about Space in Calcutta', *Public Culture*, 10:1 (1997), pp. 83–113.

8. Such a longing for the past may even exaggerate the warmth and humaneness of a more impoverished past in the midst of vastly improved material conditions. See Chua Beng Huat, 'That Imagined Space: Nostalgia for the Kampungs', in Brenda Yeoh and Lily Kong (eds), *Portraits of Places: History, Community, and Identity in Singapore* (Singapore: Times Editions, 1995), p. 223–41.

9. Raymond Williams, *The Country and the City* (Oxford: Oxford University Press, 1973), p. 35.

10. *Report of the Vidhana Soudha Enquiry Committee*, vol. I (Govt. of Karnataka, Bangalore: 1957), p. 7.

11. *Report of the Vidhana Soudha Enquiry Committee*, vol. II, part A: Evidence

of K. Hanumanthaiya, p 72. Hanumanthaiya is believed to have been greatly inspired by the Stormont building in Belfast, and the impressive drive up to the building. Interview with H.G.V. Reddy, 12 July 1999. Reddy, who was the Mysore trade commissioner to London in 1952–3, remembered Hanumanthaiya discussing his vision of cutting a similar drive through Cubbon Park to connect South Parade (later Mahatma Gandhi Road) to Vidhana Soudha: this would also have meant demolishing the Attara Kacheri which stood in between.

12. Until that time, the legislature and council had no permanent home. The Representative Assembly annually met once at the Town Hall in Bangalore and once in Mysore, while the council met on the third floor of the Old Public Offices. *Report of the Vidhana Soudha Enquiry Committee*, vol. I, p. 4.

13. Madhava Prasad, 'Back to the Present', *Cultural Dynamics* 10:2, (July 1998), 123–31, esp. p. 124. Prasad suggests that 'One could even say that it is by learning to experience this humiliation as one's own that every generation accedes to the national, that a subject becomes a national subject. The simultaneity of these two events must be noted: to experience colonial humiliation is to become a national subject, but at the same time only a national subject can feel so humiliated.'

14. There is an apocryphal tale of Kengal Hanumanthaiya's personal experience of humiliation, when a visiting Russian delegation, having gone around Bangalore, asked him 'Have you no architecture of your own? They are all European buildings.' C.D. Narasimhaiah, 'Remembering Hanumanthaiya', *Deccan Herald*, 28 July 1985.

15. Govindally Devegowda, *Sarkarada kelasa devara kelasa: vidhana soudhada mahaan shilpi kengal hanumanthaiya* (Bangalore: Kannada Kanmani Dr. Raj Samskrithika Samsthe, 1995), p. 52; Konandur Venkappa Gowda, *Nava mysooru shilpi kengal hanumanthaiya* (Bangalore: 1985), p. 177; Sundara Rao, *Bengalurina itihasa*, p. 621.

16. *Report of the Vidhana Soudha Enquiry Committee*, vol. I, p.7.

17. The conscious exclusion of the country's Islamic heritage from nationalist definitions of India's classical past has been noted, among others, by Partha Chatterjee in 'Claims on the past: the Genealogy of Historiography in Bengal', in Ranajit Guha (ed.), *Subaltern Studies: Writings on South Asian History and Society*, vol. VIII (Delhi: Oxford University Press, 1994), pp. 1–49. For a discussion of how this exclusion has worked in Mysore's history, see D.R. Nagaraj, 'The Nature of Kannada Nationalism', *Journal of Karnataka Studies*, 1 (Nov. 2003–April 2004), pp. 145–56; translated by M. Madhava Prasad).

18. We may note here that British paramountcy left the princely states of India with a very circumscribed authority, so that the princes were far from sovereign in the strict sense of the term. Indeed, the grandeur of the palaces of the restored Wodeyar princely order, as in Bangalore and Mysore, was in inverse proportion to the power of the occupants. Similarly, the forts, rather than palaces, of Hyder Ali and Tipu Sultan remain the most important public edifices of their reigns, a lasting reminder of

the constraints imposed by the period of continuous warfare while defending Mysore from the British. Taken alone, therefore, these public edifices cannot serve as a reliable index of power.

19. See Beng Huat, 'Decoding the Political in Civic Space', p. 56.

20. *Report of the Vidhana Soudha Enquiry Committee,* vol. II, p. 73.

21. Sundara Rao, *Bengalurina itihasa,* p. 624.

22. *Report of the Vidhana Soudha Enquiry Committee,* vol. I, p. 7, Emphasis mine.

23. Ibid., pp. 18–19.

24. Manor, *Political Change in an Indian State*, esp. pp. 182–7.

25. Romi Khosla, 'Including Iconography and Images in Architecture', *Journal of Arts and Ideas*, no. 7, April–June 1984, p. 5-36, esp. p. 9.

26. Ibid.

27. *Report of the Vidhana Soudha Enquiry Committee,* vol. II, annex 3, p. 5.

28. Ibid., vol. I, p. 43.

29. Ibid., vol. II, annex 3, p. 5.

30. Ibid.

31. Ibid., vol. III, annex.

32. A.P. Rao was commissioned to paint on the construction of Vidhana Soudha. T.P. Issar, *The City Beautiful*: *A celebration of the architectural heritage and city aesthetics of Bangalore* (Bangalore: Bangalore Urban Art Commission, 1988) p. 33. A documentary film was also commissioned. *Report of the Vidhana Soudha Enquiry Committee*, vol. 1, p. 157–9. The Committee declared 'the documentary is poor. Except for two or three shots, it does not exhibit the architectural features of the building. It is more or less a documentary of the inspections of the Chief Minister and the work of chiselers and workers engaged in their work. In our view the expenditure was wholly unnecessary.' p. 158. Unfortunately I have been unable to gain access to the paintings and film.

33. *Report of the Vidhana Soudha Enquiry Committee*, vol. II, p. 13.

34. Ibid., vol. I, citing the editorial in *Indian Builder*. The construction of the Eiffel Tower in 1889 produced a similar outcry from the intellectuals of Paris. Benjamin, *The Arcades Project*, pp. 161, 168.

35. *Report of the Vidhana Soudha Enquiry Committee*, vol. I, p. 16.

36. Ibid., vol. II, Evidence of J. Mohamed Imam, member, Mysore Legislative Assembly, p. 35.

37. Ibid., vol. I, p. 14.

38. A sum of Rs 23 lakh was saved by cancelling paintings, ornamental lights, and the height of the central dome. *Report of the Vidhana Soudha Enquiry Committee*, vol. I, p. 166.

39. *Report of the Vidhana Soudha Enquiry Committee*, vol. I, p. 171.

40. Ibid., vol. II, p. 73.

41. Konandur Venkappa Gowda, *Nava mysore shilpi*, pp. 198–200.

42. Ibid., p. 189. The then assistant architect of the Mysore government, V. Hanumantha Rao Naidu, however told me that the dome was a replica of a small temple at Chennapatna, which Hanumanthaiya chose as representative of the Dravidian dome. Communication from V.H.R. Naidu, 18 Oct. 2000.

43. *Report of the Vidhana Soudha Enquiry Committee*, vol. I, p. 20.

44. The website BangaloreIT.com once combined history with the new economies of information technology by melding these two architectural symbols on its home page.

45. Issar, *The City Beautiful*, pp. 32–47; Konandur Venkappa Gowda, *Nava mysore shilpi*, describes the building as the temple of the future, pp. 188–9; Ba Na Sundara Rao, *Bengalurina itihasa*, pp. 626–7 compared Mysore Palace and Vidhana Soudha, saying that the latter symbolized people's wealth. 'The Vidhana Soudha is the property of the Kannadigas. It is the most important sign of Kannada pride. The Vidhana Soudha [also] inspires pride in every Kannadiga.'

46. Govindally Deve Gowda, *Vidhana soudhada mahan shilpi,* pp. 30–46.

47. See Nair, 'The Emergence of Labour Politics in South India'.

48. At its height in 1973, the anti-price rise stir drew 1 lakh workers on to the streets, who converged on Vidhana Soudha. 'Violence Mars March on Vidhana Soudha', *Deccan Herald*, 24 June 1973.

49. *Deccan Herald*, 27 Feb. 1965; 7 May 1965; 12 April 1966.

50. In 1966, the abolition of the free water allowance to Bangalore citizens led to a spirited protest led by former mayor K.M. Naganna, who turned the lawns of Vidhana Soudha into a vast 'fasting ground'. *Deccan Herald,* 2 Feb. 1966; 21 Feb. 1966, 22 March 1966. The allowance was restored although taxes and cesses were proportionately raised.

51. For 78 days in 1981, Bangalore's public sector workers numbering 80,000 went on strike, demanding uniform wage structures in all units.

52. A militant farmers' movement in north Karnataka began demanding a series of concessions from the government in the late 1970s. Farmers' rallies were organized in the state capital in December 1980 and early 1981. The most memorable was a *jatha* organized by the Progressive Democratic Front which began from Nargund/ Navalgund, a distance of 550 km from Bangalore. The *jatha* reached on 4 Feb. 1981, and merged with thousands of industrial workers then on strike. *Deccan Herald*, 5 Feb. 1981.

53. *Deccan Herald*, 3 May 1979.

54. See, for instance, T.P. Issar, 'Keeping Out the Wedge', *Deccan Herald*, 3 June 1979; and Issar, 'Bring Back Beauty to Bangalore', *Deccan Herald*, 10 Nov. 1985.

55. *Deccan Herald*, 10 Jan. 1981. Babu Mathew, a former trade union activist associated with the All India Trade Union Congress, affiliated to the Communist Party of India, suggests that 1981 may well have been the crucial turning point in the history of political uses of the park. He said that trade unions who formed the Joint Action Front agreed that it was strategically and symbolically vital to maintain a foothold in

that space, although the police constantly limited their mobility and attempted their eviction. Interview with Babu Mathew, 8 Oct. 1999.

56. *Deccan Herald,* 2 May 1981.

57. *Report of the High Power Committee set up by the Government of Karnataka on Beautification of Bangalore* (Bangalore, 1994), p. 25. Refer to Table 3.1.

58. Ibid., p. 23.

59. Ibid. This demand was made into an order by the activist high court judge M.F. Saldanha in 1998, but was swiftly grounded by a stay order.

60. Ibid., p. 34.

61. Police Commissioner L Revanasiddaiah disallowed rallies in Cubbon Park in 1997, *Times of India*, 3 May 1997; this action was hailed as timely in the English press. *Deccan Herald*, 5 May 1997.

62. I have discussed this agitation in greater detail in Chapter 7.

63. As cited in David Harvey, *Society, the City and the Space Economy of Urbanism* (Washington: Commission on College Geography Resource Paper No. 18, 1972), p. 23.

64. This follows the distinction made by Holston in the context of Brasilia between 'élite' and 'private' space in *The Modernist City*, pp. 310–14.

65. *Times of India*, 28 July 1999. *Kannada Prabha* questioned the propriety of spending Rs 12 lakh on the construction of the gates. 'Cubbon park rakshanege 12 laksha veccha madi getu haaka beke?', 5 May 1999.

66. *Deccan Herald*, 20 August 1981.

67. In 1950, the tenants of Kagodu village in Shimoga district protested, among other things, against the unjust size of the measure used by landlords in calculating rent paid in kind. This peasant movement (of largely lower caste Deewar tenants) was supported by the Socialist Party led by Gopala Gowda, state secretary of the party. The movement was brutally suppressed by the forces of the Congress led state government, though it did put an end to the unjust extraction of free labour by landlords. M.V. Nadkarni, *Farmers' Movements in India* (Bombay: Allied Publishers, 1987), pp. 19–22.

68. Castells, *The Urban Question*, p. 185.

69. The invocation of the term Garden City bears no resemblance to the town planning efforts of Ebenezer Howard which attempted to combine the best of town and country, with limited success. Ebenezer Howard, 'The Garden City (1898)', in David R. Weimar (ed.), *City and Country in America* (New York: Appleton Century Crafts, 1962), pp. 117–278. See Hall, *Cities of Tomorrow,* pp. 86–135.

70. Bangalore has had a long history of rulers/administrators interested in its potential for horticultural gardens, ranging from the reign of Hyder Ali (1761–80), Tipu Sultan (1781–99), the commissionership of Mark Cubbon (1834–61) down to such twentieth century dewans as Mirza Ismail. Hasan, *Bangalore Through the Centuries,* pp. 211–21.

71. *Report of the Expert Committee Constituted by the Government for Submitting*

Proposals for Preservation, Restoration or Otherwise of the Existing Tanks in the Bangalore Metropolitan Area, (sometimes referred to as the Lakshman Rau Committee Report), 1988. Lakshman Rau's recommendations were overwhelmingly in favour of turning disused and even live tanks into parks and gardens. In sharp contrast was the suggestion of the N. Madhava Rau committee which strongly recommended the retention of agricultural spaces within the corporation limits. See *Report of the Bangalore Development Committee* (Bangalore, 1954), pp. 104–7. For an unsentimental depiction of the Ulsoor 'Lake'/'Kensington Park' and its attractions, see A.N. Murthy Rao, 'Kensington Park', in *Samagra lalitha prabandhagalu*, (Bangalore: Ankita Pusthaka, 1999), pp. 61–6.

72. Hasan, *Bangalore Through the Centuries,* p. 220.

73. Ibid., p. 221.

74. *Deccan Herald*, 18 May 1966.

75. He was reported as saying 'Apart from costing a lot of money, these [public water] taps were contributing to the ugliness of the city'. *Deccan Herald*, 6 April 1966.

76. *Seminar on City Architecture*, Dec. 1966 (mimeo), p. 84 (emphasis added).

77. See, however, Norma Evenson in *The Indian Metropolis* who describes architecture in Indian cities as betraying an innate disregard for urban order among Indians. 'Viewing Indian cities, one may infer Indians to possess not merely an indifference but a deep seated hatred for the physical world. Buildings are often abused in ways that suggest pent up rage that might otherwise be unleashed in a frenzy of social destruction. There seems to be some force at work that is hard to explain.' P. 267. The author here prefers a psychological identification of this 'force' as an inexplicable trait of Indians, to what might elsewhere be attributed to the functioning of a real estate market.

78. *Seminar on City Architecture*, Dec. 1966, p. 87.

79. *Bangalore Urban Art Commission, 1976–83*, A Report (hereafter, *BUAC Report*), p. 1.

80. Ibid., p. 2.

81. Ibid., p. 12. Also Annex. V, 'Extracts from Communications from Chairman BUAC to Administrator and Commissioner Bangalore City Corporation'.

82. Interview with P.M. Thacker, July 1999. Thacker designed the new Spencer's building as a 12-storeyed structure but was forced to scale his building down to five. Since then, other buildings on M.G. Road have been able to go up to a height of 13 storeys by following the rule of setbacks.

83. *BUAC Report*, p. 4–5.

84. Ibid., Annex. V.

85. Anthony D. King, *Colonial Urban Development: Culture, Social Power and Environment* (London: Routledge, 1976), pp. 134.

86. Ibid., 90–1.

87. See Hall, *Cities of Tomorrow*, p. 186.

88. *Deccan Herald*, 3 Dec. 1982 (emphasis added).

89. *BUAC Report*, p. 7.

90. Issar, *The City Beautiful*, p.168; *BUAC Report*, p. 6.

91. Letter of T.P. Issar to Edgar D'Mello, 19 March 1997 (courtesy Edgar D'Mello).

92. *Deccan Herald*, 10 Nov. 1984.

93. *Deccan Herald*, 15 Nov. 1984.

94. *Deccan Herald*, 15 Jan. 1979.

95. *Deccan Herald*, 12 Jan. 1981.

96. S.K. Karekar, 'Bangalore Beautiful: Urban Aesthetics' (Bangalore, 1987).

97. *Deccan Herald*, 22 Jan. 1981.

98. WP no. 20676 of 1983, *B.V. Narayan Reddy and Others* v. *State of Karnataka and Others*, ILR Kar. 1985.

99. Ibid., emphasis added.

100. *BUAC Report*, annex. VII A.

101. Cabinet note, C 99/83 as presented to the court, *B.V. Narayan Reddy and Others* v. *State of Karnataka and Others*, ILR, Kar 1985.

102. The Karnataka Ancient and Historical Monuments and Archaeological Sites and Remains Act, 1961.

103. *Indian Express*, 5 Feb. 1997, *Asian Age*, 31 Jan. 1997.

104. *BUAC Report*, p. 9.

105. *Report of the High Power Committee*, 1994, 33.

106. *BUAC Report*, p. 8.

107. *Report of the High Power Committee*, 1994, p. 35.

108. As in its inability to influence decisions relating to the establishment of the National Games Village at Koramangala, *BUAC Report* for 1995-6, p. 68.

109. *BUAC Report*, 69; Report, 1994, p. 34.

110. 'Custodian of Beauty Makes an Exit', *Hindu*, 27 April 2001.

111. Schorske, *Fin-de Siecle Vienna*, p. 45.

112. I am grateful to architects Raj Shetty and Edgar D'Mello for clarifying some of the ideas in this section.

113. 'Architectural Moorings', *Deccan Herald*, 9 Dec. 2001.

114. The building expected to cost Rs 80 crore, has been allotted to M/s Shirke and Sons to build; the designs were however produced by the chief architect of the PWD. 'A twin for Vidhana Soudha', *Deccan Herald*, 19 Oct. 2001.

115. Ibid.

116. Holston, *The Modernist City*, 128.

117. Communication of Raja Ramanna, M.N. Srinivas, B.V. Srikantan, and A.H. Paul, *Times of India*, 22 Feb. 1997.

118. *Times of India*, 21 Jan. 1997.

119. Karekar, 'Bangalore Beautiful: Urban Aesthetics'.

Chapter Six: Language and the Right to the City

1. 'Mob Fury Brings Bangalore to a Halt', *Deccan Herald*, 1 Aug. 2000.

2. Ibid.

3. Schools were closed for 15 days, bars and liquor stores for weeks, and cinema theatres for nearly two months.

4. 'Karnataka's Image Takes a Beating', *Indian Express*, 13 Aug. 2000; 'Riots in the New Economy', *Times of India*, 8 Aug. 2000.

5. Pradeep Belave, 'A Downhill Journey', *Deccan Herald*, 13 Aug. 2000; 'Stark Reality on Celluloid Screen', *Deccan Herald*, 21 Aug. 2000.

6. 'Kannada Chaluvali Men Stage Dharna for Raj's Release', *Times of India*, 21 Aug. 2000; 'Raj Fans to Take out Procession Today', *Indian Express*, 21 Aug. 2000; 'Massive Show of Solidarity', *Deccan Herald*, 22 Sept. 2000.

7. 'Gopal's Empty Handed Return Puts Bangalore Police on Fresh Alert', *Indian Express*, 7 Aug. 2000. Trouble was anticipated particularly in areas of west and north-west Bangalore, and some parts of the east.

8. *Indian Express*, 7 Aug. 2000. The other demands were addressed to the Tamil Nadu government: to raise the procurement price of Niligiris tea, release the five Veerappan associates from jail, and solve the problems of the Manjolai estate workers, who had been on a long strike.

9. Bargur Ramachandrappa, 'Kannadaabhimanada katuvaasthava', *Prajavani*, 31 Oct. 2000.

10. As M. Chidanandamurthy has said, 'A survey of historiography in Kannada during the 19th century clearly shows the lack of a nationalist outlook among the Kannada people, more so among the south Karnataka (old Mysore) people'. Chidanandamurthy, 'Historiography in Kannada during the 19th Century', in Tarashanker Banerjee (ed.), *Historiography in Modern Indian Languages, 1800–1947* (Calcutta: Naya Prakashan, 1987), p. 168.

11. As Bankimchandra exclaimed in *Bangadarshan* cited by Ranajit Guha, *An Indian Historiography of India: A Nineteenth Century Agenda and its Implications* (Calcutta: K.P. Bagchi, 1988), p. 47.

12. Alura Venkat Rao, *Karnataka gatha vaibhava* (Bangalore: Kannada Sahitya Parishat, [1917] 1982), esp. pp. 1–6. Also, *The Karnataka Handbook*, printed and published for the editorial board of the Karnataka Pradesh Congress Committee (Bangalore; Sreenivasa Iyengar, 1924), p. 10.

13. Kannada speakers were scattered across five administrative regions in colonial India: apart from the princely state of Mysore, the single most cohesive entity, they included Bombay–Karnataka, Hyderabad Karnataka, Madras Presidency, and Coorg. R.R. Diwakar, *Karnataka Through the Ages: From Pre-historic Times to the Day of Independence of India*, vol. II (Bangalore: Government of Mysore, 1968), p. 889.

14. Early Kannada novels were usually translations of Marathi and Bengali ones.

15. I have considered some of these initiatives in *Miners and Millhands: Work Culture and Politics in Princely Mysore* (Delhi: Sage, 1998); 'Prohibited Marriage', *Contributions to Indian Sociology*, (n.s.) 29:1&2 (1995), 157–88; 'The Devadasi, Dharma and the State', *Economic and Political Weekly*, 29:50 (1994): 3157–67.

16. Sudipta Kaviraj, 'On the Structure of Nationalist Discourse', in T.V. Satyamurthy (ed.), *State and Nation in the Context of Social Change*, vol. I (Delhi: Oxford University Press, 1994), p. 327.

17. Speaking of the Mysore Lingayat Educational Fund Associations (1905) and the Vokkaligara Sangha (1906), James Manor argues that these associations failed to become 'the new type of public organization since they were governed according to the logic of the old private politics'. Manor, *Political Change in a Princely State*, p. 46. For a list of caste associations in the early twentieth century, see Thimmaiah, *Power, Politics, and Social Justice*, p. 70–2.

18. B.M. Srikantia, *The Improvement of the Kannada Language* (Bangalore: B.M. Srikantia Memorial Foundation [1915] 1969), p. v.

19. Ibid., p. iv.

20. Ibid., p. 7 and 9.

21. Ibid., p. 18.

22. In January 2002, the Karnataka government sanctioned 300 new English medium primary schools in the state of which 150 were in Bangalore; strong objections from the chair of the Kannada Development Authority, Bargur Ramachandrappa, led to a withdrawal of the order. However, it is well known that English medium schools are supple enough to respond to the demand of the market, and resort to all kinds of subterfuge in order to exist rather than conforming to the dictates of the state.

23. See for instance, Dilip Menon, *Caste, Nationalism and Communism in South India: Malabar 1900–1948* (Cambridge: Cambridge University Press, 1994), esp. pp. 143–51. There were smaller innovations in Bangalore: in the late 1960s, several batches of volunteers of the Kannada Sahitya Prachara Samiti went around the city with pushcarts urging people to buy books rather than crackers for Diwali. 'Makkala koota in Chamrajpet', *Deccan Herald*, 10 Nov. 1969.

24. Mahadev Banakar, *Safeguards for Linguistic Minorities in India: Karnataka Sets a Model* (Bangalore: Anubhav Publications, 1982), p. iii.

25. B.G.L. Swamy, *Panchakalagopura* (1964), pp. 19–26; translation of this excerpt by Ramachandra Sharma in *Sunday Herald*, 13 May 1990.

26. Interview with N. Lakshman Rau, 22 July 1998.

27. Interview with Nittoor Srinivasa Rao, 14 July 1998.

28. Diwakar, *Karnataka Through the Ages*, p. 814.

29. S. Chandrasekhar, *Colonialism, Conflict and Nationalism* (Delhi: Wishwa Press, 1995), p. 47.

30. K. Venkatappa Private Papers, KSA. See also, Janaki Nair, 'Drawing a Line: K. Venkatappa and his Publics' *IESHR*, 35: 2, (1998), 179–210.

31. Interview with Nittoor Srinivasa Rao, 18 July 1998. Indeed, as Nittoor pointed out, it is striking that the field of Kannada literary criticism has become the monopoly of English professors: A.N. Murthy Rao, the pioneer of the Kannada essay and P. Lankesh, who ran the popular newspaper, *Lankesh Patrike*, for instance, were professors of English.

32. Chatterjee, 'Beyond the Nation? Or Within?', p. 31.

33. Thus, Kannada Shakti Kendra specifically requested the government to appoint Kannada speaking officers in Bangalore and border areas, where large numbers of other language speakers reside, presumably to ensure accurate enumeration of all populations. *Deccan Herald*, 12 Jan. 1990.

34. Pierre Bourdieu, *Language and Symbolic Power* (Cambridge: Harvard University Press, 1994), p.45. Bourdieu's chief concern is the emergence of a standardized French, that triumphs as an official language over the patois.

35. Kaviraj, 'On the Structure of Nationalist Discourse', p. 324.

36. *Deccan Herald*, 2 Feb. 1970; 3 Feb. 1970; 4 Feb. 1970; 6 Feb. 1970.

37. Alura Venkat Rao, *Karnatakatvada vikasa* (1980, p. 148) as cited in Nagaraj, 'The Nature of Kannada Nationalism'.

38. See for instance, Ra Nam Chandrasekhar, *Kannada shakthi* (Bangalore: Kannada Shakthi Kendra: 1998); also his '"Kannada jagruthi varsha" saadisideno?' (mimeo); also *Kannada-kannadiga-karnataka* (Bangalore: Kannada Pusthaka Pradhikaara, 1996). This last text draws obvious inspiration from the menacing slogan 'Hindi-Hindu-Hindusthan.'

39. I have discussed these positions briefly in '"Memories of Underdevelopment": Language and its Identities in Contemporary Karnataka', *Economic and Political Weekly*, 31.41 and 42 (12–19 Oct. 1996), pp. 2809–16. Several Kannada intellectuals (writers, teachers, journalists, and artistes) who represented the strand of 'secular politics' took a clear and uncompromising stand against the more aggressive and violent actions of several Kannada groups during the Gokak agitation (1982), the agitation against the removal of the Kannada test for Class II and Class IV employees (1984), the Thiruvalluvar episode and Cauvery riots (1991). They included writers like G.K. Govinda Rao, Marulsidappa, D.R. Nagaraj, Ki Ram Nagaraj, S. Siddalingaiah, Vijaya, Shudra Srinivas, Agrahara Krishnamurthy, and U.R. Ananthamurthy. Their stand on the riots against the Urdu telecast (1994) was less unambiguous although here too the violence against Muslims was severely condemned.

40. *Deccan Herald*, 26 March 1992.

41. Jean Racine et al., *Calcutta 1981*: there were 61 per cent Bengali speakers, 20 per cent Hindi speakers, and 9 per cent Urdu speakers in 1981, p. 111.

42. Sumathi Ramaswamy, *Passions of the Tongue: Language Devotion in Tamil Nadu 1891–1970* (Delhi: Munshilal Manoharlal, 1998), pp. 161–8.

43. At the height of the Cauvery agitation, a farmer from Bidar, a dry district far removed from the state capital said, 'Where is Cauvery? What has it to do with this backward district?' *Hindu*, Dec. 1991.

44. *Deccan Herald*, 12–13 Dec. 1991.

45. M. Chidanandamurthy, *Nanna baduku: ondu kiru chitra* (Dr M. Chidanandamurthy Gourava Samputa 'samshodana' dalli prakatagonda lekhanada mel acchu, n.d.), p. 942; see also Ve Srinivas, 'Kannada chaluvali nadedubanda daari', in *Kannada Kanmani* which describes the humiliation experienced by Ma Ramamurthy when the demand for the screening of Kannada films in Majestic was made.

46. Interview with Ra Nam Chandrasekhar, 7 and 11 Oct. 1998; see also the chapter 'Valase' in *Kannada-kannadiga-karnataka*, pp. 163–8. 'Ekathegondu savalu: antharajya valase', in *Saarthaka*, n.d., 152–62.

47. Chidanandamurthy, 'Kannadadha samasyegalu', in *Kannada-kannadiga-karnataka*, p. 51.

48. G. Narayana, 'Bengaluru nagarada mukhya samasyegalu', mimeo, 1997, p. 2.

49. Chidanandamurthy, 'Kannadadha samasyegalu'.

50. The States Reorganisation Committee (1956) acknowledged the particularly fragmented political status of Kannada speakers, who were reduced to minorities in three of the administrative divisions of colonial Karnataka.

51. Interview with Sa Ra Govindu, president, Dr Rajkumar Abhimanigala Sangha, 23 Oct. 1998.

52. *Hindu*, 14 Dec. 1993; *Deccan Herald*, 14 April 1992. A newly laid out extension came to be called 'Little Karnataka', as it had people from Bombay and Hyderabad–Karnataka, as well as old Mysore. *Deccan Herald*, 18 July 1966.

53. Ra Nam Chandrasekhar, 'Ekathegondhu savalu', p. 153.

54. Susan Lewandowski shows that Madras became a more homogeneously Tamil city as a consequence of the development of other state capitals after Independence. See Lewandowski, *Migration and Ethnicity in Urban India*, p. 75.

55. *Samyukta Karnataka*, 28 April 1962.

56. 'Kannada chaluvali nadedhu banda dari', in *Kannada Kanmani*; interview with Ra Nam Chandrasekhar, 11 Oct. 1998; 'Chidanandamurthy elevates what was perhaps no more than a small wrestling match into a historic event' says D.R. Nagaraj, commenting on the use of this episode in constructing a history of the Kannada nation. 'The Nature of Kannada Nationalism.'

57. *Deccan Herald*, 28 Dec. 1960; 20 Feb. 1962, 8 Sept. 1962.

58. Banakar, *Safeguards for Minority Languages*, p.iii.

59. *Deccan Herald*, 8 July 1994.

60. Ibid., 12 Dec. 1994.

61. Ibid., 30 Aug. 1994.

62. *Lankesh Patrike,* February–March 1996, *Hindu*, 21 Feb. 1996.

63. *Deccan Herald*, 13 July 2000.

64. *Deccan Herald*, 2 March 1996.

65. 'Takeover of Cinemas Urged', *Deccan Herald*, 19 April 1976; 'No Take over of Cinema Houses Now', *Deccan Herald*, 14 April 1976.

66. 'Why this Hindi Imposition on Bangalore TV?', *Deccan Herald*, 3 Dec. 1983; 'City TV Fans Favour Kannada and Delhi Relay', *Deccan Herald,* 9 Dec. 1983.

67. See Nair, 'Memories of Underdevelopment', p. 2813.

68. Lewandowski, *Migration and Ethnicity in Urban India*, pp. 82; 175 ff.

69. Hansen, *Urban Violence in India*, p. 47.

70. 'Raj to Head Panel on Kannada Row', *Deccan Herald*, 14 Jan. 1984.

71. 'Three Killed in Bandh Violence: Curfew Clamped on Some City Areas', *Deccan Herald*, 19 Jan. 1984.

72. A statement signed by several intellectuals made this specific charge: Go. Ru Channabasappa, Prof. G.S. Shivarudrappa, H.S. Doreswamy and Prof. M.H. Marulsiddappa released the statement on 5 Oct. 1994. People's Democratic Forum, *'Medium' for Communalism: A Report on the anti-Urdu Communal Riots* (Dec. 1994), p. 4.

73. Ibid., p. 26.

74. Muthaiah David Appavoo, *The Effect of Migration on the Churches of Bangalore* (Bangalore: CISRS, 1965), pp. 2, 10, 17.

75. Ibid., pp. 19–20: among the more exceptional churches noted by Appavoo was the St Barnabas church of HAL where workers from different backgrounds endeavoured to maintain the unity of the spirit by worshipping in four different languages. Thus, the author concludes, 'industrial life obliterated language differences' and produced a new sense of belonging. For a different reading of this phenomenon, see J.R. Henry, *A History of the Tamil Churches in Mysore Diocese*, (thesis submitted for the College Diploma of UTC, Bangalore, 1962).

76. 'Letters', *Deccan Herald*, 3 Nov. 1980.

77. 'Clash in Cathedral: Archbishop Gheraoed', *Deccan Herald*, 17 April 1981.

78. '33 Held After Disturbance in Church', *Deccan Herald*, 4 May 1981.

79. 'Writers Back Kannada Catholics Demands', *Deccan Herald*, 2 July 1981.

80. 'The Catholic Church and Language', *Deccan Herald*, 3 June 1983.

81. 'Church to Stick to Three Language Formula', *Deccan Herald*, 2 May 1988; 'Church Circular on Language Rejected', *Deccan Herald*, 4 May 1988.

82. *Samyukta Karnataka*, 18 April 1992.

83. These were the words of G.S. Siddalingaiah, president, Kannada Sahitya Parishat. 'Agitation for Kannada in Church to be Stepped Up', *Deccan Herald*, 4 June 1990.

84. Interview with Ra Nam Chandrasekhar, 7 and 11 Oct. 1998.

85. Krishna made this suggestion while inaugurating HAL's Kannada Sangha. *Deccan Herald*, 23 Aug. 1973.

86. Johnson Samuel and M. Lingaraju, 'Migrants in Bangalore', ISEC Working Paper 13, (1989), p. 13.

87. Interview of M.S.L. Rao by Dilip Subramanian, June 1981.

88. 'Posters Under Fire'; 'Uproar in Lok Sabha Over City Posters'; 'Nip it in the

Bud', *Deccan Herald*, 10 March 1981. In its hard hitting editorial, the *Deccan Herald* said 'the chauvinist call of the NSUI patterned on the Kannada Chaluvali philosophy is not only stupid and impractical but will only set one linguistic group against another in a fragile society as obtains in cosmopolitan Bangalore'.

89. Subramanian, 'The Bangalore Public Sector Strike, 1980–81, Part II', p. 852. The reference to the use of ESI funds was true: many workers made ends meet through the long strike period by claiming sickness benefits from the two ESI centres, ibid., p. 844. Predictably the ESI act was amended soon after the strike in such a way as to bar workers on strike from making sickness and disablement claims.

90. 'Posters under Fire', *Deccan Herald*, 10 March 1981

91. 'Furore Over Jobs for Kannadigas in IIM' despite land granted by state government. Also, 'Minister Clarifies IIM Affairs'. *Deccan Herald*, 25 Sept. 1973.

92. Joseph, 'Politics of Recruitment in Public Sector Undertakings', pp. 69, 168.

93. 'Kannadigas in Central Sector: Workers Dispute Official Figures', *Deccan Herald*, 16 May 1984.

94. Interview with Sa Ra Govindu, 23 Oct. 1998; interview with R. Radhakrishna, President, Jaga Mechida Maga, Dr Rajkumar Abhimanigala Sangha, 20 July 1999.

95. 'Raj Jumps Intro Fray', *Deccan Herald*, 17 April 1982; 'Rajkumar Vows to Fight for Kannada Supremacy', *Deccan Herald*, 12 May 1982; 'Stir Will Continue Till Kannada Gets Primacy—Raj', *Deccan Herald*, 17 May 1982.

96. 'Kannada Stir Turns Violent', *Deccan Herald*, 18 April 1982. The deaths in 1982 of Muslims at Chitradurga and Tamils at Kolar Gold Field (KGF) occurred as a result of police firing on those who opposed the proposed language policy: such opposition also took the form of violence against public property. For instance, the five persons from KGF who were killed in police firing had set fire to the post office and some other mining property.

97. Interview with members of Jaga Mechida Maga Dr Rajkumar Abimanigala Sangha, 20 July 1999.

98. Report of the N.D. Venkatesh Commission of Inquiry, vol. I, p. 52 (emphasis in original).

99. Steen Folke, 'Conflicts Over Water and Land in South Indian Agriculture: A Political Economy Perspective', *Economic and Political Weekly* 33.7 (1998), pp. 341–7.

100. S.G. Balekundry, 'Injustice to Karnataka in Regard to Cauvery Waters' (Bangalore, 1991).

101. *Report of the N.D. Venkatesh Commission of Inquiry*, vol. I, p. 2.

102. Ibid., pp. 59, 64.

103. *Medium for Communalism: A Report on the Anti-Urdu Communal Riots* (Bangalore; People's Democratic Forum, 1994), p. 5,7.

104. Benjamin and Bhuvaneswari, et al., 'On Valmikinagar/Azadnagar', in 'Urban Poverty and Governance in Bangalore'. An amended longer consideration is in Benjamin

and Bhuvaneswari, 'Democracy, Inclusive Governance and Poverty in Bangalore', pp. 49–53.

105. *Report of the N.D. Venkatesh Commission of Inquiry*, vol. I, p. 2–3.

106. *Indian People Human Rights Tribunal Report*, Annex. IV.

107. *Report of the N.D. Venkatesh Commission of Inquiry*, vol. I, p. 3.

108. This has also been noted in other instances of communal violence, as for instance in Ahmedabad, Surat, and Bhopal in 1993: see Mehdi Arslan and Janaki Rajan (eds), *Communalism in India: Challenge and Response* (Delhi: Manohar, 1994).

109. De Wit, 'Remote Sensing and Slums in Indian Cities', p. 58.

110. Banakar, *Safeguards for Linguistic Minorities*, pp. 31–2.

111. *Interim Report of the Committee of Legislators on the Slum Problems of Bangalore*, (draft). This reference was later deleted. p. 7.

112. *Report of the Review Committee on BDA*, vol. VIII, p. 30–1.

113. Woodruffe, 'An Adi Dravida Settlement in Bangalore India', p. 71.

114. Benjamin and Bhuvaneswari et al., 'Urban Poverty and Governance in Bangalore', pp. 75–7.

115. De Wit, *Geographical Information Systems*, p. 58.

116. *Deccan Herald*, 12 Oct. 1969.

117. *Samyukta Karnataka*, 15 Nov. 1964.

118. Anti-Hindi protests were most conspicuous in the Tamil dominated areas of the city such as Srirampuram, Ulsoor, Murphy Town, etc.

119. On the feminizing of the Tamil language, see Ramaswamy, *Passions of the Tongue*, esp. pp. 79–134.

120. 'Thayinadu prema thayi pritiashte shrestha', *Kannada Kanmani*, Nov. 1993.

121. Tejaswini Niranjana, 'Reworking Masculinities: Rajkumar and the Kannada Public Sphere', *Economic and Political Weekly* 35:47 (2000), pp. 4147–50, esp. p. 4150.

122. Interview with S. Siddalingaiah, Dec. 1999.

123. Interview with M. Chidanandamurthy, 9 Oct. 1998.

124. D.V. Gundappa Private Papers, Karnataka State Archives (KSA) Bangalore.

125. Interview with R. Radhakrishna, 20 July 1999.

126. In his recent article, Bargur Ramachandrappa discusses the futility of struggles based so narrowly on the language of cinema, arguing for a more liberal definition of culture and cultural resources. His studious avoidance of any discussion of Tamil nationalism, choosing instead to speak of Marathi, Bengali, and Malayalam successes, is however a reminder of how closely tied are the modalities of nationalism on both sides of the border. 'Kannadaabhimanada katuvaasthava'.

127. *A Mute Genocide: A Report on the Gory Incidents of Violence on Karnataka Tamils During the Black December 1991* (Bangalore: Bangalore Tamil Sangham, 1992), pp. 39, 40.

128. Ibid., p. 41.

129. 'Jati jagadalli english: asamaanathege bunadi', *Prajavani*, 16 Feb. 2002.

130. 'Do not Sacrifice Karnataka's Interests', *Hindu*, 16 Feb. 2002. This plea for protection of Kannada lay itself open to the obvious criticism that writers such as Ananthamurthy had benefited from globalization and from English translations of his writing. See, for instance, the words of the then State Information Technology Minister B.K. Chandrasekhar, 'Litterateurs' remarks lamented', *Hindu*, 23 Feb. 2002.

131. These were the words used by several Kannada intellectuals who raised their voice against the increasingly violent trend of the Gokak agitation. Letters, *Deccan Herald*, 18 April 1982.

132. 'Bhashaabhimanada hesaralli prachara tantra: krishna vishada', *Prajavani*, 22 Feb. 2002.

133. K.N. Harikumar, 'Language and Democracy: Towards a Democratic Culture in Karnataka', *Deccan Herald*, 13 Aug. 1982.

134. Maurizio Viroli, *For Love of Country: An Essay on Patriotism and Nationalism* (Oxford: Oxford University Press, 1997), p. 8.

135. Ibid., p. 175.

136. Interview with R. Radhakrishna, 20 July 1999.

137. Ramesh Bairy, 'Competing Constructions of Kannada Identity'.

138. Pamphlet of Karnataka Samata Sainik Dal, n.d.

Chapter Seven: Battles for Bangalore: Reterritorializing the City

1. The installation, of which this painting was a part, was one of three site-specific installations done for a show called *Sthalapuranagalu: Two Conversations and a Dialogue* curated by Bangalore artist Pushpamala N. It involved two other artists, B.J.Shamala and Srinivasa Prasad, who worked over a period of six months at three different sites in the city. While Shyamala chose Ulsoor Tank as her venue, Srinivasa Prasad did an installation at the Samudaya office, Basavangudi. In a city that has grown from provincial town to metropolis, said the curator in her statement of purpose for the project, 'there are chaotic signs of change, destruction, building; an enormous circulation of desire and energy and yet—[visually] no shape'. The event was intended as a reflection by artists on the visual cultures of the city.

2. The other figures were of colonial masters, near and distant, such as Edward VII and Mark Cubbon; the former maharajas of Mysore, Chamrajendra Wodeyar and Krishnaraja Wodeyar IV; national leaders such as Mahatma Gandhi, Jawaharlal Nehru, and B.R. Ambedkar; regional politicians and bureaucrats such as Visvesvaraya, Kengal Hanumanthaiah, and Devaraj Urs, and historical heroes such as Basavanna and Kempegowda.

3. Vidya Murthy, 'History in the Remaking', *Art News Magazine of India*, IV: III, pp. 74–6.

4. See Satish Deshpande, 'Communalising the Nation-Space: Notes on the Spatial Strategies of Hindutva', *Economic and Political Weekly*, 30.50 (Dec. 16, 1995), pp.

3220–7 for a pioneering attempt to theorize the social construction and meaning of space in contemporary Indian society.

5. Lefebvre, *Writings on Cities,* p. 73.

6. The ideology of beauty which envisages a city free of 'modernized and cubistic structures' air horns, spitting and littering, flyovers and graffiti, as we have seen in Chapter 6, found its most eloquent advocate in T.P. Issar, first chairman of the Bangalore Urban Arts Commission, 1976–80: 'Bangalore: Keeping Out the Wedge', *Deccan Herald* and 'Bring Back Beauty to Bangalore', *Deccan Herald*, See, also, his *City Beautiful.*

7. Lefebvre, *Writings on Cities*, p. 84.

8. *Deccan Herald*, 6 April 1970; 15 April 1970. The demand for the 'independence' of the cantonment was made by a militant Tamil group styling itself Tamil Sena, but was condemned by the most important Tamil political grouping at the time, DMK.

9. *Samyukta Karnataka*, 31 March 1994. The demand for a separate administration was raised by a DMK corporator protesting the neglect of certain areas of the cantonment such as Shivajinagar, Bharatinagar, and Shantinagar.

10. 'Let Bangalore become a City-State', *Economic Times*, 6 April 1997.

11. *Deccan Herald*, 18 Jan. 1962.

12. *Deccan Herald*, 20 Jan. 1961.

13. *Deccan Herald*, 1 Dec. 1998.

14. This has been described by Prakasa Rao and Tewari as 'binodality' with a 'crater' in between. Prakasa Rao and V. Tewari, *The Structure of an Indian Metropolis*, pp. 169–71.

15. Note on the Development of Civil and Military Station, Bangalore (n.d.) KSA.

16. Samuel and Lingaraju, 'Migrants in Bangalore', pp. 12–13; Prakasa Rao and Tewari, *The Structure of an Indian Metropolis*, p. 245.

17. The last phrase was used by V.N. Balasubrahmanyam in 'Bangalore is Where the Action Is', Paper delivered at BangaloreIT.com, 1998.

18. The five star hotel Windsor Manor is not only an architectural quotation from the colonial past, but celebrates the imperial heritage by calling its coffee shop 'The East India Company'.

19. See Chapter 5 above; see also Jayapal *Bangalore: The Story of a City.*

20. *Mysore Legislative Assembly Proceedings*, vol. 100, 24 Oct. 1949.

21. Ibid.

22. Interview with Ra Nam Chandrasekhar, 7 Oct. 1998. Chidanandamurthy, *Nanna baduku*, p. 942.

23. Remarking on the 'supreme revolution in language' that was carried out by the advent of naming streets after heroes, Walter Benjamin said 'through its street names, the city is image of a linguistic cosmos'. Benjamin, *The Arcades Project*, p. 840.

24. *Samyukta Karnataka*, 28 April 1962.

25. Even the CPI-dominated unions in the public, government, and private sectors, which were considered strong and militant, were usually led by people of Tamil and

Malayali origin, an equal cause for resentment by managements and Kannada activists. Interview with Ra Nam Chandrasekhar, 7 Oct. 1998; also Interview by Dilip Subramanian with M.S.L. Rao, BEL worker, June 1981.

26. Interview with former mayor, G. Narayana, 25 Oct. 1998. It may be no coincidence that this mayor is an active member of the Vokkaliga community, which also claims Kempegowda as a caste hero.

27. Corporation of the City of Bangalore, Proceedings, vol. 35, 21 Sept. 1964.

28. Corporation of the City of Bangalore, Proceedings, 31 Jan. 1964. p. 146.

29. *Samyukta Karnataka*, 2 Sept. 1964, 5 Sept. 1964; *Deccan Herald*, 20 Sept. 1964, 21 Sept. 1964.

30. *Samyukta Karnataka*, 29 Oct. 1964. Corporation of the City of Bangalore, Proceedings: Resolution to Remove the Cenotaph, 21 Sept. 1964.

31. *Vichara*, p. 102.

32. But not before he has had a crash course in democracy from his more intrepid friend Ranga while standing before the corporation offices. Ranga who boasts of '20 years of experience in Majestic' tells an awestruck Muthanna that there are no kings in the city, only elected representatives.

33. *Samyukta Karnataka*, 16 April 1994.

34. *Times of India*, 16 June 1995.

35. Chidanandamurthy, *Nanna baduku*, p. 942.

36. Interview with Ra Nam Chandrasekar, 7 Oct. 1998.

37. Interview of M.S.L. Rao, by Dilip Subramanian, June 1981. *Samyukta Karnataka*, 25 Jan. 1962; 25 Feb. 1964 cited Aa Na Kru talking about the insult and injustice to Kannadigas in the city.

38. Interview of M.S.L. Rao by Dilip Subramanian, June 1981.

39. 'Kannada bavuta chaluvali: rochaka itihasa', *Prajavani*, 29 Oct. 2000.

40. Interview with Ra Nam Chandrasekhar, 7 Oct. 1998.

41. *Deccan Herald*, 4 Aug. 1963; Aa Na Kru condemned Kannada actor Kalyan Kumar for acting in Tamil films. The demand began to be made for a film studio in Bangalore. *Deccan Herald*, 13 Jan. 1964.

42. *Deccan Herald*, 28 Dec. 1960; 20 Feb. 1962; 8 Sept. 1962. This was a period when vociferous demands were made for Kannada films in the city.

43. *Deccan Herald*, 5 Dec. 1966, 2 Dec. 1966.

44. See, for instance A. Srivatsan, 'Politics of Tamil Monuments', unpublished paper.

45. The agitation is referred to as the Gokak agitation after V.K.Gokak, a Kannada literatteur and Gnanpith award winner who made the suggestion in a report concerned with the status of Sanskrit in schools.

46. Chidanandamurthy, *Nanna baduku*, pp. 942–3; Ra Nam Chandrasekhara, *Kannada-kannadiga-karnataka*, pp. 74–80.

47. Interview with Sa Ra Govindu, 23 Oct. 1998. Autorickshaw drivers have

been among those who have taken an active part in establishing Kannada flagpoles near their stands at major street junctions. *Times of Indiranagar*, 2–8 Nov. 1998.

48. 'Eminent Persons Appeal to CM Against Statue', *Deccan Herald*, 24 Oct. 1991. Other place names that refused to change were: McIver Town (Shantalanagar), Austin Town (Kittel Nagar), Richards Town (C.V. Raman Nagar), Cox Town (Sarvagna Nagar), Cooke and Thomas Town (B.L. Rice Nagar), Williams Town (K.C. Reddy Nagar), Murphy Town (Hoysala Nagar), and Cleveland Town (Sri Krishna Raja Wodeyar Nagar).

49. Bairy, 'Competing Constructions', p.68ff.

50. Interview with Sa Ra Govindu, 23 Oct. 1998.

51. 'Three Killed in Bundh Violence', *Deccan Herald*, 19 Jan. 1984. Also the editorial in the same issue.

52. Interview, with Sa Ra Govindu, 23 Oct. 1998.

53. H. Narasimhaiah, 'Ayyo, abhimana shunya bengaluru', *Tereda Mana* (1974), pp. 144–50.

54. The emphasis that science too could be well learned through the medium of Kannada is critical ammunition against those who identify English with science, technology, and capitalism.

55. *Kannada-kannadiga-karnataka*, especially the chapters on migration; Ra Nam Chandrasekhar, 'Kaigarike kacheri kannada sanghagala kainkarya', unpublished.

56. A demand to direct developmental work away from Bangalore which enjoyed a disproportionate share of the state's resources has been made by Karnataka Rajya Raitha Sangha chief M. Nanjundaswamy: talk by B.K. Chandrasekhar at the Centre for the Study of Culture and Society, 5 May 1998.

57. *Deccan Herald*, 27 Sept. 1979; the Sangam claimed to have taught 11,000 people Kannada. Interview with D. Shanmughavelan, president, Tamil Sangam, 11 Oct. 1998. See *Bengaluru tamizh cankam 41am aandu sirappu malar*, 1 Sept. 1991, pp. 1–7.

58. *Deccan Herald*, 1 Oct. 1967.

59. *Deccan Herald*, 27 Sept. 1979; Interview with D. Shanmughavelan, 11 Oct. 1998.

60. Pamphlet of January 1991, *Ootru*, March 1991; April 1991. I am grateful to S. Subramanian of the Tamil Sangam for assistance with some of the Tamil reports.

61. *Ootru* announced that the statue would be unveiled on 1 Sept. 1991, followed by literary lectures. *Dinasudar*, 29 August 1991 announced plans for a 10,000 strong meeting. 'It was better to install the statue when there were so many Tamil councillors in the Corporation,' *Ootru*, April 1991.

62. *Hindu*, 31 Aug. 1991; *Dinasudar*, 30 Aug. 1991, 3 Sept. 1991; pamphlet denouncing the 'devious ways of the Bangalore Mahanagara Palike in allowing Thiruvalluvar Statue' signed by 19 Kannada organizations.

63. *Dinasudar Sanjevani*, 17 Sept. 1991.

64. *Sanjevani*, 18 Sept. 1991; for the statement by Harnahalli Ramaswamy, see *Deccan Herald*, 30 Aug. 1991.

65. Interview with Sa Ra Govindu, 23 Sept. 1998; *Dinathanthi*, 17 Aug. 1991, 'The statue must be in a public place', the Tamil Sangam submitted in court, 'because nearly 8000 had contributed to it.'

66. *Dinasudar*, 16 Sept. 1991.

67. R. Mallikarjuna BMP councillor first said that 'until Tamil Nadu puts up a statue of Basavanna, founder of [Kannada] Virasaivism, Thiruvalluvar cannot be allowed here even if he is the founder of Virasaivism in Tamil Nadu'. *Sanjevani*, 18 Sept. 1991. Legislator Vatal Nagaraj said that Kuvempu's statue must be installed in Madras. *Sanjevani*, 3 Sept. 1991. Dalit organizations made a plea for a statue of Sarvagna in Madras, (*Sanjevani*, 13 Oct. 1991) for which L.S. Seshagiri Rao claimed that permission had been sought. *Illustrated Weekly of India*, September 1991.

68. *Times of India*, 18 Sept. 1991.

69. *Deccan Herald*, 13 June 1988; 8 Oct. 1994.

70. 'Medium for Communalism', PDF, Bangalore, Dec. 1994.

71. *Dinasudar*, 6 Sept. 1991; 22 Sept. 1991; 19 Sept. 1991, 23 Sept. 1991; *Dinathanthi*, 6 Oct. 1991.

72. *Thenamudam*, 1 Oct. 1991, vol. 15, no. 10; *Dinasudar*, 27 Sept. 1991.

73. *Dinasudar*, 29 Sept. 1991.

74. *Dinasudar*, 31 Aug. 1991.

75. *Venapoonga* (n.d.)

76. *Murasoli*, Oct. 1991.

77. *Dinathanthi*, 27 Sept. 1991

78. Petition from Kannada Balaga, 30 May 1997; district revenue officer, Chennai Corporation to president, Kannada Balaga, 20 March 1998; Petition from Bangalore Tamil Sangam, 11 July 1997. The Bangalore Tamil Sangam has taken the initiative in getting a likeness of Sarvagna approved by the Kannada Sahitya Parishat in Bangalore, and in providing the estimates for its installation in Chennai: letter of Bangalore Tamil Sangam president, D. Shanmughavelan, to district revenue officer, 11 Aug. 1997.

79. *Dinasudar*, 11 Nov. 1991.

80. *Times of India*, 11 Nov. 1991.

81. *Deccan Herald*, 19 April 1982.

82. *Dinasudar*, 3 Oct. 1991.

83. Pamphlet of Karnataka Samata Sainik Dal, n.d.

84. *Deccan Herald*, 12 Dec. 1991.

85. 'Eminent Persons Appeal to CM Against Statue', *Deccan Herald*, 24 Oct. 1991.

86. *A Mute Genocide*, p. 39.

87. Interview with Ra Nam Chandrasekhar, 7 Oct. 1998.

88. Interview by Dilip Subramanian of M.S.L. Rao, June 1981.

89. Interview with Ra Nam Chandrasekhar, 7 Oct. 1998

90. *Deccan Herald*, 20 Aug. 1981.

91. *Indian Express*, 22 Nov. 1995, 'No son shall rise above the law', reports that there were 14 acts of vandalism against Ambedkar statues between 1990–4.

92. *Deccan Herald*, 13 July 1989; compare *Deccan Herald*, 15 Nov. 1995, 17 Nov. 1995.

93. See chapter 1 above.

94. Prakasa Rao and Tewari, *Structure of an Indian Metropolis*.

95. Communication from Mangaluru Vijaya, 10 Oct. 1998.

96. *Deccan Herald*, 18 Nov. 1995.

97. *Deccan Herald*, 21 Nov. 1995.

98. *Deccan Herald*, 3 Dec. 1995.

99. *Kannada Prabha*, 19 Nov. 1995.

100. PDF press release, n.d.

101. See Rekha Kaul, *Caste Class and Education: Politics of the Capitation Fee Phenomenon in Karnataka* (Sage, 1993), pp. 56 ff.

102. Of the seven medical colleges and ten engineering colleges in Bangalore, only one each is run by the government, the others being private capitation fee-based colleges. *Comprehensive Development Plan*, 1995, pp. 46–7.

103. These are the terms that frequently describe the communities which are involved in riots. There is persistent reference to the incapacity of such crowds to act on their own, egged on instead by politicans who can manipulate crowds at will. See Justice P.A Kulkarni Commission of Enquiry, *Report on Police Firings at Various Places in Bangalore City*, 28 Oct. 1987.

104. See, for instance, Naidu, *Old Cities New Predicaments*, p. 142.

105. 'A Tale of Violence', *The Week*, 21 Dec. 1986.

106. Ibid.

107. The estimates of the crowd have varied from 100 to 5000; 'An Anger Rising From Insecurity', *Telegraph*, 18 Dec. 1986.

108. 'Riots: A Test for Hegde', *Indian Express*, 17 Dec. 1986.

109. 'A Tragedy and a Few Lessons', *Hindu*, 11 Dec. 1986.

110. *WP no. 32232/98 (RES PIL GM)*.

111. Objections filed by the respondent, Government of Karnataka, *WP no. 32232/98 (RES PIL GM)*.

112. *Deccan Herald*, 6 Sept. 1998; *Times of India*, 7 Sept. 1998.

113. 'Prominent Citizens' Protest Denotification', *Deccan Herald*, 28 Oct. 1998; editorial 'Reverse the Decision', 13 Oct. 1998.

114. 'Meet to Save Cubbon Park Once and Forever', Pamphlet dated 14 Nov. 1998.

115. 'Spectacled Cobra, Blue Rock Pigeon are our Neighbours', *Hindu*, 17 Oct. 1998.

116. '65 Species of Trees Identified During Census', *Deccan Herald*, 13 Oct. 1998; 'Counting Trees to Protect Them', *Hindu*, 26 Oct. 1998.

117. 'Pushed to the Wall, Citizens Will now Take to the Streets', *Times of India*, 10 Oct. 1998.

118. *Save Cubbon Park Campaign*, Pamphlet, 23 Oct. 1998.

119. File no. 510–05, sl. no, 1–17, G&M, KSA.

120. A.N. Murthy Rao, 'Bengaluru', *Samagra lalitha prabandhagalu*, p. 222.

121. 'Old is Gold, Keep it', *Deccan Herald*, 22 Oct. 1998.

122. 'Cubbon park kabalike yathna: samskruthika kshetrada mauna pratibhatane', *Kannada Prabha*, 28 Oct. 1998.

123. 'Hash Run for Cubbon Park', *Indian Express*, 1 Nov. 1998.

124. 'How Can Rules Bend for Convenience?', *Times of India*, 26 May 1998.

125. 'Majority of Citizens vote for Lung Space', *Times of India*, 31 Oct. 1998.

126. *Deccan Herald* (photograph), 16 Oct. 1998.

127. 'Women Protest Against GO', *Deccan Herald*, 11 Oct. 1998

128. *Times of India*, 23 Oct. 1998.

129. 'Cubbon park ulivige urulu seve', *Kannada Prabha*, 16 Oct. 1998.

130. New curbs on traffic in the park are being implemented on the orders of the activist judge M.F. Saldanha, though the consensus regarding such measures is already evaporating. 'Cubbon park rakshanege 12 laksha veccha madi getu hakabeke?' *Kannada Prabha*, 5 May 1999.

131. Judgement on WPs 3223/98, 19541/99, 18287/98, and 8428–34/1998.

132. Most recent plans to expand the Karnataka Lawn Tennis Association into a club within the park, which has graver implications for encroachment on park property, have not provoked the same outrage on the part of citizens who protested the Legislators' Home. The patrons of this project include the chief minister, S.M. Krishna, as well as many other corporate icons such as Kiran Mazumdar who were part of the Save Cubbon Park Campaign. Information from Leo Saldanha; see also KSLTA (Karnataka State Lawn Tennis Association) pamphlet 'Be a Part of the Game, be a Part of an Exclusive Club'.

Chapter Eight: The 'Body Politic': Gender and the Practise of Power

1. Sundara Rao, *Bengalurina itihasa*, pp. 17–19.

2. In its structure, this folk tale follows the innumerable '*kerege hara*' songs in which the sacrifice of the pregnant woman, usually the daughter-in-law, is memorialized as helping the walls of the irrigation tank to stand.

3. See, for instance, map showing location of industries in and around Bangalore in Rame Gowda, *Urban and Regional Planning*, p. 128.

4. Gist, 'The Ecology of Bangalore', pp. 25, 27.

5. Venkatrayappa, *Bangalore: A Socio-Ecological Study*, pp. 142–3.

6. Millenium Bio Tech Policy, Bangalore, 2001.

7. Prakasa Rao and Tewari, *The Structure of an Indian Metropolis,* pp. 185–7.

8. An exception is the Lakshmipuram Slum Rehousing Project in Bangalore which was primarily undertaken by an NGO Association of Voluntary Action and Services, (AVAS) in the late 1980s. A group of 122 families existing on a 1 acre 8 *gunta* plot adjoining the prime Indiranagar area, were threatened with relocation, but efforts of the NGO along with the city corporation and HUDCO allowed *in situ* improvements to the area and also secured land tenure. In her report on this four year long effort, Anita Reddy mentions the vital role played by the Mahila Sangha, though there is no mention of the specific inputs of women, primarily domestic workers married to casual labourers, in the planning of the community or domestic space. Anita Reddy, 'Lakshmipuram Slum Rehousing Project', in *National Symposium on Planning and Development of Metropolitan* Bangalore (mimeo, BDA, 1987). For an example of the involvement of women in determining the design and use of domestic space, in post-world war Netherlands, see Wiebe E. Bijker and Karin Bijsterveld, 'Women Walking Through the Plans', *Technology and Culture*, July 2000, vol. 41, pp. 485–515.

9. Doreen Massey, 'Politics and Space/Time', in *Space, Place and Gender* (Cambridge: Polity Press, 1994), pp. 249–72.

10. Ibid., p. 260.

11. Richard Sennett, *Flesh and Stone: The Body and the City in Western Civilisation* (London and Boston: Faber & Faber, 1996), p. 24.

12. Niranjana, *Gender and Space*, p. 44.

13. V. Geeta reminds us that 'nothing captures men's relationship to [urban] space as much as the image of a man urinating unconcernedly on a busy thoroughfare, next to a girl's school building, at a street corner where buses turn, in a public park ... It is as if the public place they claim so effortlessly as their own was defined by their penis and its vagaries ... literally and ideologically ... [the mark of the phallus] ... is everywhere and always backed by the threat of violence which is no idle threat'. V. Geeta, 'On Bodily Love and Hurt', in Mary John and Janaki Nair (eds), *A Question of Silence? The Sexual Economies of Modern India* (Delhi: Kali for Women, 1996), pp. 304–31, esp. p. 320.

14. For a stricter materialist reading of the control of women see Gita Sen, 'Subordination and Sexual Control: A Comparative View of the Control of Women' in Nalini Visvanathan et al. (eds), *The Women, Gender and Development Reader*, (London: Zed Books, 1997), pp. 142–49.

15. On the flaneur in European history see Benjamin, *The Arcades Project*, p. 416–455. For an unusual look at aimless wandering or 'ganjing' in Hazratganj,

Lucknow see Imtiaz Ahmad, 'Through the Eye of the Street', in Violette Graf (ed.), *Lucknow: Memories of a City* (Delhi: Oxford University Press, 1984), pp. 273–84.

16. See for instance Mary John, 'Globalisation, Sexuality and the Visual Field', *in* John and Nair, (eds), *A Question of Silence*, pp. 368–96.

17. The enduring influence of such dichotomies in classifying male and female spaces is evident in such statements as 'It is by now well-documented that across cultures women function from confined, enclosed spaces while men have access to wider more open public spaces'. Meenakshi Thapan, 'The Body in the Mirror: Women and Representation in Contemporary India', *in* Neera Chandoke (ed.), *Mapping Histories: Essays Presented to Ravinder Kumar* (Tulika, 2001), pp. 337–64, esp. p. 340.

18. See J.G.A. Pocock, 'The Ideal of Citizenship Since Classical Times', *Queen's Quarterly* 99/1 (Spring 1992), pp. 33–55, on how the founding concept of citizenship was defined as exclusively male and property-owning. See, also, Carole Pateman, *The Sexual Contract* (Stanford: Stanford University Press, 1988), esp. pp. 77–115.

19. Pocock, 'The Ideal of Citizenship', p. 37.

20. Interview with Lakshmi Devamma, 27 April 1999.

21. For the links between gender and pavement retailing, see Prabhakar, 'KR Marukatte beedhi vyaparigala kathe', *Slum Suddhi* (April 1998), pp. 5–6; Benjamin and Bhuvansewari et al., *Urban Poverty and Governance in Bangalore*. A detailed account of life in the 'Agriculture zone' of the city in the 1950s is in Venkatrayappa, *Bangalore: A Socio-ecological Study*, pp. 130–3. In his account, women tended to the cattle and poultry while men looked after the gardens.

22. On the role of Bangalore as a major centre for the trade of fruits and vegetables, and the movement of these commodities from the three central markets to the localities, see Ismath Afshan, 'Marketing of Fruits and Vegetables in Bangalore', PhD thesis, ISEC, Bangalore, 1987.

23. Srinivas, *Landscapes of Urban Memory.*

24. The announcement of Minister for City Development V. Somanna in 1999 is a case in point. He suggested that women rather than men be issued title deeds since men often sold the houses given to them by the government and misused the money, whereas women were more concerned about the secure future of their families. 'Womenfolk Among Slum Dwellers May be Given Title Deeds', *Deccan Herald*, 3 July 1999.

25. Three case studies presented in Schenk-Sandbergen, confirm this 'Women, Water and Sanitation', in Schenk and de Wit (eds), *Living in India's Slums*, pp. 200–2.

26. Rao and Tewari, *Structure of an Indian Metropolis*, pp. 185–7.

27. STEM *Survey of Slums in Bangalore, Gender Analysis*, vol. I, Analytical Report, p. 1.

28. Mirjam Letsch, 'Poor Women in a Bangalore Slum Habitat: A Perspective', in Schenk and De Wit (eds), *Living in India's Slums*, p. 152.

29. Mertens, 'Forced Relocation of Slum Dwellers in Bangalore, India', p. 48.

30. H. Ramachandran and Daljeet Singh, 'Structures and Correlates of Home Based Manufacturing Activities in Slums', in Schenk and De Wit (eds), *Living in India's Slums*, pp. 217–37.

31. STEM, *Survey of Slums in Bangalore, Gender Analysis*, vol. I, p. 3.

32. Communication from Velliamma, 29 June 1999.

33. Benjamin, Bhuvaneswari et al., 'Urban Poverty and Governance in Bangalore', p. 190.

34. De Wit, 'Slum Perceptions', pp. 108–9.

35. *History of Bharat Electronics Employee's Union*, p. 11.

36. *IT Profile at Bangalore*, p. v.

37. *History of Bharat Electronics Employee's Union*, p. 42–3.

38. For an account of the preponderance of women in the domestic low end and IT-enabled service sector compared with men in the export driven sector of the IT industry, see S. Roethboeck, M. Vijaybhaskar, and V. Gayathri, *Labour in the New Economy: The Case of the Indian Software Labour Market* (New Delhi: International Labour Organization, 2001), p. 34.

39. *History of Bharat Electronics Employee's Union*, pp. 41, 43.

40. Interview with Babu Mathew, 8 Oct. 1999.

41. All that follows is from my article 'Finding a New Voice', *Deccan Herald*, 30 April 1999.

42. All the details of this strike are taken from my article 'When Workers Became a Rampaging Mob', *Telegraph*, 21 Aug. 2001.

43. Interview with K. Leelavathi, secretary, Garment Workers' Union, 28.7.2001.

44. Anita Gurumurthy and Lakshmi Anantnarayan, 'Verite', audit of Gokuldas Exports Factory (unpublished), 23 Dec. 1998.

45. 'Malyalikal marunattil-bangalore', *Mathrubhumi Azhachapathippu*, 31 May 1970.

46. Leelamma Anthony, 'Mary Davasia', *Sandesham* (n.d.).

47. Interview with Syed Ahmed Basheer, 24.9.01.

48. *Deccan Herald*, 12 April 1960.

49. *Deccan Herald*, 5 May 1965.

50. Leelamma Anthony, 'Mary Davasia', Interview with Syed Ahmed Basheer, 24 Sept. 2001.

51. *Saga of Our Struggle Part II, the Legal Battle* (Mysore NGOs Association, 1966), pp. 1–6; *Deccan Herald*, 7 May 1965.

52. *Deccan Herald*, 21 Dec. 1969

53. Ibid.

54. Mary Davasia, 'I Speak', (Bangalore, 1969), p. 16.

55. Ibid., p. 15.

56. The *Golden Jubilee 1920–1970* souvenir records Mary Davasia's participation

in the NGO movement pictorially, but articles which record the history have carefully skirted her substantial contributions.

57. Benjamin and Bhuvaneswari, 'Urban Poverty and Governance in Bangalore', p. 48.

58. Ibid., p. 49.

59. K. Subha, *Women in Local Governance* (Jaipur: RBSA Publishers, 1994), pp. 57–60.

60. Except where other sources are acknowledged, the information on the performance of women corporators in Bangalore is taken from a UNIFEM sponsored project on 'Gender and Urban Governance in Two Cities' conceptualised by Mary John, of which I have been a part. The study will compare the experience of reservation in the cities of Delhi and Bangalore. The data is yet to be processed and fully analysed: I have referred to some of the material from interviews with fifty-nine current and past corporators of both sexes in July–August 2002.

61. *Slum Suddhi*, Oct. 1998, pp. 1–10.

62. Subha, *Women in Local Governance*, p. 64.

63. As in the case of Pushpalata, (Rajajinagar, 1996).

64. As in the case of Ratna Gopal Reddy (Jeevanbimanagar, 1996) and Mamtaz Begum, (Shivajinagar, 2001).

65. As in the case of Mahadevamma, (Kamalanagara, 1996).

66. See also Heitzman, *Network City*, pp. 123–64.

67. 'Lal bahadur shastrinagarada bahadur kelasa', *Slum Suddhi*, Sept.–Nov. 1997.

68. For a recent comparison of the women's movements in the cities of Bombay and Calcutta, see Raka Ray, *Fields of Protest: Women's Movements in India* (Delhi: Kali for Women, 2001).

69. *Vimochana: Forum for Women's Rights* (brochure, n.d.). Although the core group at Vimochana has remained small, it has been the most visible women's right group in the city. It has initiated several activities, ranging from publication and poster campaigns, the organization of film screenings and discussions, and the running of a feminist bookshop, and most recently the training of young women as auto-mechanics.

70. In this sense, the NGOization of the women's movement, which has been noted since the 1980s in other parts of India, has a longer history in a city like Bangalore.

71. Aileen D. Ross, *The Hindu Family in its Urban Setting* (Toronto: University of Toronto Press, 1961), pp. 170–1, 262–3. Ross' sample of 157 included as many as 110 Brahmins, which makes it far from representative of families in urban settings. This has moreover, made it easier for the researcher to use several ideal–typical notions of the Brahminical family form, and particularly of the middle-class family.

72. Interview with Gowramma, 11 Nov. 1999; Donna Fernandes, 12 Nov. 1999.

73. I must emphasize that these observations would be true of dowry murders in every urban Indian setting.

74. See, for instance, Woodruffe, 'An Adi-Dravida Settlement in Bangalore', p. 22; Letsch, 'Poor Women in a Bangalore Slum Habitat: A Perspective'; Benjamin and Bhuvaneswari, also emphasize that some poor women are the sole migrants to the city, 'Urban Poverty and Governance in Bangalore', pp. 70, 76.

75. Ravindra, *Metropolitan Bangalore: A Management Perspective*, Table 11, p. 183, shows that women accounted for 32.8 and 35.1 per cent of migrants from rural areas to Bangalore city within the district, while men accounted for 27.3 and 30.9 per cent in the census years 1971 and 1981 respectively. Within Bangalore district, the 1981 census revealed that sex ratios varied from as low as 865 in Bangalore north *taluka* to 983 in Doddballapur *taluka* to provide a district average of 916 well below the state average of 963. *Bangalore District Census Handbook, 1981*, p. li. It is striking that marriage does not figure as a reason for in-migration in the brief analysis of 1981 data. In the mid 1970s, Prakash Rao and Tewari noted that marriage was the single most important reason for female migration. *Structure of an Indian Metropolis*, p. 247.

76. M.N. Srinivas, *Village, Caste, Gender and Method: Essays in Indian Social Anthropology,* (Oxford University Press, 2000), pp. 163, 177.

77. Mary John, 'The Encounters of Sociology and Womens' Studies: Questions From the Borders', *Contributions from Indian Sociology* (n.s.) 35, 2 (2001), p. 248.

78. 'City Tops in Female Fatality Rates', *Deccan Herald*, 30 Dec. 1971. Accidental deaths involving women accounted for 315 out of 695 deaths in 1969.

79. In 1976, the Karnataka government passed the Karnataka (Regulation and Miscellaneous Provisions) Bill, 'Goodbye to Wedding Gifts', *Deccan Herald*, 13 Dec. 1976.

80. See Radha Kumar, *A History of Doing: An Illustrated History of the Campaigns for Women's Rights and Feminism* (New Delhi, Kali for Women, 1993), pp. 115–26.

81. Vimochana Pamphlet number 6, 'The Murder of Laxmi and her Daughter', 18 Feb. 2000. A large group assembled at Subramanyapura Police Station to protest the death of Laxmi and her daughter Soumya by the husband and father Rangaswamy, who worked at Hindusthan Granite Ltd. There were innumerable protests organized by a range of women's groups in the early 1980s protesting women's deaths in various neighbourhoods of Bangalore.

82. Vimochana Pamphlet number 7, 'Manipal Motors: Dismiss Srikanth' demanded the dismissal of Srikanth who had allegedly harassed his doctor wife Sujatha to death for filing a case before Basavangudi Police Station under sections 498 (A) 384, 504 of IPC, along with section 3 and 4 of the Dowry Prevention act. The man was given anticipatory bail.

83. Vimochana Pamphlet number 6, 'The Murder of Laxmi and her daughter', 18 Feb. 2000.

84. Interview with Gowramma, 11 Nov. 1999; Vimochana Pamphlet Number 3, 'I Cry for Help, No One's There', 1991, recounted the stories of six women who had lost their lives, and the indifference of the courts, etc., to the problem of women. See, also, V.S. Elizabeth, 'Patterns and Trends of Domestic Violence in India: An Examination of Court Records', ICRW, 2000.

85. Interview with Gowramma, 11 Nov. 1999.

86. Even this was no more than the tip of the proverbial iceberg as these statistics were drawn from the 10 per cent of the cases reported, while the actual figures were substantially higher. Most of what follows is taken from files and records at the Vimochana office, Bangalore.

87. The Bangalore police commissioner who dismissed the statistics as an exaggeration was stunned when his own department came up with a tally of 1178 deaths of women between the ages of 14–40 in 1998!

88. *Asian Age*, 19 Jan. 1998. In many cases the homes did not even possess a 'stove'.

89. Vimochana Pamphlets number 3 and 4.

90. 'If its festival its time for more young brides to burn', *Times of India*, 13 Feb. 1998; *Rajyadalli mahileyara mele aagindagge nadeyutthiruva dowrjanya haagu varadakshine saavina bagge parishilisi antaha prakaranagalu kadime maadalu sambandapatta kaanunugalige sooktha thiddupadi haagu avugala yashasvi anushtaanakke sooktha salahegalondige varadi sallisalu rachisalaagiruva janti sadana samithiya varadi*. 1 July 1999, pp. 5, 20. 'When Brides Go Up In Smoke', *Deccan Herald*, 12 Dec. 1998.

91. See, for instance, Parvathi Menon, '"Dowry Deaths" in Bangalore', *Frontline*, 14–27 Aug. 1999.

92. *Rajyadalli mahileyara mele aagindagge nadeyutthiruva dowrjanya*, p. 8.

93. Ibid., pp. 9–10.

94. Truth Commission for Women: A Public Hearing, 15 Aug. 1999.

95. *Rajyadalli mahileyaramele aagindagge nadeyuthiruva dowrjanya*, p. 30.

96. Vimochana, 'Unnatural Death of Women in Marriage: A Campaign Diary' (Bangalore: Vimochana, 1999), pp. 25–8.

97. Interview with Gowramma, 11 Nov. 1999.

98. Vimochana Pamphlet number 3, 1991.

99. *State of Karnataka (Mahadevpura police)* v. *D.N. Vijendran* Case no. 87/ 1989, Judgement 30 Oct. 1990.

100. Thus Muniraju, who was acquitted after having stabbed his wife of 18 years, Rangamma, at the street corner, injuring her cheek, hands, and nose, was acquitted of the charge of both harassment or attempt to murder as 'It can be said the accused did not have any intention of killing Rangamma ... *He only injured her in two places, and let her off*, even though nobody was around'. NC no. 290: 1994, *Karnataka State Government* v. *Muniraju* (emphasis added).

101. Interview with Gowramma, 11 Nov. 1999.

102. Ross, *The Hindu Family in an Urban Setting*, p. 262–3.

103. Ibid., p. 137.

104. In *T. Singh* v. *State of Punjab* AIR 1970, SC 16566, the term dying declaration was defined as 'a statement made by a person as to the cause of his death or as to any circumstances resulting in his death'.

105. A conference on Dying Declaration, 16 June 2001. In his essay on dowry, Srinivas admits to being baffled by the attitude of the victim. Srinivas, *Village Caste, Gender and Method*, p. 179.

106. Faheen Taj of D.J. Halli was burnt to death within days of marriage, but police asked the mother why she wanted to ruin a young man by filing the complaint. *Hindu*, 12 June 1999.

107. See Jacobs, *The Death and Life of Great American Cities*, pp. 38–9.

108. *Indian Express*, 12 Nov. 1996.

109. 'Pageant Begins Amid Tight Security', *Hindu*, 13 Nov. 1996.

110. 'Three Events Shifted to City Outskirts', *Indian Express*, 5 Nov. 1996.

111. 'Manufacturing Consent: A Dossier on Beauty and Beauty Contests' (Bangalore: Visthaar, 1997), p. 46.

112. 'Miss World Pageant: Case for the Defence', *Times of India*, 16 Sept. 1996.

113. *Times of India*, 28 Aug. 1996.

114. *Times of India*, 29 Oct. 1996.

115. 'Belittled by Miss World? Not Me', *Times of India*, 9 Sept. 1996.

116. 'Manufacturing Consent'.

117. B.P. Das, 'The Other Side Story', mimeo.

118. 'Kannada Activists Take out Procession', *Hindu*, 23 Nov. 1996.

119. *Indian Express*, 27 Oct. 1996.

120. *Hindu*, 11 Oct. 1996. The AIMSS is a left wing organization that has long campaigned against obscenity in representations of women. Their presence in the city is visible in the many meetings and public communications, including a series of wall writings, that they organize throughout Bangalore city.

121. *Deccan Herald*, 6 Sept. 1996.

122. John, 'Globalization, Sexuality and the Visual Field'.

123. *Deccan Herald*, 25 Oct. 1996.

124. http://www.chorley2.demon.co.uk/wib.html (accessed 30 November 2003.)

125. The protest is largely, but not exclusively, attended by women.

Conclusion: Is 'Singapore' Bangalore's Destiny?

1. 'Glorious Master Plan for IT Corridor' *Hindu*, 2 Sept. 2002.

2. 'Krishna Sets Stage for the Biotech Revolution', *Times of India*, 25 Feb. 2001; 'Tax Breaks, Other Incentives Offered', *Deccan Herald*, 25 Feb. 2001.

3. D.D. Kosambi *Exasperating Essays: Exercises in the Dialectical Method* (Delhi: People's Publishing House, 1992). See also Partha Chatterjee, 'Are Indian Cities Becoming Bourgeois at Last? in *The Politics of the Governed: Reflections on Popular Politics in Most of the World* (New York: Columbia University Press, 2004), pp. 131–48. My own research, as laid out in this book, does substantiate his schematic discussion of the phases through which the post-colonial Indian city has passed, with some important differences.

4. www.blrforward.com (accessed 1 March 2003).

5. 'BDA Drive Against Illegal Structures', *Business Line*, 2 Sept, 2002.

6. 'Website Launched to Help Allottees', *Hindu*, 21 Dec. 2000.

7. 'BDA Signs MoU with France for City Development', *Deccan Herald*, 7 Feb. 2003.

8. See Beng Huat, *Political Legitimacy and Housing*.

9. The UNIFEM study on Gender and Urban Governance referred to in chapter 8 undertook a ward survey of 100 people each from eight selected wards. This is a very preliminary and superficial summary of the data that is yet to be processed.

10. 'Local Bodies Must not Rely on Government', *Hindu*, 21 Dec. 2000.

11. *Deccan Herald*, 25 Jan. 2000.

12. 'While the maiden Bangalore Summit last year was full of euphoria, the second summit concentrated on reality', said the *Times of India*, 'BATF: A small steady step for city', *Times of India*, 25 Feb. 2001. 'CM snubs politicians for opposing BATF', *Deccan Herald*, 25 Feb. 2001.

13. 'BATF Urban Initiatives: The Experiment in PPP Approach', www.blrforward.com (accessed 1 March 2003).

14. Presentation at the meeting to discuss the Infrastructure Project of the Bangalore–Mysore corridor, National Institute of Advanced Studies, 25 Sept. 1998.

15. 'Betrayed by the Bangalore Agenda Task Force', *City Reporter*, 14 Sept. 2001.

16. 'BMP Decentralizes Authority on OFC Laying', *Deccan Herald*, 25 Feb. 2001.

17. 'Biotech Park: IT Department Unfazed by UAS Rebuff', *Hindu*, 19 Sept. 2001. In a separate and equally controversial development, Venkatraman & Associates was given the contract to redesign Manickvelu Mansions for the National Gallery of Modern Art in 2001: the modalities by which this company was chosen have been questioned both by the artist community and the community of architects. See *Hindu*, 18 Aug. 2002.

18. 'Farm Department Questions UAS Decision Not to Give Up Land', *Hindu*, 22 Sept. 2001.

19. 'Police Beat up Students, Professors', *Hindu*, 27 Sept. 2001.

20. 'New Location for Bio-tech Park', *Hindu*, 2 Oct. 2001.

21. 'State's IT Dept Fed Up with Biotech Park Row', *Indian Express*, 1 Oct. 2001.

22. Interview with Ramesh Hariharan, Chief Technical Officer, Strand Genomics, 13 Nov. 2002.

23. Parthasarathy, 'Globalisation and Agglomeration in Newly Industrialising Countries', pp. 338, 387.

24. Samuel Paul, *Holding the State to Account: Citizen Monitoring in Action*, (Bangalore: Books for Change, 2002), p. 29.

25. Ibid., p. 105.

26. Chatterjee, 'Beyond the Nation? Or Within?'.

Select Bibliography

Government Reports and Official Documents

Activities and Achievements of CITB Since its Inception, i.e. from 26.1.1945 to 6.6.1973.

A. Ravindra et al., *Report of The Committee on Urban Management of Bangalore City* (Bangalore: November 1997).

Bengaluru abhivruddhi pradhikaarakke vasathi mathu nagaraabhivruddhi ilakeya vishaya samitiya maanya adhyaksharu maththu sadasyara bheti, 15.12.1995: *prashnottharagala tippani* (BDA 1995).

Comprehensive Development Plan (CDP) Report, 1985.

Comprehensive Development Plan (Revised) Bangalore: Report, vol. I and II (Bangalore, 1995).

Committee on Public Undertakings (COPU) 8th Report: Third Lok Sabha on Townships and Factory Buildings of Public Undertakings May 1965 (Lok Sabha Secretariat, Delhi).

Justice Kuldip Singh Commission of Enquiry, Report, vol. I (June 1990).

Justice N.R. Kudoor Commission of Enquiry on the Venus Circus Fire Accident Occurred in Bangalore on 7.2.1981 (Bangalore, 1982).

Kasturbhai Lalbhai, *Report on the State Owned and State Aided Industrial Concerns in Mysore* (Bangalore, 1951).

Interim Report of the Committee of Legislators on the Slum Problems of Bangalore.

Justice P.A Kulkarni Commission of Enquiry Report on Police Firings at Various Places in Bangalore City, 28 October 1987.

Memoranda of several Associations on the Retrocession of the Civil and Military Station of Bangalore to the Mysore State, KSA.

Millenium Bio Tech Policy (Bangalore 2001).

MSS Eur: New Model Housing Erected at Knoxpet by the Municipal Commission, 1923, IOL.

Rajyadalli mahileyara mele aagindagge nadeyutthiruva dowrjanya haagu varadakshine saavina bagge parishilisi antaha prakaranagalu kadime maadalu sambandapatta kaanunugalige sooktha thiddupadi haagu avugala yashasvi anushtaanakke sooktha salahegalondige varadi sallisalu rachisalaagiruva janti sadana samithiya varadi, 1 July 1999.

G.V.K. Rao, *Report on an Enquiry Conducted Under Section 64 of Karnataka Co-operative Societies Act 1959 into the Activities of Certain House Building Co-operative Societies of Bangalore City* (Bangalore, 1988).

Papers Relating to the Restoration of Jurisdiction over the Assigned Tract of Bangalore to the Mysore state (1935 ?) *KSA.*

Report of the Bangalore Development Committee (Bangalore, 1954).

Report of the Expert Committee Constituted by the Government for Submitting Proposals for Preservation, Restoration or Otherwise of the Existing Tanks in the Bangalore Metropolitan Area (Bangalore, 1988).

Report of Sri R.L. Agnohotri, One Man Commission Inquiry to Inquire into the Police Firing on 4.9.82 at Viveknagar, Bangalore City (Bangalore, 1983).

Report of Court Appointed Commissioner Prabha Murthy on Green Belt Violations: in WP 31562 of 1997 (BDA PIL) Krishna Bhat v *BDA and Others.*

*Report of the High Power Committee set up by the Government of Karnataka on Beautification of Bangalore (*Bangalore, 1994).

Report of the N.D. Venkatesh Commission of Inquiry, volume I and *II* (Bangalore, 1992).

Report of the Vidhana Soudha Enquiry Committee, vol. I, II, and III (Bangalore, 1956).

Report on Industrial Townships: Committee on Plan Projects (New Delhi: Building Projects Team, 1963).

Outline Development Plan (ODP) for the Bangalore Metropolitan Region, vol. II (Bangalore, 1963?).

Report on the Comprehensive Development Plan (CDP) of Bangalore (Bangalore, 1976),

Report of the Commission of Enquiry: Collapse of the Hotel Building Under Construction Gopal Film Theatre Complex, Subedar Chatram Road (Bangalore, 1985).

Seminar on City Architecture, December 1966, mimeo.

White Paper on the BDA, 1980–3

Non-Governmental Documents

A Mute Genocide: A Report on the Gory Incidents of Violence on Karnataka Tamils During the Black December 1991 (Bangalore: Bangalore Tamil Sangham, 1992).

Indian People Human Rights Tribunal Report (Bangalore: 1992).

'*Medium' for Communalism: A Report on the Anti-Urdu Communal Riots* (Bangalore: People's Democratic Forum, 1994).

Who Owns the Idga Maidan of Jayanagar? A Report of a Fact Finding Committee (Bangalore: People's Democratic Forum and People's Union for Civil Liberties, 1999).

Private Papers/Collections

B. Puttaiah Private Papers, KSA.

D.V. Gundappa Private Papers, KSA.

Kengal Hanumanthaiah Collection, KSA.

K. Venkatappa Private Papers, KSA.

N. Lakshman Rau Private Papers.

N. Madhav Rau Private Papers, KSA.

T.P. Issar Collection, KSA.

Articles and Papers

Anthony, Ms Leelamma, 'Mary Davasia', *Sandesham* (n.d.).

Balasubramanyam, V.N., 'Bangalore is Where the Action Is', presentation at Bangalore IT.com, November 1988.

Balekundry, S.G., 'Injustice to Karnataka in Regard to Cauvery Waters' (Bangalore, 1991).

'Bangalore: The Next Singapore?', in *Inside Bangalore: The Ideal Address, Economic Times*, Supplement, 2000.

Beals, Alan 'Change in the Leadership of a Mysore Village', in Srinivas (ed.), *India's Villages*, pp. 147–60.

Bell, Clive, 'Ideology and Economic Interests in Indian Land Reform', in David Lehman (ed.), *Agrarian Reform and Agrarian Reformism* (London: Faber & Faber 1974).

Beng Huat, Chua, 'Decoding the Political in Civic Spaces: An Interpretive Essay', in Chua Beng Huat and Norman Edwards (eds), *Public Space: Design, Use and Management* (Singapore: Centre for Advanced Studies, National University of Singapore, 1992), 55–68.

______ 'That Imagined Space: Nostalgia for the Kampungs', in Brenda Yeoh and Lily Kong (eds), *Portraits of Places: History, Community, and Identity in Singapore* (Singapore: Times Editions, 1995), 223–41.

______ 'Singapore: Management of a City State in South East Asia', in Jurgen Ruland (ed.), *The Dynamics of Metropolitan Management in South East Asia* (Singapore: ISEAS, 1997), pp. 207–24.

Benjamin, Solomon, 'Governance, Economic Settings and Poverty in Bangalore', *Environment and Urbanisation* 12.1 (April 2000), 35–51.

Benjamin Solomon and Bhuvaneswari R., et al., 'Urban Poverty and Governance in Bangalore' (2000).

Bijker, Wiebe E., and Karin Bijsterveld, 'Women Walking Through the Plans', *Technology and Culture*, vol. 41 (July 2000), pp. 485–515.

Bose Nirmal Kumar, 'Calcutta: A Premature Metropolis', *Scientific American* 213:3 (1965), 90–105.

Campbell, Tim, and Bill Wickstead, 'The Spatial Implications of Technology Development in Bangalore' (New Delhi: USAID, 1987).

Chandrasekhar Laxmi, 'Brihat samskrithika aandolana', *Samudaya 25: Samskrithika Jatha Utsavagalu* (Hubli–Dharwad: Samudaya, 2000).

Chandrashekar, Ra Nam, 'Kaigarike kacheri kannada sanghagala kainkarya' (unpublished mimeo).

Chatterjee, Partha, 'Beyond the Nation? Or Within?', *Economic and Political Weekly* 32:1&2 (1997), 30–4.

———, 'Claims on the Past: The Genealogy of Historiography in Bengal', in Ranajit Guha (ed.), *Subaltern Studies: Writings on South Asian History and Society*, vol. VIII (Delhi: Oxford University Press, 1994), pp. 1–49.

———, 'Are Indian Cities Becoming Bourgeois at Last?' *The Politics of the Governed: Reflections on Popular Politics in Most of the World* (New York: Columbia University Press, 2004), pp. 131–48.

Chatterjee, Partha, and Asok Sen, 'Planning and the Political Process in India: Duality and Differentiation', in A.K. Bagchi (ed.), *Economy, Society, Polity: Essays in the Political Economy of Indian Planning, Essays in Honour of Prof Bhabhatosh Dutta* (Calcutta: Oxford University Press, 1988), pp. 196–226.

Chaudhuri, Sachin, 'Centralization and the Alternative Forms of Decentralization: A Key Issue', in Roy Turner (ed.), *India's Urban Future* (Bombay: Oxford University Press, 1962), 213–39.

Chidanandamurthy, M., 'Kannadadha samasyegalu', in *Kannada-kannadiga-karnataka.*

———, 'Historiography in Kannada during the 19th Century', in Tarashanker Banerjee (ed.), *Historiography in Modern Indian Languages, 1800–1947* (Calcutta: Naya Prakashan, 1987).

Erappa, M. Kambali, 'Majestic Sutha ....', *Heddarigunta* (Bangalore: 1999), 1–8.

Das, B.P., 'The Other Side Story', mimeo.

Davasia, Mary, 'I Speak' (Bangalore: 1969).

de Wit, Michael, 'Geographical Information Systems Remote Sensing in Indian Cities: The Case of Bangalore' Indo-Dutch Programme for Alternative in Development (IDPAD) Occasional Papers and Reprints, 1992–8.

———, 'Slum Perceptions and Cognition', in Schenk and De Wit (eds), *Living in India's Slums*, pp. 79–112.

Deshpande, Satish, 'Communalising the Nation-Space: Notes on the Spatial Strategies of Hindutva', *Economic and Political Weekly*, 30.50 (16 Dec. 1995), pp. 3220–7.

Donaldson, Thomas, and Lee Preston 'The Stakeholder Theory of the Corporation:

Concepts Evidence and Implications', *Academy of Management Review* 20:1 (1995), 65–91.

Elizabeth, V.S, 'Patterns and Trends of Domestic Violence in India: An Examination of Court Records', International Centre for Research on Women (ICRW, 2000).

Folke, Steen, ' Conflicts over natural resources in South India—A political economy perspective', *Economic and Political Weekly* 33.7 (1998), pp. 341–7.

Garudachar, B.K., 'Bangalore Past and Present', in *Mysore Economic Journal*, May 1915.

Geeta, V., 'On Bodily Love and Hurt', in Mary John and Janaki Nair (eds), *A Question of Silence? The Sexual Economies of Modern India* (Delhi: Kali for Women, 1996), pp. 304–31.

Geethacharya, Na., 'Bengaluru—sthalanama ondu tippani', *Rajdhani* (Bangalore, 1991).

Giessen, Peter, 'Household Industries and their Market Relations: A Case Study of the Situation of Petty Commodity Producers in Bangalore, South India', mimeo, 1988.

Gist, Noel P., 'The Ecology of Bangalore: An East West Comparison' in V.K. Tewari et al. (eds), *Indian Cities: Ecological Perspectives* (Delhi: Concept Publishers, 1986), pp. 15–33.

Goh, Robbie, 'Things to a Void: Utopian Discourse, Communality and Constructed Interstices in Singapore Public Housing', Paper presented at 'City as Text: Urban Topographies and Critical Interventions', Singapore, September 1999.

Gowda, K.S. Rame, 'Fringe Area Development in Metropolitan Centres with Special Reference to Bangalore', *National Symposium on Planning and Development of Metropolitan Bangalore* (Bangalore, 1987).

Gundanna, C.K. 'Samudaayada odanaatadalli', *Samudaya 25: Samskrithika Jatha Utsavagalu* (Hubli Dharwad: Samudaya, 2000).

Gundappa, D.V., 'Bengalurinalli hotel udhyamada praramba', *Jnapaka Chitrashale*, vol. 7 (Bangalore: 1974).

______, 'The Gokhale Institute of Public Affairs: Its Birth, Growth, Prospects and Ideals', *Gokhale Institute of Public Affairs 1915–1945–1965* (Bangalore: 1965).

Gupta, Narayani, 'Urbanism in South India: Eighteenth/ Nineteenth Centuries', in Indu Banga (ed.), *The City in Indian History* (Delhi: Manohar, 1994), p. 120–47.

______, 'Urban Form and Meaning in South Asia: Perspectives from the Modern Era', in Howard Spodek and Doris Meith Srinivasan, *Urban Form and Meaning in South Asia: The Shaping of Cities from Pre Historic to Pre Colonial Times* (Hanover and London: University Press of New England, 1993), pp. 243–52.

Harvey, David, 'Society, the City and the Space Economy of Urbanism',Washington: Commission on College Geography Resource Paper no. 18, 1972.

Heitzman, James, 'Corporate Strategy and Planning in the Science City: Bangalore as "Silicon Valley"', *Economic and Political Weekly* 34.5 (30 Jan. 1999), PE 2–11.

______, 'Geographic Information Systems in India's "Silicon Valley": The Impact of Information Technology on Planning in the 1990s', mimeo, courtesy the author.

———, 'Sports and Conflict in Urban Planning: The Indian National Games in Bangalore', *Journal of Sport and Social Issues,* vol. 23.1, Feb. 1999, pp. 5–23.

Holmstrom, Mark, 'Religious Change in an Industrial City of South India', *Journal of the Royal Asiatic Society,* 1, 1971, 28–40.

———, 'Action Sets and Ideology: A Municipal Election in South India', *Contributions to Indian Sociology* (n.s.) no. II, Dec. 1969, pp. 76–93.

Holston, James, and Arjun Appadurai, 'Cities and Citizenship' *Pubic Culture* (1996), 187–204.

Hoselitz, Bert F., 'A Survey of the Literature on Urbanisation in India', in Porter (ed.), *India's Urban Future,* pp. 425–43.

Jain, Sanjeev, 'The Bangalore Lunatic Asylum.' (mimeo)

Jayaram, N., 'Sanguine Plans and Stark Realities: Limits to Planned Urban Habitat Change (the Case of Bangalore)' *Nagarlok,* 21.3 (July–Sep. 1989), 12, pp. 36–52.

Jessop, Bob, 'Cities as the New National Champions in International Competition', Paper presented at the conference 'City State and Region in a Global Order: Towards the 21st century', Hiroshima, Japan, 1998.

Jodhka, Surinder S., 'Nation and Village: Images of Rural India in Gandhi, Nehru and Ambedkar', *Economic and Political Weekly*, 37:32 (2002), pp. 3343–52.

———, 'From "Book View" to "Field View": Social Anthropological Constructions of the Indian Village', *Oxford Development Studies* 26:3 (1998), 311–31.

John, Mary, 'Globalisation, Sexuality and the Visual Field', in Mary John and Janaki Nair (eds), *A Question of Silence, The Sexual Economies of Modern India* (Delhi: Kali for Women, 1998), pp. 368–96.

———, 'The Encounters of Sociology and Women's Studies: Questions from the Borders', *Contributions to Indian Sociology* (n.s.) 35, 2 (2001), pp. 237–58.

Karekar, S.K., 'Bangalore Beautiful: Urban Aesthetics', *National Symposium on Planning and Development of Metropolitan Bangalore*. Bangalore, 1987.

Kaviraj, Sudipta, 'Filth and the Public Sphere: Concepts and Practice about Space in Calcutta', *Public Culture*, 10:1 (1997), 83–113.

———, 'On the Structure of Nationalist Discourse', in T.V. Satyamurthy (ed.), *State and Nation in the Context of Social Change,* vol. I (Delhi: Oxford University Press, 1994), pp. 298–335.

———, 'The Culture of Representative Democracy', in Partha Chatterjee (ed.), *Wages of Freedom: Fifty Years of the Indian Nation State* (Delhi: Oxford University Press, 1998), pp. 147–78.

Khosla, Romi, 'Including Iconography and Images in Architecture' *Journal of Arts and Ideas* no. 7, April–June 1984, pp. 5–36.

Kumar, Arun, 'National Housing Policy: The Implications' *Economic and Political Weekly* 24.23 (10 June 1989), pp. 1285–94.

Kumar, Radha, 'City Lives: Workers' Housing and Rent in Bombay, 1911–1947' *Indian Economic and Social History Review* 22 (1987), pp. 47–56.

Kumaran, K.S., 'Bengalurinalli swatantrya samarada smaraneeya stalagalu', in *Bengaluru nagara corporation: bellihabbada sanchike* (Bangalore, 1974), pp. 47–54.

Lambert, Richard D., 'The Impact of Urban Society upon Village Life' in Turner (ed.), *India's Urban Future*, pp. 117–40.

Letsch, Mirjam, 'Poor women in a Bangalore slum Habitat: A Perspective' in Schenk and De Wit (eds), *Living in India's Slums*, pp. 135–60.

Lynch O.M., 'Rural Cities in India: Continuities and Discontinuities' in Rao (ed.), *Urban Sociology in India*, pp. 251–71.

Madon, Shirin, 'Information-Based Global Economy and Socio-Economic Development: The case of Bangalore' *The Information Society* 13 (1997), pp. 227–43.

'Magaji dhondusa avaru', *Kempegowdanagara darshana* (Bangalore, 1980).

'Manufacturing Consent' (Bangalore: Visthaar, 1997).

Manor, James, 'Pragmatic Progressives in Regional Politics: The case of Devaraj Urs' *Economic and Political Weekly*, Annual Number 15.5, 6 & 7 (February 1980), pp. 201–13.

______, 'Structural Changes in Karnataka Politics' *Economic and Political Weekly*, vol. 12.44 (29 October 1977), pp. 1865–9.

Massey, Doreen, 'Politics and Space/Time' in *Space, Place and Gender* (Cambridge: Polity Press, 1994), pp. 249–72.

Metcalf, Thomas R., 'Architecture and Empire: Sir Herbert Baker and the Buildings of New Delhi' *in* Robert Frykenberg (ed.), *Delhi Through the Ages: Essays in Urban History, Culture and Society* (Delhi: Oxford University Press, 1986), pp. 391–400.

Millar, Jane, 'Sustaining software teletrade in Bangalore: Fostering Market Agility through Economic Competence' *Economic and Political Weekly* 35.26 (24–30 June 2000), 2253–62.

Murthy Rao, A.N., 'Kensington Park' in *Samagra lalitha prabandhagalu* (Bangalore: Ankita Pusthaka, 1999), pp. 61–6.

______, 'Bengaluru' *Samagra lalitha prabandhagalu*, pp. 217–26.

Murthy, Vidya, 'History in the Remaking', *The Art News Magazine of India*, IV: III, pp. 74–6.

Nagaraj, D.R., 'The Nature of Kannada Nationalism', *Journal of Karnataka Studies* 1 (Nov. 2003–Apr. 2004), pp. 145–156. Translated by M. Madhava Prasad.

Nair, Janaki, 'Drawing a line: K. Venkatappa and his publics.' *Indian Economic and Social History Review*, 35.2 (1998), pp. 179–210.

______, 'The Devadasi, Dharma and the State' in *Economic and Political Weekly* 29:50 (10 Dec. 1994), pp. 3157–67.

______, '"Memories of Underdevelopment": Language and its Identities in Contemporary Karnataka', *Economic and Political Weekly*, 31.41 and 42 (12–19 Oct. 1996), pp. 2809–16.

———, 'Singapore is not Bangalore's Destiny', *Economic and Political Weekly*, 35.18 (29 April 2000), pp. 1512–14.

———, 'Contending Ideologies? The Mass Awakener's Union' *Social Scientist*, 22: 7–8 (July–August 1994), pp. 42–63.

———, 'Predatory Capitalism and Legalised Land Grab: Karnataka Land Reforms' *Economic and Political Weekly* 31.5 C (1996), pp. 251–2.

———, 'Prohibited Marriage' *Contributions to Indian Sociology* (n.s.) 29.1&2 (1995), pp. 137–86.

———, 'From Devadasi Reform to SITA: Reforming Sex Work in Mysore state, 1892–1937', *National Law School Journal*, Special Issue, 1993, pp. 82–94.

Narasimhaiah, H., 'Ayyo, abhimana shunya bengaluru', *Tereda Mana* (1974), p. 144–50.

Narayana, G., 'Bengaluru nagarada mukhya samasyegalu' (mimeo, 1997).

Pani, Narendar, Tara Anand, Vinod Vyasulu, 'Impact of Colonialism on the Economic Structure of Indian Cities: 1800–1900' in Vinod Vyasulu and Amulya K.N. Reddy (convenors), *Essays on Bangalore*, vol. I (Bangalore: KSCST, 1985), pp. 1–34.

Parry, Amanda, 'Law and Urban Change in an Indian City' in Edesio Fernandes and Ann Varley (eds), *Illegal Cities: Law and Urban Change in Developing Countries* (Zed Books, London and New York, 1998), pp. 89–103.

Pendakur, V. Setty, 'Elaboration of the Transport System' in Kernial Singh Sandhu and Wheatleaf, Paul (eds), *Management of Success: The Moulding of Modern Singapore* (Singapore: ISEAS, 1989), 399–419.

Pocock, D.F., 'Sociologies: Urban and Rural' in Rao (ed.), *Urban Sociology in India*, pp. 18–39.

Pocock, J.G.A., 'The Ideal of Citizenship Since Classical Times' *Queen's Quarterly* 99/1 (Spring 1992), pp. 33–55.

Prakash Gyan, 'The Urban Turn' in *Sarai Reader 02: Cities of Everyday Life* (Delhi: CSDS, 2002), p. 2–7.

Prasad, Madhava, 'Back to the Present' *Cultural Dynamics* 10:2 (July 1998), pp. 123–31.

Prasanna, Subbarayan and Vathsala, V.S., 'Development Sequences and the Planning Continuum in Bangalore Metropolis' (unpublished paper, 1983).

Ramachandran, H., 'Slumming of a Metropolis' in Vyasulu and Reddy (ed.), *Essays on Bangalore*, vol. 2 (Bangalore, KSCST, 1985).

———, and Daljeet Singh, 'Structures and Correlates of Home Based Manufacturing Activities in Slums' in Schenk and De Wit (eds), *Living in India's Slums*, pp. 217–37.

———, 'Greening of a Metropolis: An analysis of open spaces in and around Bangalore' (Bangalore: ISEC Working Paper, 1982).

Ramachandrappa Bargur, 'Bengaluru nagara enba ondu halli' in B. Srinivasaraju (ed.), *Prabandhagalu* (Bangalore: Kannada Sahitya Akademi, 1992), pp. 65–72.

Rao, Harihara Srinivasa, 'Bengalurina haleya peteya garadigalu' *Itihasa darshana* (Bangalore, 1996).

Rao, M. Bhaskara and M. Johnson Samuel, 'Growth of Bangalore: Population and Industrialisation' (Bangalore: ISEC Working Paper, IPD 368).

Rao, Ramachandra S.K., 'Bengalurina samajika nele' in *Bengaluru nagara corporation bellihabbada sanchike* (Bangalore, 1974), pp. 39–46.

Reddy, Anita, 'Lakshmipuram Slum Rehousing Project' in *National Symposium on Planning and Development of Metropolitan* Bangalore (Bangalore, BDA, BDA 1987).

Saberwal, Satish, 'Indian urbanism: a socio-historical perspective' *Contributions to Indian Sociology (*n.s.) 11:1 (1977), pp. 1–19.

Samuel, M. Johnson and M. Lingaraju, 'Migrants in Bangalore' (Bangalore: ISEC Working Paper 13, 1989).

Sangundayya S.G., 'Bengaluru' *Ekantha maththu ithara prabandhagalu* (Bangalore: Kamadhenu Prakashana, 1993).

Schenk-Sandbergen, Loes, 'Women, Water and Sanitation in the Slums of Bangalore: A Case study of Action-Research' in Schenk and de Wit (eds), *Living in India's Slums*, pp. 187–216.

Sen, Gita, 'Subordination and Sexual Control: A Comparative View of the Control of Women' in Nalini Visvanathan et al. (eds), *The Women, Gender and Development Reader* (London: Zed Books, 1997), pp. 142–9.

Shekhar, V. Keerthi, 'Sociography of Satellite Towns', in R. Ram Mohan Rao and S. Simhadri (eds), *Indian Cities: Towards the Next Millenium*' (Jaipur and Delhi: Rawat Publications, 1999), pp. 49–79.

Sinha, Pradip. 'Calcutta and the currents of history' in Sukanta Chaudhuri (ed.), *Calcutta: the Living City*, vol. I, *The present* (Calcutta: Oxford University Press, 1990), pp. 31–44.

Srinivas M.N., 'Village studies and their significance' in D.N. Majumdar (ed.), *Rural Profiles (1)* (Lucknow: Ethnographic and Folk Culture Society, 1955), pp. 87–100.

———, 'The industrialisation and urbanisation of rural areas' in Rao (ed.), *Urban Sociology in India*, pp. 488–99.

Srinivas, Smriti, 'Hot Bodies and Cooling Substances: Ritual and Sport in a Science City' *Journal of Sport and Social Issues* 23.1, February 1999, pp. 24–40.

Srinivas, Ve. 'Kannada chaluvali nadedubanda daari' *Kannada Kanmani* (1996).

Srivatsan, A., 'Politics of Tamil Monuments' (mimeo).

Stein, Burton 'Towns and Cities: the Far South' in Tapan Raychaudhuri and Irfan Habib (eds), *The Cambridge Economic History of India*, vol. 1, c. 1200–1750 (Hyderabad: Orient Longman, 1984), pp. 452–8.

Subbaiah, M., 'Apple Cultivation in Bangalore', *Mysore Economic Journal* (June 1915).

Subramanian, Dilip. 'The MICO Strike: A Retrospective' *Economic and Political Weekly*, vol. 15:22 (31 May 1980), pp. M59–68.

______. 'Bangalore Public Sector Strike: A Critical Appraisal' *Economic and Political Weekly* 32: 15 (12 April 1997), pp. 767–78, 32.16 (19 April 1997), pp. 843–53.

______. 'Bangalore Public Sector: The Unofficial Strike, 1981 *South Indian Studies*, 3 (January–June 1997), 89–143.

Southworth, Michael, and Balaji Parthasarathy, 'The Suburban Public Realm: Its Emergence, Growth and Transformation in the American Metropolis' *Journal of Urban Design*, vol. I, no. 3, 1996, pp. 245–63 and vol. II, no. 1, 1997, pp. 9–34.

Thapan, Meenakshi, 'The body in the mirror: Women and Representation in Contemporary India', in Neera Chandoke (ed.), *Mapping Histories: Essays presented to Ravinder Kumar* (Tulika, 2001), pp. 337–64.

Upadhyaya Shashi Bhushan, 'Cotton Mill Workers in Bombay, 1875–1918: Conditions of Work and Life' *Economic and Political Weekly* 25.30 (28 July 1990), PE 87–99.

Venkatachalam, Lakshmi, 'Urban Planning Processes: A Critique of the Master Plan Concept' (mimeo n.d.)

Vagale, L.R., 'The Green Belt: Can it check the growth of Bangalore?' in *National Symposium on Planning and Development of Metropolitan Bangalore* (Bangalore: 1987), pp. 13–14.

Venkatesh, M.G. and C.R. Bhat, 'Samudaya nadedhu bandha dari' *Samudaya 25: Samskritika Jatha Utsavagalu* (Hubli Dharwad: Samudaya, 2000).

Yeoh, Brenda, 'Municipal Sanitary Ideology and the Control of the Environment in Colonial Singapore' in Alan H. Baker and Gideon Biger (eds), *Ideology and Landscape in Historical Perspective: Essays in the Meanings of Some Places in the Past* (Cambridge: Cambrdige University Press, 1992), pp. 148–72.

Books

A Guide to Bangalore and Mysore Directory (Bangalore 1905).

Anthappa Swami D.I., *Britisharu baruvudakku munche bengaluru maththu suththamuththalalli kristadharmada ugama* (Bangalore: Catholic Kristhara Sahitya Sangha, 2000).

Appavoo, Muthaiah David, *The Effect of Migration on the Churches of Bangalore* (Bangalore: CISRS, 1965).

Asian Institute of Urban Development, *A Medium Term Development Plan for Bangalore City* (Bangalore, 1988), mimeo.

Ballhatchet, Kenneth, *Race, Sex and Class under the Raj: Imperial Attitudes and policies and their critics 1793–1905* (Hyderabad: Orient Longman, 1979).

Banakar, Mahadev, *Safeguards for Linguistic Minorities in India: Karnataka Sets a Model* (Bangalore: Anubhav Publications, 1982).

Benjamin, Walter, *The Arcades Project*. Translated by Howard Eiland and Kevin McLaughlin. Cambridge Mass and London: Belknap Press of Harvard University Press, 1999).

Beng Huat, Chua, *Political Legitimacy and Housing: Stakeholding in Singapore* (London and New York: Routledge, 1997)

______, *Communitarian Ideology and Democracy in Singapore* (London and New York: Routledge, 1995).

Bishop Brenton T. Bradley, *Visions and Victories in Hindustan: A Story of the Mission Stations of the Methodist Episcopal Church in Southern Asia* (Madras: Methodist Publishing House, 1931).

Bopegamage A., *Delhi: A Study in Urban Sociology* (Bombay: University of Bombay Press, 1957).

Bose Nirmal Kumar, *Calcutta 1964: A Social Survey* (Bombay: Lalwani Publishing House, 1968).

Bourdieu, Pierre, *Language and Symbolic Power* (Cambridge Mass: Harvard University Press, 1994).

Buch, M.N., *Environmental Consciousness and Urban Planning* (Hyderabad: Orient Longman 1993).

Buchanan, Francis, *A Journey from Madras through the countries of Mysore, Canara and Malabar*, vol. I (Originally published, London: 1807; Reprint: Asian Educational Services, 1988).

Castells, Manual, *The Urban Question: A Marxist Approach,* Translated by Alan Sheridan (London: Edward Arnold, 1977).

______, *The Information Age: Economy, Society and Culture: The Rise of Network Society*, vol. I (London: Blackwell Publishers, 2001).

______, *The Power of Identity*, vol. II (London: Blackwell Publishers, 2000).

______, *End of Millenium* (London: Blackwell Publishers, 2000).

______ and Peter Hall *Technopoles of the World: The Making of 21st Century Industrial Complexes* (London and New York: Routledge, 1994).

Chandavarkar Rajnarayan, *The Origins of Industrial Capitalism in India: Business Strategies and the Working Classes in Bombay 1900–1940* (Cambridge: Cambridge University Press, 1994).

Chandoke, Neera (ed.), *Mapping Histories: Essays presented to Ravinder Kumar* (Delhi: Tulika, 2001).

Chandrasekhar, S., *Colonialism, Conflict and Nationalism* (Delhi: Wishwa Press, 1995).

Chandrasekhar, Ra Nam, *Kannada-kannadiga-karnataka, kannada shakti* (Bangalore Kannada Shakthi Kendra, 1996).

Chatterjee, Partha (ed.), *Wages of Freedom* (Delhi: Oxford University Press, 1998).

Chaudhuri Sukanta (ed.), *Calcutta: The Living City Volume I: The Past; Volume II: The Present and Future* (Calcutta: Oxford University Press, 1995).

Chidanandamurthy, *Nanna baduku: ondu kiru chitra* (Dr. M. Chidanandamurthy Gourava Samputa 'samshodana' dalli prakatagonda lekhanada mel acchu, n.d.).

Davis, Mike, The *City of Quartz: Excavating the Future in Los Angeles* (London: Verso, 1990).

______, *Ecology of Fear: Los Angeles and the Imagination of Disaster* (New York: Vintage Books, 1999).

Devegowda, Govindally, *Sarkarada kelasa devara kelasa: vidhana soudhada mahaan shilpi kengal hanumanthaiya* (Bangalore: Kannada Kanmani Dr Raj Samskrithika Samsthe, 1995).

Dirom, Major, *A Narrative of the Campaign in India, which terminated with the war with Tippoo Sultan in 1792* (London: 1793).

Diwakar, R. R., *Karnataka Through the Ages: From Pre-historic times to the Day of independence of India*, vol. II (Bangalore: Government of Mysore, 1968).

Dossal, Miriam, *Imperial Designs and Indian Realities: The Planning of Bombay City 1845–1875* (Delhi: Oxford University Press, 1996).

Fernandes, Edesio and Ann Varley (eds), *Illegal Cities: Law and Urban Change in Developing Countries* (Zed Books: London and New York, 1998).

Ferroli, D., *The Jesuits in Mysore* (Kozhikode: Xavier Press, 1955).

Frykenberg, R.E. (ed.), *Delhi Through the Ages: Essays in Urban History, Culture and Society* (Delhi: Oxford University Press, 1986).

Gooptu, Nandini, *The Politics of the Labouring Poor in early 20th century India* (Cambridge: Cambridge University Press, 2001).

Gowda, K.S., *Urban and Regional Planning: Principles and Case Studies* (Prasaranga, University of Mysore, 1972; revised and enlarged, 1986).

Gowda, Konandur Venkappa, *Nava mysooru shilpi kengal hanumanthaiya* (Bangalore: 1985).

Graf Violette (ed.), *Lucknow: Memories of a City* (Delhi: Oxford University Press, 1997).

Guha, Ranajit, *An Indian Historiography of India: A Nineteenth Century Agenda and its Implications* (Calcutta: K.P. Bagchi, 1988).

Gupta, Narayani, *Delhi Between Two Empires: 1803–1931: Society, Government and Urban Growth* (Delhi: Oxford University Press, 1998).

Hall, Peter, *Cities of Tomorrow: An Intellectual History of Urban Planning and Design in the Twentieth Century* (London: Blackwell, 1995).

Hamilton, Walter, *Geographical, Statistical and Historical Description of Hindustan and the adjacent countries*, vol. 2 (London: 1820).

Hansen, Thomas Blom, *Urban Violence in India: Identity Politics, 'Mumbai' and the Postcolonial City* (Delhi: Permanent Black, 2001).

Hanson, Susan, and Geraldine Pratt, *Gender, Space and Work* (London: Routledge, 1995).

Harvey, David, *Social Justice and the City* (Baltimore: Johns Hopkins University Press, 1973).

Hasan, Fazlul, *Bangalore Through the Centuries* (Bangalore: Historical Publications, 1970).

Heyne, Benjamin, *Statistical Fragments of Mysore* (London: 1805).

History of the Bharat Electronic Employee's Union and Bharat Electronics (Bangalore: BEEU, 1993).

Holmstrom, Mark, *Bangalore as an Industrial District: Flexible Specialisation in a labour Surplus Economy?* Pondy Papers in Social Sciences, 14 (Pondicherry: Institut Francais de Pondichery, 1994).

Holston, James, *The Modernist City: An Anthropological Critique of Brasilia* (University of California Press, 1989).

Irving, R.G., *Indian Summer: Lutyens, Baker and Imperial Delhi* (New Haven: Yale University Press, 1981).

Issar, T.P., *The City Beautiful: A Celebration of the Architectural Heritage and City Aesthetics of Bangalore* (Bangalore: Bangalore Urban Art Commission, 1988).

Iyer, K.V., *Deyada Mane*. Sunday Herald, 13 May 1990.

Jacobs, Jane, *The Death and Life of Great American Cities* (New York: Vintage Books, 1992).

Jaypal, Maya, *Bangalore: The Story of a City* (Chennai: East West Books, 1997).

Johns, Michael, *The City of Mexico in the Age of Diaz* (Austin: University of Texas, 1997).

Joshi, Chitra, *Lost Worlds: Indian Labour and its Forgotten Histories* (Delhi: Permanent Black, 2000).

Kalia Ravi, *Chandigarh: The Making of an Indian City* (Delhi: Oxford University Press, 1988).

Kaul, Rekha, *Caste, Class and Education: Politics of the Capitation Fee Phenomenon in Karnataka* (Delhi: Sage, 1993).

King, D. Anthony, *Colonial Urban Development: Culture, Social Power and Environment* (London: Routledge, 1976).

Kosambi, D.D., *Exasperating Essays: Exercises in the Dialectical Method* (Delhi: People's Publishing House, 1992).

Kumar, Radha, *A History of Doing: An Illustrated History of the Campaigns for Women's Rights and Feminism* (New Delhi, Kali for Women, 1993).

Lefebvre, Henri, *The Production of Space*. Translated by Donald Nicholson Smith (Oxford, Blackwell Publishers, 1991).

———, *Writings on Cities*. Translated and edited by Eleanore Kofman and Elizabeth Lebas (Oxford: Blackwell Publishers, 1996).

Lynch, Kevin, *The Image of the City* (Cambridge, Mass: MIT Press, 1992).

Mackenzie, Roderick, *A Sketch of the War with Tippoo Sultan* in two volumes (Calcutta, 1793).

Manor, James, *Political Change in an Indian State: Mysore* 1917–1955 (Delhi: South Asia Books, 1978).

———, *Power, Poverty and Poison: Disaster and Response in an Indian City* (Delhi: Sage, 1993).

Marx, Karl, *Capital* Volume One, Introduced by Ernest Mandel and translated by Ben Fowkes (New York: Vintage Books, 1977).

Masselos, Jim, *Towards Nationalism: Group Associations and the Politics of Public Associations in Nineteenth Century Western India* (Bombay: Popular Prakashan, 1974).

McAuslan, Patrick, *The Ideology of Planning Law* (London/New York: Pergamon Press, 1980).

Menon, Dilip, *Caste, Nationalism and Communism in South India: Malabar 1900–1948* (Cambridge: Cambridge University Press, 1994).

Morris, Morris D., *The Emergence of an Industrial Labour Force in India: A Study of the Bombay Cotton Mills, 1854–1947* (Bombay: Vikas Publishing House, 1965).

Mumford, Lewis, *The City in History: Its Origins, its Transformations and its Prospects* (New York: MJF Books, 1989).

Mysore Dasara Exhibition Handbook, 1953.

Nadkarni, M.V., *Farmers' Movements in India* (Bombay: Allied Publishers, 1987).

Naidu, Ratna, *Old Cities, New Predicaments: A Study of Hyderabad* (Delhi: Sage, 1990).

Nair, Janaki, *Miners and Millhands: Work, Culture and Politics in Princely Mysore* (Delhi: Sage, 1998).

Nandy, Ashis, *An Ambiguous Journey to the City: The Village and Other Odd Ruins of the Self in the Indian Imagination* (Delhi: Oxford University Press, 2001)

Narasimhaiah, S.K., *The founder of Bangalore or Magadi Kempe Gowda and his ancestors, successors and collaterals* (Bangalore: Vokkaligara Sangha Press, 1924)

Narayan, R.K., *Mysore* (Mysore, 1944).

Niranjana, Seemanthini, *Gender and Space: Femininity, Sexualisation and the Female Body* (Delhi: Sage Publications, 2001).

Norma, Evenson, *The Indian Metropolis: A View Toward the West* (New Haven: Yale University Press, 1989).

Oldenburg Veena Talwar, *The Making of Colonial Lucknow: 1856–1877* (Princeton: Princeton University Press, 1984).

Patel Sujatha and Alice Thorner (eds), *BOMBAY: Metaphor for Modern India; BOMBAY: Mosaic of Modern Culture* (Bombay: Oxford University Press, 1995).

Paul, Samuel, *A Report Card on Public Services in Indian Cities: A View from Below* (Bangalore: PAC, 1995).

Pott, Janet, *Old Bungalows in Bangalore* (London: Published by the author, 1977)

Prakasa Rao, V.L.S. and Tewari, V.K., *Structure of an Indian Metropolis* (Bombay: Allied Publishers, 1979).

Racine Jean et al. (eds), *Calcutta 1981: The City, its Crisis and the debate on Urban Planning Development* (Delhi: Concept Publishing House, 1990).

Ramachandran, R., *Urbanisation and Urban Systems in India* (Delhi: Oxford University Press, 1989).

Ramaswamy, R., Sumathi, *Passions of the Tongue: Language Devotion in Tamil Nadu* 1891–1970 (Delhi: Munshilal Manoharlal, 1998).

Rangaswami, Su (ed.), *Karnatakada devalayagalu* (Bangalore: 1994).

Rao, Ba Na Sundara, *Bengalurina itihasa: sthaapaneyinda hididhu swarajya labhisuvavarege* (Bangalore: Vasanth Sahitya Granthalaya, 1985).

Rao, Hayavadana, C. (ed.), *Mysore Gazetteer: Compiled for Government* (New Edition), vols I–V (Bangalore, Government Press, 1927–30).

Rao, M.S.A. (ed.), *Urban Sociology In India: Reader and Source Book* (Hyderabad: Orient Longman, 1974).

Rao, Narayana, P.S., *The Bangalore Municipal Corporation: Problems and Finances* (Corporation of the City of Bangalore, 1970).

Rao, Rammohan and C. Simhadri (eds), *Indian Cities: Towards the Next Millenium* (Jaipur and Delhi, Rawat Publications, 1999).

Rau, M.P. Somasekhara, *Growth of Local Self Government in Bangalore (*Bangalore: GIPA, 1964).

Ravindra, A., *Metropolitan Bangalore: A Management Perspective* (Bangalore: Times Research Foundation, 1992).

Raychaudhuri, Tapan, and Irfan Habib (eds), *The Cambridge Economic History of India,* vol. 1, c. 1200–1750 (Hyderabad: Orient Longman, 1984).

Rice, Lewis, *Mysore: A Gazetteer compiled for Government* (Revised Edition), vol. II (London: Archibald Constable and Company, 1897).

Ross, D. Aileen, *The Hindu Family in its Urban Setting* (Toronto: University of Toronto Press, 1961).

Salar E. Hind, Special Number on Mysore, 1938.

Sarai Reader 01: On the Public Domain (Delhi: CSDS, 2001).

Sarai Reader 02: The Cities of Everyday Life (Delhi: CSDS, 2002).

Sarai Reader 03: Shaping Technologies (Delhi: CSDS, 2003).

Sarai Reader 04: Crisis/Media (Delhi: CSDS, 2004).

Sarin, Madhu, *Urban Planning in the Third World: The Chandigarh Experience* (London: Mansell Publishing Limited, 1982).

Sassen, Saskia, *Global Cities: London, New York, Tokyo* (Princeton: Princeton University Press, 1991).

Schenk, Hans and Michael De Wit (eds), *Living in India's Slums: A Case Study of Bangalore* (Delhi: Manohar and IDPAD 2000).

Schorske, Carl, *Fin-de-Siecle Vienna: Politics and Culture* (New York: Vintage Books, 1981).

Seminar on City Architecture, December 1966 (mimeo).

Sennett, Richard, *Flesh and Stone: The Body and the City in Western Civilisation* (London: Faber and Faber, 1996).

______, *The Uses of Disorder: Personal Identity and City Life* (New York and London: W.W. Norton and Co, 1992).

______, *The Conscience of the Eye: The Design and Social Life of Cities* (New York and London: Norton and Company, 1992).

______, *The Fall of Public Man* (London and Boston: Faber and Faber, 1993).

______, *The Corrosion of Character* (New York and London: W.W. Norton and Co., 1998).

Simo, Fr Anthony, *History of the Archdiocese of Bangalore*, vol. I (St Francis Xavier's Cathedral, Bangalore, no date).

Singh, R.L., *Banaras: A Study in Urban Geography* (Banaras: Nand Kishore and Brothers, 1955).

______, *Bangalore: An Urban Survey* (Varanasi: Tara Publications, 1964).

Sinha, Pradip (ed.), *The Urban Experience: Calcutta, Essays in Honour of Prof. Nisith R. Ray* (Calcutta: Riddhi-India, 1987).

Sinha, Surajit (ed.), *Cultural Profile of Calcutta* (Calcutta: Indian Anthropological Society, 1972).

Spence, Jonathan, *The Search for Modern China (*New York and London: WW Norton and Company, 1990).

Spodek, Howard and Doris Meith Srinivasan (eds), *Urban Form and Meaning in South Asia: The Shaping of Cities from Pre Historic to Pre Colonial Times* (Hanover and London: University Press of New England, 1993).

Srikantia, B.M., *The Improvement of the Kannada Language* (1915; reprinted, Bangalore: B.M. Srikantia Memorial Foundation, 1969).

Srinivas, M.N., *Village Caste, Gender and Method: Essays in Indian Social Anthropology (*Oxford Unversity Press, 2000).

———, *India's Villages* (Bombay: Asia Publishing House, 1963).

Srinivas Smriti, *Landscapes of Urban Memory: The Sacred and the Civic in India's High Tech City* (Minnesota and London: University of Minnesota Press, 2001).

Staley, Elizabeth, *Monkey Tops (*Bangalore: Tara Publications, 1981).

Stephens, J.M., *Plague Proof Town Planning in Bangalore, South India* (Madras: Methodist Publishing House 1914).

Thimmaiah, G., *Power, Politics and Social Justice: Backward Castes in Karnataka* (Delhi: Sage Publications, 1993).

Tremewan, Christopher, *The Political Economy of Social Control in Singapore* (New York: St Martins' Press, 1996).

Unnatural Deaths of Women in Marriage: A Campaign Diary (Vimochana, Bangalore, 1999).

Van wersch, Hubert, *The Bombay Textile Strike: 1982–83* (Bombay: Oxford University Press, 1992).

Varshney, Asutosh, *Ethnic Conflict and Civic Life: Hindus and Muslims in India* (Delhi: Oxford University Press, 2002).

Venkatrao, Alura, *Karnataka gatha vaibhava* (1917; reprinted Bangalore: Kannada Sahitya Parishat, 1982).

Venkatrayappa, K.N., *Bangalore a Socio-Ecological Study* (University of Bombay, 1957).

Viroli, Maurizio, *For Love of Country: An Essay on Patriotism and Nationalism* (Oxford: Oxford University Press, 1997).

Visvesvaraya, M., *The Bangalore City and Its Future* (Bangalore: Bangalore Press, 1953).

Vyasulu, Vinod and A.K.N. Reddy (convenors), *Essays on Bangalore*, vol. I–IV (Bangalore: KSCST, 1983).

Williams, Raymond, *The Country and the City* (Oxford: Oxford University Press, 1973).

Yeoh, Brenda and Lily Kong (eds), *Portraits of Places: History, Community, and Identity in Singapore* (Singapore: Times Editions, 1995).

Zukin Sharon, *The Cultures of Cities* (London: Blackwell Publishers, 1996).

Theses and Dissertations

Aundhe, Sanjeev, 'A Comparative Study of Three models for Evaluating Urban Infrastructure Projects' (IIM Bangalore, 2001).

Bairy, T.S. Ramesh, 'Competing Constructions of Kannada Identity: A Study of Two Organisations' (M.Phil. Thesis, University of Hyderabad, 1996).

Joseph, T.M., 'Politics of Recruitment in Public Sector Undertakings: A Study of the Nativist Movement in Bangalore' (Ph.D. Thesis, ISEC, 1994).

Mertens, Rosita, 'Forced Relocation of Slum Dwellers in Bangalore, India: Slum Dwellers, Landlords and the Government' (M.A. Thesis Submitted to Vrijeuniversiteit Amsterdam, 1996).

Nair, Janaki, 'The Emergence of Labor Politics in South India: Bangalore, 1900–1947' (Ph.D. Thesis, Syracuse University, 1991).

Parthasarathy, Balaji, 'Globalisation and Agglomeration in Newly Industrialising countries: The State and the Information Technology Industry in Bangalore, India' (Ph.D. Dissertation, University of California, Berkeley, 2000).

Sudarshan, P., 'Relocation of Slum Dwellers: A Case Study of Sanjay Gandhi Nagar in Bangalore' (M.Phil. Thesis, University of Hyderabad, 1998).

Thippaiah, P., 'Informal Sector and the Urban Poor in a Metropolitan Area: A Case Study of Bangalore' (Ph.D. Thesis, ISEC, Bangalore, 1994)

Gertrude Woodruffe, 'An Adi-Dravida Settlement in Bangalore: A Case Study in Urbanisation' (Ph.D. Thesis, Radcliffe College, Cambridge Mass, 1959).

Cases

Achaiah Chetty v. *State of Mysore* AIR 1962 Mys 218 (V49 C73).

A.K. Ahmed v. *Special Land Acquisition Officer*, KLJ 1974 (2).

Annayya and others v. *State of Karnataka and others* 1988 (2) KLJ.

B.S. Muddappa and others v. *State of Karnataka and others*, KLJ 1989 (2).

Bangalore District Central Bank Employee's Co-operative Society Ltd v. *BDA and another* KLJ 1989 (1).

G. Gurubasappa v. *SLAO, City Municipality and others,* AIR 1959, vol. 46.

H.N. Nanje Gowda and another v. *State of Karnataka and others* 1996 (3) KLJ 39 (DB).

IBM World Trade Corporation v. *Assistant Commissioner and Competent authority and another* KLJ 1979 (2).

Assistant Commissioner and competent authority v. *IBM World Trade Corporation,* KLJ 1981 (2).

K.C. Raju Reddy v. *Commissioner, BDA* 1995 (4) KLJ.

Kalyan Co-operative Housing Society v. *BDA/BCC/Bapujinagar Attiguppe Site Owners' association and 10 others* (BDA Law office).

Kanthamma and others v. *State of Karnataka and another*, KLJ 1984 (2).

KGNS Sangha, Avalahalli Bangalore South Taluk v. *Kota Srinivasa Murthy* (since deceased) by LRs and others 1998 (1) KLJ, 227 (DB).

Land Acquisition Officer CITB v. *Narayanaiah K.*, KLJ 1976 (2).

M. Maniklal v. *State of Mysore*, MLJ, 1968 (1).

M.S. Narayanappa v. *Special Land Acquisition Officer, CITB* Bangalore, AIR 1966, vol. 53.

M/s Revajeethu Builders and Developers and Others v. *S. Vasudeva and Others*, 1991 (1) KLJ 522 (DB).

Major General M.K. Paul and others v. *Bangalore City Corporation*, KLJ 1994 (2) 158.

Mrs Behroze Ramyar Batha and others v. *Special Land Acquisition Office, Bangalore and others*, KLJ 1992 (1).

M.S. Shakthivelanagara Gudisala Nivasigala Kshemabhivriddhi Sangha v. *State of Karnataka and others*, 1997, 920 KLJ 379.

Muniswamy Reddy and Ningamma Trust and another v. *State of Karnataka and others*, 1995 KLJ (6) 55B (DB).

Narasimha Murthy v. *State of Mysore*, 1967 (1) MLJ.

Narayan Raju v. *State of Karnataka and others* KLJ 1988 (3).

Narayan Reddy v. *State of Karnataka*, 1991 (3) KLJ 545 (DB).

NC no. 290: 1994, *Karnataka State Government* v. *Muniraju*.

NC no. 319 of 1994, *Karnataka State Government* v. *Nawab Jan*.

Residents' of MICO Layout II Stage and others v. *JSS Mahavidya Peeta Mysore and others* (1997) (4) KLJ 442.

S.S. Darshan v. *State of Karnataka*, KLJ 1995 (4). (DB).

S.G. Heble and Others v. *BDA and others* 1997 (7) KLJ 352.

Special Land Acquisition Officer CITB v. *J.B. Kempanna Setty Charities*, MLJ 1972 (2).

Special Land Acquisition Officer CITB v. *Chikkaboranna*, AIR 1968, vol. 55.

State of Karnataka (Mahadevpura Police) v. D.N. Vijendran Case no. 87/1989, Judgement, 30 October 1990.

Subbanna v. *State of Karnataka* 1996 (5) KLJ 190 (DB).

Union of India and others v. *Narsappa and others*, MLJ, 1970 (1).

V. Lakshmipathy and others v. *State of Karnataka and others*, KLJ, 1991 (2) 453.

Vishwa Bharati House Building Co-operative Society Limited v. *Bangalore Development Authority*, KLJ 1990 (1).

Vishwabharati House Building Co-operative Society v. *BDA* KLJ LJ 1989 (3).

WP 13148/1998, *Vijayanagar East Tax Payers' Association (regd) RPC Layout Vijayanagar and four others* v. *State of Karnataka and others* (BDA Law Office).

WP 28241/1995, *Model Housing Co-operative Society Limited* v. *Basaveshwaranagar and BDA* (BDA Law Office).

WP 8378 of 1992. *N. Kannan* v. *Government of Karnataka and others* (mimeo).

WP no. 11976/84 for Sy. No 345 of Banaswadi (BDA Law Office).

WP no. 16660/1998. *K.G. Vijayakumar* v. *State of Karnataka and others* (BDA Law Office).

WP no. 20676 of 1983, *B.V. Narayan Reddy and others* v. *State of Karnataka and others*, ILR Kar 1985.

Bangalore City Municipality v. *Sub Division Officer, Bangalore and others* MLJ, vol. 27 (1946).
T. Adinarayan Shetty v. *Special Land Acquisition Officer* AIR 1954, Mys 71, vol. 41.
H.N. Nanje Gowda v. *State of Karnataka* 1996 (3) KLJ 39 (DB).
Union of India and others v. *Narsappa and others,* MLJ 1970 (1).
V. Lakshmipathy and others v. *State of Karnataka and others,* KLJ, 1991 (2) 453.

Interviews

A. Ravindra, May 1999.
Babu Mathew, 8 October 1999.
B. Krishna Bhat, 13 August 1999.
B.K. Chandrasekhar, June 2000.
Donna Fernandes, 12 November 1999.
G. Narayana, 25 October 1998.
Gowramma, 11 November 1999.
K. Leelavathi, 28 August 2001.
Lakshmi Devamma, 27 April 1999.
Lakshmi Venkatachalam, 3 March 1999; 13 August 1999.
M. Chidanandamurthy, 9 October 1998.
Members of Jaga Mechida Maga Dr. Rajkumar Abimanigala Sangha, 20 July 1999.
M.S.L. Rao, by Dilip Subramanian, June 1981.
N. Lakshman Rau, 22 July 1998; 29 September 1998.
Nittoor Srinivasa Rao, 15 May 1998, 14 July 1998.
Parvathiamma, 26 May 1999.
P.M. Thacker, July 1999.
Ra Nam Chandrasekhar, 7 and 11 October 1998.
R. Radhakrishna, 20 July 1999.
Sa Ra Govindu, 23 October 1998.
Shaikh Pir Sahib, May 1999.
S. Siddalingaiah, December 1999.
Syed Ahmad Basheer, 12 September 2001.
Veera Sundari Amma, 5 July 1999.
Vinay Baindur, 29 September 1999.

Newspapers

Deccan Herald 1960–2000
Prajavani 1998–2000
The Hindu 1998–2000
Times of India 1998–2000
Indian Express 1998–2000
Samyukta Karnataka 1963–98
Lankesh Patrike 1975–98

Index

Abbe Dubois 36
Abercrombie, Patrick 158–9
Adarshnagar 259
Adi Dravida 5, 261
Adi Parashakthi shrine 157
Adimoolam, Mari Muttu 316
Aditi Technologies 337
Agram 30
Air Force Parade Grounds 327
Akkipet 81
All India Anna Dravida Munnetra Kazhagam (AIADMK) 249
All India League for Revolutionary Culture 328
All India Mahila Samskrutika Sanghatane 329
All India Trade Union Congress (AITUC) 255, 265
Alura Venkata Rao 238, 243
Amalgamated Planning area 160
Amarjyothi House Building Society 184
Ambedkar, B.R. 4, 214, 288, 290
  statue 217, 272, 287–9
Ambedkar Bhavan 290
Ambedkar Medical College 289–90
Ambedkar (Vidhana) Veedhi 201–2, 213, 222–4, 227–8, 231–3
Amco Batteries 83
American 14
  cities 11
  sociologists 11
Anand, M.C. 110
Ananthamurthy, U.R. 266, 286
Andhra Mahasabha 239
Andhra Pradesh 247, 250
Anglo Indian 58, 65, 75
Anjanappa Gardens 55, 81
Annamma Devi 32
Apex Garments 309
Arab Lines 48
Arabic 63
Arcot Srinivasachar Street 64, 70
Arkavathi river 27, 31
Arlepet 45, 62, 81
Armenians 56
Arokiaswamy, Reverend 253
Ashoknagar 192
Ashraya scheme 144

Asoka Pillar 276
Attara Kacheri 57, 205–6, 210
extension of 223–6
Aundhe, Sanjeev 102–3
Austin Town 196
Avalahalli 231
Ayudha Puja 2
Azadnagar 87, 150, 259

Babasanpalya 156
Bachchan, Amitabh 327–8
Amitabh Bachchan Corporation Limited (ABCL) 327–8, 330
Bairagis 35
Bairy, Ramesh 268
Baker, Herbert 223
Balepet 34
Balija merchants 34
Ballapurpet 35
Banakar, Mahadev 249, 261
Banappa Park 57, 70, 213
Banaras 7, 10
Banaswadi 152
Banawara 28
Bandaya literary movement 110
Bande Squatter Settlement 259
Bandipura 264
Bangalore Agenda Task Force (BATF) 15, 77, 79, 118, 123, 179, 334–40, 344
Bangalore Summit 123
Bangalore Blue Grape 60, 182
Bangalore Brewery 66
Bangalore City Chikpet House Building Society 184
Bangalore City Corporation (BCC) 77, 114, 128, 131, 140, 190, 220, 274–7, 283
Bangalore City Planning Area Zonal Regulations (Amendment and Validation) Bill, 1996 175
Bangalore Development Authority (BDA) 90, 114, 121, 131–3, 135, 148, 151, 153, 156, 160, 169, 172–99, 306, 333, 335–6
Bangalore Development Committee 128, 159–60
Bangalore Disturbances
(1928) 63, 70–3, 75
(1931) 73, 75
Bangalore Environment Trust 196
Bangalore Hunt 58–60
Bangalore Literary Union 14
Bangalore Mahanagara Palike (BMP) 114, 195, 299
Bangalore Metropolitan Region (BMR) Structure Plan 134
Bangalore Metropolitan Task Force (BMTF) 176, 195, 199
Bangalore Mysore Infrastructure Corridor 268
Bangalore Steam Woollen Mills 45
Bangalore Tamil Sangam 237, 265, 283–6
Bangalore Trades Association 75
Bangalore University 107, 282
Bangalore Urban Art Commission (BUAC) 103, 172, 214–28, 283
Bangalore Urban Management Committee (1997) 125
Bangarappa, S. 218, 287
Bania traders and merchants 44
Basava 34
Basavalingappa, B. 107–8
Basavanappa, G. 172
Basavaraj, Nalini 314, 316
Basavangudi 33, 50–1, 56, 90, 196–7, 288
Masjid Committee 197
Basaveshwaranagar 259
Bavoor (Begur) 28
Baweja, Vandana 92
Beals, Alan 5, 149
Beera Devaru 33
Begur Hobli 161
Beladide Noda Bengaluru Nagara! 22
Bellary Road 156

Beng Huat, Chua 13
Bengali 238, 241
Bengaluru 23, 26–30, 32, 34–5, 38, 40–1, 46
Benjamin, Solomon 19, 87, 126, 146, 259, 261, 306, 313
Benjamin, Walter 14, 97, 271
Bhaktavatsala, M. 226
Bharat Earth Movers Limited (BEML) 113
Bharat Electronics Limited (BEL) 89, 96, 113, 127–8, 138, 182, 255–6, 265, 306
Bharat Heavy Electricals Limited (BHEL) 82–3, 256
Bharatinagar 197
Bhat, Krishna B. 183, 188–9
Bhonsle, Shahji 30
Bhuvaneswari Raman 19, 87, 259, 261, 306, 313
Bidar 110
Bijapur 27, 29, 38 205,
Binnamangala 147, 153
Binny and Co. 45
Binny Mills (Bangalore Woollen, Silk and Cotton Mills) 69–70, 81, 85, 150
Binnypet 55, 150
Biocon 337
Birdwood, George 42
Bisilu Maramma temple 34
Bismillahnagar 197
B.K. Mariappa's Charities 67
Bharatiya Janata Party (BJP) 317
Blackpally 36, 47, 52–3
Blighty's Tea Rooms 65
Bombay 1, 5, 7, 8, 10, 14, 21, 79, 251
  Marine Drive 14
  Municipality 10
'Bring Back Beauty to Bangalore' 273
Bommasandra 86
Border Security Force 327
Bose, Nirmal Kumar 7
Bose, Subhash Chandra, statue of, 217
Bourdieu, Pierre 242
BPL strike 113, 269, 308–9
BPL Karmikara Sangha 308
B.R. Ambedkar Birthday Scheme 191
Brahmins 29, 30, 51, 53, 64–9, 73–4, 97
Brasilia 11
Briand Square 253
Brigade Group 337
Brigade Road 83, 97–8, 158, 222
British rule 9, 10, 35, 38, 41, 46, 57, 62, 320
  Army 23, 57
  conquest of Mysore 34, 36
  Empire 23, 295
  residents 167
Broadway 305
BTM Layout 179, 183
Buchanan Francis 40
busa agitation 107–8
Byatarayanapura 136, (north) 148
Byrasandra 196
Byrasandra Tank Bed (BTB) area 143–4, 152, 192, 194

Calcutta 1, 7, 21, 80, 130, 245, 294
Canally (Kanalli) 28
Cantonment, or Civil and Military Station Bangalore 26, 28, 36–7, 42, 44–8, 53, 56–8, 62–3, 65–7, 69, 73–7, 90, 160, 166–7, 274–5, 278, 282, 287, 294–5, 330
  demographic profile 45
  disturbances 73
  industrial activity 44
  Muslims 75
  notables 67
  railway station 54
  water supply 51
Casba Hale Bengaluru 28
Caste
  and church 252
  and citizenship 273, 297

and city space 18, 273, 287, 300
and industrial worker 255–6, 287
and inequality 266
and language agitation 111, 265
and neighbourhood 113–14, 345
and patronage 66–8
and planning 9, 21, 51–5, 288
and public life 64–6, 69–70, 74, 107, 304
and rural society 4
and trading 44
and urban village 148, 150
and water allocation 258
associations 238, 283, 303, 317
geographies of 287–9
leaders 35, 72
lower caste assertion 107–8, 290, 293
panchayat 5
symbols 286–90
temples in Old City area 34–5
textile production c. 1800 40
Castells, Manual 12–13, 198, 218
Cauvery river 258, 268, 286
riots 112, 146, 236, 287
water dispute and agitation 236, 245, 247, 258, 286
cenotaph 275–9
Cenotaph Road 277
Central College, 239–40
Central Reserve Police Force (CRPF) 327
Centre for Informal Education and Development Studies (CIEDS) 319
Centre of Indian Trade Unions (CITU) 308
Challaghatta 83, 186
Tank Bed 186
Chalukya style (architecture) 204
Chalukyan capitals 223
Chamaga Raya Swamy Devasthanam 33
Chamrajpet 50, 53, 67, 69, 196
Chandigarh 1, 9
Chandra Layout 314
Chandrakala, P.N. 317
Chandrasekhar, Laxmi 110
Chandrasekhar Ra Nam 247, 278
Chatterjee, Partha 164, 241, 273, 344
Chennai 122, 245, 247, 272, 280, 283, 285
Chennai Kannada Balaga 285
Chennapatna 40
Chennigaraya Swamy temple 33
Chicago school 11, 223
Chidanandamurthy M. 243–4, 246, 252, 263–4, 278
Chik Lal Bagh 32, 70
Chikmagalur 110, 268
Chikpet 45, 64
Chile 331
China 61
Chingleput 261
Chinnappa Gardens 60
Chinnasamudram 30
Chitradurga 40
Cholas, 27, 286
Chowdiah T. 264
Christian 66, 150, 158, 252, 254
Christianity 34, 36, 252
Church Street 337
Churchill, Winston 204
'City Beautiful' 220, 222–3, 227
Citizen's Action Group 196
Citizen's Voluntary Initiative for the City (CIVIC) 116–18, 190, 196
City of Bangalore (Old) 23, 26, 34, 36–8, 56, 77
hotels 64
market
Municipal Council 53
Municipality 74
railway Station 32
City Improvement Trust Board (CITB) 90, 128, 131, 169, 172–3, 221
Civic Amenity (CA) sites 153
Coca Cola 337
Columbo arrack 66
Commercial Street 97

Comprehensive Development Plan (CDP 1974) 125, 130, 143, 159
(1985, revised 1995) 135, 160, 182, 193
Congress 64, 69, 72, 106, 123, 204–5, 207, 213, 256
Exhibition 96
Congress I 317
Constitutional Amendment, 74th 134
Coorg 213
Correa, Charles 223
Cottonpet (earlier Arlepet), 55, 69, 213
Cox Town 54
Cubbon, Mark 167
statue 271, 295
Cubbon Park 14, 42, 60–2, 70, 190, 201–3, 212–13, 215–16, 218, 224, 226–7, 233, 279, 293–7
Cubbonpet 27, 35, 57
C.V. Raman Nagar 314

Dakhni 63
Dakshinacharya, Sangeet Vidwan 64
Dalit movement 290, 318
Dalits 169, 213, 217, 286–91
Dalit Sangarsh Samiti (DSS) 110, 213, 288–9
Dalit unity 265, 268
Dasgupta, Sanjoy 135
Davasia, Mary 303, 310–12
Davis, Mike 11, 135, 163,
Deccan Herald 154–5, 266, 291
Delhi 1, 9, 10, 27, 161, 201, 204, 210, 223
Deo Enquiry Committee 206–8, 210, 212
Depressed Classes 67
Desai, N.H. 215
Deshadapet 38
Devamma, Lakshmi 303–5
Devangas 34
Devarajeevanhalli (D.J. Halli) 44, 197
Devaraj Urs 161, 172–3, 256
statue, 217
Deve Gowda, H.D. 118, 175, 318
D'Mello, Edgar 225
De Wit, Michael 306
Deve Gowda, Govindally 212
Dharmambudhi Tank 31, 32, 56, 70
Dharmaraya Temple 34, 36
Dharwar 244
Dhondusa Magaji 67–8
Diamond District 92
Diaz, Porfirio 11
Diwakar, R.R. 264
Doddabommasandra Jalahalli 182
Doddballapur 35, 40, 113
Dodd Bylakhana 83
Doddpet 34, 38, 45
Dollars Colony 119, 133
Doopanahalli 37
Doopasamudra 30
Doordarshan 322
Doreswamy, H.S. 268
Dossal, Mariam 10
Draupadi 36
Dravidian style (architecture) 204–5
Dravidian culture and identity 265, 286–7
movement 262
Dravida Kazhagam 279
Dravida Munnetra Kazhagam (DMK) 262–3, 279
Durvaninagar 89, 95, 137, 139

East India Company 40
East Parade Church 36
Easter 253
Edward VII 271, 279, 287, 295
Electronic City 86, 87, 91, 121, 135, 333
Electronic Research and Development Establishment (LRDE) 293
Elevated Light Rail Transport System (ELRTS) 102–3
Emergency years (1975–7) 97, 108, 110, 172

Employees' State Insurance Scheme 255
England 27, 59
English language 63–4, 239–45, 250, 253, 264–6, 274, 278–9, 282, 287, 291–2
  people 23
  press 247
Essays on Bangalore 18
Eurasian 62, 66
European
  Catholics 56
  city 11
  people 58, 62, 65–6, 75
  squatters 166
  troops 44

Feast in the House of Levi 271
Fernandes, Michael 256
Field Marshal Cariappa Road 158
Folke, Steen 258
Foucault, Michel 241
Fraser Town 53–4, 62, 67, 119
  Papareddipalya 54, 62, 119
  Pulakesinagar 62, 119

Gajjalawar 35
Gandhi, Indira 110
Gandhi, M.K. 4, 204, 212,
  statue 215, 271, 293, 294
  Road 103 215, 222, 291–2
Ganesha (Ganapathi) 73, 196
  associations 317
  Chathurthi 114, 158
  Galabhe or Hindu–Muslim Garshane (clashes) 70
  'Galate' Ganesha temple 63
  processions 8
Gangamma Chery 143,
Gangaram, K. 108
Gangas 27
Gangenahalli/Ganganagar 147
Ganigarpet 33
Garden City 160, 219
Garimella, Annapurna 157
Garudapura 148
GATT Virodhi Okkuta 278
Gavi Gangadhareswara temple 33, 68
Geddes, Patrick 5, 158
General Bazaar 36
General Post Office 24, 201, 203, 223–4, 227–9, 232–3
Gidda Gowda Tank 30
Giessen, Peter 143
Giri, V.V. 220
Girinagar 322
Gist, Noel 17, 85
Gokak agitation/chaluvali 111–12, 245, 256–7, 261, 266
Gokak V.K. 253
Gokaldas Exports Factory 309
Gokhale Institute of Public Affairs (GIPA) 68, 105–8
Gokhale, Gopalkrishna, 105
Gopalkrishna temple 35
Goripalya 197
Government of India 42
Govindu, Sa Ra 247, 257, 263, 280, 282
Gowda, Gopala 210, 217
  Vritta 215
G.V.K. Rao Committee Report 183
Gowda, Lalitha Srinivas 315
Gowda, Padmavati Gangadhara 299, 315
Gowda, Rame K.S. 125, 147
Gowda, Sheela 297
Gowramma 321
Great Britain 61
Gubbi 40
Gujarati 63
Gundappa, D.V. (DVG) 32, 64, 68–9, 97, 106, 108, 264, 266
Gundu Rao, M. 217, 287
Gupta, Narayani 9, 62
Gurappanapalya 197

Hall, Peter 223
Handijogis 151
Hansen, Thomas Blom 8, 251
Hanumantha temple 35
Harikumar, K.N. 266
Hanumanthaiya, Kengal
building of Vidhana Soudha, 203–12
statue 217
Hariharan, Ramesh 341
Harvey, David, 12
Hash House Harriers 295
Hatarahalli 5
Hazrat Sayyad Shah Mohiuddin Quadri (Kambal Posh) 35
Hazrat Tawakkal Mastan Shah 35
Hegde, Ramakrishna 173, 185, 187–8, 217, 251, 256–7, 268
Heitzman, James 27, 85, 126, 133, *Network City* 19
Hesarghatta 28, 231
Tank 30
Heuze, Gerard 7
Heyne, Benjamin 40
Highway Anjaneya 156
Hindi 242, 244
anti-Hindi agitation 279
Hindu Jagaran Vedike 252
Hindu 10, 46–7, 69, 70, 72–3, 150, 158, 196, 284
traders 44
Hindu Coffee Club 64–5
Hinduism 10, 279
Hindusthan Aeronautics Limited (HAL) 81–3, 89, 113, 119, 127, 247, 255–6, 278
airport 15
layout 133
Sanitary Board 138–40
Hindusthan Machine Tools (HMT) 82–3, 89, 113, 127–8, 255–6, 307
Hindutva 251
HMT Watch Factory 82–3, 128
Holmstrom, Mark 5, 85, 148
Holston, James 11, 13, 166
Home, Robert 56
Hommadevahalli 161
Hoskote Town Municipality 139
Hosur Road 100
Hosur-Sarjapur Road Layout 187
House Building Co-operative Societies (HBCS) 90, 132, 161, 169, 183–4, 199
Hoysalas 27
Hoysala style (architecture) 204
Hudson Church 49
Hunter, James 56
Hyder Ali 35, 38, 40, 46, 57, 60
Hyderabad 8, 122, 247, 272, 280, 296

Imperial Tobacco Company (earlier Peninsular Tobacco factory) 45, 81
Indian Builder 210
Indian Economic Association 6
Indian Institute of Science 65, 341
Indian People's Human Rights Tribunal 259
Indian Sociological Association 6
Indian Space Research Organisation 224
Indian Telephone Industries (ITI) 81–2, 89, 95, 113, 127–8, 255–6, 307, 323
notified area 128, 139–40
notified area committee 140
township 136–40
Indiramma 313
Indiranagar 15, 147, 157, 190
Infantry Road, 337
Infosys Foundation 337
Infosys Technologies 79, 134, 338
Infrastructure Leasing and Financial Services 102
International Instruments 83
International Tech Park 86, 91–2, 212, 333

Irwin, Lord 204
Ismail, Mirza 72
Issar, T.P. 222–4
Information Technology (IT)
capital 338
Corridor 87, 92, 135, 333, 341
Department 340
Enabled Services 18, 86
industry 12, 19, 86, 91, 118, 122, 135, 161, 242–3, 274, 307, 334–5
jobs 85–6, 133, 307, 334
Park 231
Township 135
Iyer, K. Narayanswami 69
Iyer, K.V. 35
Iyer, Dewan Seshadri 50
Iyer, Guruswami 65

Jacobs, Jane 325
The Death and Life of American Cities 11
Jadahally 30
Jaga Mechida Maga Dr Rajkumar Abhimanigala Sangha 264, 267
Jagadeesh, B.V. 337
Jain, Sanjeev 56
Jains 10
Jairaj, K. 118,
Jakkarayanakere 142,
Jallianwala Bagh 277
Janaagraha 15, 334–5, 340, 345
Janardhan 109,
Janata Dal (S) 314
Janata Meal (Sriramulu Meal) 97
Jaraganhalli 304
Jayachamarajendra Road 143
Jayanagar 144, 188, 194, 196–7, 220, 322
Nagarika Committee 197–8
JB Exports 309
Jeevan Bima Nagar 315
Jerome Jayakar 118, 335
Jesuit 28, 36
Jigani 28, 160
J.L. Morrison 307
Jodhka, Surinder 4, 5, 10
John, Mary 320, 329
Johns, Michael 11
Joint Action Front (JAF) 256
Jurong Consultants 333

Kacharakanhalli 151
Kadalekai Parishe 2, 6
Kadu Malleswara temple 33
Kadugondanahalli (KG Halli) 197, 288
Kagodu Satyagraha 217
Kailasam, T.P. 65
Kalasipalya 57
Kalia Ravi 1
Kalikamba temple 35
Kalipuram 243
Kalkur, Ramesh 271
Kalyan Kumar 249
Kalyananagara Layout (HRBR Layout) 30, 151–2
Kalyani Gardens 190
Kamakshipalya 259
Kamalanagar 315
Kanavi, Chennavira 2
Kanchi 28, 249
Kanchi Thalaivan 249
Kankanpalya 220
Kannada Bhavan 271–2
Kannada Bhuvaneswari 263, 265, 280
Kannada
and the language of liturgy 252–4
Chaluvali 243
department of 239–40
films and film industry 249–50, 264, 276, 279
flag 258, 279–80
language and literature 63, 75, 110, 234–5, 238, 239–52, 263–6, 274–5, 278, 280–2, 290

movement 111, 237, 240, 247–8, 250, 254, 257, 263–4, 266–7, 276, 278–9, 280–1, 284–5, 287, 318
nationalism 135, 237–8, 241, 243, 247, 249, 251, 265, 268, 279, 282, 292
people 238, 267–8, 279, 282, 286–7
sanghas 137, 255–7, 279–80
Kannada and Culture Department 239, 289
Kannada Chaluvai (Vatal) Paksha 279, 328
Kannada Chaluvaligaru 245, 279
Kannada Development Authority 239, 282
Kannada Paksha 279
Kannada Pulakesi Sangha 283
Kannada Puthra 312
Kannada Rajyothsava 114, 265, 280
Kannada Sahitya Parishad 63, 238
Kannada Sahitya Sammelan 266
Kannada Shakthi Kendra 105, 111–12, 243–6, 252, 278, 282
Kannada Writers' and Artists' Guild 110
Kannadiga 111, 234, 246–7, 253–8, 262–7, 269
Kannan N 145, 152
Karaga 2, 3, 35–7, 72, 304
Karanji Tank 30
Karanth, B.V. 109
Karekar, S.K. 224, 232
Kari Amman 30
Karithimannahalli 150
Karnataka 28, 75, 79–81, 103, 110–11, 123, 134–5, 172, 182, 185, 187, 201, 204, 212–13, 217–18, 235–7, 241–5, 247–8, 250–1, 253–5, 257–9, 261–2, 264–9, 311–13, 317, 319, 327
Bombay–Karnataka 213
Hyderabad–Karnataka 213
(unification) Movement 244, 280
Urban Agglomerations 124, 130, 147,
Karnataka Catholic Christhara Sangha 253
Karnataka Film Directors' Association 249
Karnataka Film Producers' Association 249
Karnataka High Court 174
Karnataka Housing Board (KHB) 131, 143–4, 191
Karnataka Kolageri Nivasigala Samyuktha Sanghatane 191
Karnataka Rajya Raitha Sangha 98, 265, 286, 329
Karnataka Ranadheera Padhe 111
Karnataka Samata Sainik Dal 268, 286
Karnataka Samyuktha Ranga 248
Karnataka Slum Areas (Improvement and Clearance) Act, 1973 172
Karnataka Slum Clearance Board 131, 146, 172
Karnataka State Tourism Development Corporation (KSTDC) 186–7
Karnataka Town and Country Planning Act 1961 159
Amendment Act (1999), 175
Amendment Bill (1998), 176
Karnataka Vimochana Ranga 247, 265, 268, 281
Karnatakatva 251
Karunanidhi, M. 243, 262
Kashmir 264
Kasi Visveswara Temple 34
Katiawari traders and merchants 44
Kattupaiyur 261
Kaveryamma/Kaateriamma 153
Kaviraj, Sudipta 202, 216, 238, 333
Kempambudhi Tank 30
Kempamma 33
Kempapura Agrahara 30
Kempegowda I 28, 30, 32–3, 153, 212, 276–7, 299–300
statue 276, 277

Kempegowda II (Immadi) 30, 33
Kempegowda Road 56, 131, 224
Kemp Fort 153
Kengeri 28
  Satellite Town 140
Kentucky Fried Chicken 98, 267
Kerala 239, 311–12
Kerala Samajam 255
Keralites 251
Khader Sharief Gardens 60
Khan Bahadur Hajee Ismail Sait 67
Khan, Abbas 71–5
Khan, Sanjay 249
Khande Rao 46
Kharge, Mallikarjun 264
Khilafat 69
Khosla, Romi 206
Kinetic Honda 330
King, Anthony 48, 222
Kirloskar Electric 83
Kittur Rani Chenamma 284
Kodihalli 186
Kolar 286
Konkani 245
Koramangala 15, 83, 197, 300
  Tank Bed 186, 192
KR Market 104, 146, 259, 261, 303–5
K.T. Appanna's Hotel 64
KGF (Kolar Gold Field) 110
Kosambi, D. D. 335
Kowdenahalli 136,
Krishna Rao Aa Na (Aa Na Kru) 248, 276
Krishna, S.M. 15, 79, 118, 123, 176, 231, 255, 315, 334, 339
Krishnan, M.S. 119
Krishnarajasagar Dam 207
Krishnarajpuram (KR Puram) 60, 136, 138–40,
Krishnaswamy, C.G. 109–10
Kuldip Singh Commission of Inquiry 188
Kulkarni, Vivek 118
Kumar, Nita 10
Kumara Krupa 155
Kumaran, K.S. 70
Kumbalgud 28
Kurubarpet 81
Kutch 40

Labbes 42
Laggere 145–6, 214, 305
Lakshmamma 299–300
Lakshmipuram 243
Lal Bahadur Shastri Nagar 318
Lalbagh 60, 61, 97, 143, 303
Land Reforms Act, 1974 172, 175
Langford Town 47
Lankesh, P. 286
'Layout' Krishnappa 119
Layout Range 149
Le Corbusier 9
Lee, Standish 50
Lefebvre, Henri 12, 26, 122, 130, 133, 167, 346
  The Production of Space 20
Legislators' Home 293–4
Lele, Jayant 7
Letsch Mirjam 305
Lewandowski, Susan 251
Lingaiah, J. 124
Lingayats 51, 66,
  Nagarth Lingayats 67
London 12, 124, 160, 223
Los Angeles 11
Lourdes convent 35
Lucknow 9–10
Lutyens, Edwin 223
Lynch, Kevin 201

Mackenzie, Roderick 40
Madivala 197
Madras City 79, 250–1, 261

Madras Presidency 42, 63–5, 69, 75, 213, 248–9, 274–5
Madurai 29
Magadi 28
Magadi Road 243
Mahadevamma 315
Maharaja Mills 81, 305
Maharashtra 42
Mahila Jagran 329
Mahila Sangarsh Okkuta 328
Mahila Udyog Sahakara Sangha 138
Majestic 146
Malayalam 36, 245, 264
Malayalis 251, 255, 264, 312
Mallasandra 231
Malleswaram 50–1, 90, 119, 192, 288, 317–18
Mamtaz Begum 317
Manickam B. 205, 208.
Manjappa, Kadidal 206
Manor, James 18
Maran, R.S. 237, 286
Marathas and the control of Bangalore 35
dominions 40
Marathi 63, 238, 241, 244–5, 251
Mariyappanapalya 169, 172
Marwari traders and merchants 44
Marxist sociologists and method 12
Mass Awakener's Union 56, 65
Mass Rapid Transit System 102–3, 124
Mass Rapid Transport System (MRTS) 103
Massey, Doreen 12, 300
Mathew, Babu 307
Mavalli Tiffin Rooms 65, 97
Mayor Muthanna 277–8
Mayurvarman, Kadamba King 249
Mazumdar, Kiran 118
Mehta, Dinesh 122
Mekhri Square 49
Melwani, Ravi 153
Mertens, Rosita 142, 190–1
MICO Layout 197
Miller Committee Report 73
Miller's Tank 30–1, 192
Mirza Oval 49
Miss World Contest, agitation against 303, 327–30
Model Dairy Farm 82
Modern Hindu Hotel 65
Moodelliar Arcot Narainswamy 44
Motor Industries Company Limited (MICO) 63, 85
Mount Joy 50
Mudaliars 42, 44
Mudaliar, Rai Bahadur Annaswamy 67
Mudaliar, Rai Bahadur Maigandeva 67
Mudaliar, Shanmugham 44
Mughal 9, 35, 38
Muharram procession 8
Multani bankers and merchants 44
Mumbai 284, 328
Mumford, Lewis 11, 151
Muniraju, Vijaya D. 314
Murphy Town (Knoxpet) 54, 280, 288
Murthy Rao, A.N. 23, 295
Muscat 40
Muslims 67, 69–74, 111, 144, 158, 194–8 244, 251–2, 258–9, 290–2, 306, 313
Muslim dominated ward 317
Muslim Welfare Association 195–6
Muthyalpet 35
Mysore Bank 208
building 24, 26,
Square 24–5, 69, 70, 213
Mysore City 27, 35, 65, 240, 245, 251, 291–2
Jagan Mohan Palace 208,
Palace (Amba Vilas) 65, 205, 264
Station 264
Mysore Civic and Social Progress Association 67
Mysore Economic Conference 238

Mysore Housing Board 136
Mysore, Kingdom or Province of, 27–9, 35, 38, 40, 46
  and Wodeyars 38
  conquest by British 29, 36
Mysore Labour Housing Act (1949) 128
Mysore Labour Housing Corporation 128
Mysore Mills 81
Mysore Road 259
Mysore State 17, 42, 46 56, 60, 63, 66, 75, 91, 167, 203–8, 213, 220, 238, 243, 248, 258, 275–6, 311
  administration 64
  Brahmins 73
  Diocese 251
  Government of 149
  officials 50
  Police 70
  Resident (British) 51
Mysore Social Service League 68

Naganna, K.M. 106, 117
Nagappa 269
Nagappangudi 35
Nagar 40
Nagaraj, D.R. 109, 243–4, 263, 270, 286
Nagaraj Ki Ram 109, 286
Nagaraj Vatal 243, 245, 249, 279
Nagarathnamma, Bangalore 50
Nagarhole 264
Nagarik 196
Nagarths 40
Nagarthpet 45, 50, 62
Nagarur/Heggadadevanapura 161
Nagawara tank system 31
Naidu, Kunnaswamy 67
Naidu, Ratna 8
Naik, Lalitha 289
Namhalli 5
Nandy, Ashis 1, 2,
Nanjundaswamy, M. D. 286, 329
Narasimhaiah H. 282
Narasimharaja Square 277
Narayan, R.K. 46
Narayan's Hotel 240
Narayana, G. 247, 277
Narayana, K.V. 109
Narayana Murthy, N.R. 118, 134, 265
Narayanpur B. Panchayat 139
Nargund-Navalgund 213
Nariman Disturbances, (1937) 25
National Games Complex 186, 192
Naxal movement 4
Nehru, Jawaharlal 1, 4, 9, 203, 217, 220, 288
Nehru, Motilal 210
Nesargi, Pramila 283
New Government Electric Factory (NGEF) 82
  layout 133
New York 12
Nijalingappa, S. 106, 117, 220, 283, 311
  statue 227
Nilekani, Nandan 79, 118, 339
Niranjana, Tejaswini 263
Niranjana, Seemanthini 301
Nizam's dominions 40
NMKRV 321
Non-Brahmin movement 251
Non-Gazetted Officers' (NGO) Forum 213, 311–12
Non-Governmental Organisations (NGOs) 114, 144, 193, 319, 344
Non-Resident Indian (NRI) 133, 187–8
  Housing Association (NRIHA-K) 187–8
North Arcot 261
Nrupathunga Road 277

Old Madras Road 136, 156, 337
Old Taluk Cutcherry Road 34
Oldenburg, Veena 9, 10
Outer Ring Road 121
Outline Development Plan (ODP) 159, 161

Padalkar, Sharad 92
Padarayanagutta 150
Padarayanpura 150–1
Padmavathi, G. 315
Pai, Dayanand 186–7
Pallavas 249
Pampa Mahakavi Road 57
Pandavas 36
Paramanand's *Shiva Bharat* 38
Paris 9, 14, 124, 133
Parsis 67
Parthasarathy, M.A. 103, 222, 228
Parthasarathy, Balaji 341
Parvathiamma 142–3
Parvathypuram 143
Patalamma Garden 143
Patel, J.H. 250
Patil, Chandrasekhar 286
Patil, Veerendra 124
Pattabhiramanagara 314
Paul, Samuel 116, 344
Peenya Industrial Estate 87, 146, 307–9, 317
People's Democratic Forum 252, 328
People's Protection League 65
Peoples' Human Rights Tribunal 259
Persian 63
Pillana Gardens 60
Pinakini S. 27
Pit Colony 55, 81, 192
Planning Commission 6
Poornia's Choultry 35
Poura Samiti 106, 117
Prajavani 154–5
Prakashnagar 315
Prasanna 109
Prasanna, Subbarayan 115, 125
Prestige Group 161–2
Prince Albert 32
Public Affairs 105–8
Public Affairs Centre 116–17, 318, 344–5
Public Utility Building 222
Pune 122
Punjabi 63
Pushtu 63
Puttaiya, B. 67
Puttenahalli 304

Queen's Road 59
Queen's Sappers and Miners 53
Queen Victoria 63
statue 62, 215, 271–2, 278–9, 287, 293–6, 332

Radhakrishna 264, 267
Raghu, Pratima 314–15
Raheja's Group 162, 215, 293
Raitha Horata Jagrithi Committee 121
Rajagopalachari, C. 97
Rajajinagar 89, 119, 128, 169, 192
Rajasthani 63
Rajkumar Abhimanigala Sangha 111–12, 246–7, 249 252, 257, 265, 267–8, 280, 286
Rajkumar 92, 234–5, 237, 245, 257, 263–4, 268–9, 277, 280, 282, 287
Ramachandra, H. 141, 305
Ramachandrappa, Bargur 2, 109, 237, 239, 286
Ramamurthy Ma 248, 279
Ramamurthynagar 139–40
Ramanathan, Ramesh 118, 336
Ramanavami 276
Ramaswamy, Sumathi 245
Ramayana 249
Ranasingpet 81
Ranganathswamy temple 35
Rao, Bhima 71, 72
Rao, Narahari 50
Rao, C.N.R. 282
Rao, M.S.A. 4, 10
Rao, Narayana P.S. 74
Rao, Narayana V.S. 73

Rao, Prakasa V.L.S. 18, 87, 131, 141, 147, 300, 305
Rao, Suryanarayana 119, 139
Rapid Action Force 327
Rashtriya Sevika Samiti 316
Rashtriya Swayamsevak Sangh (RSS) 317
Rau, N. Lakshman 140, 240
Ravindra A. 86, 114, 124–5, 196, 318
RBI Colony Welfare Association 194–5
Reddy, H.G.V. 187–8
Reddy, K.C. Raju 121
Reddy, Chinappa 161
Reddy, B.V. Narayana 208
Reddy, K.C. 203, 205
Reddy, Padmini, 314–15
Reddy, Ramaswamy 153
Reddy, Ratna Gopal 315–16
REMCO-BHEL House Building Society 184
Representative Assembly, Mysore 75
Residency, British 47
Resident of Mysore 51
Revajeethu Case 188–9
Rice Lewis 31, 46–7
Richards' Town 53–4
Richmond Town 47
RMV II Stage 174–5, 179
Ross Aileen 325
Rudrappa Garden 259
Russell Market 37, 292, 303, 305

Saberwal, Satish 6
Sadashivanagar 283
Sagar, Ramanand 249
Saldanha, Michael 174, 296
Sampangi Tank 30, 58, 143, 192
  Gopalappa Gardens 143
Sampigehalli Area 62
Samudaya 105, 108–10,
Sangeen Jama Masjid 35
Sangliana H.T. 103
Sanjay Gandhinagar 146
Sankey, Richard 42, 293
Sankey's Reservoir 31
Sanmathi, women's organization 294
Sanskrit 266
Santa Clara 135, 334,
Sardar 313
Sarin, Madhu 9
Sarjapur
Sarojini Mahishi Commission 111, 256–7
Sassen, Saskia 12
Sastry, Sitarama 70–1
Savandurga 28, 60
Save Cubbon Park Campaign 293–7
Scheduled Castes and Tribes 160–1, 191, 346
Schorske, Carl 200–1, 228
Sen, Asok 164
Sena, Shiv 7, 8
Senji 29
Sennett, Richard 11, 13–14, 32, 152, 157
Seshadri Road 67
Seshadri S.V. 105
Shaivism 33
Shaivite temple complexes 33
Shamanna T. R. 106, 117
Shantakumari N. 317
Sharma, Ramachandra 65, 286
Sharma, Shivadatta 224
Sharma, Thi Tha 70
Shashikala 329
Shiv Sena 7, 8, 251
Shiva Kumar, D.K. 317
Shiva temple 34
Shivaji statue 283–4
Shivajinagar 35, 37, 47, 151, 214, 291, 305, 317
Shivanagar 315
Shivaram, Bharati 316
Shivaram, M. 65
Shoolay 47
Shoolay Coffee Room 66

Siddaiah Puranik 247
Siddalingaiah S. 109–10, 263, 286
Siddapura 143, 190
Siddikatta 45, 62
Siluvepura 265
Silver Jubilee Park 214
Simla 264
Singapore 11, 13, 79, 103, 123–4, 160, 163–5, 333, 336, 347
Singapura 30, 346–7
Singh, K.S. 264
Singh, Rutna 67
Singh, R.L. 7, 17–18, 28, 83,
Singh, Daljeet 305
Sinha, Surajit 7
Sitaramanjaneya temple 34
Sivanasamudram 28
Slum Dwellers' Association 145
social muncipalism 18, 105, 303, 318
Society of Jesus 35
Someswara temple 33
Somanna, V. 317
Sommer, Robert 216
Sondekoppa Gate 38
South Arcot 261
Southern Karnataka Region (SKR) Concept Plan 134
Sri Krishna Temple 157
Sri Lakshmi Narasimha Charities (Janopakari Doddann's Charities) 67
Sri Rameswara Temple 53
Sri Varasiddhi Vinayaka Temple Building Committee 158
Srikantia, B.M. 238–9
Srinagar 315
Srinivas, Smriti 304
Srinivas, M.N. 4, 232, 320
Srinivas, Shudra 109
Srinivasa Rao, Nittoor 65, 240–1
Srirampuram Labour Housing Colony 56, 81, 169
Sriramulu, D. 97
Srirangapatnam 40
St Luke's Church 36
St Mark's Church 47
St Mary's Basilica 35, 37
St Xavier's Cathedral 253
STEM Report (1991) 141
Strand Genomics 341
Subbalakshmi, M.S. 276
Subbanarasimhaiya, A.R. 105
Subrahmanyam, H.V. 71–2
Subramanian, Dilip 85, 113
Sudarshan, P. 145
Sufis 35
Sugreeva temple 35
Sultanpet 63, 70
Sunnakal Tank 83
Sundara Rao, Ba Na 20, 50, 57, 72, 299
Supreme Court 174–5, 191, 325
Swabhimana 114, 318
Swagath slum 143–4,
Swamy B.G.L. 239

Talaghatapura 28, 161
Tamil Nadu 5, 27, 169, 235, 243, 245, 247–51, 258–9, 261–2, 269, 279
Tamil
  films 249–50, 264, 269, 279
  language 63, 241–2, 245–6, 252–4, 263–4, 274, 278, 287
  nationalism 234–5, 244, 262, 279
  organizations 237
  people 36, 67, 111, 143–4, 194, 235–7, 243–4, 250–3, 255, 258–9, 261–5, 267, 276, 286–7, 291
  region 28
Tamil National Liberation Front 235
Tamilians 276, 279
Tamilotsava 276
Tamilttay 263
Tanks 27–32, 219, 220
  diggers 34, 36, 38, 42, 62
Taramandalpet 35, 62